THE OXFORD HISTORY OF ENGLAND
OF ENGLAND

Edited by SIR GEORGE CLARK

THE OXFORD HISTORY OF ENGLAND

Edited by SIR GEORGE CLARK

THE
WHIG SUPREMACY
1714–1760

By

BASIL WILLIAMS, F.B.A.

SECOND EDITION
REVISED BY
C.H. STUART
Student of Christ Church, Oxford

OXFORD
AT THE CLARENDON PRESS

Oxford University Press, Ely House, London W.1

GLASGOW NEW YORK TORONTO MELBOURNE WELLINGTON
CAPE TOWN SALISBURY IBADAN NAIROBI LUSAKA ADDIS ABABA
BOMBAY CALCUTTA MADRAS KARACHI LAHORE DACCA
KUALA LUMPUR HONG KONG

FIRST PUBLISHED 1939
REPRINTED WITH CORRECTIONS 1942, 1945, 1949, 1952
SECOND (REVISED) EDITION 1962
REPRINTED WITH CORRECTIONS 1965

PRINTED IN GREAT BRITAIN
AT THE UNIVERSITY PRESS, OXFORD
BY VIVIAN RIDLER
PRINTER TO THE UNIVERSITY

PREFACE TO THE SECOND EDITION

PROFESSOR BASIL WILLIAMS, the author of this book, died on 5 January 1950. The success and popularity of the book were due to many qualities, but most of all to the uncommon sympathy and insight which he brought to the England of the first two Georges. Although he was successively a professor in three universities in three different English-speaking countries he did not become an academic teacher until he was over fifty. Before that time he had been, among other things, a clerk in the house of commons, a soldier in a colonial war, a parliamentary candidate, and the loyal friend of some of the most remarkable men of his time. He saw the eighteenth century in the light of this rich experience.

The preparation of this second edition has presented an editorial problem of some delicacy. When *The Whig Supremacy* was written Sir Lewis Namier had already made his main contributions to the knowledge of this period, but in the ensuing years and largely through his influence research has been active, expecially in the fields of parliamentary and party history. Mr. Stuart, in addition to such other revision as was needed, has taken into account the results of this research. While making the appropriate corrections he has been careful to disturb the original text as little as possible and to preserve its individual flavour. As in the volumes of this series which have been revised by their own authors, the new matter is not marked as such; but where Mr. Stuart expresses opinions which it is necessary to distinguish from those of Professor Williams the initials 'C.H.S.' are added to the footnotes. A revised Bibliography, by another contributor who remains anonymous, refers the reader to the new literature of the subject.

G. N. C.

PREFACE TO THE FIRST EDITION

M Y preface is entirely one of thanks: thanks to my wife for her judicious reading of the manuscript; to the many learned friends, indicated in the notes to some of the chapters, who have corrected my deficiencies in certain subjects; to my former colleague, Dr. D. B. Horn of Edinburgh University, for suggestions, inspired by his profound knowledge of eighteenth-century history, on the proof-sheets; and above all to the general editor of the series, Professor G. N. Clark, for proposing to me a subject which has been a constant delight, and for the patience and acumen with which he has so willingly supervised my labours.

B. W.

London
Lady Day, 1939

REVISER'S PREFACE

MY preface, like the author's, is one of thanks; and of thanks, above all, to the general editor of the series, Sir George Clark, for his patience in enduring the many delays in my work. I have also to thank my colleagues on the Governing Body of Christ Church for granting me leave for two terms during which the greater part of this revision was completed. But for such understanding of this period as I possess and for the interest in it which grows in me still I must thank my own tutors, Sir Keith Feiling and Sir John Masterman, who launched me in the study of the eighteenth century. To alter the work of another man is delicate and difficult; I have throughout attempted to do justice to Professor Williams and to show a proper concern for his honour and fame. Yet, as Hardwicke once observed to Newcastle: 'Posterity will do . . . justice; . . . nobody ought to rely upon their contemporaries for such retribution.'

C. H. S.

Oxford
Lady Day, 1961

CONTENTS

V. SOCIAL AND ECONOMIC LIFE OF THE ENGLISH PEOPLE

VI. SETTLEMENT OF THE DYNASTY
STANHOPE'S MINISTRY 1714–21

VII. THE SETTLEMENT OF THE DYNASTY
WALPOLE'S MINISTRY 1721–42

VIII. THE ARMY AND THE NAVY 1714–60

IX. CARTERET AND THE PELHAMS

X. SCOTLAND AND IRELAND

CONTENTS

XI. THE COLONIES AND INDIA

b

CONTENTS xvii

XIII. THE GREAT COMMONER

XIV. SCIENCE AND HISTORICAL RESEARCH

XVI. LITERATURE

LIST OF MAPS

NOTE ON DATES

DURING part of this period two calendars were in use in this country. Until 31 December 1751 the Julian or Old Style was the legal calendar, which was eleven days behind the Gregorian or New Style used in all other European countries except Russia, where the Julian calendar continued to be used until the twentieth century, and Turkey, which had a Mahommedan calendar of its own. Moreover, until the end of 1751 the legal beginning of the year in Great Britain was Lady Day, 25 March, not 1 January as in other countries. But to obviate confusion between the two calendars, until 1752 it was a common practice in Great Britain to date letters by both styles, e.g. $\frac{23 \text{ January}}{3 \text{ February}}$ 1714/5, 1/12 April 1716. By Lord Chesterfield's Act of 24 George II, cap. 23 (1751), 'An Act for regulating the commencement of the year and for correcting the Calendar now in use', the Julian calendar was superseded by the Gregorian in this country. By this Act the day following 31 December 1751 became 1 January 1752 (not 1751); and, in order to correct the error of eleven days in the Julian calendar, the eleven days between 2 and 14 September were omitted from the calendar for that year, the day after 2 September 1752 being called 14 September (the succession of days of the week thus not being interfered with).

Unless otherwise indicated the dates of the month in this volume are given according to the Old Style before 1752. Dates of the year are given according to the New Style throughout, e.g. the date of the battle of Toulon is given 11 February 1744—not 11/22 February 1743/4.

Dates of Birth and Death of Persons mentioned in the volume

In order to save an accumulation of footnotes, the years of the birth and death, whenever ascertainable, of all persons mentioned in the text have been inserted after their names in the index.

MAPS

1. ENGLAND AND WALES DIVIDED INTO DIOCESES

As shown in Appendix 3 of *First Report from H.M. Commissioners to consider state of Established Church, &c.* H.C. Paper 54, 19 March 1835.

In this map the counties are indicated by numbers and the bishoprics by letters.

In this list of bishoprics is added the value of the sees and their cathedral offices as given in *A List of the Archbishops, Bishops, Deans, and Prebendaries in England and Wales, in His Majesty's Gift. With the reputed Yearly Value, of Their respective Dignities, 1762,* to be found in *Correspondence of K. George III,* ed. Sir J. Fortescue, 6 vols., 1927, i. 33–44.

Index
letter
on map

Counties indicated by numerals

AA *Canterbury* Abp. £7,000; Dean £900; 12 Prebendaries each £350 (9 in King's gift, 3 in Abp.'s).
D *York* Abp. £4,500; Dean £600; Prebends of York and Southwell all in Abp.'s gift.
U *Bath and Wells* Bp. £2,000; Dean £600; Prebends in gift of Bp.
W *Bristol* Bp. £450 and residentiary of St. Paul's and Rectory of Bow *in commendam* together worth £1,100; Dean £500; 6 Prebends each £200 in gift of Lord Chancellor.
C *Chester* Bp. £900 and rectory of Stanhope *in commendam* worth £600; Dean £250; 6 Prebends in Bp.'s gift.
B *Carlisle* Bp. £1,300; Dean £300; 4 Prebends in Bp.'s gift.
V *Chichester* Bp. £1,400; Dean £300; Prebends in Bp.'s gift.
A *Durham* Bp. £6,000; Dean £1,500; 12 valuable Prebends in Bp.'s gift.
T *Exeter* Bp. £1,500; Dean £500; Prebends in Bp.'s gift.
Q *Ely* Bp. £3,400; Dean £450; 8 Prebends in Bp.'s gift.
M *Gloucester* Bp. £900 and a rich Durham Prebend *in commendam*; Dean £450; 6 Prebends, 5 in Ld. Chan.'s gift, 1 annexed to Mastership of Pembroke, Oxford.
K *Hereford* Bp. £1,200; Dean £260; Prebends in Bp.'s gift.
G *Lichfield and Coventry* Bp. £1,400; Dean £450; Prebends in Bp.'s gift.
H northern part ⎰ *Lincoln* Bp. £1,500; Dean £800; Pre-
P southern part ⎱ bends, &c., in Bp.'s gift.
S *London* Bp. £4,000; Dean £1,800; 3 residentiaries each £800.
R *Norwich* Bp. £2,000; Dean £500; 6 Prebends, 5 in gift of Ld. Chan., 1 annexed to Mastership of Catherine Hall, Cambridge.
N *Oxford* Bp. £500 and Deanery of St. Paul's £1,800 *in commendam*;[1] Dean £900; 5 canons (2 attached to professorships) each at £400.
O *Peterborough* Bp. £1,000 and vicarage of Twickenham *in commendam*; Dean £400; 6 Prebends in Bp.'s gift.
Z *Rochester* Bp. £600 and Deanery of Westminster £900; Dean £450; 7 Prebends, 6 in gift of Ld. Chan., 1 annexed to Provost of Oriel, each worth £180.
V *Salisbury* Bp. £3,000; Dean £900; Prebends in gift of Bp.
X *Winchester* Bp. £5,000; Dean £600; 12 Prebends each £250 in gift of Bp.
L *Worcester* Bp. £3,000; Dean £500; 9 Prebends £220 each (1 annexed to Lady Margaret Professor at Oxford).
   [*Windsor* Dean £900; 12 Canons at £450 each.]
F *St. Asaph* Bp. £1,400; Dean and Prebend in gift of Bp.
E *Bangor* Bp. £1,400; Dean and Prebends in gift of Bp.
I *St. David's* Bp. £900 and Vicarage of Greenwich and Rectory of St. Anne's, Soho, *in commendam*; no Dean; Prebends, &c., in gift of Bp.
  Llandaff Bp. £500 and Canonry of Windsor at £450; cathedral dignities in gift of Bp.

1. Northumberland	27. Cardigan
2. Cumberland	28. Pembroke
3. Durham	29. Carmarthen
4. Westmorland	30. Brecknock
5. Lancashire	31. Radnor
6. Yorkshire	32. Herefordshire
7. Anglesey	33. Glamorgan
8. Carnarvon	34. Monmouth
9. Denbigh	35. Gloucestershire
10. Flint	36. Worcestershire
11. Cheshire	37. Oxfordshire
12. Derbyshire	38. Buckinghamshire
13. Nottinghamshire	39. Bedfordshire
14. Lincolnshire	40. Hertfordshire
15. Merioneth	41. Middlesex
16. Montgomery	42. Essex
17. Shropshire	43. Cornwall
18. Staffordshire	44. Devonshire
19. Leicestershire	45. Somersetshire
20. Warwickshire	46. Dorsetshire
21. Rutland	47. Wiltshire
22. Northamptonshire	48. Berkshire
23. Huntingdonshire	49. Hampshire
24. Cambridgeshire	50. Surrey
25. Norfolk	51. Sussex
26. Suffolk	52. Kent

[1] The Deanery of St. Paul's is also attributed to the bishop of Lichfield, probably an error, as that bishop was fairly well paid.

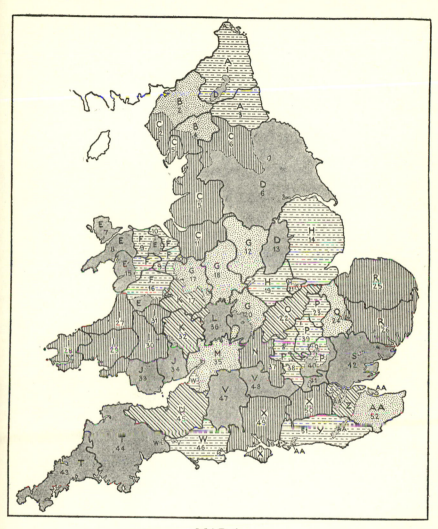

MAP 1

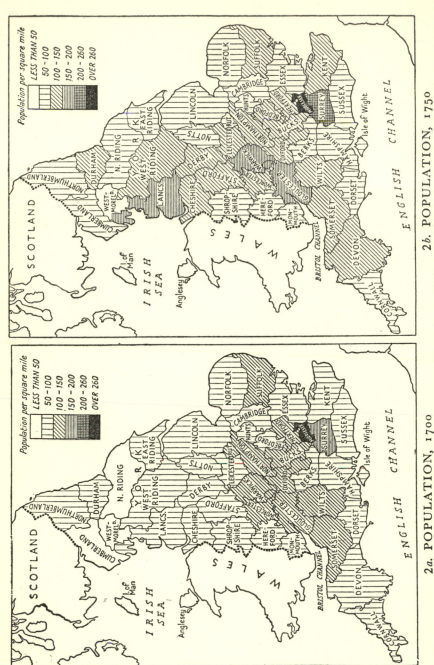

2b. POPULATION, 1750

2a. POPULATION, 1700

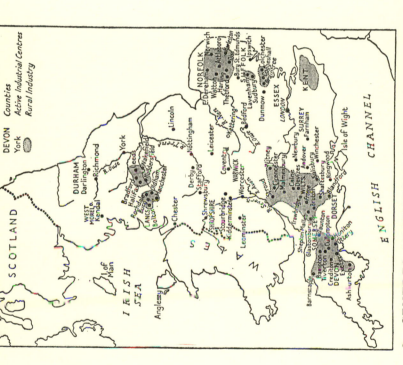

2c. CENTRES OF ENGLISH WOOLLEN TRADE
AT BEGINNING OF EIGHTEENTH CENTURY

A Plan of the CITIES of LONDON & WESTMINSTER and the BOROUGH of SOUTHWARK, &c.

Scale 1¼ inches to 8 miles

3. EIGHTEENTH-CENTURY LONDON EARLY IN GEORGE III'S REIGN

KEY TO THE CITIES OF LONDON AND WESTMINSTER

References to Streets, &c.

1. Tiburn Road
2. Oxford Street
3. Broad St. Giles's
4. High Holborn
5. Lincolns Inn Fields
6. Lincolns Inn
7. Fleet Market
8. Fleet Ditch
9. Hyde Park Corner
10. Piccadilly
11. Hay Market
12. Charing Cross
13. St. James's Park
14. Treasury
15. Strand
16. Drury Lane
17. Temple Barr
18. Butcher Row
19. Wytch Street
20. Soho Square
21. Grosvenor Square
22. Hanover Square
23. Berkeley Square
24. St. James's Square
25. New River Head
26. Pall Mall
27. Admiralty
28. Leicester Square
29. Grays Inn Square
30. Queen's Square
31. Covent Garden—Market
32. Royal Mewse
33. Long Acre
34. Bloomsbury Square
35. Red Lion Square
36. Chancery Lane
37. Cavendish Square

References to Buildings, &c.

A. Queen's Palace
B. St. James's Palace
C. White Hall
D. Palace Yard
E. Savoy
F. Somerset House
G. Temple
H. Bedford House
I. British Museum
K. Foundling Hospital
L. St. Peter's Abbey
M. Middlesex Hospital
N. Chesterfield House
O. Lambeth Palace
P. Queen Ann's Squ.
Q. Portman Square

KEY TO THE BOROUGH OF SOUTHWARK

References to Streets, &c.

1. Fish Street Hill
2. Grace-church St.
3. Bishops-gate Street
4. Norton Folgate
5. Shoreditch
6. Cheapside
7. Poultry
8. Cornhill
9. Leaden-hall Street
10. High Street
11. White Chapel
12. Mile end old town
13. Lombard Street
14. Fenchurch Street
15. Tower Hill
16. Minories
17. Goodman's Fields
18. Rosemary Lane
19. Ratcliff Highway
20. Wapping
21. Moorfields
22. Artillery Ground
23. Charter house Sq.
24. St. Martins le Grand
25. Aldersgate Street
26. Pick Axe Street
27. Goswell Street
28. Old Street
29. Foster Lane
30. Red Cross Street
31. Golden Lane
32. White Cross Street
33. Old Jury
34. Coleman Street
35. Dowgate Hill
36. Wallbrook
37. Cannon Street
38. Great East Cheap
39. Hoxton Square
40. Spittle Square
41. Brick Lane
42. Devonshire Square
43. Houndsditch
44. Mark Lane
45. Tower Street
46. Thames Street
47. The Borough
48. Blackman Street
49. Tolley Street
50. St. Olave's Street

References to Buildings, &c.

A. St. Paul's Cathedral
B. Monument
C. Mansion House
D. Tower
E. Bethlem Hospital
F. Haberdashers' Hosp.

4. ROADS AND NAVIGABLE RIVERS OF ENGLAND

Navigable parts of rivers are indicated by double lines; roads by single lines based upon the Ordnance Survey Map of seventeenth-century England, with the sanction of the Controller of H.M. Stationery Office

I

INTRODUCTORY

THE period of the first two Georges seems an oasis of tranquillity between two agitated epochs: before it, a century of revolutionary unrest hardly stayed even by the glorious twelve years of Anne; following it, the long reign of George III with its uneasy adjustments, at home and in America, barely completed when all the energies of the nation were called for the quarter-century of struggle with France for security—almost for existence. Between 1714 and 1760 the English people, wearied with struggles and sated with glory, was content to stabilize the results of the Revolution under a dynasty for which it had no love and accept an oligarchic system of government which for the time being seemed exactly suited to its needs. It was an age of stability in politics, in religion, in literature, and in social observances, a stability needed to enable the nation to recover its poise after more than a century of excitement. Thus the period has a rare unity of its own and seems to concentrate in itself all the faults and merits that we are apt to think of as specially characteristic of the whole eighteenth century. Common sense is the highest virtue, enthusiasm is distrusted; individual enterprise is encouraged, communal effort neglected; the boundaries between the different classes of society are well marked and not easily overstepped, while the Englishman of every class is famous for his insular self-satisfaction and his contempt of the foreigner. In some respects it may seem a humdrum age, but its stability is not the stability of inertness, for, under cover of its orderliness, ideas and movements were originated that found fuller expression in later years. And after all it was the support of these practical, common-sense Englishmen that enabled Pitt, the greatest child of the period, to end it in an unforgettable blaze of glory.

For political purposes the era of the first two Georges may be roughly divided into two parts. The first dates from 1714 to the fall of Walpole in 1742, a period within which two great statesmen, Stanhope and Walpole, established the dynasty and the whole Revolution system on so firm a basis that they remained immune from serious danger, internal or external, for the rest of the era. Thus secure, two statesmen, Carteret in fumbling fashion, Pitt with unerring vision of aims and means, were able to devote themselves for the next twenty years to the task of extending the bounds of empire and giving England that influence and position in the world to which her internal stability entitled her. But, as in all historical generalization, the boundaries between these two periods cannot always be exactly maintained. In the Stanhope–Walpole period, though the interest is predominantly domestic, the internal development of the country is often subject to external influences, while the foreign policy and the wars, so important in the second part of this history, cannot be fully understood without constant reference to the internal jealousies and intrigues of the whig oligarchy mainly responsible for the direction of affairs.

Naturally, to understand the life of a nation at any period, the main stream of political narrative must suffer continual interruptions to explain particular aspects of that life. We need for this period to know how far the new system of government, especially as elaborated by Walpole, fitted in with old constitutional traditions, how far with the newer doctrines derived from the Revolution, first explicitly set forth by Locke, and adopted by the whigs as the orthodox creed; how far too facts corresponded with theory, often more wide apart in England than in any other country. What was the theoretical power of the king, what his real power, where the two houses of parliament stood in relation to one another and the nation, how the internal government of the country was carried on and its foreign policy directed: these are all questions of special importance during a period when the constitution was being evolved, either so skilfully or so unconsciously it is often hard to say, but in such wise that with hardly any drastic change it has developed from a predominantly oligarchic system to the present almost unfettered democracy.

Political and even the more restricted parliamentary history must necessarily loom especially large for the period from 1714 to 1760, when the debates in both lords and commons rose to an importance and created an interest in the cultivated world rarely equalled in our history, and when with diarists and letter-writers, like Hervey, Walpole, and even Bubb Dodington,

Hardwicke, Egmont, and, above all, the duke of Newcastle, we
have such abundant material for calling up the political passions
of the time and re-creating the political scene. But the picture of
the age would be very defective if it represented only the interests
of those concerned in politics, especially since it was an age in
which politics had singularly little effect on the daily lives of the
great mass of the nation. How, apart from politics, did the
limited class of whom we hear almost exclusively in the pages
of Hervey and Walpole employ their opulent leisure? How
fared the poor and the solid middle class in town and country?
What was the trend of thought in theology, science, law, literature, and art? How were trade and commerce carried on, what
the industries and methods of agriculture? These are some of the
questions which also in their turn fall to be answered, all the
more so since in several of these provinces the beginnings of
change appear, notably in religious outlook, in agriculture, and
in industry, as well as in art and literature, which in the succeeding century produced almost revolutionary effects.

It is no exaggeration to say that in the political sphere the
undisputed domination of Locke's[1] political ideas provides the
most obvious thread of unity for this period. For both the theory
and the system of government during the reigns of the first two
Georges were a direct result of the Revolution settlement, which
would never have had the importance it gained in succeeding
years had it not been for Locke's interpretation of it. It is no
doubt true that the settlement in itself was a compromise between two conflicting parties, adopted, in the English way, to
meet the special difficulties of the moment; but the principles
latent in it were erected into a political system by Locke, the
evangelist of whig doctrine. England, indeed, for want of a
written constitution has always depended more on the deduction of such commentators as Locke than on legal enactments
for the preservation and development of its system of government.

The transitory union of whigs and tories which had effected
the Revolution and its great charter, the Bill of Rights, was
soon dissolved, for it had been due solely to the personality of
James II. The whigs, indeed, had consistently questioned the
king's claims to unrestrained authority, the tories, loyal to king
and church, had joined them only when they found the two

---

[1] See vol. x in this series *passim* for a further account of John Locke's works, &c.

loyalties incompatible with a Roman catholic king. During
William's reign the tories, it is true, were hard put to it to justify
their old doctrine, the Divine Right of Kings and Non-Resist-
ance, but under Anne and after the death of James II they had
not the same difficulty and many of them looked, after her
death, to the restoration of her brother to his legitimate rights.
In its extreme form their doctrine found expression in Sir Robert
Filmer's *Patriarcha*, which traced the right of monarchs to
absolutism to the divinely ordained 'Fatherly and Sovereign
Authority of Adam' and concluded that 'Men are not naturally
free'. The whigs found in Locke's two great works on civil
government and toleration an effective antidote to the tory
thesis, and all their statesmen from Stanhope to Chatham
adopted his creed as their political Bible.

Locke's first *Treatise on Civil Government* is a lengthy and somewhat laboured confutation of Filmer's absurdities, negligible
now, necessary even then only because 'the Pulpit', as he says,
'of late years, publickly owned his Doctrine and made it the
Current Divinity of the Times'. In the second treatise, *An Essay
concerning the True Original, Extent, and End of Civil Government*,
Locke expounds his own theory. He bases his whole structure on
the assumption that civilized society is the result of a voluntary
contract made by men in a state of nature establishing a representative authority to enforce rights and guarantee security
which had hitherto depended on their own individual exertions.
This assumption, no more susceptible of direct proof than his
adversary's, as he himself admits, is the weak link in his chain
of argument; but once it is granted his argument is unimpeach-
able. For on his assumption all authority in the state is derived
from the voluntary contract of its members and limited by its
terms. Hence any infringement of the contract by the authority
so constituted *ipso facto* nullifies it, and the community is thereupon entitled to resist and at need depose that authority.
Throughout the *Essay* he never alludes to the Revolution in so
many words, but in no uncertain language justifies its results.
The government can be dissolved when 'the supreme Executive
Power [i.e. James II] neglects and abandons that charge. . . .
When a King has Dethron'd himself and put himself in a state
of War with his People, what shall hinder them from prosecuting him who is no King?' In such an issue the final judgement
'will always remain in the Community'; and when, 'by the

Miscarriages of those in Authority it [their power] is forfeited; upon the Forfeiture of their Rulers, or at the Determination of the Time set, it reverts to the Society, and the People have a Right to act as Supreme, and continue the Legislative in themselves, or place it in a new Form, or new hands, as they think good.'

With such arguments as these Locke brought out the implications of the Bill of Rights even more outspokenly than its authors themselves would perhaps have admitted; and he impressed on Englishmen a larger sense of responsibility for the actions of their government than was the case with any other nation during this half-century. He even gave an impulse to the demand voiced later by Chatham to make this responsibility more effective by a reform of the system of parliamentary representation, by abolishing such abuses as he describes in this passage: 'We see the bare Name of a Town, of which there remains not so much as the ruines, where scarce so much housing as a Sheepcoat, or more Inhabitants than a Shepherd is to be found, send as many Representatives to the grand Assembly of Law-makers, as a whole County numerous in People, and powerful in Riches.'

In some respects, on the other hand, his influence was restrictive, perhaps in no respect so much as in his insistence on the rights of property. 'Civil society, the chief end whereof is the Preservation of Property'; 'The great end of Mens entering into Society being the enjoyment of their Properties in Peace and Safety'—such sentiments meet us at every turn and serve him even as an excuse for justifying in certain cases the status of slavery.[1] In emphasizing this merely protective duty of the state Locke was no doubt expressing the whig revulsion from the paternal interference with the lives of the people and their rights of property so dear to James I and his successors. On the other hand his teaching encouraged a whig oligarchy to regard one of the chief objects of government to be the protection of their own rights of property and to adopt an attitude of neglect or indifference to social evils affecting the lower classes of society. In fact the functional view of society, implying the duty of the state as well as of individuals to remedy such evils, which was so predominant at the close of the nineteenth century, was

[1] These quotations from Locke's *Second Treatise* can be found in paragraphs 134, 157, 219, 239, and 241.

entirely ignored by Locke and his followers in this respect, such as Blackstone, Kames, Hutcheson, Hume, and Adam Smith. The sole object of society and civil government in their view was to preserve rights and to ignore almost entirely the functions or duties of citizens. By this theory all the stress was laid on the privileges of property-owners until it became doubtful if the really poor had any rights at all theoretically. To Locke the cost of the poor was 'a growing burden on the Kingdom', due to 'a relaxation of discipline and a corruption of manners'; and he advocated seizing all the sound idle poor up to the age of fifty to serve on His Majesty's ships, for the maimed and those over fifty to be sent to houses of correction for hard labour and not too much comfort: those willing to work were to be set to jobs lucrative for their masters and presumably for the benefit of the country.

But with all the limitations involved in his theory of government Locke's emphasis on a sense of responsibility and on freedom for the whole community implicitly paved the way for revolt against these very limitations. 'Freedom of Men, under Government', he writes in the *Essay*, 'is to have a standing Rule to live by, common to everyone of that Society and made by the Legislative Power erected in it. A Liberty to follow my own Will in all things, where that Rule prescribes not, not to be subject to the inconstant, uncertain, unknown, Arbitrary Will of another Man.'

Far more inspiring and liberating than his *Essay* is the noble first *Letter on Toleration*. Here he dwells on what till the end of the seventeenth century was even less understood than civil liberty—religious liberty. Locke's earnest, even impassioned arguments for toleration may seem obvious to us, but came almost as a new light to his generation and to eighteenth-century England. So far no government, broadly speaking, had treated religion as anything but an affair of state, one might almost say of policy. *Une foi, une loi, un roi*, the explicit maxim of Louis XIV, though not everywhere put so crudely, was as much the norm for the puritans[1] of Old and New England, or for the Great Britain of Laud and Charles I, as for the most bigoted Roman catholic countries. Almost revolutionary therefore

---

[1] An exception should perhaps be made for the independents; but even they when in power showed little tolerance to Roman catholics and anglicans, for political reasons.

seemed Locke's dictum that 'the whole jurisdiction of the magistrate reaches only to civil concernments . . . it neither can nor ought in any manner to be extended to the salvation of souls. For no man could, if he would, conform his faith to the dictates of another. All the life and power of true religion consists in the inward and full persuasion of the mind; and faith is not faith without believing.' Accordingly he declares that 'the business of laws is not to provide for the truth of opinions but for the safety and security of the commonwealth and of every particular man's goods and person. . . . Truth certainly would do well enough if she were once made to shift for herself.' To the objection that some religious beliefs may be harmful to the commonwealth, he admits that this may be so in a few cases such as the belief that faith should not be kept with heretics or that the protection and service of another prince must be preferred to that of one's own country, or, again, a belief that denies the being of God, since no covenants or oaths are binding on those who hold such an opinion. For these purely secular reasons, therefore, he grants that atheists should not be tolerated, nor Roman catholics, it would seem, in so far as they hold the first two opinions, though to their purely religious beliefs he would be as tolerant to Roman catholics as to any. But the argument that secret dissenting conventicles are suspect of conspiring against the state he brushes aside with scorn. If it is so, he asks, 'Who are they that are to be blamed for it, those that desire, or those that forbid their being public? . . . There is one thing only which gathers people into seditious commotions, and that is oppression. . . . If solemn assemblies . . . be permitted to any one sort of professors, all these things ought to be permitted to the Presbyterians, Independents, Anabaptists, Arminians, Quakers and others with the same liberty', nay even Jews, Mohammedans, or pagans should not be excluded from civil rights. And so he concludes: 'God Almighty grant . . . that the Gospel of Peace may at length be preached and that civil magistrates, growing more careful to conform their own consciences to the law of God, and less solicitous about the binding of other men's consciences by human laws, may . . . promote universally the civil welfare of all their children . . . and that all ecclesiastical men, who boast themselves to be the successors of the Apostles, . . . may apply themselves wholly to promote the salvation of their souls! Farewell.'

Such were the principles on which the whole political system of men like Stanhope and the elder Pitt were explicitly based, while even more opportunist statesmen such as Walpole and the lesser politicians of the whig party in power were more or less consciously influenced by Locke's doctrines. Even the tory opposition for their own purposes implicitly acknowledged them in their attacks on the government, while the majority of the population, who probably had never heard of Locke, accepted his theories as a current commonplace. As a result no other country in Europe, not excepting even Holland, had more real toleration for differing religious views than England: in none other had the common man so proud, even insolent, a conception of his own rights and of his part in deciding on any matters of public policy that seemed to affect him. The law in England was then incredibly brutal in some respects and in many others defective; but at any rate it was not supplemented, as in most other countries, by irresponsible and undefined claims of the administration against the legal rights of even the meanest in the community. Again, in no other country during this period could a popular movement have brought about, against the wishes of the most powerful minister of the century, the Spanish war of 1739, or have insisted, against the king's strong prejudices, on calling upon a Pitt to save the country in the early days of the Seven Years war.

The prevalence of Locke's principles also helps to explain the very restricted area claimed by government during this period as a special sphere for its activities. During the seventeenth century the Stuart kings had a passion for ordering the lives of their subjects, and, both before and after the Revolution, parliament found much scope for legislation in countering or remedying the encroachments of the Crown. Again, from the time of George III onwards a renewed period of active legislation begins; America, India, social and political evils like the slave-trade, the state of the poor, begin once more to stir the conscience of the community and to call for remedy from parliament. But the reigns of George I and George II have perhaps the scantiest crop of important legislation in our parliamentary records; for apart from remedial measures for the dissenters or to secure the stability of the government against rebels or turbulent mobs inflamed by excessive gin-drinking, there were comparatively few other acts placed on the statute-book. This was only to be expected in an age when the chief function of government was held to be 'the preservation of Property', and when absolute freedom of contract, however oppressive such a system might be to the weaker members of society, was regarded as essential in a free community.

But within this limited sphere parliament and the politicians rendered an inestimable service to future generations, concentrating on two main objects: first, to maintain unimpaired and even to enlarge the liberties secured at the Revolution and, secondly, by unceasing vigilance in foreign policy to preserve and extend all the advantages of external trade and expansion which had been won so dearly in Marlborough's wars. In these two provinces no other period in our history can show such keen and well-informed debates or such masters of parliamentary craft and eloquence as the reigns of the first two Georges.

The absence of any constructive legislation to remedy the social ills of the age, and indeed of any appreciation of its need, is largely responsible for the bad name this first half of the eighteenth century has obtained as lacking in ideals and immersed in gross material aims. But such a judgement leaves out of account other aspects of the period at least as important as the political. *Laisser-faire*, with all its social disadvantages, especially in an age such as this was becoming, of more organized labour under capitalized direction, does at least promote strong and racy individuals in all classes of the community. One need only read Smollett and Fielding or look at Hogarth's pictures to see what richly diversified and what independent, self-relying characters were to be found scattered all over this England of ours, some indeed unpleasant but all of them full of juice. It was an age in which the privileged families were creating a high standard of culture and intelligent living not divorced from public spirit, in which the adventurous poor had every chance of exciting adventures and even of rising to prosperity by the use of their wits. It was an age in which the sturdy middle-class merchants, whigs to a man, and even worse in the estimation of George III and Dr. Johnson, were consolidating our commercial supremacy in this country, in India, the West Indies, and America, and, caring for no man whether English lord or Spanish guarda-costa, producing the wealth which made possible Pitt's victories and later the quarter-century of struggle against France.

Nor can an age be called materialistic or humdrum which could produce such outstanding personalities: Stanhope, Walpole, Carteret, Pitt among the statesmen, with Bolingbroke, the fallen angel in their midst, unresting in his efforts to recover his heaven of place and power; lawyers such as Blackstone, Hardwicke, and Murray; Chesterfield and Horace Walpole as arbiters of social and political propriety; Swift, Pope, Defoe, Prior, Steele, Addison, Gay, Fielding, Smollett, Richardson, and Sterne among the writers; in philosophy, theology, scholarship, Bentley, Butler, Berkeley, Clarke, Hume, Law; evangelists and philanthropists such as the Wesleys, Whitefield, Oglethorpe, and Coram; Hogarth, Reynolds, Gainsborough, Handel, and Garrick in the arts; Dr. Johnson, who in any age would have stood out as one in authority; not to speak of such minor portents as the all-pervasive duke of Newcastle or Bubb Dodington who raised toadyism to almost sublime proportions; and notable women such as Queen Caroline, the great Sarah of Marlborough, Lady Mary Wortley Montagu, and Kitty, duchess of Queensberry, most enchanting of roguish charmers.

THE ENGLISH SYSTEM OF
GOVERNMENT UNDER
GEORGE I AND II

GEORGE LEWIS, elector of Brunswick-Lüneburg and arch-treasurer of the Empire, was already well set in his fifty-fifth year when he came to rule Great Britain. He came from a country with institutions and a form of government as different as could be conceived from those of his new realm. The original Guelf duchy of Brunswick-Lüneburg had, as so often happened in Germany, been divided up between 1267 and 1285 among various branches of the ducal family: by 1634 most of these branches had died out, leaving only two, those of the dukes of Lüneburg with its capital at Celle and of Kalenberg with its capital at Hanover. In 1641 George, duke of Kalenberg, who was also heir presumptive to the larger duchy of Lüneburg, made a will declaring that, after his succession to Lüneburg, no further division of either duchy should be legal, that the two should never be under the same ruler, and that the nearest heir could always exercise the option of choosing Lüneburg. All his four sons were in turn dukes of Kalenberg and the two eldest successively dukes of Lüneburg. The youngest, Ernest Augustus, husband of Sophia, James I's granddaughter, and father of our George I, formed the project of uniting the two duchies in his own line. To compass this he persuaded his second brother, George William, the only one who seemed likely to have issue, to agree never to marry and that, despite their father's will, the two duchies should eventually be united in Ernest Augustus and his line. George William so far kept his word that he limited his matrimony to a morganatic union with the Frenchwoman Eleanor d'Olbreuse, but, to make assurance doubly sure, Ernest Augustus in 1682 married his son George Lewis to Sophia Dorothea, the only offspring of that union. It was an unhappy marriage and twelve years later, after the birth of his two children,[1] George Lewis divorced his wife and

---

[1] George Lewis's children were a son, George (II), and a daughter, Sophia, later queen of Prussia.

shut her up in a fortress for the rest of her life. In 1698, on the death of his father Ernest Augustus, George Lewis had become duke of Kalenberg and in 1705 on George William's death, duke of the reunited duchies of Lüneburg and Kalenberg; but he still kept his capital at Hanover.[1]

Already in 1692 the electorate of Brunswick-Lüneburg, popularly known as Hanover, had been created by the emperor as a reward for aid sent by Ernest Augustus against the Turks in 1683 and 1685. George Lewis had to wait till 1708 for formal admission to the electoral college and till 1710 for the title of arch-treasurer of the Empire, after further services to the emperor in the French wars at the end of the seventeenth and beginning of the eighteenth centuries. But after 1692 his mother Sophia, heiress by the Act of Settlement of 1701 to the Crown of England, was always known as the electress of Hanover. George Lewis himself did not of course succeed to the parliamentary title of heir to the Crown till the death of Sophia, two months before that of Queen Anne.

In addition to the two main duchies of Kalenberg and Lüneburg other small territories, the princedoms of Göttingen and Grubenhagen, the countships of Hoya and Diepholz, and the dukedom of Lauenburg, had become attached to the electorate on various pretexts: the neighbouring bishopric of Osnabrück, alternating between a Roman catholic ruler and a member of the protestant Guelf family, was held by George I's brother from 1716 to 1728, in 1761 by George III, and from 1763 to 1803 by his son Frederick, duke of York. The territories of Bremen and Verden, conquered by the Danes from Sweden, and valuable as commanding the lower reaches of the Elbe and Weser, were on the point of being added to the electorate when George came over to England; and Hadeln, an enclave in the territory of Bremen, was absorbed by 1731. The total area of

---

[1] The royal arms from 1714 to 1801 were quarterly: (1) the Lions of England impaling the Lion of Scotland; (2) The French fleur-de-lys; (3) the Irish harp; (4) the arms of Hanover, to wit, *Per pale* and *per Chevron* (i) *Gules*, two Lions *passant guardant*, in *pale*, *or* (for Brunswick); (ii) *or*, *semée* of Hearts, a Lion *rampant azure* (for Lüneburg); (iii) *gules*, a Horse *courant argent* (for Westphalia); and over all an inescutcheon *gules*, charged with the golden crown of Charlemagne. The white horse was not a popular addition to the fleur-de-lys, the harp, and the lions of England and Scotland crowded into one quartering. The black cockade introduced by the Hanoverians, as opposed to the Stuarts' white cockade, may still be worn by the servants of peers, and of court and government officials. For illustration see T. Willement, *Regal Heraldry*, 1821.

the electorate with its dependencies was some 8,500 square miles, with a population of three-quarters of a million.[1] All these various territories comprised within it still retained a shadow of local autonomy with their separate little landtags of knights, prelates, and burgesses, but it was a mere shadow. In reality the electorate was governed despotically from Hanover, through ministers responsible only to the elector, who was supreme lord of the army and dictated internal and external policy. It was a kindly, paternal despotism over subjects who gave no trouble but much affection to their ruler, and never ventured to criticize him or his policy. The foreign interests of the electorate were almost entirely confined to north-eastern Europe, especially the big neighbours, Brandenburg-Prussia and the Baltic powers, Sweden, Denmark, and Russia. Otherwise the new arch-treasurer of the Empire was mainly concerned with his chief, the emperor. Grateful for his recent elevation to the electoral dignity, he soon looked to him also with hopeful anticipation for imperial confirmation of his recent acquisitions, Bremen and Verden.[2]

The despotic nature of the elector's rule was apparent in the 'Order of Government' issued by George I just before his departure for England.[3] In his absence all matters *pure militaria*, such as army organization, the appointment and dismissal of officers, and military justice were still to remain directly under the elector without the interposition of any minister: the routine administration of the army was indeed left to the departments, but even there the elector's pleasure was to be taken on all important matters. So was it with civil affairs: the ministers left in Hanover had to take the elector's pleasure on every important and many unimportant questions; the elector signed all pardons and alone could sanction the prosecution of highly placed Hanoverians. In foreign affairs the ministers were allowed no responsibility except in the grave emergency of actual invasion, and the envoys abroad had to send duplicates

[1] C. T. Atkinson, *History of Germany*, p. 47, estimates the population of the electorate at little over half a million.

[2] For an account of the component parts of the electorate of Hanover and their history see Ernst von Meier, *Hannoversche Verfassungs- u. Verwaltungsgeschichte*, 2 vols., Leipzig, 1898. For the diplomatic confusion of all these little Brunswick-Lüneburg states before their union see L. Bittner and L. Gross, *Repertorium der diplomatischen Vertreter*, I, *1648–1715*, Berlin, 1936, pp. 64–65.

[3] See Meier, i. 156 sqq., and A. W. Ward, *Great Britain and Hanover*, pp. 51 sqq.

of all dispatches to London; nor could ministers sanction any expenditure greater than 50 thalers (about £12), or appoint any departmental officials except their own copyists; and they themselves were appointed arbitrarily by the elector. During the whole period of the king-electors, 1714–1837, in addition to a Hanoverian envoy accredited to the king of Great Britain, one of the Hanoverian ministers was in attendance on him as elector and with two secretaries constituted the German chancery which issued to Hanover the elector's rescripts. The first of these Hanoverian residents was Hattorf from 1714 to 1737,[1] the two others in George II's reign were Steinberg (1738–49) and Ph. Adolf Munchausen (1749–62); and naturally, in spite of their long absence from Hanover, they had a large say in Hanoverian administration. It is also worth noting that George I and his four successors as electors also paraded the royal title, but as kings of England never used the electoral title. In fact in England Hanover was officially treated as a foreign country.

But for the elector himself, Hanover was a pleasant little dominion, with its cosy *gemütlich* little capital at Hanover, its agreeable summer residence at Göhrde, where immense battues attested the precision of the electoral gun, and the orangeries the skill of the electoral gardeners. In Hanover there was no nonsense about troublesome parliaments, but an easy-going people, content with an easy-going paternal government ordering everything as seemed best. No wonder George Lewis was not nearly so convinced of the honour his new English subjects had conferred on him as they were when they called him from these pleasant ways to rule over a self-opinionated, often turbulent population, under the eyes and largely in the power of a critical parliament. He had never even taken the trouble to learn their language and might possibly never have taken over their crown had he not, like William of Orange, thought that England might be of use to him in his foreign politics. Indeed he took the earliest opportunity to show that he preferred his old electorate to his new kingdom, and absented himself from England as often and for as long as he could, an example followed by his son George II, who was thirty years old before he came to live in England.

[1] Hattorf did not exercise ministerial functions until a year or so after 1714. See A. W. Ward, op. cit., pp. 60–61, and 77.

Contrast this idyllic existence in Hanover, where there was not too much business to disturb George's regular pleasures, and where no voice was raised against his commands, with the elaborate system of government he found in England, a system chiefly designed, as it must have seemed to this simple autocrat, to provide at every turn checks to thwart his will.

The king's personal power had been in certain respects seriously curtailed by the legislation of William III's and Anne's reigns. His religion was defined for him, and the religion of his wife; he was forbidden to give office or a peerage or grant lands to a foreigner, even naturalized; his power of creating new ministerial posts was barred by the proviso that such ministers could not represent his views in the house of commons. Without the leave of parliament he could not, whatever the emergency, raise a regiment or a tax or suspend a law, or, when he came to the throne, leave the country even to visit his beloved electorate. Though he still appointed the judges, he had lost that effective control over their decisions which the Stuarts had found so useful, since he could no longer dismiss them at his own good pleasure. The fact, too, that the Hanoverian kings would never have come to the throne at all had they not been specifically chosen by parliament diminished their prestige and to some extent their authority. Thus since George I's accession no sovereign has refused assent to a bill passed by both houses. William and Mary and Anne had no doubt reigned by parliamentary authority out of the regular order of succession, but Mary and Anne were both of British stock and daughters of an undeniably legitimate king; and the fiction that their half-brother the Pretender, the nearest heir to the throne, was supposititious, which had helped their acceptance by the country, was now entirely abandoned. Thus something of that sacred *aura* of majesty which still attached to dynastically legitimate kings was lost to the Hanoverians; and it is significant that they never attempted to exercise the royal gift of touching for the king's evil claimed from time immemorial even to the reign of Queen Anne. The openly expressed preference of both George I and George II for their German possessions as compared with England also detracted from their English subjects' enthusiastic loyalty and tended to diminish their authority.[1]

[1] George II, when pressed to return to England from Hanover almost on the eve of the Seven Years war, replied, 'There are kings enough in England. I am

Nevertheless it would be a great mistake to imagine that the 'constitutional kings' George I and George II were as devoid of personal power and initiative as our constitutional monarchs have been since 1837. Queen Victoria and her successors have had no power to carry out their personal views except so far as they happen to coincide with those of parliament as expressed by their responsible ministers. Victoria and her son and grandson undoubtedly had great influence on some of the decisions taken by ministers, partly because they all had great experience in affairs of state and had the unique advantage of knowing the secrets of all administrations, partly because they were persons with views of their own which they had every opportunity of impressing on their advisers; but, unless they were able to convince, they were powerless. This is much less true of our monarchs in the eighteenth century. There were certain provinces of government in which, even if their power was not uncontrolled, they had as a rule the preponderating voice. Paradoxical as it may at first sight appear, they still had considerable financial power. The king's civil list was, it is true, voted for him by parliament, but, once voted, it was for life and moreover was used, not only, as today, for the king's personal and household expenses, but also for many of the purposes, such as the civil service, for which money is now voted, after parliamentary criticism, annually. Thus a fruitful source of power to the king arose from the large amount of money he had at his disposal for pensions, either on the English or the Irish establishment, to favourites or politicians whose votes he wanted to secure, and for the purpose of influencing parliamentary elections. George II, indeed, unlike his successor, gave such a minister as Newcastle considerable discretion in suggesting the best uses to which this method could be put, but even he sometimes took his own line, and in all cases had a personal hold on the recipient's grateful loyalty. Again many of the chief ministers, including the secretaries of state, though partly paid by fees and perquisites, were dependent on the king's civil list for the rest of their emoluments and so retained something of their original position as the king's personal servants, both in fact and in popular estimation. Thus it will be

nothing there, I am old and want rest and should only go to be plagued and teased there about that D——d House of Commons.' B.M., Add. MS. 32857, f. 553, Holderness to Newcastle, 3 Aug. 1755.

remembered that when Pitt, at the height of his power and popularity, spoke to the cabinet of his having been called by the people to assist the state, Granville reminded him that when he talked of being responsible to the people he talked the language of the house of commons, and forgot that at that board he was responsible only to the king.[1] Granville's saying, 'Give any man the Crown on his side and he can defy everything', was indeed disproved in his own case, but it contained an element of truth in the eighteenth century. In the actual choice of ministers the first three Georges, and to a less extent their two immediate successors, had far more power than our kings have today. George I, following Anne's example in the case of Shrewsbury, appointed all his first ministers solely on his own responsibility, helped only by the advice of his German counsellors; later, on his own initiative, he dismissed Townshend from his post of secretary of state; and he gave orders to the admiral in command of the Baltic fleet without the knowledge of his English advisers. George II's determination to stick to Walpole for some time after the voice of parliament and people was manifestly against him provoked indeed this protest from Egmont.

'Tis a solecism in our constitution to leave the same powers in the Crown which it had when more absolute, now that the subject has grown more powerful, for there will be eternal differences . . . between the Crown and people. The king will say, 'I won't or I will do this, and I insist on my prerogative,' but the Parliament will say, 'Sir, you have the prerogative indeed but 'tis an abuse of your prerogative, and if insisted on, this matter in question will ruin us; therefore, if you are obstinate we will distress you, you will have no supplies; you are ill advised, and we will know who advised you so!'[2]

But the protest went no farther than Egmont's private diary, though in fact the king shortly afterwards had to accept Walpole's resignation after several defeats in the house of commons. George II, again, named Pelham as first lord of the treasury as an act of personal choice.[3] He was also believed to have been

[1] This famous comment appears in the *Annual Register* for 1761, p. 44. It is generally attributed to Burke and is a gloss on Granville's remarks. See below, p. 370, and *English Historical Review*, xvii. 690–1.

[2] *Hist. MSS. Comm., Egmont Diary*, iii. 241.

[3] See below, p. 246, n. 1. The often repeated tale that George II made this choice on the advice of Walpole, then Lord Orford, is without foundation. The king was in Hanover when the decision was taken. But it does appear that Pelham

in the habit of consulting Granville behind the backs of his ministers, after he had been forced to dismiss him;[1] he was compelled to admit Pitt to a minor post in the ministry only after most of his ministers had resigned on the question, and, in spite of the evident wishes of the people and the house of commons, for long set his face against admitting him to the secretaryship. Indeed throughout his reign he treated ministers whom he disliked with studied want of confidence, and always had the final decision as to their appointment or dismissal. This amount of royal control over ministers was still possible since the implications of the Revolution that the only effective control over the executive lay in the conception that the whole body of ministers should represent the general feeling of the house of commons were not yet realized. It was not till the nineteenth century that political opinion passed beyond the stage of preventing the king in his executive capacity from doing certain things declared to be illegal, to that of compelling him to act according to the wishes of parliament in everything by ensuring that his ministers formed an executive committee bound to do nothing counter to those wishes. Among the interesting constitutional developments of this period is the gradual and almost unconscious tendency towards a greater solidarity in ministries as representing public opinion, and a corresponding diminution in the king's personal authority.[2] But the victory had not been won by 1760 as may be seen by George III's proceedings during his first twenty years.

Two departments of government the early Hanoverian kings regarded as especially subject to their direct control, the army and foreign affairs. Both George I and George II fancied themselves as soldiers, so naturally clung to the traditional conception of the king as supreme over the armed forces of the realm, and they always retained army patronage in their own hands.[3] Their interest in the army was chiefly directed to the

had obtained a promise of the reversion of Wilmington's office before George left the country. See J. B. Owen, *The Rise of the Pelhams*, pp. 159–61, and 165–71.

[1] See below, p. 258, n. 3.

[2] [Professor Williams seems here to exaggerate the growth of solidarity in ministries during this period. After Henry Pelham's death ministries became less united than in the previous thirty years. On the dangers of deducing constitutional progress from temporary situations see Namier, *England in the Age of the American Revolution*, p. 51. In the footnotes below the work of Namier referred to as op. cit. is that named in n. 3. C.H.S.]

[3] See Namier, *Structure of Politics at the Accession of George III*, 1st edn., p. 37.

details of army organization specially associated with the secretary at war, the reason no doubt why George II would not hear of Pitt for that office, since it would involve his frequent attendance in the closet. The last of our kings to command an army in the field was George II at Dettingen, a battle in which he showed great personal courage but little strategic insight. This desire to have a personal authoritative voice in army organization was the prerogative least willingly given up even by the Georges' great descendant Victoria, who at times gave considerable trouble to her ministers by her claim to have the last word in matters affecting 'my army'.

In foreign affairs there was more justification for the sovereign's interference in the early eighteenth century. As electors the first two Georges were well versed in German and eastern European questions, then beginning to assume an importance they had never hitherto held for England, and except for Stanhope and Carteret and, at the end of the period, Pitt, they never had ministers who could approach them in understanding of such matters. Unfortunately George I had personal grievances against his son-in-law of Prussia, and also against the Tsar Peter, and both he and his son were inclined to attach attention, excessive in the eyes of their English subjects, to the interests of Hanover even when these interests clashed with those of England. But on the whole the very important part they took in foreign affairs was beneficial to English interests. Thus it was owing to the king, even more than to Stanhope, that, in view of the Russian aggression on Mecklenburg in 1716, the valuable alliance with France of 1716 was concluded so swiftly, when delay might have proved fatal. Again George II, in co-operation with Carteret, took a more intelligent view of England's interests in the war of 1740–8 than either Walpole or the fumbling secretaries of state who followed Carteret.

Nevertheless the personal union between Great Britain and Hanover, which lasted from 1714 to Queen Victoria's accession in 1837, was anomalous and at times the cause of considerable friction. In spite of all the precautions taken in the act of settlement,[1] it proved impossible entirely to rule out the influence of Hanoverian interests on English policy. In the early years of his reign George I made no scruple in promoting those interests by the added power and prestige he had attained as

[1] See this *History*, vol. x, pp. 190–1 (2nd edn.).

king, and the English ministers had a hard struggle to hold their own against Bernstorff[1] and other Hanoverian ministers. In 1719, however, Stanhope finally defeated Bernstorff and secured the alliance with Prussia, opposed by the Hanoverians, in support of his northern policy; at the same time he obtained from the king a decision 'not to suffer his Germans to meddle in English affairs, he having forbidden them to presume so much as to speak to him about them'.[2] Still it was impossible for England to neglect entirely the interests of the electorate ruled over by her king. Whenever England was at war the somewhat defenceless electorate was an easy prey to France and other continental neighbours, and the need of protecting Hanover could hardly be overlooked, a need which, until Pitt came into power in 1756, was apt to deflect the natural course of British policy. Moreover the frequent visits of George I and II to the electorate, often highly inconvenient for the easy and rapid conduct of business, and their evident predilection for their Hanoverian interests and subjects were extremely unpopular and gave the parliamentary opposition ample scope for blaspheming and to the populace excuses for rioting.

George I had been only two years on the throne when he became so much impressed by these difficulties that in 1716 he drew up a will whereby after his death, whenever any of his successors had two sons, the elder should retain the Crown but hand over the electorate to his next brother for himself and his male heirs. In 1719 he submitted this proposal to a committee presided over by the chancellor, Lord Macclesfield, for their advice. But though this committee pointed out the serious difficulties involved in the scheme even in England, and the need of imperial consent, he still persisted with the idea, adding to the will a codicil with further provisions in 1720. George II,[3] on coming to the throne, did his best to suppress the scheme; he obtained the copies of the will lodged by his father in the keeping of the duke of Wolfenbüttel and of the emperor and sent them with his own copy to be lodged in the arcana of the Hanoverian Records, where they are still to be found. Nevertheless

---

[1] Andreas Gottlieb von Bernstorff, 1649–1726.

[2] See Williams, *Stanhope*, pp. 371, 419, and *Hist. MSS. Comm. (Carlisle)*, xv. vi. 23.

[3] George II himself in 1725, when prince of Wales, according to Lord King's Diary (quoted by Campbell, *Lord Chancellors*, iv. 618), considered a scheme for excluding his elder son Frederick from the English throne and sending him to rule Hanover, and for the second son William to succeed as king.

even George II seems to have been so much impressed by the unpopularity of his Hanoverians in 1744, owing to the favour he showed them in the Dettingen campaign, and once more in 1757, after the Convention of Klosterseven, in withdrawing Hanover from further participation in the Seven Years war, that in both years he ordered his Hanoverian council to consider the possibility of such a severance of the electorate from England. But nothing further was done in the matter. At any rate such a separation was a constant topic for discussion during the reign of George II. Walpole had a long conversation with Hervey about it in 1737, and in 1741 he asked the Speaker Onslow what would be thought in the house of commons if the proposal were made, to which Onslow replied that it would be regarded as a message from heaven.[1] Frederick, prince of Wales, was no doubt told about the scheme by his grandfather, and in the testament he left to his son George (III) expressed hearty approval of it. But the scheme was probably impracticable, however popular it might have been in England, owing to the almost insuperable difficulties that would have arisen in the Empire in securing any alteration of the established rights of succession in the electorate.[2]

Henry Pelham was wont to assert that when parliament was against him he might get his way by royal support, when the king disapproved he sometimes got his way by relying on parliament, but that against king and parliament he was powerless. This opinion is obviously better founded than Granville's quoted above, and may indeed be taken as a very fair statement of the relative strength of king and parliament during the period 1714–60.

At other times in our history parliament as a whole has been more representative of the nation and during the nineteenth century exercised more actual power, but it never perhaps had more prestige than in this first half of the eighteenth century.

[1] See Coxe, *Walpole*, ii. 571–2.

[2] Professor Michael, in his pamphlet *Personalunion v. England u. Hannover* . . . and in his *Englische Geschichte*, iii. 518–28, iv. 523–7, has thrown much light on the subject; and his account has recently been supplemented and to some extent corrected by R. Drogereit's *Testament König Georgs I.* . . . (in *Niedersächsisches Jahrbuch für Landesgeschichte*, B. 14, 1937). See also R. Sedgwick's edition of Hervey's *Memoirs*, xxxiv–xxxv, for Prince Frederick's testament to his son. Lord Macclesfield's report to the king on the subject in 1719 is in B.M., Stowe MS. 249. See also Plumb, *Walpole*, ii. 157.

True it did not represent more than a fraction of the nation, but it did represent fairly accurately those elements in the nation which then counted in the national life, the great landowners and the country gentlemen to whom Walpole was wont to appeal as representing the sound sense of the nation, lawyers of historical fame such as Yorke and Murray, great merchants of London and Bristol, directors of the powerful East India Company, successful planters from the colonies like Beckford, men like Steele, Addison, Glover, Lyttelton, and Chesterfield, esteemed as much for their political services as for their acknowledged literary eminence, a galaxy of orators and expert debaters, Walpole, Carteret, Pulteney, Chesterfield, Henry Fox, Murray, and Pitt, rarely equalled in our parliamentary annals. In no other age have parliaments taken themselves more seriously as the supreme council of the nation, not inferior in power, dignity, and wisdom to the Roman Senate in its palmiest days; rarely have their debates been more keen and their absorption in business more complete than in these fifty years; certainly between 1714 and 1760 little fault was found with parliament as an institution, and it was generally accepted at its own valuation as the principal organ of the nation's will.

Of the two houses of parliament the house of lords no longer held quite the dominating position which its services at the glorious Revolution and the assertion of its claims against both king and house of commons had given it during the reign of King William and the early years of Anne. But it was by no means as unimportant constitutionally during this period as it has now become. One source of its strength is to be found in its comparatively small numbers which, between 1714 and 1760, remained at the almost constant figure of 220, 26 of whom were bishops.[1] This limited assembly inevitably acquired an *esprit de corps* and a sense of responsibility much more difficult to attain by the present unwieldy body of peers, whose average attendance at debates is proportionately much smaller than in the eighteenth century. Nor is it surprising that in George I's reign the peers welcomed, while the house of commons rejected, a Peerage Bill which, by making the house of lords practically a closed body, would have immensely increased its strength.

[1] This total also includes the 16 representative peers from Scotland. Exact numbers for 1714, 1719, 1728, and 1759 were 213, 220, 221, and 214. See A. S. Turberville, *The House of Lords in the Eighteenth Century*, 1927, pp. 4–5.

A further source of strength arose from its composition. Chiefly owing to their vast landed possessions, the peers individually had a personal importance in the country almost inconceivable at the present day. Their wealth and power over their tenants and dependants not only gave them local prestige, but also some control over the house of commons itself by their influence in county and borough elections. This personal importance of the peers as such is reflected in the ministries of the period, which always contained a much larger proportion of members of the house of lords, especially in the higher posts, than of commoners. The house of lords, then as now, had judicial as well as legislative and deliberative functions, but the importance of the first was in some respects greater than today. Divorce was then impossible without an act of parliament, and the bills for divorce were always initiated in the house of lords while the addresses of counsel and evidence of witnesses were held before one of its committees: by the time the lords had finished with a case there was little left for the commons to do but to pass the bill as sent down to them. Then the house of lords was the highest court of appeal in the land, and by no means uniformly, as had become the custom and finally the law by the nineteenth century, confined the exercise of this jurisdiction to its legal members: in cases arousing special interest lay and spiritual peers, besides the lawyers among them, were wont to exercise their right of taking part in the proceedings. Thus in 1733 on the appeal of Bentley against a decision of the king's bench in favour of the bishop of Ely, Carteret took a leading part in favour of his friend Bentley, while the bishop's case was warmly upheld by his brother of Bangor, and after a spirited debate in which many bishops and lay peers took a part, the decision was reversed by 28 against 16. Again the not infrequent custom of sending for the judges in Westminster Hall to consult them on legal points not only on appeals but on questions arising in the ordinary course of legislation illustrates the lords' determination to maintain their prerogative as supreme guardians of the law. But in no more ceremonial form could the prestige and power of the house of lords be made patent to the world than in the brilliant and dignified ceremonies of an impeachment. In George I's reign there were no less than five such ceremonies and one in the reign of George II, in addition to the trial on indictment by the house of three rebel lords in

1746, which was conducted with the same solemnities as an impeachment.[1] These trials, held in Westminster Hall with the peers attending as judges in their gorgeous scarlet robes under the presidency of a lord high steward, were well calculated to fire the imagination of the public and impress it with the dignity and responsibility of the peerage as the highest assemblage in the kingdom.

In its capacity as a legislative and debating assembly the house of lords, though definitely inferior in power to the house of commons, still retained great authority by its proceedings; and its support was carefully nursed by each successive ministry. The dignity of impoverished peers was enhanced by grants from the civil list and they were expected to be correspondingly amenable; new peerages were never created except as a return for service to the party in power either in parliament, at court, or in county business; the twenty-six bishops, all appointed or promoted mainly for their sympathy with the ministerial policy, could almost invariably be reckoned on to support their makers, if not their Maker;[2] the election of the sixteen Scottish representative peers was also arranged for by such managers for the government as Lord Islay. But the docility of these fifty or so members of the upper house thus influenced was by no means general; and the house as a whole put its claims as 'hereditary great council of the Crown', to use Carteret's expression, even above any rights that might be claimed by the commons. It never, for example, specifically admitted the claim that all aids and supplies were 'the sole gift of the Commons . . . which ought not to be changed or altered by the House of Lords'. In fact on two occasions, in 1726 and 1740, the opposition peers, on the ground that their lordships were 'the hereditary guardians of the liberties and properties of the people',[3] claimed that they were as much entitled as the commons to receive a royal message for supplies to meet a national emergency.

None was more forward on the second occasion, in 1740,

---

[1] Besides the five individual impeachments under George I of Oxford, Bolingbroke, Ormonde, Strafford, and Macclesfield, seven rebel lords were impeached after the '15. See below, p. 163. The single impeachment under George II was of Lord Lovat in 1747 who was tried separately from the other rebel lords. See below, p. 256.

[2] Hanbury Williams made this point in 'Old England's Te Deum' addressed to the king, when he wrote 'The Holy Bench of Bishops throughout the land doth acknowledge thee . . .'.

[3] *P.H.* viii. 518. This phrase was the earl of Strafford's in 1726.

than Carteret, a peer almost from his birth, to assert the lords' privileges in their extreme form. He called on the house[1] 'to reassume and exercise its ancient right of being his Majesty's great and chief council. . . . My lords, we must enquire; the whole kingdom expects it at our hands. . . . I have not learned from old books, but in this House I have learned . . . from my lord Halifax, my lord Somers, my lord Cowper [i.e. the giants of the house of lords' palmiest days] I have learned that we sit here in three capacities . . . as a legislative council, as a jurisdictive council, and as the great council of state. In this last capacity we ought to give our advice to our sovereign upon all important occasions.' As a minister he gloried in his own 'vigorous constitution to support the fatigue of unseasonable hours' when defending the king's measures in the small hours of the morning in 'His Majesty's great and chief council'; and rejoiced that 'a spirit of virtue and liberty [was] beginning to prevail among the young lords of this House', keen in initiating debates. He claimed at least an equal duty with the house of commons 'to examine any position relating to the public security'; and when a message even on supply sent to the commons was not also sent to the lords, 'if such things are over-looked,' he thundered, 'this House will come to be an empty room with a great coal fire, a few bishops and two judges and the Lords walking into the court of Requests to know what Message hath been sent to the Commons separately'.

Debates conducted in this spirit by some of the most influential men in the country, with a display of classic eloquence very different from the conversational, almost casual, tone in which the peers of today usually conduct their business, could not be ignored even by the most powerful minister. At that time, too, though ministers could generally carry measures or resolutions of which they approved by a majority in the house of lords, a minority had an effective method of elaborating and making known their arguments against the decision of the majority by written protests, recorded in the journals. These protests are not only the most authoritative evidence for succeeding generations of the course of debate, on one side at any

---

[1] [Professor Williams has in the remainder of this paragraph conflated a number of Carteret's speeches of 1740 with the addition of one phrase from a speech of 1744. The passages can be found in *P.H.* xi. 451, 468, 631, 682–3, 926, and xiii. 551. C.H.S.]

rate, but at the time were used as a means of influencing public opinion. For, despite standing orders to the contrary, they were not infrequently published by the protesting lords themselves, whereas the majority had no such effective method for making known their point of view.[1]

The house of commons was certainly more catholic in the interests it represented than the house of lords, but even there the great landowners had a large share, direct or indirect, in its composition. The eighty English county members, elected on the comparatively wide 40s. freehold qualification,[2] often claimed for themselves to be the truest representatives of popular opinion; but this view is subject to large reservations. The mere fact that the voting was open created caution in voters dependent for their living or for favours on the great men who could ascertain how they voted. Few voters indeed were not susceptible to influence from local magnates, bishops, and local clergy or government patrons, and so they felt their independence restricted. The candidates for election were generally fixed upon by small cliques of local magnates and country gentlemen; often indeed one of the local families, such as the Pelhams of Sussex or the Courtenays of Devon, held an almost prescriptive right to provide one of the county members. Such, too, was the expense of organizing and corrupting the comparatively large county electorates, that, except in years of acute controversy such as 1734, amicable compromises between conflicting claims were frequent, and contested elections rare. At the same time it is certainly true that the county members as a whole did represent the local feeling of the country gentlemen. They almost invariably belonged to the county they represented and had its interests at heart; and, being proud of their local connexions, had little to ask of the government and on most questions took an independent line. Their type can best be understood, not from the chronicles of the keen politicians such as Hervey, Walpole, Dodington, and their like, but from the coarse, unvarnished descriptions, redolent of the soil, of such angular, self-sufficient country squires and parsons as are to be found in Fielding, Smollet, or even Sterne. Their prime

---

[1] Much useful information has been collected on the house of lords by A. S. Turberville, *The House of Lords in the Eighteenth Century*, 1927. For the paragraph above see particularly pp. 21–23 and 27–29.

[2] This qualification included leaseholds for life, rent charges, &c. See E. Porritt, *Unreformed House of Commons*, 2 vols., 1903, i. 22–23, and Namier, l.c., p. 82.

interests were local, their estates, their dependants, their duties as country justices, and not least their dogs and horses, their hunting and shooting; so they were not very regular attendants at Westminster unless some especially important matter was toward. It was only a Walpole who was able to bring these country gentlemen as a body to Westminster to reject the Peerage Bill by telling them that unless they did so they would lose all chance of joining the exclusive caste of peers; or a Pitt to inspire them with a nobler zeal for public affairs and persuade them to desert 'their hounds and their horses, preferring for once their parliamentary duty'.[1]

The borough members did on the whole represent wider interests. They also reckoned many of the landed gentry in their number, but in addition there were merchants and lawyers, shipowners, contractors, officers of the army and navy, government officials, representatives of the big corporations such as the East India and the South Sea Companies, and wealthy adventurers like old Thomas Pitt who regarded a seat in the house as a good investment. But they did not represent wide constituencies. In 1760 there were only twenty-two boroughs that had more than 1,000 voters, and it has been estimated that the total electorate of the 203 cities and boroughs in England was no more than 85,000.[2] Nor did the great majority of these borough members represent anything more than their personal interests or those of their patrons. A few of the larger constituencies, such as the City, Westminster, Bristol, Liverpool, returned members to represent the civic interests; and even there it was generally found useful to have at least one member chosen for his ability through ministerial connexions to secure contracts or commercial advantages for the town. The smaller boroughs had a bewildering variety of electoral systems; election by the corporation, by freemen of the borough, by those paying a poor-rate, or by burgage-tenants, systems having this at least in common that they lent themselves readily to bribery and gerrymandering methods. Certain small boroughs were frankly the property, for electoral purposes, of patrons who could sell or give the representation to whomsoever they pleased.

[1] Richard Glover, *Memoirs*, &c., quoted in Basil Williams, *W. Pitt, Earl of Chatham*, i. 292.
[2] See Namier, op. cit., pp. 100 and 102. The whole of his chapter on the electoral structure of England is relevant.

The influence of the ministry in elections was another factor
to be reckoned with in the composition of the house of commons.
In the first place the forty-five members for Scotland were
elected on such a narrow basis[1] that it was easy for the ministry,
as in the case of the sixteen representative peers, to be assured
of at least a majority among them. Ministers also had exceptional means of influencing elections in England. All of them
belonged to the class with useful local connexions, and many
of them, like Newcastle, had one or more pocket boroughs to
which they could nominate the members: it was indeed more
to his boroughs than to his powers of intrigue that Bubb Dodington owed his importance and even for a time held a post in
the ministry. Moreover the wide patronage at the disposal of
the more important ministers was a valuable electoral asset.
The great number of places in the dockyards or in the customs
or excise, especially in the largely represented southern counties, were normally used to secure amenable voters. In the disposal of ecclesiastical patronage account was almost invariably
taken of the recipient's political views: while to secure the
goodwill of the electoral magnates in counties or boroughs there
were valuable sinecures or grants from the civil list or the secret
service fund[2] to be disposed of. All that was needed was to have
one man to canalize these various sources of influence and direct
them to the one end of securing government majorities; and
during this whole period successive ministers were fortunate in
having that one man in the duke of Newcastle, who, whatever
his other shortcomings, was a genius at electoral management.
He had the initial advantages of great personal wealth, which
he spent lavishly in the whig interest, the control of seven
boroughs, and a decisive voice in the choice of candidates for
at least four counties, besides influence in many other counties
and boroughs through his wide family connexions; and as time
went on, the lay and clerical patronage which his colleagues were
content to leave with him.[3] Above all he had an intense delight in organizing, down to the minutest details, electioneering

---

[1] See below, pp. 271–2.

[2] [The value of this fund should not be exaggerated; Namier, op. cit., p. 290,
concluded that it was 'a mere supplement to places and other open favours'.
C.H.S.]

[3] [See Namier, op. cit., p. 13, on Newcastle's political influence and in particular
on its predominantly 'official' nature derived from his position as a minister of the
Crown. C.H.S.]

campaigns not only in his own territories but also wherever he or his colleagues could exercise pressure through their friends or by the judicious use of ministerial rewards and punishments. In every election from the first in George I's reign in 1715 to the first in George III's, forty-six years later, he took a prominent part, not only in his own special counties, Sussex, Nottinghamshire, Yorkshire, and Lincolnshire, but soon as general agent for the government throughout the country. As early as 1719, when he was only twenty-six, he was consulted as a high authority on electoral prospects by Stanhope; and even then was so confident of being able to ensure a majority as to discountenance Stanhope's unfortunate proposal to extend the Septennial Act. His chief triumph was perhaps the election of 1734, when the ministry entered the contest under the shadows of Walpole's failure with his excise scheme, in spite of which Newcastle's unflagging industry in the constituencies during a year of preparation was rewarded by a comfortable majority for the ministers.[1]

But though a powerful and well-connected minister like Newcastle, with ample means of patronage and persuasion at command, was always able to secure a majority at elections in favour of the predominant whig views, and subsequently to influence members by favours and pensions, it must not be imagined that the house of commons was a merely subservient assembly. The ties of party were much less tightly drawn in those days than today, and, apart from the 'country party' already referred to as proud of their independence and inclined to take a line of their own on important questions, the ministerial majority was not one compact body but a conglomeration of groups apt at times to be fissiparous. The great art of government as understood by Walpole and his friends and successors was to keep in a good temper the Bedford group, the young Patriot group, and such bands of jackals as came to the call of Dodington and his likes; but occasionally one or

---

[1] I have given an account of Newcastle's part in this typical election campaign in *English Historical Review*, xii. 448 ff. For the election of 1727 see L. B. Realey, *Early Opposition to Sir R. Walpole*, Lawrence, Kansas, 1931, pp. 226–32, and for Newcastle's activities in it H. Nulle, *Journal of Modern History* (U.S.A.), Mar. 1937, and in that of 1741 see C. Perkins, 'Electioneering in Eighteenth-Century England', *Quarterly Journal of University of Dakota*, Jan. 1923. [Professor Williams's work on the election of 1734, which was completed more than sixty years ago, has now been largely superseded. C.H.S.]

more of these groups would break away and cause difficulties. Moreover when really momentous issues came up, on which the country felt strongly, such as the Peerage Bill, the Excise Bill, the Spanish war of 1739, and the management of the Seven Years war, no electoral devices or private persuasion of members were of avail. On such issues the house of commons showed a sturdy independence and even a sensitiveness to public opinion not common with the cast-iron majorities of later days. The debates were pitched at a high level, debates in which argument really told and of which the issue could hardly be predicted till the actual division. In a word, though the house of commons of this period cannot be called truly representative of the whole population, it could rise to a sense of responsibility worthy of its claims to independence.

This responsibility of parliament, and especially of the house of commons as the dominating power in the constitution, cannot be better illustrated than by the fact that from 1714 onwards the royal veto on bills passed by both houses ceased to be exercised. In the Stuart days such veto was hardly needed by the kings, since they had a reserve force for exercising their will against that of parliament in the dispensing and suspending powers they claimed. But after the Revolution, since nothing in the Bill of Rights or the Act of Settlement specifically impaired the right of veto, its use by the first two sovereigns under the new dispensation was never questioned. William III exercised the royal veto on several occasions and Anne once, in 1707, on a Scottish Militia Bill; but this was the last instance. The saying, 'The King can do no wrong' signified to the Stuart kings that they were above the law; with the development of the Revolution theory it had come by 1714 to mean that the king in his official capacity can do nothing at all except on the responsibility of ministers holding the confidence of parliament and particularly of the house of commons. Thus, although the king still appointed his ministers, the house of commons had in effect gained the right of a negative voice on their tenure of office; and in these circumstances it was obviously absurd to expect any minister to take responsibility for a royal veto on a bill passed by parliamentary majorities.[1]

[1] [Professor Williams seems here to exaggerate the extent of parliamentary control over ministers. For a discussion of this point see R. Pares in *Eng. Hist. Rev.* lv. 136 sqq. and, more sympathetic to Professor Williams's view, J. B. Owen, *Rise of the Pelhams*, pp. 35–40. C.H.S.]

But the growing interest of the general public in parliamentary proceedings found little response in either house; indeed both lords and commons took active steps to suppress the means of satisfying it by forbidding reports of their proceedings. Although at election times peers and candidates for the lower house professed great deference to the electors' views, at other times they regarded themselves as the unfettered judges of the public interest. Pulteney in a debate of 1738 declared that 'to print or publish the speeches of gentlemen in the House looks very like making them accountable without doors for what they say within'; a crude expression of the same opinion clothed later by Burke in more majestic language, 'Your representative owes you', he told the electors of Bristol,[1] 'not his industry only but his judgement; and he betrays, instead of serving you, if he sacrifices it to your opinion. . . . Parliament is a *deliberative* assembly of *one* nation, with *one* interest,—that of the whole; where, not local purposes, not local prejudices ought to guide, but the general good, resulting from the general reason of the whole.' Strangers were admitted only on sufferance to the debates and on the objection of a single member could be expelled. In 1738 two duchesses and three other peeresses had the doors of the house of lords shut in their faces during an important debate on the Spanish question; in this case, however, the ladies would take no denial and by a stratagem made their way triumphantly into the house, luckier than the peers' sons and members of the house of commons ignominiously hustled out in 1770 by the peers themselves. So great, however, was the interest of the public in parliamentary proceedings that Boyer in his *Political State of Great Britain*, and the *London Magazine*, *Gentleman's Magazine*, and *Historical Register* provided reports of important debates. But since such reports were treated by both houses as a breach of privilege they had to be made up surreptitiously by Johnson and others and the identity of the speakers decently veiled under fictitious names; nor indeed were keen controversialists like Chesterfield averse on occasion to sending out versions of their speeches in pamphlet form. In 1747 indeed the house of lords brought up to their bar the editors of the two magazines for reporting debates in the house and terrified them so effectually that thenceforward until 1770 the records of lords' debates are singularly meagre.

[1] Speech at conclusion of poll, 1774, Burke's *Works*, Bohn edn., i. 447.

There was indeed a danger that parliament, and especially the house of commons, by the immunity from criticism against itself and the extension of the privilege that it claimed might become almost as irresponsible an authority as the Stuart kings. In 1721, for example, the house of commons committed to Newgate the printer of a Jacobite pamphlet without a trial and by simple resolution, though no privilege of theirs was involved. It expected a man censured by itself to receive the Speaker's reprimand on his knees as a mark of respect to its authority.[1] Even its own composition was to a certain degree decided by the majority in the commons, since from 1727 to 1770 disputed returns were decided by the whole house on party lines: indeed Walpole made a defeat on an election petition his excuse for resigning in 1742. Fortunately by 1770 the scandal of such party decisions in deciding on the electors' wishes had become so great that a more impartial tribunal than the whole house was substituted.[2] About the same time the difficulties experienced in the Wilkes case and of printers brought up for breach of privilege led shortly to the abandonment both of superannuated claims about the publication of debates and of the illegal pretensions of the commons to interfere with the rights of electors.

Although the king still exercised, as we have seen, considerable freedom in the choice or dismissal of his ministers, this freedom was limited by the implied or explicit sanction of a parliamentary majority. George I appointed his first ministers, but he could not have kept them in office had not his first parliament of 1715 supported them; he dismissed Townshend in 1717, but the strength of Townshend and of his brother-in-law Walpole, who had thereupon resigned, was so great in parliament that he was obliged to reinstate them three years later. Carteret was a favourite minister of both George I and George II, but he had no parliamentary following, and both kings in turn had to get rid of him owing to the opposition of those

[1] The house found itself in a quandary in 1751 when the Hon. Alexander Murray refused to kneel to receive his sentence of imprisonment, saying that 'when I have committed a crime, I kneel to God for pardon; but knowing my own innocence, I can kneel to no one else'. The house accordingly committed him to prison for the rest of the session, but when in the following session the case was brought up again, it was rather relieved to find that he had absconded to the Continent. The story is told in Coxe, *Pelham*, ii. 182–6, 199–202.

[2] See *Oxford History of England*, xii. 139.

ministers on whose parliamentary majority they had to depend. Pitt was long kept out of responsible office partly by Newcastle's jealousy, partly owing to the king's prejudice against him, but finally had to be given power because the house of commons was becoming unmanageable without him.[1]

Ministries of today derive their strength first from their corporate responsibility for the conduct of affairs, and secondly as representing the views of a definite and homogeneous party in the house of commons. During this period ministries had little corporate responsibility, nor could they, as a rule, rely on the support of a homogeneous party. Each minister was responsible solely for his own department to the king, and indirectly to the house of commons: he had no concern with the administration of other ministers nor they with his. Such a system was more practicable then that it would be today, because the number of ministers whose functions were essential in carrying out a general policy was much more restricted, being practically limited to the first lord of the treasury, the two secretaries of state, and the lord chancellor. The first lord was obviously important, since financial policy depended entirely on him, especially as, during most of this period—the twenty-one years of Walpole's ministry and the eleven of Pelham's—he was also chancellor of the exchequer. The lord chancellor kept his colleagues straight on matters of law and legislation and the legal limitations of their functions. But the chief burden of government fell on the two secretaries of state;[2] for they alone were the source of executive orders. From them came all instructions to envoys abroad, to the lord lieutenant of Ireland, to colonial governors; not a ship could be moved, not a regiment march without orders from them to the admiralty or the military authorities; they were the sole link between the centre and such local authorities as lords lieutenant, justices of the peace, and mayors of cities and boroughs; and in emergencies they could themselves issue warrants and examine witnesses.[3] Other

---

[1] [See above, p. 30, n. 1. Professor Williams once again appears to underestimate the extent to which the king's chief ministers in quiet times managed parliament simply by reason of their position as ministers. C.H.S.]

[2] For three short periods there was a third secretary for Scotland; the duke of Montrose from Sept. 1714 to Aug. 1715; the duke of Roxburgh Dec. 1716 to Aug. 1725; and the marquess of Tweeddale from Feb. 1742 to Jan. 1746. It will be noted that, whenever Scottish affairs became specially important or difficult, they were transferred to the other two secretaries. See below, p. 272.

[3] For the very close touch between the secretaries of state and the local

ministers derived their importance not so much from their offices as from their personality, experience in affairs, wisdom in counsel, or even influence at court, such as Granville as lord president of the council, Hervey as lord privy seal, Anson as first lord of the admiralty, or Grafton as lord chamberlain. How little corporate responsibility was felt by ministers is evident from the fact that they sometimes took opposing sides in debate. On the Marriage Bill the secretary at war, Fox, and the chancellor, Hardwicke, attacked one another bitterly; Fox again coalesced with Mr. Paymaster Pitt against their colleague Robinson, a secretary of state; Legge when chancellor of the exchequer refused to pay the subsidy negotiated with Hesse-Cassel by his immediate chief Newcastle, and Pitt when secretary of state attacked Legge in turn on the budget.[1] Nor did changes in the ministry usually affect any but those immediately concerned. The resignations forced by Walpole on Carteret and Townshend, and the resignations or dismissals of Granville (as Carteret had by then become), Bedford, Sandwich, Robinson, and Fox under the Pelhams caused no sympathetic resignations. In fact when Newcastle and Hardwicke persuaded nearly the whole ministry to resign with them in 1746 they regarded it as a quite exceptional triumph over the king.[2]

A great element of strength in modern ministries is in the office of prime minister, who is not only the acknowledged head of the cabinet, but also the head and chief representative of the party of the house of commons which keeps that ministry in power. The slow evolution of the office of prime minister during the eighteenth century is due partly to the want of a clear definition of parties, partly to the absolute responsibility of each minister for his own office during most of that period, and also no doubt to the popular fear of substituting for an arbitrary king one too-powerful subject. The term 'prime minister' or even 'premier' is indeed heard, first in the reign

authorities, especially in times of danger or disturbances, see P.R.O., S.P. Dom. 35. i, and ibid., Entry Book 117 for the period 1714–15. Constant reports are sent in to them from all over the country and they send specific orders about searching or arresting suspects, calling out the armed forces to suppress riots or disturbances, &c. See also Williams, *Stanhope*, pp. 180–3, for further details. See below, pp. 55–56.

[1] See Basil Williams, *W. Pitt, Earl of Chatham*, ii. 52–57. (In subsequent notes this book is referred to as *Chatham*.)

[2] For a discussion of Newcastle's exploitation of the idea of collective resignations see R. Pares, *George III and the Politicians*, pp. 95–97.

of Anne of Godolphin and Marlborough, and more commonly as a term of opprobrium to Walpole, who in fact more nearly approached being a prime minister in the modern sense. But, so far as can be ascertained, in Pitt's great ministry neither he, nor Newcastle as first lord of the treasury, was ever called prime minister. Nor indeed did the resignation of the real head of the ministry, in the case of Pitt, involve a disruption of that ministry.[1]

But although the collective responsibility of ministries was hardly recognized as it is today, the growth of parliamentary criticism and interference with the actions of the executive since the beginning of the seventeenth century had long impelled the king to secure himself by seeking the collective advice of ministers more in touch with parliament than himself. Even Charles I had tried, in the early days of the Long Parliament, to protect himself against parliamentary criticism by forming such a body of advisers; Charles II had made several such attempts, notably through the Cabal ministry and by Temple's abortive scheme. William III had gone a step farther when, contrary to his own inclination, which was to pick out ministers to advise him irrespective of their political views, he had been constrained to follow Sunderland's advice and accept a ministry almost entirely composed of men in sympathy with the majority of the house of commons. Queen Anne's first ministry was composed of tories and whigs, who could more easily co-operate since the dominating question on which both then agreed was the war with France. But, as the parties gradually became divided on this issue, she was forced in 1708 to consent to a purely whig administration, since by that time Godolphin and Marlborough, originally tories, had found that for their war policy they could depend only on the whigs. Similarly in 1710, when the tories had a majority, partly on the church question but chiefly on the issue of peace, a tory ministry was formed without any whig admixture.

With the development of ministries more or less homogeneous politically, the old function of the privy council as the sovereign's chief consultative body became superseded. For the

[1] For discussions on the use of the term 'prime minister' in this period see Michael, *The Beginnings of the Hanoverian Dynasty*, i. 100, 163, and Williams, *Stanhope*, pp. 254–7, and *The Times Literary Supplement*, 6, 13, and 20 Mar. 1930.

privy council, being composed of men of varying political views, became obviously unfitted to decide on measures put forward by advisers of the Crown tending more and more to belong to one party only. At the same time it was still necessary to co-ordinate the activities of ministers, each independent in his own department, and to formulate some general policy for the administration. The system adopted therefore by William III and his successor was to substitute for the privy council as an advisory body on policy a committee of the Crown's chief ministers and officers of state for the time being, while the privy council gradually became, as it is today, a body used merely to ratify formally decisions already taken. The new committee, entitled the cabinet council or cabinet, was still presided over by the sovereign, and contained all the great officers of state, including the archbishop of Canterbury, the lord chamberlain, the lord steward, master of the horse, groom of the stole, master general of the ordnance, besides the purely political ministers, the treasurer or first lord of the treasury, secretaries of state, first lord of the admiralty, chancellor, president of the council, lord privy seal, and occasionally, at the will of the sovereign, peers without office whose advice was regarded as useful. Thus after the fall of Walpole, Pulteney (Lord Bath) though holding no office, was 'of the Cabinet Council' until 1746 after his abortive attempt to form a ministry, and during Pitt's great ministry both Hardwicke, no longer lord chancellor and with-out any office of state, and Lord Mansfield, the lord chief justice of the King's Bench, attended cabinet meetings. The discussions were informal and no record was kept even of de-cisions except in a note made by one of the secretaries of state. Occasionally also it was found advantageous to summon to attend the cabinet meetings others besides the regular members when matters concerning them were being discussed. Thus in 1706 we hear of a cabinet council under the queen's presidency to which General Stanhope was summoned to give his views and receive orders on the Spanish campaign; and in 1740 Admiral of the Fleet Sir John Norris was 'called in as an auxiliary when anything was under deliberation relative to our present mari-time war with Spain'.[1] But although policy was settled at cabinet councils the cabinet still assumed no corporate re-sponsibility for its advice or for the measures taken on that

[1] *Lord Hervey's Memoirs* (Sedgwick), iii. 925.

advice. Acts of administration were still solely within the control of the individual ministers concerned, subject to their responsibility to the Crown and their liability to account for their actions to parliament.

How gradual was the recognition of a cabinet council's place in the constitution and of its exact functions may be seen from a debate in the house of lords as late as 1753. The debate arose on the examination by the cabinet of two witnesses, Fawcett and Murray, in regard to difficulties about the education of the young prince of Wales. In this debate the duke of Bedford declared that 'a cabinet council is not recognized in our constitution; it is a state-expedient borrowed from France. In their own persons only, these lords [i.e. members of cabinet] are respectable.' Against this view Lord Chancellor Hardwicke justified the cabinet's legality on the ground that its 'existence was on record in the Journals of Parliament'; and he was supported by Lord Bath, who declared it 'perfectly constitutional and . . . its proceedings . . . not unprecedented', quoting an instance of his own examination by a cabinet council under Queen Anne.[1]

Thus the cabinet, like so many other important institutions in the English political system, began quite informally; and even today it has no formal recognition in the law, unless the establishment of a cabinet secretariat may imply such formal recognition. Its membership was never fixed, nor was attendance of all its members ever expected or indeed needed. The great household officials, the archbishop, and even some of the political ministers rarely attended the meetings; on the other hand the treasurer, or first lord of the treasury as the case might be, the secretaries, the chancellor, and generally the lord president, as representing the working and responsible members of the ministry, were nearly always present; and the king naturally presided over what had become his chief advisory council. But already in Anne's time the more influential ministers were beginning to find that preparation for the solemn cabinet sessions in the queen's presence could usefully be made by private consultation among themselves; and such small *conciliabula* were recognized to the extent of being called committee of council, lords of the committee, or simply councils.

---

[1] For this debate see Coxe, *Pelham*, ii. 259–63, relying largely on Horace Walpole's *Memoirs*; see also p. 341 below.

Sometimes too policy was discussed at still more informal gatherings at Mr. Harley's house and elsewhere, attended by such unofficial advisers as Swift. But in neither case are such meetings to be confused with the now established cabinet councils in the royal presence.

Soon after the accession of the Hanoverian dynasty, however, the more formal cabinet meetings in the royal presence were replaced by the purely ministerial meetings. At first indeed George I followed the practice of William and Anne. Nine days after landing in England he presided over a meeting of the new whig cabinet, and he may have done so eight or nine times within the next four years, notably when Wyndham's arrest was sanctioned in 1715 and in the following year when foreign troops were summoned to suppress the rebellion. But after 1718 he entirely ceased attendance: he could not understand discussions in English, few of his ministers could express themselves readily in French, only one perhaps in German, so, to the mutual advantage of both sides, the cabinet ministers discussed their policy in English by themselves and presented their decision, baldly stated in French, to the king for his approval. George II, who understood and could express himself in English, had, when guardian of the realm in 1716, presided at cabinet meetings, but when he came to the throne in 1727 was content to accept a now established practice and, except on one or two special occasions, to follow his father's example. Constitutionally the change was important. As was pointed out by the acute Prussian envoy Bonnet, since the king never heard the pros and cons of a policy debated but merely his ministers' decisions, his power was materially diminished and theirs correspondingly increased.[1]

The want of formality in cabinet meetings, all the more apparent when the king ceased to attend them, made it easier for the more influential ministers to dispense with the services of their less important colleagues when discussing the most important business. The full cabinets of the Georges, though the actual work of government was immeasurably smaller than it is today, were hardly less numerous than those of the twentieth

[1] See Michael, iii. 559 sqq. [Professor Williams here remains loyal to the traditional explanation for the withdrawal of the monarch from cabinet meetings, an explanation which Sir Lewis Namier characterized as 'a crude and . . . exploded legend'; see below, p. 40, n. 1. C.H.S.]

century, varying from a membership of thirteen in 1717 to seventeen in 1757. In that year the duke of Newcastle gives a list of the full cabinet council, including the archbishop of Canterbury, lord chancellor, lord president, lord privy seal, lord steward, lord chamberlain, chancellor of Scotland, master of the ordnance, two secretaries of state, chancellor of the exchequer, lord lieutenant of Ireland, lord chief justice, first lord of the treasury, first lord of the admiralty, keeper of the great wardrobe, master of the horse, and groom of the stole.[1] Obviously such a large body, containing such non-political persons as the archbishop, the lord chief justice, and six court officials, was little qualified to give a judgement on the conduct of the war, or on foreign policy, normally the chief matters of business before the early eighteenth-century cabinets; and its functions appear to have been chiefly to hear the king's speech before its delivery to parliament or to advise the king on death sentences. Accordingly the custom grew up for a small body of effective ministers—the first lord, the two secretaries, the chancellor, and such others as the lord president, when Granville held the office, and any other minister whose department was concerned—to meet regularly and come to decisions which might or might not be submitted *pro forma* to rarer meetings of the full cabinet. Indeed by the middle of the century Newcastle had elaborated a definite system of an inner cabinet or *conciliabulum*,[2] as he called it, which practically decided on policy, while membership of the outer cabinet became little more than an honorary distinction. In December 1754, for example, Newcastle, needing Henry Fox's help in the house of commons, but fearful lest he should become too powerful, admitted him only to the outer cabinet. The following September, however, he was forced to make him secretary of state, a post carrying with it a seat in the inner cabinet. But it would be a mistake to find in the distinction between outer and inner cabinet anything more than an informal arrangement for temporary convenience. The cabinet itself was, and still is, a body with no legal powers; it always was in the past, and no doubt still is, a body liable to be influenced in its decisions by the result of

---

[1] B.M., Add. MS. 32997, f. 146, quoted in *Amer. Hist. Review*, Oct. 1913, by E. R. Turner, who does not include the keeper of the great wardrobe.

[2] Other designations were the 'Efficient' Cabinet, the 'King's Principal Servants', 'the Lords whom the king entrusts with his private correspondence'.

preliminary consultations in private between a few of its more important members.[1]

During the reigns of the first two Georges special arrangements had to be made for carrying on the government of the country during those kings' frequent absences in Hanover. Excluding the period between 1 August and 18 September 1714, before George I came over to assume his English Crown, these kings were absent from the realm, during the forty-six years of their reigns, on nineteen occasions for periods generally of about six months.[2] On one such occasion George I appointed his son the prince of Wales 'guardian of the realm', and during Queen Caroline's lifetime she was appointed four times to the same office. During the other fourteen absences a council of regency entitled 'lords justices' was substituted for the single guardian. These lords justices were composed of the whole cabinet with the addition, on the last occasion in 1755, of the duke of Cumberland. The powers of the guardian or lords justices were strictly limited: they could make no treaties or alliances with foreign powers on their own authority, nor could they grant titles or pensions or make civil and military appointments without special leave from the absent king. In fact one can trace in George I's and II's limitations on the regent's authority the same anxiety lest their personal power should be diminished as was displayed in the Hanoverian 'Order of Government'.[3] The conduct of foreign affairs was always during these absences kept by the king even more stringently than usual in his own hands. He invariably took with him to Hanover a secretary of state,[4] on one occasion both; to the secretary in Hanover the English envoys at foreign courts had to send duplicates of their ordinary dispatches and their even more important private and confidential letters to him alone. Thus during the king's absence in Hanover the lords justices, i.e. the

---

[1] Notably in a recent emergency (Oct. 1938). [Professor Williams here adopts an old-fashioned view of the development of the cabinet. The division between the outer, or nominal, cabinet council and the inner 'efficient' cabinet, however informal and temporary in origin, was of lasting significance. The inner cabinet, freed of both the king and the high officers of state, was the body from which the modern cabinet derives. The nominal cabinet 'faded away until it sank into an anonymous grave'. See Namier, *In the Margin of History*, pp. 105–14. C.H.S.]

[2] George I was absent seven times and George II twelve times.

[3] See above, p. 13.

[4] On one occasion the elder Horace (or Horatio) Walpole deputized for the secretary of state.

cabinet council, were left with hardly any voice in foreign affairs unless, as in the case of the Hanau and Worms negotiations in Carteret's time, exchequer payments were involved; in fact they had little to do besides carrying on the internal administration, a light business except in times of civil strife.

These frequent absences of the two first Hanoverians abroad did not tend to the smooth working of the government. In the first place the meeting of parliament was on several critical occasions postponed owing to the absence of the king, notably in 1720 after the bursting of the South Sea Bubble; for both Georges steadily refused to allow their representatives in England to summon parliament in their absence. The absence of George II in Hanover at the very time when the young Pretender landed in Scotland in 1745 was a serious handicap to the government, and was particularly resented by the loyal population. Even in more normal times, business was apt to be delayed, owing to the length of time letters took between Hanover and England, and difficulties occurred which could easily have been removed by a few moments' personal talk between the king or the secretary in attendance and his colleagues in London. An instance of such a difficulty was the delay in London about the completion of the Triple Alliance in 1716, a delay which resulted in the break-up of the ministry and would probably not have occurred had the king and Stanhope been able to discuss the matter with Townshend and Walpole. Again, the sojourns at Hanover were a fruitful source of ministerial intrigue. At a time when the king, especially George I, was a decisive factor in foreign policy and had a considerable voice in domestic appointments, the secretary in attendance at Hanover had a great pull over his colleagues in London if he had a mind to grind his own axe; for, as Pelham told Newcastle, the way to rule the king was to attend him on his trips abroad. In 1723 the mutual jealousy of the two secretaries, Townshend and Carteret, was such that both went to Hanover with the king, leaving Walpole to perform the duties of secretary at home; but in this instance Carteret's journey profited him little, for Townshend, with the help of his powerful brother-in-law in England, entirely worsted his rival. Carteret's second journey abroad as minister in attendance, in 1743, gave him for the time being almost absolute control over foreign policy. But in the end, by the animosity this policy aroused not only among his colleagues but also in the house of commons, this journey also proved his undoing. Even Newcastle, in spite of his natural timidity at crossing the sea and sleeping in strange and unaired beds, preferred in 1748, 1750, and 1752 to risk these dangers rather than give his brother secretary a chance of pouring insidious poison into the king's ear at Hanover. In fact almost the only three periods when the king's absence did not create difficulties for the government were between 1729 and 1736; for then his capable queen, Caroline, was left guardian of the realm, and Walpole, with her support, was quite able to hold his own against any schemes that might be hatched in Hanover. But even then these prolonged absences were exceedingly unpopular in England, especially the eight months in 1736, which were spent in dalliance with Mme de Wallmoden (Lady Yarmouth). Ribald notices were posted on the gates of St. James's Palace, such as: 'It is reported that his Hanoverian Majesty designs to visit his British Dominions for three months in the Spring', and another, 'Lost or strayed out of this house, a man who left a wife and six children on the parish; whoever will give any tidings of him to the churchwardens of St. James's Parish, so he may be got again, shall receive four shillings and sixpence. N.B. This reward will not be increased, nobody judging him to deserve a Crown.' In court circles verses were handed round, such as,

> The King, this summer having spent
> Amoribus in teneris,
> Desires his loving Parliament
> To meet him Die Veneris.[1]

The first two Georges, it may be admitted, were never personally popular in England. Their highly inconvenient journeys to the beloved electorate, the twist given to our island politics by their Hanover connexion, and their gruff and ungracious demeanour to their English subjects were causes of constant complaint. Nevertheless, whatever may have been the disposition of Scotland, England never showed any inclination to send them back to Hanover; the absence of any widespread enthusiasm for the Jacobite cause in 1715, 1719, and 1745 is sufficient evidence of this. For under these Georges—perhaps

---

[1] *Hist. MSS. Comm. (Carlisle),* xv. vi. 175. George II visited Hanover between May and Sept. in 1729 and again in 1735. In 1736 he set out towards the end of May but did not return until the middle of Jan. 1737.

even because of their aloofness—the Englishman enjoyed to the full his cherished privilege of grumbling, he felt his religion to be secure, and he certainly had a greater amount of personal and political freedom than would have been the case under the alternative dynasty.

III

ENGLISH LOCAL GOVERNMENT AND THE LAW

ONE of the features which distinguished England in the eighteenth century not only from the England of today, but even from most of the other countries of Europe at the time, was the very small part taken by the central government in the local administration of the country. In France or Prussia, for example, though there may have been divergencies in local customs or even in local taxation, the king, through his intendants in the one case, or his well-organized civil service in the other, had eyes everywhere to report to him and enable him to keep a tight control over the details of local government. In the England of today, in spite of an impressive appearance of local democratic government, a constant and meticulous supervision over the local bodies' activities and expenditure is exercised by parliamentary criticism and legislation, by the treasury and by such ministers as the home secretary, the ministers of health, education, labour, transport, power, agriculture, and the president of the board of trade. But in the England of the eighteenth century the parish, the borough, and the county, the three units of local administration, were practically autonomous in the exercise of the functions imposed upon them by ancient custom, parliamentary legislation, or conciliar decree of the Tudor period. It is true that the ancient parochial self-governing institutions, as well as the chief county officials, who were appointed and could be dismissed by the Crown, had new duties imposed upon them from time to time by legislation, such as the restriction of excessive gin-drinking by the lower classes, or new methods of dealing with the poor; but in the normal exercise of their old or new functions the local authorities were left almost entirely to their own devices and the burden of carrying out parliamentary decrees was alleviated by no assistance from the central government. It would not indeed be far from the truth to say that the secretaries of state, the only ministers responsible for the internal state of the country, never interfered with local administration except in time of civil strife or rebellion.

An historical scrap-book is perhaps the best description that can be given of the various haphazard methods—they cannot be dignified with the name of a system—of local government in England during the eighteenth century. Here and there we find survivals of Anglo-Saxon customs, more frequently of officials and institutions dating from Norman or Angevin times, a strong admixture of Tudor centralizing methods with less happy experiments on the same lines by the Stuarts, and finally a reversion, as a result of Revolution principles, to something like the local autonomy, of Anglo-Saxon times. Every one of these periods provides examples of its characteristic institutions, the sheriff and shire of Anglo-Saxon times, the manor court and privileged corporation of feudal days, the justice of the peace as developed by the Tudors, the gradual concentration of local power in the close corporation of Stuart days and the continuation of this process according to the principles of aristocratic, or at least oligarchic, liberty dear to the Revolution whigs. The result is an amazing hotch-potch of authorities and conflicting institutions, on all and every one of which parliament tended periodically to impose new duties with hardly any provision for the due performance of these or any of the older functions. The astonishing thing is that these heterogeneous institutions somehow seemed to work, all the more astonishing since nearly all the officials concerned in their working were, nominally at least, unpaid, and on the whole displayed a zeal and efficiency remarkable in the half-educated class from which most of them were drawn. This is only one of many instances in our history of our conservative habit of retaining old institutions and adapting them, more or less successfully, to meet the entirely new and often more liberal needs of a progressive society.

Again just as the central government of the eighteenth century, though in form democratic, was in reality predominantly oligarchic, so in local affairs the forms of self-government to be found in the parish, the manor, the shire, and the chartered boroughs, though equally democratic in theory, resulted in the main in a government of the local oligarchies. These democratic forms may have been successful in promoting local self-consciousness and pride, but contributed little to the education of the humbler majority in the methods of self-government; nor did the Crown's power of patronage, which was great, really secure to the Crown much influence in local affairs. Even the overriding authority of the justices of the peace appointed directly by the Crown did not in practice give the central government much control over the affairs of the county.

By the eighteenth century the popular assemblies of the shire and the hundred, from which the house of commons itself may have drawn its origin, had practically disappeared, their only vestige still left in the shire being the right of the freeholders to come together to vote for their representatives in parliament. In all the 9,000 odd ecclesiastical parishes of England and Wales, on the other hand, the institutions were in theory, sometimes even in practice, democratic. Here the vestry meeting was the normal organ of government. These vestries met in the parish church, generally under the chairmanship of the parson, elected the churchwardens who were responsible for the fabric and appurtenances of the church, for the due performance of their duties by the clergy, and for the moral conduct of the parishioners; they also sanctioned the rates for these and other purposes. None but ratepayers had the right of attending vestry meetings, so that in small country parishes sometimes the only vestrymen were the squire and parson, a few farmers, and the inn-keeper, the majority of the population being labourers not liable to a rate and having no voice in the proceedings. Nor in all cases were all the ratepayers allowed to take part. For in certain districts, especially in London and the northern counties, in contrast with the more usual open vestries of all ratepayers, close or select vestries of only the chief landowners or the more influential ratepayers, either by ancient custom or by usurpation, had assumed all the functions of the local council. Moreover in many respects the autonomy of the parish had been whittled away by the overriding powers of the justices of the peace imposed by Tudor legislation which was being constantly added to in the succeeding centuries. The parish, for example, though the legal unit for the upkeep of roads in its vicinity and for the maintenance of its poor, had hardly any say in either the finance or the conduct of these activities. For both purposes the justices of the peace, not the vestry, struck the rates which the parish had to pay; again, though the vestry might suggest names for the office of surveyors of the highways, the justices appointed them, as they did the overseers of the poor, entirely on their own responsibility. Even the parish constable, charged with the arrest of village misdemeanants and lodging them, perhaps, in the stocks, was appointed either by the justices or by a manor court and in the northern counties was entitled to levy a rate for his expenses on his own authority. In spite, however, of these restrictions on their powers, there are instances, even in the eighteenth century, of public-spirited vestries in certain populous parishes, such as Liverpool and Leeds or some of those in London, assuming duties corresponding to those of an energetic municipality of modern times for the improvement and good government of the parish.

But the vestry was not the only assemblage which still dealt with local affairs. In many rural parishes and in many towns, such as Westminster and the ancient liberty of the Savoy and some even of the importance of Birmingham and Manchester, the ancient manorial court baron and court leet of feudal origin still exercised authority for certain purposes. The steward of the lord of the manor still presided at these courts, and though a jury of the principal inhabitants could propose to him candidates for such offices as those of constable, pig-ringer, ale-conner, hayward, &c., the steward made the final selection.[1] The court baron in country districts still dealt with the use of common and waste-lands and even with the rotation of crops, while the court leet, more important in manorial towns, dealt with the suppression of nuisances, enforced personal obligations, and acted as a small debts court. In certain cases the lord of the manor had either lost his rights by neglect or sold them to the freeholders of the manor, but even in those cases the ancient feudal courts often survived and carried on their functions. In such cases sometimes the parish vestry still officiated side by side with the court leet, sometimes the two were in practice merged into one body.

But these survivals of ancient democratic institutions in the vestry and the parish were to a great extent fictitious, owing to the control exercised over all the activities of the shire, with the one exception of the autonomous municipalities within it— of which more anon—by officials nominated by, and technically responsible only to, the Crown.

---

[1] This was not true of Birmingham where 'the Lord of the Manor had . . . let slip all his authority . . . except the formal presiding of his Steward'. Webb, *Local Government*, ii. 158.

These officials were the lord lieutenant, the sheriff, and above all the justices of the peace. The only county official not appointed by the Crown was the coroner, elected then, as now, by the freeholders of the county and responsible, as today, only for inquests and treasure-trove inquiries. The lord lieutenant was invariably a local magnate, usually a peer, or in a few cases a commoner belonging to one of the great county families, such as an Edgcumbe[1] for Cornwall, a Herbert for Shropshire, or a Lowther for Westmorland; with the lieutenancy he generally, though not invariably, combined the office of *Custos Rotulorum*. In the latter capacity he was supposed to preside over the quarter sessions of the justices, the successor of the old shire court, but hardly ever did, though he still appointed the one paid official of that body,[2] the clerk of the peace; as lord lieutenant he took command on an emergency of all the local forces, appointed deputy lieutenants and after 1756 the officers of the militia, and had a voice, though not so great then as today, in submitting to the Crown the names of those he recommended for the county magistracy.[3] His importance lay partly in the patronage and local influence he wielded, partly in his duty of summoning and commanding the local forces in time of civil tumult or rebellion. As a rule the lords lieutenant took these duties lightly, but occasions might arise when they became of importance. Thus during 1715 we find the young Lord Carteret and the duke of Newcastle, recently appointed lords lieutenant of Devon and Nottingham respectively, going down to their counties on the look-out for signs of rebellion.[4] Later in the century Pitt had to rely largely on the sympathetic co-operation of the lords lieutenant for the organization and smooth-working of the ancient territorial force, previously moribund, which he revived by his Militia Act of 1757. A zealous parliamentarian such as the duke of Newcastle, who was lord lieutenant of Middlesex as well as of Nottingham, and for two years of Sussex also, found plenty of scope for his electioneering activi-

[1] Edgcumbe had been raised to the peerage in 1742 before he became lord lieutenant of Cornwall in 1744.
[2] The clerk of the peace had no salary but was entitled to 'customary fees'. See Webb, i. 304 and 503.
[3] See below, p. 50.
[4] Although Carteret was active in the West Country during the '15 his appointment as lord lieutenant of Devon did not come until 1716. See Ballantyne, *Carteret*, pp. 25–26.

ties in the patronage and influence he had from his office in those counties. Accordingly care was taken to appoint as lords lieutenant only those likely to support the political views of the ministry in power and to remove those guilty of flagrant opposition in parliament. During William's and Anne's reigns several lords lieutenant were superseded for political reasons, as were several who held tory views on the accession of the Hanoverians. But no such drastic removal of these officials was ever seen as in the early years of George III when Newcastle, Rockingham, Temple, and several others were summarily replaced by those more sympathetic to the new dispensation.

By the eighteenth century the sheriff had long been shorn of the great power he possessed during the Norman kings' reigns as the king's permanent representative in the county; and it was now only an annual office. During this year the sheriff's main functions were honorary and expensive, such as attending and entertaining the judges on circuit; his remaining effective duty of presiding over the county court was left to an under sheriff. He was still legally entitled to call up the *posse comitatus* of the county, i.e. all able-bodied males over fifteen years of age except peers and clergy, to suppress tumults and arrest dangerous criminals; but even during the rebellions of 1715 and 1745 no use seems to have been made of this right.

Compared, however, with the lord lieutenant and the sheriff, mainly ornamental in their functions, in normal times the chief organs of local government were the justices of the peace. Their effective institution as judges in petty cases dates from the time of Edward III; but their real importance begins with the Tudors.[1] To their petty jurisdiction in the counties were added numerous functions which brought them into closer touch with the privy council. They acted as intelligence officers to report the state of their districts to that body and as local agents to transmit its orders and ensure the due observance of the laws about religion and good order. They also had definite administrative duties imposed upon them with regard to the upkeep of the highways and the new poor laws. With the decay of conciliar government in the course of the seventeenth century they still retained, in addition to their judical functions, their administrative duties, and in that and the eighteenth century were

---

[1] For the functions of the justices of the peace in Elizabethan times see vol. viii in this series, pp. 212–13 (2nd edn.).

continually having new such duties imposed upon them by legislation; but by that time they had ceased, except, as noted below, in times of civil disturbance, to have such close touch with the central government and become virtually uncontrolled in the exercise of their functions. Thus instead of being mainly agents of an almost autocratic government, they acquired virtual independence as the local oligarchies of the districts. This oligarchic tendency was still more emphasized by legislation of 1732 and 1744 which raised the qualification for justices of the peace from an estate of the value of £20 per annum to one of £100,[1] and by a relaxation of the rule that one of every two justices acting together should be learned in the law.[2] Commissions of the peace were periodically issued for each county by the lord chancellor when he wanted to add new justices to the roll, or to remove existing justices not considered suitable.[3] The recommendations for additions to the list were still made to the chancellor by ministers, local M.P.s, or county magnates, and it was not till the end of the eighteenth century that the recommendations were left exclusively to the lords lieutenant. How strictly social rank as well as the necessary qualification was considered by the chancellor may be seen in Hardwicke's refusal, even on Walpole's request, to include the organist of St. James's, Piccadilly, in the commission for Middlesex on the ground that the other J.P.s might object to consorting with a mere organist.[4] By the end of the century the power of the justices had been further entrenched and it was laid down as a rule by Lord Eldon that once a justice a man was always a justice and could not be removed from the commission except on legal conviction of an offence.

In the eighteenth century the power of these justices in urban as well as rural districts was immense, since they combined

[1] These acts were primarily intended to check the abuses resulting from the appointment of impecunious justices. See Webb, i. 324 n.

[2] The modern use of the word *quorum* arises from the phrase in the Elizabethan commissions of the peace *quorum aliquem vestrum* (i.e. those learned in the law) *unum esse volumus*. [The *quorum* clause had become 'a mere form' as early as 1689— all justices being named in each commission as members of it. Professor Williams seems here, as elsewhere, to exaggerate the conscious movement towards oligarchy. See Webb, i. 302–3. C.H.S.]

[3] See in Campbell, *Lives of Lord Chancellors*, iv. 373–7, an interesting minute from Lord Cowper to the king explaining the principles which guided him in appointing or removing the justices. This practice did not continue; 'after the first quarter of the 18th century, it became extremely rare'. Webb, i. 380.

[4] Webb, i. 325 n.

administrative with judicial functions, thus signally refuting Montesquieu's contemporary theory of the complete separation of such powers in the British constitution. When the county justices met in quarter sessions they could give orders and strike rates for the repairing of bridges, the upkeep of jails and houses of correction, they could fix wages, license trades, deal with disorderly houses, and make levies for parish needs; there was no appeal from their decisions in these matters, nor had the general body of county inhabitants or ratepayers any say in what concerned them so closely. The same court also dealt judicially with cases of felony and even treason, and also with civil cases, aided by a jury for which the qualification in England had been raised in 1693 from £4 to £10 annual value of land.[1] In the special sessions of the hundreds the justices of each hundred in the county had entire control, after 1729, of licences for public houses and other local duties such as, in 1745, that of recruiting men for the army; and judicially they dealt with non-jury cases. But the daily lives of the villagers or townspeople were probably more affected by the power of the petty sessions of two justices or even of the single J.P.s. The petty sessions appointed the overseers of the poor and the surveyors of highways, and could order the removal of those likely to be charged on the rates from the district and see that every villager provided his quota of forced labour on the roads;[2] they fixed the parish poor rate and audited the local officials' accounts; but any two justices not even belonging to the district could be used for these purposes, so that no regular system was current. This strange tribunal also controlled the licensing of public houses until 1729, when owing to the abuses of its administration this duty was transferred to the special sessions. Sometimes, too, quarter sessions delegated to these petty sessions the duty of dealing with gaming and disorderly houses and of suppressing nuisances: they also regularly dealt summarily with minor offences; while if a third justice was added they could even sentence a man to seven years' transportation for rick-burning.[3]

---

[1] The qualification in Wales was raised to £6 at the same time. These new qualifications were at first imposed for short periods and regularly re-enacted. They were made perpetual in 1733.

[2] In fact the statutory forced labour for roads was more honoured in the breach than the observance. See S. and B. Webb, *Story of King's Highway*, pp. 28–30.

[3] This was by an act of Charles II's reign. But these justices could only exercise this power if the accused chose to be tried immediately. See Webb, i. 299 n.

Lastly, the single J.P. could, 'on his own view' without any trial, fine or send to the stocks a man for swearing, being drunk, or committing an offence against the stringent game laws;[1] he had plenary jurisdiction over defaulting parish officers; on mere suspicion of an offence he could exact security; on an information of bastardy he could send the erring mother to the house of correction, and he could order a vagrant to be whipped 'until his back be bloody'.

The justices were in fact the local despots. It is true their actions could be questioned at quarter sessions or even before the judges of assize, but this was a serious business not likely to be undertaken by the simple, uneducated folk of little means chiefly subject to their jurisdiction. Most of them, no doubt, were benevolent despots like Addison's Sir Roger de Coverley or Fielding's Squire Allworthy, though even he, such was his zeal for village morality, could exceed his legal rights: 'however,' says Fielding, 'as his intention was truly upright, he ought to be excused *in foro conscientiae*; since so many arbitrary acts are daily committed by magistrates, who have not this excuse for themselves'.[2] Nor could a more public-spirited justice be found than Gibbon's friend, Squire Holroyd of Sheffield Place. Finding that the parish officers, in league with the farmers, were using the poor rates to pay the wages and rent of their labourers and domestic servants, he took over the office of overseer himself and put an end to these abuses. He restricted the poor rates to the use of the aged and infirm and abolished the custom of paying for parish feasts out of the rates, thereby reducing the district levy from 4s. to 1s. 6d. in the £.[3] On the other hand many of the justices described in the literature of the period are bullying despots with hardly a touch of human feeling, intent only on currying favour with the rich and powerful and oppressing the humbler folk who are unable to bribe them. For, as lawyer Scout remarked to Lady Booby in *Joseph Andrews* (iv. 3), 'the laws of this land are not so vulgar to permit a mean fellow to contend with one of your Ladyship's fortune'. Such is Mr.

[1] Offences against the game laws were 'as a rule' tried by two justices, only occasionally by one. See Webb, i. 598.

[2] W. S. Holdsworth, *History of English Law*, x. 145, quotes several examples of admirable county J.P.s, such as Charles Selwyn in Surrey, Bayley in Lancashire, and Sir G. O. Paul in Gloucestershire. [Only the first of these was active before 1760.]

[3] The story is told by Arthur Young, *Journal . . . Eastern England*, iii. 143-5.

Justice Thrasher who commits Amelia's husband to prison, because he 'had too great an honour for Truth to suspect that she ever appeared in sordid apparel' (*Amelia*, i. 2), such too are the justice who deals with Beau Jackson in *Roderick Random* and the peculiarly vile specimen in *The Adventures of a Guinea*. It may be admitted that the examples chosen by the authors of such novels were exceptional, but at any rate they illustrate the undoubted fact that these justices, whether in town or country, had powers over the population which made it possible for them to become the almost irresponsible tyrants of the neighbourhood.

But the manor, the parish, and the commission of the peace for the shire with the other shire officials do not exhaust the complicated list of authorities dealing with local government in this period. In addition there were some two hundred municipalities scattered about the country, cut off entirely from the normal shire system. These autonomous municipalities had been created at various times, generally by charter from the king, which granted wide powers of government either to the body of freemen or to a close corporation within their respective areas. Such chartered bodies, though sometimes concurrent with, generally tended to absorb the powers of the vestry or vestries within their borders, and in addition had special powers of their own. They could enact by-laws, exact market fees, administer lands, ports, fisheries, sometimes outside their own borders, and exercise police duties. But their most notable privilege was their exemption from the jurisdiction of the county authorities. The lord lieutenant's authority, it is true, nominally ran in these chartered boroughs, but his functions were so diminished as to be normally of no importance. The sheriff had no jurisdiction in them; and above all they were either entirely or partially exempt from the authority of the county justices, for they had the privilege of appointing their own municipal justices of the peace, who could in all cases act in their single capacity or in petty and special sessions, and in the majority of boroughs had the right to hold quarter sessions. In one respect the municipal justices were even more independent than their brethren of the shire, for, being appointed justices solely in respect of their municipal office, they could not be removed by the Crown.

Thus local government in the eighteenth century, with some

appearance and a few vestiges of democratic influence, was essentially at the mercy of these justices of the peace, unpaid and largely irresponsible agents increasingly drawn as the century progressed from the upper or upper middle classes. The question arises how far this loose system of local administration through semi-independent justices working as isolated units in the different shires and boroughs and parishes was able to present some sort of consistent method throughout the country. The legislation which governed their activities gave them vast discretion both as judges and administrators, and undoubtedly the exercise of their functions depended largely on the idiosyncrasy of the single justices or on the views of a majority on the county bench at quarter sessions. But some consistency was maintained by the method of their appointment which ensured that they generally belonged to the ruling political party; grave aberrations of justice could be corrected by the judges of assize; and above all the secretaries of state were in constant communication with them, receiving reports from their districts and issuing orders for their conduct in times of disturbance or emergency. In spite, too, of acts of injustice by self-opinionated or venal justices, this system of local government was generally accepted, largely because the majority of the population were quite content to be ruled by their 'betters', and the justices as a class formed a family party with the oligarchic majority that ruled in parliament. And on their side the justices, apart from bad exceptions, were in the main public-spirited men animated by a horse common sense, a pride in their duties, and a paternal interest in the poorer neighbours who looked to them for guidance and correction.

The further question arises how was the connexion between the central government and the local authorities maintained in a century when there were no specialized government departments to deal with local affairs, and when there was no Scotland Yard and hardly any police worth the name in town or country. Short of dismissal, rarely exercised except for political reasons, there was no means whereby the central government could exercise any direct control over the lords lieutenant, responsible for the county levies, or the county magistrates with their wide and largely irresponsible powers: the chartered municipalities were in practice subject to no control. The lords lieutenant, all being prominent members of the local aristocracy, could exercise some control over justices and, being carefully chosen for their loyalty to the government of the day, could generally be depended on for that purpose by the secretaries of state in times of difficulty. In normal times, it is true, the other local authorities were practically independent of the central government. Within the limits of their wide jurisdiction the justices of the peace were uncontrollable, and only if they exceeded their rights could their actions be reviewed in the king's courts, if their victims, as was rarely the case, had the means or the knowledge required to justify a complaint. At the same time both the country justices and the municipal authorities still retained the tradition handed down from Elizabethan times that they were the eyes and ears of the privy council, and generally took a pride in reporting to that body directly or to the secretary of state any occurrences in their districts that seemed to threaten the safety or tranquillity of the realm; generally, too, they showed commendable zeal in carrying out, in cases of riot or rebellion, orders sent to them from Whitehall. A safeguard for the established system also existed in the power of the lord chancellor to issue a new commission of the peace for any county, in which the names of suspect or inefficient justices might be omitted and those of more trustworthy county gentlemen added; but though new names were periodically inserted the omission of existing justices was very rarely found necessary. A study of the 'Domestic Entry Books' during the Georgian period shows how very close, in times of trouble, was the correspondence between the centre and the localities. The lord mayor of York writes in August 1714 to the secretary of state about the measures taken to ensure a peaceable succession for George I; Maidstone J.P.s report to him in the same month the evidence they have secured of a Jacobite plot; Hampshire J.P.s consult the regency whether bail should be allowed to a suspicious character they have committed to jail. Sometimes private persons give information as to local difficulties. Thus in October 1714 eleven of the gentry of the East Riding write to complain to the secretary of state of their lord lieutenant's suspicious neglect of his duties. A cattle dealer at Portsmouth writes to the lords justices to complain of riotous interference with his cattle-loading, and their secretary at once orders the mayor to put a stop to these riots. On their side the secretaries of state, especially during the troubles of 1715–16, are in constant correspondence with lords lieutenant and mayors of cities as to measures they should take to suppress riots and arrest disturbers of the peace or Jacobite plotters. They are specially vigilant in giving directions to mayors and customs officials of the southern ports as to the detention of travellers with or without passes or the liberty to be given them to proceed freely on their business; they order the lords lieutenant of all the southern coast counties to examine all foreign ships, they summon the lord lieutenant and the deputy lieutenants of London and Middlesex to confer with them on measures for the security of the capital, and are lavish in their praise or blame of local magistrates for zeal or remiss-ness. In case of serious disturbance or a threat of disturbance at Chester or Oxford, for example, the secretaries on their own authority order the secretary at war to send troops to keep order. The bishop of London is ordered to stop Jacobite prayers in Aldersgate Street, and constant references are made to the attorney-general as to the advisability of prosecuting men reported on locally as possible plotters. The secretaries of state themselves often had suspicious characters brought before them for examination, and the under-secretaries, on appointment, were placed on the commission of the peace to enable them also to examine and commit suspects.[1]

Clearly, although the relations between the local and the central authorities were not established in the Georgian era on the explicit legal basis they are today, the secretaries of state, especially in times of emergency, exercised supreme and un-questioned control over the local authorities, partly through their authority over the armed forces of the Crown, partly owing to the king's right of appointment or dismissal of lords lieutenant and J.P.s, but mainly owing to the general accep-tance of the common-sense principle that the central govern-ment must be mainly responsible for the general security of the kingdom.[2]

The *Commentaries on the Laws of England*, delivered at Oxford by Blackstone in 1758, but not published till 1765, are a land-

[1] The 'Domestic Entry Books' and 'General Correspondence' are full of examples of the close connexion between the secretaries of state and the local authorities, especially in troubled times. See above, p. 33, n. 3.

[2] S. and B. Webb's monumental work on *English Local Government* is invaluable for conditions in the eighteenth century, particularly vols. i and ii dealing with *Parish and County* and *Manor and Borough*. Josef Redlich, *Local Government in England* (edited by F. W. Hirst), 2 vols., 1903, is also suggestive.

mark in our legal history.[1] No such comprehensive account of our system of law from its origins had yet appeared, nor so exact a survey of the state of the law and the law courts up to and including the first half of the eighteenth century. In spite, too, even because of, Blackstone's intense admiration of the British constitution—'so wisely contrived,' he says, 'so strongly raised, and so highly finished [that] it is hard to speak with that praise which is justly and severely its due'—still more for his lucid and urbane exposition, his *Commentaries* are still the best history of English law from the standpoint of his contemporaries and for our purpose in this connexion.[2]

Already by the eighteenth century, as Blackstone says, in the 'distinct and separate existence of the judicial power . . . consists one main preservative of the public liberty'.[3] For the judges, though appointed by the Crown, were no longer subject to its influence in their decisions, since they could not be removed except on an address from both houses of parliament. It is true that on a demise of the Crown their tenure was held to cease unless they were reappointed by the new king: in fact, when George I came to the throne, on the advice of the new whig chancellor, Cowper, some changes were made in the bench;[4] but no such changes were made on the accession of George II or of George III; and George III himself, at the beginning of his reign, promoted the act abolishing this rule. Thus the complete independence of the judges was fully secured; and when Walpole and the chancellor, Macclesfield, in 1722 tried to induce Chief Justice Pratt to alter a judgement he had given favour of Richard Bentley, he refused to do so.[5]

[1] In 1753 Blackstone had begun giving private lectures on the law at Oxford. Thanks to the munificent bequest from Charles Viner for a Vinerian professorship of law, accompanied by scholarships and fellowships for law students, he was elected to that professorship in 1758. My quotations from the *Commentaries* are taken from the fourth edition, published in 1770, notable for the changes made in vol. i, pp. 163 and 170, as a result of the Wilkes case.

[2] A successor of Blackstone as Vinerian professor, Sir William Holdsworth, has brought his great *History of English Law* to the end of the eighteenth century, which is covered by vols. x–xii. To that work, and to his kindness in suggesting alterations in the first draft of this section, I owe mainly my acquaintance with the most recent and authoritative view of legal conditions in this period. For a defence of Blackstone against Bentham's and others' criticism of his complacent satisfaction with the English constitution and law see Sir William's vol. xii, pp. 727–31. [Note of 1939].   [3] *Commentaries*, i. 269.

[4] See an interesting note in Campbell, *Chancellors*, iv. 349–50, on the changes Cowper proposed. The chief justice of the common pleas and two other judges were accordingly superseded.   [5] Campbell, *Chief Justices*, ii. 184.

Nevertheless, reform was still much needed in the judicial system, which, in the course of our history, had grown up hugger-mugger from the various courts set up for particular purposes, many whereof were by this time obsolete. There were three common law courts. The king's bench, with its chief justice and three puisne judges, was still the chief tribunal for important criminal prosecutions, but by this time also, by the use of legal fictions, entertained cases of private litigants. These cases were originally the province of the common pleas, with another lord chief justice and three other puisne judges. The court of exchequer, where the chief baron had three other barons to assist him, was first instituted to decide cases affecting the royal revenue, but, again by the use of legal fictions, now also dealt with civil cases between private parties. Thus all these three ancient tribunals in practice now dealt with many similar cases and were apt to give varying decisions. Most of the criminal work, except the more important cases, was done at assizes, which were attended by judges from all these three courts. The chancellor, on the other hand, was purely an equity judge to deal with matters not envisaged by the common law of England. He was assisted in his equity jurisdiction by the master of the rolls, and had under him eleven masters in chancery to take charge of money lodged in court by litigants and report on matters he might refer to them. The court of exchequer also, besides its common law work, had an equity jurisdiction parallel to that of the chancellor. In addition to these royal courts, the counties palatine of Durham, Lancaster, and Chester[1] and the royal franchise of Ely held special privileges whereby they exercised an extensive common law and equitable jurisdiction: the bishop of Durham even issued his own writs. The ancient county courts to decide on small civil cases had now fallen into disuse; but courts of conscience were being established during this period in London and a few other trading towns to relieve the king's courts of trivial disputes about sums up to 40s. or in some cases £5. The ecclesiastical courts at Doctors' Commons still dealt with tithes, marriage and divorce, and also, by a singular anomaly not found even in 'popish countries', with the probate of wills. The admiralty court, also at Doctors'

---

[1] Chester had its chief justice. Sir Joseph Jekyll, M.P., later master of the rolls, and Sir John Willes, later chief justice of the common pleas, were the only notable holders of this office.

Commons, was especially important in war-time, owing to the number of prize-cases, and it gained a great reputation, even in enemy countries, for the fairness of its decisions. There were also two chief justices in eyre, for the north and the south of the Trent, but, though they still drew salaries,[1] they had no functions since the virtual supersession of the Forest Laws after the reign of Charles II.

For appeals there was a medley of jurisdictions. High courts of delegates, judges appointed *ad hoc*, heard those from the ecclesiastical courts; those from the admiralty court went before commissioners of appeals, consisting chiefly of the privy council. The court of exchequer chamber, differently constituted from the court of exchequer, and composed of the justices of the common pleas besides the barons of the exchequer, heard those from the king's bench; while another form of the court of exchequer chamber, with the chancellor presiding over the justices of the king's bench and common pleas, heard appeals from the court of exchequer itself. The king's bench, with its 'very high and transcendent' jurisdiction, as Blackstone calls it, kept 'all inferior jurisdictions within the bounds of [its] authority', and was especially a court of appeal by writ of error from the court of common pleas.[2] The house of lords, besides being the original court before which peers accused of treason or felony were tried,[3] was also the supreme court of appeal from other tribunals. When the house was acting as a judicial body all the lay peers still exercised the right of voting; and, though the judges were called in to give their opinions on legal points that might arise, they had no vote on the decision: in fact, the only peer learned in the law during nineteen years of this period was the chancellor Hardwicke, who thereby was the sole lawyer to decide on appeals from his own jurisdiction.[4] When the great seal was entrusted to a lord keeper, without a peerage, though

[1] The chief justice in eyre for the north of the Trent seems to have drawn only £100 per annum, but his colleague for the south as much as £1,666. 13s. 4d. See *Calendars of Treasury Papers, passim*. Among the holders of these agreeable sinecures in this period were three dukes and several earls.

[2] *Commentaries*, iii. 42–43. For a full account of all the various courts see ibid. iii, chaps. iv–vi, particularly pp. 40–45, 56, 69–73, 78, 81–82, 437, and 442.

[3] On these occasions the house of lords sat under the chairmanship of a lord high steward appointed to 'regulate and add weight to the proceedings'. See *Commentaries*, iv. 260.

[4] After Murray was raised to the bench as Lord Mansfield in 1756, at the same time as Hardwicke ceased to be chancellor, this anomalous condition ceased.

he acted as Speaker of the lords, he had no vote in that house. Sir Robert Henley, for example, was only lord keeper without a peerage from 1757 to 1760, when he got his peerage as Lord Northington, but he was not made chancellor till 1761.

Besides this somewhat confusing medley of jurisdictions there were many obsolescent processes of law still available for the litigant. Two of the strangest were the ancient wager of battle, which Blackstone says was resorted to as recently as Elizabeth's days and was still legal;[1] the other was the old Saxon wager of law, hedged round with obstacles, but still available in small-debt causes, whereby a man, by bringing eleven other men to swear to the same story as himself, could prove his case without reply.[2] An instance in the reign of George II is quoted even of a man pressed to death by the horrible torture of the *peine forte et dure* for refusing to plead on a charge of felony.[3] There was also the form of indictment entitled Appeal of Murder brought not by the Crown but by some near relative of the victim, the consequence of which was that the king himself was barred from pardoning the convicted murderer. In 1724 and 1729 cases of appeal of murder were brought by the brothers of murdered women against their husbands, and in both cases resulted in convictions and hangings. The last such case was apparently in 1730, when the widow of a Fleet prisoner brought such an appeal against a jailer of the Fleet; but in this case a verdict of not guilty was returned.[4] The old privilege, benefit of clergy, for felons presumed to be able to read,[5] was still recognized at common law, but it was being gradually whittled down. Instead of the mild branding and whipping ordained for such learned felons, hard labour and then transportation for seven years were substituted in this period. Finally, the plea became so absurd that in most of the numerous acts of the eighteenth century imposing new penalties for felony the proviso 'without benefit of clergy' was inserted. Even that cherished guardian of our liberties, the Habeas Corpus Act, was found to have a loophole of escape for authoritarian lawyers. In 1757

[1] It was not abolished till 1819; see Holdsworth, l.c. i. 310.
[2] *Commentaries*, iii. 337–45.
[3] *State Trials*, xxx. 767, 828; see also *Commentaries*, iv. 320.
[4] The case is reported in *State Trials*, xvii. 383–462; and see Holdsworth, l.c. ii. 363.
[5] Even the reading test was abolished in Anne's reign. See *Commentaries*, iv. 363–4.

a man illegally pressed for the army had been confined in the Savoy, but could obtain no remedy from Lord Mansfield in the king's bench by the speedy procedure of the act of 1679, since no criminal charge was exhibited against him. Pitt at once got a bill passed in the commons to remedy the defect, but the lords were persuaded by Hardwicke and Mansfield to reject it; nor was the difficulty removed till 1816.[1] Again the judges still upheld the Stuart doctrine as to the jury's rights in libel cases, restricting its verdict to the fact of publication and the truth of the innuendos (i.e. the naming of the persons aimed at in the publication), reserving to themselves the decision as to its libellous character. Yorke, when attorney-general, strongly upheld this view, which was countenanced by two chief justices, Raymond and Lee. In 1752, however, Pratt, afterwards Lord Camden, as counsel for the defence, circumvented this ruling by persuading the jury to give a verdict of not guilty in a libel case, on the obviously false grounds of non-publication.[2] Pitt, who hated lawyers, once expressed the opinion that 'the constitution may be shaken to its centre and the lawyer will sit calm in his cabinet. But let a cobweb be disturbed in Westminster Hall, and out the bloated spider will crawl in its defence',[3] certainly an unjust opinion if the whole work of Hardwicke and Mansfield as judges in chancery and the king's bench be taken into account.

None the less the only definite reforms in the law enacted by parliament during this period were the substitution in 1731 of English for Latin in indictments, so as to make the jargon of the law more intelligible to laymen, a reform opposed by many lawyers, including Chief Justice Raymond, and lamented by Blackstone himself; the abolition of witchcraft as a crime in 1736; the grant of counsel to those impeached of high treason in 1747; and the reform of the marriage law by Hardwicke's act of 1753. But even in this last instance, though the scandal of the Fleet marriages was done away with, new restrictions

---

[1] See *Chatham*, ii. 37–40, and Yorke, *Philip Yorke, E. of Hardwicke*, iii. 1–19 and 42–52, for a more favourable view of the lawyers' arguments; and Holdsworth, l.c. ix. 119–21, for a full discussion of this point.
[2] See Yorke, ibid. i. 86–87; Campbell, *Chief Justices*, ii. 207–9, 227–8; id., *Chancellors*, v. 24–25. See also below, pp. 332–3.
[3] See *Chatham*, i. 174. This image of the law as a spider seems also to have been used by Fox in the debates on the Marriage Bill. See *Hardwicke*, ii. 65 and iii. 462.

were imposed on dissenters and Roman catholics.[1] On the other hand this period saw an enormous increase in the crimes to which the death penalty was attached. By the end of George II's reign no less than 160 felonies had been declared worthy of instant death, among them being such minor offences as sheep-stealing, cutting down a cherry-tree, being seen for a month in the company of 'Egyptians' (gypsies), and petty larcenies from dwelling-houses, shops, or the person.[2] The absence of any effective system of police for the protection of property,[3] rather than innate brutality, was no doubt the cause of this savage legislation by the governing classes, to whom property was almost more sacred than human life, in the mistaken view that such severity would prove an effective deterrent. But Johnson, Goldsmith, and even Blackstone[4] himself had serious doubts as to the virtue of capital punishment for this purpose. In the first place the very brutality of the punishment tended to uncertainty in the law, owing to the frequent pardons granted to the convicted felons, either absolutely or subject to transportation. Moreover, there is little doubt that one result of this indiscriminate severity was an increase in crimes of violence, on the principle, 'you may as well be hanged for a sheep as for a lamb'; for if a thief suppressed his victim's evidence by killing him, he risked no greater punishment than for his theft.

In the actual practice of the law there were many abuses which had to wait long for a remedy. Blackstone, in his introductory lecture, deplores the absence of any adequate provision for the teaching of the law.[5] At Oxford, until Blackstone began giving lectures privately in 1753, there was little interest in the subject: nor is that surprising when in that year Newcastle, ignoring Murray's recommendation of Blackstone, appointed as professor of civil law one Jenner, a party hack, likely to be useful to him at elections. The inns of court, founded for the instruction of law students, had long abandoned that function,

[1] See below, p. 137.
[2] The picturesque capital felony of associating with gypsies was of sixteenth-century origin (5 Eliz., c. 20); sheep-stealing and tree-cutting were added to the capital list during this period, but the petty larcenies had been included under William III.
[3] See below, p. 133.
[4] *Commentaries*, iv. 9, 10, 18; Holdsworth, xi. 563.
[5] Blackstone did not do this with much vigour; as Gibbon observed, he touched on this neglect 'with the becoming tenderness of a pious son who would wish to conceal the infirmities of his parent'. See Holdsworth, xii. 728.

merely requiring them to keep terms for five years, eat dinners, and, at the perfunctory examinations preliminary to being called to the bar, recite a certain number of Latin sentences.[1] The custom of reading in barrister's chambers had not yet arisen, so that the only training young barristers could acquire was by studying the somewhat jejune legal textbooks of the day, attending the courts at Westminster, or working in an attorney's office, as was the case with Lords Macclesfield and Hardwicke. Particularly keen students sometimes took a legal course at Leyden. Boys educated at Lichfield grammar school, where Johnson was a pupil, seem to have become especially proficient in the law: the headmaster, Hunter, indeed was celebrated for having flogged seven judges, including two chief justices of the common pleas, Willes and Wilmot.

Many of those who attained high eminence on the bench were notorious for feathering their nests with great profit to themselves and their families. Of the chancellors, Lord King beside his ordinary emoluments was content with a pension of £6,000[2] and £1,200 extra from the hanaper,[3] to compensate him for the ending of the sale of offices, while Hardwicke's salary of above £7,000 was greatly augmented by fees, besides the reversion of a rich tellership of the exchequer for his eldest son. Macclesfield's salary was only £4,000, but in addition he received a lump sum of £14,000 on appointment and a tellership for his son also. Unfortunately Macclesfield, not content with this competence, made a practice of selling master-ships in chancery for exorbitant sums, ranging from 1,500 to 5,000 guineas—'guineas', as his agent in these transactions once put it, being 'handsomer' than pounds. He was also culpably lax in supervising the masters' methods of dealing with the funds lodged with them by litigants in chancery, many of which they misappropriated, partly to recoup themselves for these large bribes exacted by the chancellor on their admission to

[1] Even the fixing of the number of terms to be kept was not agreed until 1762. See Holdsworth, xii. 22–25. W. Herbert, *Antiquities of the Inns of Court and Chancery*, 1804, pp. 172–81, has an interesting account of the ancient 'readings' and 'mootings' for the training of barristers, long disused by the eighteenth century; also of the various inns of court.

[2] £6,000 in those days was, of course, worth much more than the present chancellor's salary of £12,000.

[3] The hanaper (hamper) was the chancery office where writs relating to private suitors were kept, the Petty Bag where the Crown writs were kept. In both cases, of course, these writs were a source of fees. See *Commentaries*, iii. 48–49.

office. So notorious had these bribes and this embezzlement of chancery funds become by 1725, when the total deficit is said to have amounted to £100,871. 6s. 8d., that Macclesfield was impeached and sentenced to the Tower until he had paid a fine of £30,000, which he managed to find within six weeks.[1] Of another chancellor, Robert Henley, Lord Northington, though he was only too glad to accept the unexpected offer of the great seal without bargaining, perhaps the most notable characteristic was, as with Eldon, his 'one great taste—if a noble thirst should be called by so finical a name—an attachment to port-wine, strong almost as that to Constitution and Crown; and indeed a modification of the same sentiment. It is the proper beverage of a great lawyer—that by the strength of which Blackstone wrote his *Commentaries* and Sir William Grant modulated his judgements, and Lord Eldon repaired the ravages of study and withstood the shocks of party and of time.'[2] Horace Walpole adds a touch in illustration of this chancellor's amiable weakness. A smart gentleman came to see him, 'when the Chancellor happened to be drunk', to announce his election as a governor of St. Bartholomew's Hospital. But when the spokesman began a solemn oration congratulating his 'lordship on his health and the nation on enjoying such great abilities', Northington stopped him short, crying, 'By God, it is a lie! I have neither health nor abilities; my bad health has destroyed my abilities.'[3]

On the whole, however, the judges in this period were honourable, competent in the law, and firm in their decisions. Of the chief justices of the king's bench, Lord Raymond and Lord Hardwicke were the strongest before William Murray, Lord Mansfield, who began his notable term of office, lasting thirty-two years, in 1756; but most of Mansfield's great decisions and reforms in that court were made in the following reign. Sir John Willes, though personally disreputable and able, it was said, to talk only about law and lewdness, proved a good chief

[1] See Campbell, *Chancellors*, iv. 535-58, and Holdsworth, i. 440; xii. 205-6. Previous chancellors had by custom taken fees on the admission of masters, but not on such a scale or with such undignified bargaining. *State Trials*, xvi. 767 sqq., has a full account of the trial, and *Hist. MSS. Comm., Portland*, vi. 1-8, has gossipy letters to Lord Oxford about it.

[2] Quoted in Campbell, *Chancellors*, v. 177, from the *Quarterly Review*, on *Lords Stowell and Eldon*.

[3] H. Walpole, *Letters*, to Hertford, 29 Dec. 1763.

justice of the common pleas, and would have got the great seal in 1757 instead of Henley had he not put his demands too high. His successor at the common pleas, Sir John Eardley Wilmot, was excellent on the bench, but was of so retiring a disposition that he three times refused the chancellorship, once in 1757 and twice in 1769.[1] Of the chancellors, Talbot showed promise of becoming a notable chief of the equity bench, but he died prematurely after only four years of office. His successor Philip Yorke, earl of Hardwicke, during his nineteen years on the 'marble seat'[2] in Westminster Hall, proved himself one of our greatest chancellors.

Hardwicke as a judge showed none of the faults of which he was accused as a somewhat time-serving and over-cautious politician. He started with the great advantage of being as familiar with the common law as with equity, not only from his experience at the bar as solicitor and attorney-general, but also as chief justice during the four years of his friend Talbot's chancellorship. Thus equipped with an intimate knowledge of both branches, he was able, as chancellor, to complete the work of Nottingham and his successors in harmonizing the relations between equity and the common law, and rendering them not—as had been the case in the days of Ellesmere and Coke—antagonistic, but supplementary to one another. When he said in one of his judgements, 'Aequitas sequitur legem', he was explaining the same view as that expressed later by Maitland, that 'equity had come not to destroy the law but to fulfil it. Every jot and every tittle of the law was to be obeyed, but when all this had been done something might yet be needful, something that equity would require.'[3] Since Elizabeth's day there had been great chancellors before Hardwicke—Ellesmere, Bacon, Coventry, Nottingham, and Somers—but none of his predecessors had established the equity branch on so secure a basis, as an assistance to the common law side and to supplement its lacunae, as he did in his memorable term on the

[1] Mansfield also refused the chancellorship three times, in 1756, 1757, and 1770, not from a retiring disposition, but because he did not wish to exchange for a post of uncertain tenure one which was permanent and for which he was supremely fitted.

[2] 'In sede marmoreâ; ubi cancellarii sedere sunt assueti' is quoted from a record of 36 Ed. III by W. Herbert, l.c., p. 77. Hardwicke was wont to speak of this 'marble seat'.

[3] Quoted by Holdsworth, xii. 602.

F

bench. He was not, indeed—like his Scottish correspondent Lord Kames, and that great judge, another Scotsman, Lord Mansfield—in favour of amalgamating the two branches to the extent of having law and equity administered in the same tribunals. Yet his work tended to facilitate their partial amalgamation, effected more than a century after his death. As has been well said of him: 'Just as Coke laid the foundations and erected some part of the edifice of the modern common law, so Hardwicke laid the foundations and erected a large part of the edifice of modern equity.'[1]

His success as a judge was largely due to his quick apprehension of the changing conditions of his time and of the need for the law to provide for these new conditions. In this spirit he dealt with the new problems arising from the union with Scotland, not only by his legislation dealing with the clans after the '45,[2] but also in dealing with appeals to the house of lords from the Scottish courts. With his sound knowledge of the Roman civil law and of the ancient feudal system of land-tenure in Scotland, he was able, in one of his most important Scottish judgements, as the Scottish judge, Lord Kames, put it, 'not . . . from ignorance of the law of Scotland . . . [to make an] innovation . . . necessary in order to make a perfect equality between the two nations with respect to the punishment of treason'.[3] In England, by the time he came to the bench, the increasing prosperity of the country and the growing expansion of trade and commerce were bringing up for decision in the law courts an entirely new branch of questions, such as trade agreements, the banking system, bills of exchange, insurance policies, and so on. On such questions, to a large extent ignored by the common law, Hardwicke realized the need of laying down, through his more elastic chancery branch, principles on which the rising commercial community could rely. It is true his mercantile work was not nearly so comprehensive or so important as that achieved by Mansfield; but at any rate he had shown the way. Though ready to make decisions applicable to cases of exceptional hardness, his great aim in these, as in all his judgements, was to establish general rules applicable to

---

[1] Holdsworth, l.c. xii. 284.
[2] See below, pp. 281–3.
[3] In this instance Campbell, *Chancellors*, v. 61–62, is unfair to Hardwicke; see Yorke, *Hardwicke*, ii. 483.

future cases, and so gradually to establish a code of precedents to guide his successors. Three notable men of the century, as different from one another as possible—Mansfield, Burke, and Wilkes—each separately remarked on hearing some of his judgements: 'Wisdom herself might be supposed to speak.' He himself, in elucidating the law or formulating new rules, always had before him his favourite maxim: 'Certainty is the Mother of Repose, and therefore the Law aims at Certainty.'[1]

[1] Yorke, *Hardwicke*, ii. 413–555, though animated, as the whole work is, by an engaging inability in the author to find any flaw in his ancestor's composition, has the most exhaustive account of the chancellor's legal achievements. Holdsworth, l.c. xii. 237–97, gives a more critical and authoritative view of him. For Hardwicke's correspondence with Lord Kames see A. F. Tytler, *Memoirs of H. Home of Woodhouselee*, 3 vols., 1814.

IV

RELIGION AND THE CHURCHES

By the eighteenth century the medieval idea of the church as, if not the superior, at any rate the equal and independent of the lay state, had disappeared in England as it had in France and to a greater or less extent in other countries. In France Louis XIV, by his Gallican policy, his extirpation of heresy, and his control of the *feuille des bénéfices*, had made the church one of his most powerful instruments for the internal control of the country. In England the Tudors and Stuarts had indeed failed in the hopeless task of bringing all their subjects within their own special form of church discipline; but at any rate they had succeeded in making the church a formidable instrument of state policy. This system had been continued, though with a slightly different bias, since the Revolution, and had been extended to Ireland: Scotland alone since the union had been perforce allowed to go her own way. But at no time in our history was the Anglican church, both in England and in Ireland, so completely Erastian and so entirely subservient to the purposes of civil government as in the eighteenth century.

This end was partly attained by the civil disabilities imposed upon those who did not conform with the observances of the established church. The Roman catholics, indeed, by a series of enactments dating from Elizabeth's time to within the first quarter of the eighteenth century, were legally little better than pariahs. Their priests could be fined £200 and were liable to the penalties of high treason for saying Mass; their schoolmasters, not approved by the bishops, could be fined 40s. a day and their harbourers £10 a month; their laymen could have an oath denying even the spiritual authority of the pope tendered to them by any two J.P.s, and on refusal were liable to the penalties of recusancy, which included a fine of £20 a month for not attending church, inability to hold any office, keep arms in their houses, maintain suits at law, travel over five miles without a licence, or be an executor, guardian, doctor, or lawyer; by the legislation of Charles II's reign no Roman catholic could sit in parliament or on corporations, nor could he hold any civil, military, or naval office under the Crown; by an act of William III the nearest protestant kin could claim their lands from Roman catholic heirs; and by acts passed in George I's reign the landed property of Roman catholics was subjected to special disabilities, including a double land tax.[1] Protestant dissenters were more mildly treated: they were allowed by William and Mary's Toleration Act of 1689 to build conventicles and, on registration, to worship there as they pleased. But even they had serious disabilities: they could not sit on corporations unless they qualified by taking the Sacrament in an established church, a provision made more stringent by the tories' Occasional Conformity Act of 1711; they could not hold a commission in the army or any office under the king; under the Schism Act of 1714 the tories had even tried to make it impossible for them to educate their children.[2] The quakers among them, though no longer actively persecuted as in the last century, were constantly being sold up or imprisoned for refusing to pay tithes. The Jews could hold no public offices or landed estates except by special act, nor could they be naturalized, and, though they were allowed to worship as they pleased, as late as 1743 a legacy devised for a Jewish seminary was disallowed by Lord Chancellor Hardwicke.[3] Until 1753, when Hardwicke's Marriage Act made a special exception for Jews and quakers, no marriage was legal unless celebrated by an Anglican clergyman. To the English universities none but professed churchmen were admitted to degrees throughout the century.[4]

[1] Maude Petre, *The Ninth Lord Petre*, N.Y., 1928, pp. 86 sqq., has a good account of the penal laws against the Roman catholics. See also C. Butler, *Historical Memoirs of . . . Catholics*, 4 vols., 1819–21, ii. 64–71 and iv. 225–9. See below, p. 74, on the lax enforcement of these laws, and also N. Sykes, *Edmund Gibson*, pp. 292–5.

[2] See vol. x of this series, pp. 232, 247 (2nd edn.).

[3] See below, p. 74 and n. 1. This case (*Da Costa* v. *Da Paz*) was heard in Dec. 1743 when Hardwicke pronounced against the legacy; in May 1754 he further ruled that the Crown should direct the legacy to some other charitable use, whereupon the greater part of the money was handed over to the Foundling Hospital. See Holdsworth, viii. 409; Yorke, *Hardwicke*, ii. 471; and *English Law Reports*, xxi. 268 and xxxvi. 715–16.

[4] At Oxford dissenters were not admitted even as undergraduates; at Cambridge they could matriculate and pass the examination, but could not proceed to degrees. See Olive M. Griffiths, *Religion and Learning* . . ., Cambridge, 1935, pp. 33–34. For the Marriage Act see pp. 136–7 below.

The distribution of the population among the various creeds is not easy to discover with any accuracy owing to the absence of trustworthy statistics. A return

One of the objects of this penal legislation had originally been to induce dissenters from the established church to find refuge therein: a very few Roman catholics, of whom the most notable was the eleventh duke of Norfolk in this century, did indeed come over to Anglicanism; seceders from the protestant dissenters were not so unusual and included two of the most eminent bishops of this age, Butler and Secker. But the main object of all these laws was to protect the church and state from attack.

Now, however, the protestant dissenters' attitude at the Revolution and their zeal for the Hanoverian succession, especially during the '15, made it impossible for the whigs, at any rate, to regard them as anything but a bulwark to the new civil dispensation. So the toleration begun in William's reign was further extended during the long whig régime inaugurated with George I. To enable the dissenters to be admitted more freely to corporations as an antidote to tory office-holders predominant in many country districts, the Occasional Conformity Act was repealed, and to restore their right to educate their children in their own schools the Schism Act was also repealed in 1719. Stanhope, a real liberal, would have gone further and repealed the clauses as affecting them in the Test and Corporation Acts, but finding the church too strong for such an attack on the ark of its covenant, had contented himself with an Act for Quieting and Establishing Corporations,[1] whereby dissenters duly elected to corporations, whose tenure of office had not been questioned for six months, were freed from any further obligation to take the Sacrament. Even Walpole, more concerned with his own

to an Order in Council of William III gives 2,477,254 as belonging to the church of England, 108,676 to the various protestant dissenting bodies, and only 13,856 to the Roman catholic; but only freeholders are included. According to Skeats, *History of Free Churches*, their numbers do not appear to have increased during our period; statistics, indeed, of Presbyterian chapels show that they must have greatly decreased, for at the beginning of the eighteenth century they numbered 500, whereas by 1812 there were only 252 (see Griffiths, l.c., p. 150); the Roman catholics, estimated at nearly 28,000 in 1714, did not exceed 60,000 by 1780 according to Berington's *State and Behaviour of English Catholics*, but that figure probably includes others besides freeholders. The total number of Jews in England during the first half of the eighteenth century was small, no more than 6,000 in 1738 and 8,000 in 1753 according to authorities quoted by G. B. Hertz, *British Imperialism in Eighteenth Century*, 1908, p. 63. For statistics of numerical decline of dissenters during this period see C. E. Fryer, 'Numerical Decline of Dissent' in *American Journal of Theology*, xvii. 2 (April 1913), 232–9.

[1] This act was passed in 1718 (5 Geo. I, c. 6) and is printed in part in Horn and Ransome, *English Historical Documents*, x. 394–5.

parliamentary security than Stanhope, tried to conciliate the dissenters in 1723 by the *Regium Donum*, a grant at first of £500 and subsequently of £1,000 per annum for their ministers' widows; in 1728[1] he introduced his first Indemnity Act, valid for twelve months, whereby the qualifying Sacrament could be taken after instead of before election to a corporation. Except for seven or eight intermissions these acts continued annually for 100 years till the Test and Corporation Acts were repealed.[2] But it was still easy to stir up popular feeling against the dissenters, in spite of their valiant support of the whigs, as was evident from the rabbling of dissenting chapels, no less than of Roman catholics, during the '15; for the high church cry of 'the church in danger' long remained effective with the more ignorant. Walpole himself, though fully conscious of the dissenters' services to the dynasty and the whigs, resolutely refused to repeal the Test and Corporation Acts in their favour.[3] Sometimes, indeed, the laws against dissenters were used for the basest purposes of gain. In 1742 the city of London, when anxious to raise funds for the new Mansion House, conceived the ingenious scheme of passing a by-law that any one declining nomination for the office of sheriff should be fined £400 or, if he refused to serve, £600, and then for several years in succession nominating and electing conscientious dissenters, known to be unwilling to qualify by taking the Communion in church. By 1754 the corporation had raised no less than £15,000 by these fines, when a series of lawsuits was brought against it by the dissenters, lawsuits not finally decided till 1767 by Lord Mansfield, who contemptuously told the corporation that they evidently wished 'not so much' for the dissenters' 'services as for their fines', and gave judgement against them on the ground that nonconformity was not a crime in the eyes of the common law of England.

But the full iniquity and absurdity of the legislation against

[1] This was 1 Geo. II, c. 23. In 1727 a similar act had been passed (13 Geo. I, c. 29), but only indemnifying 'persons on board the fleet or beyond the seas'.

[2] The years of intermission were 1730, 1732, 1744, 1749, 1750, 1753, and 1757. Dr. Sykes gives 1734 instead of 1732 in *Sheldon to Secker*, p. 102, but this is incorrect as 7 Geo. II, c. 10, demonstrates. It seems that 1814 was also a year of intermission. See T. Bennett, 'Hallam and the Indemnity Acts', in *Law Quarterly Review*, xxvi (1910), 400–7. See also N. C. Hunt, *Two Early Political Associations*, pp. 120–9.

[3] See Michael, iv, 473–81, and Sykes, op. cit., pp. 102–3, for his resistance to their entreaties in 1732, 1736, and 1739, and his negotiations with Hoadly on that subject in Hervey, i. 121–32. For further discussion see Hunt, op. cit., ch. 8.

the dissenters was illustrated in 1715 and 1745. At both these crises they rose almost to a man in defence of the government. Their ministers urged them from the pulpit to enlist, many raised and commanded detachments to fight the rebels, and even the quakers sent flannel to Cumberland's soldiers for their winter campaign. Yet after the victory their only reward was an Act of Indemnity for those who had transgressed the law by serving in the commissioned ranks. As Fox put it in 1790: 'During the rebellions of 1715 and 1745 . . . they cheerfully had exposed their persons, lives and property in defence of their King and country. . . . For this gallant behaviour all the retribution they ever obtained was an act of indemnity—a pardon for doing their duty as good citizens in rescuing their country in the hour of danger and distress.'[1]

The quakers, a class apart from other dissenters since they not only objected to taking an oath but also refused to pay tithes, had to be separately dealt with. Already under William III an Affirmation Act had been passed for their benefit, but it did not satisfy their scruples. In 1722,[2] however, a more satisfactory form of affirmation was passed, and made perpetual in 1749. Their grievance against tithes, however, was not met, for Walpole's bill to relieve them in 1736 was defeated by Gibson and other bishops in the house of lords, who stirred up the clergy with a spate of anti-quaker pamphlets. A special hardship was in the method of distraint used for unpaid tithes, not by the cheap process through two justices of the peace, but through the costly exchequer and ecclesiastical courts, where the fees mounted so high that for tithes worth £8, £7, and 14s. 6d., the total expenses amounted to £61, £237. 5s., and £84. 10s. 6d. respectively; and one Daniel Hollis, for a tithe debt of a few shillings, had £700 distrained on him in the fifty years he was in prison from 1709 to 1758 for this debt.[3]

It was even harder to obtain relaxation from the more savage restrictions on the Roman catholics. Stanhope indeed

---

[1] *P.H.* xxviii. 393–4 (2 Mar. 1790). [Professor Williams followed the version of this passage given by Skeats, op. cit., p. 423 n.; here the *Parliamentary History* is followed, which in any case Skeats claimed as his authority. C.H.S.]

[2] The conventional date for this act is 1721, but it did not pass the Lords until June 1722. Skeats, p. 318.

[3] See J. Gough, *History of the People called Quakers*, 4 vols., 1790, iv. 161, 181, 197, 278 sqq., 420. For the bishops' part in exciting the inferior clergy see Sykes, *Gibson*, pp. 163–6, and, for a more critical analysis, Hunt, l.c. ch. 6.

made an effort in that direction in 1718–19, but failed, partly
from the uncompromising attitude of some of the Roman
catholics themselves, but chiefly owing to the widespread fear
of papist machinations against the constitution. The Pretender
had found considerable support in 1715 from papist families,
and the suspicion that the papists had designs not only against
the dynasty but also against the establishment seemed in some
measure confirmed by Stanhope's and Craggs's negotiations with
them in 1719; for though representatives of the chief catholic
families, Stonors, Blounts, and Howards, were quite ready to
sign a binding promise of allegiance to George I, the ultramontane element obstinately refused to retract the claim set up by
Sixtus V in Elizabeth's reign, that a pope had power to release
the subjects of an heretic monarch from any promise of fealty.[1]
The fear of catholic machinations at times of unrest was widespread, and at such times the full penalties of the law were
exacted from papists. Thus in the North Riding alone of Yorkshire in 1716 not less than 350 persons were brought up before
the quarter sessions and convicted of recusancy.[2] Again the
strength of anti-papist feeling was illustrated in 1722, when
Walpole found no difficulty in persuading parliament to impose
further disabilities on the papists on the pretext of Layer's and
Atterbury's plots. But such legislation was always defended
solely on civil grounds. When, in 1723, Dubois protested against
the special levy of £100,000 on Roman catholics, Carteret
replied that it was imposed 'ni à cause de la différence de religion, ni par un principe de persécution qui confonde les inno-
cents avec les coupables, mais en conséquence des principes
qui ont soutenu la dignité de la couronne et la liberté de la
nation depuis le temps de la Reine Elizabeth'; and defended the
special levy on the ground of the papists' disloyal activity in
1715 and 1722.[3] It was the same with the Jews. When Newcastle
in 1753, as a slight acknowledgement of the great services
rendered by Gideon[4] and others of their community during the

---

[1] For an account of this negotiation see Hon. C. Howard, *Historical Anecdotes
of some of the Howard Family*, 1817, pp. 137–40; see also P.R.O., S.P. 43/57, and
B.M., Stowe MSS. 121, and Basil Williams, *Stanhope*, pp. 395–8, and Michael,
Quadruple Alliance, pp. 59–63.
[2] *Hist. MSS. Comm.* xiii. vi. 179–85.
[3] *Dipl. Instructions, France, 1721–7*, pp. 36–38; *Hist. MSS. Polwarth*, iii. 199, 202.
[4] Sampson Gideon, 1699–1762, much consulted by Walpole and Pelham for their
financial policy. Although he brought up his children as Christians he never himself joined the church.

'45, had passed an act permitting them to obtain naturalization by special acts, the mob agitation, fostered on the eve of an election by the baser politicians, appeared to Newcastle's timorous mind so formidable that he repealed the act in the same year.[1]

But it is only fair to admit that, bad as all this discriminating legislation was, its victims did not suffer so much hardship in ordinary times as the law prescribed. The Jew Gideon and many of his co-religionists had few practical grievances to complain of and were socially anything but pariahs. This was still more the case with the dissenters, who were as a rule recognized as valuable members of the community and were normally untrammelled in their worship, their schools, and their business activities. Defoe, himself of course a dissenter, notes with glee in his *Tour* evidences of his co-religionists' numerous and thronged meeting-houses in such places as Hull and Newcastle, in Devonshire and in London; and at Southwold he contrasts the 27 worshippers in the church accommodating 5,000–6,000 with the meeting-house full to the doors with a congregation of 600–800. As for the Roman catholics, savage as were the laws against them and never even partially alleviated till Savile's Relief Act of 1778, the country at large, by the admission of Roman catholic writers, was much better than its laws. The penal clauses against priests and laity for saying or hearing the Mass were rarely put into force during this century. We hear indeed of one priest, Matthew Atkinson, who died in Hurst Castle in 1729 after thirty years' imprisonment, and of some priests, including a bishop, James Talbot, being indicted early in George III's reign for this offence; but in those cases no conviction seems to have followed: J.P.s, eager as some of them were to display zeal or exercise power, rarely, except during actual rebellion, used their right of tendering the obnoxious oath to papists: nor were there many instances of catholics' lands being claimed by protestant kin, so strong was all decent feeling against the practice. Typical instances of this accommodating spirit are given by Defoe, writing in George I's reign, when anti-catholic feeling was fairly active. The cathedral city of Durham he found 'full of Roman Catholicks, who

---

[1] For the condition of the Jews in this century see A. M. Hyamson, *History of Jews in England*, 1908, chap. xxviii, and for the Jew Naturalization Act controversy see Hertz, l.c., pp. 60–109.

live peaceably and disturb no Body and no Body them; for we
. . . saw them going . . . publickly to Mass'; and to St. Wini-
fred's Well in Flintshire 'numbers of Pilgrims resort . . . with
no less Devotion than Ignorance. The Priests that attend here
. . . are very numerous . . . and good Manners has prevail'd
so far, that however the Protestants know who and who's
together; no Body takes notice of it, or enquires where one
another goes, or has been gone.' This practical toleration is
fully confirmed by the Swiss César de Saussure, in his account
of his sojourn in London between 1725 and 1730.[1] On the other
hand, the exclusion of Roman catholics from all public offices
or representation was looked on as almost the ark of the covenant, and no responsible politician would have ventured to
propose a change. The inherited tradition about the horrors of
the Spanish inquisition, revived as a stimulus to war with Spain
in the 1730's, Louis XIV's treatment of the huguenots, and
living people's remembrance of the danger of a Roman catholic
revival under James II, all served to keep alive the fear of
papist power. To Pitt himself, exceptionally liberal and tolerant
though he was for his age, the very name of catholicism was
almost as a red rag to a bull. 'The errors of Rome', he declared,
'are rank idolatry, a subversion of all civil as well as religious
liberty, and the utter disgrace of reason and of human nature.'[2]
Even today a large part of the population has not lost that
fear. The alarm and excitement caused by the growth of Roman
catholicism and the creation of a Roman territorial hierarchy
revealed its strength in the last century, and anti-catholic riots
in Glasgow, Edinburgh, and Merseyside show that in our own
times the prejudice is not dead.

Such an attitude of mind towards the Roman catholics, and
in a less degree towards the dissenters, quite accounts for the
strong position given to the established church in the political
system of the eighteenth century. The non-jurors, who refused
to recognize the protestant succession, at first seemed likely to
question the position of the establishment effectively, and still
had some strong personalities among them; such were Hickes,
'bishop of Thetford', Charles Leslie, Thomas Baker, and Law.
But they reckoned only 20,000 adherents at most, and even these

[1] See César de Saussure, *A Foreign View of England in the Reigns of George I and
George II* (1902), pp. 327–8.
[2] *Chatham*, i. 276.

were split up, so that with the passing away of their leaders they became of no account.[1] On the other hand, the establishment was regarded as a church militant with the special duty of keeping the whig party in power and preserving the whig conception of the state as enunciated by Bishop Gibson: 'the Protestant Succession, the Church Establishment, and the Toleration'. The established religion was indeed regarded by most politicians, and many churchmen too, of the eighteenth century, first as a safeguard for the whig system of government, and especially as a valuable form of police control over the lower classes. Aristocrats like Shaftesbury, Chesterfield, or even Bolingbroke might safely be left to their free-thinking propensities, so long as they abjured extreme tory doctrines in the state and were careful not to contaminate the poor by too popular a presentment of their heresies. As Fielding, with blunt irony, puts it in his *Proposal for . . . an effectual Provision for the Poor for amending their Morals and for rendering them useful members of the Society*, 'heaven and hell, when well rung in the ears of those who have not yet learnt that there are no such places, . . . are by no means words of little or no signification'; and he calls in aid of this view the words of no less a divine than Tillotson: 'magistrates have always thought themselves concerned to cherish religion, and to maintain in the minds of men the belief of a God and another life, [as acknowledged by atheists who say it was] at first a politic device and is still kept up in the world as a state-engine to awe men into obedience.'[2] It is not, therefore, surprising that bishops were mainly chosen for their sympathy with whig doctrines and their capacity for enforcing them in the house of lords and their dioceses. Deaneries, prebends, canonries, and rich benefices were chiefly used either to increase the incomes of the less well-endowed bishoprics or to provide the scions of the great whig families, whom it was wise to keep in good humour, with—to quote one so favoured—'a pretty easy way of dawdling away one's time: praying, walking,

---

[1] Hickes died in 1715. There followed a long ritualistic conflict among the non-jurors which was not ended till 1732. As their later historian observed, 'internal dissensions contributed largely to the decline of the Non-juring cause'. J. H. Overton, *The Non-jurors*, p. 309. [I have not been able to trace Professor Williams's source for his estimate of the number of non-jurors in this period. It was certainly declining throughout and had 'greatly diminished' by 1745. See T. Lathbury, *History of the Non-jurors*, p. 386. C.H.S.]

[2] Fielding, *Complete Works*, ed. Henley, xiii. 186.

visiting;—and as little study as the heart could wish'. The rank and file of the clergy, miserably paid as a rule, were dependent on their bishops or on wealthy patrons for promotion to richer benefices;[1] to many such the temptation was strong to neglect their spiritual duties in order to forward the political views of their superiors in their parishes.

Ever since the Revolution the selection of bishops had been chiefly based on political grounds. When the whigs came into their long lease of power in 1714 they found much leeway to make up, for Anne, with her high church principles, had done her best to pack the bench with tories such as Dawes, Hooper, and Manningham, or even Jacobites, such as Atterbury. Throughout the reigns of the first two Georges the process was reversed. Walpole at first relied almost entirely for his choice of whig bishops on the advice of Gibson, himself an irreproachable whig, whom he had translated from Lincoln to London in 1723. In 1736, however, he quarrelled with Gibson and handed over the ecclesiastical patronage to Newcastle, who found the business so congenial that he kept control of it for nearly thirty years:[2] in fact when he died in 1768 there were few bishops on the bench who did not owe acknowledgement to him as their maker; fewer still who had not been promoted largely for their staunch whig principles. George I himself, though far more tolerant than any of his ministers save Stanhope, seems to have taken little part in the actual choice of bishops; but in the next reign both George II and Queen Caroline took considerable interest in ecclesiastical patronage. Caroline indeed prided herself on her theological discernment, and both as princess of Wales and as queen had regular meetings in her closet to discuss religious and philosophical questions with Leibnitz up to his death in 1716, Clarke,[3] Butler, Berkeley, Sherlock, and Hoadly, and even with Roman catholics such as Hawarden and Courayer. She would have liked to make Clarke a bishop, but was overruled by Gibson, who suspected Clarke of Arian opinions, and she was chiefly responsible for elevating to

[1] Sterne was among the luckier inferior clergy, for besides being a prebend of York he had amassed three livings which enabled him to live decently, 'a becoming ornament of the church, till his Rabelaisian spirit . . . immersed him into the gayeties and frivolities of the World'. Sterne's *Works*, 1794, i, p. x.

[2] On Newcastle as an ecclesiastical minister see N. Sykes in *Eng. Hist. Rev.* lvii. 59–84, and D. G. Barnes in *Pacific Historical Review*, iii (1934), 164–91.

[3] Rev. Samuel Clarke, 1675–1729, Boyle Lecturer and theologian.

the bench Secker, Sherlock, Potter, and the two greatest of the Georgian bishops, Berkeley and Butler.[1] Her husband had no such theological interests, but he too occasionally circumvented Newcastle's control of the *feuille des bénéfices*, and, during Newcastle's brief absence from Pitt's first ministry in 1757, made a general post of transfers, including the promotion of Hutton from York to Canterbury. Moreover, during both reigns the king managed to establish an almost prescriptive right to at least a deanery, if not a bishopric, for the royal chaplains taken with him to Hanover, though the wily Newcastle at times made up for this by picking out the Hanover chaplain from his own protégés. Blackburne of Exeter and York, Wilcocks of Gloucester and Rochester, Thomas of St. Asaph, Lincoln, and Salisbury, Johnson of Gloucester and Worcester, all reached the first rung on the episcopal ladder by a trip to Hanover; while on one occasion George I personally nominated Baker to the see of Bangor simply as a consolation for not having gone to Hanover as intended.[2]

Though there were a few Georgian bishops of whom any church might have been proud, the usual qualification for that office was political service or the support of powerful patrons in the whig party. Hoadly's four successive bishoprics, Bangor, Hereford, Salisbury, and Winchester, were the reward for his political pamphlets even more than for his Bangorian sermon; Potter, the son of a linen-draper, would hardly have risen to the primacy had he not first paid his court to Harley and at the propitious moment found salvation in whig circles; Gibson, a distinguished scholar, might not have risen above a college living had he not dedicated some of his works to Somers and Archbishop Tenison; Pearce of Bangor and Rochester first stepped on the ladder of promotion through a chaplaincy to Lord Chancellor Macclesfield, and later gained the favourable notice of Queen Caroline through the patronage of Lady Sundon. Willes earned his see of Bath and Wells by his labours as 'decypherer' of intercepted dispatches.

It will be observed that hardly any of these bishops remained in their first bishoprics; indeed the task of satisfying ambitious

[1] The part played by Queen Caroline in ecclesiastical promotions should not be exaggerated. For a balanced statement of her achievements in this sphere see Sykes, *Gibson*, pp. 141–2.
[2] N. Sykes, *Church and State . . . in the 18th Century*, pp. 39, 151–4.

divines was by no means concluded when they were once established on the bench. For there was a regular hierarchy of bishoprics, reckoned not by their spiritual or even political importance, but by the more mundane considerations of income and convenient distance from the metropolis. The plums of the profession, besides Canterbury and York at £7,000 and £4,500 respectively, were Durham at £6,000, Winchester £5,000, London £4,000, with Ely, Salisbury, and Worcester ranging from £3,400 to £3,000.[1] A bishop generally had to begin with one of the poorer sees, such as Bristol—valued by Secker in 1734 at only £360 and grumbled at even by Butler—Oxford, and Rochester; or one of the Welsh bishoprics, three of the four miserably paid and all in remote and 'barbarous' dioceses. It is true that these poorly paid bishops almost invariably had their incomes supplemented by deaneries, prebends, or rich benefices held in commendam,[2] but their chief ambition was generally translation to one of the richer dioceses, an ambition which sometimes took up more of their attention than their spiritual duties. Fortunately Newcastle, master of translation as well as of appointment, took a perfect delight in the intricate game of satisfying such claims by performance or dilatory promises. The poorer bishoprics suffered especially from this custom of translation owing to their brief tenure, especially in the case of the four Welsh sees: in fact, of the fifty-six bishops appointed to these four sees during the century after the Revolution, no less than thirty-nine were translated, often within a few years or even months of their appointment.[3]

Newcastle and other ecclesiastical patrons naturally expected a political quid pro quo from bishops so appointed or translated. Nor were they generally disappointed. Two of the northern bishops, Nicolson of Carlisle and Herring of York, took a large part in organizing their dioceses to resist the Jacobite risings of 1715 and 1745, calling men to arms, raising money, and reviewing troops: the fiery Nicolson was actually present at a skirmish near Penrith, and Herring in 1745 raised no less than £40,000 from Yorkshire for the government; while at Cloyne, in Ireland, the saintly Berkeley composed his letter to the Roman catholics

[1] These figures are for 1762; see Correspondence of K. George III, ed. Fortescue, i. 33–44, cited above in key to Map 1.
[2] i.e. to draw the revenues of a benefice, to which an incumbent was not appointed.
[3] See Sykes, Church and State, pp. 356–7.

which did much to restrain the Irish from joining the rebellion. But purely party services were more in demand, especially at elections. In the election of 1734, minutely described in Newcastle's correspondence,[1] Archbishop Wake and Bishops Hoadly, Sherlock, and Gibson all exercised pressure on the Sussex clergy at the duke's request. Hare, the bishop of the diocese, was reported as being ready to do all he could for the duke's candidates 'if it does not appear to be by way of a job', offered to put up their voters at his palace, where they would have well-aired beds, liquors, and breakfast, and though admitting that 'it can't be expected they [his clergy] should act all alike', promised that if any of them acted 'a rude, violent or factious part' he would be 'sure to remember it upon occasion'. At a later date, when Johnson, whose party allegiance was not entirely above suspicion, was translated from Gloucester to Worcester, Newcastle took care to exact an assurance from him that he would serve the government's interest in his new diocese. With such examples from their fathers in God, it is not surprising that the country clergy found it to their advantage to throw all their influence on the government side. Apart from such activities in their dioceses, no small part of the bishops' duty was deemed to be attendance in the house of lords during the session. The archbishop of Canterbury had a peculiarly close connexion with the government, since he had an official seat on the full cabinet council and was invariably a member of the regency councils during the king's frequent visits to Hanover: and so, like his medieval predecessors, he had a voice in the decision of secular policy. The bishops' votes were of special importance to the government in an age when party solidarity was less certain and close divisions more common than in the house of lords of today. In the division, for example, on Stanhope's bill for repealing the Schism and Occasional Conformity Acts the ministry required every one of its eleven supporters on the bishops' bench, two of William III's, three of Anne's, and six of George's, as against the fifteen bishops, most of them appointed by Anne, who voted against the measure.[2] But by the first decade of George II's reign the bench had been so well packed that most of the twenty-six could be regarded as normal supporters of the government. Even so a fairly full attendance from them was needed; in fact, in 1733, Walpole was twice

[1] See *E.H.R.* xii. 448 sqq., and above, p. 29, n. 1.   [2] Sykes, op. cit., p. 35.

saved from defeat in the lords only by the votes of twenty-four of the twenty-five bishops present.

This duty of attendance in London during half the year was some excuse for the comparatively lax observance of their pastoral duties by many of the bishops; for, owing to the difficulties and duration of journeys to and from the capital, occupants of remote sees could hardly be expected to visit them during the session. Again for the same reason the four or five summer months were hardly sufficient to enable bishops of such vast dioceses as Lincoln or York, for example, to carry out all the necessary ordinations, confirmations, and visitations of parishes every year. Probably, indeed, the majority of the bishops performed these formal duties as conscientiously as was possible, and certainly there was very little to complain of in that respect during the episcopates of Wake at Lincoln, White Kennett at Peterborough, Benson at Gloucester, or Drummond at York. But there were some scandalous exceptions, such as Blackburne, who does not appear to have conducted any confirmations personally during his tenure of York,[1] while Hoadly set foot in his diocese only once during his six years as bishop of Bangor, and not at all during his two years at Hereford. Nor were some of the bishops even respectable in their habits. Hoadly had the reputation of being a glutton—and his smug, well-fed appearance in the portrait by Hogarth bears out this view—and Gilbert of York of being 'like a pig of Epicurus', while Blackburne, though probably maligned by Horace Walpole as the keeper of a seraglio, was a great, roistering, ex-naval chaplain, who shocked even one of his vicars by calling for pipes and liquor in the vestry after a confirmation.

Perhaps the worst aspect of the ecclesiasticism of this period was the great gulf fixed between episcopal princes of the church, with all their state and comparative luxury, and the humble country parsons under their jurisdiction. Of the 10,000 benefices in England during the early part of the eighteenth century nearly 6,000 had revenues of less than £50 a year, 1,200 of them at under £20.[2] These humble and ill-paid pastors and their wealthy fathers in God rarely saw one another, and even when they did, the social distance between them was so great that

---

[1] But in 1737 Benson confirmed nearly 9,000 persons at Halifax and Ripponden. Sykes, p. 124.

[2] See M. G. Jones, *Charity School Movement in Eighteenth Century*, 1938, p. 66, n. 1.

little human intercourse was possible. This distance between the ranks and the predominantly secular aspect of the church was emphasized by the suppression of the convocation of the clergy in the two provinces. In the sixteenth and early part of the seventeenth century the convocations had been active bodies, dealing with the canons of the church and other religious questions, and useful for ventilating the complaints and aspirations of the whole clerical body. But when, at the Restoration, the convocation's privilege of voting clerical subsidies was taken away and parliament asserted its right to decide on canonical, liturgical, and church disciplinary questions, they lost their importance in the eyes of the state, and were not allowed to sit for business till 1700. Unfortunately, when they were convoked in that year, though that of York was innocuous, the convocation of Canterbury proved a veritable bear-garden under the stimulus of the firebrand Atterbury. The lower house quarrelled with the house of bishops, disputed the archbishop's rights as president, and enunciated extreme high-tory doctrines. Finally, in May 1717, when the lower house attacked Hoadly, bishop of Bangor, for his notorious sermon, both convocations were prorogued by the ministry, not to meet again for business till 1741, when once more they were prorogued owing to the renewal of the old disputes. After that, convocations did not meet till 1855. However just may have been the causes, this suppression of convocation had unfortunate results on the religious life of the church. The least disadvantage was that complained of by bishops Newton and Gibson that the clergy thereby lost a 'school of oratory' where embryo bishops were trained 'to a facility and readiness of speaking in the debates of a higher assembly'. Far more serious, especially at a time when the bishops and cathedral clergy were so much cut off from their poorer brethren in the country parishes, was the loss of the one opportunity for the higher and lower clergy to meet and discuss the doctrinal and practical questions affecting them all. As it was, there was no common policy in the church for dealing with such new problems as Wesleyanism, hardly even a common religion, and certainly little feeling of common interest between the wealthy bishops and pluralists and the humble village parsons. The suspension of convocations, necessary as it may have seemed to the politicians of the day, whose main concern was not to disturb sleeping dogs in church or state, was one of the causes of the lethargy and want of spirituality not unjustly imputed to the English church of the eighteenth century.

By a strange paradox, though the workaday religion preached and practised by the mass of the clergy, both established and dissenting, has rarely been so uninspiring as in this century, yet few ages in our history have been so prolific in serious thought about the fundamentals and justification of the whole scheme of Christianity, and especially of the established church itself. Not only the establishment but Christianity itself was felt to be on trial; and though most of the discussions showed little real apprehension of the spiritual side of religion, at the same time they served a purpose in clearing the ground for the more earnest spiritual stirring of the succeeding century. They also produced the works of three great writers and one mighty movement in the church, which alone would make the first half of the eighteenth century memorable in English ecclesiastical history.

The religious thought of this period, no less than its political theories, was largely dominated by the ideas and arguments of Locke. Breaking away from Descartes's 'innate ideas' as a justification for belief in God, he maintained that the mere fact that man has a clear perception of himself is quite enough evidence, apart from the special revelation in the Bible, that an eternal God implanted facilities in us whereby we attain this self-consciousness. From this fundamental need of a God to explain man's perceptions and his very existence Locke argued in his *Reasonableness of Christianity* that, though Christianity was not very different in its moral teaching from other creeds, it was specially deserving of credence because it gathered all moral teaching into one co-ordinated body of rules, and because Christ's gospel was more helpful to the vulgar than all the wisest philosophers' arguments. From Locke's first proposition are derived the deistical views so prevalent in the theological thought of the early eighteenth century, from the second, the utilitarian arguments so much employed to combat deism and support Christianity.

The first of the school of deists may be said to be Lord Herbert of Cherbury, in the seventeenth century: in our period also deism attracted aristocrats such as Shaftesbury, author of the *Characteristicks of Men*, and Bolingbroke. The latter's pretentious philosophy is of no more importance in theology than in politics, but Shaftesbury's *Inquiry concerning Virtue*, published in 1698, really started the controversy in its later phase. He identified God with the harmony of nature and defined virtue as an agreement with this universal harmony, to which we are impelled by a moral sense implanted in us by nature and so in no need of the divines' stimulus of future rewards and punishments. But the most important work of this school, against which orthodox arguments were mainly directed, was Tindal's *Christianity as old as the Creation*. To Tindal all religion was to be found in natural religion, based as that is on reason, which must be the ultimate test even of the revelation claimed as the proof of Christianity. Morality, the chief aim of all religions, was essentially the same in them all, so what, he asked, was the good of all the petty observances foisted by revealed religion on natural religion; and if Christian revelation was the only means to true happiness, how could a beneficent Creator have left such as the aboriginal natives of America without this revelation? Other deists began questioning the evidence for the Bible stories, one of them, Woolston, probably insane, being left to die in prison for declaring the resurrection to have been an imposture. Mandeville, in his *Fable of the Bees*, promulgated a kind of inverted deism by his theory that 'private vices are public benefits', since all men were naturally vicious and selfish, and virtue was merely imposed by crafty men for their own ends; a thesis which found an adversary in the Glasgow professor, Hutcheson, a forerunner of the utilitarians.

During George I's reign and the first decade of George II's deism called forth a host of pamphlets and treatises of very varying merit in defence of Christianity. Samuel Clarke, Queen Caroline's favourite divine, was one of the first in the field; he was followed by Waterland and Conybeare, supported by the dissenters Isaac Watts, Chandler, and Pope's 'modest Foster', who tackled the most formidable of the deists, Tindal; while poor Woolston, who had questioned Christ's miraculous powers, was set upon by no less than twenty adversaries. Among these were Bishop Smalbroke, who made the ingenious calculation about the legion (6,000) of devils expelled from one man into a drove of pigs, that each pig received no more than three devils, whereby he obtained the nickname of 'split-devil Smalbroke'. More effective was Sherlock's[1] *Tryal of the Witnesses*, which

---

[1] Thomas Sherlock, 1678–1701, bishop of Bangor, Salisbury, and London (1748–61).

had an immense vogue and was considered by its realistic form of a judicial trial to have entirely pulverized Woolston's arguments against the resurrection. The three great writers, however, Law, Butler, and Berkeley, who may be said to have given the quietus to deism, require separate treatment later.

One important result of the deistic controversy was that it compelled theologians to examine in a more critical spirit the evidence for revelation. The Bible had hitherto been accepted by all Christian sects as inspired and not open to question. Samuel Clarke, though not a deist, had stimulated the movement by his unorthodox views on the Trinity, and was accused of Arianism. In fact the heresies of Arianism, Sabellianism, and the sixteenth-century Socinianism, all of them either unitarian or denying the equality of Christ and the Holy Spirit with the Father, were dangerously prevalent in the church and dissenting bodies. Among the first to attempt a critical examination of Biblical evidence was Anthony Collins, a friend of John Locke. He was followed by Whiston, a disciple of Newton, but now best known for his translation of Josephus: for his Arian doctrines he was deprived of his Lucasian professorship, but he earned the vicar of Wakefield's approval by his view that 'it was unlawful for a priest of the church of England, after the death of his first wife, to take a second'. Middleton, author of the *Life of Cicero*, indirectly threw doubt on the Biblical miracles by his criticism of the powers reputed to have been exercised by the early fathers. Finally Hume, in his section 'Of Miracles' in *The Enquiry concerning the Human Understanding* (1748) argued that 'no testimony for any kind of miracle has ever amounted to a probability, much less to a proof'; and declared that 'a miracle is a violation of the laws of nature'. Hume went even further in his *Natural History of Religion* of 1757, and in his posthumously published *Dialogues concerning Natural Religion*, showing that the deists' arguments against revealed religion were just as valid against their substitute natural religion, and led to complete scepticism about the ordered foresight of any Supreme Being.[1] Nor was any serious attempt made to combat this scepticism till Paley, in the last decade of the century, brought out his *View of the Evidences of Christianity*.

Even that ark of the whig covenant, the established church,

---

[1] For a further discussion of Hume's philosophy see below, pp. 429-30.

was called into question during this sceptical century, and that not only by dissenters like Watts and Towgood, or non-jurors like Leslie, but by implication even by a prince of that church. Locke indeed, in his *Letter concerning Toleration*, had defended the establishment purely on the grounds of expediency, as compared with other forms of Christianity; but it was left to Hoadly, bishop of Bangor, to take away the last shred of excuse for such an institution. Hoadly was a practised pamphleteer, who on the accession of George I was made a royal chaplain as a reward for his valiant service to the whigs against Atterbury and the high church party in the previous reign; and in 1715 he was made bishop of Bangor. Though he neglected his episcopal duties, he again did valiant service for the government in his *Britannicus* letters against Atterbury in 1722 and his tract defending Walpole's foreign policy in 1726; but he is chiefly remembered for his pamphlet *A Preservative against the Principles and Practices of Non-jurors* and his sermon preached before the king in March 1717, which started the famous Bangorian controversy. In the pamphlet he asserted that a title to God's favour did not depend on any particular method of religious observance, but on sincerity in the conduct of the conscience and of actions. In the sermon, on the text 'My kingdom is not of this world', he declared that Christ was the sole law-giver to his subjects and that the laws of Christ, being sanctioned by no earthly reward or penalty, but by the future joys or pains of heaven or hell, were not subject to interpretation by any mundane authority. Nor was he afraid of drawing the conclusion that for priests, instead of those of Christ's kingdom who accepted His laws, to set themselves up as interpreters of those laws was to substitute priestly rule for that of God over His church. In fact he divested the church of all doctrinal or disciplinary authority. The most lasting effect of this sermon was to precipitate the suspension of convocations to avoid the scandal of a direct attack by the lower house of Canterbury on a bishop. It also initiated a controversy in which 53 writers produced some 200 pamphlets, 12 of which were from Hoadly's own pen. Effective answers to Hoadly came from Law, the non-juror, and from Sherlock, the bishop's old rival at Cambridge, who pointed out that his arguments 'cancelled all our obligations to any particular communion' and led directly to deism. Twenty years later the final blow to Hoadly's position was delivered by

Warburton,[1] already known for his *Divine Legation of Moses*, a somewhat paradoxical defence of revealed religion against the deists, in his *Alliance between Church and State*. In this work he had two main objects, first to refute Hoadly's denial of a visible church having authority within its own sphere, and second to justify the established church of England in alliance with and under control of the state. He admits that the church is a voluntary association, but necessary for the corporate attainment of the objects of religion; and though he goes as far as Hoadly in denying any authority to priests as mediators between God and man, he reasonably asserts the need of authority in the church to deal with those who do not conform with the objects of the association. His defence of the establishment is an elaboration of Locke's idea that this is the most convenient arrangement for both state and church. It suited the civil authority to have the support of religious sanctions in its government of society: it suited the church equally to have the prestige of the civil government to protect its dignity and, if necessary, enforce its decisions. But Warburton admitted, as Locke had implied, and as Paley later explicitly stated, that the state church must be chosen, not for the superiority of its doctrine, but because its adherents were the majority of the population; and he hardly flinched from the corollary that, were any other religious body later to become a majority, it would be difficult to deny its claims to be the established church. Tests for political office he defended on the ground that the church of the majority must be supported against attack from a hostile minority: at the same time, he, like Hoadly and Locke, was all for tolerance of protestant dissenters, since the Revolution the faithful allies of the whigs.

This treatise is a typical product of an eighteenth-century bishop. It conveys, as has been said, 'the lowest theory of an established religion that could be framed. . . . It degrades the clergy to the rank of a body of police, and the Church to a mere office of Government.'[2] It must indeed be admitted that the church of England during the eighteenth century is not an inspiring spectacle. Latitudinarian to a degree which makes it difficult to find any theological justification for its existence, at

---

[1] William Warburton, 1698–1779, bishop of Gloucester, friend of Pope, and a prolific writer.
[2] Skeats, p. 418.

its highest it was an efficient instrument of statecraft, at its lowest it was a nest of pluralists and mundane divines. It contained no doubt many saintly and vigorous servants of the gospel, such as Thomas Wilson, the noble and self-sacrificing bishop of Sodor and Man, Bishop Martin Benson of Bristol, and parish clergy such as Fletcher of Madeley, Venn of Huddersfield, Grimshaw, a predecessor of Mr. Brontë at Haworth, John Berridge of Everton, and the devotional writer James Harvey.

The historian[1] of the free churches during this period gives a somewhat unfavourable view of their activities and suggests that they, like the established church, had spent most of their vigour in the heroic combats of the seventeenth century and were relaxing in the sun of comparative security. Superficially, there seems much to say for this view. For, although the free churches still had some notable preachers and writers such as Bradbury,[2] Lardner, Neal, Doddridge, two more Calamys, and Isaac Watts the hymn-writer, it is certainly true that they seem to have diminished in numbers in the course of the century.[3] Various reasons account for this decrease. The original presbyterians had, until driven out by Charles II's legislation, always regarded the church of England as a mother, however erring a mother she might be, and their eighteenth-century descendants not infrequently returned to the fold, some to recover the full rights of citizenship, others for social reasons, others again, Butler for example, from deep spiritual conviction. Many again, and these some of the most thoughtful, such as Priestley, Richard Price, Philip Furneaux, were impelled, by the development of free thought so marked in many of the presbyterian communities, to adopt Arian, Socinian, or frankly unitarian views. This tendency was much encouraged by their educational system, which fostered vigorous speculation and a development of doctrine, affording a strong contrast to the religious and intellectual apathy of so many of the established clergy and their flocks. This educational system, partly in their own academies, partly in the universities open to them, was deservedly famous and in many respects ahead of that given in the schools and universities open only to churchmen. In nothing indeed was

[1] Skeats, l.c.
[2] It was he who, shortly after Queen Anne's death, preached from the text: 'go see now this cursed woman and bury her, for she is a king's daughter'. Skeats, p. 274 (2 Kings ix. 34).
[3] See above, p. 69, n. 4.

Calvin's teaching more exactly followed in the eighteenth century by these English presbyterians than in their care for the best education procurable. In addition to the classics, French, Italian, history and political theory, English literature, inductive, instead of the old Aristotelian, logic, and above all science were included in the curriculum of many of these academies, such as Morton's at Stoke Newington, where Defoe was taught, Doddridge's at Northampton, Dr. John Taylor's at Warrington, and Samuel Jones's at Tewkesbury, where, too, besides the dissenters Chandler, Edmund Calamy, and Toland, Bishop Butler and Archbishop Secker were educated. Here, too, free discussions on politics and even on the fundamentals of religion were encouraged in the liberal spirit of Dr. John Taylor, who told his students to keep their minds 'always open to evidence . . . and freely allow to others the inalienable rights of judgment and conscience'. Since the students at these academies were mostly excluded from entry into the English universities, they were encouraged to go to the more vigorous universities of Edinburgh and Glasgow, Utrecht and Leyden; and well-to-do dissenters maintained a fund whose expenditure often reached £2,000 per annum to help the poorer scholars there with bursaries. Naturally this enlightened system of education encouraged a free spirit of inquiry among the dissenters. The harsh narrow creeds of the seventeenth century gave way, especially under the influence of Dutch theologians and Scottish philosophers, to a more humanistic view of religion; and though such heresies as Arianism, Socinianism, and unitarianism gained much ground among these chapel folk, at any rate there was less stagnation and apathy than was common in the established church and more well-thought-out beliefs.[1]

On the other hand, no one among the dissenters stands out as do those three great doctors of the established church, Butler, Berkeley, and Law. These hold a place apart, not only in the eighteenth century but in the long history of that church.

Joseph Butler was the son of a well-to-do dissenting tradesman, and after he had decided to enter the church of England, was fortunate in having many years for quiet reflection, first

---

[1] A good account of the presbyterians in this century and of their educational system is in Olive M. Griffiths, *Religion and Learning, A Study of English Presbyterian Thought . . .*, 1935.

as preacher at the Rolls Chapel, the birth-place of his *Fifteen Sermons*, and then at the quiet but well-endowed country rectory of Stanhope in Weardale. Here he had leisure for ten years to attain his great object in life, 'to prove to myself the being and attributes of God', a period of quiet thought and deep reflection which resulted in *The Analogy of Religion, Natural and Revealed, to the Constitution and Course of Nature*, published in 1736. The greatness of Butler consisted partly in the statesmanlike fairness of his method of arguing: he was always prepared to face unwelcome facts, and, as Mr. Gladstone points out, was ready to admit that we must be content, as in all practical matters, 'with the kind and amount of evidence which falls far short of demonstration', and that this very lack of demonstration is just part of our probation. But in answer to the deists he was conclusive in showing that the natural arguments for their all-powerful creator were beset with even greater difficulties than those taken for the revelation of Christ. His chief merit, however, is his vindication of the authority of conscience as opposed to that of self-interest as the main criterion of right, and his intense belief that God is, that He is just and good, and that He is Love, cares for man and seeks to redeem and save him. Butler, too was no mere theorist in this view of Christianity, strangely spiritual for his age. He was a great supporter of home and foreign missions, charities, and hospitals; and he insisted on the need for a more vital spirit in the church, partly by means of decent and reverent ceremonial, but above all by prayers and visitations and by the education of children in the love of God. He had his limitations, no doubt. It is quaint to see how a man, capable of such high thoughts as Butler, is still a child of his time and touched by the prejudice of his day. When Wesley came to speak to him about methodism, which in many ways came near his own spiritual ideals, he exclaimed testily, 'Sir, the pretending to extraordinary revelations and gifts of the Holy Ghost is a horrid thing, a very horrid thing.' But then the whole trend of his mind was against 'enthusiasm' and all for a religion based on truth and arrived at entirely by hard reasoning, not by vague sentiment or appeals to the emotions.

No greater contrast can be imagined than that between Butler and the other great doctor of the eighteenth-century church, George Berkeley. Butler, the favourite of fortune, had all the ease and leisure he required for his one great object in life, 'to prove to myself the being and attributes of God'; but he was denied that power of limpidly presenting the results of his massive reasoning or that charm of style most fitted to win adherents easily to his conclusions. Berkeley's, on the other hand, was a restless and adventurous nature, full of schemes for active benevolence to his fellow men in both hemispheres. A much-travelled man, he was one of those who cared nothing for the riches of this world except so far as they enabled him to carry out his beneficent schemes. Of these the best known was his project for the foundation of a college at Bermuda for training missionaries to the Indians and reforming the manners and morals of the colonists of America.[1] Full of enthusiasm at the *Prospect of Planting Arts and Learning in America*, he hopefully foretold that

> Westward the course of empire takes its way;
> The four first Acts already past,
> A fifth shall close the Drama with the day;
> Time's noblest offspring is the last.

To this object he devoted the income of his rich deanery of Derry, a legacy of £3,000 from Swift's Vanessa, and the subscriptions that his persuasive enthusiasm extracted from well-wishers such as Lord Egmont. Walpole had promised him the necessary grant to complete his plans; and in the faith of it he set sail to Rhode Island, only to find that the grant was not to be forthcoming. After three years of vain waiting in America he returned to England. He was given as a consolation the bishopric of Cloyne, a remote diocese of Ireland, where he remained for almost the rest of his life,[2] busied with good works, such as reforms for the social state of Ireland or the advocacy of tar-water for the cure of human ailments. But he is famous chiefly for his philosophical and theological speculations, most of which were published before he went to Cloyne. Berkeley was a platonist and an idealist, whereas most of the theologians of this century were more inclined to the hard logical reasoning of Aristotle. He went so far against the deist view of God standing aloof from the world, as to argue that 'as the visible world has no absolute existence, being merely the sensible expression

[1] See also below for the Bermuda scheme, p. 323.
[2] He died at Oxford in the house in Holywell known as 'The Cardinal's Hat', once a 'colony' of New College.

of Supreme Intelligence and Will, each man has actually the same kind of evidence that God exists—and in a much higher degree—which he has that a fellow man exists when he hears him speak'.[1] To Berkeley nothing except minds existed, save as a perception of the mind; and the explanation of our certainty of the permanence of an outside world was that 'all objects are eternally known by God, or, which is the same thing, have an eternal existence in His mind', and He produces ideas in our minds on a constant, though arbitrary plan. This theory gains persuasiveness by the charm and beauty of diction with which it is set forth, principally in the *Dialogues between Hylas and Philonous*, published in 1713, and also in the *Alciphron*, a dialogue written during his sojourn at Rhode Island and cast in the Platonic mould. This opens with a resigned allusion to the miscarriage of his Bermuda scheme, tempered by the opportunity which 'this distant retreat, far beyond the verge of that great whirlpool of business, faction, and pleasure which is called the *world*', gave him for 'reflections that make me some amends for a great loss of time, pains, and expense'; and he thus describes the scene of the dialogue, in words that recall the Buddha's choice of 'a pleasant spot and a beautiful forest' as the scenery most 'soothing to the senses and stimulating to the mind': 'We walked under the delicious shade of . . . trees for about an hour before we came to Crito's house, which stands in the middle of a small park, beautified with two fine groves of oak and walnut, and a winding stream of sweet and clear water.' Even if we cannot accept all Berkeley's arguments against the free-thinkers in this Dialogue, Alciphron and his more worldly friend Lysicles, we cannot fail to be impressed with the spirituality and moral earnestness of his creed, so refreshing after the rather arid common sense of most eighteenth-century thinkers and theologians, or enchanted with the sheer beauty of thought and language in the exposition of his philosophy. Take, for example, these passages setting forth one of the cardinal ideas of his creed:

The Author of Nature constantly speaks to the eyes of all mankind, even in their earliest infancy, whenever the eyes are open in the light, whether alone or in company: it doth not seem to me at all strange that men should not be aware they had ever learned a

---

[1] A. C. Fraser in *Works of George Berkeley*, ii. 8.

language begun so early. . . . Things which rarely happen strike; whereas frequency lessens the admiration of things, though in themselves ever so admirable. Hence, a common man, who is not used to think and make reflections, would probably be more convinced of the being of a God by one single sentence heard once in his life from the sky than, by all the experience he has had of this Visual Language, contrived with such exquisite skill, so constantly addressed to his eyes, and so plainly declaring the nearness, wisdom, and providence of Him with whom we have to do.[1]

Eighteenth-century epitaphs, especially to bishops, are apt to be unduly fulsome, but Berkeley deserves the noble words engraved on a marble tablet at Christ Church, Oxford:

> Seu Ingenii et Eruditionis laudem
> Seu Probitatis et Beneficentiae Spectemus
> Inter primos omnium aetatum numerando.
> Si Christianus fueris
> Si Amans Patriae
> Utroque nomine gloriari potes
> Berkleium vixisse.[2]

The third great spiritual writer of our period, William Law, was not, like the other two, a bishop; he was not even a beneficed clergyman, for being a non-juror he lost a fellowship at Emmanuel College, Cambridge, and a college living, though he still remained in communion with the established church instead of joining the separate non-juring schism. He was tutor for a time to Edward Gibbon's father and remained some ten years in that family, but from 1740 he lived retired from the world near Stamford with Gibbon's aunt Hester and another pious woman, Mrs. Hutcheson, founding schools for the poor and alms-houses, and devoted to religious meditation. Earlier he had published three of the best refutations of Hoadly's, Mandeville's, and Tindal's heretical views, and also two manuals of practical ethics and religion, the best known being his *Serious Call to a Devout and Holy Life*. This is concerned with the practical question of how to live according to Christ's teaching—not by ceremonial devotions but by a new principle of life, a change of temper and aspiration. It had an immense influence

[1] Berkeley, *Alciphron*, iv. §§ 11, 15.
[2] On Berkeley, in addition to his own works, see Professor Sorley's chap. xi in vol. ix of *Cambridge History of English Literature*.

on such varied characters as Dr. Johnson, who declared that it turned him to the religious life which became so marked a characteristic in him, George Lyttelton, the statesman, who read it through in bed before he got to sleep, even Gibbon, who said that 'if he finds a spark of piety in his reader's mind he will soon kindle it to a flame', and the anonymous vicar who, after years of vain struggle, brought his parish to godly ways by distributing copies of the *Serious Call* to every household. This is not to be wondered at considering the book's logical power, its racy wit, its homely and effective stories such as those of Flavia and Miranda or of Ouranius, and the delightful style in which the author's contagious devotion is expressed. Later, in his retirement, he fell under the influence of Boehme, the religious mystic, and published two books, *An Appeal to all that Doubt* and *The Way to Divine Knowledge*, which justify for him the title of 'our greatest prose mystic'. In these books he expounded the view that mystic attainment depends on the will or desire to get into harmony with God; when once we are united with God our errors cease, coming as they do from our division from God; for there is nothing evil in God, of Whom man's soul partakes. His mysticism for a time influenced the Wesleys and Whitefield, though they parted from him, as they came to think that his mysticism did not partake enough of Christ. But he had a lasting influence on the evangelical revival not directly the outcome of methodism. Law, therefore, much more than Butler and Berkeley, started the tendency to that personal and devotional religion which gradually, towards the end of the eighteenth century, began to supersede the formal and purely Erastian religion prevalent in the greater part of that age.[1]

Apart from these few great men and the sprinkling of some devoted country parsons, the established church, throughout the century, was more of a political system tinged with the minimum of Christian doctrine than a living example of faith animating the community. Benevolence, it is true, was an active force in this period, as is testified by the number of hospitals, alms-houses, and charitable doles instituted in London and the provinces.[2] It was also an age which saw the feeble

[1] On Law see Dr. Caroline Spurgeon's chapter on 'Law and the Mystics' in *Cambridge History of English Literature*, vol. ix. See also J. H. Overton, *William Law*, pp. 111–13.
[2] See M. G. Jones, *Charity School Movement*, and below, pp. 137 sqq.

beginnings of a more humanitarian spirit in the treatment of prisoners, or in provision for the indigent and infirm associated with such names as those of Oglethorpe, Henry Fielding, and Dean Tucker, who was, however, thought to be too much of an economist to obtain a bishopric. But very little of this spirit was due to the impulse of the church. For, in the orderly and comfortable religion in vogue, polite society looked askance at anything savouring of enthusiasm.[1]

But at this very period sprang from, but not of, the church itself a new movement which appealed directly to the consciences of the mass of the people and gave them a living, enthusiastic faith. This living hope was brought to millions not touched by the ministrations of the regular clergy. At Oxford in 1729 Charles Wesley founded his Holy Club of a few earnest Christians, named methodists in derision, who met together to discuss religion, attended church daily, and partook of the Holy Communion once a week. Soon they were joined by Charles's more famous brother John, elected Fellow of Lincoln from Christ Church, and also by the younger man George Whitefield of Pembroke. Feeling the call to stir up their fellows to realize the need of personal salvation, of which they themselves were so acutely conscious, they dedicated their lives to missionary work. First the two Wesleys and later Whitefield went forth to Oglethorpe's new colony of Georgia, with the same objects as Berkeley's, to evangelize the Indians and to preach the gospel to the new colonists. The Wesleys' efforts were not entirely successful there, and resulted in disputes with the Georgia trustees; Whitefield was more tactful, founded an orphan college at Savannah, and several times revisited America, where he died in 1770.

But the main work of the Wesleys and Whitefield was in England, where all three had been ordained priests of the established church. Whitefield was the first to adopt the open-air method of preaching so characteristic of early methodism, simply because he found himself excluded from the Bristol and Bath pulpits by the incumbents, horrified at his unfashionable

[1] White Kennett, dean and then bishop of Peterborough, in many respects an admirable churchman, one of the founders of the Society for Propagating the Gospel in Foreign Parts, nevertheless, when preaching at court, threatened the sinner with punishment 'in a place which he thought it not decent to name in so polite an assembly'. See Pope, *Moral Essays*, iv. 150: the 'soft Dean Who never mentions hell to ears polite'.

directness and 'enthusiastic' methods of preaching, with their almost hysterical effects on the crowds that came to hear him. Wesley also was looked on as dangerously enthusiastic in his sermons and was likewise warned off sacred edifices, but he was much more doubtful about so novel an experiment, 'having been all my life (till very lately)', he said, 'so tenacious of every point relating to decency and order that I should have thought the saving of souls almost a sin if it had not been done in a church'. But after he had been inhibited from preaching in his diocese by Butler, he was persuaded by Whitefield to attend one of his mass meetings of miners, bereft of all spiritual help from the regular clergy, at Kingswood near Bristol. This decided him, for he was convinced by the effects of his friend's preaching that this was the only way of reaching the great mass of the people; and thenceforward he took to the fields also.

In 1740, however, the two great evangelists parted company. Whitefield adopted the Calvinistic creed of 'election', or predestined salvation, and became more and more estranged from the church of England; Wesley held to the Arminian view that salvation was open to all who found faith in Jesus Christ and so left an opening for free will. He also remained steadfast to the church of England, in spite of a growing desire of the majority of his followers to ordain their own ministers and form an entirely separate organization. Whitefield felt the ties to the old church far more lightly, like his notable patroness Selina countess of Huntingdon who eventually also was obliged to carry on her 'Connexion' outside the church in buildings still to be seen, somewhat decayed, in places so wide apart as Bath, Pilt-down in Sussex, and near the High School Yards at Edinburgh. Whitefield was certainly the more prominent of the two in the early days of the methodist movement,[1] partly owing to the greater eccentricity of his preaching, though Dr. Johnson's verdict that 'he did not draw attention by doing better than others, but by doing what was strange' is palpably unjust. Even as late as 1772 he and his followers, rather than Wesley, figure principally in Graves's[2] *Spiritual Quixote*, an able and not entirely unsympathetic satire on the methodist movement. But though the two leaders differed, they always remained in

[1] See, for example, Fielding's *Joseph Andrews*, i. 17, first published in 1742.
[2] Richard Graves had been an exact contemporary of Whitefield at Pembroke, Oxford.

brotherly affection to one another; and Wesley, at Whitefield's dying request, preached his funeral sermon.

John Wesley, aided by his brother Charles, chiefly remembered for his hymns, was not merely a great preacher, but a marvellous organizer. Every moment of his long life was carefully mapped out in order to find time for his great journeys—he is said to have travelled 250,000 miles on horseback in fifty years; for his sermons, of which his average was fifteen a week; for his organizing activities; and especially for his own private devotions of two hours regularly every day. This studied economy of his time evoked Dr. Johnson's humorous protest: 'John Wesley's conversation is good, but he is never at leisure. He is always obliged to go at a certain hour. This is very disagreeable to a man who loves to fold his legs and have out his talk as I do.'

John Wesley's greatness consisted not only in his power as a preacher, but also in his initiation of the vast system by which his teaching was to be kept alive and vigorous. He and Whitefield were not indeed the first to 'look upon all the world as my parish' and to refuse to regard it as trespassing to invade the parishes of brother-clergymen in order to awake their somnolent parishioners to the living Gospel. The same system had already been started in the even more neglected parishes of Wales by Howel Harris and Daniel Rowlands, who within a few years had turned an almost pagan Principality into the intensely methodist country that it still is. But Wesley surpassed all his contemporary revivalists first by his well planned system of circuits for his lay preachers. Of these the most notable was John Nelson, the Yorkshire mason, whose influence over the working-classes, especially in Cornwall, owing to the Yorkshire common sense, homely wit, and intense pathos of his preaching, is said to have been equal to that of Wesley himself; and, like Wesley and Whitefield, he suffered unbelievable outrages from some of the baser clergy and the mobs they instigated. The methodist doctrines reached even the prisons, according to Smollett, whose turnkey at Clerkenwell prison complained that since Humphrey Clinker entered the place there had been 'nothing but canting and praying . . . [and] the gentlemen get drunk with nothing but your damned religion'. Wesley also organized his followers by his 'tickets' of membership, the weekly meetings of ticket-holders for mutual confession, and the quarterly 'love-feasts' he instituted. Already in 1744 he had formed his central organization at a conference at the Foundry, his headquarters in London, and to the end of his long life kept the control of this organization in his own hands. He had difficulties with his followers, who increasingly desired to break away from the church of England and form an entirely distinct body; but as long as he lived he resisted this successfully, and only after his death came their final breach with the church.

One of the most interesting contemporary accounts of the methodists' views and aspirations, as well as of the charges brought against them, is to be found in Lord Egmont's *Diary* for 1739. The entries relate solely to Whitefield, but at that early date he and Wesley were still at one, so they illustrate fairly the ideas and methods of both. On Tuesday, 5, and Friday, 8 June of that year Egmont and his wife heard two of Whitefield's sermons, the first on Woolwich Common and the second on Charlton Green, overlooked by a summer-house at the end of Egmont's garden, to which the family and neighbours were invited, 'to partake of the curiosity'. In each case the proceedings opened with a psalm sung by the crowd, followed by 'a long pathetic prayer' and a sermon from Whitefield, who 'preached by heart with much earnestness and spreading his arms wide and was at no loss for matter or words, and the people were very attentive'. After the second sermon Egmont called Whitefield into the house and offered him refreshment, whereupon a long discussion took place as to his doctrines and methods. Whitefield denied the stories put about by his enemies that he set up for working miracles, encouraged his adherents to rise fasting from the table, so disappointing 'their carnal appetites', allowed women to preach, taught that all things should be in common, had made many run mad, or had declared in one of his sermons that if what he said was not due to the inspiration of the Holy Ghost then Christ was not true. He was willing, he said, to preach in church, but was excluded by the 'common clergy [who] do not preach the true doctrine of Christ'; he was not, however, sorry to preach in the fields, because there he got a chance of speaking to many, such as reprobates, who never went to church and who, coming to hear him by curiosity, sometimes went away converted. Dissenters, too, who also would not go to church, willingly heard him in the fields. He insisted that the doctrine he taught was that of the church of England and of the 39 Articles. Only the free Grace of God could save us without the help of good works, for by the sin of Adam all were under sin and would be damned, were it not for the free and gracious sufferings of Jesus Christ; and everybody by praying could obtain this free grace. But though good works alone would not save us, we may assure ourselves that without good works we have not the necessary faith, for good works were the evidence of this faith. Egmont's verdict after this conversation was that he found in him 'only . . . an enthusiastic notion of his being capable of doing much good, and perhaps he thinks he is raised up for that purpose; for the rest I believe him perfectly sincere and disinterested, and that he does indeed work a considerable reformation among the common people, and there is nothing in his doctrine that can be laid on to his hurt'.[1] Later, too, when the Georgia trustees took umbrage at Whitefield's proceedings in America, Egmont defended him on the ground that though 'a great enthusiast, [yet] enthusiasts were always sincere though mistaken, and did not consist with hypocrisy'.[2]

The church of England, though no kindly mother to her two great sons, Wesley and Whitefield, may yet claim some little merit for their work. Both were brought up in her creed and both began their work under her tutelage. Some at least of her clergy followed them; some of the cultivated laymen like Egmont, a very devout churchman, could recognize the good in their work; while twice, in 1741 and 1744, after Wesley had begun his 'enthusiastic' preaching in the fields, Oxford University invited him to deliver university sermons. Wesley himself never lost his love and loyalty to George Herbert's 'dear Mother', the church of England. But certainly their work for religion was almost entirely outside the church, work which brought about the regeneration of a living faith in England.

[1] *Hist. MSS. Comm.*, . . . *Diary of 1st Earl of Egmont*, 1923, iii. 64, 67–69.

[2] Ibid., pp. 127–8. Not all indeed of Egmont's fellow aristocrats took so broad-minded a view. Four years later the 'haughty' duchess of Buckingham wrote as follows to Selina countess of Huntingdon: 'I thank your ladyship for the information concerning the Methodist preachers. Their doctrines are most repulsive, and strongly tinctured with impertinence, and disrepect towards their superiors. It is monstrous to be told that you have a heart as sinful as the common wretches that crawl the earth. I cannot but wonder that your ladyship should relish any sentiments so much at variance with high rank and good breeding.' Quoted by V. Gibbs in *Complete Peerage*, ii. 400.

They appealed to the vast mass of their countrymen who had, most of them, either never been inside a church in their lives, or, if they had, were untouched by the formal services they found there—the poor, the degraded, no less than the honest working folk, repelled by the cold, lifeless, and perfunctory ministrations of the beneficed clergy. Mr. Richardson himself, most respectable of printers and authors, bears testimony to the work of the methodists in helping those impervious to other religious influences. 'Mrs. O'Hara', he writes in *Sir Charles Grandison* (volume v, letter 12), 'is turned *Methodist*. . . . Thank God she is anything that is serious. Those people have really great merit with me, in *her* conversion.—I am sorry that our own Clergy are not as zealously in earnest as they. They have really . . . given a face of religion to subterranean colliers, tinners and the most profligate of men, who hardly ever before heard either of the word or thing.' The movement came too at a time when it was most needed, on the eve of the industrial revolution, when great communities were springing up in the sordid surroundings of the new factories, with no provision for any spiritual teaching save that given by the travelling methodists, whose chief business it was to seek out and feed the souls of such neglected people. They alone brought them any alleviation from the degrading misery of their work-a-day lives, and helped to make them the deeply religious and self-respecting people which the lower middle class of factory workers and shopkeepers of the manufacturing areas had become by the nineteenth century.

Some credit, too, for the success of methodism may be given to the general sense of fairness in the English people. Intolerant, brutally intolerant, we may sometimes be at first to strange and little understood movements, such as methodism or the Salvation Army, which do not seem to fit into our ordered system; but when the new movement has proved its sincerity by steadfastness in face of persecution and its value by the fruits it brings forth, then it has won its liberty. Not so long ago a distinguished foreigner was standing in delighted appreciation in front of a poor little meeting-house in a mean street, belonging to some obscure sect. 'Such little tabernacles as this', such was the gist of his comment, 'are the best evidence of your greatness as a nation. They are evidence of the independence of judgement which every man can exercise as to his beliefs: they are also evidence of the toleration which, in the long run, the whole community gives to every opinion and every form of enthusiasm which can prove honesty of purpose and sincerity.'

NOTE. On this chapter I have had the advantage of comments from Mr. H. W. B. Joseph and Professor Kemp Smith. [Note of 1939.]

V

SOCIAL AND ECONOMIC LIFE
OF THE ENGLISH PEOPLE[1]

WE are fortunate in having two remarkable records of the state of England at the opening and close of this period of our history. First we have Daniel Defoe, the supreme journalist, interested in every aspect of the national life, who between 1724 and 1726 published his *Tour through Great Britain*,[2] describing the social and economic conditions of the whole island during the reign of George I. To supplement Defoe at the end of the period we have Arthur Young, the practical farmer and indefatigable observer, whose *Six Weeks' Tour through the Southern Counties of England and Wales*, *Six Months' Tour through the North of England*, and *Farmer's Tour through the East of England*, undertaken in the first decade of George III's reign,[3] are mainly concerned with agricultural investigations, but also contain valuable information on rates of wages, cost of provisions, and other industrial and social matters. At the outset, the mere physical difficulties of travel encountered by both men over the abominable roads and tracks of the period[4] give us an insight into one of the elementary obstacles to efficient government, internal trade, and even the interchange of social amenities in the eighteenth century. Of the two the earlier, Defoe, is the less vociferous in his complaints, partly because his main object is to dwell on all the best aspects of British civilization, partly because he is much impressed by the few stretches of

[1] The social and economic conditions in Scotland and Ireland are dealt with in Chap. X.

[2] The text quoted of Defoe's *Tour through the Whole Island of Great Britain* is that published by G. D. H. Cole in 2 vols. in 1927. [I have retained the text of these quotations as given by Professor Williams but I have altered the page references to fit the Everyman edition (1928) prepared by G. D. H. Cole from the same text, as this edition is more generally available. C.H.S.]

[3] Arthur Young made his tours in the south in 1767, in the north in 1768, and in the east in 1770. See preface to *Farmer's Tour through the East of England*; the editions quoted are of 1768 (south), 1771 (2nd edn., north), 1771 (east).

[4] At the beginning of this period the roads had very little improved since Elizabeth's day. See *Oxford History of England*, viii. 263-4 (2nd edn.).

comparatively good turnpike roads over which he was able to
ride. But even he has nothing good to say about the roads
passing through the thick clay of the Midlands north of Dun-
stable, or of the Sussex roads on which 'an Ancient Lady . . .
of very good Quality . . . [was] drawn to Church in her Coach
with six Oxen; nor was it done in Frolick or Humour, but
meer Necessity, the Way being so stiff and deep, that no Horses
could go in it'. He too regrets that no living workmen can be
found to imitate the Romans' 'noble Causeways and Highways' still standing in some parts of the country, 'perfect solid
Buildings' on their deep-laid foundations.[1] Young, though turnpike acts had multiplied in the intervening years, is much less
restrained in his denunciations. Of the turnpike roads in the
south of England he picks out only six short stretches as good;
of the others, 'it is a prostitution of language to call them turn-
pikes'. In his exhaustive commentary on the northern roads he
finds rather more good patches, but of the rest one is 'vile, a
narrow causeway cut into ruts', others 'execrably broke into
holes . . . sufficient to dislocate one's bones, a more dreadful road
cannot be imagined', while as for the cross-roads some are 'fit
only for a goat to travel'.[2] A fruitful cause of the rapid deteriora-
tion even of the best-laid roads was the constant use of them by
droves of stock. Every year some 40,000 Highland cattle came to
be fattened on the Norfolk pastures and, when in condition, were
driven by road to the London market; while 30,000 black cattle
from Wales were herded annually to the south-east of England
to swell the total arriving at Smithfield. Geese and pigs went the
same way, and every year 150,000 turkeys gobbled and waddled
their way along the road from Ipswich to London.[3]

Even the turnpike roads, indifferent as many were, remained
almost a rarity up to the middle of the century. From Saxon
times it had been the duty of individual parishes to keep in
repair the sections of road within their boundaries, partly by
a levy on the rich, partly by the forced labour of the poorer
parishioners; and naturally such work was perfunctory. Only
towards the end of the seventeenth century was this system
beginning to be superseded by turnpike trusts, which were incorporated by acts of parliament. These trusts were composed of

[1] Defoe, Everyman edition, i. 129; ii. 119.
[2] See *Southern Tour*, p. 249, and *Northern Tour*, iv. 424, 427-8, 433.
[3] S. and B. Webb, *Story of the King's Highway*, pp. 67-68.

county justices and others who undertook the repair and up-keep of stated tracts of road, recouping themselves by tolls levied on travellers over those parts of the highway. But it was not till after the '45 had made manifest the shortcomings of the roads for the rapid transport of troops pitted against the High-landers travelling light that these turnpike trusts became more efficient and fairly general, increasing rapidly from about 160 in 1748 to about 530 in 1770.[1] One of the great pioneers in this road-making age was John Metcalf, 'Blind Jack of Knares-borough', who was responsible for 180 miles of good roads in Yorkshire and Lancashire.[2] Even as late as 1752, however, the Great West Road, after the first 47 miles out of London, was still for 220 miles under the old parish system. In fact, until well into George III's reign the state of the roads and the means of communication were so poor that a great deal of the inland transport of goods, such as pottery, cloth, even coal, had to be done by pack-horses; and even they found difficulties. At the end of the century Francis Place, who was born in 1771, still remembered the road from Glasgow to London as a narrow causeway as far as Grantham, described in 1739 as so narrow that a train of pack-horses meeting another had to go into the ditch till the other had passed. Even today the remains of pack-horse travel may be noted in the high raised paths outside some old farms at a convenient height for unloading saddle-pack goods.

Owing partly to the badness of the roads, partly to high turnpike charges, the cost of transport was enormous: even for the 36 miles stretch from Liverpool to Manchester the cost of conveying a ton of goods was £2, while from London to Leeds it amounted to £13. Such exorbitant charges were so highly resented that in 1726, 1732, 1749, and 1753 formidable turnpike riots occurred in various parts of the country with destruction of toll-bars and toll-houses. Still by 1766 some of the roads had been so much improved that the 'flying coach' from Manchester and Liverpool was able to accomplish the

---

[1] S. and B. Webb, l.c. p. 124. In the Highlands of Scotland General Wade, at the government's expense, had already constructed 259 miles of road and 40 bridges between 1726 and 1737; and after the '45, 800 more miles with 1,000 bridges were made there, again by soldiers. H. Hamilton, *Industrial Revolution in Scotland*, p. 229. See below, pp. 281 and 284.

[2] John Metcalf became blind at six years old, but fought at Falkirk and Culloden, rode races, and was a great road- and bridge-builder.

journey to London in less than three days. In some degree, too, the difficulties of road transport were being gradually relieved by the development of water-transport. To an increasingly larger extent goods were being borne by coasting vessels to and from the numerous ports then used for the purpose.[1] Much, too, was being done to make the rivers more navigable for the boats which transported goods to and from these ports, by deepening and widening their channels and sometimes by a system of locks. In fact, by 1727 there were already some 1,160 miles of navigable rivers fit for inland transport.[2] Moreover, by the end of George II's reign the way had been shown for a cheaper and even quicker transport of heavy goods by the opening of the duke of Bridgewater's Canal, the first of a network of waterways to be available to the fast-growing industries in Yorkshire, Lancashire, and the Midlands.[3]

The main industry of the country during the first six decades of the eighteenth century was still agriculture, including sheep and cattle raising. Arthur Young, indeed, calculates[4] that in the 1760's, exclusive of landlords, clergy, tradesmen working for farmers, and the parochial poor, 2,800,000, not far from half the total population, were supported by agriculture. How profitable good land was may be seen from some of the instances quoted by Defoe and Young. The former mentions one 're-markable pasture-field' at Aylesbury let to a grazier for an annual rental of £1,400, and a meadow on the Avon near Amesbury let for £12 an acre 'for the grass only'; and he waxes lyrical on 'the best and largest oxen and the finest galloping horses' of the North Riding, on the cornfields of Cambridge-shire, Bedfordshire ('best wheat in England'), Monmouth, and Hampshire; on the great pasture-lands of Norfolk and Suffolk, Romney Marsh, Somerset, and the Fen country.[5] Arthur Young is more specially concerned with the improved methods of farmers introduced since Defoe's day. He is enthusiastic about Lord Townshend's discovery of the value of turnips

[1] For list see pp. 121–3.
[2] See T. S. Willan, *River Navigation in England, 1600–1750*, Oxford, 1936, p. 133. This book has some useful maps of navigable rivers; and Defoe's numerous references to the importance of river-transport are set forth in an appendix.
[3] See, on roads, S. and B. Webb, l.c. *passim*, and P. Mantoux, *Industrial Revolution in the Eighteenth Century*, revised edn., translated by M. Vernon, 1935, pp. 115–23.   [4] *Northern Tour*, iv. 417–20.
[5] Defoe, l.c. i. 58, 79, 125, 187, 211, 270; ii. 14, 52, 95, and 113.

planted on a large scale[1] as a cleaning crop and as an encouragement to cattle to manure the ground, and about the four-course rotation of wheat, turnips, barley, and clover crops also introduced by 'Turnip Townshend' and his brother-in-law Walpole. Pastoral economy was indeed almost revolutionized by Townshend's practice of keeping sheep and cattle in good condition throughout the winter by turnips; whereas formerly, for want of winter food, beasts had to be killed off and salted almost wholesale, and the well-to-do alone could count on some fresh meat from their pigeon-cotes. Young records too with approval the improved system of sowing by hoe and drill, especially for the cultivation of grasses for cattle, such as clover, sainfoin, and lucerne, the enlightened farming methods of the great Yorkshire landowners, Rockingham, Darlington, Holderness, and the reclamation of barren moorland by Mr. Danby of Swinton. Altogether no less than two million acres of new land were brought into cultivation by these and other progressive farmers before the end of the century.[2] At the same time Robert Bakewell of Dishley, though only a tenant-farmer, was creating a revolution in the scientific breeding of cattle, to be followed later in the century by the still more famous Coke of Norfolk. During this period, indeed, England was not only self-supporting in the main articles of food, but was able to export a great deal of its wheat and dairy produce. The export of corn was even stimulated by bounties whenever the home-price of corn fell below 48s. a quarter, which was a high price, since the average price for the whole period between 1713 and 1764 was only 34s. 11d. a quarter, and in some years was as low as 32s. (1719), 31s. 9d. (1723), 30s. (1731), 24s. 4d. (1732), 25s. 11d. (1733), 22s. 9d. (1743–4), 25s. 2d. (1745), and 31s. (1755); the only serious shortages in this period were in 1728 when the price rose to 49s. 11d., in 1740 to 46s. 5d. or even 59s. in some districts, and 1757 when the Eton price was 55s., but in the north as high as 72s.[3] During the years 1721 to 1741 the excess

---

[1] See Pope, *Imitations of Horace*, ii. 2. 272–3:

> The other slights, for women, sports, and wines,
> All Townshend's turnips, and all Grosvenor's mines.

[The field-cultivation of turnips and the four-course rotation of crops had, in fact, been practised in Norfolk since the late seventeenth century. See J. H. Plumb in *Ec. Hist. Rev.* 2nd series, v. i. 86–89, C.H.S.]

[2] R. Prothero, *English Farming, Past and Present*, 4th edn., 1927, p. 154.

[3] Ibid., pp. 148 and 440–1, gives the wheat prices at Eton year by year. They were not, however, uniform throughout the country, especially in bad years, when

of exports over imports of corn amounted to 9,290,689 quarters, and in the year 1738 alone to as much as 923,459 quarters; and it was not till 1765 that England ceased to export and began importing corn, nor till 1773 that the system of bounties on exported corn was finally abolished.[1]

One great obstacle to improved methods of farming, especially pasturage on a large scale, was the old strip system of cultivation in the open field. In the fifteenth and sixteenth centuries a good deal of inclosure of lands hitherto held on this system had been carried out by rich landowners to the detriment, it was claimed, of tillage as compared with pasturage, as well as to the rights of smallholders; this process, though to a much smaller extent, continued during the seventeenth century.[2] But in the eighteenth century the need of improved methods of agriculture on a large scale and the political influence of the great landowners gave a great impetus to the inclosure system. Hitherto, inclosures had been effected chiefly by the use of rights claimed by landowners over their copyhold tenants, sometimes even by a straining of the law; the results being generally legalized by enrolment of a chancery decree. In this century parliament itself intervened by giving full legal sanction by statute to inclosures.[3] A landlord who wished to inclose land, hitherto held on the open-field system, in which the villagers had rights not only of raising crops but also of pasturage, commonage, and wood-cutting, proposed an Inclosure Bill which was referred to local commissioners for adjusting compensation for such rights. At such inquiries the promoter with his local influence and the legal assistance at his command could generally make his own terms for compensating the villagers to be turned out of their former rights. The award thus

some districts had to pay much higher than others, no doubt owing to difficulties of transport. For example, in 1727, when the Eton price was 38s. 6d., in the north it was 32s. 11d., in 1740, 46s. 5d. and 59s. respectively, and in 1757, 55s. and 67s. or even 72s. Ashton and Sykes, *Coal Industry*, pp. 116–22, give northern prices differing from Prothero's. Egmont, *Diary*, i. 122, notes that with corn 'under five shillings a bushel the farmers cannot live'.

[1] N. A. Brisco, *Economic Policy of Walpole*, 1907, p. 183. As late as 1763–4 100,000 quarters of English wheat, valued at £160,000, were exported to Naples; R.O., S.P. 93, 21.

[2] See *Oxford History of England*, viii. 252 sqq. (2nd edn.) and ix. 279–81 (2nd edn.); also Mantoux, part i, chap. iii, and Hammond, *Rise of Modern Industry*, pp. 81 sqq.

[3] There appear to have been only eight Inclosure Acts passed during the seventeenth century, two in James I's reign, four in Charles II's, and two in William III's. See *Return of Inclosure Acts, Parliamentary Papers*, 1914, vol. lxvii.

concluded was rarely questioned in the subsequent proceedings in parliament. At first this new process was sparingly used. Only two Inclosure Acts were passed in the twelve years of Anne's reign; between 1714 and 1720 only five. But in the succeeding twenty-year periods of the century the pace began to quicken, with 67 in 1721–40, 204 in 1741–60; then, as corn-prices rose, no less than 1,043 Inclosure Acts were passed between 1761 and 1780, and 901 for the period 1781–1800. It is noticeable, too, that whereas in Tudor times the object of inclosures was mainly to secure large pasture-lands, in the eighteenth century the object was mainly to increase the size of arable farms which could be more profitably devoted to corn than the small tenures absorbed in them. Thus, as Prothero points out, the parts most affected by the inclosure system during the century were the corn-growing districts of the east, north-east, and east midlands, whereas the Welsh counties and such English counties as those round London, and Hereford, Shropshire, and Westmorland were very little affected.[1]

There is no doubt that this inclosure system powerfully stimulated the agricultural development of the country. Instead of a population of small peasants cultivating the land by antiquated and wasteful methods and often producing just their own bare subsistence, England was gradually being divided into large farms on which less wasteful and more progressive methods of raising crops, cattle, and sheep could be employed by men who had the capital and knowledge for turning the land to its best uses. And this improved use of the land was all the more necessary at a time when the population was beginning, with the more rapid development of industry and commerce, to increase beyond its almost static condition in preceding centuries. On the other side of the picture, however, must be put

[1] For the figures quoted above see *Return of Inclosure Acts*. Mantoux, p. 146, gives different figures, 3 for 1702–14; 68 for 1720–40; 194 for 1740–60; 1,066 for 1760–80; and 793 for 1780–1800. Unfortunately no statistics of the acreage inclosed by these acts are given in this return for the period before 1801. H. Levy, *Large and Small Holdings*, p. 24, estimates the area enclosed, 1702–60, at 400,000, and in the next 50 years at 5,000,000 acres. Among the counties with the largest number of inclosures during the century are Leicester with 139, Lincoln 220, Yorkshire, E. Riding, 123, W. Riding 164, N. Riding 72, Derbyshire 84, Gloucestershire 87, Northants. 146, Nottingham 97, Somerset 76; whereas all the Welsh counties had only 26 inclosure acts between them, Devonshire only 3, Essex 5, Kent 2, Westmorland 14. For the incidence of inclosures see Prothero's comment in *English Farming*, p. 167.

the hard fate of the thousands turned adrift from their cherished rights in the land. Many, no doubt, were still employed in the inferior status of hired labourers on their landlords' increased estates, but even those had no security of occupation. Many had not that alleviation owing to the greater economy in man-power of the new methods of farming. Such had no alterna-tives but to sink into the ranks of pauperism, or else drift into the towns to seek employment in the depressing surroundings of the growing factory system. Indirectly too, the new methods of farming on a large scale tended to extinguish the independent yeoman class, mostly free-holders with 100 acres or less. Finding themselves unable to compete with the big landowners who had profited from inclosures, they often sold their own holdings to become tenant-farmers of larger farms.[1] Some, indeed, of those whose families had been driven out of their holdings by such competition—men like Strutt of Derby, Wilkinson, Craw-shay, Abraham Darby of Coalbrookdale, and the first Sir Robert Peel—proved leaders in the new industrial movement: but they were the minority of the yeoman class.

As early as 1770, before the inclosure movement had reached its height, Oliver Goldsmith in his *Deserted Village*, and es-pecially in the dedication to Reynolds, bears witness to its evils. Even Arthur Young, at first an enthusiastic advocate of inclosures for the benefit they brought to farming without detriment, as he then thought, to the poor, by the end of the century had largely modified his view. In 1768 he had even argued for the benefit of large farms to the labouring poor: 'the vulgar ideas, of great farms depopulating the kingdom, are here proved from facts to be false.' But thirty years later, realizing the moral, no less than the material, degradation suffered by the poor cottagers thus displaced, he earnestly pleaded for a vast scheme of allotments and cottages for such landless peasants. 'The poor', he wrote, '. . . may say and with truth, "Parliament may be tender of property: all I know is that I had a cow and an Act of Parliament has taken it from me." ' But he spoke to deaf ears, and the Inclosure Acts even multiplied during the first part of the nineteenth century.[2]

---

[1] See Levy, p. 29, for disappearance of yeoman class in the period 1760–1815.

[2] See *Northern Tour*, iv. 254, and Hammond, *Village Labourer*, pp. 83–84. For in-closures in the eighteenth century and their useful results for farming in England see Prothero, *English Farming*, pp. 148–67, and especially H. Levy, *Large and Small*

Next to agriculture, the greatest industry in England during our period was still the woollen trade, which depended
largely on the pastoral industry of sheep-rearing. Defoe even
suggests that Wiltshire was originally chosen by the manufacturers as the principal seat of their craft 'because of the
infinite numbers of sheep which were fed at that time upon the
downs and plains of Dorset, Wilts, and Hampshire, all adjoin-
ing'. By the eighteenth century the western counties of Devon,
Gloucester, and Somerset were running Wiltshire close in wool
manufacture. The other two great wool-manufacturing counties were Norfolk—at Norwich alone, says Defoe, no less than
120,000 people were so employed—and the West Riding of
Yorkshire, which by the middle of the century was already
ousting its eastern and south-western competitors from the
primacy.[1] John Kay's invention of the fly-shuttle in 1733 enormously increased the rapidity of weaving. But the weavers had
to wait another thirty years for Hargreaves's invention of the
spinning jenny to speed up the process of spinning wool enough
to keep pace with the flying shuttle. For hosiery, concentrated
chiefly at Nottingham and Leicester, an Englishman, William
Lee, had invented the stocking frame in 1589. At first discouraged by Elizabeth and James I, by the eighteenth century
this invention was so well established that the number of frames,
estimated at 8,000 in 1727, had increased to over 13,000 by
1750.[2] In fact, except in some of the home counties, there was
hardly a county in England in which woollen goods in some
form were not made. The great marts for woollen cloths were:
in London, at Blackwell Hall, sold by Richard II to the City in
1397 and converted into 'the greatest woollen cloth-market in
the world';[3] the serge-market at Exeter, where it was said
£100,000 worth of serges were sometimes sold in a week, and
the cloth-market at Leeds, 'a prodigy of its kind', according to
Defoe, where the sales were even greater.[4] In addition, there

Holdings, pp. 1–39, who also brings out the resulting hardships on the cottier and
yeoman classes. He points out that by 1811 the families of Great Britain occupied in
agriculture had been reduced to 35·2 per cent. as against 44·4 per cent. interested in
trade or commerce. For other authorities see the Bibliography, p. 460.
  [1] As early as 1742 Fielding noted 'the decay of the woollen trade' in the south-
western counties. See Joseph Andrews, iv. 12.
  [2] See Defoe, i. 62, 221, 271–2, 281–2; ii. 203–4; E. Lipson, Economic History of
England, ii. 104–9; Mantoux, pp. 211–13.
  [3] B. Lambert, History and Survey of London, 1806, ii. 543.
  [4] See Defoe, i. 222; ii. 204.

was the September fair at Stourbridge near Cambridge, famous not only for its hops and wool sales but also for the woollen cloths from Yorkshire, Lancashire, Norfolk, and the west country. These vast sales of woollens were not solely for the internal trade, of which English manufacturers had the monopoly, but also for export. Already in 1700, out of a total value of exports amounting to £6,477,402, woollen goods accounted for nearly half, £2,989,163, in addition to those valued at some £5,000,000 absorbed at home; by 1760, when the total value of exports had risen to £14,694,970, the woollens sent to foreign markets had nearly doubled at £5,453,172.[1] The national pride in this great industry is well reflected in Dyer's poem *The Fleece* (1757):

> Lo, in throngs,
> For ev'ry realm, the careful factors meet,
> Whisp'ring each other. In long ranks the bales,
> Like war's bright files, beyond the sight extend.
> . . . Pursue,
> Ye sons of Albion! with unyielding heart,
> Your hardy labours: let the sounding loom
> Mix with the melody of ev'ry vale.[2]

It was only fitting, too, as Mantoux remarks, that the highest dignitary in parliament should be seated on a woolsack.

The other great English industries in soft goods were silk and cotton, linen being by the middle of the century the almost exclusive product of Scotland and Northern Ireland.[3] Silk, in a statute of 1721, is described as 'one of the most considerable branches of the manufactures of this kingdom'. Its sudden importance since the Revolution was due partly to the immigration of some 30,000 Huguenot weavers, partly to the stringent prohibition of silk articles from France and the bounties given on the export of English silk, largely also owing to the enterprise of John Lombe in smuggling over designs of a secret silk-throwing machine from Italy in 1716. From these designs in 1718 his brother Thomas, subsequently a sheriff of London and knighted, was able to erect similar machines on the Derwent, which in fifteen years brought him a fortune of £120,000.

---

[1] Lipson, ii. 188; Brisco, p. 178.
[2] Book iii, ll. 340–3, 396–9.
[3] In Defoe's time (ii. 260) the coarse linen called huckaback was still being manufactured at Warrington.

In 1732 parliament voted him £14,000 for the surrender of his patent, which was thus made accessible to his rivals, chiefly concentrated at Spitalfields and Macclesfield, with smaller establishments at Derby, Coventry, and Stockport. In this case also the supply of the raw material was sometimes apt to lag behind the producing capacity of the looms. Still, at the beginning of George III's reign a single employer kept 1,500 workers busy at his looms in London, Dorset, Cheshire, and Gloucestershire; at Macclesfield another 2,500 silk weavers were employed, besides hundreds more at other centres.[1]

The manufacture at Manchester of cotton goods, though known to Camden in Elizabethan times, was a comparatively new industry on a large scale, and its competition was beginning to be resented by the woollen and silk workers. At first the outcry was directed against imported cotton. When, at the end of the seventeenth century, the use of 'fine painted callicoes' from the East was introduced by Queen Mary, they were considered, says Defoe, so 'Greivous to our Trade, and Ruining to our Manufactures and the Poor' that an act prohibiting their importation was passed in 1700. This act appears to have failed in its purpose, partly because Manchester was beginning to imitate the eastern products; and in 1721, owing to the riots of the Spitalfields weavers in 1719 against the wearers of printed calicoes, a more stringent act was passed extending the prohibition to home-printed cottons. But, in spite of opposition, the manufacture of cotton goods and fustian, a mixture of cotton and linen, increased rapidly in the favourable climate of Bolton and Manchester; in 1736 the ban on printing was removed for home-made fustian, though it was not till 1774 that it was removed for the pure cotton product. Between 1701 and 1751, apart from the home consumption, the value of cotton goods exported had nearly doubled.[2] Its chief markets were the West Indies and the American colonies; and even in 1769, in spite of the reduced trade due to the troubles with America, Arthur Young found that three-quarters of the Manchester cotton goods still went to America, and that no less than 30,000 workers were being employed at the looms.[3] It was not, however,

---

[1] Mantoux, pp. 197 sqq.; Lipson, ii. 100–4. For the number of Huguenot immigrants see Lipson, iii. 60.
[2] 1701—£23,253; 1751—£45,986. Lipson, ii. 93–97; iii. 39–44; Defoe, i. 165–6.
[3] *Northern Tour*, iii. 192–4.

till Whitney's invention of the cotton gin in the last decade of the century that the vastly increased supply of raw cotton enabled the industry to develop as it did in the nineteenth century.

Though England was more than holding her own in agriculture and the manufacture of soft goods during this period, her era of prosperity in iron and steel, so notable in the succeeding century and a half, had barely begun. In fact, at the beginning of the eighteenth century the industry was showing signs of decline. It is true some 200,000 men are said to have been employed in 1719, but among these were, no doubt, included the 45,000 metal workers engaged in the Birmingham 'toy' trade, making nails and other small gadgets.[1] This decline was not due to any lack of native ore, but to the depletion of the forests which supplied the charcoal then considered essential for reducing the iron ore into a metal fit for working. Defoe was almost alone in his characteristically optimistic view, that there were no signs of decay in our woods, '. . . the Three counties of Kent, Sussex, and Hampshire . . . being one inexhaustible Store-House of Timber never to be destroy'd, . . . and able at this time to supply [besides charcoal for the blast furnaces] Timber to rebuild all the Royal Navies in Europe'. But, in fact, ever since Elizabeth's time, anxiety had been felt at the gradual destruction of the forests in Sussex and elsewhere in order to supply charcoal. So serious, indeed, was becoming the dearth of wood for charcoal that by 1720 only 59 blast furnaces, producing some 18,000 tons of pig-iron per annum, were at work in England. Sussex, hitherto famous for its iron, had only 10, the Forest of Dean and the Sheffield district 11 each, the others being dotted about in small numbers in Kent, Hampshire, South Wales, Shropshire, Yorkshire, and the Furness district. In 1727 and 1752 two important ironmasters actually migrated to the wilds of the Highlands, where they had no advantage for their industry save dense forests.[2]

[1] J. F. Rees in *Economica*, v. 140; J. S. Ashton, *Iron and Steel in Industrial Revolution*, p. 104; Brisco, p. 179.

[2] Defoe, i. 125; Ashton, pp. 17, 35, 235–8. Ashton shows that this is a serious underestimate of the number of furnaces and of the amount of their production. The first of these Highland furnaces was established by the Backbarrow Company at Invergarry in Inverness-shire, but, owing to the cost of working, lasted only nine years; the second, at Taynuilt in Argyllshire, was more successful, lasting over

I

The processes in the iron industry as carried out at this period were three. First came the casting stage. In the blast furnace the crude ore was deoxidized, and carburized iron produced. The carburized iron was tapped from the blast furnace in a liquid condition and either run directly into ladles and poured into moulds whence, when cooled and set, it was taken out in its final form as cast-iron grates, pots, &c.; or the liquid iron was run into a main channel formed in a bed of sand called the 'sow', connected with D-shaped furrows or 'pigs', and when the metal had cooled the 'pigs' were detached from the 'sow'. In the next stage the crude pig-iron underwent a second process of purifying in the finery and chafery and conversion into square blocks called 'blooms', which were hammered, rolled, and slit into 'bar-iron'.[1] Thirdly, this bar-iron formed the raw material of the smith, who hammered and fashioned it on his forge into wrought iron. At the beginning of the eighteenth century the only fuel used for the first two processes, at the blast furnace and during conversion into bar-iron, was charcoal: coal, of which there was no dearth in the country, had hitherto been found unsuitable, since its sulphurous fumes, mingling in the furnace or the finery with the molten iron, made the metal brittle and unworkable. For the smith's work on wrought iron, coal or coke was perfectly suitable. Thus, owing to the deficiency of charcoal for the furnaces, there was not enough native-made bar-iron to supply even the 128 forges in the country. In spite, therefore, of the immense deposits of native iron ore, two-thirds of the bar-iron used by our smiths had to be imported from Sweden and other foreign countries to the tune of some 17,000–20,000 tons a year.[2] When, therefore, as in the years 1716–18, relations between England and Sweden were strained and the Swedish supply was cut off, the forges were hard put to it to obtain enough iron; nor were the attempts to encourage a supply from the American colonies particularly successful.[3]

100 years to 1866. A third, in Strathspey, lasted less than ten years. Hamilton, *Industrial Revolution in Scotland*, pp. 151–3.

[1] See Ashton, pp. 233–4, for an interesting seventeenth-century account of these processes.

[2] Ibid., p. 111. These figures apply to 1720. By 1737 imports of bar-iron were running at over 24,000 tons a year 'of which about three-fourths came from Sweden'. Ibid., p. 238.

[3] The average annual importation from America, 1751–5, was only 3,335 tons;

Obviously the chief hope for the development of the iron industry lay in the discovery of some method of overcoming the defects of coal fuel in the first two processes of production. As early as the first half of the seventeenth century, Dud Dudley, in charge of his father's Worcestershire iron works, claimed to have successfully employed coked coal; but, if he did, his secret died with him. In 1727 the notorious William Wood of the 'half-pence'[1] took out a patent for a coal process in the blast furnace, but on trial his products were found useless. Before that, however, in 1709 Abraham Darby had succeeded, by the use of coke at his works at Coalbrookdale in Shropshire, in producing iron good enough for casting;[2] still the process remained for long only in the experimental stage, and does not seem to have become generally known for many years afterwards. Darby's son Abraham the second, about 1750, improved on his father's process, mainly, probably, by the more careful selection of coal suitable for coking and by increasing the strength of the blast necessary to dissipate the sulphurous fumes. With the invention by Henry Cort, some thirty years later, of the puddling process, in which common coal, instead of coke, could be employed in refining pig-iron, the modern methods of producing iron were in principle completed. In the puddling furnace the coal is burnt in a separate chamber and only the flames produced are allowed to come into contact with the pig-iron which is in process of being converted into wrought iron. As a result, the sulphur in the fuel is mainly converted into sulphurous acid gas before coming into contact with the iron, and its deleterious action is therefore much reduced. The other impurities in the pig are removed during the stirring action carried out by the so-called puddlers or stirrers. The bloom of crude iron produced in the puddling furnace undergoes further treatment by hammering, and is rolled in the rolling mills into bars or plates. By these new methods of using coke or even coal in increasing quantities for smelting, furnaces on a much larger scale became possible and required larger and more powerful bellows. Abraham Darby the second in 1743 was perhaps the first to use Newcomen's steam-engine, perfected in

in 1761–5 it was 3,107, as compared with 27,954 and 40,919 tons respectively from foreign countries. Ibid., p. 123.

[1] See below, pp. 300–3.

[2] See *Oxford History of England*, x. 50 (2nd edn.).

1720, to pump up the water-power needed to drive an effective blast into his furnace; in 1761 John Roebuck installed in his newly established Carron works a still more powerful bellows worked by Smeaton's cylindrical blowing machine. Even, however, with the development of such labour-saving machinery, employers were slow in putting steam or even water-power to its full use. Arthur Young, for example, when he visited Crowley's ironworks in 1768, complains that there is too much manual work; 'an anchor', he says, 'of 20 tons may, undoubtedly, be managed with as much ease as a pin', by mechanical handling.[1]

Almost contemporaneously with the improved methods of producing iron, the steel industry was also reformed. Up to the middle of the eighteenth century the steel used in the industry was iron refined and hardened by the absorption of carbon from the charcoal with which it was packed in the furnace. The steel so produced was, however, still wanting in the hardness required for making steel instruments with a fine edge. But the need, as in so many instances of manufacturing inventions during this century, though unaccompanied by any special scientific training, stimulated the inventive power. Benjamin Huntsman, a Doncaster clock-maker, requiring a material better fitted for delicate clock-springs, in 1750 contrived a method for making a purer and harder steel. Filling a crucible with small pieces of ordinary steel and adding to them a special flux, of which he kept the secret, he sealed the crucible and subjected it to an intense heat for five hours in a furnace; and in the result he obtained a steel of the required purity and hardness. The Sheffield steel-makers were at first suspicious of the new method, till they found it eagerly adopted on the Continent. They then persuaded Huntsman to settle among them and supply them with his product, whereby Sheffield was able once for all to establish its leadership in the steel trade. Walker of Rotherham, originally a nail-maker in a small way, who by a subterfuge obtained Huntsman's secret, turned the discovery to such good account that he increased the value of his products from £900 in 1747 to £11,000 in 1760.

These improvements in the iron and steel trade had not produced any large increase in the output by the end of George II's reign, for a general appreciation of their importance was of

[1] *Northern Tour*, iii. 11. Young erroneously calls him Crawley.

slow growth. To Smollett, as late as 1771, the new art, introduced by the Darbys half a century before, 'of clearing [coal] in
such a manner as frees it from the sulphur that would otherwise render the metal too brittle for working', seemed worthy of
Squire Bramble's surprised attention on his visit to the Carron
works.[1] In 1769, however, Watt had patented his first engine,
though manufacture was not started till some years later,
whereby the power and rapidity of production were vastly
increased. The stage was now set for the great leap in iron and
steel production that signalized George III's reign. All the
other preparations had been made in the preceding fifty years.
In addition to the important iron concerns, such as the Foleys'
of Stourbridge, the Crowleys' near Newcastle, the Backbarrow
Company's in the Furness peninsula, already established at the
beginning of the century, the Darbys at Coalbrookdale, the
Guests at Dowlais, the Bacons at Merthyr Tydvil, the Wilkin-
sons at Bersham and Broseley were now ready with their forges
and foundries; the model Carron works, started by Roebuck,
Garbett, and Cadell in 1759, two years later were already producing 40 tons a week.[2] But such figures seem trivial compared
with those of the last quarter of the century. To take an instance
—the Coalbrookdale works, which in the first Darby's time were
thought to be doing well with an annual output of 500–600
tons, by the end of the century were producing 13,000–14,000
tons per annum. The total output of English pig-iron, barely
20,000 tons in 1720, had risen to 68,000 in 1788, to 125,400 eight
years later, and by 1806 to 250,000 tons, more than twelve
times the amount at the beginning of the eighteenth century.
It should be noted, too, that most of the improvements and inventions, originated in the first half of that century, had been
to the benefit of the easier and more rapid process of the foundry
as compared with the forge: in fact the chief productions of the
English metal-workers were no longer of wrought-iron or steel
from the forge, but cannons, cylinders, and engine-parts, besides
the older fire-grates and iron pots cast in the foundry.[3]

[1] *Humphrey Clinker* (letter of 28 Aug.).
[2] [I cannot find Professor Williams's authority for this figure. Hamilton, l.c.,
p. 160, shows that in 1767 it was hoped to achieve the production of 70 tons a week
with four furnaces at work. As only two furnaces were operating by the end of 1760
production may have reached 35 to 40 tons a week then. C.H.S.]
[3] For this section Mantoux, pp. 277–312, and Ashton are invaluable. I have also
been fortunate enough to obtain suggestions from Professor Sir Thomas Hudson

Closely connected with the new methods of the foundry was the coal industry. At the beginning of the century coal was already used for brewing, distilling, brick-, tile-, and pottery-making, the manufacture of glass, nails, hardware, cutlery, brass and lead smelting, and in the iron-masters' forges. But it was only with the discoveries of the Darbys and others that the use of coal became more general in the iron industry. Throughout the eighteenth century the bulk and weight of coal and inadequate means of transport made it essential that the industries which used it should be established near the coal seams or in places whither it could easily be transported by water. The same transport problem applied to coal for domestic firing. Sussex, for example, and other counties not well supplied with ports had to depend almost entirely on wood for domestic purposes during most of the century. Defoe[1] mentions Newcastle, Sunderland, Swansea, Neath, Tenby, and Whitehaven as coal-exporting districts and in addition Clackmannan in Scotland; but in his account of Staffordshire he does not speak of any coal-mines; and, though he picks out the coal of Wigan and Bolton as specially suitable for households, he admits that, owing to the cost of transport, it was rarely seen in London. By Arthur Young's time the increased need of coal for the foundries and other industries and the gradual improvement of transport by road, river, and canal had made its use more general; and he specially notes as an advantage for Wedgwood's new potteries the abundance of coal opened up in Staffordshire. But even so the slow expansion of the coal trade in the eighteenth by contrast with the nineteenth century may be seen from estimates showing that the total production of $2\frac{1}{2}$ million tons of coal in 1700 increased to only about 6 millions in 1770 and to 10 millions by the end of the century.[2] Collieries then, as today, were generally on land belonging to great landowners such as the Lowthers, the duke of Norfolk, Lord Dudley, the Delavals, Lumleys, and Lambtons in the north-east, who by the eighteenth century found it most profitable to lease them either for a rent or royalties on production, besides the heavy charges they made

Beare, who tells me that he himself had experience of 'puddling' when learning the engineer's craft. For the Carron works H. Hamilton, *Industrial Revolution in Scotland*, pp. 155-61, may be referred to. [Note of 1939].

[1] Defoe, ii. 55, 57, 250, 266-7, 273.

[2] Ashton and Sykes, *Coal Industry in the Eighteenth Century*, p. 13; *Northern Tour*, iii. 253.

for granting way-leaves over their land from the pit-head to the port or depot.[1] The actual work in the pits was even more laborious and dangerous than it is today, in spite of the comparatively shallow workings—a Cumberland pit 489 feet deep, for example, was exceptional.[2] The pumping apparatus was primitive, and in 1725 a 'fire-engine' for draining a coal-pit was regarded as noteworthy;[3] and there were still few of the modern contrivances of hoists and rails for the trucks. There were no safety lamps or efficient means of ventilation to obviate the effects of choke-damp and fire-damp; and explosions, such as that described in 1726 by Defoe,[4] which destroyed some sixty workers, were not uncommon.

Throughout the century Newcastle and Sunderland were the main sources of 'sea-coal', as it was called, for domestic purposes, especially for London. In 1727, according to Defoe, some 30,000 miners and 10,000 seamen and lightermen are said to have been employed in hewing and conveying from those ports the 400,000 chaldrons[5] of coal required for the London market. This industry was valued not only for the coal, but also as providing in its fleet of colliers 'the great Nursery for our Seamen':[6] so important was it that the threat of an attack on Newcastle by the rebels in 1715 was enough to divert Carpenter from his pursuit of Forster's levies in the west.[7] Both in Newcastle and in London there was an elaborate organization of the coal trade. The coal was conveyed from the pits to the wharf on the Tyne, where a close corporation of 'fitters' or 'hostmen' took it over, loading it into 'keels' for transhipment to the 'cats' or 'hayboats', as the coal ships were called. These 'hostmen' were so powerful that they to a large extent controlled the price of pit coal and the amount to be delivered from each pit, and for a time even the shippers. In the Thames another close corporation of lightermen had the monopoly of unloading the 'cats' and delivering the coal to Billingsgate market, where sworn 'meters'[8] appointed by the City took another fee for verifying

[1] See *Hist. MSS. Comm., Portland*, vi. 104, for the heavy charges made for the five miles' way-leave from the Chester-le-Street Colliery to Sunderland.

[2] Ashton and Sykes, p. 10.

[3] *Hist. MSS. Comm., Portland*, vi. 103.   [4] Defoe, ii. 249.

[5] Lipson, ii. 113, 139. The London chaldron weighed 28½ cwt.; the Newcastle chaldron 53 cwt. Ashton and Sykes, pp. 249–51.

[6] Lipson, ii. 117.

[7] I. S. Leadam, *Political History of England 1702–60*, p. 253.

[8] The 'meters' were only appointed to verify weights on land in 1746 and were

the weight or bulk of the coal sold to the retail dealers or 'woodmongers'. It is hardly surprising that, with all these pickings in transit, the amount of coal that cost about 13*s.* at the most in Newcastle should be priced at anything from £2 to £4 in the London market.[1]

The pottery industry of the Staffordshire Five Towns, one of the many depending on a good supply of coal, was entirely revolutionized in 1759, when Josiah Wedgwood[2] opened his works at Burslem. Hitherto English pottery had been rough and crude, carelessly and inefficiently manufactured, and difficult to distribute owing to the dearth of good road or river transport. Wedgwood had begun working in the Potteries at the age of nine; he had subsequently been apprenticed and soon mastered the various branches of the craft. But he also had higher ambitions, taught himself languages, studied Greek and Etruscan antiquities and vases—his second factory he called Etruria —developed a turn for science and invention, and even became an F.R.S. in later life. Having established himself at Burslem, he was not content with the common clay of the district. He procured fine clays from Cornwall, Devon, and Dorset, and flints from the Thames for glazing, and was the first to introduce an engine-lathe for turning. Within a few years he had started producing his famous cream-coloured ware, and even for his cheaper pottery for common use he insisted on careful workmanship and beautiful modelling. Almost at once the new ware caught the public taste; and when Arthur Young visited his factory, barely ten years after it had been opened, he found 10,000 people employed there, whereas forty years earlier there were only about 4,000 inhabitants in all the Five Towns. These 10,000 workers included, besides grinders, washers, throwers, and engine-men, specially skilled craftsmen in painting, modelling, and gilding, all at high rates of wages, one expert modeller even earning as much as £100 a year. Already, too, the best Wedgwood ware was finding a market in America, the East Indies, and throughout Europe, especially in France.[3] For the

additional to the so-called 'sea-coal meters' who verified amounts on transhipment into the lighters. Ashton and Sykes, l.c., p. 208.

[1] Ashton and Sykes, p. 252. See Lipson, ii. 128–41, on the organization of the coal trade.

[2] Josiah Wedgwood began working as a potter at Burslem in 1739.

[3] A. Young, *North of England*, iii. 252–5.

domestic trade in his cheaper ware better means of internal communication were essential: accordingly Wedgwood was foremost in promoting better roads and canals as outlets from the Five Towns. Few even of the great inventors of the eighteenth century achieved a greater and more permanent success for their special industries than this master-potter, the founder of a lineage still prominent in English life. For he not only produced pottery of the highest repute in his own workshops, but set a standard to which all the other producers of the district were forced to approximate.[1]

Foreign trade and shipping were naturally stimulated, partly by Walpole's prudent fiscal policy, but principally by the progress made in native industries during this century. In shipping and port facilities London remained supreme, both for the export trade and, as Defoe says, 'by the immense Indraft of Trade to the City of London'. In the Pool alone he counted on one day no less than 2,000 sea-going ships; while, apart from the royal navy's docks and shipbuilding yards, the merchant service had 25 wet and dry docks and 33 shipbuilding yards in the Thames above Greenwich.[2] At the beginning of the century Bristol was unquestionably next in importance. Agricultural produce and woollen goods from the midland and south-western counties and metal-work from Birmingham and the Severn and Wye districts were brought there for export, and it was the headquarters of the wine trade with Spain and Portugal; Bristol ships, too, almost monopolized the lucrative slave trade with the West Indies. But already in Defoe's time Liverpool, 'one of the Wonders of Britain', was threatening to outdo Bristol. When Defoe first visited Liverpool in about 1680 it was already 'a large . . . and . . . thriving town'; ten years later he found it rapidly increasing, and by 1724 he estimated that its size and population had doubled since 1690.[3] Liverpool's opportunity had come in the seventeenth century when the Dee had begun to silt up at Chester, since, almost next door, the estuary of the Mersey provided an admirable land-locked harbour

[1] For an account of the sulphuric acid industry see below, p. 387.
[2] Defoe, i. 43, 348. See also Sir J. Broodbank, *History of the Port of London*, 1921, who describes (i. 67–69) the Great Wet (Howland) Dock at Rotherhithe constructed about 1700 and then regarded as a marvel.
[3] Defoe is not always reliable for estimates of population, but Mantoux, pp. 109 sqq., estimates the population at 5,000 in 1700, 10,000 in 1720, and 26,000 by 1760.

between the Wirral peninsula and the mainland of Lancashire. By 1734 this harbour had been improved by the wet-dock or basin, and its importance increased by the development of the Manchester cotton trade and by its proximity to the Furness and Yorkshire iron and cloth industries. Already, though not yet equal to Bristol, it was beginning to take a large share of the Irish and Welsh trade and even to send its ships round Scotland to take a part in the Baltic trade; by 1730 it was encroaching on Bristol's monopoly of the slave-trade, later to become its special preserve, and it was importing Virginian tobacco. By the first decade of George III's reign it had definitely superseded Bristol as the second port in the kingdom, with its docks and shipping superior to any in England.[1]

But apart from these three great ports, a large number of smaller ports, now almost derelict owing to the concentration on the most favourable localities made possible by better means of internal communication, were still active in the eighteenth century. It is true the series of wars before 1713 had stopped the trade of many of these smaller ports, but they soon revived with the peace and the growth of industry during Stanhope's and Walpole's ministries, so that in 1739 it could be said that 'there was not a seaport, and scarce an inland town in England, that was without adventurers who exported quantities of goods, and did business directly with most of the trading companies in Europe and America'.[2] Besides the well-established ports of Newcastle and Sunderland, Hull, Grimsby, Yarmouth and Harwich, Portsmouth, Southampton, and Plymouth, such new ports as Neath, Swansea, and Whitehaven were beginning to flourish owing to the development of coal and iron, while there was still vigorous life, both in trade and shipbuilding, in the smaller ports of England: Stockton and Whitby, Gainsborough, Lynn, Shoreham and Arundel, Poole, Weymouth, Dartmouth, Fowey, Falmouth and Penzance, Minehead and Bideford, to most of which little is now left but fishing or pleasure craft and the memory of former adventure and prosperity.[3]

Some measure of the increase of industry and prosperity during this period may be obtained from the Custom House

---

[1] For the ports and trade of Bristol and Liverpool see Defoe, ii. 69, 255–8; A. Young, *Northern Tour*, iii. 216 sqq.; C. R. Fay, *Great Britain from Adam Smith to the Present Day*, 3rd edn., 1932, pp. 156–7; Mantoux, pp. 107–11; Lecky, i. 197–8.

[2] Brisco, p. 205, citing a pamphlet of 1739.

[3] See above, p. 105.

figures of the value of imports and exports which steadily increased from £5,792,422 (imports) and £7,696,573 (exports) in 1714, to £8,948,700 (imports) and £14,694,970 (exports) in 1760. The much higher increase in the value of exports, which was nearly doubled in this period, as compared with the slight increase in imports was then regarded as an additional indication of prosperity. But there are no figures to show what must have been the much greater increase in internal trade during this period, or the increased earnings due to the greater amount of English tonnage, chiefly employed in the carrying trade, which rose from 421,431 tons in 1714 to 609,798 in 1750 during the peace, and which even in 1760 during the war was 471,241 tons.[1]

Any estimate of the population during this century must be founded on inference or even guess-work, since there was no official census until the year 1801. A bill for Registering the Number of the People was indeed introduced in 1753, but met with violent opposition in the commons as a 'project . . . totally subversive of the last remains of English liberty . . . an abominable and foolish measure'[2] calculated to reveal our weakness to our enemies; and, though it actually passed the commons, it found its quietus in the house of lords. Those who attempted to form estimates of the population were therefore reduced to such indications as were to be gleaned from parish registers,[3] bills of mortality, and returns of the house-duty, from which ingenious writers like Dr. Price[4] tried to deduce the number of inhabitants from the amount of taxes paid for different-sized houses. So uncertain were the facts that many people, including Shelburne, thought the population was decreasing during the century; but most of those who had studied the available indications, including Arthur Young from his careful observation of agricultural and industrial conditions throughout the country, took

[1] These figures are taken from G. Chalmers, *Estimate of Comparative Strength of Britain*, 1782, table at p. 37. The figures for Scotland, first available only in 1756, are not included. See also C. Whitworth, *State of Trade*, 1776; Brisco, p. 205; and Lipson, ii. 187–90 and iii. 139. Chalmers gives totals for exports and for the balance of trade; the import figures are deduced from those. Whitworth's figures are slightly different—£5,929,227 and £8,361,638 for imports and exports in 1714, and £9,832,802 and £15,579,073 for 1760.

[2] *P.H.* xiv. 1320, 1329.

[3] An uncertain guide, as they mainly recorded church of England baptisms, marriages, and burials, though many nonconformists' burials were also included. There were also some nonconformist registers.

[4] Richard Price, 1723–91, a prolific writer on morals, politics, and economics

a more optimistic view. A fairly safe estimate is that at the beginning of this period the population of England and Wales numbered some 6,000,000, and by 1760 had increased to about 7,000,000; by 1801, as we know from the figures of the first official census, it had risen to 9,178,980.[1]

Those who believed that the population was decreasing were probably misled by the gradual drift of population from the lowland south, without taking into account the corresponding increase of population in the highland zone of the western midlands, Lancashire, and Yorkshire, which went on throughout the eighteenth century.[2] This remarkable change of relative density in the population was due to the need for the coal, metals, and water-power of this highland region, which resulted partly in the growing concentration of the metal industries in the midlands, partly in the great development of the cotton trade in Lancashire and of the woollen manufacture in Yorkshire, that was steadily depriving Norfolk and the great south-western clothiers of their primacy. In 1700 far the most populous part of England was south of a line drawn from Bristol to the coast of Suffolk; by 1750 the districts north-west of a line drawn from Bristol to Durham were filling up rapidly; while by 1801, were it not for the 900,000 inhabitants of the London district, the population of the north-west would have been largely in excess of the southern portion.[3]

Not the least of Arthur Young's services to our knowledge of economic conditions in this period are the detailed statistics he gives of wages and cost of provisions, household necessities, and rents of the labouring classes. These statistics, it is true, were collected in 1767, 1768, and 1770,[4] but are also generally applicable to conditions throughout George II's reign, during

[1] See Webb, *English Poor Law*, part i, p. 156.
[2] For the characteristics of the lowland and highland zones of Britain see in this series vol. i, pp. 1–14.
[3] Mantoux, pp. 359–62, gives four interesting maps showing the relative density of population in 1700, 1750, 1801, and 1901, the last differing little from that of 1801, which already shows the great manufacturing areas stabilized. The first two of these maps are reproduced at the beginning of this volume.
[4] See especially *Eastern Tour*, iv. 301–7, and *Northern Tour*, iv. 274–322. [I have not been able to find the figures Professor Williams here cites for London. At one point Young gives prices for 'Feversham' which he says are 'the London prices'; but these are $1\frac{3}{4}d.$ for bread, $4\frac{1}{2}d.$ for cheese, $4\frac{1}{4}d.$ for an average of meats, and 9d. for butter. See *Eastern Tour*, iv. 302, 304. C.H.S.j

which, and for some years later, the prices of labour and of
necessities remained fairly stable. As might be expected in a
country with such bad means of communication, the variation
in prices and wages in different parts is notable. In the north
and west of England both seem to have been lower than in
the south; but Young is chiefly impressed by the influence of
London, Cobbett's 'Great Wen', in raising the price of labour
in its immediate neighbourhood, quite disproportionately, as
he believes, to the slightly higher price of some provisions.
Bread there at 2*d.* a lb. and cheese at 3½*d.* were, he says, as
cheap as anywhere in the south, and meat at 4*d.* a lb. only 1*d.*
dearer than in the cheapest part: the most important difference
was in the price of butter at 8*d.* compared with prices as low as
5½*d.*–6¾*d.* in other parts. But the relatively high wages for
London craftsmen, averaging 3*s.* a day from 1720 onwards, and
for labourers, which rose from 1*s.* 8*d.* to 2*s.* between 1700 and
1735, as compared with 1*s.* 6*d.* to 2*s.* for craftsmen and from
10*d.* to 1*s.* 6*d.* for labourers in other parts of the country,[1] were
probably due, not so much to the debauchery and extravagance
of the Londoners, as Young and others declared, but to the
demand in London for better workmen and also to the greater
irregularity of employment there in certain trades. In the north
Young found the average prices appreciably lower than in the
south, with bread at 1¼*d.*, cheese 3*d.*, butter 6*d.*, meat 3*d.*; and
correspondingly the weekly wage for agricultural labourers
7*s.* 1*d.*, compared with 7*s.* 9*d.* in the south. 'Manufacturers', as
the workmen in trades such as cloth-making, potteries, ironworks, collieries, &c., were called, generally had higher wages,
ranging from 15*s.* a week earned by Newcastle colliers to 7*s.* 6*d.*
by lead-miners,[2] women from 6*s.* 6*d.* in the potteries to 3*s.* 3*d.* in
a stocking-factory, and children from 4*s.* in a lace factory to
1*s.* 8*d.* in a Leeds cloth-factory,—the average wage for 'manufacturers' in the north working out at 9*s.* 6*d.* for men, 4*s.* 7*d.*
for women, and 2*s.* 8*d.* for children. The employment of children
in factories, which later became such an abuse, was only a
development of the home-industry practice. Defoe, for example,

[1] These average wages are taken from E. W. Gilboy, *Wages in Eighteenth Century
England*, pp. 219–23. For her more detailed analysis see pp. 8 sqq., 92 sqq., 148 sqq.
See also p. 127, n. 2, below.

[2] Forty years earlier Defoe (ii. 162) found a lead-miner in Derbyshire earning
only 5*d.* a day, and his wife 3*d.*; i.e. 4*s.* a week between the two of them, 'and
that not always'.

when visiting the valleys round Halifax, packed with houses each producing its own separate lengths of cloth, kersey, or shalloon, noted the 'Women and children . . . always busy Carding, Spinning &c. so that . . . all can gain their Bread, even from the youngest to the antient; hardly anything above four Years old, but its Hands are sufficient to itself'.[1]

The weakest point in Young's analysis of economic conditions is that he nowhere attempts an exact correlation between the labourer's wages and his household expenses, though he gives indications which permit of rough deductions. For example, the agricultural labourer, at the lower average wage of 7s. 1d. per week, would earn in a full year no more than about £18. 10s. From this amount house-rent, firing, and repair of tools, which Young estimates at about £3 altogether, had in many cases to be deducted; and even if the man's own food could be put at as low a figure as £9—the amount given by Young for the keep of farm-servants boarded by the farmer himself—precious little can have been left over for his wife and family and for his own and their clothes. On the other hand, in most parts the wife and family generally earned something by labour in the fields; there were perquisites such as free beer or cider and even meals at harvest and hay-making times; occasionally, too, the farmer allowed the labourer to build himself a house on waste land or gave him a cottage rent-free, besides wood-cutting rights for firing. Young, indeed, comes to the complacent conclusion that the wages he records are 'high enough for maintaining the labouring poor in that comfortable manner in which they ought certainly to live', but adds significantly, '*also nearly to exclude parish assistance*'.[2] In fact the system of supplementing wages from poor-rates had begun at least as early as 1730, when Egmont notes this use of them in making 'sundry sorts of our work cheap by beating down the price of labour';[3] and forty years later Young notes the alarming increase of the poor-rates by about 64 per cent. within the previous eighteen years.[4] There is no doubt that in years of specially bad harvests and high prices, such as 1710, 1740, 1756, and 1766, there was intense distress and even actual starvation among the working classes —in spite of Young's optimistic view that high prices make

[1] Defoe, ii. 195.   [2] *Eastern Tour*, iv. 313 (my italics).
[3] *Hist. MSS. Comm., Egmont Diary*, i. 91.
[4] *Eastern Tour*, iv. 349.

'manufacturers' industrious and their families easy and happy, whereas in times of cheapness the men spend half their time in ale-houses, leaving their families to starve.[1]

A useful addendum and corrective to Young's conclusions as to comparative wage and price values may be found in two detailed studies by Mrs. Elizabeth Gilboy, based to some extent on Young's figures, but principally on a scientific study of a mass of records and statistics not available to him.[2] Taking the year 1700 as the datum point at 100 per cent., her tables indicate that during the fifty years from 1714 to 1763 inclusive the average cost of living in London was 98 per cent., and the average money wages and real wages (based on price values) 115 and 118 per cent. respectively, while in Lancashire money wages averaged 127 per cent. and real wages over 130 per cent. during the same period.[3] Remarkable, too, is the variation of actual wages that she brings out between London, the West Country, and Lancashire, as shown by the annual average of a labourer's income (family's earnings excluded):

	London	West Country	Lancashire
	£ s.	£ s.	£ s.
1700 . .	25 0	17 10	11 5
1725 . .	27 10	17 10	13 15
1750 . .	30 0	17 10	15 0
1775 . .	30 0	18 15	22 10
1790 . .	30 0	20 0	26 5

To these budgets women and children added considerably in the north, in the west to a less extent, and in London hardly at all.

On the whole Mrs. Gilboy's investigations led her to the conclusions that in the cities and their immediate surroundings (not only in London, as Young thought) wages were highest, but that in London they began to decline in real value in the

[1] *Northern Tour*, iii. 189, quoted by Lipson, iii. 481–2.
[2] *Wages in Eighteenth Century England* (Harvard), 1934, pp. 219–20; 'Cost of Living and Real Wages in 18th Century England' (*Review of Economic Statistics*, vol. xviii, 1936). The only copy of this *Review* which I found available in London is at the London School of Economics: even the British Museum has no copy of it. I am indebted to Mr. Wadsworth of Manchester University for these references. [This *Review* is now more readily procurable. C.H.S.]
[3] The exact averages for London are 97·98, 114·6, and 117·88; for Lancashire, 126·8 and 130·5.

late 40's of the century, whereas in Lancashire they rose almost continuously in value till late in the 60's; in the west, on the other hand, owing partly to the losses of the western wool-trade from the growing competition in the north and for other reasons, the state of the labouring man became progressively worse. But she agrees with most of the other authorities, from Adam Smith and Malthus to Prothero and the Webbs, that the eighteenth century marks on the whole a rise in the standard of living of the working classes.

What of the general state of society in this period? One of its most marked characteristics was the great cleavage between the well-to-do 'persons of fashion and fortune' and the poor or 'lower order of the people'. It has not always been so in modern times. Under the Tudors, Shakespeare indeed, reflecting the spirit of his age, loved a lord or a duke of Milan, and kings abound in his plays; but he was equally at home with the simple rustics of Arden, the Christopher Slys and Bottoms, the common soldiers of Henry V's army or Falstaff's pot-boys. In the next century, too, the rebellion brought all classes into close contact, and Pepys's diary makes it evident that the Restoration did little to re-erect class barriers. Today even more is it true that the barriers between classes of the community are fast disappearing. But in the eighteenth century, with the increased prosperity that came after the treaty of Utrecht, wealth, even more than gentle birth or public services, became the touchstone that separated the class that counted in the community, 'their betters' as Fielding calls them,[1] from the destitute 'mob' or even from the wage-earning poor, who were thought lucky to be protected by the rich. As Thomson, apostrophizing Britannia, wrote:

> Thy Country teems with wealth,
> And Property assures it to the swain,
> Pleas'd and unwearied in his guarded toil.[2]

The rise to power of Pitt himself was regarded as a portent by his friend Glover, who spoke with wonder of this 'private gentleman of a slender fortune, wanting the parade of birth or title . . . [being] considered as the only saviour of England'.[3]

---

[1] *Voyage to Lisbon.*
[2] Thomson, *Summer*, ll. 1454–6.   [3] See below, pp. 375–6.

There were no doubt a few of those admitted into polite society, Dr. Johnson, Oglethorpe, Hay, Coram, Hanway, and others, not to mention Wesley and Whitefield, who took a serious interest in their poorer brethren and tried to improve their lot either spiritually or materially; but these were rare exceptions. As a rule the poor were regarded as a class apart, to be ignored except when their hardships made them boisterous. This attitude is reflected in the literature of the period; as in Pope's indignant lines:

> 'God cannot love (says Blunt with tearless eyes)
> The wretch he starves'—and piously denies:
> But the good Bishop, with a meeker air,
> Admits, and leaves them, Providence's care.[1]

Gray, half apologetically, when in his one great poem he speaks so feelingly of the humble peasants, the village Hampdens and the mute inglorious Miltons, begs 'Grandeur' not to

> hear with a disdainful smile
> The short and simple annals of the poor.

Gay's *Beggar's Opera* was indeed an incursion into the affairs of low life, excused by its latent satire and never repeated; and perhaps even Fielding's low-born scoundrel *Jonathan Wild* was tolerable to his generation mainly because that hero was one of the blood-suckers of the rich. Fielding, too, though there was doubtless a spice of irony in his remark that masquerades, assemblies, and places of amusement should not be denied to the higher classes, since 'pleasure always hath been, and always will be, the principal business of persons of fashion and fortune. . . . To the upper part of mankind time is an enemy, and . . . their chief labour is to kill it'; yet there is no irony intended in his conclusion that the legislature should sternly repress all such amusements for the poor, since to them 'time and money are almost synonymous', and all temptation should be removed from them 'to squander either the one or the other; since all such profusion must be repaired at the cost of the public'.[2]

[1] *Moral Essays*, iii. 102–3. This was written shortly after the exposure of the scandal of the Charitable Corporation, established nominally to relieve the poor by lending them money on pledges, but really to enrich its projectors, one of whom remarked to the investigating committee, 'Damn the poor'. 'Every man in want is knave or fool' was another apophthegm attributed to the directors of this charity.

[2] *An Inquiry into . . . the late increase of Robbers. The Writings of Henry Fielding*, ed. Henley, xiii. 27–28.

The lot of the poor was indeed hard during the eighteenth
century. Even the capable and hard-working among them had
often, as we have seen, a hard struggle to make both ends meet;
want of work or the temptations of an ill-governed Alsatia, such
as the poorer parts of London, drove many to drunkenness
and crime; while the infirm or the unfortunate who could not
get regular work were at the mercy of a system, not perhaps by
intention callous, but rendered so largely by defects of administration. As Gonzales, an intelligent Portuguese visitor to England in 1730, remarks: 'The legislature has provided abundance
of excellent laws for maintenance of the poor, and manufactures sufficient to employ them all; and yet by indolent
management, few nations are more burdened with them, there
not being many countries where the poor are in a worse condition.'[1] The principal defect, indeed, of the poor-law system in
the eighteenth century lay in the difficulties and vagaries of its
local administrators in whose hands the main statutes relating
to the poor left all responsibility. By the act of 1597 overseers of
the poor in each parish had power to levy a rate to support their
poor; by that of 1662 anybody below the status of property-
owner not originally 'settled' in the parish could be removed to
his own parish unless he gave security to the justices that he
would never come on the rates; in 1692 the justices were given
a controlling power over the expenditure of the overseers, but
that measure seems only to have increased the rates. In 1723
parishes were empowered to establish workhouses in which
able-bodied paupers were made to work and the infirm fed at
the parish expense: an act which, by insisting on the workhouse
test, seems to have temporarily checked the rise in poor-rates.
By various Vagrancy Acts of increasing severity passed between
1597 and 1744 'rogues, vagabonds and sturdy beggars' were
liable to be whipped 'until bloody' and then sent on to their
original parishes or lodged in a house of correction. Until
1662, indeed, some control over the vagaries of parish officers
had been exercised by the supervision of the privy council;
but after that date the local authorities of the 15,000 parishes
and townships[2] in the country were left entirely to their own

---

[1] Pinkerton's *Voyages and Travels*, 1808, ii. 144.
[2] For this number see Webb, *English Local Government* (*English Poor Law*, part i),
vii. 150, and for the Vagrancy Acts, id., p. 355. See also Prothero, *English Farming*,
p. 435.

discretion, at the very time when the development of industry and commerce and the growing tendency of the poorer classes to migrate in search of work rendered some more national system of control essential. The overseers of the poor were unpaid officials, often ignorant and unwilling workers; many were corrupt and all imbued chiefly with the desire 'to save the parish harmless' of new-comers who, however able and industrious at first, might some day come on the rates: at the same time the methods of relief were often extravagant, and already the so-called 'Speenhamland' system of supplementing low wages by parish doles was being anticipated in many parishes.[1] The rising cost of poor-rates throughout the country, estimated in 1695 by Davenant at £665,362,[2] in 1753 by Fielding at £1,000,000, and in 1776 by a committee of the house of commons at £1,500,000, was causing alarm and encouraging a harsh view of the poor. Locke, for example, thought poverty due to 'a relaxation of discipline and a corruption of manners', Defoe attributed the increase of the indigent poor to laziness, and Arthur Young, until he became wiser with age, to a growing taste in the labouring classes for such new-fangled luxuries as tea and sugar.

Perhaps the most lamentable aspect of the poor-law system was its treatment of pauper children, especially in London. Here the system was for the overseers to send these as infants either to the workhouse or to parish nurses for a fee of 2s. 6d. or less a week. Most of these infants were utterly uncared for and many actually starved to death. A committee of the house of commons in 1716 found that of 1,200 children christened in the one parish of St. Martin's-in-the-Fields, three-quarters died within the year, while a return of infant mortality among parish children from sixteen parishes of London for the years 1750–5 showed the following terrible results:

Born and received	Discharged	Dead	Remained alive in 1755
2,239	1,074	1,097	168

Another gives the percentage of children dying in London

[1] See above, pp. 126–7.
[2] Davenant's figure applies to the end of Charles II's reign; by 1695, when he wrote, he thought the total 'much higher'. See Lipson, iii. 485. Fielding's figure is given in his *Proposal*, see Henley, edn. cit., xiii. 141.

under five years of age as 74·5 per cent. between 1703 and 1749 and 63 per cent. between 1750 and 1769, most of those dying being probably pauper children.[1] The pauper children who survived from this holocaust were hardly better off, for, as soon as possible, they were apprenticed to learn a trade under some master for a premium ranging from £2 to £10. The apprentice-ship lasted till the age of twenty-four, and though some masters taught their apprentices to be craftsmen and treated them decently, there was practically no control over the many inhuman wretches who starved and beat them and taught them no trade except that of stealing.[2]

In many ways London, as far as the poor were concerned, was the plague-spot of England. Already, according to Smollett, it contained, by the first decade of George III's reign, 'one-sixth part of the natives of this whole extensive kingdom', and was still growing so rapidly that soon 'the whole county of Middlesex will be covered with brick'.[3] Unfortunately the new houses were almost entirely for the accommodation of the wealthier classes, while the poor were still left to swarm in the old insanitary rabbit-warrens that disgraced the capital. Moreover, except for the port-workers, the Spitalfields silk-weavers, builders, and a few skilled optical and scientific instrument makers, and the watchmakers, who were world-famous, London had no important industry: the rest of the numerous labouring class were employed chiefly at tailoring, seamstress work, shoemaking, laundering, book-binding, printing, coach-making, and shop-keeping, all rather seasonal trades, very busy when the rank and fashion were in town but with long spells of dullness at other times. The wages and prices were high compared with other parts of England, but not high enough to make up for the periods of slack trade, while the hours were inordinately long, sometimes from 6 a.m. to 8 or even 9 p.m.,[4] and there were very few holidays except just at Easter, Whitsuntide, and Christmas, and on the eight 'hanging days' at Tyburn. On the other hand, there was a large idle or criminal class who earned a precarious

[1] From a table in J. Hanway, *Letters on Importance of Rising Generation*, 2 vols., 1767, i. 80–81.
[2] The subject of the poor is admirably discussed by Dorothy Marshall, *English Poor in the Eighteenth Century*, 1926. For the premiums paid see Webb, p. 197.
[3] *Humphrey Clinker* (Letter to Dr. Lewis of 29 May).
[4] These details are of the tailoring industry in London. See Lipson, iii. 403–5. For other industries in London see Lipson, ii. 58–59.

subsistence by their misdirected wits, and whose existence was fostered by the absence of an efficient police-system, the ill-lighted streets,[1] and the horrible rookeries full of brothels and 2d. a night lodgings off Holborn, Long Acre, St. Martin's Lane, Petty France, the Haymarket, Clare Market, and Covent Garden. Of Drury Lane Gay wrote in 1716:

> O! may thy virtue guard thee thro' the roads
> Of Drury's mazy courts, and dark abodes,
> The harlots' guileful paths, who nightly stand,
> Where Katherine Street descends into the Strand.[2]

Another of the terrors of London was the fear of being suddenly seized by the licensed press-gangs for the navy or by the unlicensed kidnappers of labour for the plantations. How vivid such terrors might be is illustrated by the case of James Watt. During the year he was working in London and living on 8s. a week he hardly ever dared stir out of doors for fear of being seized for a man-of-war or for service in America.[3]

One of the worst curses of London was drunkenness. During the eighteenth century the licensing laws, owing to the slackness or corruption of the licensing J.P.s, had become almost a dead letter. In 1722 no less than 33,000,000 bushels of malt were used for brewing, representing a 36-gallon barrel of beer for every man, woman, and child of the population.[4] But the devastation caused by excessive beer-drinking was as nothing compared with the sudden epidemic of gin-drinking specially notable in London during the first half of the century. The tax on French brandy after the Revolution made it almost

---

[1] In one respect the London of the eighteenth century had an advantage over the London of today in the greater use made of the Thames as a highway. London was then much more centralized on the river, and to those who could afford the watermen's charges the Thames was much preferable to the narrow dirty streets. These watermen were an important fraternity: for their benefit the actor Doggett in 1716 founded the race for Doggett's Badge still rowed annually on the anniversary of George I's coronation.

[2] *Trivia*, iii, ll. 259–62.

[3] H. W. Dickinson and R. Jenkins, *James Watt and Steam-Engine*, 1927, p. 14.

[4] S. and B. Webb, *History of Liquor Licensing*, pp. 17, 18. The Englishman's thirst for beer was of long standing. Maitland's apostrophe to beer in his *Domesday Book and Beyond*, pp. 439–40, will be called to mind: 'And who shall fathom that ocean? Multum biberunt de cerevisia Anglicana, as the pope said. . . . The economy of the canons of St. Paul's was so arranged that for every 30 quarters of wheat that went to make bread, 7 quarters of wheat, 7 of barley and 32 of oats went to make beer. The weekly allowance of every canon included 30 gallons. . . . Perhaps to every mouth in England we must give half a gallon daily.'

unprocurable, except as a smuggled article, by the poor; on
the other hand, the 'patriotic distillers' of English gin paid so
small a duty that the very poorest could afford the liquor sold
at unlicensed 'dram-shops'. By 1736 there were 6,000–7,000
of these dram-shops in London alone, and wages were often
given to workmen in the form of cheap gin. Parliament made
several vain attempts to restrict the traffic: in 1729 by a tax
of 5s. on the gallon and of £20 for the retailer's licence, and
again in 1736 by a still more drastic measure of Sir Joseph
Jekyll's, raising the tax on a gallon to £1 and on the retailer's
licence to £50; but the severity of this measure simply led
to its complete evasion, informers being intimidated by the
populace[1] and the justices either from fear or corruption neglecting to levy the duties. In fact between 1734 and 1742 the
sale of gin had increased from 4,947,000 to 7,160,000 gallons.
In 1743 the government itself passed a bill repealing Jekyll's
act, abolishing his prohibitive duty on retail sales, slightly increasing that on manufacture and reducing the retailer's licence
fee for bona-fide taverns and ale-houses to a modest £1, in the
hope, expressed by Carteret, that these licence-holders might
take care that illicit houses should not remain open. This act
answered some of Carteret's hopes, but a further concession to
the distillers in 1747 only increased the evil. At last, however, in
1751 the public conscience was thoroughly aroused, partly by
Fielding's *Inquiry*, still more by Hogarth's *Gin Lane*, which gave
ocular and in no way exaggerated demonstration of the ravages
of this horrible gin traffic. From north, south, east, and west of
England petitions against the iniquitous traffic came to parliament demanding effective legislation; and in the same year an
act was passed strengthening that of 1743 and effectively stop-
ping illicit sales. By the end of the reign the evil had been at last
brought within measurable bounds.[2]

[1] Carteret speaking in the house of lords in 1743 says that one such informer was
'upon the point of being . . . destroyed when one of the greatest persons in the
nation . . . opened his doors to the distressed fugitive and sheltered him from a
cruel death'. *P.H.* xii. 1357 (22 Feb. 1743).

[2] The attention devoted to honest English beer as opposed to the supposed dram-
drinking habits of the French may in the patriotic fervour of the Seven Years war
have had something to do with this improvement. See Wright, *Caricature History*,
1848, i. 294–6. See also Lecky, *History of England in Eighteenth Century*, 1883, i.
476–82. On all the above see Webb, pp. 22–39. The act of 1751 (24 Geo. II, c. 40)
was further strengthened in 1753 (26 Geo. II, c. 30) so that by 1758 the sale of gin
had fallen to 1,849,370 gallons.

It was a brutal age, illustrated by many even of its amusements, such as bull-baiting, cock-fighting and cock-throwing, badger-baiting and goose-riding, and the popular spectacle of public hangings, amusements which encouraged what Fielding calls the 'barbarous custom . . . peculiar to the English' of insulting and jesting at misery.[1] In such an age the brutality of punishments hardly excites wonder. They included the pillory and whipping, burning in the hand, transportation, and hanging even for the most trivial thefts.[2] Prisons, it is true, were rarely used for convicted offenders, but mainly for the detention of prisoners before trial, and above all for debtors. They were often horrible places, for though all prisons were, in legal theory, royal, most were in the possession of local bodies or even of private persons under no effective supervision by the Crown.[3] These public bodies or private owners generally farmed them out to wardens who appointed the jailers and made what they could out of the prisoners. There were fees payable to the 'turnkey' on entry, fees for beds, fees for putting on or taking off irons, fees on discharge from jail.[4] The buildings themselves were often so crowded that people of both sexes were herded into one room; they were so insanitary that in some of them jail-fever, a malignant form of typhus, was almost endemic. The Black Sessions of 1750 at the Old Bailey were long remembered for the deaths among others of four of the six judges, two or three of the counsel, one of the under-sheriffs, and several jurors, a total of some forty who all caught the jail-fever during the sessions.[5] Not the least evil were the debtors' prisons, of which the Fleet and the Marshalsea were the most notorious. In 1716 as many as 60,000 debtors, some for the smallest sums, were stated to be imprisoned in England and Wales: the Marshalsea alone had 700–800, of whom a parliamentary committee of 1719 reported that 300 had died in less than three months.[6] In 1729 public attention was directed to the horrible conditions under which debtors were confined, by the report of Oglethorpe's committee on the Fleet prison under the charge of one Bambridge, a veritable monster in human form.[7]

---

[1] *Voyage to Lisbon* (26 June 1754).   [2] See above, p. 62.
[3] See Webb, *English Local Government*, vi (*English Prisons*), 1–4.
[4] Ibid., pp. 5–8.   [5] Ibid., p. 20, n. 1.
[6] [I have not been able to find Prof. Willams's authority for these figures. C.H.S.]
[7] Hogarth's picture of Bambridge appearing before Oglethorpe's committee is in the National Portrait Gallery.

He and several of his murderous subordinates were fortunately dismissed as a result, but at their trial he and his underkeeper were acquitted of the murders and felony of which they were charged, largely, as it appears, because of the impossibility of obtaining enough legal evidence from their subordinates. In another case, however, to which the poet Thomson drew attention—

> Drag forth the legal monsters into light,
> Wrench from their hands oppression's iron rod,
> And bid the cruel feel the pains they give—[1]

one of the culprits was found guilty but fled from justice.[2] Other committees were set up to inquire into prisons in 1735 at the instigation of William Hay, and in 1754 again by Oglethorpe, which led to some slight amelioration in conditions; various Insolvent Acts were passed to release certain classes of debtors from prison; and an act of 1759 made creditors liable to pay a groat a day for the support of their debtors in prison; but it was largely inoperative. The fact was that it was nobody's business to see that prison conditions were made tolerable, and no great improvement was apparent until Jonas Hanway and Howard had really aroused general public feeling in George III's reign. But at any rate some alleviation of the imprisoned debtors' conditions resulted from Oglethorpe's inquiry, and still more from his appeal for public subscriptions to pay off the debts of some of those imprisoned and to settle them in his new colony of Georgia in 1732 (see below, pp. 309–10).

Specially associated with these debtor prisons, though not confined to them, were the so-called Fleet marriages. Drunken and down-at-heel parsons, many not even in regular orders, haunted the purlieus of these prisons or taverns and other shady resorts, offering to marry for a small fee any couple brought before them. Many were the stories of unfortunate heiresses and other girls abducted and married under duress to scoundrelly adventurers, or of young men plied with liquor and paired off with Drury Lane trollops by these ruffians. One Fleet parson is said to have earned £75. 12s. in one month by the traffic, another to have solemnized 6,000 such marriages yearly. At last in 1753 the abuse was tackled by Lord Chan-

---

[1] *Winter*, ll. 379–81.

[2] See Campbell, *Lives of Chief Justices*, ii. 204–5. *State Trials*, xvii. 375; Holdsworth, xii. 438–9. The reports of Oglethorpe's committee are in *P.H.* viii. 708–49.

cellor Hardwicke in a Marriage Bill enacting that no marriage was valid unless solemnized by an anglican clergyman after the banns had been cried for three successive Sundays in the parish church. The only exceptions admitted were for the royal family, Jews, and quakers, but not for dissenters or Roman catholics. Nobody in the commons seems to have objected to the hardship on dissenters and Roman catholics;[1] but Charles Townshend, who meditated an advantageous match, and Henry Fox, especially, who had made a runaway match with a daughter of the duke of Richmond, attacked the chancellor with a ferocity to which he was not slow to reply in kind. Finally, however, the bill was passed.[2]

Dark though the age was for the unfortunate poor, there were already signs of a revolt, which became more insistent in the second half of the century, against the view, largely due to Locke and most of the economists, that poverty was almost a crime and that at any rate the poor deserved all they got. For the defects of the poor-law, especially those arising from its narrow parochial administration, remedies were being sought by spreading the responsibility over wider areas, where ampler provision with greater economy could be more easily attained. A promising beginning was made at the close of the seventeenth century at Bristol. John Cary in 1696 obtained an act setting up a corporation of the poor, representative of all the wards and parishes of the city, with a common fund which enabled it to set up a spacious workhouse where lodging and food were given to the infirm; the able-bodied set to work; and pauper children trained for employment. William Hay, a friend of the duke of Newcastle's, encouraged similar undertakings elsewhere,[3] and Henry Fielding, in his *Proposal . . . for the Poor* of 1753, advocated a county workhouse to hold 5,000 at Acton Wells in Middlesex at a cost of £100,000, which would, he believed, repay itself by the profit from the work of the industrious poor, and by keeping out of mischief the more unruly. In many respects his proposals for the conduct of such an establishment are in advance of the age, notably in the wise charity of his plea that 'shame should be as little as possible . . .

---

[1] But the duke of Bedford made this point in the lords.
[2] See Yorke, *Hardwicke*, ii. 58–71; H. Walpole, *Memoirs of George II*, ii. 336–53; Sir G. Trevelyan, *Early History of C. J. Fox*, pp. 13–17; and above, pp. 61–62.
[3] Hay's efforts were without success. See Webb, *Local Government*, vii. 265–6.

mixed' with any necessary correction of the unruly, since shame
made men callous. Fielding had the more right to speak since
his fatal illness, which drove him to the *Voyage to Lisbon*, was due
to his exertions as a magistrate in suppressing the gangs of
robbers and murderers infesting London during the winter of
1753.[1] A few years later the Nacton House of Industry was
started in Suffolk, on similar lines to Fielding's *Proposal*, by
Admiral Vernon and other county magnates, and at first, at
any rate, was a great success. When Arthur Young visited it in
1770, he was delighted with its high, airy situation, the good
wholesome diet and warm clothing given to the inmates, the
separate apartments for married couples, single men and lads,
and single women and girls, the infirmary and surgery, and the
spacious workrooms for spinning, weaving, &c. He was also
impressed with its economical management, enabling the poor
to be better cared for at less expense, and he noted that as a
result four other such houses of industry had been started in
Suffolk and one in Norfolk.[2]

But such experiments, successful as they were at first, too
often, when the first enthusiastic founders lost their interest or
died out, degenerated into the soulless institutions described by
Crabbe in 1783:

> There Children dwell who know no Parents' care;
> Parents, who know no Children's love, dwell there!
> Heartbroken Matrons on their joyless bed,
> Forsaken Wives, and Mothers never wed,
> Dejected Widows with unheeded tears,
> And crippled Age with more than child-hood fears;
> The Lame, the Blind, and far the happiest they!
> The moping Idiot and the Madman gay.[3]

It was not indeed that men of goodwill and capacity were
deficient in the England of the first two Georges—one has only
to recall the names of philanthropists such as Thomas Coram,

[1] Even the king himself suffered from their unwelcome attentions. As he was
walking alone in the garden of Kensington Palace, he was accosted by a robber who
relieved him of his watch, money, and shoe-buckles. See the *Greville Memoirs*,
1938, v. 147. For Fielding's *Proposal* see Henley, edn. cit., xiii. 131–94, particularly
pp. 145, 169, 178, and 190.
[2] Young, *Eastern Tour*, ii. 178–83. By 1785 there were thirteen 'houses of industry'
on the Nacton pattern.
[3] *The Village*, i. 232–9, quoted by Webb, p. 246.

who founded the Foundling Hospital;[1] Oglethorpe, who brought
to light the iniquity of debtors' prisons and saved many from
their misery by taking them over to Georgia; the Russia merchant Jonas Hanway, who introduced the umbrella and organized charitable institutions; William Hay, and many others. But
theirs were at best individual efforts; and, owing largely to the
political theories of the time, there was no systematic and continued attempt to deal with such problems of local government
as the prevention of crime and of dire distress. It was only after
another seventy years had passed, bringing with them the
metamorphosis of a scattered and mainly rural population into
a more closely knit and mainly urban population, that England
began to realize the need of tackling such problems as a whole
instead of leaving them to the slipshod methods of local Dog-
berrys or to the unco-ordinated efforts of a certain number of
public-spirited philanthropists.

Before, too, such a revolutionary idea could establish itself,
the general education of the community had to be raised. Since
Tudor times the education of the ruling classes, and probably
even that of the less well-to-do classes, had sadly degenerated.
The Tudor monarchs were all well versed in languages and
were scholars who had studied history and statecraft in theory
as well as in practice; and their courtiers followed suit; and
at any rate the middling classes had grammar-schools and such-
like, still influenced by the revival inspired by Erasmus, Colet,
and More. But by the eighteenth century the education given
to those who could gain entry into Eton, Winchester, or Westminster consisted in little more than a formal exactitude in the
Latin and Greek classics, with a very perfunctory training,
given on holidays, in French, mathematics, and geography.
History, the best preparation for public life, appears to have
been entirely neglected in these great schools, as was science,
'the knowledge of external nature', as Johnson calls it, which
was left to the dissenting academies.[2] But at least Eton and

[1] The charter for this hospital was obtained in 1739; children were first admitted
to a temporary home in 1741; the hospital itself was opened in 1745.

[2] Johnson, though recommending history as an important study, entirely
approves of the omission of science from the curriculum. 'Physiological learning',
he says, 'is of such rare emergence, that one may know another half his life, without
being able to estimate his skill in hydrostaticks or astronomy. . . . Our intercourse
with intellectual nature is necessary; our speculations upon matter are voluntary
and at leisure.' *Lives of the English Poets* (Milton), i. 147 (1779 edn.).

Westminster produced statesmen with a fairly exact knowledge of the classics and a faculty for apt quotation from them, men such as Stanhope, Pulteney, Carteret, Pitt, and Walpole himself. But it is doubtful if even this much can be said of the two universities. At both the main subjects of instruction were the classics and theology, taught and examined with hardly any change from the system of the middle ages. Of the two seats of learning, Cambridge, with its giants Bentley and Newton at the beginning of our period, was the less sunk in lethargy. It was beginning to specialize in mathematics, and produced theologians and scholars such as Edmund Law,[1] Whiston, Waterland, Samuel Clarke, and Middleton, whose views, often unorthodox, stimulated thought. Oxford, on the other hand, could hardly claim more than one great teacher, Blackstone, who gave his notable lectures at All Souls at the end of George II's reign. For the sons of the rich, privileged as Gentlemen (or Fellow) Commoners, both universities were mainly an occasion for luxurious or riotous living, with a few such exceptions as Pitt and Carteret, who, however, almost apologized for his industry. The poor scholars such as Johnson, or the still humbler servitors or sizars such as Whitefield and Potter, a future archbishop, at Oxford, Sterne and Isaac Milner,[2] the mathematician, at Cambridge, had more inducement to study and to profit from the few good tutors such as Wesley must have been at Lincoln and Waterland at Magdalene. But at neither university was either the obsolete curriculum or the dons, mostly die-hard, port-drinking tories even at Cambridge, likely to stimulate intelligent interest in public affairs. It is significant that at neither university do the professors of history, instituted by George I in 1724 for the express purpose of training public servants, appear to have given any lectures during this period. To find men taking the most enlightened views on social conditions and animated with the greatest public spirit one would have had to look mainly in the ranks of the dissenters, whose special schools had advanced beyond the old dry methods, and who were driven, owing to religious tests at Oxford and Cambridge, to the more enlightened Scottish or Dutch universities.[3]

[1] Edmund Law, 1703–87, professor of moral philosophy and later bishop of Carlisle, not to be confused with William Law of the *Serious Call*.
[2] Milner did not matriculate at Cambridge until 1770.
[3] See above, pp. 88–89.

While for those of middling means like Johnson there were numerous grammar-schools with endowments[1] or private schools with low fees, such as Johnson himself started, at the beginning of the century there were few facilities for the really poor of the labouring class to obtain more than the mere rudiments, if even that. Here and there a village schoolmaster, whose fees probably could be reckoned in pence, would be found with a real gift for teaching and a love for his pupils such as Goldsmith's:

> The village all declared how much he knew;
> 'Twas certain he could write, and cypher too;
>
> .   .   .   .
>
> Yet he was kind, or if severe in aught,
> The love he bore to learning was in fault.[2]

But such were probably rare, and the amount they taught or their pupils had time to learn, before at a tender age they were set to work, was limited.[3] It was not indeed that there was a want of desire for knowledge, but a dearth of opportunity. No doubt there were many such as the boy rowing Johnson and Boswell to Greenwich: Johnson had admitted to Boswell that in certain cases 'learning cannot possibly be of any use; for instance this boy rows us as well without learning, as if he could sing the song of Orpheus to the Argonauts, who were the first sailors'; and turning to the boy, 'What would you give, my lad, to know about the Argonauts?' 'Sir (said the boy), I would give what I have.'[4]

To a very limited extent, indeed, the opportunity desired by Johnson's rowing boy was supplied by the charity schools, started by the Society for Promoting Christian Knowledge at the end of the seventeenth and greatly increased during the first thirty years of the eighteenth century. By 1723 no less than 1,329 such schools had been established throughout England, but after 1730, owing to religious and political difficulties, the increase was not nearly so marked. In England, unlike Scotland and Ireland, the schools were entirely managed by local

[1] Some 128 grammar-schools are said to have been established in England and Wales during the eighteenth century: see M. G. Jones, *Charity School Movement*, 1938, p. 18.

[2] *The Deserted Village.*

[3] And often remained so till within living memory. Only the other day an old man in Kent told me that at the age of six he was put to rook-scaring, his pay being 4d. a day, but no pay for his work on Sundays. [Note of 1939.]

[4] Boswell's *Johnson* under 30 July 1763.

142 SOCIAL AND ECONOMIC LIFE

committees of subscribers, the S.P.C.K. merely acting as an advisory body which provided the initial stimulus to local effort. The most numerous and best-managed schools were in London and some of the larger towns, such as Bristol, where the subscribers, being people of substance, not only provided adequate funds to pay for the buildings and teachers, but in some cases clothed the children and started them in life as apprentices to a trade. In most country districts, owing to the poverty of the clergy and peasants and often to the indifference of the squires, the schools were sparse and far less efficient. But in all these schools the curriculum was very limited, being confined to religious instruction, reading and writing, and, for specially bright boys, simple arithmetic, with needlework for the girls. The main object was, in fact, to establish social discipline among the poor and '*condition* the children for their primary duty in life as hewers of wood and drawers of water'.[1] For underlying the subscribers' benevolence was generally the fixed determination to do nothing to break through the rigid class system and to keep the poor in their place, in fact, to regard these schools 'as a shield and defence against the specific religious, political and social perils of the age'.[2] In Wales, on the other hand, the movement was far more democratic, the teachers were largely unpaid volunteers, and old and young flocked eagerly to the benches to learn to read the Bible and their own literature: in fact, the schools stimulated the great religious and political awakening of that country, so remarkable in the eighteenth century.[3]

In England it was not only in book-learning that the labouring classes had a stunted growth, but they were discouraged in every way from discussing their own grievances or acting as a corporate body to redress them. By law wages could still be fixed by the justices in session, and no doubt they consulted only the masters, not the labourers, for their decisions. These assessed wages were, no doubt, often exceeded, but that was mainly due to scarcity of labour. It is true also that friendly societies and benefit clubs increased largely during the eighteenth century among the more intelligent workmen of the towns—by

[1] M. G. Jones, *Charity School Movement*, 1938, p. 5. This book gives a well-documented and interesting account of the movement in the eighteenth century.
[2] Ibid., p. 343.
[3] Ibid., pp. 321-5. The educational movements in Scotland and Ireland are dealt with in Chap. X below.

1797 there are said to have been 600 of them in London alone;[1] but any attempt by such associations to combine for the purpose of improving wages and conditions of labour were sternly repressed. The general attitude of economists and of the government was that workmen should not be too well paid, as that was bad for trade, and that 'nothing but necessity will enforce labour'.[2] When in 1721 some 7,000 journeymen tailors of London as an organization demanded higher pay and shorter hours, parliament passed an act declaring combinations of workmen for such a purpose illegal, enacting penalties on masters and men for giving or taking higher wages than those fixed by the justices, and obliging unemployed journeymen to accept work at the wages offered. Two years previously, when the keelmen of Newcastle had struck for higher wages, a regiment of soldiers and a man-of-war were sent by the regency to overawe them.[3] Again, in 1726, when the weavers and wool-combers of Devon and Somerset tried to enforce their demand for increased wages by rioting and loom-breaking, another act was passed forbidding such combinations and declaring it criminal to quit employment: but the right of combinations among employers was left untouched.[4] In 1758 Lord Mansfield denounced as illegal a strike of the Manchester check-weavers against the length of cloth, the price of weaving, and the employment of 'illegal' workmen; and in 1759 the rigours of the law were threatened on the worsted weavers for trying to regulate the system of apprentices and other grievances with their employers. In spite of these severe measures, strikes and riots of dissatisfied workmen, notably the Spitalfields weavers in London and the coal-miners of Newcastle, were not uncommon, but were generally suppressed by the military in the interests of the employers. Every obstacle, indeed, was placed in the way of the working classes anxious to improve their condition; and they had to wait nearly three-quarters of a century before they achieved any sensible improvement. By that time a larger pro-

---

[1] Lipson, *Economic History*, iii. 391–2, citing Eden, *The State of the Poor* (1797).

[2] Mantoux, p. 70, n. 3, quoting a pamphlet of 1764.

[3] Michael, *Englische Geschichte im 18ten Jahrhundert*, iv. 196–9. Lipson, iii. 404–5; see also E. R. Turner in *American Historical Review*, xxi (1916).

[4] See Lipson, *History of the Woollen and Worsted Industries*, pp. 120–2. Nevertheless, a year later, when the workmen petitioned the king against the combinations of their masters, the Privy Council intervened to settle the dispute. See Lipson, *Economic History*, iii. 395–6.

portion of the more fortunate and better-educated members of society were taking an interest in their condition; and they themselves were being influenced by equalitarian ideas spread by the French Revolution and by agitators of their own class such as Cobbett and Place,[1] by the diffusion of good and cheap literature through such men as Brougham, and not least by the mitigation of the savage combination laws in 1824. Then at last the working classes were able to make their voices heard and even to influence the legislators in parliament.

The great middle class above the labouring poor ranged in the country from squires and J.P.s to yeomen and parsons, often the lowest in that grade; in the towns it comprised more or less substantial citizens engaged in business and the professions. From this class came the only civil or spiritual authorities with whom the poor ever came into direct contact, in the persons of J.P.s, members of corporations or clergy; from this class, too, came the majority of voters nominally responsible for electing members of the house of commons, very few of course coming from the class below. Their lives were generally spent in their own small towns or country-side, within which their outlook was mainly confined. Travel was too irksome or expensive for most to pay more than one or two visits to the great world of London, and such visits rarely repaid them. Squire Western was frankly bored with his journey thither in pursuit of his errant daughter, and though Squire Bramble, more serious-minded and better educated, found much of interest in his long journey through a large part of the island, he was glad enough to find himself back at Brambleton Hall, and declared 'it must be something very extraordinary that will induce me to revisit either Bath or London'.[2] They had, of course, their compensations at home. The country squires and J.P.s were the despots, beneficent or otherwise, of their neighbourhood, the parsons, whether men of noble charity like Adams or rogues like Trulliber, could indulge their oddities as they pleased: a Squire Western could eat and drink heavily in the intervals of his fox-hunting or shooting, Matthew Bramble looked forward to taking 'the heath in all weathers . . . [with his] excellent fowling-piece', and even

---

[1] Place, it is true, became an employer in later life, but he had been through the mill in his youth.

[2] He even went to a levee at the duke of Newcastle's. For quotations see *Humphrey Clinker*, Letter of 28 Nov.

Richardson's tiresome George Selby could visit his neighbours and inflict on them his jokes to his heart's content. In the country towns, where those comfortable, square-built eighteenth-century houses still predominate and indicate the growing prosperity and good taste of the period, they formed pleasant little societies of their own, and had their distractions in occasional routs and assembly balls, periodical fairs and wandering theatrical companies; Bath and Nottingham, indeed, had their own theatres before George III came to the throne.[1] Defoe has much to say of the 'Polite Conversation' of the gentry about Bury St. Edmunds and of the 'very good Company' to be found at Ipswich of 'Persons well-informed of the World, and who have something very Solid and Entertaining in their Society'; of Maidstone, 'where a Man of Letters, and of Manners, will always find suitable Society'; and farther north, of the 'Ladies . . . Bright and Gay' and 'the Illustrious Company' to be seen at the Nottingham races; and of Yorkshire generally, 'in spite of the pretended Reproach of Country breeding, the Ladies of the North are as handsome and well dress'd as are to be seen either at the Court or the Ball'. At the fashionable watering-places, such as Bath and Tunbridge Wells,[2] the local gentry had the opportunity of meeting all the great and lovely of the land, and even to less popular resorts such as Epsom, Scarborough, and Brighthelmstone the Londoners were beginning to find their way. By the end of George II's reign, indeed, though the remoter country districts were still isolated and the unquestioned domain of the local potentates, the majority no doubt rough and rude like Squire Western, but with a minority of cultured and beneficent men such as Allworthy (Allen of Bath), the country towns were gradually absorbing, in their own individual way, something of London's politer culture.

To turn lastly to the small coterie of the really ruling class: by the eighteenth century this class was beginning to include not merely the old aristocracy and county families, but also the *novos homines* such as the Pitts, the Beckfords, the Clives, the Childs, the Yorkes, who had acquired wealth and gained

[1] *Johnson's England*, i. 212. The theatre at Bath opened in 1750 and that at Nottingham in 1760.

[2] A contemporary print of Tunbridge Wells in 1748 shows Dr. Johnson, Colley Cibber, Garrick, Richardson, Speaker Onslow, Lyttelton, Mr. Pitt, and the fair Miss Chudleigh in company there. See *Chatham*, i. 197. For Defoe's comments see i. 46, 49, 115; ii. 148 and 235.

influence through commerce, adventure, eminence in the professions, or speculation. Indeed, it is notable that England and
Scotland were almost the only countries in Europe, not excepting
Ireland, where trade or business was then regarded as an
honourable profession fit for gentlemen. But even so the class
remained extremely limited. Everybody who counted at all in
society or the government of the country was known to everybody else in the same circle: men or women not known to such
hardened society Londoners as Horace Walpole or George
Selwyn would be outcasts. One cannot, for example, conceive it
possible for anybody in this society having had the experience
of the late Lord Rosebery, who said of one prime minister that
he never expected to see anybody whom he did not even know
by sight appointed to that great office. Nearly all the members
of this select clique were well-enough off to be untroubled by
money cares; while those of the nobility in straitened circumstances seem to have regarded it as quite natural, like Lord
Essex, to take foreign embassies or colonial governorships or
even to ask for and accept royal pensions from the secret service
fund to enable them to uphold their dignity. As Lord Hardwicke remarked, 'I look upon such pensions as a kind of obligation upon the Crown for the support of ancient noble families,
whose peerages happen to continue after their estates are worn
out.'[1] Of a majority of them it may be said that they took their
duties in parliament and as local magnates no less seriously than
their pleasures. It is true that, except for those who took an
active part in administration, these duties of attending the
houses of parliament or of taking their share in local affairs as
lords lieutenant, and promoting elections either in their own
favour or for the benefit of their party, were not unduly onerous.
Sometimes, too, they might even be tempted by a sudden thaw
in February to neglect their parliamentary duties, in order 'to
get the little fox-hunting which the season allows'. But certainly
the standard of public service of such men as Stanhope, Townshend, Walpole, Newcastle and his brother Henry Pelham,
Pulteney, Carteret, Pitt, Mansfield, and Hardwicke was as high
as that of statesmen in any age, most of them devoting practically the whole of their time to the public.

Apart from politics, the life of polite society in the reigns of
the first two Georges must have been as agreeable as such life

[1] See Namier, *Structure of Politics* (1st edn.), p. 278.

can ever be. With sufficient means and a position which needed no self-assertion on their part to uphold, its fortunate members fell easily into the habits of elegance and urbanity which form one of the notes of the select society of that age. They could indulge their taste in splendid and commodious mansions and fantastically laid out gardens, built or planned for them by architects and landscape-gardeners unsurpassed in catering for these special tastes.[1] The brothers Pelham could repair

> To Clermont's terraced height, and Esher's groves,
> Where in the sweetest solitude embraced,
> By the soft windings of the silent Mole,
> From courts and senates Pelham finds repose.[2]

Temple could gather his Boy Patriots, Pitt, Lyttelton, and the rest, in the

> Fair, majestic Paradise of Stowe,[3]

with its gardens, busts, and temples; and at Cliveden by the Thames Prince Fred played the genial patriot with Bolingbroke, Pulteney, and the rising poets. They could travel with ease—sometimes even in war-time, so polite was the cosmopolitan society of the day—and polish their manners or sharpen their wits at foreign courts or at the supper-table of Mme du Deffand and her rivals' salons. At home, if they were in disgrace at the court of St. James's, where at any rate the queen's pungent good sense, George II's surly ill-manners, and Hervey's back-biting innuendoes were always amusing, they could seek the freer and more literary circle to be found at Leicester House where, instead of Walpole's cohorts of placemen and bishops, they found most of the poets and wits of the day. They could mingle without loss of dignity with the shopkeepers and little milliners, or the country sightseers, such as Matthew Bramble and his party, at Ranelagh or Vauxhall, or, when their generous living required precautions against the gout, mix with their own fellows as well as people of less *ton*, such as the Chudleigh and her tribe, or plausible tuft-hunting rogues at the Wells or Bath. Conversation and letter-writing were practised as an art by men like Chesterfield and Horace Walpole, and

---

[1] See below, pp. 411–13, for building and landscape gardening.
[2] Thomson, *Summer*, ll. 1429–32.
[3] Thomson, *Autumn*, l. 1042.

society verses by many, though by none so well as by Hanbury Williams, whose *Isabella or the Morning* gives an idea of the vapid talk at a duchess's morning reception. Then there were Hervey, Bubb Dodington, the jackal of this urbane society, and Horace Walpole himself to chronicle for future generations the political and social talks, the intrigues and gossip in which they themselves were often the principals. Even when my Lord Granville was too gouty to go abroad from his house, the wisdom and wit of his talk were so much appreciated that 'he used to sit at home and receive such visitors as his high station and lively conversation attracted at all hours of the day . . . and by thus staying at home [he] saw the ministers that were out as well as those that were in'. As, too, in all ages when polite conversation is at a premium, women took a leading part in this society. Apart from the frailer beauties, the Elizabeth Chudleighs and the Anne Vanes,—masterful dowagers such as Carteret's mother, 'the old dragon' Countess Granville, Sarah of Marlborough, or the 'haughty duchess' of Buckingham,[1] blue-stockings, such as the classical scholar Mrs. Carter, Mrs. Vesey, Lady Mary Wortley Montagu, and her duller namesake Mrs. Montagu;—great ladies assured of their own beauty and charm, Kitty, duchess of Queensberry, Marlborough's daughter the duchess of Montagu, Molly Lepel (Lady Hervey), Lady Suffolk, the lovely Gunning sisters—all these held sway not only over men's hearts but also their intellects.

No doubt this polite society was in many respects selfish and self-indulgent: by its monopoly of social and political power and its sublime conviction that it alone possessed the right and capacity of leadership, it no doubt continued the subordination and even prevented the development of the classes below far longer than was their due. At the same time, with all their selfish pleasures, they not only elevated the standard of good taste in art, literature, and music and above all in urbanity of conduct and conversation, but set an example as a class of public spirit and public duty. It was this consciousness of civic

[1] See above, p. 99, n. 2. The duchess of Buckingham plumed herself, according to Horace Walpole with little justification, on being James II's illegitimate daughter and used to weep on his tomb at St.-Germain. When her son died she asked Sarah of Marlborough to lend her Marlborough's funeral car. 'It carried my Lord Marlborough,' replied Sarah, 'and shall never be used for anybody else.' But honours were even, for the Buckingham retorted, 'I have consulted the undertaker, and he tells me I may have a finer for twenty pounds.' H. Walpole, *Reminiscences*, ix.

duty which in the long run eased the inevitable change in their relations to the classes then of little account, and made such a change much easier than was possible in the countries where aristocracies had no purpose in society beyond amusement and military glory.

VI

THE SETTLEMENT OF THE DYNASTY—STANHOPE'S MINISTRY 1714–21

ON the day of Queen Anne's death the most prominent tory leaders—Ormonde, Bolingbroke, Bathurst, Wyndham,[1] and Atterbury, bishop of Rochester—met at Lord Harcourt's house to consider their course of action. Atterbury bluntly declared that two things must be done: (i) aid sought from Louis XIV; (ii) James III's accession proclaimed, with Ormonde in command of a military force. He added that

he would at the Royal Exchange read, in his lawn sleeves, the Proclamation. Upon this Lord Bolingbroke said that all our throats would be cut. To which the Bishop reply'd that if a speedy resolution be not taken, by God all will be lost. Lord Bolingbroke harangued upon this subject, and the Bishop fell into a great passion and said that this pusillanimous fellow will ruin our country; so he quitted them.[2]

Thus the Jacobites lost their last chance, even then a small one, of carrying the country by surprise. Had a deliberate vote been then taken of the British population there seems no doubt that a majority would have supported the Hanover succession. The whigs to a man would have voted for it as the only sure guarantee of the Revolution system in church and government. A large body of tories would also have voted the same way: for the Revolution itself was quite as much the work of high-flying church tories who feared for their religious security under a Roman catholic king as of whigs who saw in it their political

[1] Sir William Wyndham, 1687–1740, had been secretary at war and chancellor of the exchequer successively in Anne's last tory ministry. He was a faithful friend of Bolingbroke, who on his dismissal from the Pretender's service in 1716 addressed to him in the following year the famous letter repudiating all further connexion with the Jacobites. Wyndham thereafter became the most respected and able of Bolingbroke's new party of Patriots opposed to Walpole but loyal to the Hanoverian dynasty.

[2] Add. MS. 35837, f. 509, cited in A. S. Foord, *His Majesty's Opposition*, Oxford, 1964, p. 44.

salvation, while the Act of Settlement itself was passed by a tory majority. Bolingbroke, no doubt, for his personal ends, would have welcomed the Stuart king, whom he hoped to guide politically. But he had a better sense of the feeling of the English people than the bishop: 'England would as soon have a Turk as a Roman Catholic for King', he said. His refusal to go with Atterbury to proclaim James III at the Royal Exchange was due not to cowardice but to a sense of its futility.

At the same time the absence of serious resistance to the immediate succession of George I was not an unmixed advantage to him and his successor. The minority supporting James III's rights was a compact and pertinacious party consisting not only of the small[1] but devoted phalanx of papists, who had everything to gain from a Roman catholic king, but also of a considerable number of tory squires and high anglicans like Atterbury, who believed that adequate safeguards for their religion could be secured from James and were convinced that in breaking the legitimate line they would commit a deadly sin. Had they made the attempt when the throne was vacant in 1714, they would at least have felt that they had put their convictions to the test under the favourable circumstances of a tory ministry in power and an unoccupied throne. As it was, their failure to make the effort at such a time gave a rankling feeling of frustration to the legitimist party without revealing its inherent weakness. It was tempted to regain self-respect by sporadic attempts in less favourable conditions, when the new dynasty was established and supported by all the resources available to a whig ministry in power. Hence, though, as events proved, there was never any serious danger to the dynasty, the continual plotting of the Jacobites, which flared up in 1715, 1719, and 1722, and their readiness to use any complications in foreign policy, as in 1725, to advance their cause, gave constant anxiety to the government during the whole of the reign of George I.[2] Had the issue been decided once for all in 1714, it is more likely that the Jacobites would have realized their weakness and whig ministers have been less nervous of their activities; nor probably would there have been the same

[1] Estimated at nearly 28,000 by C. Butler, *Hist. Memoirs respecting English Catholics*, iv. 253–4. Michael suggests 25,000, *Quadruple Alliance*, p. 58, n. 1.

[2] This anxiety continued, though in a less intense form, until after the 1745 rebellion. Fears of a Jacobite rising in the fifteen years before this were often exaggerated by the government for political purposes. See below, p. 185.

persistent exclusion of the tories from the government for the next thirty years.

There was little, it must be admitted, to encourage loyalty in the character and proceedings of the first two Hanoverian kings. George I was fifty-four when he landed in England, George II only ten years younger when he succeeded his father, both with characters well set in the German mould. The father delayed coming over to England till seven weeks had passed since Queen Anne's death:[1] neither of them took any pains to conceal his preference for the electorate, where he was a real ruler, to the Crown hedged in with constitutional restrictions. George I never paid his new subjects the compliment of learning their language; his son spoke it, indeed, but with an atrocious accent. Though their English subjects had been willing to condone the light-hearted infidelities of Charles II with mistresses who at any rate amused and charmed the populace, and even the gloomy and less patent irregularities of James II, they had, during Anne's virtuous reign, become accustomed to the observance of the decencies at court and were shocked at the grossness of George I's amours. The place of his divorced and imprisoned wife Sophia Dorothea was supplied by three mistresses. First of these was the Baroness von Schulenberg, later duchess of Kendal, whose scrawny figure was likened to a hop-pole by the ribald populace; her leading rival was the Baroness Kielmansegge, later countess of Darlington, a lady of opulent charms; finally, there was Kielmansegge's sister-in-law Countess von Platen, the youngest and least unpleasing of the three.[2] George II, though less promiscuous, had not the same excuse for infidelity, as he had one of the ablest and most devoted wives in Europe.

George I landed at Greenwich on 18 September 1714, accompanied by Mme Kielmansegge and a whole train of courtiers, including his private secretary Robethon and his two

---

[1] George had intended to come sooner, on Bothmer's advice, but he delayed in order to arrange the government of Hanover during his absence. Michael, *Hanoverian Dynasty*, pp. 58, 71–72.

[2] Perhaps the only being for whom George I really cared was his daughter Sophia Dorothea, queen of Prussia. 'Souuennés vous cependent toujour de moy ma chere Fillie et sojés asseurée que je vous aimeres toujour tendrement', a phrase which occurs in one of his letters to her (published in *Eng. Hist. Rev.* lii. 492–9), throws an unusually soft light on his grim personality. Details of George I's mistresses are to be found in the *Complete Peerage* under 'Kendal' and 'Darlington'. Kielmansegge's enormous bulk occasioned her nickname 'The Elephant and Castle'. Von Platen was married to Kielmansegge's elder brother.

chief Hanoverian ministers, Bernstorff and Goertz. Even before he arrived the new king had indicated in what political quarter he reposed his trust. Immediately after the queen's death the Hanoverian envoy had produced before the privy council the list, as previously drawn up by George, of lords justices who were to act as regents until his arrival. Of these, four only were tories, all of them known for their support of the new dynasty: the other fourteen were whigs. Even among these were three important omissions: Somers, who had been ill, and, more significant, Marlborough, known to have recently corresponded with his nephew Berwick at the Pretender's court, and Marlborough's son-in-law, Sunderland. One of George's first instructions to the lords justices was to dismiss Bolingbroke from his office and seal up his papers, for no one had been more indignant than the elector at Bolingbroke's Restraining Orders to Ormonde in 1712;[1] Ormonde himself likewise was deprived of his office of captain-general. An active correspondence had been carried on between Hanover and London as to the formation of a new ministry; but in this the lords justices had no part, the task being entrusted mainly to Bothmer, the experienced Hanover agent in England, in correspondence with Jean de Robethon in Hanover. For some years to come this man Robethon was to hold a key position in English politics, to the growing indignation of British politicians. He was a French Huguenot refugee well versed in English politics and sufficiently interested in English literature to have translated into French Pope's *Essay on Criticism*. He had been in the confidential service of both Portland and William III and skilfully used this opportunity of acquiring great influence with the leading whigs; he also had a wide knowledge of continental politics and personalities. Born to intrigue, he was content to remain in the background, where his influence was more effective than it would have been in a more prominent position. In Hanover he had merely been Bernstorff's private secretary, and was chosen by George to accompany him to England in the same capacity to himself. In the choice of ministers, most of whom were unknown to him personally, the king was guided almost entirely by Bothmer and Robethon, who, after consultation with the leading whigs, had the list ready for his formal approval.

On landing at Greenwich the king was received by all the

[1] See *Oxford History of England*, x. 233 (2nd edn.).

notables of the kingdom except Ormonde and Bolingbroke, whose presence would obviously have been unwelcome. To most of the others George was gracious, but on Oxford he pointedly turned his back, while Marlborough, though reinstated in his post of captain-general, and honoured by an hour's private conversation, was soon made to feel that his days of influence were over. A few days later the list of the new ministry was published. Except for Shrewsbury, a trimming politician, called in to break up the whig junta in 1710, who for some weeks retained his post as lord treasurer, and the lord president, Nottingham,[1] a Hanover tory, all the new ministers were whigs. Among the many propositions put forward to Bothmer by the leading politicians and forwarded by him to the king had been the idea of a mixed ministry to include other Hanover tories such as Bromley and the Speaker, Hanmer; but George had decided against this.[2] The leading member of the administration was generally taken to be Townshend, secretary for the northern department. His main public service had hitherto been as negotiator at Gertruydenberg, but his eminence in the whig party was probably due to his association with his abler brother-in-law Robert Walpole, who for the time being was content with the obscure but lucrative office of paymaster. Cowper, a sound whig but rather impracticable as a colleague, was made chancellor. Sunderland, much to his disgust, was put on the shelf as lord lieutenant of Ireland. Another disappointed office-holder was Viscount Halifax (Montagu), who, though promoted to an earldom and given the Garter, did not attain his ambition of the lord treasurer's staff, which, early in October, Shrewsbury exchanged for that of chamberlain.[3] Shrewsbury was the last to hold the historic office of lord treasurer, which

---

[1] Nottingham had previously advised Bothmer (a) to set up a whig ministry, (b) to conduct a strict inquiry into the conduct of Anne's last ministry, but (c) to maintain the tory character of the church and notably his own Occasional Conformity Act; see Michael, *Hanoverian Dynasty*, pp. 91–92. Cowper also drew up a paper for George I, *An Impartial History of Parties* (printed by Campbell, *Chancellors*, iv. 421–9, see also ibid., pp. 347–9), strongly urging a preponderating whig element in the new ministry.

[2] Berwick in his *Mémoires* regards it as a mistake of George I not to have included more tories in his first ministry, as he might thus have united the people in his favour, but he was not prepared to gamble on tory loyalty. See Williams, *Stanhope*, p. 153; Berwick, *Mémoires*, t. lxvi, p. 226. Compare Foord, op. cit., p. 48.

[3] Up to 30 Sept. (O.S.) Stanhope was still writing to Shrewsbury as lord treasurer; his first letter to the lords of the treasury was on 13 Oct. (O.S.), R.O., S.P. Dom. E.B. 117.

was replaced by a treasury board, presided over by Halifax as first lord. The more dignified and authoritative office of lord treasurer was suppressed, probably to prevent any minister obtaining such predominance over his colleagues as Oxford had and Bolingbroke aspired to, and also to emphasize the equal responsibility of all ministers directly to the king. The chief surprise in the new ministry was the appointment of General Stanhope as secretary for the southern department. His main ambition had been, and, in spite of his defeat and capture at Brihuega, still was for supreme military rank; but since his return from captivity he had distinguished himself by his resource and enthusiasm as a leading debater for the whigs in the tory parliament, and in the queen's last year had taken a prominent part in organizing active support for the Hanoverian succession.[1]

The almost complete exclusion from the ministry of the tory party, which still had a majority in both houses of parliament, and that without a word of criticism on constitutional grounds, clearly indicates that the king's right to appoint ministers on his own responsibility was still generally accepted. The new ministry was, however, not called upon to put its security of tenure to the test, since the old parliament, which had been called together by the lords justices for a few days to transact mainly formal business, was dissolved without further meeting on 5 January 1715.

The royal proclamation of 15 January summoning a new parliament was more like an electioneering manifesto than an impartial call on the electors freely to exercise their choice, for it contained an attack on the late ministry, and called on the electors to choose as members only 'such as showed a firmness to the Protestant succession, when it was in danger'. The Pretender published a counter-proclamation which gave little help to his cause, since he insinuated that the late ministry had supported his claims, and, while reasserting his fidelity to Roman catholicism, gave the vaguest assurances of protection to the church of England.[2] The election, especially with the powerful backing that a ministry in office could give to its supporters,

---

[1] Horatio Walpole, Robert's brother, claimed the credit for suggesting Stanhope as Townshend's colleague, but he probably owed his office much more to the influence of his old acquaintance Robethon.

[2] *Hist. MSS. Comm., Stuart Papers*, i. 343.

resulted in a majority estimated at 150 for the whigs.[1] Even with this advantage, so swift a revulsion from the tory enthusiasm of four years before may seem surprising. But in both elections the same desire for peace and tranquillity probably accounts for the results. In 1710 the country had become weary of the state of war almost continuous since 1689 and was alarmed at the menace to the church so skilfully suggested by the tories, who promised peace abroad and security for the church at home; by 1715 a tory ascendancy would probably have meant renewed civil war, while the Hanoverians' quiet assumption of power seemed to promise stability for the future.

When the new parliament met in March 1715, the ministers, backed, if not driven, by their whig majority, determined to clinch their victory by effectively depriving their chief adversaries of all power in the future. The impeachments then undertaken against Bolingbroke, Oxford, Ormonde, and Strafford[2] for their part in the treaty of Utrecht were the last of that series of purely political impeachments revived in the seventeenth century by parliament as the only weapon, apart from an act of attainder, then available against servants of the king. Since none of these tories enjoyed the confidence of George I their impeachment was unnecessary but it was natural that the whigs should be tempted to retaliate on their opponents for the obloquy and persecution they had themselves suffered between 1710 and 1714, and to secure their own supremacy by the obliteration of their most eminent rivals.

Certainly, the action taken against the four tory ministers effectively clipped their pinions during a critical period for the dynasty. After a somewhat inconclusive examination by a committee of the papers of Bolingbroke, Strafford, and Prior, the superseded plenipotentiary at Paris, the commons resolved to lay articles of impeachment for treason against Bolingbroke, Oxford, and Ormonde, and for high crimes and misdemeanours against Strafford. Bolingbroke and later Ormonde saved their adversaries further trouble by escaping to France and taking service under the Pretender, so they were declared traitors and their estates and civil rights forfeited by acts of attainder. The

[1] About 160 tories were returned at this election. See K. G. Feiling, *The Second Tory Party*, p. 15.
[2] Thomas Wentworth, Baron Raby and 3rd earl of Strafford (1672–1739), had been one of the chief negotiators at Utrecht.

impeachment of Strafford was soon dropped as of a man of no importance: Oxford was kept in the Tower for two years, but then, on the failure of the commons to put in an appearance against him, was acquitted by his peers in July 1717. The two years in the Tower had kept him out of the way during the rebellion, and, though he occasionally spoke in the house of lords after his acquittal, he was a broken man and could do no harm. Ormonde, a futile grandee, served the Hanoverians best by remaining in the Pretender's service. In 1723 Bolingbroke, who had soon been discarded by the Pretender and realized his inadequacy, was contemptuously allowed by Walpole to return to England and two years later had his estates restored to him; but he was never allowed to resume his seat in the house of lords. He had to carry on his opposition by subterranean intrigues with discontented whigs and the heir to the throne from his country house by the Thames at Battersea or his friend Pope's villa higher up the river at Twickenham.

When Bolingbroke arrived in Paris in March 1715 he found the Jacobites there all agog with preparations for restoring the throne of his fathers to James III. Their hopes were high. In England, where George I had at first been received with acquiescence, if not with enthusiasm, there were already signs of growing opposition. The king's aloofness and his train of Hanoverians were adversely commented on even by his supporters. Sporadic riots and disturbances were causing anxiety to the government, whose armed forces, during the first half of 1715, did not exceed 16,000 men.[1] Ormonde, who remained in England till August, and Mar[2] were almost ostentatiously preparing the ground for revolt, especially in the predominantly tory counties in the west of England. The growing unpopularity of the Hanoverians and the increasing favour of Ormonde and the high church tories, if not the Pretender himself, were so vigorously manifested by riotous mobs in London, Oxford, Staffordshire, and other parts of the country that parliament hurriedly passed the Riot Act increasing the power of magistrates to deal with unlawful assemblies.[3] Abroad, the Bourbon powers, in spite of their undertakings at Utrecht, notoriously favoured

[1] Only some 8,000 of these were available for the defence of Great Britain. See Williams, *Stanhope*, p. 176; Michael, *Hanoverian Dynasty*, p. 146.

[2] John, sixth or seventh earl of Mar, titular duke; 'Bobbing John'; for and against the Union, for and against the Pretender at various times.

[3] See Smollett, *History of England from Revolution to death of George II*, iii. 107–8.

the Jacobites. Louis XIV, though forced by the treaty to refuse James an asylum in France, winked at his sojourn at Commercy,[1] barely over a hundred miles from Paris, in the client state of Lorraine; and allowed the queen mother, Mary of Modena, to hold her court, a nest of Jacobite intrigue, at St. Germain. Without overtly recognizing the Pretender, and unable in the state of French finances to advance him any money, Louis suggested to his grandson of Spain to contribute 400,000 crowns towards a Jacobite rising, and allowed his minister Torcy to advise the Jacobite leaders and even to transmit their letters to friends in England through the French diplomatic couriers. In Berwick, a marshal of France and his own half-brother, James also had a loyal supporter and wise counsellor.

But to a politician of Bolingbroke's experience these advantages seemed more than outweighed by the folly and incompetence of James and his most favoured courtiers. James may have been worthy of respect for his staunch loyalty to the religion in which he had been brought up and for which his father had lost a throne, when he might have imitated the politic opportunism of his great-grandfather. But unfortunately this loyalty to his faith, natural, as he wrote in one of his proclamations, to one born and bred in it, degenerated into mere bigotry and made him the slave of priests and his still more bigoted mother; and even his most robust supporters in England would have distrusted him more, in spite of his tepid promise of protection to the English and Scottish churches, had they known of his secret assurances to the pope that, once restored to the throne, he would do his utmost to restore the true religion also. It was not entirely his fault that, as is generally the fate of exiled pretenders, he was encompassed by 'those busy flies that buzz all day about me', as Bolingbroke described the second-rate intriguers and the meddlesome, chattering women, many of them as ready to betray James's plans for money as to convey to him tainted information. But he seemed to prefer such flatterers and such muddlers as Middleton,[2] Ormonde, and Mar to the wiser counsels of men such as Berwick,[3] Torcy, or even

---

[1] Professor Fieldhouse in *Eng. Hist. Rev.* lii. 289, gives an account of the vain efforts even of the tory ministry to get the Pretender removed to an asylum farther away from England or his French base.

[2] Charles, second earl of Middleton, titular earl of Monmouth, secretary of state to James II in exile and till 1713 to the Old Pretender.

[3] In a fit of pique at the refusal by his half-brother, Marshal Berwick, of the chief

Bolingbroke; and characteristically at a critical period of preparation for the 1715 rebellion wasted time discussing the colour of the wax and the exact form of words for the patents he issued granting spurious titles or employment in his service.

With Bolingbroke's acceptance of office as his secretary of state in July 1715 a ray of light is suddenly cast upon the gloomy correspondence in the Stuart papers. Bolingbroke indeed was not the man to persist in a course which proved unexpectedly difficult, but he had knowledge of affairs, ingenuity, and fitful energy, and above all some appreciation of English conditions, so lacking in the Pretender's entourage. He was convinced that success was to be found only in 'the purse and strength of England' rather than in the 'undertaking spirit of Scotland';[1] and for that reason deplored Ormonde's sudden flight to France in August, for there was no one else in England prepared to organize a rising,[2] and still more Mar's precipitate raising of the standard of revolt in Scotland on 6 September, just when he was planning an expedition under James himself to the south coast. But he made the best of a bad job; he arranged for a ship to be ready in each of the four available French ports to carry over James to assume command of his supporters in Scotland, and was indefatigable in scraping together money from Spain as well as from Marlborough,[3] Shrewsbury, and other English well-wishers. In spite, too, of the premature rising in Scotland, he stuck to his point that England above all must be won, especially by proclamations 'to speak to the passions of men, which is, I presume, the only way of influencing them'. But even there he found an insurmountable obstacle in James's bigotry. Drawing on his long experience as a party leader, in his draft proclamations for the army, navy, city of London, and universities as well as in a general manifesto to the English people, he insisted on the need of 'some popular paper'. His

command in Scotland, he ordered Bolingbroke to have no more dealings with one he termed 'a disobedient subject and a bastard too'.

[1] When he was still a minister of Queen Anne Bolingbroke had told James that 'il ne compte pour rien les secours qu'il pourroit tirer des Écossois et des Irlandois' (*Eng. Hist. Rev.* lii. 451–2).

[2] Evidence of the widespread preparations for a Jacobite rising in the west of England and of the sudden collapse of these plans on the flight of Ormonde are given in Sir Charles Petrie's article on 'Jacobite Activities in South and West of England, 1715', *R. Hist. S. Transactions*, iv. xviii. 85–106.

[3] See *Hist. MSS. Comm., Stuart Papers*, i. 357, 401, 407, 412. Marlborough's contribution totalled £4,000.

arguments for this course show his brilliant foreseeing mind. He says, 'since the decay of the monarchy and the rise of popular power', the only way of counteracting whig schemes was to 'combat them at their own game by frequent and popular appeals' calculated to arouse the people from 'desponding submission to Hanover, to exert themselves in your cause'. But James would have none of this. From Bolingbroke's drafts he cut out all reference to the church of Ireland, a promise to re-establish the churches of England and Scotland in 'all those rights that belong to them', and allusions to Charles I, as 'the blessed martyr' and to the 'blessed memory' of Queen Anne, phrases regarded by the high church tories as a test of legitimacy. Indeed he forestalled Bolingbroke's protests by having his own emasculated versions printed in Lorraine and distributed forthwith.

One of Bolingbroke's troubles lay in the extreme difficulty of getting into touch with James personally. At Paris the English government had one of their most vigilant watch-dogs in the ambassador, Lord Stair. By his admirably organized system of intelligence he knew almost all the Jacobite plans and hampered even Bolingbroke's activities. The short distance between Paris and the Pretender's headquarters in Lorraine made it easy for Stair's spies to keep a watch on travellers and abstract suspicious correspondence. In fact Bolingbroke himself only once ventured to travel there to confer with his master; and all correspondence had to be carried on in cipher or by such cant-words as 'Lady Mary' for England, 'Nelly' for Scotland, which in truth deceived nobody. Money for arms and equipment was scarce. Above all the death on 1 September 1715 of Louis XIV, the Pretender's best friend in Europe, was a crushing blow to the cause. His successor, the Regent Orleans, though at first not unfavourable, soon found reasons for keeping on good terms with the new dynasty in England. Even when, with the regent's tacit consent, James, who, whatever his faults, did not lack personal courage, embarked from a French port in December, it was only to find Mar's force in Scotland already defeated and dwindling.[1]

[1] Much information about Bolingbroke's difficulties, the Pretender's ideas, and the preparations for the invasion is to be found in *Hist. MSS. Comm., Stuart Papers*, i, and Berwick, *Mémoires (Collection des Mémoires relatifs à l'histoire de France*, Petitot et Monmarqué, t. lxvi, 1828). See also Professor H. N. Fieldhouse's note in *Eng. Hist. Rev.* lii, on Bolingbroke's relations with the French envoy, d'Iberville, and on the

Apart from their own internal difficulties the Jacobites were ill-matched against the Hanoverian king's determined and united ministry in England. The two secretaries of state, Stanhope and Townshend, were a pair hard to beat for energy and enterprise in acquiring information of Jacobite plans and taking measures against them. Fortunately, by 15 July they had ample information from Stair of the Pretender's plans. A squadron was at once dispatched under Byng to keep watch on the French Channel ports; twenty-one new regiments were added to the standing army, the western ports and nests of Jacobites such as Bath and Oxford secured by garrisons. An attempt was made to preserve the loyalty of Scottish lairds by an act of Stanhope's requiring them to give security for their good behaviour on pain of losing their estates;[1] and ample power over suspects was given to the government by the suspension of the Habeas Corpus Act for six months. In September, when the Jacobites' plans had matured, the government struck: the arrest was ordered of Sir William Wyndham, five other members of the house of commons, and two peers for promoting a rising in the west, and Argyll was sent with a small force to deal with Mar's insurrection in Scotland. Still the main body of troops was retained in England, where Stanhope, in this respect at one with Bolingbroke, judged the crucial decision must be taken.[2]

These timely precautions were justified by the event. Ormonde made two attempts, in October and December, to land on the Devonshire coast, but on both occasions, finding no such support as he had hoped for, retired ignominiously to France. In the north-east of England a small force of Jacobites organized by Thomas Forster and Lords Derwentwater and Widdrington, after failing to surprise Newcastle, crossed the border, where it was reinforced by a body of Lowlanders under

reasons for his flight to France. Berwick's *Mémoires* are valuable for the insight they give into the futility of the Pretender's court and advisers.

[1] This was the so-called 'Clan Act'. Its immediate result was the reverse of its purpose; of some sixty suspected persons summoned to Edinburgh only two obeyed. See Hume Brown, *History of Scotland*, iii. 163; Michael, op. cit. i. 156.

[2] For the effective measures taken by Stanhope and Townshend to suppress Jacobite activities in the country see P.R.O., S.P. Dom. Entry Book 117, and Williams, *Stanhope*, pp. 175 sqq. with the authorities there quoted. Wyndham evaded the officers sent to arrest him but subsequently gave himself up. Of the others, both peers, Lansdowne and Dupplin, were successfully arrested, but two of the members of the commons, Kynaston and Forster, escaped, the one overseas and the other to lead the rising in the north-east.

the Scottish Lords Kenmure, Nithsdale, Carnwath, and Wintoun, and another party of Highlanders, under Mackintosh of Borlum, with Lord Nairne, detached by Mar. After some aimless wanderings in the Scottish Lowlands Forster decided to try his fortune in the Jacobite north-west of England, and reached Preston in Lancashire with a force of some 4,000–5,000, where he was easily surrounded and induced to capitulate on 13 November by Stanhope's generals, Wills and Carpenter, some 1,600 prisoners being captured and the rest dispersed. As it proved, the most formidable rising was in Scotland. Mar, with a small body of Highlanders, had raised the standard of revolt at Perth on 6 September. He was opposed by Argyll, at first with only 1,300 men to watch Stirling, the key to the Highlands, and to defend Edinburgh while the northern lairds Sutherland and Lovat were sent to gather their loyal clans at Inverness to cut off Mar's rear. Unsuccessful raids were made by the Jacobites on the capital and other strongholds on the Forth; but by November Mar's strength had increased to 10,000 and he advanced towards Dunblane to try conclusions with Argyll who still had only some 3,300 men. But although the battle of Sheriffmuir, fought on the same day as that of Preston, was tactically indecisive, it proved the end of Mar's activities. He retired to Perth, where the Pretender still found him after landing at Peterhead at the end of December. By that time Argyll had been reinforced by 6,000 Dutch troops landed in England in accordance with the guarantee in the Barrier Treaty of 1713, and some Swiss mercenaries. Even so he proved unwilling to advance[1] and was superseded in February 1716 by Cadogan, who ruthlessly hunted down the dispersing remnants of Mar's force, already abandoned by both Mar and the Pretender, who took ship for France on 4 February.[2] By April 1716 the rising had been entirely suppressed both in England and in Scotland; and by the end of the year the danger of renewed Jacobite plots on the Continent had been very much diminished. The Pretender, on his return from Scotland, was no longer allowed by the Regent Orleans to live so near Paris and the Channel ports as Lorraine, and was forced to take refuge first in the

[1] Argyll held back partly because of the severe weather and partly because he wished the government to consider Mar's request for terms.

[2] James's precipitate return to France was due to no want of courage, but simply to give his already defeated followers more chance of making favourable terms.

papal city of Avignon, and in 1717, after the Triple Alliance had been concluded, beyond the Alps. Meanwhile he had ignominiously dismissed from his service Bolingbroke, almost the only man amongst his adherents abroad with any sense of statesmanship or organizing capacity. 'Il faudroit être dépourvu de tout bon sens pour ne pas voir la faute énorme que le roi Jacques faisoit en chassant le seul Anglais capable de manier ses affaires', is Berwick's scathing comment on his brother's folly.[1]

Thus the English government could afford to be comparatively merciful, according to the standards of the time, in its punishment of the rebels. Only twenty-six of the captured officers suffered the death penalty; of the rank and file taken prisoner at Preston and in Scotland[2] only about one in twenty, some 700, were brought to trial and sentenced to be indentured for seven years' service on the West Indian plantations. Some of the chief rebel leaders at Perth, including Mar himself, the earl marischal and his brother, James Keith, had escaped to France; Forster and Mackintosh broke out of Newgate. But the seven English and Scottish lords who were captured were tried before their peers and sentenced to death. Great pressure was thereupon put on the government for a reprieve, a course advocated by a majority of five in the house of lords itself. In the end the sentences of all but three, Derwentwater, Kenmure, and Nithsdale, were commuted to imprisonment.[3] In the next session, of 1717, further clemency was legalized by the Act of Grace whereby the three lords still in the Tower, Carnwath, Widdrington, and Nairne, besides some hundred other rebels under sentence of death or confined in English and Scottish prisons, were released: an unprecedented and certainly wise and politic treatment of rebellion. On the other hand the ministry was not unnaturally purged of its doubtful members. There had already been some changes during 1715. Shrewsbury, who had contributed to the Pretender's campaign fund, had resigned in July. On the death of Halifax and the dismissal of his successor

[1] See Berwick, *Mémoires*, lxvi. 259–62. For further details of this Jacobite rebellion see Williams, *Stanhope*, pp. 175–93.

[2] In view of § 19 of the Act of Union a special act had to be passed for the trial of these prisoners at Carlisle, since it would have been difficult to get juries to convict in Scotland.

[3] Wintoun's trial and sentence did not take place till after the execution of Derwentwater and Kenmure on Tower Hill, 24 Feb. 1716: he escaped from the Tower, as did Nithsdale, who was rescued by his wife before the day of execution.

Carlisle in October, Walpole had left the pay office and become first lord of the treasury and chancellor of the exchequer. Now in March 1716 the tory Lord President, Nottingham, who had moved the Address to the king for mercy to the rebel lords, and three of his relations were dismissed from their posts.

The ministry, unhampered by tory or trimming colleagues, and for the first time composed entirely of whigs, thereupon set about strengthening their own tenure of power. Their first measure was to prolong the existence of the sitting house of commons with its safe whig majority. By the provisions of the Triennial Act the general election was due in 1718, but the disturbed state of the country as a result of the Jacobite rising and the danger of further outbreaks in the turmoil of a general election afforded strong arguments to the ministry for proposing the Septennial Bill. Thereby the possible duration of the existing house of commons and of all future houses was to be extended for four years, so that the danger from contested elections throughout the country would be staved off till 1722. Nobody denied that parliament could alter the Triennial or any other past act for the election of succeeding houses of commons; but a very effective argument brought up by the opponents of the measure was that it was flagrantly unconstitutional for members elected for only three years to prolong their own tenure for four years longer. However, as ministers pointed out, the emergency to be dealt with was immediate and must be dispelled by dealing with the existing house of commons; the bill was passed without difficulty in both houses and on 7 May 1716 became law. But *facilis descensus Averno*: three years later Stanhope and Sunderland, as a bribe to members of the house of commons to pass the Peerage Bill, proposed to repeal the Septennial Act and even further extend the duration of the 1715 parliament; but fortunately, chiefly owing to Newcastle's arguments, this dangerous proposal was dropped.[1]

The Septennial Act was the last important measure passed by the united whig ministry, which, within a year, split asunder, partly for personal reasons, but chiefly owing to differences on foreign policy.

[1] For a fuller discussion of this proposal see Williams, *Stanhope*, pp. 410–14 and Appendix, pp. 459–63; see also above, p. 22.

In 1714 the Hanoverians had found England without a friend in Europe. Her old allies, the emperor and the Dutch, were sore at having been left in the lurch at Utrecht; Sweden, also a nominal ally, was interfering with her vital trade for naval stores in the Baltic; Russia, the new power in the East, was an uncertain quantity; while France, in spite of Bolingbroke's attempts at an unnatural alliance with her, was showing favour to the Pretender and refusing to destroy 'the cursed sluices at Dunkirk'[1] that had proved so formidable to our shipping in the last war. England's isolation was the more perilous since there were all the makings of a renewed war in Europe. Spain and the emperor had made no peace and were still wrangling on petty points of dignity as well as on the Utrecht settlement of Italy, with which Victor Amadeus of Savoy was also dissatisfied. The northern war between Sweden and Russia and her other neighbours showed no signs of abating and, whereas previously of small concern to England, had become of at least indirect concern to her owing to the elector of Hanover's quarrels or connexions with Sweden, Denmark, Poland, Prussia, and Russia.

In this state of Europe it was obviously dangerous for England to remain friendless. No time therefore was wasted by George and his whig ministry in attempting to renew contact with our old allies, the Dutch and the emperor. On the very day after the king's coronation, Stanhope, chosen for this purpose owing to his close connexion with the emperor during the war in Spain, had been dispatched to The Hague and Vienna. His first business was to compose differences between the two powers as to the Barrier fortresses to be held by the Dutch as a condition for the emperor's possession of the Low Countries, and then to renew treaties with both. He succeeded at least in clearing up misunderstandings, and within little more than a year the Dutch had agreed to a renewal of the treaty of guarantee and alliance with England (February 1716) and a Barrier treaty with the emperor (November 1716). In May 1716 the emperor, threatened by a Turkish war, made the treaty of Westminster with England, guaranteeing the Hanoverian succession in exchange for a guarantee of his own gains by the treaties of Utrecht and Baden. A further success for the whigs' policy were new and more favourable treaties with Spain

---

[1] Bolingbroke's phrase.

(December 1715 and May 1716) removing some of the difficulties of the commercial provisions of Utrecht. In 1715 and 1716 also, in contrast to Bolingbroke's ineffective remonstrances with Charles XII, vigorous measures had been taken to protect our Baltic trade from Swedish attacks by the dispatch of fleets under Admiral Norris to convoy our merchantmen.[1]

The arch-enemy, France, the chief hope of Jacobite plotters, still remained. But here also, after the death of Louis XIV in September 1715, there seemed a prospect of accommodation. His successor, Louis XV, was an ailing child of five and, if he died without issue, the Crown, by virtue of the treaty of Utrecht, would devolve on the Regent Orleans; but Philip V of Spain, in spite of his solemn renunciation, still cherished his claim as the nearest lineal heir; so it became Orleans's chief preoccupation to secure his own treaty rights. Hardly had he obtained the regency when he made an approach to Stanhope to obtain the reinsurance of those rights by England in return for a further guarantee by France of the protestant succession. Stanhope was disposed to consider the proposal, but soon cooled off owing to the support given by France at the end of the year to the Jacobite cause. The regent indeed, partly owing to the strong feeling in France in favour of the Pretender, partly, while the issue was doubtful, from fear of committing himself too far on the other side, had turned a blind eye to the Jacobite preparations in France and allowed the negotiation with England to drop. But no sooner was the success of the Hanoverian cause made manifest than he resumed his advances, which were then received with more suspicion, especially as England had now found allies in the Dutch, the emperor, and even Spain. But it so happened that in July 1716 Stanhope was accompanying the king on his first holiday to Hanover. On his way through Holland he was waylaid by Dubois, Orleans's principal adviser, a wily priest who invited Stanhope to see his collection of pictures and rarities, the ostensible purpose of his visit to The Hague. Three interviews between the two ministers removed some of Stanhope's scruples, and it was agreed that Dubois should come secretly to Hanover to resume the discussions. By the last week in August the draft treaty was settled:

---

[1] This was partly the result of George I's Hanoverian interests in the Baltic. See Williams, *Stanhope*, pp. 231–4; and below, p. 174. On the Spanish treaties see J. O. McLachlan, *Trade . . . with Old Spain*, pp. 69, 73.

thereby the succession to the thrones of England and France as stipulated at Utrecht was solemnly guaranteed, the fortifications and sluices of Dunkirk and its subsidiary fort Mardyk were to be destroyed; and the Pretender was to be forced to leave Avignon and cross the Alps into Italy; it was also decided to invite the Dutch to become parties to the treaty. It was then left to the regency council and ministers in London to fill in details and prepare full powers for the signing of the treaty at The Hague. At this point, however, difficulties arose.

When the king left London he had appointed his son guardian of the realm under restricted powers, with Townshend and Walpole as his chief advisers. George I, however, had always been jealous of his son; and when Sunderland, dissatisfied with his unimportant position in the ministry,[1] came on a visit to Hanover, he seems to have stimulated this jealousy by reports of the prince's affable ways with the people and the devotion of the two ministers to his interests. The king's suspicions were further aroused by the long delays in completing the treaty and some bungling in the London office about the full powers. Furthermore, by the end of September the king and Stanhope had a special reason for haste. The tsar Peter, hitherto co-operating with Denmark and Hanover against Sweden, had suddenly landed troops in Mecklenburg in which George I had interests, and there was a threat of the combined support of Peter and Charles XII for another Jacobite raid on England. An immediate alliance with France owing to her close connexions with Sweden and good relations with Russia seemed, therefore, essential to avert this sudden menace; and, as the delays continued, Townshend was summarily dismissed from his post and offered instead the lord lieutenancy of Ireland, the post usually reserved for unsatisfactory or disappointed politicians. In November 1716 the treaty was signed by the French and English plenipotentiaries and converted into a Triple Alliance by the accession of the Dutch in the following January. For the next fourteen years this Triple Alliance remained one of the main factors in English diplomacy, and indeed it lasted nominally till 1744. It was especially valuable to England in

[1] He had by then exchanged his office of lord lieutenant for that of privy seal. His excuse for leaving the country was his ill health and his ostensible destination was Aix not Hanover. See Williams, *Stanhope*, pp. 241–2, and J. H. Plumb, *Sir Robert Walpole*, i. 222–3.

securing immunity from any serious Jacobite danger during the whole of its duration: it also enabled the two rival protagonists in the war of the Spanish succession to co-operate with marked success in averting another serious European war between the powers dissatisfied with the Utrecht settlement.

In April 1717 Townshend, who had only grudgingly accepted the vice-royalty while awaiting the king's return from Hanover, was finally dismissed for further disagreement with Stanhope's foreign policy. This would have mattered less had not his brother-in-law Walpole insisted on also retiring from his financial posts. With them Methuen, Pulteney, Orford, and Devonshire also resigned from the ministry, which was reconstituted under Stanhope and Sunderland. At the end of the year Walpole and the other disobliged whigs found a rallying-point in the heir to the throne himself. George I had not forgiven his son for his efforts to win popularity during his own absence in Hanover; when therefore the prince openly insulted the new lord chamberlain, the duke of Newcastle, for claiming the right of standing godfather to the prince's newly born son, the king took it as a personal affront, expelled him from the court, and forbade his courtiers to pay their respects to him. Thereupon Walpole and his section of the whigs made a point of attending his levees, and so widened the breach between themselves and their former colleagues as well as the king himself.

This first cleavage of the whig party so soon after its triumph in 1714 did no permanent harm to the dynasty. On the contrary in the long run it strengthened it. Hitherto the king's choice of alternative ministers had been limited to the tories, many of them tainted by Jacobitism: now there were ministers out of office as whig and as devoted to the dynasty as those in office. These men and their successors in the next reign turned naturally to the Hanoverian heir to the throne, rather than to the Jacobite Pretender, as the patron of their opposition. While this development aggravated the constant tension between the king and his heir, it made possible the practice of loyal opposition under which politicians, however critical they might be of measures proposed by ministers, were always prepared, if called upon, to serve the throne loyally. Indeed, such opposition was normally practised by excluded politicians with the purpose of forcing themselves back into the king's notice. In course of time this was accepted by tories, but for over a generation they suffered from the fact that both ministerial and opposition whigs, when in office, made common cause by identifying them with the Jacobites.[1]

In the ministry as reconstituted under Stanhope and Sunderland the former was unquestionably the leading spirit. This is the more remarkable because Sunderland had far greater experience in politics, having been a leader of the whigs in Anne's time, and was, moreover, consumed with political ambition. But he was never quite trusted by the king or at Westminster. Stanhope on the other hand—*impiger, iracundus et acer*, as he might be described—had no special bent for domestic politics and still regarded a military career as the summit of his ambition. His impetuosity and want of experience indeed led him into mistakes sometimes in dealing with internal questions. On the other hand, in foreign politics his comprehensive grasp of European conditions and of England's essential interests, his tact and self-control in dealing with foreign allies or opponents, and the blunt honesty of his diplomacy gave him an ascendancy rarely equalled by any of our foreign ministers. This ascendancy was the more remarkable since it had peace alone as its object and its result. The long epoch of comparative security in external relations which enabled Walpole quietly to consolidate the country's internal prosperity on a sound basis was mainly due to Stanhope's achievements in foreign policy. It is a tribute to Stanhope's transparent honesty of purpose that Sunderland, a jealous and ambitious man, never seems to have questioned his virtual leadership.[2]

In domestic affairs the reconstituted ministry pursued much the same policy as before, at first with diminished authority, since they now had against them many of their former whig allies led by Walpole, the ablest debater and tactician in parliament. For a year Stanhope, although finance was not his strong point, took the offices resigned by Walpole; then he returned to his former duties as secretary of state. At the exchequer he did

---

[1] Whig ministers were, on occasions, prepared to exploit the tories for their own ends. Stanhope and Sunderland negotiated with them when in office; Walpole allied with them when out of it. See Williams, *Stanhope*, pp. 258 and 421–3; Michael, *Quadruple Alliance*, pp. 17 and 302–4; Plumb, *Walpole*, i. 249 and 251.

[2] Stanhope's ascendancy sprang from his possession of the confidence of the king, and Sunderland's reluctance to challenge it reflects his understanding of this important political factor. See Williams, *Stanhope*, p. 257.

little more than carry through, with some amendments, the scheme already prepared by Walpole for funding the debt at a lower rate of interest and establishing a sinking fund for the gradual paying off of capital.[1] To proposals mainly drafted by himself Walpole could hardly put up much opposition; but thereafter for the next two years he took a violent, often factious, line against the government's measures. Amongst these was the repeal of the tory acts against protestant dissenters, the Occasional Conformity and Schism Acts of 1711 and 1714. George I, in his first declaration to the privy council, had already promised to take all protestants not belonging to the church of England under his royal protection, and shortly afterwards had made a similar declaration to a deputation of some hundred nonconformist ministers.[2] Stanhope himself and many of his supporters were on principle for religious toleration; apart from this the dissenters deserved encouragement for the loyal support they gave to the dynasty during the rebellion and their staunch adherence to whig principles. It was to the advantage of the whigs that they should be allowed to educate their children in their own excellent schools and sit on corporations without vexatious interference.[3] Toleration for good dissenting whigs was all very well for a whig ministry, but toleration for Roman catholics was another matter; and it is to Stanhope's credit that he even attempted to modify the savage anti-Roman catholic laws by negotiations with the leading Roman catholics. He failed, partly owing to popular prejudice, partly owing to the uncompromising obstinacy of the Roman catholics themselves.[4] Other less happy proposals to secure whig predominance were to bring Oxford and Cambridge, then considered forcing-grounds of toryism rather than of sound learning, under direct government control, and even, in order to preserve the whig majority in parliament, to prolong the existing parliament beyond seven years,[5] as well as the more famous Peerage Bill.

[1] On the results of this sinking fund see below, pp. 186–87.

[2] Michael, ii. 103–4 (or *Quadruple Alliance*, pp. 49–50).

[3] See *Oxford History of England*, x. 24 (2nd edn.), and also above, Chap. IV.

[4] The persecution of protestants in some of the German states at this time had aroused great feeling in England and made any concession to English Roman catholics more difficult. See Williams, *Stanhope*, pp. 395–8, and for a full account of the continental dispute, K. Borgmann, *Der deutsche Religionsstreit der Jahre 1719/20*, Berlin, 1937.

[5] For these two proposals see Williams, *Stanhope*, pp. 399–403, 456–8; and 410–14, 459–63. See also p. 164 above.

The ostensible motive for the Peerage Bill of 1719 was to prevent any such wholesale creation of twelve peers as the tory government had made in 1712 in order to secure a majority for their peace policy in the house of lords. At the time such an innovation had been regarded, even by the tories, as at best an unpleasant necessity, 'unprecedented and invidious' as Boling-broke himself described it later; by the whigs it had been stigmatized as an unconstitutional abuse of the royal preroga-tive. But the drastic measure proposed by Stanhope and Sun-derland was even more unconstitutional, since its main object was to secure a permanent majority in the lords for their own ministry. For, owing to the split in the whig majority and the favour shown by the prince of Wales to Walpole's section, they feared that on his accession to the throne he might destroy their own majority in the lords by a similar creation of new peers, and accordingly so framed the measure that the royal prerogative of creating peers would be curtailed almost to vanishing-point. In addition to the 26 bishops the house of lords then consisted of 178 English peers and 16 representative peers elected for each parliament from the peerage of Scotland. The proposal was, except for princes of the blood and to replace extinct peerages, to restrict the creation of new English peerages to six; while, instead of the 16 Scottish representatives, 25 Scottish peers were to be nominated as hereditary lords of parliament.[1] In practice this scheme would have made the house of lords the dominating oligarchy in the state, impervious to the influence of either king or commons, and perpetuating its existing pro-ministerial com-position. The bill, introduced into the lords in the first session of 1719, naturally found favour in that house owing to the immensely increased power it would give to the existing English peers, while even the 16 Scottish representative peers were attracted by the prospect of being included among the 25 im-movables. But before its final stage was reached the clamour against it from the outside induced Stanhope to withdraw it for the time being. But in the second session of 1719, after ministers had more carefully prepared the ground, the bill was reintro-duced and once more passed easily through the lords, only to meet its Cannae in the commons. Here Walpole, at last finding a worthy cause on which to oppose Stanhope, carried the day

[1] On the death of an hereditary Scottish lord without heirs his place was to be filled by one of the remaining Scottish peers.

against it by his common-sense appeals to members who hoped some day to become peers themselves.[1]

This defeat taught the ministers that it would be folly to keep up the vendetta with Walpole and his friends: so in April 1720 not only were the two sections of the whigs reconciled by the readmission of Walpole and Townshend to office, but a truce was also patched up between the king and the prince of Wales.

Evidently Stanhope had not been happy in his ventures in domestic policy, partly owing to his long absence abroad in the last reign and his unfamiliarity with parliamentary government, partly because he relied too much on the sinister and intriguing disposition of his ally Sunderland. On the other hand, in the field of foreign policy he was one of the greatest of our ministers. The reconciliation he had effected with the emperor by the treaty of Westminster in 1716 and the Triple Alliance with France and the Dutch of 1717 were only the first instalments of his great scheme for restoring real peace in Europe, not only by clearing away the misunderstandings and removing the sources of quarrel latent in some of the provisions of the treaties of Utrecht, Rastadt, and Baden, but also by settling the affairs of the north where war had been proceeding since 1700.

As soon as he had made the alliance with France in 1717 he set himself, with the help of his new associate Orleans, to avert the danger of renewed war between the emperor and Philip V of Spain, whose conflicting ambitions in Italy and obstinate refusal to recognize one another's titles were a constant menace to the peace of Europe. Apart from Philip V's ambition to recover Spain's lost provinces of the two Sicilies, his new wife Elizabeth Farnese, as the nearest in succession to both the Farnese of Parma and the Medici of Tuscany, on the imminent failure of their male lines, put forward the claims of her son Don Carlos to Tuscany as well as to her native Parma. The emperor on his side wished to add Sicily to Naples and at all costs to keep Spanish princes out of the Italian Peninsula. A compromise was arranged between Stanhope and Orleans whereby Don Carlos was to have the reversion of Parma and

---

[1] For a full discussion of the Peerage Bill and its implications see Turberville, *House of Lords in the Eighteenth Century*, pp. 169 sqq. The selected Scottish peers are listed by Plumb, *Walpole*, i. 276, n. 2.

Tuscany, while the emperor was to give up Sardinia to Victor Amadeus of Savoy and receive in exchange Sicily, which had been assigned to Savoy at Utrecht. The emperor, taken up with a Turkish war and in need of allies, agreed to this arrangement which was embodied in the treaty of the so-called Quadruple Alliance of August 1718.[1] In this treaty was a proviso that, failing Spain's agreement, the allies should coerce her, if necessary by arms, to accept these terms.

Spain, in fact, would not hear of acceding to a treaty which would benefit the emperor almost more than herself. Whereupon Stanhope, perhaps the first example of a perambulating foreign minister, himself made two visits to Paris to secure Orleans's consent to this proviso, and even proceeded to Madrid to urge acceptance of the treaty on Philip and his minister Alberoni.[2] The moment was ill chosen, for one of the most imposing Spanish fleets launched since the Armada had actually started to secure Sicily and Naples by force of arms; and the Spaniards were so assured of success that they would listen to no arguments nor even the offer of the return of Gibraltar. On the other hand, Stanhope had already sent Byng to the Mediterranean to obstruct the Spaniards' designs on Naples and Sicily, and had barely quitted Spanish soil on his return before news came of the destruction by Byng of the great Spanish fleet at Cape Passaro.

A short war then ensued against Spain. A French army, assisted by a small English squadron, invaded the north of Spain and caused some damage to the dockyards; Alberoni provided Ormonde with a squadron to attempt an invasion of England, equipped a small expedition of Jacobites to invade Scotland, and tried to stir up Sweden and Russia to assist. But Ormonde, with his usual ill luck, had his squadron dispersed and battered by a storm, while the Jacobite force was defeated at Glenshiel. These reverses during 1719, combined with the death of Charles XII in December 1718, persuaded Philip and Elizabeth to throw up their hands, dismiss Alberoni, and in January 1720 grudgingly to accept the terms laid down in the Quadruple Alliance. The trouble, however, was by no means

[1] The Dutch republic, designed to be the fourth party to this Alliance, never actually came into it.

[2] Stanhope was in Paris in July, in Madrid in Aug., and back again in Paris in Sept. of 1718.

over. On his visit to Madrid two years before, Stanhope had offered Philip the return of Gibraltar for immediate acceptance of the terms proposed; and now Philip, backed by the regent, assumed that this conditional offer still held good. But, though Stanhope and the ministry generally attached little importance to Gibraltar as compared with friendly trade relations with Spain, the nation and the house of commons would not hear of its surrender. Stanhope had to travel again to Paris to make the regent understand that the offer was no longer open since Spain had persisted in hostilities, and after Stanhope's death Philip had to content himself, in June 1721, with a letter from George I promising to consider the cession 'with consent of my Parliament . . . at the first favourable opportunity', thus in fact postponing it to the Greek Calends.

While occupied mainly with Spain Stanhope had also been keeping a vigilant eye on the Baltic powers. At the outset of the reign he and Townshend had taken a firmer line than Bolingbroke with Charles XII's attempts to prevent our merchants trading with Baltic ports conquered from him by Peter the Great. Every year squadrons were sent to escort the traders and soon found themselves committed to hostile acts, first against Sweden and then against Russia. George as elector had special interests in the north, since he claimed Sweden's territories of Bremen and Verden, partly purchased by him from Denmark, partly occupied by his own troops. He also had a quarrel with Sweden's chief enemy Peter, who had sent troops into Mecklenburg, where he had interests. These quarrels, at first purely Hanoverian, developed into an English quarrel when in 1717 Gyllenborg, the Swedish minister in England, was discovered to be carrying on intrigues with the Jacobites; and his papers, which were seized and published in 1717, revealed a widespread plot to restore the Pretender, a plot involving not only Sweden but also Peter, and supported by Alberoni. The squadrons to the Baltic were given stringent orders to 'burn, sink and destroy' Swedish men-of-war and keep a vigilant watch on those of the tsar.[1]

But with the death of Charles XII at the end of 1718 came a sudden revolution in Baltic politics. Sweden, exhausted by

---

[1] Little came of these warlike orders, one Swedish cruiser being captured. See Michael, *Hanoverian Dynasty*, pp. 308–9; J. F. Chance, *George I and the Northern War*, pp. 217–18.

twenty years of continuous war, and no longer under the spell of her imperious master, had no other desire than to make peace with her numerous enemies, Russia, Poland, Denmark, Hanover, Prussia. The only question was with which group of enemies she should make peace first, in the hope of rescuing at least some of her lost provinces from the other. Russia, her most formidable enemy, was only too anxious to make peace with her since she had acquired all the Swedish provinces she needed in the Baltic; equally anxious were Hanover and Prussia to secure by treaty their conquests of Sweden's north German provinces. England had no direct interest in conquests; on the other hand, Stanhope was chiefly anxious to prevent Russia from obtaining complete control of the Baltic.

Stanhope's policy, therefore, was to induce all the Germanic powers concerned to co-operate in securing a joint peace with Sweden and to leave Russia out in the cold. His first difficulty was to bring Prussia into line with Hanover. In spite of the close family relationship[1] of the two monarchs petty quarrels and personal jealousies caused an almost endemic state of feud between them during most of George I's and George II's reigns. This would have mattered less had it not so often affected Anglo-Prussian relations. One of these periods of mutual pique between the two kings, accentuated by the personal interests of the chief Hanoverian minister Bernstorff, was making co-operation specially difficult when it was most needed in 1719. Stanhope, however, by a combination of tact and decision, not only managed to reconcile the two touchy monarchs, but also to put a stop, once for all, to Bernstorff's interference with English politics. A treaty was concluded committing the joint interests of both countries to the English ambassador at Stockholm, who was to secure George I's retention of Bremen and Verden and Frederick William's of Pomerania and Stettin.

Carteret, Stanhope's ablest pupil in diplomacy, was sent as ambassador to Stockholm, where he did his work well. He arrived in July 1719 to find the Russians raiding the countryside almost up to the gates of the capital and the Swedes prepared to save themselves by accepting almost any terms from the tsar; but he soon gained the confidence of the young queen and a section of her advisers by promising immediate help from Norris's fleet and by his vigorous diplomatic methods. Within

[1] George I was Frederick William's father-in-law.

little more than a month he had attained the main object of his mission by treaties securing Bremen and Verden for Hanover, Stettin and western Pomerania for Prussia, and free commerce for English ships in the Baltic, in return for promises of a subsidy and the help of the fleet against Peter. In the course of the next twelve months he even succeeded in negotiating a treaty between Sweden and her hitherto irreconcilable enemy Denmark, so that she could concentrate all her energies against Russia, the Baltic power most feared by England. Stanhope also saw to it that France, in spite of her traditional policy to secure Sweden's influence in the empire through such possessions as Bremen and Stettin, should also guarantee these treaties. Unfortunately during 1720 England was unable to make effective her promise to help Sweden to recover from Russia some at least of her former Baltic provinces, owing to Norris's caution and the failure of his fleet to deal with the swarm of light Russian raiders that could always evade the heavier English men-of-war. Accordingly, by the treaty of Nystad in 1721, Sweden was obliged to cede to Russia all these Baltic provinces except Finland. As far as English trade was concerned, this result was not so detrimental as Stanhope had anticipated. Russia did not seriously interfere with it, and within thirteen years came the first of a series of favourable commercial treaties between the two nations.

Stanhope himself did not live to see the disappointment of his hopes for preventing Russia's domination in the Baltic; and his last months in office were saddened by the scandals and confusion that resulted from the bursting of the South Sea Bubble, though he himself had had no part in it.

In January 1720 Sunderland, then first lord of the treasury, impressed no doubt by the success of Walpole's partial funding scheme carried through by Stanhope in 1717, welcomed a proposal from the South Sea Company to take over on what appeared to be exceedingly favourable terms the whole of the national debt with the exception of that part held by the Bank of England and the East India Company. This involved over £30,000,000 of the total national debt then standing at £51,000,000. After some competition with an offer from the Bank, parliament was induced to accept the Company's revised proposal to incorporate the agreed three-fifths of the national debt in its own capital, to pay more than £7,000,000 forthwith for this privilege, and accept from the government 5 per cent. interest on the sum incorporated until 1727 and 4 per cent. thereafter. The Company on its side expected to recoup itself partly by its profits from the South Sea trade and its *Asiento* concession, but chiefly from the rise in value of its own shares. The result was a fantastic gambling in these shares, which rose from 130 per cent. in January to a peak of over 1,000 per cent. in the last week of June, soon followed by a fever of speculation in the hundreds of schemes set afoot by optimistic or dishonest company promoters. By September the bottom had fallen out of the market, first owing to the alarm induced by the Company's attempts to suppress these rival speculations, which had scarcely been checked by the proclamation of the government's so-called Bubble Act in June, and finally when South Sea shares themselves fell rapidly from 780 to 180 per cent. at the end of the month. A wild panic ensued, speculators from all classes of society were ruined by the thousand, and an outburst of indignation arose on all sides against the Company, the government, and even the king. Among the principal people accused of receiving bribes from the Company in the form of shares for little or no consideration were two of the king's mistresses, the baroness von Schulenberg, recently created duchess of Kendal, and Madame von Platen,[1] Aislabie the chancellor of the exchequer, Stanhope's cousin Charles, also on the treasury board, the postmaster, Craggs, and his son, a secretary of state, and, probably with less justice, Sunderland himself.[2]

Walpole's chance came with the bursting of the South Sea Bubble. He had not himself foreseen the dangers of the South Sea scheme in which he had speculated with some small profit at an early stage. So far from anticipating the crash he had been willing to subscribe during the summer of 1720 and had incurred considerable losses. Nor when the Bubble burst in September was he at once regarded in the City or by his ministerial colleagues as the man to stem the disaster. His initial intervention, when he took a leading part in the negotia-

[1] The Schulenberg had been granted an Irish peerage as duchess of Munster in 1716 in spite of her strong wish for an English title. It was not until 1719 that she was created duchess of Kendal. This was at the instance of Sunderland who hoped to secure her support at court against Townshend and Walpole whom she held responsible for her earlier disappointment.

[2] Details of the South Sea scheme and its collapse may be found in W. R. Scott, *Joint Stock Companies to 1720*, i. 408–38 and iii. 288–360.

tions to secure the support of the Bank of England for the South Sea Company, was ineffective, after which he retired abruptly to Norfolk. This strategic retreat, although probably not inspired by thoughts of political advantage, was the turning-point in his fortunes. It at once dissociated him from the ministry and drew attention to his existence. By the middle of October he was by general consent regarded as the only minister capable of restoring public confidence.

When parliament met in December he had a scheme ready; this was the work of Robert Jacombe, an under-secretary in the ministry and Walpole's banker. Its main feature was to transfer eighteen millions of South Sea Company stock in equal shares to the East India Company and the Bank of England. In fact the measure, which was permissive, was not put into operation, but its acceptance by parliament and the three companies concerned helped to restore confidence.[1] On the question of dealing with the chief offenders who misled the public or enriched themselves by accepting favours, Walpole was all for 'letting sleeping dogs lie', the more so, perhaps, because he saw that his own rise to supreme power would only be possible if he courted the king by protecting his favoured ministers.[2] Early in February 1721 Stanhope, the greatest of the existing ministers and untouched by even a breath of scandal, died suddenly after a passionate reply to an attack by the duke of Wharton in the house of lords; he was succeeded by Walpole's faithful brother-in-law Townshend. Craggs, the other secretary of state, died of smallpox soon after and a month later his father killed himself. In March, Aislabie, who had already resigned as chancellor of the exchequer, was expelled from the house of commons, and Sunderland, the author of the South Sea scheme, though acquitted of corruption, could no longer remain first lord of the treasury. In April Walpole succeeded to both these offices, but his supremacy was not yet complete. Sunderland, now groom of the stole, remained a powerful rival retaining the confidence of the king and control of the secret service money.[3]

[1] The final settlement between the South Sea Company and the Bank of England was fixed by statute in 1722 (8 Geo. I, c. 21). See Clapham, *The Bank of England*, i. 88.

[2] From this time Walpole was known as the Skreen or the Skreen Master General. His own speculations were sufficiently doubtful to make an inquiry undesirable. For this whole crisis see Plumb, *Walpole*, i. 293–358.

[3] In 1750 Hardwicke, in a letter to Newcastle, referred to Sunderland's ability to 'remove from one office to another still retaining the character and influence of prime minister'. Yorke, *Hardwicke*, ii. 96.

For twelve months the struggle between them was evenly balanced. Then, in April 1722, Sunderland died. Walpole was now supreme, the arbiter of English policy for the next twenty years—the first of our prime ministers in fact if not in name.

It was fortunate for England that the way for Walpole's great ministry of peace and financial reconstruction was paved by the six and a half years' work of a foreign minister of such integrity and outstanding vision as Stanhope. Finding England without a friend and exposed to danger of foreign war and internal rebellion, Europe still a prey to war in the north and on the brink of renewed war in the south, he almost alone, by his personal exertions, had made her practically the arbiter of Europe's peace. He paved the way for a settlement of the disputes between Spain and the emperor, laid the foundations of a more equitable and even national structure for Italy, restored peace to the north, and above all instituted that close co-operation of England with France that for nearly twenty years of Walpole's rule stood him in good stead and enabled him to develop the country's peaceful activities without risk of invasion or Jacobite insurrection.

VII

THE SETTLEMENT OF THE
DYNASTY—WALPOLE'S MINISTRY
1721–42

W ALPOLE was the very essence of rough English common sense; and therein lay his strength. His family,
which claimed to have settled in Norfolk at the time of
the Conquest or even before,[1] had produced a long succession
of worthy country squires immersed in local duties and interests,
or in public affairs as members of parliament. He himself, the
third son in a family of nineteen, had been sent to Eton and
King's, where he learned enough Latin to converse with
George I and to make apt, if inaccurate, quotations in the house
of commons. Recalled by his father, on the death of his two
elder brothers, to the family estate at Houghton, he was set to
learn the business of a country squire—to manage the property,
to take his share in county business, hunt and shoot with his
neighbours, and, not least, to stand up to his drink like a man:
'Come, Robert,' said his father to him, 'you shall drink twice,
while I drink once; for I will not permit the son, in his sober
senses, to be witness to the intoxication of his father.' Thus
early he learned to know and play his part in the pursuits,
pleasures, and prejudices of the masterful country gentry who
formed the majority in the eighteenth-century house of commons; there, too, he acquired that practical, unsentimental
common sense and that gift of leadership which came as second
nature to the squire Allworthys and, in grosser guise, the squire
Westerns of the age. To the end of his life, it was said, he
always opened his bailiff's letters about hunting, coursing, and
local news of Norfolk before those dealing with affairs of state;
and he boasted that at his own table 'he always talked bawdy,
because in that all could join'.[2] Family pride led him to rebuild
the old country home at Houghton, 'to fill the mind', in the
words of an old guide-book, 'with everything that magnificence

---

[1] See A. Collins, *Peerage of England* (Sir E. Brydges ed.), 1812, s.v. 'Orford'.
[2] Boswell's *Johnson* (under year 1776).

can inspire'; or, as the second Lord Oxford put it more unkindly:[1] 'it is neither magnificent nor beautiful, there is a very
great expense without either judgement or taste'. He then filled
up its saloons with gigantic casts of the Laocoon, the Tiber
and the Nile, and the Gladiator, and its walls with the vast
collection of pictures, including, besides Snyder's 'Markets'
and the works of such fashionable Italians as Guido and
Domenichino, others more agreeable to our modern taste, which
later became the pride of Catherine the Great's galleries at the
Hermitage. But in themselves the gracious arts meant nothing
to him. The only writers he patronized were those who wrote
pamphlets in support of his policy; he subjected the drama to
severe censorship; and all the poets fled to the ranks of the
opposition, except those like *Night Thoughts* Young, who flattered
him in such lines as:

> My breast, O Walpole, glows with grateful fire.
> The streams of royal bounty, turn'd by thee,
> Refresh the dry domains of poesy.

He entered parliament in 1701 as member for Castle Rising
and one year later was elected for King's Lynn, which he
represented for forty years. During his first twenty years in
politics he gave ample proof of his staunchness to whig principles
and friends. In 1710 Harley besought him to join his tory
ministry, but he preferred to suffer in the Tower for his obstinate
whiggery; again in 1717 he resigned from the ministry rather
than desert his brother-in-law Townshend, while in the following year he stoutly rejected offers from Stanhope which would
have secured his return at the expense of his friends.[2] This long
experience of political vicissitudes had, however, taught him the
danger of revolutionary adventures and to take as his guiding
principle *quieta non movere*: it had also, unfortunately, led him to
hold and express that cynical view of political morality which
did much to discredit parliament in the public eye and to
create that climate of opinion in which radical criticisms were
later to flourish.[3] Nor, when he had once attained the supreme
position in the state, would he brook any rival. Being himself a
first-rate man of business, he looked on his ministry in the light
of a business firm, which must have one undisputed head,
himself. Thus he gradually eliminated, or sought to render

---

[1] *Hist. MSS. Comm., Portland*, vi. 160–1.
[2] See Plumb, *Walpole*, i. 265.   [3] See vol. xii of this series.

impotent, all who by their talents could have competed with him, Pulteney, Carteret, Chesterfield, even Townshend, not to speak of his old opponent Bolingbroke, or Mr. Pitt, that 'terrible cornet of horse', so that towards the end of his career he had reduced his ministry mainly to a set of second-rate men. But almost to the very end he retained his mastery of the house of commons: no minister before or since, except perhaps Palmerston, has ever had so quick a perception of the average members' moods and of the limitations within which he could enforce upon them his will. This was largely because at first he confined himself to the domestic politics he understood so well, leaving foreign affairs to Townshend. He soon indeed came to realize the essential connexion between foreign and domestic policy, and after he had driven out Townshend in 1730 tried to keep both in his own hands. But in the end the task proved beyond even his abilities.

In the early years of his ministry the fear of a Jacobite revival was the mainspring of his policy. Glenshiel in 1719 had already warned him that the 1715 fiasco had not yet damped the ardour of the dynasty's opponents. Again in April 1722, before he had been a year in office, confidential information was sent to him by Dubois of another Jacobite plot to seize power as soon as the king had started for Hanover. The news leaked out, and for a brief space there was a panic and a run on the Bank of England.[1] But Walpole soon restored confidence by his prompt measures. He persuaded the king to postpone his journey, called up the Guards to camp in Hyde Park, and ordered a search of the mails and of suspects for incriminating letters, which gave evidence of a widespread plot. In May, Kelly, a secretary of Atterbury, was lodged in the Tower, and by August there was enough evidence to warrant the arrest of the bishop himself; Layer, an active plotter, Lord North and Grey, Lord Orrery, the duke of Norfolk, and others soon followed them to the Tower. At Layer's trial in November the main details of the plot were laid bare. The inevitable Ormonde in Spain, Dillon, an Irish Roman catholic commanding a French regiment, and others were to provide arms, men, and money for an expedition

---

[1] A. Andréadès, *History of the Bank of England*, translated by Christabel Meredith, 1909, p. 149.

to be joined by the Pretender from Rome; at home arms were to be distributed to sympathizers; the Tower, the Bank of England, and the Royal Exchange were to be seized; King James III was to be proclaimed and George I and his chief ministers arrested. Layer's part in the scheme was fully proved and he was sentenced to a traitor's death.[1] But Walpole was not content with such small game; he was determined once for all to strike terror in the Jacobite ranks. When the new parliament met in October he got the Habeas Corpus Act suspended for a year, and passed a discriminating act against Roman catholics and non-jurors imposing on them a special tax of 5s. in the £. The pretext put forward for this unjust exaction—a complete reversal of Stanhope's wiser attempt to reconcile the Roman catholics to the dynasty by removing some of their legal restrictions—was the expense caused to the nation by their friends' participation in the plot.[2]

His greatest stroke he reserved for the idol of the country clergy, the Pretender's most formidable supporter in England, Atterbury, the learned, the eloquent bishop of Rochester and dean of Westminster, the friend of Oxford and Bishop Trelawney, of Swift, Pope, and Gay. Walpole had first tried to bribe him by offering the rich see of Winchester at its next vacancy,[3] but in vain: now he must be crushed. But though his sympathy with the cause was notorious, the evidence for his share in this Jacobite plot was weak, depending almost entirely on the interpretation of cant terms and fictitious names in the intercepted correspondence. Swift, for example, was able to make great play with the dog Harlequin, admittedly sent by Mar to Atterbury, but spoken of in the letters as sent to 'Jones' or 'Illington', cant names for the chief plotter. So for want of convincing evidence Walpole had to follow the bad precedents in Strafford's and Fenwick's cases of a bill of pains and penalties, which required only presumptive evidence. Atterbury was

[1] No less than three respites were given to Layer, in the hope that he might reveal further evidence of the plot, especially against Atterbury. But little could be extracted from him, and he was finally executed at Tyburn in May 1723. His trial is given at length in *State Trials*, xvi.

[2] This at least was the excuse given by the secretary of state, Carteret, in answer to the protests of the catholic powers against such discrimination (*Hist. MSS. Comm., Polwarth*, iii. 199–200, 202–3). Speaker Onslow, on the other hand, spoke of the disastrous effect of making everybody take oaths of loyalty to escape the tax (*Hist. MSS. Comm.* xiv. ix. 403).

[3] See Beeching, *Francis Atterbury*, pp. 278–9.

indeed allowed to call evidence—his friend Pope for one was called to prove that the bishop had no time for plotting—to be represented by counsel, and to speak in his own defence. But when Walpole was cross-examined by Atterbury on the credibility of the Crown witnesses, the bishop, according to Onslow, used 'all the art his guilt would admit of to perplex and make Mr. Walpole contradict himself; but he was too hard for the bishop upon every turn, although a greater trial of skill this way scarce ever happened between two such combatants, the one fighting for his reputation, the other for his acquittal'. In spite of a most eloquent and artful speech from Atterbury, the bill depriving him of all his preferments and sentencing him to perpetual banishment was passed in May 1723 by a majority of 40 in a house of 126.[1] On landing at Calais, the first stage of his lifelong exile, Atterbury was told that Bolingbroke had just arrived there on his way back to England: 'Then I am exchanged', said Atterbury with a smile.

Atterbury's condemnation may have been defective on the strict rules of evidence, but, as we now know from the Stuart papers, was substantially justifiable; and on the principle of *salus reipublicae suprema lex* it was a great success for Walpole's policy. During the rest of his long ministry England was never troubled with Jacobite plots of a serious nature. This was partly because of Walpole's own constant vigilance. Bolingbroke's return and the restoration of his estates in 1725, obtained by a heavy bribe to the duchess of Kendal, he had not been able to prevent, but he took care not to allow him to sit again in the house of lords. A strict watch was kept on the movements of suspects at home, and one of the main duties of English ministers abroad, from the ambassador in Paris down to a little resident such as Horace Mann at Florence, was to report on any signs of Jacobite activity in the countries to which they were accredited.[2] Among the chief reasons indeed for Walpole's consistently pacific policy was his fear of armed support to the Pretender from

---

[1] A long but not always accurate account of the proceedings is given in *State Trials*, xvi. Atterbury's speech is more correctly given in his *Correspondence*: and the encounter between him and Walpole is entirely omitted, but is recorded in *Hist. MSS. Comm.* xiv. 462–3. Useful information about the main plotters is found in *Williamson's Diary*. Camden series III, vol. xxi.

[2] A Baron de Stosch, who signed his reports 'John Walton', was also employed unofficially to report on the activities of the Pretender and the papal curia 1722–31. See *Brit. Diplom. Representatives, 1689–1789* (R. Hist. Soc.), p. 80.

abroad. Jacobitism also had its uses as a bogy to the ground-
lings, especially at election times; and by identifying all tories
with Jacobites Walpole created a tradition, that died hard, of
disloyalty attaching to all but his own supporters.[1] How little
he really believed in any strong feeling in the country for the
Pretender may be seen in his private letter to Townshend in
1725, when the emperor and Spain were said to have promised
support to the Pretender:

if [he wrote] we are to be engaged in a war, . . . 'tis to be wished
that this nation may think an invasion by a foreign power, or an
evident design of such an invasion, the support of the pretender,
and the cause of the protestant succession, are the chief and principal motives that obliged us to part with that peace and tranquillity,
and the happy consequences thereof, which we now enjoy.[2]

During the first years of his ministry Walpole was able to
devote himself to the reorganization of the country's finances,
content to leave foreign policy in the hands of his brother-in-
law Townshend. This he did with the more confidence since
in 1724 he and Townshend managed to get rid of the other
secretary Carteret, Stanhope's pupil, now the leader of Sunderland's faction within the ministry and their most formidable
rival. Carteret indeed was useful to them at first, since his presence in the ministry reassured Orleans and Dubois as to the
permanence of Stanhope's system of close alliance, but when
these successively died in 1723 and were succeeded by Orleans's
enemy the duc de Bourbon, this reason for Carteret's presence
in the ministry was no longer valid. On the other hand Carteret's growing favour with the king made him appear a dangerous rival, to be got rid of as soon as possible. Carteret played
into their hands by engaging in a foolish intrigue at the French
court in favour of the king's two junior mistresses, Lady Darlington and her sister-in-law, the countess von Platen,[3] which
antagonized the more powerful duchess of Kendal. Walpole and
Townshend found an excuse for interfering with Carteret's own
province in the incapacity of his ambassador at Paris, Schaub,
who was deeply engaged in this intrigue. They persuaded the

[1] A generation later Bute deplored the whigs' ability 'to tip the rascal and
Jacobite to any man that opposed' them. See R. Sedgwick, *Letters from George III
to Lord Bute*, p. xxviii.　　　　　　　　　　[2] Coxe, *Walpole*, ii. 486.
[3] For George I's mistresses see above, p. 152. The baroness Kielmansegge
achieved her position as countess of Darlington in 1722.

king to send over Horatio, Robert's brother, nominally on a special mission, really to supplant Schaub; and on his report Schaub was dismissed.[1] Carteret could then do no less than accept his transfer to Ireland and was replaced as secretary by Newcastle, Walpole's docile henchman. Townshend and Walpole thereby became supreme in the cabinet.

In Walpole's view, after he had struck his resounding blow against internal Jacobite intrigue, the best security for the dynasty was a prosperous and contented people resting on a sound basis of industry and commerce. At first, therefore, he devoted his whole attention to the economic policy on which his greatness as a minister is founded.

His principal care was to set the national finances in order. In 1723 he introduced the treasury practice, still current, of paying off the exchequer bills issued to anticipate the yield of taxes voted by parliament as soon as the revenue came into the treasury, instead of allowing them to earn interest for a whole year. More important was the use to which he put the sinking fund established on his own initiative in 1717. At the end of 1714 the national debt had stood at over £54 million at varying rates of interest up to 9 per cent., involving an annual charge of £3,351,358. By 1727 the capital of the debt had been reduced by £6½ million and the interest to a uniform 4 per cent.; and in that year Walpole was able to raise a loan at 3 per cent., which ten years later for a short time reached a premium of 7 per cent. The elasticity of the finances is well shown by the fact that, though by temporary borrowing the total debt stood at £48 million in 1734,[2] by 1739, the last year of peace, it had been reduced once more to only £46 million and the annual charge to no more than £2 million. This result was partly due to the funding of all public debts completed by Sunderland's arrangement with the South Sea Company in 1720, partly to Walpole's arrangements, after the crash, but above all to the confidence given to investors by his sinking fund.[3] Had this fund been confined to its strict purpose the national debt might

[1] For this incident see *British Diplomatic Instructions*, iv. *France 1721–7*, R. Hist. Soc. 1927, pp. 47–53, xvi–xviii, and Coxe, *Walpole*, i. 180–8.

[2] Michael, iv. 598.

[3] See above, pp. 170, 176, 178, n. 1. See also Brisco, *Economic Policy of Walpole*, pp. 31, 40, 60.

well have been paid off within a comparatively short period; but it proved too great a temptation even to so rigid an economist as Walpole as a means of financing extraordinary expenditure or covering the deficit involved in a reduction of taxation. In 1727, for example, he took the extra £100,000 he needed to increase the new king's civil list to £800,000 from the sinking fund; again in 1733 he made good from the same source the deficit of £500,000, arising from the reduction of the land tax from 2s. to 1s.; and thereafter he made no scruple in using the fund to supply deficiencies in taxation. Indeed, he came to regard the sinking fund mainly as an instrument of government quite as useful for lightening taxation or meeting sudden exigencies as for reducing the debt. In 1737, when Sir John Barnard[1] proposed a further reduction in the interest of the debt and that the corresponding increase in the sinking fund should be used to redeem annuities and abolish certain specific taxes, Walpole opposed him on two grounds, first that by earmarking the sinking fund for certain specific purposes its proved use as a resource in emergencies would be hampered, and secondly that the bondholders and annuitants would have a legitimate grievance in being deprived of a valued source of income. In fact, whereas in the unsettled days of 1717 the size of the national debt and its high rate of interest were a source of anxiety, twenty years later, thanks to Walpole's own careful and economical management of the national finances, it had come to be regarded, especially by small annuitants and investors, as a safe and remunerative investment, and had thereby become an actual safeguard to the established order.[2]

In his treasury policy and management of the debt Walpole followed, and improved upon, the whig system inaugurated by Charles Montagu in the seventeenth century. In his revenue policy he was himself a pioneer of that sound system followed by Peel and Gladstone in the next century of using the taxes not merely as a source of supply but as a means of fostering the national industries. It is true his theory of the best means of helping the nation's economic development differed in one

[1] Sir John Barnard, 1685–1764, merchant, alderman, and M.P. for London; much respected by Walpole for his financial ability.
[2] Delafaye, the under-secretary, writing to Waldegrave in Paris on the state of the finances in 1732, says, 'Let the opposers say what they will, the generality of people must have a good opinion of that government whom they are so desirous to trust with their money.' Coxe, *Walpole*, iii. 125.

important respect from that of his two great successors. But then the circumstances were very different. Peel and Gladstone came at a stage when English industry and commerce were so well established that freedom from all governmental shackles appeared the only need for further expansion. In Walpole's time, on the other hand, our industry and commerce, though already developing, still seemed in need of protection from foreign competition. But his form of encouragement to the economic revival was based, not only on avowedly protective measures, but also largely, as was theirs, on a simplification and lightening of the fiscal burdens on industry and on a peaceful foreign policy.[1]

His first task was to simplify the complicated system of taxation that had grown up since the middle ages and thereby remove many sources of confusion. The two direct taxes then in existence were the land tax and the house duty. The land tax had been introduced and its incidence stereotyped in 1692,[2] when the value of all landed property was definitely assessed, rather to the advantage, it was complained, of the tory landholders in the west and north as compared with the mainly whig proprietors in the south and east of England. It was a convenient tax, as every rate of 1s. on the assessed value could be calculated to bring in a round £500,000. Walpole disliked the tax, partly because it was a tax on a limited class and he believed that every man should be taxed in proportion to the benefit he received from the community, partly because he was anxious to conciliate the mainly tory landholders; had he had his way with the excise scheme of 1733 he would have abolished it altogether. At any rate he always kept it as low as possible, reducing the levy from 3s. to 2s. in his first budget, and even to 1s. in 1732 and 1733, and raising the maximum, 4s., only in 1727, 1740, and 1741, years of war.[3] The other direct tax was the house duty of 2s., with additional charges according

---

[1] [Walpole's general economic outlook was probably less forward-looking than Professor Williams here suggests. Certainly, throughout this period 'Parliament still legislated in many economic and social matters' with a wide paternalistic purpose. See Sir George Clark, *The Wealth of England 1485-1760*, pp. 176-7, and see below, p. 192. C.H.S.]

[2] This is the conventional date always given for the introduction of the land tax: in fact it was introduced in Feb. 1693 (1692 o.s.). See W. R. Ward, *Land Tax*, p. 3.

[3] In 1728 and 1729, when there was trouble with Spain, the rate was fixed at 3s.

to the number of windows: this tax Walpole, though not fond of it, kept on, probably because of the ease of collection.

Apart from these direct taxes the other main sources of revenue were the excise and customs duties, the excise being levied internally, mainly on such necessaries as malt for brewing, candles, leather, soap, and salt, the customs on imported goods at the port of entry. The excise duties gave better returns to the revenue, as they were levied by excise officers who could demand evidence of payment from retailers; but they were unpopular owing to the inquisitorial visits of the excisemen. It was easier to evade customs duties owing to the activity of smugglers, whose 'free-trade' was highly profitable to themselves[1] and popular with the purchasers of their cheap brandy, tea, and other luxuries. Walpole found the whole customs system in need of reform. The official rate-books of the value and duty leviable on each taxable article had not been revised since 1660, and much had to be left to customs officers' guesswork or the importer's dishonest undervaluation. Another complication arose from the number of duties to which many articles were liable.[2] In his first three budgets Walpole made a thorough revision of the system. He issued a new Book of Rates, up to date and in many cases showing one inclusive duty on an article, instead of the confusing list of varying subsidies. In a great many cases he reduced the almost prohibitive tariffs: the duty on pepper, for example, was reduced from $1s.\ 11\frac{1}{2}d.$ to $4d.$, and that on many raw materials needed for industry he either greatly reduced or abolished altogether. He also set himself,

---

[1] Fielding, in his *Voyage to Lisbon*, quotes the case of a smuggler who made £40,000 out of the business, but who 'did not long escape the sharp eyes of the revenue solicitors and was . . . soon reduced . . . to confinement in the Fleet'.

[2] Brisco, *Economic Policy of Walpole*, p. 132, gives an example of the duties on pepper:

						s.	d.	
(1) old subsidy of 1660			.	.	.		$\frac{1}{2}$	per lb.
(2) new	„	1698	.	.	.	1		„
(3) $\frac{1}{3}$	„	1703	.	.	.		$\frac{1}{3}$	„
(4) $\frac{2}{3}$	„	1704	.	.	.		$\frac{2}{3}$	„
(5) old impost			.	.	.		3	„
(6) new duty		.	.	.	.	1	6	„
Total		.	.	.	.	1	$11\frac{1}{2}$	„

Adam Smith, *Wealth of Nations*, book v, chap. 2, gives a lucid explanation of the various subsidies.

with less success, to tackle the problem of smuggling which caused so much loss to the revenue, and was even a national danger in time of war. Admiral Vernon, for example, writing in November 1745, declared that at Deal there were 200 young smugglers, 'many keeping a horse and arms to be ready at all calls', 400 at Dover, and 300 each at Ramsgate and Folkestone, who, besides running over some £1,000 a week 'in the smuggling way', gave away important information to the French about our naval expeditions.[1] He increased the severity of the customs laws and the powers and numbers of the customs officers; but these measures had little result except to give added venom to his opponents' attacks on the increased patronage thereby accruing to the treasury. More and more, therefore, he inclined to the more effective excise system, unpopular though it was, as the best protection to the revenue.[2]

In 1723 he made his first experiment in developing the bonded warehouse system, first started on a modest scale for pepper in 1709.[3] By this system imported goods on landing were taken to a government warehouse and kept there till actually required either for re-exportation or for sale to retailers in England. Goods re-exported paid no duty, those intended for domestic consumption paid an excise duty only when they were taken out for retail sale. The importer stood to gain, since he no longer had to pay duty on a whole cargo at once and wait, perhaps for months or longer, to recover it on re-export or from internal buyers: the exchequer also gained by the effective check on smuggling, since the duty was paid as an excise tax, the receipt for which could be demanded from the retailer of dutiable goods. In 1723 Walpole applied this system to imported tea, coffee, cocoanuts, and to chocolate made in Great Britain[4] with such good results that, though he had reduced the duties on all these articles, within seven years the exchequer returns on them had

[1] Quoted in Clowes, *The Royal Navy*, iii. 16.

[2] Egmont in his *Diary* (*Hist. MSS. Comm.*), ii. 236, cites the opinion of a contemporary M.P. that Walpole was not really anxious to stop smuggling, as the fines and forfeitures on convicted smugglers amounted annually to some £200,000, which went directly 'into the king's purse unaccountable to parliament', but Walpole's whole policy contradicts this assertion about him.

[3] This system was extended to cover tea and coffee in 1711, but only permissively. See 8 Anne, c. 7, and 10 Anne, c. 26; Brisco, op. cit., p. 120.

[4] The importation of ready-made chocolate was prohibited. Home-manufactured chocolate could only be sold at approved premises and was subject to the new duty of 1s. 6d. per pound. This act (10 Geo. I, c. 10) was effective from midsummer 1724.

increased by £120,000 per annum. Encouraged by this success, ten years later Walpole proposed, by his famous excise scheme, to extend this warehouse plan to wine and tobacco, calculating that by the enhanced revenues—£200,000–300,000 on tobacco alone—he would be able to abolish the land tax altogether. But this time the opposition was too strong for him. For six years the persistent attacks in the opposition paper *The Crafts-man*, inspired by Bolingbroke and Pulteney, and showers of pamphlets had left him comparatively unscathed; but in the hated name of excise his opponents found an ideal battle-cry.[1] It was put about that the new scheme was only the beginning of a plot to impose an excise tax on every article of consumption by means of an army of excise men scouring the countryside and prying into every shop, nay every home: even the land-owners, who were to profit by the scheme, looked askance on the project as they preferred the existing small rate on their under-valued lands to the future risks of a restored tax based on a fresh valuation. In the face of such widespread opposition Walpole found his majorities dwindling in the house of com-mons and, bowing to the storm, withdrew the bill after the second reading. Not till forty years later did Adam Smith's *Wealth of Nations* revive interest in the warehouse and excise scheme and encourage Pitt to reintroduce it, with benefit to the merchants as well as to the revenue of the country.

Besides his economical management of the national finances, which in itself promoted the country's prosperity, Walpole also gave more direct encouragement to the national trade and industry. When he took office he found the export trade in some cases hampered by heavy duties or even prohibition. In the first king's speech for which he was responsible, in October 1721, he clearly laid down his economic policy 'to make the exportation of our own manufactures, and the importation of the commodi-ties used in manufacturing of them, as practicable and as easy as may be; by this means, the balance of trade may be preserved in our favour, our navigation increased, and the greater num-bers of our poor employed'.[2] Early in his ministry he abolished all duties on the export of agricultural produce and of over a hundred manufactured articles that found a ready market

[1] In the act of 1723 Walpole had wisely excluded the word 'excise': the new taxes had there been described as 'inland duties'.
[2] Coxe, *Walpole*, i. 163.

abroad; he even gave bounties for the exportation of grain, spirits, silk, sail-cloths, refined sugar. On the other hand, he took off the import duties on such raw materials as dyes, undressed flax, raw silk needed for home industries. Between 1724 and 1731 he also revived the traditional idea of qualitative regulations for manufactured goods, then rather falling into desuetude, by legislation, which finds an analogy in our modern 'national mark' system, to keep up the standard of English manufactures, especially those destined for the foreign market; a fixed quality and fixed measurements, for example, were laid down for bales of broadcloth and serges, for linen, sailcloth, and bricks and tiles. With the same object he also promoted the more disputable forms of paternal legislation. The prevalent theory was that cheapness of manufacture, and especially low wages for the workmen, was essential for a successful export trade; so in 1721 and 1726 acts were passed for the regulation of wages by the justices of the peace and to prohibit combinations of workmen to secure better pay or conditions of labour. Home industries in their turn were protected by tariffs or even prohibition against competition, not only from foreign, but even from Irish and colonial manufactures. Thus, to protect English hatters, hats from America were forbidden; to enforce the law against the exportation of woollens from Ireland the navy was employed in revenue work in the Irish Channel.[1] In theory at least Walpole was hardly in advance of his age, which looked on the colonies as a milch-cow for the English market. Sugar and tobacco, raw materials for English manufacturers, naval stores for the benefit of the navy the colonies were indeed encouraged to produce, but exclusively for the English or colonial market; but the colonies were not allowed, except in some special cases, to trade directly with foreign countries. When the powerful sugar-planters of Jamaica found the North American colonies bartering their lumber and horses for sugar from French, Dutch, and Danish colonies, they demanded redress from Walpole. The result was the Molasses Act of 1733 imposing prohibitive duties on foreign-grown sugar landed in America, and giving protection to Jamaica sugar re-exported to the Continent from England. But Walpole was wiser in practice than in theory, for, owing to protests from America, he allowed the act to remain almost a dead letter on his favourite principle

[1] See p. 297.

quieta non movere. In 1739, when urged to impose direct taxes on the colonies, he replied: 'I have old England set against me, do you think I will have new England likewise?'; and in the same year he even allowed the sugar colonies to trade directly with south European countries instead of through the mother country. Walpole's common sense never allowed him to drive abstract theories to death.[1]

During the first five years of his ministry Walpole had been quite content to allow his brother-in-law Townshend to direct foreign policy and even to regard himself as the senior partner in the Townshend–Walpole association. The main business during this period was to complete the territorial arrangements agreed upon in the Quadruple Alliance by Stanhope and Dubois. This was by no means an easy matter. For, though Spain had acceded to these arrangements in 1720, fresh difficulties had arisen. France and Spain had taken the opportunity to renew the family connexions by a double marriage contract between a daughter of the regent and Philip's heir and between Louis XV and the little infanta, whose tender years, however, made it necessary in their case to postpone the consummation. One result of this Bourbon connexion was to give France, which in Stanhope's time had been very much under England's direction, the lead in the Anglo-French alliance. At the same time the emperor, freed from the Turkish menace by the treaty of Passarowitz in 1718, began to make difficulties about granting the investitures of Parma and Tuscany to Don Carlos, as had been agreed by the Quadruple Alliance,[2] or allowing garrisons on his behalf to enter those duchies; he even antagonized his English and Dutch allies by allowing his Ostend Company to trench on the preserves of their lucrative East India Companies.[3] At the congress of Cambrai, which after two years' delay met finally in January 1724, France and England undertook to mediate on behalf of Spain with the emperor about these and other difficulties, but after six months of discussion nothing had been

---

[1] For further details of these fiscal measures see S. Dowell, *History of Taxation and Taxes in England*, 4 vols., 1884, ii, chap. iii; C. R. Fay, *Great Britain from Adam Smith to Present Day*, 1932, pp. 25 sqq.; W. Kennedy, *English Taxation 1640–1799*, 1913, chap. vi; Brisco, l.c., *passim*.

[2] The emperor claimed feudal suzerainty over Parma and Tuscany, hence the need of imperial patents of investiture before Don Carlos could take them over.

[3] See below, pp. 196–7.

decided. Apart from trivialities the main point at issue was as to the immediate admission of garrisons, either neutral or Spanish, to secure Don Carlos's rights. Finally Spain, despairing of any result from all this talk, decided in November 1724 to short-circuit the proceedings by a secret negotiation direct with Vienna. The envoy chosen for this mission was Ripperda, a Dutch adventurer, formerly sent as envoy to Madrid by the republic, who when his mission was terminated had returned to Spain, changed his religion, and secured employment from King Philip.[1] His instructions were not only to secure the admission of Don Carlos with adequate garrisons into the duchies but, by a complete volte-face of policy, to form a close alliance with the imperial house by the marriage of Don Carlos and his brother Don Philip with the Archduchess Maria Theresa and her sister. Vienna was not very forthcoming, and the negotiation would probably have been dropped had it not been for an unforgivable insult offered to Philip and Elizabeth by the duc de Bourbon.

The infanta affianced to Louis XV had in 1722 been sent to France to be educated, but was still only seven by March 1725, whereas Louis himself was then old enough to marry. Just then Louis was taken ill and was even thought to be dying.[2] His first minister Bourbon alarmed, not so much for his royal ward, as at the prospect of the childless king being succeeded by his enemy the young duc d'Orleans, swore that if Louis recovered he should be married forthwith, and, without a word of warning, brusquely announced to Philip that he was returning the infanta to her parents.[3] Philip and Elizabeth, outraged by such an insult, sent the French ambassador packing, recalled their own from France, and ordered Ripperda to enter into a treaty on any terms with the emperor. At the same time they declined to accept the French any longer as mediators at Cambrai and offered the sole mediation to England.

Horatio Walpole almost alone advocated England's acceptance of this offer, arguing that in the circumstances France could

[1] See G. Syveton, *Une cour et un aventurier au 18ᵐᵉ siècle; le baron de Ripperda*, 1896, pp. 60–64.
[2] The infanta had been born on 30 Mar. 1718. Louis's illness was in Feb. 1725. It was violent rather than dangerous; he had eaten too many chocolates.
[3] Bourbon had been considering the return of the infanta during 1724. Louis's illness finally decided him. See J. Dureng, *Le Duc de Bourbon et l'Angleterre*, pp. 236–46, 496–511; A. M. Wilson, *French Foreign Policy . . . 1726–43*, pp. 29–33.

hardly take offence and that in the interest of our valuable trade with Spain it would be of inestimable advantage to earn thereby her goodwill. Walpole and Townshend, on the other hand, had no doubt about rejecting it, partly because hints had already reached them from Spain of Ripperda's secret negotiations, but chiefly in order to rivet France more closely to the alliance which had already proved so useful and to recover the lead which we had lost since Stanhope's day. 'France', Horatio Walpole was told, 'will stand more in need than ever of the king's assistance, and consequently will be obliged to act everywhere in the most perfect concord with His Majesty.'[1] And so it proved, even though George I wisely rejected, on the score of religion, the marriage proposed by Bourbon of Louis XV with the prince of Wales's daughter Anne.

Meantime Ripperda had not been idle and on 30 April 1725 secured, on the best terms he could, the signature of three treaties with the emperor. By the first, the ostensible, treaty Philip agreed to guarantee the Pragmatic Sanction, the main object of all the emperor's diplomacy, whereby, in default of a male heir, all the Habsburg possessions were to devolve on his daughter Maria Theresa; by the second the emperor promised to use his good offices for the recovery by Spain of Minorca and Gibraltar, but with no obligation to fight for them; on the other hand, by the third he was given special trade privileges with Spain and a promise of support from Philip for his new Ostend trading company already viewed with hostility by England and Holland, with no corresponding advantage to Philip except that one of the archduchesses might possibly be given to Don Carlos. In fact Philip gained nothing more than he was already entitled to by the Quadruple Alliance but undertook new and onerous engagements to the emperor. But Ripperda by his vague boastings managed to convince Europe that there were secret clauses affecting France and England, especially in regard to support of the Pretender. He said enough about his secret plans to create alarm in England and France and cause them to seek further support against the threatened combination.[2]

[1] *British Diplomatic Instructions*, iv, *France*, p. 98.
[2] It seems clear that neither of the two treaties of Vienna, of Apr. and Nov. 1725, contained a specific clause about the Pretender. But his use as a weapon against England was so obvious that such a clause was presumed to exist, and its supposed form was actually reported from Madrid to Walpole and Townshend. See the discussion in Michael, iii. 410–15, 595, and in *E.H.R.* xii. 798–800; see also

England and France had somewhat different motives for opposing this new alliance. France dreaded another encircling movement portending an era of struggle such as had strained her energy for centuries against the allied Habsburgs of Spain and Austria. England had more immediate cause of apprehension from Ripperda's vapourings. The fear of foreign support for the Pretender was never far distant from the minds of English statesmen, and though Walpole may have privately pooh-poohed the danger,[1] he was prepared to make the most of it in public utterances. But our main preoccupation was trade. Alarm was felt at any such threat as seemed implied in the treaties of Vienna to our special privileges under the treaties of 1667, 1713, 1715, and 1716 with Spain. These treaties gave us rights of trade with Spain and also the Asiento or contract for supplying slaves to the Spanish West Indies and the privilege of sending an annual ship to the fairs at Cartagena and Vera Cruz. Even more serious was the support apparently promised by Spain to the emperor's Ostend Company.

The emperor had at first regarded the Spanish Netherlands, allotted to him at Utrecht, as more of a burden than an advantage, owing to their remoteness from his other dominions and his obligation to pay out of their revenues for the Barrier fortresses manned by the Dutch: in fact he would willingly have exchanged them for Bavaria had it not been for English and Dutch opposition. In 1714, however, some foreign adventurers conceived the idea of starting a trade with the East from the port of Ostend, the only Flemish port not closed by treaty, and in 1715 and 1716 had experimented with a few ships that returned with valuable cargoes. Both the Dutch and English East India Companies at once protested against these interlopers on the ground that by the treaty of Münster and § 26 of the Barrier treaty of 1715 Philip II's veto on any interference by the Flemings with Castilian trade rights in the East or West had been confirmed. Prince Eugene, the absentee governor of the Low Countries, was himself against the trade, for which he did not think it worth while antagonizing the English. But in 1720 Ker of Kersland, a Scottish adventurer, and John Colebrooke, 'a cunning man and a perfect master in the art of stock-

---

Chance, *The Alliance of Hanover*, p. 141; Syveton, op. cit., p. 148, n. 1; Dureng, op. cit., pp. 355-7. For the text of the November treaty see Syveton, pp. 283-94.
[1] See above, p. 185.

jobbing', proposed to the emperor himself a scheme for creating a chartered company with the lure of 3–6 per cent. of the profits for the depleted imperial treasury. Accordingly in December 1722 the emperor granted a charter to the Imperial and Royal Company of the Austrian Low Countries with trading rights to the Indies, China, and Africa. The Dutch and English were at once up in arms: protests were lodged at Vienna by both governments, and parliament declared it criminal for an Englishman to have any part in the venture. Owing to the competition from the Ostenders the shares and profits of the older Dutch and English companies went down in value; and when it was discovered that Spain had engaged to help the new venture, both these companies called on their governments for immediate action. France was not so directly affected by the menace to Indian trade, but owing to her new dependence on England had to follow in her wake.[1]

From Townshend, still the guiding spirit in foreign affairs and always suspicious of Austrian designs, the English merchants found a ready response, for he was seriously alarmed, not only at this sinister combination of Spain and the emperor, but also at the prospect of a hostile fleet based on Ostend as a menace to our Channel trade and even to our shores. He immediately set to work securing allies on the Continent; and, thanks to the vague rumours of help offered to the Pretender and the alarm caused by the Ostend Company's activities, received over-whelming popular support, expressed in a resolution of the house of commons that the treaty of Vienna was 'calculated for the entire destruction of the chief branches of the British trade'.[2] Accompanying George I to Hanover in the latter half of 1725 Townshend was master of the diplomatic situation and set himself to make a network of alliances specially directed against the emperor. The first treaty was with Frederick William of Prussia, with whom in 1723, following Stanhope's example in 1719, he had already negotiated another reconciliation with his father-in-law. This treaty of Charlottenburg of 1723, which was defensive in form, had been concluded largely because Frederick William and George I feared a Franco-Russian alliance which,

---

[1] For the Ostend Company see M. Huisman, *La Belgique commerciale sous Charles VI; la compagnie d'Ostende*, 1902; Hertz, 'England and the Ostend Company' in *E.H.R.* xxii. 255; J. F. Chance, *The Alliance of Hanover*, passim.

[2] *P.H.* viii. 508.

in the former's phrase, might 'bridle Germany'.[1] Townshend saw the treaty in a wider setting as a military alliance which would put:

into the scale with his Majesty the whole force and strength of Prussia, at least three score thousand men, excellent troops. Before this the power of Great Britain lay only in its fleet, which tho' strong . . . yet, as everybody saw . . . that we had no land forces to spare, the respect our Fleet carryed could not spread its influence so far as was necessary. But now . . . His Majesty is become Master, as it were, of so mighty a Land force, he will not only be more secure, but also more respected both in the North and the South.[2]

A subordinate factor in the Prussian decision was the hope of Frederick William and, more particularly, of his queen that their double marriage scheme would be advanced. By this George I's grandson, Prince Frederick, was to marry a Prussian princess, and Prince Frederick of Prussia was to marry a daughter of the prince of Wales. In fact, owing to subsequent differences between the two testy and quarrelsome monarchs, the scheme was never fulfilled, Townshend nevertheless succeeded by the treaty of Hanover of 3 September 1725 in bringing France into this political and military alliance. By that treaty the three powers guaranteed one another's possessions against the designs attributed to the Vienna allies, and agreed, though in studiously vague terms, to resist any attack on Gibraltar or Minorca, the encroachments of the Ostend Company, and the persecution of protestants in the empire, the special bribe to Frederick William being a guarantee for his succession to Juliers and Berg.[3] Working on this foundation Townshend eventually secured accessions to the alliance of Hanover from the Dutch in August 1726 and in the following year from Sweden and Denmark; previously, in March 1726, he had concluded a subsidy treaty with Hesse-Cassel for 12,000 troops.

On their side the Vienna allies had not been idle. Alarmed by the treaty of Hanover, the emperor, in a second treaty of

---

[1] See J. F. Chance, 'The Treaty of Charlottenburg', *E.H.R.* xxvii. 52–77.

[2] Townshend to Walpole, 18 Oct. 1723, Stowe MS. 251, f. 57, quoted in Dureng, p. 78. Compare *British Diplomatic Instructions*, iv, *France*, pp. 47–49.

[3] Owing to the failure of direct heirs to the Neuburg line, then ruling the two duchies of Juliers and Berg, there was a long-standing dispute between the Prussian and Bavarian claimants to the succession. Finally Frederic II of Prussia gave up his claims to them. See Dureng, pp. 331–42, *Recueil des Instructions, Prusse*, 350, 355 sqq., and 'Foreign Policy of Walpole', *E.H.R.* xv. 675–6.

Vienna of 5 November 1725, had given more definite hopes to Spain of help in recovering Gibraltar and Minorca and even as to the marriage, so much desired by Philip and Elizabeth, of Don Carlos with Maria Theresa in return for Spain's renewed promise of support for the Ostend Company; and the two allies had gone so far as to envisage a partial dismemberment of France as a result of a successful war. In August 1726 Russia, unsuccessfully angled for by France and England, definitely joined the emperor in an alliance which proved fairly constant for a century. Another success for imperial diplomacy was Frederick William's volte-face in October, when he deserted the Hanover allies for the emperor, partly from pique at the difficulties made by George I about the double marriage, partly because he was foolish enough to prefer Charles VI's unreliable promise about Juliers and Berg[1] to that of England and France. The emperor also secured the important support of the Rhenish electors of Cologne, Trier, and Mainz, besides Bavaria and Wolfenbüttel,[2] important for their strategic positions against France. By May 1727 it was reckoned that the Vienna allies could muster some 387,000 land forces, composed of 200,000 imperialists, 60,000 Spanish, 70,000 Prussian, 30,000 Russian, and 27,000 troops from German princes; and the Hanover allies 160,000 French, 30,000 Danes, 15,000 Swedes, 22,000 Hanoverians, 26,000 English, 12,000 Hessians, and 50,000 Dutch—a total of 315,000. But the inferiority of the latter in land troops was more than counterbalanced by the great superiority of the English and Dutch navies over that of Spain.[3]

But these formidable preparations were hardly brought to the test. Actual hostilities broke out only between England and Spain, and those on a small scale. Ripperda's boastful menaces, after his return to Spain at the end of 1725, especially against England, called for elementary precautions, such as the dispatch of a squadron to the West Indies under Admiral Hosier to

---

[1] The emperor had already promised his support to the Wittelsbach claimant of these duchies. Frederick William was also influenced in his decision to desert the Hanover allies by his knowledge of the emperor's alliance with Russia. He had himself signed a defensive alliance with Russia in Aug. 1726. Chance, op. cit., p. 413.

[2] Bavaria and Wolfenbüttel subsequently changed over to the side of the Hanover allies, but only after preliminaries of peace had been agreed upon.

[3] These calculations are based on Hervey's *Memoirs*, i. 64–65, which agree very closely with those drawn up by Marshal Berwick, Add. MS. 32750, f. 235. See 'Foreign Policy of Walpole', *E.H.R.* xv. 696–7.

intercept the galleons and trade fleet, on which the payment of the subsidies promised to the emperor depended, and of another under Sir John Jennings to blockade the Spanish coast. Ripperda himself, proving an incompetent administrator, was dismissed in May 1726 and, taking refuge in the house of the English ambassador Stanhope,[1] made a full confession to him of the secret articles in the treaties of Vienna and of his own designs for supporting the Pretender. But the king and queen abated none of their arrogance, and in February 1727 opened the trenches against Gibraltar. At first the emperor was equally bellicose. His ambassador in London, Palm, was instructed to protest in the most insulting language to the king about his speech to parliament against the emperor's 'usurped and extended exercise of trade and commerce' at Ostend, and even to publish this protest 'to the whole nation', an insult as much resented by the opposition as the ministry,[2] and for which he was forthwith ordered to leave the country. But this bellicose humour of the emperor soon cooled down. Owing to Hosier's blockade none of the Spanish galleons had been able to reach Spain with the treasure promised him to fill up his depleted exchequer and pay the subsidies due to his German allies. So he soon showed himself willing to hearken to pacific overtures from France and England.

In June 1726 the duc de Bourbon, whose clumsy diplomacy had precipitated the breach with Spain, had been dismissed and succeeded by the king's old tutor Fleury, who had already reached the ripe age of seventy-three. During the seventeen more years that remained to him of life and office Fleury's aims were first to keep France at peace, and secondly to regain for France her diplomatic ascendancy in Europe, and in particular to restore the intimate family connexion with Spain. At first he was well content to abide loyally by the English alliance, and as long as Sir Robert's brother Horatio Walpole remained ambassador in Paris—until 1730—few serious difficulties occurred between the two nations. But from the outset he made it clear that the lead in the alliance held by Stanhope and to a less extent by Townshend should for the future remain with

[1] William Stanhope, a distant cousin of the first Earl Stanhope: created Baron Harrington 1730; secretary of state 1730–41; an earl 1742, again secretary of state 1744–6, and subsequently viceroy of Ireland 1746–50.
[2] A point well brought out in Michael, iv. 55.

himself. As soon, therefore, as he found the emperor more inclined to peace, he promoted negotiations which resulted in the
Preliminaries of 31 May 1727. Walpole on his side was only too
ready to acquiesce in this settlement with the emperor. He had
been much troubled by the course of Townshend's negotiations
in 1725, as they seemed to make the emperor rather than Spain
our chief objective, whereas he believed that such a policy was
only playing France's anti-Habsburg game and might leave us
without a friend in Europe. He also blamed Townshend for
neglecting Portugal, our most useful ally against Spain, and for
antagonizing Russia by his extravagant policy of subsidizing
Sweden, now almost valueless as an ally. The rising opposition
in the house of commons also found the Hanover treaty a good
object of attack, whereof Walpole, not Townshend, had to bear
the brunt; so he began thenceforward to take a more decided
part in foreign policy.

By the Preliminaries of 1727 England lost all occasion for
quarrel with the emperor, since he agreed to suspend the Ostend
trade for seven years—it being understood that it should never
be revived. Two years later Spain, by the treaty of Seville with
England and France, restored to England all her trading privileges, and in return England and France were to help her to get
Spanish garrisons into Parma and Tuscany. Then the emperor
made more difficulties about the garrisons, refusing to admit
them unless he obtained a guarantee for his Pragmatic Sanction,
to which France was inexorably opposed. Finally, after Spain,
wearied with the discussions, had repudiated the treaty of
Seville, Walpole cut the Gordian knot. In 1730 Townshend,
the determined adversary of the Habsburg connexion, had
resigned after serious differences with Walpole and was succeeded by William Stanhope, created Lord Harrington for his
successful negotiation with Spain. Thenceforward he and the
other secretary, Newcastle, were quite content to follow Walpole's dictates. In March 1731 Walpole made another treaty of
Vienna with the emperor. On his side the emperor agreed to
abolish the Ostend Company entirely and to admit the Spanish
garrisons in return for England's guarantee of the Pragmatic
Sanction and a mutual guarantee of the two countries' possessions. In October English and Spanish fleets conveyed 6,000
Spanish troops to the duchies and in December Don Carlos
arrived at Leghorn. So closed for a time the long controversy

about the Italian duchies inaugurated by the Quadruple
Alliance.

This treaty of Vienna was notable for two reasons, first as a
definitive victory for Walpole's views on foreign policy, secondly
as marking the end of the close alliance with France inaugurated
by Stanhope in 1717 and the return of England to William III's
old system of close co-operation with the emperor and the
Dutch. The treaty of 1717 did not indeed formally lapse till
1744, but after 1727, when Fleury promoted Chauvelin to the
post of foreign minister, the French and English policies tended
more and more to diverge. Chauvelin himself was frankly anti-
English and was found very useful to Fleury as a foil to himself.
Horatio Walpole and his successor Lord Waldegrave would
first go to Chauvelin, who expressed his views with blustering
brutality: they would then complain to Fleury who soothed
their ruffled feelings with a flow of mellifluous words that in
essence amounted to little less than Chauvelin's uncompromising frankness. Even England's vigorous action against Spain in
1727 was criticized, and, later, disputes were continually arising.
At one time it was about the Dunkirk and Mardyk conditions
of Utrecht, at another the ownership of certain West Indian
islands, St. Vincent, St. Lucia, Tobago, and Dominica, or the
French forts in Canada menacing the New England settlers, or
the activities of French recruiting officers in Ireland, or, on the
other side, the English interlopers' activities in West Indian
waters. Some of these were comparatively trivial questions, but
cumulatively they added fuel to the flame of national antipathies.

It is an illustration of the firm hold obtained by Walpole on
the government of the country that the sudden death of his old
master George I in June 1727 had made no difference to his
position. George II had a grudge against him because, when he
resumed office in 1720, he had successfully urged a reconciliation between him and his father, and then seemingly used this
as a pretext for deserting his court. Accordingly, the new king
at first proposed to commit the treasury to Sir Spencer Compton,
an amiable nonentity. But, finding Compton unable without
Walpole's help to draw up the speech from the throne or make
provision for the new civil list, and also influenced by his
remarkably able wife, Queen Caroline, George had wisely committed the government once more to Walpole. In Queen Caroline Walpole for the next ten years found his ablest coadjutor,

especially in managing the king. Walpole and the queen would agree upon all important decisions in the first instance, and then the queen would discuss them with the king, leading him to believe that Walpole's policy was his own choice. As long as this curious partnership lasted Walpole's position at court was almost impregnable, but on her death in 1737 it was much more difficult for him to be certain of guiding George in the right path, for he was a choleric, conceited little man who liked to think that decisions rested with himself.[1] Walpole indeed, according to Newcastle, felt the queen's death as 'the greatest Blow that ever he received' and thought of retiring. 'But a concern for His own Honor, the Good of the Publick, a Regard for his Friends, and a desire to comply with the dying Requests of the Queen, has determined him to engage and go on, and indeed He thinks He has no Choice: the Goodness of the King to Him, and the King's Service, make Him not His own Master.'[2]

The removal of Carteret as secretary of state was followed by the exclusion of his supporters in the government; Macclesfield, Cadogan, and Roxburgh all fell in 1725 and with their going Walpole seemed free of serious opposition within the ministry.[3] But in that year, just when he was beginning to take a greater interest in foreign politics, a field in which he was more open to criticism than in his domestic measures, an opposition party began to be organized of malcontents chiefly created by Walpole's own jealousy of any possible rivals. Behind the scenes his old rival Bolingbroke, carefully cut off by Walpole from any direct connexion with parliament, was still at hand. Uxbridge was not so far from Westminster but that a hackney coach could make the journey without discomfort; and the

---

[1] Walpole had previously maintained his interest with Queen Caroline while she was still princess of Wales and this, in Onslow's opinion, accounted for the early re-establishment of his power in the new reign (see *Hist. MSS. Comm.* xiv. 516). But George II was never a mere figurehead. He retained some political initiative and reserved decisions in respect of the granting of peerages and of army and household appointments. Professor Pares suggested that 'politicians did not mind leaving' these decisions to the king, but Walpole does not seem to have shared this view. See R. Pares, *George III and the Politicians*, p. 63, and cf. Hervey's *Memoirs*, iii. 771.

[2] Add. MS. 32690, f. 445.

[3] For Carteret's removal see above, pp. 185–6. Macclesfield was impeached for corrupt administration as lord chancellor; Cadogan was replaced as master general of the ordnance by Argyll; Roxburgh's office as secretary for Scotland was suppressed. On these events and the development of the new opposition to Walpole see Realey, *The Early Opposition to Sir Robert Walpole*, pp. 137–42, 156–85.

spacious Bolingbroke house with its pleasing gardens made a very commodious cave of Adullam. Here the new-formed party of patriots often met. At first its leading members in parliament were William Pulteney, its ablest debater, with his brother Daniel, and Sir William Wyndham, still a tory but brought over by Bolingbroke to the dynasty. In the house of commons Shippen[1] and his small band of irreconcilable Jacobites helped with their speeches if not their votes. Within the next fifteen years the ranks of this opposition were constantly being increased by whigs turned out of office or favour by Walpole's impatience of criticism. Townshend himself had retired to the country to cultivate turnips, but others were more pugnacious. Carteret, on his return from Ireland in 1730, illuminated their councils by his comprehensive knowledge of foreign politics; in 1733 they were reinforced by Chesterfield, Bolton, and not least by Cobham with his following of 'Boy Patriots', Lyttelton, the Grenvilles, and Cornet Pitt; still later the great duke of Argyll broke with Walpole and joined them. Soon after his arrival in England in December 1728 Frederick, prince of Wales, who, as usual with the Hanoverian heirs, had a feud with his parents, became the nominal centre of this opposition. Encouraged by the 'Patriots', he quarrelled openly with his parents, demanding a higher allowance after his marriage in 1736; and in the following year he made the breach irreparable by allowing his friends in the opposition to bring forward the question of his allowance in parliament, and then by carrying off his wife, in the pains of labour, from the parental home.[2] To this galaxy of political stars were added nearly all the wits and men of fashion, merry ladies such as Kitty, duchess of Queensberry, and the formidable dowagers Sarah of Marlborough and Carteret's mother, Lady Granville; and above all most of the literary talent of the day—Swift, Pope, Gay, Arbuthnot, Glover, and Fielding—who put the case for the opposition with far greater conviction and effect than did Walpole's hired pamphleteers for the government. One of the most powerful weapons of the 'Patriots' was *The Craftsman*, a periodical started in December 1726 and run for ten years by Nicholas Amhurst. Bolingbroke and Pulteney were its most effective contributors, and by its

---

[1] William Shippen, 1673–1743, an uncompromising tory, sent to the Tower 1718 for a speech reflecting on George I, but highly respected for his honesty in the house.

[2] For Frederick, prince of Wales, see also below, pp. 338–40.

virulent attacks on Walpole's excise scheme of 1733 it had a large part in forcing him to withdraw the measure; while its persistent and well-reasoned attacks on Walpole's foreign policy stimulated the public indignation against Spain which resulted in the war of 1739. Other opposition periodicals, only less effective than *The Craftsman*, were *Fog's Weekly Journal* and *Common Sense*, to both of which Chesterfield lent his mordant pen. For long, however, Walpole, who cared little for literature and fashionable wit, was able to despise his enemies and their manœuvres. In the house he could generally hold his own, partly by reason of his favour at court and his alliance with local magnates which combined to bring him electoral victories in 1727 and 1734; partly by his skilful use of sinecures and places to create a body of regular supporters sufficient in normal circumstances to carry through government measures;[1] but above all by his own consummate skill in debate and use of practical arguments most fitted to the understanding of the rough country squires and hard-headed business men who formed the large independent section of the commons whose support was as essential to a successful minister as that of the Crown. Moreover, the opposition was disunited and afraid of going to extremes. Bolingbroke, indeed, in spite of the defeat of the Excise Bill in 1733, after Walpole's victory at the polls in 1734 gave up the contest in despair, took no further active part in politics, and retired to France to write essays on history and *The Patriot King*.[2] There was one man, however, of whom Walpole was instinctively afraid, the 'terrible cornet of horse', the future Great Commoner. Deprived of his cornetcy for an audaciously ironical speech in 1736 on the prince's loving parents, Pitt, unabashed, soon turned to the more congenial tasks of spokesman for the increasingly important community of traders and of denouncing Walpole's foreign policy.

After the treaty of Vienna of March 1731, however, Walpole

---

[1] [This body of regular government supporters numbered about 150. Its size and composition is discussed at length in J. B. Owen, *The Rise of the Pelhams*, chap. ii. Although it was far from being a majority of the whole house of commons, its regularity of attendance greatly eased the conduct of business for ministers. C.H.S.]

[2] His departure may also have been due to the discovery by the government that he was carrying on a secret correspondence with the French ministers; Pulteney himself, in a letter to Swift, wrote that Bolingbroke's presence was more of a hindrance than a help to the opposition. See Vaucher, *Crise du ministère Walpole*, pp. 62–65.

seemed at the height of his power. With the queen his devoted supporter, the king, under her influence, well in hand, and a ministry under his own absolute sway, he had satisfied Spain and recovered the emperor as England's ally; and no open breach had yet appeared in the relations with France. Nevertheless this spectacular triumph marks the beginning of his fortunes' decline. Two years later he had to drop the excise scheme, his first great rebuff in domestic politics, and abroad England's influence, secured by Stanhope's Triple Alliance, was visibly dwindling with the first Family Compact between France and Spain and the treaty of neutrality entered upon by Holland with France. This weakening of England's continental influence was accentuated by the Polish Succession war, in which Fleury, always professing the most pacific principles, was induced to take a hand on behalf of the French king's father-in-law, Stanislaus. Little was done for Stanislaus, but France gained the reversion of Lorraine, Don Carlos exchanged Parma and Tuscany for the Two Sicilies, and the emperor, further weakened on the eve of another war with Turkey, merely obtained the barren consolation of a French guarantee for the Pragmatic Sanction.

The most serious result for England was that she was left without an ally, with France pursuing her own policy and the emperor sore at her desertion in his time of need. When attacked on the Rhine and in Italy by France, Spain, and Savoy, the emperor had appealed to England to honour her guarantee, by the treaty of 1731, to protect his dominions if attacked. Walpole, however, on the flimsy pretext that Holland remained neutral, refused to honour the obligation, and was politely edged out by Fleury from the negotiations for peace;[1] so that England, accustomed since 1717 to have the chief voice in European councils, was left impotently to acquiesce in this final accession to France's territory and the serious weakening of the emperor, the only ally she could have looked to in Europe. Walpole himself rejoiced that no English life had been lost or English shilling spent in a war that did not directly concern the country; but his abstention was not only a dereliction of a national obligation but also had contributed to the strengthening of France, our main enemy, and the weakening of our only

---

[1] Walpole's unsuccessful efforts to have a say in the negotiations for peace are well brought out by P. Vaucher, *Robert Walpole et la Politique de Fleury*, Paris, 1924, pp. 160–227. See also A. M. Wilson, op. cit., pp. 257–64.

ally, Maria Theresa, in the forthcoming conflict between England and France. The statesmen of Vienna never thereafter quite trusted us, even as allies in the next war.[1]

One year, in fact, after the treaty of Vienna of 1738, Walpole found himself driven into a war with Spain without an ally or even a friend in Europe. The causes for this war had long been gathering force. Spain had never ceased resenting the privileges exacted by England at the peace of Utrecht: the Asiento or monopoly of the slave-trade with the Spanish West Indies, the South Sea Company's annual ship with English goods for sale at the great fairs at Vera Cruz or Cartagena, and above all the confirmation of England's conquests of Minorca and Gibraltar, the last likened by Philip V to a thorn in his foot. The Spaniards also complained of the South Sea Company's delays in rendering their accounts and of the fraudulent overloading of the annual ship. Other grievances were the swarms of unlicensed English traders constantly carrying on a contraband trade with the Spanish West Indies, English settlers illegally collecting salt on the Tortugas islands or cutting logwood on the coast of Honduras, and boundary disputes with Oglethorpe's colony of Georgia established in 1732.[2] On their side the English had been accumulating grievances. The South Sea Company complained of the vexatious delays of the Spanish officials in issuing the permit for the annual ship, and of their ships and effects being impounded as soon as hostilities opened in 1718 and 1727, notably the *Prince Frederick* in the latter year, although by treaty ample time should have been allowed to the Company to remove them after the outbreak of war. English merchants generally resented the so-called 'right of search' exercised by *guarda-costas* licensed by the Spanish governors to stop illegal smuggling. Often these *guarda-costas* were little better than pirates, attacking all English ships they met in West

---

[1] Professor Michael in his fourth volume appears to think that Walpole was justified in not honouring the engagements taken in the treaty of Vienna (1731); but for the reasons given above I venture to differ from his great authority. Moreover, he himself admits, pp. 345-6, that the Polish war was not essentially one about Poland, but an attempt by France to destroy the European balance by the ruin of the Austrian monarchy. He seems to me also to attach too much importance, as an indication of English influence on the Continent, to our dispatch of a fleet to protect Portugal on the occasion of a trivial Hispano-Portuguese dispute in 1735 (Michael, iv. 419-25). [See also the discussion of this problem by Sir Richard Lodge in *R.H.S. Transactions*, iv. xiv. 141-73. C.H.S.]

[2] On Georgia see below, pp. 309-10.

Indian waters, even those plying between English colonies, on mere suspicion of smuggling intent. They would either bring them into Spanish ports where judges could always be found to confiscate ships and cargoes on the flimsiest pretexts,[1] or seize the cargoes themselves on the high seas and turn the ships adrift. Between 1713 and 1731 no less than 180 English ships are stated to have been thus illegally confiscated or pillaged;[2] accusations were also freely made that captured English sailors were handed over to the tender mercies of the inquisition. The most notorious case was that of Captain Jenkins in 1731, who told the house of commons seven years later that his ship had been completely pillaged, even of its nautical instruments, and turned adrift, but not before he himself had been bound to the mast and had an ear torn off. When asked what he did then, he asserted that he 'committed his soul to God and his cause to his country', words as efficacious in stirring up warlike feeling as the 'contemptible little army' of two centuries later.[3]

By 1738 these various disputes, and especially the tales of losses and outrages committed on the high seas under the Spaniards' plea of a 'right of search', had created such indignation in parliament and outcry in the country that Walpole himself, pacific as he was, could not ignore them. In April, after an inquiry and strong resolution by the house of commons, Benjamin Keene,[4] our minister in Madrid, was ordered to demand from the Spanish court compensation for illegal captures and that strict orders should be sent to the West Indies to stop English ships being molested. To back up these demands a squadron was sent to the Mediterranean, and letters of reprisal against Spanish ships offered to our merchants.[5] As a result the Spaniards agreed to a joint commission to investigate complaints

[1] The mere possession, for example, of 'pieces of eight' or other Spanish coins was treated by the Spanish guarda-costas and admiralty courts as evidence of illicit trading, though this coinage was in general use throughout the English and French, as well as the Spanish, West Indies.

[2] See P.R.O. Spain 106, Proceedings of Commissioners to Discuss Trade Grievances with the Spaniards 1730–4. Other estimates of losses are to be found in the diplomatic correspondence of the duke of Newcastle in the Record Office and British Museum. [Only 20 ships were seized between 1733 and 1737. See J. O. McLachlan, *Trade and Peace with Old Spain*, p. 92. C.H.S.]

[3] See also below, pp. 314–15, for these trade disputes with Spain.

[4] Benjamin Keene, minister 1727–39, ambassador 1748–57, at Madrid; K.B. 1754.

[5] It had already been decided to reinforce the squadron in the West Indies in Feb. See H. W. Richmond, *The Navy in the War of 1739–48*, i. 5.

on both sides and assess damages, and in January 1739 the commissioners' report was embodied in the Convention of the Pardo. This Convention showed on balance a sum of £95,000 as compensation due to England. This sum was arrived at by an offset of £60,000 claimed by Spain for the sinking of the Spanish fleet at Passaro and of £45,000 for prompt cash, to the £200,000 admitted by the Spanish commissioners to be due to England. But even this £95,000 was to be conditional on a payment of £68,000 claimed by Spain from the South Sea Company for arrears: so that the utmost England could get was whittled down to £27,000 out of the original total of £200,000. Moreover, the crucial questions of the right of search and of the boundaries of Florida and Georgia had not been settled and were to be remitted to a further commission.

Walpole himself was still against war; he believed that much as the right of search might be abused by the Spaniards they had a prima facie justification for trying to stop the illicit traffic admittedly carried on by English and colonial traders with the Spanish colonies. He believed, too, that Spain, having once admitted by her offer of £95,000 that she owed redress for the *guarda-costas'* excesses, might come to a reasonable arrangement for preventing excesses in the exercise of this right of search. 'A war with Spain,' he declared, 'after the concessions she has made by this very Convention, would on our parts be unjust, and, if it is unjust, it must be impolitic and dishonourable.'[1] Above all he dreaded being involved in a war with France, then apparently at the height of her power, and likely owing to her engagements by the Family Compact of 1733[2] and from self-interest to come in with Spain. But in the end he had to yield, not so much to the opposition in parliament, which, after a great speech from Pitt against the Convention[3]—condemned by 'your despairing merchants' . . . 'by the voice of England'—had stultified itself by seceding from the house, as to his colleagues in the ministry, particularly Newcastle, who were alarmed at the growing unrest of the trading community. The traders indeed, whose case was voiced by Pitt, dimly perceived that the expansion of our trade and even of our colonial empire was at stake

[1] *P.H.* x. 1291.
[2] These ties were strengthened by the marriage of Don Philip and Louis XV's eldest daughter in Aug. 1739. See below, p. 232.
[3] *P.H.* x. 1283.

P

on this issue and were clamorous for a sharp lesson to Spain. Accordingly Haddock's orders to return from the Mediterranean, issued on the first news of the Convention, were revoked, Norris was appointed to command a fleet in home waters, and in July Admiral Vernon, one of the opposition most vociferous against the Convention, was sent to take command in the West Indies.[1] War was not actually declared till 19 October 1739 amidst the rejoicings of the mob, the ringing of bells, and the prince of Wales toasting the multitude from a city tavern.[2]

Hardwicke, in a letter to Newcastle, gives a pathetic picture of the old warrior for peace at a cabinet meeting when the orders had been sent to the admirals before war was actually declared.

> Sir R. W. [he writes] began in a strain of melancholy and complaints,—I don't mean personal but relating to things and circumstances. I endeavour'd to show him that his difficulties arose chiefly from a fixed opinion in many and from a suspicion in some of his Friends that nothing would be done against Spain. . . . That as things were come to a Crisis, and Spain had broke the Convention, that was a new event upon which even He might take a vigorous part without contradicting any opinion or measure he had avow'd before . . . He allow'd a great deal of this and I really think is determin'd to act with vigour to a certain degree.[3]

But his heart was not in it and the vigour which had sustained him for over twenty years of power was fast ebbing away. 'This war is yours,' he said to Newcastle after it had been in progress for a year, 'you have had the conduct of it—I wish you joy of it.'[4] This was true enough, but, that being so, it would have been more dignified of him to have retired at once, better too for the direction of the war. Instead he lingered on in the ministry, a hindrance rather than a help to the conduct of the Spanish war and of the still more difficult situation brought about in Europe by Frederic of Prussia's sudden raid into Silesia. After the election of 1741, when the ministerial majority was diminished, he at last resigned in February 1742 after an

---

[1] For Vernon's instructions see below, p. 234.

[2] On the origins and rights of this war two somewhat different points of view are expounded by Professor Temperley in *Trans. of R. Hist. Soc.*, 3rd ser., vol. iii, and by Mr. Hertz in *British Imperialism in the Eighteenth Century*.

[3] 'Walpoliana' in *Hardwicke State Papers*, ii. 7. Quoted in Yorke, *Hardwicke*, i. 222–3.

[4] See Yorke, op. cit. i. 251, Newcastle to Hardwicke 25 Oct. 1740, quoted in Coxe, *Walpole*, i. 638.

adverse vote, not on a matter of high policy, but on the representation of Chippenham.[1]

To resign not on any great issue but on a matter affecting representation in parliament had indeed a certain appropriateness. For Walpole was above all a great house of commons man; and not the least of his services to England was to teach that house to be the real ruling element in the state. Since the beginning of the seventeenth century, no doubt, the house had become the mouthpiece of the people's grievances and was often effective in removing them. But as late as William III's reign it still regarded its function mainly as that of a critic, sometimes a very querulous critic, of administration and had not yet conceived that its main concern should be to assist in carrying on the king's government. Even during the first two decades of the eighteenth century, though growing in power, it had not correspondingly grown in a sense of responsibility. Walpole, during the debates on the Peerage Bill, by his masterly conversion of a lukewarm house to a real senate consulting about the republic, first perhaps gave it that sense of authority; and by his long tenure of office confirmed it in that sense. For he was the first chief minister in normal times to look on the house of commons, not the house of lords, as his proper place. 'I have lived long enough in the world, Sir,' he said in one of the Spanish debates, 'to know that the safety of a minister lies in his having the approbation of this House. Former ministers, Sir, neglected this, and therefore they fell; I have always made it my first study to obtain it, and therefore I hope to stand.'[2] By such an attitude he immeasurably raised the prestige of the commons. Before his time there would have been little point in the greeting to his old rival Pulteney, as the two newly created earls met for the first time in the house of lords: 'You and I, my lord, are now two as insignificant men as any in England.' In his management of the house he may occasionally have trusted too much to the regular supporters of the ministry;[3] but at any rate he always paid it the compliment of luminous explanations of his policy and was influenced by good arguments even from his opponents. An interesting illustration of this accessibility to argument

[1] Walpole's decision to resign was taken before his defeat on the Chippenham election petition. See Owen, op. cit., pp. 33, 87.

[2] *P.H.* xi. 224 (21 Nov. 1739).

[3] See above, p. 205 and n. 1.

occurred in the debate on the salt tax which he reimposed in
1732, on the ground that the most equal and most general tax
was the least burdensome and most just; but in the course of the
debate he was so much impressed by the arguments of his opponents as to the injustice to the poor of such a tax on a necessary
of life that he entirely revised his view and thereafter went on
the principle that taxes on the luxuries of the rich were a juster
method of raising revenue.[1]

To sum up, Walpole was one of our greatest finance ministers:
he was a great peace minister, 'averse to war,' as it was said of
him, 'from opinion, from interest and from fear of the Pretender.
. . . If (he said) there was a war the King's Crown would be
fought for in the land. . . . The chief light in which he considered
the army and navy was that of a support to Civil i.e. Ministerial
Power':[2] and, above all, he was a great house of commons man.

[1] See Brisco, op. cit., pp. 120–1.
[2] P. Yorke, 2nd Earl of Hardwicke, 'Walpoliana', London, 1783, p. 7.

VIII

THE ARMY AND THE NAVY 1714–60

THE Spanish War of 1739, forced so light-heartedly by popular opinion upon an unwilling minister, was only the prelude to a struggle for dominion, lasting all but a quarter of a century, between England and the Bourbon powers. Nominally interrupted in 1748, the struggle still persisted, if not in Europe, in Asia and America, during the eight succeeding years before war was again declared in due form. Long before the issues between England and Spain had been decided, they had been lost sight of in the far larger interests brought into the contest by the general upheaval of Europe and England's rivalry for empire with France: indeed neither at Aix-la-Chapelle in 1748, nor at Paris in 1763, were the original causes of dispute with Spain so much as mentioned.

The country was ill prepared in 1739 for the long struggle before it. During all the years of peace since 1714, barely interrupted by the Jacobite invasions of 1715 and 1719 and the minor hostilities against Spain in 1719 and 1727, the army, regarded as a menace to a free constitution, had been kept at little more than the minimum required for internal police purposes and its discipline had deteriorated; and even the navy, especially in the higher commands, had been allowed to fall into slack ways. In fact neither the military nor the naval forces were prepared even for a struggle with the decadent power of Spain, still less for the European Armageddon which was to come.

The army, unemployed for a quarter of a century, except to suppress riots or for the relatively small operations of 1715 and 1719, was neither popular nor efficient. The old seventeenth-century fear of a standing army as a menace to civil liberties was as deep-seated as ever. The national pride in its achievements during Marlborough's earlier campaigns had evaporated even before the end of his military career; and with peace the civil population's apprehensions of 'a burthensome and useless army at home' had been revived by both political parties. At the death of Anne, apart from the three regiments still in Flanders, the strength of the army at home had been reduced to less than 8,000, while even the Irish establishment, paid for by Ireland, was only about 5,000 strong. Under the menace of Jacobitism the British army was perforce raised to 36,000 in 1716,[1] but in the succeeding years it was steadily reduced so that by 1718 it totalled 16,300 and in 1721, 12,400. During Walpole's ministry, between 1722 and 1738 it stood normally at between 16,000 and 17,700, with slight increases in 1726–8 and 1734 owing to continental unrest. During the war-period 1739–48 the numbers rose from 35,900 to a maximum of 74,000 in 1745, then dropped to a uniform 18,857 till 1754, after which the Seven Years war brought them up to a maximum of 67,776.[2] These small numbers are the more noteworthy since, in the absence of any organized police force, the soldiers were normally called out to suppress riots or even strikes of discontented workmen. Of Walpole himself it was said that, since 'the chief light in which he considered the army and navy, was that of a support to Civil, i.e. Ministerial, Power; he was reproached by his enemies with being more attentive to the Civil than Military subordination of it'.[3] Nevertheless, almost every year the ministry's modest demands were met with opposition in parliament, led by the sturdy tory Shippen, and often supported by the opposition whigs. The result was that in times of foreign invasion or even civil strife England was in the humiliating position of having to borrow regiments from the Irish establishment, normally kept at 12,000 strong, or hire troops from the Dutch, Hanover, or the Landgrave of Hesse-Cassel to defend her own soil.

With public opinion so antagonistic to a standing army, it is hardly surprising that in peace-time its discipline and morale were low. The recruits obtained by voluntary enlistment—for, except in war-time, the army did not, like the navy, depend on the press-gang—were chiefly drawn from the scum of the population, especially as the conditions of service were anything but attractive. At first sight indeed the pay appeared to be relatively good, with 3s. 6d. per week for a private and 7s. for a sergeant in the infantry, and 9s. 11d. and 15s. 9d. for similar ranks in

[1] Besides the twenty-one new regiments raised in 1715 (see above, p. 161) a further thirteen were raised on the Irish establishment in 1716 and disbanded the next year. See C. Dalton, *George I's Army*, i. xx–xxiv, xxxi, xxxviii.
[2] For the annual figures from 1720 see C. M. Clode, *Military Forces of the Crown*, i. 398. For the figures for 1718 see Dalton, i. xlvii.   [3] 'Walpoliana' l.c., p. 7.

dragoon regiments. But with deductions for diet, billets, &c., and in the cavalry for the farrier, horse-provender, &c., the net pay worked out at no more than 6*d*. and 1*s*. per week respectively in the infantry, and 1*s*. 2*d*. and 7*s*. in the cavalry; and even out of these pittances further deductions could be claimed by the colonel for medicines, shoes, gaiters, &c. The soldiers, too, were abominably housed. The only barracks of any size in England were at the Tower and the Savoy and at Hull, although all garrisoned towns had small barracks for their handfuls of 'invalid' gunners; Scotland was slightly better off with barracks at Edinburgh Castle and quarters dotted about the Highlands to overawe the population.[1]

This dearth of barracks was of set purpose; for in 1741, when a proposal was made in parliament to build more barracks, it was dropped for the reasons suggested by Wade, that 'the people of this kingdom have been taught to associate the idea of barracks and slavery so close together', and by Pulteney, that 'if the soldiers were all kept in barracks the people would be insensible of their numbers', whereas, if they were billeted out in the country-side, the people would be 'sensible of the fetters which are preparing for them . . . [and] put an end to . . . too numerous an army . . . before it be too late'.[2] This system of scattered billets, sometimes in as many as six separate villages for one unit, made the training and discipline exceedingly difficult, and was also most unpopular with innkeepers compelled to lodge, feed, and supply with small beer each foot-soldier billeted on them for 4*d*. a day. The chief method of securing discipline, at any rate until a better type of officer had been evolved in the latter days of George II, was by barbarous floggings or other forms of torture, under which the death of culprits was not uncommon. That desertion was frequent is hardly surprising.

In the long period of peace the officers had deteriorated as much as the men: in fact in 1746 Chesterfield with some justice called the army 'the worst-officered . . . in all Europe'.[3] Most of

---

[1] In Ireland there was no such dearth of accommodation, for the Irish parliament made no difficulty in providing barracks.

[2] See *P.H.* xi. 1442, 1448, cited by Clode, l.c. i. 223 and 234; Wade was, of course, arguing in favour of the erection of barracks and deploring the popular cry against them.

[3] *Private Correspondence of Chesterfield and Newcastle*, R. Hist. Soc. (Sir Richard Lodge ed.), p. 113.

those trained under Marlborough, Stanhope, or Galway were either dead or past work. A large proportion of the newer officers, drawn from noble or wealthy families, brave enough when it came to fighting, simply neglected their duties in peace-time or even absented themselves from an irksome station. When, for example, Minorca was besieged in 1756, no less than thirty-four officers, including the colonels of the four regiments quartered there, were found to be absent from their posts. Few indeed of the junior officers took their profession as seriously as Wolfe who in 1751 deplored 'the prevailing ignorance of military affairs', or Cornet Pitt who, on receiving his commission, laid in a stock of military treatises and set himself to master the principles of strategy and tactics. Most of them, says Mauvillon,[1] who was in personal contact with them during the Seven Years war, 'do not trouble their heads about the service; and understand of it, very *very* few excepted, absolutely nothing whatever, . . . and this goes from the Ensign to the General'. Among the worst evils of the system were the custom of selling and purchasing commissions for each successive grade, and the 'parliamentary solicitations' for promotion by junior officers elected to the commons, a scandal deplored by Chesterfield, Pitt, and even Newcastle. The officers' pay, especially in the higher ranks, was relatively good, but to recoup themselves for the cost of commissions they had to rely on allowances they were entitled to draw from the men's pay or from the pay of fictitious men nominally on the strength of the regiment. For the colonel, indeed, a regiment was regarded as a source of wealth, for, besides such allowances, he drew bounties for re-cruiting and profits from clothing the men and dealings with army contractors, &c. In fact the colonel almost looked on the regiment as his private property; and it is characteristic of the system that until 1753[2] regiments were known, not by official numbers and titles, but by the names of their colonels. In these circumstances, so high were the prices of commissions to the higher grades, that poor men without influence, unless they had an opportunity of distinguishing themselves in action, often had to remain through life in the lower ranks of lieutenant or

---

[1] Quoted by Carlyle, *Frederick the Great*, Bk. xx, Ch. 7.
[2] [This date is given by Fortescue, *History of the British Army* (2nd edn.), ii. 592, but Dalton, l.c. ii. v, shows that the regimental numbers were 'served out' in 1751 and listed in 1752. C.H.S.]

captain. Sterne's father, for example, obtained his commission as an ensign in 1710 and died in the West Indies in 1731 still only a lieutenant; and Fielding (*Tom Jones*, vii. 12) mentions a lieutenant, 'now near sixty years of age', who had obtained that rank under Marlborough.

The central administration of the army was equally unsatisfactory. The secretary of state was responsible for plans of campaign and orders for the movement of troops; but the routine details of army administration were committed to various subordinate departments. The secretary at war settled billeting areas, sent out marching orders, issued commissions, obtained through the secretary of state and signed by the king, and at one time arrogated to himself the right of granting leave to officers without reference even to their colonels; the board of ordnance was solely responsible for military stores and, such as they were in this period, for the engineer and artillery branches of the army;[1] the paymaster issued the pay of the army, was responsible for Chelsea Hospital and army pensions, and paid out to foreign rulers subsidies for hired troops; and, until Pitt's time, he made big profits by investing on his own account the large sums voted for these purposes. The want of co-operation between these departments and their slack methods account for many military failures during this period; and it was not till Pitt came into power in 1756 and knocked their heads together that satisfactory means were found for equipping and manning expeditions promptly and efficiently.

But even before Pitt's time some improvements had been made. Both George I, with some reason, and George II, with less, plumed themselves on their military knowledge and capacity, and insisted on having a decisive voice in the organization and direction of the army. The duke of Cumberland, too, though barely twenty-four when first made commander-in-chief,[2] initiated several useful reforms, in spite of the fact that, like his father, he attached undue importance to the cut of uniforms and the frippery of military dress.[3] George I conceived

[1] See below, p. 220, for the strength of the Engineers. 'It is', says Fortescue, ii. 598, 'almost an extreme assumption to assert their existence except in name.'

[2] Cumberland was appointed commander-in-chief in Mar. 1745, a month before his twenty-fourth birthday. See below, p. 250.

[3] Horace Walpole says unkindly of him that he was 'as intent on establishing the form of spatter-dashes or the pattern of cockades as on taking a town or securing an advantageous situation'.

a 'great aversion' to the system of purchase of commissions,[1] and though unable entirely to break through the obstacle of vested rights, insisted on laying down a definite tariff for commissions and requiring evidence of the purchaser's soldierly fitness.[2] Cumberland reformed abuses of the army in the field, limiting the number of private carriages for officers,[3] insisting on the control of leave by the regimental authorities, and raising the tone of the army by his attention to proper discipline and encouragement to keen and humane young officers such as Howe, Wolfe, Monckton, Murray, Lawrence, Coote, and Forde, who were given their opportunity under Pitt.[4]

But the drill and tactics of the British army were still by the end of this period not so advanced as those of some of the continental armies, notably the Prussian. The Prussian army in 1740 had had little experience of war, but had been formed into a perfect instrument for that purpose, not only by Frederick William's care in filling up the ranks with well-chosen recruits, but still more by the revolutionary methods of drill and tactics introduced by Leopold of Anhalt-Dessau ('the old Dessauer'). He it was who invented the iron ramrod, the equal step, the barrack-square words of command, still largely in use, and adopted Marlborough's methods of moving from line into column and vice versa, later called the 'Prussian manœuvre' from its regular use in the Prussian army, before other armies had made it their regular practice. Frederic the Great had even improved on this system by his oblique columns of attack enabling him rapidly to attack the enemy's front and also to envelop his flank; and by his improvement in cavalry tactics. The whole idea of the new system was rapidity of action: 'Good shooting, quick loading, intrepidity and vigorous attack', as it was summarized by Leopold, who brought the Prussian infantry to the pitch of firing 5 rounds a minute, compared with the 2–3 rounds in other armies.[5] Already in the war of the Austrian

[1] Clode, ii. 606, quoting a letter of the secretary at war of Mar. 1717.

[2] This was a great advance on Anne's permission to grant an ensigncy to an infant, 'for the support of his mother and family'. Though this was granted 'in consequence of the loss of his father and uncle who died in the service...'. Clode, ii. 610.

[3] George II himself was a great sinner in this respect: in the Dettingen campaign his equipage is said to have consisted of 662 horses, 13 Berlins, 35 wagons, and 54 carts. Add. MS. 32700, f. 154.

[4] Cumberland, however, was not impeccable in his judgement; for among his favourite officers were Hawley and Braddock.

[5] [It is doubtful whether the Prussian infantry achieved a rate of more than

Succession these new tactics had saved the day for Frederic at Mollwitz, Hohenfriedberg, and Kesselsdorf, as well as later at Rossbach and Leuthen; and the Prussian army was soon recognized as having obtained the supremacy enjoyed by the Swedes in the seventeenth century. The British army was still, and for long afterwards, far behind. There was a general want of system in drill and organization, each battalion being a law to itself in composition of columns and barrack-square usages; and any improvements made were regimental rather than applicable to the whole army. No doubt many keen young officers, some of whom would attend Prussian manœuvres during the peace years 1748–56, made improvements in drilling their own men, but no general rule was established. The best training was acquired by those who formed part of the composite army in Germany, commanded during the Seven Years war by Prince Ferdinand of Brunswick, a general chosen by Frederic himself from his own staff. One of these officers was David Dundas,[1] a twenty-three-year-old lieutenant, who served as assistant quartermaster under Ferdinand from 1758 to 1759. He took notes during this period and often thereafter went to study the Prussian methods at manœuvres; but it was not till 1788 that he published his book on the *Principles of Military Movement chiefly applied to Infantry*, which entirely revolutionized the British system of drill and tactics in time for the revolutionary and Napoleonic wars, a book in which he quotes (pp. 198–206) Prince Ferdinand's *Orders for the Marches and Movements of the Army*, a model of clear and comprehensive regulation.[2]

But before our mid-eighteenth-century wars certain other improvements had been made in the British army system. Of these the most important was the development of the artillery arm. Already in 1716, on Marlborough's advice, the place of the

four rounds a minute in the field. See E. M. Lloyd, *History of Infantry*, p. 155. Nor, according to Fortescue, was the splendid British fire-discipline of the Seven Years war the consequence of the adoption of Prussian methods. See Fortescue, ii. 599. C.H.S.]

[1] (Sir) David Dundas, 1735-1820, later commander-in-chief 1809–11. He continued in Germany for the campaigns of 1760–1 as aide-de-camp to Colonel Eliott, later Lord Heathfield.

[2] These orders are printed side by side with those of Marshal Broglie to demonstrate 'the sameness of principle which directed the conduct . . . of both generals'. See, besides Dundas's book, above quoted, E. M. Lloyd, *Review of History of Infantry*, pp. 154–79; *Encyclopaedia Britannica*, 1910, xiv. 524–6; Carlyle, *Frederick the Great*, Bk. iv, Ch. 2.

ephemeral trains of artillery was taken by two permanent companies; and in 1722 Albert Borgard,[1] a Dane who had served under William III and Marlborough in Flanders and under Galway and Stanhope in Spain, was placed in command of these companies, which in 1727 were raised to four with the title of Royal Regiment of Artillery. Finally in 1741 Woolwich Academy was founded to train 40 gentlemen-cadets;[2] and by 1761 the Royal Regiment had been increased to 31 marching companies: 3,200 of all ranks. One great source of strength in the regiment was that commissions depended solely on merit and not on purchase; another was the magnificent training their colonel was able to give it. By the time of the Seven Years war the regiment, armed with light and heavy 3-, 6-, and 12-pounders and howitzers and 24-pounders, had, as it proved at Minden, Warburg, and other engagements, become one of the finest artillery corps in the world. An engineering school, also established in 1741 to train the engineer officers' corps formed in 1717, was not so successful. By 1759 the corps was only 61 strong and had no men attached to it, the company of miners, 200 strong, being attached to the artillery branch. Either the teaching or the officers trained must have been exceedingly poor, for the engineers' work on the various expeditions to which they were attached was almost beneath contempt. On the other hand, in spite of the hardships and savage punishments to which they were liable in peace-time, the infantry and cavalry soldiers on active service proved at Dettingen, Fontenoy, Minden, and Quebec that they had lost none of the spirit, fire-discipline, and steadiness for which they were so remarkable under Marlborough. This was no doubt due partly to the better type of officers that emerged as the war progressed to supersede incapable martinets such as Braddock and Hawley, partly also because in war-time a better type of recruit came into the ranks. Normally the press-gang was not used to fill up the army, which depended for recruits partly on volunteers enlisted by the

---

[1] A. Borgard, 1659–1751, had already distinguished himself in the Danish and Prussian armies before he entered the English service at the age of 33, with the reputation of being 'one of the most experienced artillery and engineer officers in the world'. He was no less remarkable for his disinterestedness as colonel of the artillery in refusing to accept the usual perquisites of the office. Besides his skill in lethal fireworks he was an adept in 'pleasant fireworks', and was responsible for the illuminations and fireworks on the Thames to celebrate the treaty of Utrecht.

[2] This number was raised to 48 in 1744.

regimental officers, partly on the criminals and debtors released from prison on condition of joining the army. Acts passed during the two wars between 1739 and 1763, however, allowed impressment of paupers from the parishes on payment of bounties to the parish authorities.[1] But so great was the enthusiasm for war in 1739 that many of the better-class men flocked to the colours as volunteers, and such men were encouraged by an act passed in 1744 offering them a bounty of £4 to enlist for three years instead of for the life-long service required of normal recruits.[2] The introduction, too, of light companies for scouting and skirmishing duties, such as were Wade's Highlanders and the Riflemen inaugurated by Amherst and Wolfe, broke down some of the stiff barrack-square tradition and gave scope for individual daring and initiative. Lastly, the medical and sanitary services for soldiers in the field or in hospital were enormously improved by the exertions of John Pringle, who served as an army doctor under Stair and Cumberland between 1742 and 1748.[3]

But in spite of increases in the army and improvements in its training during the actual periods of war, the prejudice against a large standing army still remained; and, apart from this, the needs of the navy, and the smallness of the available population, made it impossible for England to rely solely on her own manpower for home defence as well as continental campaigns. For most of this period indeed, even when we were not involved in continental wars, the home army had to be supplemented by foreign mercenaries for the defence of our own shores. In 1715 and 1719 Dutch troops had to be brought in, Dutch and Hessians in 1745, and in 1756 Hessians and Hanoverians to crush the rebels or guard our shores against foreign invasion. It was not until Pitt came into office and introduced his Militia Bill that the foreign auxiliaries could be sent back to the Continent and the militia levies trained to take over part of the burden of home defence. But for our continental expeditions even Pitt was fain to follow the example of all his predecessors and employ

---

[1] These acts were passed in 1745 and 1756, 18 Geo. II, c. 10, and 29 Geo. II, c. 4.

[2] This act was 17 Geo. II, c. 15. A similar measure was passed in 1757, 30 Geo. II, c. 8, with a bounty of £3 per volunteer; this also continued the measure of impressment passed the previous year (see note 1 above). For all four acts see Clode, l.c. ii. 17–18, and Fortescue, l.c., pp. 581–3, for an inaccurate summary.

[3] See below, pp. 392–93.

hired troops from German principalities to bring our armies abroad to sufficient strength for effective action.[1]

There was never the same difficulty in supplying the needs of the navy. A long succession of victories and adventurous enterprise at sea, dating from at least as far back as the battle of Sluys, had made the nation sea-conscious and proud of its navy as the safeguard for our inviolability. Quite apart, too, from considerations of home defence, the politically powerful commercial community demanded a strong navy to protect its trade and the overseas colonies on which so much of that trade depended. In peace-time the normal number of seamen voted by parliament was 10,000, sinking below that in four years only:[2] in years of war or threat of war the least number voted was 12,000, but generally from 40,000 to 70,000, at which the personnel of the navy stood in 1760–2. In addition to the pay of the seamen sums ranging from £30,000 in 1736 to £200,000 in each of the years 1756–62 were voted for construction and other expenses of the navy.[3]

Another advantage that the navy had over the army was that it necessarily was exercised in sea-service in peace-time as well as in war, so that its officers and men never fell into quite such slack habits as were almost inevitable for an army during a prolonged period of peace. From 1715 to 1721 a fleet was annually sent to the Baltic, and again in 1726–7, partly for commerce protection, partly for active measures against Swedes or Russians; a Channel fleet was always in being and squadrons regularly kept watch in the Mediterranean and on the west coast of Spain, and in the West Indies, where indeed Hosier's and his successor's fleet spent nearly three pestilential years, 1726–8, blockading Porto Bello and Cartagena.

But in spite of these opportunities of active service for the fleet, all was not well with our naval defences at the opening of the war in 1739. The fleet numerically, it was true, was superior

[1] For all the foregoing paragraphs see Fortescue, *History of British Army* (2nd edn. 1910), ii. 1–54, 571–602, and C. Dalton, *passim*, and Clode, *passim*.

[2] 7,000 for 1722, 8,000 for 1732–3 and 1751, but in the last instance Pitt made so strong a protest against the reduction that in 1752 the normal 10,000 was restored. See p 335 below.

[3] W. L. Clowes, *The Royal Navy*, iii. 5, gives the number of seamen voted for each year from 1715 to 1762, as well as the sums voted for other naval expenses. No 'extra' sums were voted in 1722–9, 1734–5, 1739–49, or 1753; for each of the three years 1715–17 more than £200,000 was voted.

to that of Spain, but not by any means to the combined fleets
of Spain and France, which might at any moment take part
against us, as they actually did even before war between England
and France was declared in 1744. This was the more serious
since, unlike Spain and France, we had to depend almost
entirely on the navy for defensive and offensive operations, the
army, even when reinforced by subsidized troops, being numerically no match for the large armies of the Bourbon powers.[1]
Nor, in spite of improvements in naval architecture introduced
in 1719, 1733, 1741, and 1745, were our men-of-war, ship for
ship, as seaworthy or effective in gun-fire as the best produced
in the French and Spanish dockyards.[2]

The actual administration of the navy was almost as chaotic
as that of the army, being also divided between separate departments with very little inter-communication. General orders for
the movements of the fleet came from a secretary of state;
the board of admiralty, stationed in Whitehall or St. James's
Square,[3] was responsible for its state of preparedness and for
detailing the ships and squadrons necessary for carrying out the
secretary of state's orders; the navy office in Seething Lane dealt
with personnel, victualling, uniforms, &c.; the navy pay office
was in Old Broad Street; the sick and wounded board, which
was established in 1740, was on Tower Hill, and separate boards
of commissioners superintended each of the royal dockyards.
The first lord of the admiralty from George I's accession until
1742 was always an admiral, Sir Charles Wager[4] holding the
office when war broke out in 1739, and there were generally
two or more admirals on the board. But on the fall of Walpole
Lord Winchilsea became first lord of a board manned by officials almost as ignorant of naval matters as himself; nor was it
till he was superseded by the duke of Bedford in 1744 that

---

[1] Of the 124 ships of 50 guns or more in our navy in 1739, only 80 were fit for
service. Opposed to these were 41 Spanish and about 50 French ships, but these
were not concentrated. On land, at that date, whereas our scattered army was under
30,000 strong, the Spanish had one of 130,000, the French of over 300,000. See
Richmond, *The Navy in War of 1739–48*, i. 14, 15.

[2] See Clowes, iii. 8–12; Hannay, *Short History of R. Navy*, ii. 81–82.

[3] Between 1722 and 1725 the old admiralty building in Whitehall was being
rebuilt and the board found a temporary home in St. James's Square. See Clowes,
iii. 2.

[4] Sir Charles Wager, 1666–1743, captured a treasure-fleet at Cartagena in 1708,
commanded in the Baltic 1726 and off Cadiz 1727–8; first lord of admiralty
1733–42.

Anson was brought in to contribute some naval experience. Thereafter till 1762 either Anson or Boscawen was always on the board, Anson himself being first lord, except for a few months' interval, from 1751 to 1762, greatly to the advantage of the training, organization, and fighting spirit of the navy.

The fleet was manned predominantly by the press-gang, which recruited by force from the sea-faring populace. In addition able-bodied seamen were induced to volunteer by the offer of bonuses ranging from 20s. to 100s.[1] Some such forcible or pecuniary inducements were needed to procure the men for a service attended with such hardships and with poor prizes. The pay offered them was but 19s. to 24s. a month,[2] and for most of this period even that scanty sum was not payable until their return to England, when it was still liable to deductions by agents, the navy pay department, or even their own officers. Among the many reforms, however, for which Anson was responsible was an act of 1758[3] which ensured prompt payment of wages, allowed the seamen to assign part of their wages to their families, and stopped the exactions of agents. The food on board was often scanty and of the poorest quality,[4] made up for by over-generous allowances of liquor, each man being entitled to a gallon of beer a day in home waters, a quart of wine in the Mediterranean, and half a pint of raw spirits on the West Indian station, until Vernon[5] introduced the now familiar grog (so named from his well-known grogram cloak) of a quart of water mixed with the half-pint of spirits. The men's quarters, too, were unbelievably cramped and insanitary, and their treatment on some ships by junior and even senior officers atrociously brutal. The insanitary quarters and bad food were a prolific source of scurvy and, in tropical climates, of deadly fevers, which often took toll of more than half a ship's crew;

---

[1] An act raising the bounty to 100s. was passed in 1741 (14 Geo. II, c. 38), after protests in the commons against a more stringent form of impressment through the justices. *P.H.* xii. 26–143.

[2] These were the rates fixed in 1653 and apparently left unaltered for the succeeding century. See Clowes, ii. 98, 236.

[3] This act (31 Geo. II, c. 10) was largely the work of George Grenville as treasurer of the navy.

[4] Orders were frequently given for the men to be put on 'six upon four' (i.e. three-quarter) rations owing to the inadequate supply. *Hist. MSS. Comm.*, *Ducane*, xii. On the other hand Hosier off Cartagena, finding that the bread was 'on the decay' ordered a 'whole allowance . . . for a quicker expense'. Ibid., pp. 32, 35.

[5] Edward Vernon, 1684–1757, M.P. for Ipswich. See below, pp. 234–6.

how bad the medical service was may be seen even from the perhaps exaggerated account in *Roderick Random*.[1] The naval officers' sea-training, on the other hand, was pretty thorough. They came to sea between the ages of twelve and fourteen, either on the king's nomination as 'king's letter boys' ('volunteers per order'), or in the capacity of servants to captains or admirals as 'volunteers'. After passing through the ranks of able-bodied seamen and midshipmen for periods up to six or seven years, they obtained the rank of third lieutenant after passing before a board of naval officers a fairly stiff practical and theoretical examination.[2] In 1733 a naval academy was opened at Portsmouth for forty of the 'volunteers per order', where they were put through a more systematic training.[3] On board the junior ranks of the officers were herded together in barely less cramped quarters than the men, the only roomy cabins being monopolized by the captains and admirals. They indeed lived in great state with their cooks, servants, volunteers, and chaplain to attend on them.[4]

At the beginning of this period neither officers nor men had any distinctive uniform to promote an *esprit de corps*. The men, indeed, had all their clothes burned, for sanitary reasons, when they were thrust on board by the press-gang, and had to obtain slop clothes of varying patterns, chiefly red breeches or trousers, grey jackets, striped waistcoats, and checkered shirts, delivered by contractors, the price being deducted from the men's pay. The officers could, and did, deck themselves in any finery they chose until 1748, when standard patterns of uniforms were introduced by George II.[5] As contrasted with the small pay given to

[1] Thanks to the scientific skill and enthusiasm of J. Lind great improvements were made in naval hygiene during this period. See pp. 392–3.

[2] The Hon. Sam. Barrington, after serving for over five years as a 'volunteer' without pay, had to produce to a board of captains his journals and certificates from his previous commanders and to pass a stiff examination in the practice and theory of navigation before obtaining his commission. See *Barrington Papers* (Navy Records Soc.), 1937, i. 4–5.

[3] The Order in Council establishing the new academy was issued in 1729. See E. P. Statham, *The Story of the Britannia*, 1904, pp. 6 sqq. This system of training was not popular and the forty places were seldom filled. See Michael Lewis, *A Social History of the Navy*, p. 144.

[4] Hogarth's picture in the Royal Maritime Museum, of 'Lord George Graham in his Cabin', with his cook, his negro, his chaplain, his jovial toady, and his dogs, illustrates a fashionable captain's easy life on board.

[5] See Clowes, iii. 20; *Hist. MSS. Comm., Ducane*, pp. 22–23, 28–29; and especially G. E. Manwaring, *The Flower of England's Garland*, 1936, pp. 156–91. I am also indebted to Mr. Manwaring for other suggestions on this section. [Note of 1939].

the sailors and junior officers, the latter receiving only £73–91 per annum, the senior captains were entitled to £365 with allowances and the admirals from £640 to £1,825 also with allowances.[1] The contrast was all the more glaring in the distribution of prize-money in accordance with a declaration of the king in 1744 that the value of all prizes taken by the navy should be the property of the officers and crews of the captors. Many of the admirals, such as Wager, became rich men from the prize-money they obtained, while the men had to be content with mere pittances. For example, as a result of the prizes taken during the capture of Havana in 1762, Sir George Pocock the admiral and Lord Albemarle the general each obtained no less than £122,697. 10s. 6d., the captains in the fleet each £1,600. 10s. 10d., the petty officers £17. 5s. 3d., and each seaman and marine only £3. 14s. 9¼d.[2] No wonder that at Trafalgar an Irish sailor was found praying that the enemy's bullets should be distributed on the same scale as the prize-money— the lion's share to the officers.[3]

By 1739 nearly all the senior officers in the service had seen their best days. The system of promotion to flag-rank was still strictly by seniority, and, as the number of admirals was then limited to nine, most of them were old men with out-of-date experience and lacking in vigour. Wager, the first lord of the admiralty, and Norris, the commander-in-chief of the channel fleet, had both attained flag-rank in 1707, and by 1739 were aged respectively seventy-three and seventy-nine; Mathews, after nearly twenty years of retirement from sea-service, was, unfortunately for the country and himself, made a vice-admiral at the age of sixty-six and entrusted with the command of the Mediterranean fleet in 1742, in succession to Haddock, his junior by ten years; nor did Lestock, Mathews's mutinous second in command, do anything to merit his promotion: in fact Vernon, fifty-five when he was suddenly made a vice-admiral in 1739, was almost the only one among the seniors who really distinguished himself in his command. From 1743, however, this bad system of flag-promotion was altered by gradually increasing the number of admirals, and in 1747 by getting rid of the

[1] These rates of pay, which were fixed in 1700, were calculated on a daily basis. In the cases cited above junior officers received 4s. to 5s. a day, captains £1 a day, and admirals from £1. 15s. to £5 a day. See Clowes, ii. 235 and iii. 20.

[2] See Clowes, iii. 18, 249.

[3] Quoted by Hannay, ii. 386.

superannuated captains' claims by promoting senior captains to the flag-list on half-pay.[1]

Fortunately the opportunity of war encouraged a band of younger men who began to illustrate this century as one of the most glorious in our naval annals. Foremost among them, as the trainer and inspirer of this finer breed of sailors, must be placed George Anson. His voyage round the world illustrates, not only the defects of the admiralty system of 1739–40, but more especially what one quiet, efficient, and determined man could accomplish despite the system. One of the government's original plans in 1739 was that two squadrons should set forth, one under Commodore Anson eastwards to Manila, the other under Commodore Cornewall to the same tryst but westwards round the Horn, with orders to both to pick up any galleons or other Spanish treasure-ships and otherwise 'vex' the Spaniards on their way. Cornewall's part was then dropped and Anson left to circumnavigate the globe alone, starting round Cape Horn. But so much time was wasted by the admiralty in furnishing instructions and completing the complement of ships and men for Anson's squadron that the Spaniards got wind of the intended surprise and had ample time to prepare for its reception. The instructions dated January 1739/40 did not reach Anson till 28 June, and even then there were intolerable delays in providing him with the ships, crews, soldiers, and stores he needed. Of the 300 sailors which Admiral Balchen was to send him to complete his complement only 170 could be spared; instead of Bland's regiment and three independent companies promised to provide his storming parties,[2] he was allotted 500 invalids from Chelsea, of whom all those able to walk disappeared in Portsmouth, leaving only 259 almost bedridden men to embark.[3] Finally he got off on 18 September, just about three months too late to catch the favourable season for rounding the Horn. Anson's flagship was the *Centurion* of 60 guns with a crew of 400, and accompanying him were two 50-, one 48-, one 28-gun ships and a sloop of 8 guns, with two pinks as victuallers.

[1] The first officers so promoted on half-pay were captains dating from 1713. Clowes, ii. 20.

[2] There was as yet no permanent establishment of marines, companies being raised for war purposes and disbanded thereafter. In 1755, 50 companies of marines were formed intended to be always available for service afloat; during the Seven Years war these were expanded until they numbered 18,000 men. Hannay ii. 144.

[3] Not one of these lived to see England again.

Fortunately the more powerful Spanish fleet sent to intercept him was later still in starting, missed him off the east coast of South America, and was destroyed by storms. In the appalling passage round the Horn the squadron was scattered, Anson being the first to arrive in June 1741 at the island of Juan Fernandez, hitherto erroneously charted, whose rare visitors included Alexander Selkirk in 1704 and his rescuer, Woodes Rogers, privateer and finally colonial governor.[1] Here Anson was re-joined by the *Trial* sloop, of 8 guns, the *Gloucester* of 50, and the *Anna* pink: two of his ships had been forced to put back to Brazil; one alone, the *Wager* of 28 guns, was broken up on the rocks and only four of its company got back to England.[2] But scurvy had proved even more fatal than the storms off Cape Horn, for at Juan Fernandez the crews of the *Centurion*, *Gloucester*, and *Trial* had by its ravages been reduced from the 961 with which they started to 335. Nevertheless, after refitting, Anson captured a treasure-ship and a town on the coast of Peru, and reached Macao in China after more sufferings. Anson himself had been struck down by scurvy, and the two other ships had to be scuttled and the crews transferred to the *Centurion*. One more prize, the galleon *Nuestra Senora de Cabadongo*, with a crew of 600 and heavily armed, was captured off the Philippines, and finally Anson with the *Centurion* reached Spithead on 15 June 1744 after a voyage of three years and nine months. The captured treasure, worth over £500,000, was carried to London in a triumphal procession recalling the days of Elizabeth.

This adventurous voyage was valuable not chiefly for its material achievements or for the comparatively slight damage it inflicted on the Spaniards, but above all for the magnificent courage shown by the seamen, and the wonderful example set by Anson himself during the whole expedition. Unlike many of the commanders of that era he made himself one with his men, helping to carry the sick to land, working at carpentry or any odd job ashore, and inspiring officers and men with his example. During the voyage he took careful notes of these comparatively uncharted seas and coasts, picking out, for

---

[1] See Manwaring, pp. 105-7. Dampier, who piloted Rogers, had visited the island twice in the 1680's.

[2] Some of the crew, who had mutinied after the wreck, reached Lisbon via Brazil. See Clowes, iii. 321-2.

example, the Falkland islands as a suitable base for our fleets; and throughout he was a model of good seamanship and cheerful courage as well as of a noble courtesy to prisoners, unexpected by the Spaniards, more accustomed to the rough brutalities of some of our buccaneers. But the greatest benefit that he conferred on the navy and his country by this voyage was the training he gave to the young officers of the squadron who accompanied him, and the care he took that their merit should be recognized.[1] Charles Saunders, Peircy Brett, Denis, Augustus Keppel, Hyde Parker, J. Campbell, Byron, all of them his pupils, and admirals all sooner or later, lived to illustrate the spirit imbibed from this great commander.[2] Even in the portraits of these admirals and some of their contemporaries, Vernon, Hawke, Boscawen, Rodney, one is at once struck with their keen, wiry, and alert figures and countenances, as contrasted with the heavy, well-fed appearance of their immediate predecessors, such as Norris, Haddock, Rooke, and even Cloudesley Shovel, one of the best of the old breed.

This more adventurous spirit in the younger men brought to the front in the two major wars of George II's reign is well illustrated by the gradual modification in practice of the *Fighting Instructions* for the fleet dating from 1703, and really based on Russell's *Instructions* of 1691. The underlying idea of these *Instructions* was to keep the fleet together when opposed to an enemy of approximately equal strength, and to prevent individual action by attempts of ships separately to break through the enemy's line and so weaken the general massed attack. This object was good as far as it went, but in practice the result was a slackening of individual initiative even when the enemy's fleet was inferior—as occurred in the battle of Hyères (or Toulon) of 1744,[3] and still more notably in Byng's action off

---

[1] Anson himself was made a rear-admiral on his return, but returned his commission until such time as the admiralty confirmed the commission as captain of the *Centurion* he had given during the voyage to Peircy Brett.

[2] In 1748 R. Walter, chaplain on the *Centurion*, published *A Voyage Round the World by George Anson*, compiled from notes taken on the voyage and information from Anson himself. It is only from occasional hints that one gathers from it the great part taken by Anson himself, a reserved man, not given to self-advertisement. Walter's authorship was disputed after his death by one Robins, with little justification. A model of the *Centurion*, made on Anson's orders in 1746, is to be seen in the National Maritime Museum, Greenwich.

[3] This failure was also apparently due to Lestock's ignoring of Mathews's signals, which were in conformity with the *Instructions*; see below, pp. 247–8.

Minorca in 1756[1]—and a wooden conformity to regulations by commanders too intent on 'safety first' and fearful of exercising their own discretion in abnormal circumstances. Fortunately in practice men like Vernon, Anson, Hawke, and Boscawen introduced bolder methods and encouraged, by *Additional Instructions*[2]—notably Anson's of 1747 and Boscawen's of 1759— tactical initiative in their subordinates. Anson, in his long watch in the Bay for de la Jonquière's fleet in 1747, kept his fleet practising manœuvres for a month, and, when de la Jonquière at last appeared, changed the correctly formal line into a general chase, in which each English ship was left to its own devices. Hawke, in his engagement five months later with Létanduère, successfully carried out the same tactics, and at Quiberon showed the new spirit in the navy by his remark to his pilot: 'You have done your duty in showing me the danger, now you will obey orders and lay me aside the *Soleil Royal*'; a remark to be capped by the rejoinder of Boscawen, 'wry-necked Dick' as the men called him,[3] to the officer who called him up at night, saying, 'Sir, there are two large ships which look like Frenchmen bearing down on us, what are we to do?'— 'Do, damn 'em, fight 'em', as he came up on deck in his night-shirt.

[1] See Mahan, *Sea Power in History*, pp. 286-7. [In Byng's action the opposing fleets were virtually of equal strength since the French inferiority of one ship of the line was made up by their superior weight of guns. Corbett argues strongly against the suggestion, here adopted by Professor Williams on the powerful authority of Mahan, that Byng was 'hidebound in the stereotyped *Fighting Instructions*'. See Corbett, *Seven Years War*, i. 115-23. C.H.S.]

[2] See *Navy Records*, 1905, *Fighting Instructions 1580-1816*, with Julian Corbett's valuable Introduction. Anson's *Additional Instructions* have not survived, but Corbett shows that they were in existence by the time of his action against de la Jonquière in 1747. On Vernon see Richmond, i. 40-42, 112-13, and *Navy Records*, 1958, *Vernon Papers*, ed. B. L. Ranft.

[3] [This was because he carried his head on one side; he was also known as 'Old Dreadnought' from the name of the ship he commanded as a young captain. The story of his rejoinder to his officer of the watch, given above, while 'possibly true' is 'unsupported by any evidence'. See *Dictionary of National Biography*, under 'Boscawen'. C.H.S.]

IX

CARTERET AND THE PELHAMS

For more than two years after 1739 Walpole remained nominally in control during the initial stages of the war with Spain and of the continental war set going by Frederic of Prussia's sudden invasion of Silesia. By temperament a man of peace, he lacked the gifts for waging successful war, nor could he find them in the group of mediocrities he had gathered round him. He had now to pay the penalty for his ruthless rejection of all his ablest ministers, Pulteney, Carteret, Townshend, Chesterfield. For guidance on foreign affairs he had to depend chiefly on the dim lights of the duke of Newcastle. The chancellor, Hardwicke, his only colleague with any political insight, had no turn for executive action, and had been appropriated by Newcastle as his special crony and adviser. Instead of Chesterfield, one of the ablest of his opponents, whom he might have had for the asking, he brought Hervey, formidable in satire but a light-weight in council, into the cabinet as lord privy seal. For an essentially naval war with Spain, his chief professional adviser was Wager, first lord of the admiralty, an old man long past his work; the other veteran, Sir John Norris,[1] called in to advise, though even more advanced in years, had a better conception of naval strategy and a more active mind, but was rarely able to bring the discussions in the regency or the cabinet to the point of decisive action. To add to the difficulties in the way of prompt decisions, during 1740 and 1741 George II refused to forgo his beloved sojourns in Hanover, absences which involved further delays in correspondence. Lastly Walpole himself had lost grip and the power of imposing his will even on matters which he deemed essential, such as the primary duty of safeguarding the kingdom against invasion. 'What, may not one poor ship be left at home?' he exclaimed in a painful scene recorded by Newcastle, who had proposed denuding the home fleet for the ill-conceived expedition to Cartagena; but, on

[1] Sir John Norris, c. 1660–1749, in command in Baltic 1715–16 and 1718–19, admiral and commander-in-chief 1734.

Newcastle's persisting, he gave up the struggle: 'I oppose nothing, I give into everything, and yet, God knows, I dare not do what I think right . . . I *dare not*, I *will not* make any alterations. . . . Let them go, let them go.'[1] Such an outburst only confirms the impression derived from Hervey's reports and Norris's diary, as to the almost incredibly trivial and inconclusive discussions in the regency and the council as to the manning of the navy, plans of operation, instructions to the admirals, and the equipment of the fleets.[2] Even Newcastle himself is fain to admit that 'it is thought by some that I take too much upon me and spend the time of the Regency in unnecessary discourse'.[3]

A cabinet such as this was not fitted to deal with the difficult strategic problems that arose. A war with Spain was bound to be almost entirely naval, its objects being to harass the enemy's trade and to seize some of the Spanish colonies in America or the Philippines. For these ends it was necessary not only to attack Spain's commerce and possessions on the high seas, but also to keep a watchful eye on her ports, so as to blockade her fleets and prevent her trade coming to harbour. There was also the attitude of France to be taken into account. From the very outset this was a matter of serious concern to the ministry. Fleury had taken an early opportunity of declaring that he would not view with indifference any conquest by England of Spanish possessions: the Family Compact of 1733 had been strengthened by the recent marriage of Don Philip of Parma with Louis XV's eldest daughter and active negotiations were said to be proceeding between the two crowns for trade and even territorial advantages to Spain and France at England's expense.[4] It was known too that there was considerable activity in the dockyards of Brest and Toulon, which might portend a substantial reinforcement for Spain both in the Atlantic and the Mediterranean.

By 1740, indeed, the fatal results of Walpole's policy of leaving the emperor in the lurch during the war of the Polish Succession

---

[1] Coxe, *Walpole*, i. 637. See also Yorke, *Hardwicke*, i. 248.
[2] See Hervey, *Memoirs*, iii. 927 sqq., and H. W. Richmond, *The Navy in the War of 1739-48*, i. 31-37, 73-86, quoting from Norris's Diary in Add. MSS. 28132-5.
[3] Add. MS. 35406, f. 274. Printed in Yorke, i. 237.
[4] Add. MS. 32800, ff. 132, 262; 32802, f. 176. See also A. M. Wilson, *French Foreign Policy . . . 1726-43*, pp. 318-26; *British Diplomatic Instructions*, vi, *France*, pp. 219-20, 227, 236.

were only too apparent. The power and prestige of our most dangerous enemy, France, had been immensely enhanced by her unhampered military successes in Germany and Italy and her acquisition of the reversion of Lorraine by the treaty of Vienna of 1738, while our chief continental ally, the emperor, had been weakened and estranged. Nor was that all, for a year later the emperor, after a brief war with the Turks, had been jockeyed by the French ambassador, Villeneuve, into the treaty of Belgrade, whereby he gave up nearly all the Austrian gains from Turkey by the treaties of Carlowitz of 1699 and Passarowitz of 1718; while France, by the capitulations of 1740, had regained her political and commercial dominance in Turkey. That acute observer, Frederic II, at the beginning of his *Mémoires*, though not blind to the weakness of Louis XV's personal government, points out that in 1740 France, 'respectée au dehors'—owing to the prestige she had thus acquired, her well-trained army of 130,400 regulars and 36,000 militia, her fleet of 80 men-of-war and its 60,000 sailors, and her revenue of 60,000,000 crowns—'était l'arbitre de l'Europe'.[1]

When the war began Admiral Haddock,[2] based on Port Mahon, had no more than ten ships of the line with which to watch the Spanish coast from Cartagena on the east, past Cadiz on the west to the northern ports of Santander and Ferrol; and with such a force naturally he had much ado to blockade a Spanish fleet of thirteen ships reported to be in Cadiz and to intercept the Spanish trade with the West Indies.[3] In the Western hemisphere Commodore Brown had eight ships to patrol West Indian waters and protect the American coast colonies. The home fleet under Admiral Norris, formidable in numbers, but desperately under-manned and ill equipped, had not only to provide against invasion but to supply reinforcements for Haddock and the West Indies, besides watching Brest. Early in the course of hostilities the first Spanish treasure-ships were snug in Santander a month before the squadron sent from England to intercept them was aware of their safe arrival. Similar mismanagement delayed Anson's departure on his voyage round the Horn for three critical months.[4] One small

---

[1] Frédéric II, *Mémoires*, 2 vols., Paris, 1866, i. 24–25.

[2] Nicholas Haddock, 1686–1746, distinguished at Vigo 1702, Passaro 1718.

[3] Haddock's solitary success against the Spaniards was his capture of two rich treasure-ships, said to be worth £200,000, in Oct. 1739 (23 and 29 Sept. O.S.).

[4] See above, p. 227.

success, however, marked the opening phase of the war, but for this the ministry could take little credit. During the numerous debates in the commons on Spanish outrages one of the most pertinacious critics of the government's inaction was Captain Edward Vernon,[1] who had insisted on Spain's weakness and declared that with six ships he could capture Porto Bello, a favourite nest of the hated *guarda-costas*. Taken at his word in July 1739 he was promoted vice-admiral and given eight ships, reduced before he reached the West Indies by detachment for other services to five.[2] His instructions required him only to burn the shipping in Spanish ports such as Porto Bello;[3] but, though its fortifications looked formidable enough, Vernon by a bold and well-conceived attack captured it on 22 November 1739 after only two days' fighting. This first success made Vernon the hero of the hour, especially with the opposition; he was thanked by both houses, medals were struck in his honour, mugs and public houses decorated with his effigy, and the freedom of the City conferred on him when he returned two years later.

Vernon himself, one of the most enlightened sailors of his day, advised the ministry to be content with a formidable fleet in West Indian waters, 'by which means, let who will possess the country, our Royal Master may command the wealth of it', instead of attempting further conquests by costly land expeditions in an unhealthy climate.[4] Nevertheless Whitehall insisted on a joint naval and military expedition to capture Spanish strongholds—Cartagena or Cuba itself—in the West Indies. The best chance of success for such a policy was a prompt dispatch of the expedition before the Spaniards had time to repair their defences: instead of which more than a year passed before Vernon received the necessary naval and military reinforcements.

---

[1] See above, p. 224.

[2] Brown joined him with one ship in time for the attack on Porto Bello, so that its capture was achieved with the exact force he had called for. Richmond, i. 46.

[3] Richmond, i. 41.

[4] Vernon to Newcastle, 31 Oct. 1739; it seems doubtful whether Newcastle revealed this advice to his colleagues, see Richmond, i. 44, 101–2. On his return to England Vernon, resolved to tell the king 'what no ministry would tell him, for they flatter the king in his passions', took the opportunity of half an hour's audience to assure him that his 'security lay in being master of the sea, and that when he ceased so to be, his land army could not preserve him'. The king was 'not pleased, answering that soldiers were necessary'. *Hist. MSS. Comm., Egmont Diaries*, iii. 280.

Newcastle, responsible for giving orders to the fleet, when asked by Hardwicke to explain the delay in sending off Ogle with the reinforcements for Vernon, replied: 'You ask me, why does not Sir Chaloner Ogle sail? I answer because he is not ready. If you ask another question, Why is he not ready? To that I cannot answer.'[1]

The fleet of 30 of the line,[2] with 10,000 soldiers aboard, assembled under Vernon's command in January 1741, was the largest yet sent by any power to the West Indies, but almost from the outset seemed doomed to the fate of the Athenian expedition to Syracuse. It was a calamity that Lord Cathcart, in command of the troops, died on arrival at Dominica and was succeeded by General Wentworth, an obstinate and inexperienced officer without imagination or initiative. Two months were spent in preparations before Cartagena was reached.[3] Vernon and his fleet did more than their share in reducing the forts commanding the harbour, and making easy the landing of the soldiers, but Wentworth wasted invaluable time laying out camps, preparing batteries, and advancing with elaborate precautions, instead of rushing the outlying forts which the Spaniards abandoned on the first attack, and finally, when a clear road to the city was open, allowing himself to be held up by a puny fort through the incompetence of his gunners. Meanwhile the men were dying like flies in the unhealthy climate, and after this last unnecessary delay Vernon was obliged in April to re-embark, the force reduced, chiefly by fever, from 8,000 to 3,500. After resting and refitting at Jamaica in July he persuaded Wentworth to make an attempt on Santiago de Cuba, but here again the general's pedantic obstinacy and want of initiative during four months led to a similar fiasco. One more attempt, to capture Panama by troops which were to be landed at Porto Bello on the other side of the isthmus, was abandoned by Wentworth in April 1742 'before a soldier's foot had been put on shore'.[4] At the end of the year, when events on the Continent had thrown the original quarrel with Spain into the shade, both Vernon and Wentworth were recalled to England, and no

[1] Add. MS. 35406, f. 253 (3 Oct. 1740). See also Yorke, *Hardwicke*, i. 250.
[2] Reduced at once to 29 when the *Augusta* lost her rudder leaving harbour. See Richmond, i. 106, n. 2.
[3] Much of this delay was caused by Vernon's uncertainty as to the whereabouts of the French squadron in the West Indies. See Richmond, i. 110.
[4] Richmond, i. 132.

further expeditions on the grand scale were attempted in the West Indies.[1]

Meanwhile in Europe the preparations for the French fleet in Brest and the massing of the Spanish squadrons in Ferrol during 1740 had been causing justifiable alarm in England. In April a small squadron under Sir John Balchen was sent to watch Ferrol but was recalled the next month. In June, Ogle's detachment from Haddock's fleet, which had been cruising off Cadiz, was also recalled. These ships together with such others as could be got ready for sea formed the home fleet under Sir John Norris who was now ordered to put to sea to prevent the junction of the French and Spanish fleets or any attempt at the invasion of England on behalf of the Pretender; for rumours were afoot that the duke of Ormonde, that stormy petrel of the Jacobites, was hovering about the neighbourhood of Ferrol. But months were spent in sending Norris orders and counter-orders and in contriving means to man his fleet; and, when all was ready, he was kept in the Channel by contrary winds till news came in September that both the Brest and Ferrol fleets had come out and sailed to the West Indies. He was then ordered to strike his flag and return to the council. The next month the fleet, now under Ogle's command, sailed to reinforce Vernon, taking the troops for the Cartagena expedition in escort. Fortunately the French and Spanish fleets did not coalesce, so that Vernon was not forced to deal with their overwhelming joint force.[2]

Already by the end of 1740 Frederic's sudden attack on Silesia indicated that the war would not long be confined to a duel between England and Spain. It had also at one blow shattered the Pragmatic Sanction, that edifice of cards so painfully built up for more than twenty years by the Emperor Charles VI to safeguard his young daughter Maria Theresa's undisturbed succession to the Habsburg possessions. Since 1713, when it was first promulgated, every state in the empire, including Prussia and Hanover, and almost every other ruler in Europe, including those of France, Spain, and England, had solemnly promised by treaty to observe the Pragmatic Sanction. But

---

[1] Richmond, i. 101–37, gives the best account of this disastrous campaign.

[2] Richmond again, i. 73–97, is useful for details of the English council's bewilderment and changes of plan.

hardly was the emperor in his grave before Frederic of Prussia and the electors of Bavaria and Saxony found excuses for repudiating their engagements, and when the hunt was up pretexts came easy to France and Spain for doing the like. Fleury himself indeed was for peace and for honouring France's obligations incurred so recently as 1738 for the valuable *quid pro quo* of Lorraine; but he was getting old and, like Walpole, losing grip.[1] Meanwhile the hot-heads of the court, led by Belleisle, were clamouring for a final reduction of the hereditary enemy to impotence. Belleisle was given full rein, and in his notable tour through Germany[2] secured alliances for France with various princes of the empire, including Frederic himself, with the object of securing the election of Charles Albert of Bavaria as emperor and partitioning the Habsburg dominions in Germany. Spain followed suit with claims on the Habsburg possessions in Italy. Maria Theresa in her distress called for aid from Holland, Russia, Savoy, and England. The Dutch were slow to move; Russia was preoccupied with a Swedish war and with dynastic troubles; Charles Emmanuel of Savoy was open to the highest bidder for his co-operation.

England had guaranteed the Pragmatic Sanction by the treaty of Vienna of 1731, but her relations with the emperor Charles VI had been sensibly cooler since Walpole's desertion of him during the war of the Polish Succession. Now, however, she had every inducement to respond to Maria Theresa's appeal for help when her own enemies, France and Spain, were joining the combination against the queen. Apart from that, too, a generous feeling of sympathy had manifested itself in England for the gallant young woman, beset by a hungry crowd of claimants bent on profiting from her weakness. Walpole, not too willingly, was obliged to bow to the popular feeling, and in April 1741 proposed a vote of £300,000 as a subsidy to Maria Theresa. At the same time a contingent of Danish and Hessian troops in England's pay was to go to support her.[3] George II, as elector of Hanover, was naturally disposed to look with a jealous eye on his neighbour Frederic's aggrandizement, and was only too ready at first to support his victim. But when the beloved

[1] Part of Fleury's weakness arose from the loss of his hold on Louis XV.
[2] Amusingly described by the duc de Broglie in *Frédéric II et Marie Thérèse*, 2 vols., 1883, i. 273 sqq.
[3] This contribution of 12,000 troops represented England's obligation under her guarantee of the Pragmatic Sanction.

electorate was threatened by French troops, he hastily concluded a treaty in September for the neutralization of Hanover and even agreed not to cast his electoral vote for Maria Theresa's husband Francis of Lorraine.[1] Walpole for his part persuaded the young queen in the following month to agree to the convention of Klein-Schnellendorf with Frederic, whereby for the cession of Silesia she obtained a breathing-space.

After Walpole's belated resignation in February 1742 he had enough influence in the closet to secure a government composed largely of men of his own choice.[2] From the old ministry still remained Newcastle and his brother Henry Pelham, Hardwicke, Harrington, and the duke of Devonshire. Pulteney, his chief opponent in the commons, developed scruples about accepting a place and was persuaded to lose all influence by taking a peerage as earl of Bath. At the treasury Walpole was succeeded as first lord by his former rival Spencer Compton, now earl of Wilmington, a nonentity, and as chancellor of the exchequer by Sandys, the 'motion-maker' against him, of whom little further was heard. The only important change was the return of Carteret to his old office as secretary of state. None of these new ministers was anxious to press the charges against him of corruption and bribery so freely bandied about in recent debates and pamphlets; and the earnest young men of the Cobham group, Pitt, Lyttelton, and the Grenvilles, carefully excluded from office, were obstructed in their endeavours to produce evidence of the charges against him in the fishing inquiry set up by the house of commons.[3]

For nearly three years Carteret in foreign policy was virtually 'sole minister', as Pitt denounced him in his philippics. During this period, and indeed for the rest of George II's reign, foreign affairs overshadowed those domestic interests which Walpole

[1] George II eventually voted for Charles Albert of Bavaria, who was crowned emperor in Feb. 1742.
[2] [The extent of Walpole's influence in remodelling the ministry is hard to assess. Owen points to the unfortunate absence of evidence on this problem in the Newcastle and Hardwicke papers and offers alternative solutions to it. At one point he argues that it was 'doubtless after full consultation with Walpole' that the king acted and that together they 'clearly outmanœuvred their opponents'. Subsequently he states that it was the Pelhams' 'plans for the reconstitution of the administration' which 'succeeded beyond their most sanguine hopes'. See Owen, *The Rise of the Pelhams*, pp. 88, 91, 94, 122. C.H.S.]
[3] For further details of the ministerial reorganization and the committee of inquiry into Walpole's actions see *Chatham*, i. 87–92, and Owen, l.c., pp. 87–125.

had made his special concern, and Carteret seemed to possess all the gifts needed for a great foreign minister. Not only a Greek and Latin scholar, he could read and converse in all the European languages that mattered for diplomacy, French, German, Spanish, and Scandinavian. In his brilliant missions to Stockholm and Copenhagen in 1719 he had proved his diplomatic skill and initiative, and had shown himself a forceful foreign secretary in 1721–4, till jockeyed out by the intrigues of Walpole and Townshend. With George II he found favour by his intimate knowledge of the constitution and complicated politics of the Holy Roman Empire;[1] and he was well justified in boasting, in answer to a presumptuous young peer who had ventured to lecture him on the constitution of the Empire, of 'my long acquaintance with the constitution of the Empire, which I understood before the noble lord, who has entertained you with a discourse upon it, was in being'.[2] But this favour of the king in the end proved his undoing, as he believed that, 'Give any man the crown on his side, and he can defy everything.'[3] Too aristocratic to stoop to party manœuvres, he infuriated his supporters by refusing to meet them at the Feathers Tavern, replying that 'he never dined at taverns'. To his colleagues in the ministry he showed the same aloofness, often refusing even to let them know to what he was committing them. Like a true Cornishman, indifferent, as is said, to what the rest of England was doing or thinking, he scorned the necessary condescensions of statesmen to secure the co-operation of fellow ministers, parliament, or people. Even foreign rulers, except the king of France, he was inclined to treat with the same haughty disdain, Frederic II bitterly observing in 1742 'qu'on traite les autres (princes) en petits garçons'.[4] But, at least, to start with, he gave a resolute direction to the country's policy, which in the nerveless hands of Walpole's dying ministry had lost all grip or definite aim. France, though still nominally at peace with Maria Theresa, had invaded Germany with a large army and occupied Prague; Frederic, after repudiating the convention of Klein-Schnellendorf, again attacked and defeated

---

[1] George II genuinely recognized and admired Carteret's outstanding capacity. In 1745 he described him as 'a man of the greatest abilities this country ever bred'. See Owen, p. 274.   [2] *P.H.* xii. 1061 n., 1085 (1 Feb. 1743).

[3] H. Walpole to Mann, 26 Nov. 1744.

[4] Friedrich, *Correspondenz*, ii. 160 n. This phrase comes from a dispatch written by Podewils expressing agreement with Frederic's ideas.

the Austrians at Chotusitz; Haddock in the Mediterranean had not been strong enough to interfere with the transport of a Spanish army to North Italy under the protective aegis of the French fleet from Toulon; Hanover's neutrality had bereft England of her only ally.

Carteret, who had 'adopted the principle that nothing in the world was impossible; and had found it his experience in life, that one had only to keep that principle before one and stick to it, if one wanted to arrive at a successful issue',[1] soon brought about a new spirit in the conduct of foreign affairs. He raised the subsidy to Maria Theresa from £300,000 to £500,000, persuaded George II to abandon the neutrality of Hanover[2] and, since as elector George professed himself too poor to pay his Hanoverian troops, took them, as well as a contingent of Hessians, into English pay. He brought to a favourable conclusion long-drawn-out negotiations with Russia by the treaty of December 1742, whereby Russia was to provide 12,000 men and England twelve men-of-war if either were attacked by a third power in their wars with Sweden and Spain respectively.[3] Above all, after reminding Frederic that he would 'much deceive himself if he thought the king would be . . . brought to abandon the liberties of Europe by the danger with which his German dominions might be menaced, since he could firmly rely on the weight and power of these kingdoms',[4] he secured his acceptance of the treaty of Berlin in July 1742,[5] thus once more freeing Maria Theresa from her most formidable enemy; and by the treaty of Westminster in the following November he obtained a defensive alliance with Frederic which he hoped would guarantee Hanover against French raids. The queen was also relieved of another enemy by Commodore Martin's threat, watch in hand,[6] of a bombardment of Naples unless Don Carlos

---

[1] J. C. Adelung, *Pragmatische Geschichte Europens*, Gotha, 1763, III. i. 294.

[2] Later admitted by Newcastle to be 'the best thing he ever did'. See Lodge, *Studies in 18th Century European Diplomacy*, p. 3, n.

[3] Martens, *Recueil des Traités: Russie–Angleterre* ix; *Royal Hist. Soc. Trans.* III. xiv. 169. P.R.O. Russia, 63, for correspondence with Tyrawley. See also *E.H.R.* xliii. 354–74.

[4] Add. MS. 22531, f. 7. This is taken from Carteret's instructions to Hyndford of Mar. 1742, which are quoted at length in Basil Williams, *Carteret and Newcastle*, pp. 127–8.

[5] Sometimes spoken of as the treaty of Breslau, where the preliminaries were settled in June.

[6] [Coxe said that Martin delivered his ultimatum 'laying his watch on the table'. Armstrong made this 'with watch in hand' and Professor Williams accepted the

agreed within half an hour to refrain from helping his brother
Don Philip in north Italy. But even to Carteret the obstinacy
of the Dutch at first proved insurmountable. He had sent an
army of English, Hanoverians, and Hessians under Lord Stair
to the low countries to create a diversion against the French for
Maria Theresa, but it needed a Dutch contingent to make it
effective. Even a personal visit from Carteret could not move the
Dutch to action in 1742; and for want of them this pragmatic
army, as it was called, never stirred from its quarters for the
whole of that year.

Until 1744 France was no more officially at war with England
than she was with Maria Theresa: nevertheless there was
nothing to prevent French and English armies meeting in battle
purely as auxiliaries of the Bavarian emperor or the queen of
Hungary respectively. Carteret, however, realized, as no one
else did, except perhaps Pitt, that France was the real enemy.
'Vous voudriez donc, milord, nous obliger à une paix honteuse',
said the French envoy to him in 1742; to which Carteret cheerfully replied, 'Sans doute, et c'est mon unique préoccupation
depuis que je suis dans les affaires: et je me flatte même d'y
réussir.'[1] With this object he had detached Frederic from the
combination against the queen. With the same object he did his
utmost to detach the emperor from his French allies and gain
Charles Emmanuel, king of Sardinia, for Maria Theresa as a
firm supporter in Italy, hoping thereby to crush the Bourbons in
their two main spheres of operations. Unfortunately Frederic,
in his own interests and as a claimant to a predominant place in
the empire, had other views. He had been willing enough to
accept French aid to enable him to establish himself in Silesia
and dispossess the Habsburgs of their German pre-eminence;
and having secured his immediate object he had no further use
for the French in Germany. But he was equally opposed to any
interference in German affairs from Carteret's motley pragmatic army—reinforced at last in 1743 by a Dutch as well as an
Austrian contingent—especially if it tended to restore the Habsburg dominance. So, in spite of their recent treaties, Carteret
and Frederic were at cross purposes during 1743 and 1744.

improvement. Martin's own account, cited by Richmond, seems to indicate
that he did neither. See Coxe, *House of Bourbon*, iii. 335; Armstrong, *Elisabeth
Farnese*, p. 365; and Richmond, i. 214–15. C.H.S.]
   [1] Friedrich, *Correspondenz*, ii. 301–2.

1743, however, was Carteret's *annus mirabilis*, in which it looked as though he would carry all before him. On 27 June the pragmatic army was set in motion under the direct command of the king, with Carteret as minister in attendance. From its camp at Aschaffenburg on the Main it marched out, some 37,000 strong, along the right bank of the river to join up with the 6,000 Hessians and 6,000 Hanoverians encamped at Hanau. The French army of between 60 and 70,000 under marshal Noailles was on the left bank of the river marching parallel with and keeping George's army in view. Half-way to Hanau, on the king's side of the river, lay the village of Dettingen protected by woods to the north and by a marshy ravine crossing the road by which the king was advancing. Noailles sent his nephew Grammont with 23,000 men across the river on pontoons to occupy the village, with strict injunctions not to go forward to the ravine, while he himself bombarded the pragmatic army from the southern bank. On arriving before the French position at Dettingen George halted his army for three hours, when Grammont, losing patience, abandoned his favourable position and launched a cavalry attack across the marshy ravine. After breaking through a regiment of dragoons the French cavalry was held up by George's infantry on the left of the allies. Thereupon the king, dismounting and 'sword in hand', led the English and Hanoverian infantry on the right against the advancing French infantry routed them and put them to flight across the Main, where many were drowned. In this battle the French loss was some 4,800, double that of George's army; but, having no supplies for his troops, the king had to hasten on to Hanau, leaving his wounded to the care of the French. Nevertheless Dettingen had the result of forcing Noailles to recross the Rhine for the defence of his own country. Carteret in his paean of triumph addressed to Newcastle naturally made the most of an engagement which was the last in which an English king took part in person, and gave special prominence to the king's valour.[1] In England George II gained

---

[1] Add. MS. 22536, f. 87. Carteret himself was dissatisfied with the style of this dispatch, written hurriedly from camp, and said of it: 'Here is a letter, expressed in terms not good enough for a tallow-chandler to have used', Boswell's *Johnson* (for the year 1780). There is a good description of Dettingen in Arneth, *Maria Theresia*, ii. 259–61. [See also Coxe, *Pelham*, i. 65–71, Fortescue, *History of the British Army*, ii. 93–102, and Rex Whitworth, *Field Marshal Lord Ligonier*, Oxford, 1958, pp. 73–76. There is much confusion in these authorities about the numbers engaged. C.H.S.]

a short-lived popularity by this action, soon dissipated, however, by the tales reported from the front of his partiality for his
Hanoverian troops. Nor was the flagging popularity of the
king and of his army revived by any fresh victories; for this was
the first and last exploit of the pragmatic army, which, it was
thought, when reinforced by the 12,000 at Hanau, might well
have given a final blow to Noailles. Carteret indeed, for the
rest of his time on the Continent, was too much taken up with
negotiations with the emperor and the king of Sardinia to have
time to plan more warlike adventures.

At the moment all seemed propitious for uniting the emperor
with the rest of Germany and so getting rid of France from the
empire—all except Frederic II, who had been left out of account.
Already before Noailles's retreat across the Rhine the French had
been driven out of Prague, and Maria Theresa's troops had even
expelled Charles VII from his Bavarian possessions. So beset
was the emperor that he could not even enter his imperial city
of Frankfort without the goodwill of Carteret and the pragmatic army. Shortly after the battle Prince William of Hesse,
brother of the king of Sweden, who had recently been appointed
by the emperor as his emissary to George II,[1] came to meet
Carteret with peace proposals on his behalf. Throughout 1742
he had been trying to get Carteret to persuade Maria Theresa
to yield to the emperor's demands for a portion of her Austrian
dominions, with the unalluring bait of the emperor's mediation
between England and Spain; early in June 1743, when the
emperor's fortunes had already begun to decline, he had
brought less exacting proposals to Carteret and George II
during their sojourn in Hanover on the way to the pragmatic
army, but was told that, beyond an assurance of safety in
Frankfort for the emperor and his family, no promise could be
made. At Hanau, where he met Carteret after Dettingen, he
brought still further reduced terms from a much-chastened
emperor, who agreed to dismiss his French allies on condition
that Maria Theresa should restore Bavaria to him and that,
since he had no resources, George II should provide him with
an allowance to support his imperial dignity. Throughout the
negotiations Carteret insisted that nothing could be concluded
without Maria Theresa's consent and gave little hope of an early
return of Bavaria, but promised that the king would do the best

[1] See Lodge, l.c., pp. 14–15.

he could for the emperor when his French allies had been dismissed. He even offered, as an earnest of sincerity, to pay the emperor 100,000 crowns forthwith and 200,000 more within forty days subject to the scheme being approved in London. Prince William, however, haggled over the immediate payment of 100,000 crowns on behalf of the emperor so that, even before Carteret received the adverse decision of his colleagues in London, the negotiations collapsed, no money was paid out, and no further meetings took place. Thus in fact nothing came of this diplomatic interlude. For Maria Theresa was not yet willing to give up Bavaria, while the English ministry calculated that it would be much better to allow the French to waste their money on the fugitive emperor than to bolster him up with a subsidy from the English taxpayer. The worst result of the incident was the estrangement of Frederic II, who had been kept out of a negotiation, in which as a leading German ruler he claimed a voice, and who, in the following year, returned to the fray against Maria Theresa.[1]

Far more important than the negotiation at Hanau was the next task Carteret set himself, to establish a firm alliance between Maria Theresa and Charles Emmanuel of Savoy, for in this was involved the balance of power not only in Italy but in the Mediterranean. Our fleet had not prevented two Spanish expeditions landing in Italy in 1741 and 1742, and with Don Carlos already established at Naples and the prospect of the other Infant Don Philip turning the Austrians out of Milan and Tuscany, the Mediterranean and even Minorca and Gibraltar might be entirely at the mercy of Bourbons in France, Spain, and Italy. So far Maria Theresa with the help of Savoy had kept head against the Spanish invaders of north Italy, and Commodore Martin, by his threat to bombard Naples, had prevented Don Carlos from helping his brother. But the

---

[1] For Prince William's various negotiations with Carteret, see Add. MSS. 22527 and 22536. Egged on by Frederic II in the following year, Prince William published his account of the Hanau business, casting all the blame on Carteret. Sir Richard Lodge (*Eng. Hist. Rev.* xxxviii. 509 sqq., and *Studies in European Diplomacy*, pp. 1–30) argued that Carteret was never in earnest about this negotiation, but merely played with Prince William until he had concluded his more important negotiation with Sardinia. As proof of Carteret's insincerity he suggests that Vienna was never informed of the emperor's terms, a point dwelt on by Frederic II and Prince William in their subsequent attack on him. But in fact Vienna was informed, as appears from a copy of Carteret's letter to William forwarded to Vienna on 8 Aug. 1743 and to be seen in the Vienna Archives, *Berichte, England*, 1743, no. 91. See also Owen, l.c., pp. 162–5, and *E.H.R.* xlix. 684–7.

convention of 1742 between Maria Theresa and Charles Emmanuel was subject to the curious proviso that the latter might at a
month's notice repudiate it when he chose, and France was now
tempting him by the dazzling offer of the Milanese to change
sides and support Don Philip. Meanwhile the Austrian ministers were haggling over the terms for converting the convention
into a firm treaty of alliance. At this point Carteret, though the
business really pertained to Newcastle's department,[1] intervened
in his masterful way. Taking charge of the triangular negotiations being carried on by the representatives of Maria Theresa,
Charles Emmanuel, and George II at Worms, he set himself to
persuade the Austrians to offer adequate immediate gains from
portions of their own territory to counterbalance the larger, but
only prospective, offer made by France. Finally, on Charles
Emmanuel's threat that he would accept the French offer,
Carteret persuaded the Austrians to agree to the treaty of
Worms with Savoy under England's guarantee (13 September
1743). Besides territorial gains at the expense of the Austrians
and Genoa Carteret promised Charles Emmanuel that his
subsidy of £200,000 from England should be continued until
the end of the war;[2] he made a similar promise to Maria Theresa
about her English subsidy of £300,000 and agreed that England should guarantee to her territorial compensation for the
loss of Silesia—telling her envoy Wasner with characteristic
bluntness that, as she held Bavaria, she had better stick to it
and say nothing about it.[3] In its immediate object of keeping
Charles Emmanuel faithful to the anti-Bourbon alliance Carteret's diplomacy was successful. But on the other hand it precipitated the treaty of Fontainebleau, whereby France, hitherto
merely a benevolent observer, made a close alliance with Spain
and enabled her for a time to gain the upper hand in Italy.
Moreover, as in the case of the 100,000 crowns offered to
the emperor at Hanau, Carteret's unconditional promise of
£300,000 to Maria Theresa was repudiated by the cabinet:[4]

[1] Austria was within Carteret's province but Savoy was not, so that neither had
exclusive claims to the negotiation. See Lodge, pp. 48–49.

[2] This £200,000 was originally taken from the £500,000 voted for the support of
Maria Theresa, who claimed therefore that it was her contribution. See above,
p. 240.

[3] The fullest account of the Worms negotiations is to be found in A. F. Přibram,
Oester: Staatsverträge, England, i. 597–630. See also Lodge, pp. 31–79.

[4] P.R.O. *Treaty Papers*, 115, for cabinet minute of 24 Nov. 1743. Printed in
Yorke, *Hardwicke*, i. 323–5.

Frederic II also was further alienated by the guarantee of compensation for Silesia, and he found another grievance in the omission of the treaty of Berlin among those formally confirmed. This alienation of Frederic was indeed the most unfortunate result of Carteret's diplomacy; indeed Frederic's sudden invasion of Bohemia in August 1744 was mainly due to his apprehensions caused by the Hanau and Worms negotiations.

This treaty was the last of Carteret's independent ventures. On his return to England in the autumn of 1743 he found himself hampered at every turn by his colleagues in the cabinet and the object of violent attacks in parliament. Already, on the death of the innocuous Wilmington at the end of June, the king had passed over Carteret's friend and nominee Lord Bath, and replaced him at the head of the treasury by Newcastle's brother, Henry Pelham.[1] Carteret, as was his wont, took the rebuff magnanimously and wrote a cordial, even affectionate, letter of congratulation to Pelham.[2] None the less it was a serious blow to his position in the cabinet, where his jealous colleague Newcastle was more strongly entrenched than ever with the support of his brother and his crony Hardwicke, who were, next to Carteret, the two ablest ministers. The cabinet as a whole had long been alienated by his 'obstinate and offensive silence' about his negotiations in Germany and gave him little help against his opponents in parliament. The most persistent and effective attacks on his policy, and especially on his taking the hated Hanoverian troops into English pay, were made in the house of commons, where Pitt surpassed even himself in his invectives against the 'Hanover troop-minister', 'an execrable, a sole minister, who had renounced the British nation and seemed to have drunk of the potion . . . which made men forget their country'.[3] It is unfortunate for Carteret, and incidentally for the delectation of later generations, that he could not meet Pitt and his other tormentors on the same ground, but had to defend himself in the house of lords, where the only opponent

[1] Pelham later superseded Sandys as chancellor of the exchequer, thus uniting once more the two offices of his master Walpole. [Carteret had not expected Bath to apply for the succession to Wilmington; when he did so, he felt bound in honour to support his claims with the king. See Owen, pp. 162–8. C.H.S.]

[2] Printed in Coxe, *Pelham*, i. 85.

[3] [Both these phrases were recorded by Philip Yorke in his parliamentary journal, the one from the debate of 19 Jan. 1744, the other from that of 1 Dec. 1743. See *P.H.* xiii. 465, 136. C.H.S.]

almost worthy of his steel was Chesterfield.[1] Here Carteret, almost unsupported by his colleagues, more than held his own in debate. When formal objection was taken to the Hanoverian grievance being brought up a second time in the same session and much time wasted on discussions about procedure, Carteret brushed aside all technicalities and welcomed the motion, remarking, 'I am, indeed, enabled by the happiness of a very vigorous constitution to support the fatigue of unseasonable hours; nor shall I feel any inconvenience from attending this debate beyond midnight . . . nor do I need any time for premeditating arguments which crowd upon me faster than I can utter them.'[2] He exposed as mendacious gossip the stories about favouritism to the Hanoverian troops, and the sneers at the pragmatic army's inactivity after Dettingen: 'if we have not slaughtered our enemies, we have obliged them to destroy themselves; if we have not stormed towns and citadels we have compelled those that had taken possession to evacuate them.'[3] Above all he insisted on his policy of seeing in France the 'enemy which equally in peace and war endeavours our destruction', with whom even the times of friendship are 'only an intermission of open hostilities'; but though we must take vigorous measures against them, we will not 'irritate our enemies with unnecessary provocations, [and should] imitate the French in mixing politeness with hostilities'.[4]

Soon, however, the country had graver matters than Hanover grievances to think of. The French, though still nominally at peace with us at the beginning of 1744, had given shelter in Toulon to a Spanish fleet intended to convey more troops for Don Philip in Italy. Haddock had retired from the command of our Mediterranean fleet in 1742 and been succeeded by Mathews,[5] ten years his senior, who was also accredited diplomatically to Charles Emmanuel. His chief business, however, was to watch the French and Spanish fleets as they came out of Toulon. In February 1744 they came out, and were followed in pursuit by Mathews with a slightly larger fleet. Unfortunately

---

[1] A famous pamphlet of 1742 *The Case of the Hanover Troops* was attributed among others to Chesterfield as well as to Pitt.   [2] *P.H.* xiii. 551 (27 Jan. 1744).
[3] Ibid. xiii. 120 (1 Dec. 1743). Noailles indeed had hastily recrossed the Rhine into France after Dettingen.   [4] Ibid. xiii. 122, 125.
[5] Thomas Mathews, 1676–1751, retired as a captain in 1724. Commissioner of the navy at Chatham 1736. Returned to service and promoted vice-admiral 1742. See above, p. 226.

Mathews and his second-in-command, Lestock,[1] were hardly on speaking terms. In the van some gallant work was done by Mathews himself and two of his captains, Cornewall of the *Marlborough* and Hawke of the *Berwick*; but Lestock with his detachment in the rear ignored his orders, which he professed not to understand, and took no part in the fight; nor did Mathews follow up the retreating enemy, who suffered little loss. This disgraceful failure aroused intense indignation in the nation and, on the demand of the commons in the following year, the two admirals, nine of the captains, and four lieutenants were tried by court martial; as a result, Mathews and several of the captains were cashiered, but Lestock, from his position perhaps the most in fault, was honourably acquitted.[2]

This battle of Hyères or Toulon, as it was called, was fought on 11 February 1744. Less than a fortnight later, on the 21st, England itself was scared by the appearance of Roquefeuil's Brest fleet off Dungeness, and the imminent danger of invasion by a still nominally friendly power.[3] For some months Marshal Saxe had been making secret preparations at Dunkirk for a Jacobite invasion which was to be covered by Roquefeuil's fleet; but the ministry had fortunately obtained an inkling of these plans[4] and had Norris on the watch with a superior fleet, which would probably have crushed Roquefeuil had not violent easterly gales, besides playing havoc with the Dunkirk flotilla of transports, driven the French fleet out of the Channel before Norris could come to grips with it. It was not, however, till March[5] that the absurdity of hostilities between powers nominally at peace was ended by formal declarations of war by Louis XV and George II and Louis XV and Maria Theresa against one another.

[1] Richard Lestock, *c.* 1679–1746.

[2] All the lieutenants and two of the captains were acquitted. Of the others two were placed on half-pay and five were cashiered, but only one of these permanently. Two other captains were to have been tried but one died and the other absconded. As between the admirals Clowes says 'Mathews blundered but his intentions were good. Lestock clung tightly to the dead letter of his duty, but his intentions were contemptible.' Clowes, iii. 103–6.

[3] Roquefeuil anchored off Dungeness on the night of 21 Feb. Norris did not have confirmation of this until the evening of the 23rd. See Richmond, ii. 72, 82.

[4] News of the sailing of the Brest fleet and of the arrival of the Young Pretender in France reached London on the same day—1 Feb. 1744. See Richmond, ii. 62.

[5] According to the New Style the French declaration was issued on 31 Mar., the English on 11 Apr.

But though the threat of a Jacobite invasion and open war with France had aroused the spirit of the nation, the ministry seemed quite incapable of rising to the occasion. Whereas Marshal Saxe, France's most brilliant general, was sent to conquer the Low Countries, they could find nobody better to command the motley and quarrelsome pragmatic army of English, Dutch, Austrians, and Hanoverians opposed to him than Marshal Wade, a good soldier in his time but now over 70, gouty, and exhausted by a few hours on horseback. For a time the allies escaped danger, as Saxe had to divert a large detachment to meet the Austrians invading Alsace. Then came another turn of the wheel. In May Frederic, alarmed at Maria Theresa's success and fearing for his possession of Silesia, had formed the Union of Frankfort, to which France adhered,[1] with the object of restoring Bavaria to Charles VII and securing his rights as emperor; in August he invaded Bohemia and captured Prague in September. Maria Theresa had therefore to recall her troops from Alsace, but even so failed to retain Bavaria: she also had to weaken her forces in Italy, with the result that Saxe was free to resume his conquest of the Low Countries, and the 'Gallispans', as the French and Spanish invaders of Italy were called, began to get the upper hand there also. In fact the great system of alliances contrived by Carteret, now Earl Granville,[2] with his treaties of Berlin, Westminster, and Worms was crumbling to pieces, largely through his own arrogant independence of action. The Pelham–Hardwicke clique, supported by most of the less important members of the cabinet, who resented his masterful dictation, seized the opportunity to indite a memorandum to the king demanding his dismissal. George II would willingly have kept him, for Granville was the minister after his own heart, sympathizing as he did with the king's ambition to play a leading part in imperial politics, and as ready as George himself to put his upstart cousin of Prussia in his place. But finally on 23 November 1744 George perforce accepted Granville's resignation.[3]

Granville's resignation enabled the Pelhams to bring some

---

[1] The French took an active part in organizing the Union and this adherence took the form of a guarantee of Silesia to Frederic. See C. T. Atkinson, *A History of Germany*, pp. 149–50.

[2] Carteret's mother, Lady Granville, died 18 Oct. 1744, whereupon he succeeded to the earldom.

[3] For the memorandum presented to the king on the need of change in foreign

new blood into the ministry. Harrington, their ally as president of the council, succeeded to Granville's office; places were found for several of the opposition, including even the Jacobite Sir John Hynde Cotton,[1] with Pitt's friends Lyttelton and George Grenville. Pitt himself, who had done more than anybody to upset Carteret, the king would not admit into this 'Broadbottom Administration' as it was called. This was scarcely odd considering Pitt's diatribes against the Hanoverian troops and veiled sarcasms even against the Royal Person. However, the almost equally obnoxious Chesterfield was allowed to have the government of Ireland and the admiralty board was strengthened by Hardwicke's son-in-law, Anson.[2] But neither was the policy of the government changed nor its success any greater in 1745. The obnoxious Hanover troops were no longer, it is true, to be directly paid for by England, but Maria Theresa was granted a larger subsidy in order to hire them and employ them as before in the mixed army of English, Dutch, and Austrians opposed to Saxe in Flanders. As commander-in-chief Wade, the septuagenarian, was superseded by the king's second son, Cumberland, a youth of barely 24.

The allied army numbered about 50,000, just over half that of Saxe, which contained the pick of the French regiments.[3] To save Tournai, one of the strongest places in the Low

policy and other incidents leading to Granville's resignation, see Coxe, *Pelham*, i. 154–90; Yorke, *Hardwicke*, i. 318–72; Owen, *Rise of the Pelhams*, pp. 223–38. [George II's final decision to accept Granville's resignation is usually ascribed to the advice of Orford and this is accepted by the most recent authority (Owen, l.c., p. 237). But it seems doubtful whether this was so. According to Coxe the king's appeal to Orford was made in the first instance at Granville's instigation. Suspecting this, Orford was reluctant to leave Norfolk, particularly as Pelham confirmed his suspicions. When the king persisted Orford at last set out for London and sent a letter supporting the Pelhams. But this letter can hardly have had much influence, as Dr. Plumb (its discoverer) says it was returned unanswered; it also appears to have arrived after the decision had been taken. See Coxe, *Walpole*, iii. 601–6; *Pelham*, i. 189; J. H. Plumb, *Chatham*, p. 29. C.H.S.]

[1] In 1742 the king had vetoed the inclusion in the ministry of Cotton as a tory and a Jacobite. But his Jacobitism was much modified by this time. Even in the 1730's his whig friends thought he had 'too good sense to be a thorough *jure divino* man'. See K. Feiling, *The Second Tory Party*, p. 29.

[2] [The essence of these ministerial changes was to reverse the compromise settlement of 1742. The followers of Granville and Bath, who had been taken in then to the exclusion of the rest of the opposition, were now expelled and their places allotted to converts from among those previously excluded. For further details and discussion see Owen, pp. 244–7. C.H.S.]

[3] The full strength of the opposing armies was about 50,000 to 98,000, but the effective number engaged was more like 44,000 to 76,000. See *E.H.R.* xii. 527, n. 13.

Countries and Saxe's first objective, the allied army advanced to Fontenoy, where the French army was drawn up in a well-prepared position to receive them on 11 May, and whither Louis XV and the dauphin had come to witness the expected victory. The centre of the French position was at the village of Fontenoy, commanding the glacis up which the allies had to advance; thence their line extended westwards to Antoing on the Scheldt and in a north-easterly direction to the well-protected Bois de Barry: for further precaution Saxe had fortified the line with artillery redoubts at intervals. To the Dutch and Austrians was assigned the attack on the line between Fontenoy and the Scheldt, but they soon took shelter from the murderous fire directed on them; the British, led by Cumberland himself, advanced between Fontenoy and the wood and bore the brunt of the fighting. After marching as if on parade under enfilade and frontal fire without returning a shot the British infantry halted on the crest of the glacis. There Lord Charles Hay, commanding the foot guards, advanced towards the French lines, drank to them from his brandy-flask, and said: 'We are the English guards and hope you will stand till we come quite up to you and not swim the Scheldt as you did the Main at Dettingen.'[1] There for nearly four hours the British infantry withstood infantry, cavalry, and artillery attacks, gradually making ground towards the French lines, until at last, overwhelmed by numbers and a final charge by the Irish brigade, the remnants were led back to safety by the duke. It was a defeat, but for the British a glorious defeat. A month later Tournai fell, then Ghent, Bruges, Oudenarde, Ostend, the British base, and Nieuport; and Saxe was master of Flanders. By October Cumberland himself and all the British troops had been recalled to England to fight the Young Pretender, leaving only 6,000 Hessians as our contribution to the allied army.

Charles Edward, the Young Pretender, deputed by his father to represent him, was now just twenty-five. High-spirited and adventurous, handsome and with winning ways, more like those of his great-uncle than his father's or grandfather's, he had that royal touch which accounts for the enthusiasm he aroused among his rough Highlanders and for the glamour that still

[1] See Carlyle, *Frederick the Great*, Bk. XV, Ch. 8, who also quotes Voltaire's different version of this story.

surrounds his name after more than 200 years have passed. It is true he was often ill-judged in counsel, but that is often glossed over by those who remember his piteous wanderings or that stirring proclamation on behalf of his father at Perth: 'Though we acknowledge some obligations to the French Monarch, we shall not do anything that is not becoming to a king, and an English King. . . . You may rest assured that I put my faith in no other arm than the justice of my cause and in the justice and the affection of my people.' He missed perhaps the best chance of success in 1744, through the storm of February that had dispersed Roquefeuil's fleet and put a stop to Saxe's well-appointed expedition from Dunkirk,[1] whereupon the French government, doubtful of effective support from the English Jacobites, had found the conquest of Flanders an easier and more profitable undertaking. But Charles Edward was all the more determined to make an attempt by himself, and even professed to think his chances of success better if he did not start under the aegis of England's secular enemy. For the next year he was holding meetings and discussing plans with his Jacobite friends and scraping together as much money as he could for the enterprise, with the benevolent if not active acquiescence of Versailles. By the summer of 1745 his plans were laid. Chartering two ships, the *Doutelle*,[2] in which he and his 'seven men of Moidart' embarked, and the *Elisabeth*, a well-armed privateer, to convey the arms and ammunition he had collected, he left Nantes on 22 June (O.S.) 1745; after waiting twelve days off Belle Île he was joined by the *Elisabeth* and together they sailed for Scotland on 5 July. Off the Lizard Captain Brett of the *Lion* met them and after a furious fight for five hours with *Elisabeth* disabled her so severely that she had to limp back into Brest with her precious cargo of arms. On 23 July (O.S.) Charles Edward himself landed on Eriskay island, and two days later on the Moidart peninsula, as he said himself, 'without men, without money, with but seven friends of my own'.[3] Though he set

---

[1] See above, p. 248.

[2] The correct name was *Du Teillay*, but in Scottish records the ship is always spoken of as *Doutelle*.

[3] The 'seven men of Moidart' were Tullibardine, Strickland, Sheridan, George Kelly, Sir John and Æneas Macdonald, and O'Sullivan. [The dates of the Pretender's movements are much confused by the use of the two styles. By the New Style he embarked on 2/3 July, sailed from Belle Ile on 16 July, encountered the *Lion* on 20 July, and arrived on Eriskay on 3 Aug. C.H.S.]

foot in the country of the Macdonalds, hereditary foes of the Campbells, he was at first coldly received, until at length Macdonald of Clanranald and 'Young Lochiel' of the Camerons came forward to support him with 900 clansmen. On 19 August, three days after a first Jacobite success in the capture by the Macdonalds of 80 men of the Royal Scots on their way to Fort William, the Stuart standard was solemnly raised at Glenfinnan in the presence of some 900 Highlanders.

News of the Young Pretender's landing in July did not reach London till the second week in August and found the government quite unprepared. The king was in Hanover and did not return until the last day of the month. One of the regency's first acts was to issue a proclamation offering £30,000 for the apprehension of Charles Edward, which had no other result than to bring forth a similar proclamation from him offering the same sum for the 'Elector of Hanover'. Most of the king's troops were in Flanders, whence they had to be hastily recalled, together with 6,000 Dutch troops[1] to protect the country. In Scotland itself there were some 3,750[2] regulars, scattered in garrisons, under the command of Sir John Cope. Ministers were specially ill-informed about Scotland, for Tweeddale, the Scottish secretary of state, was at odds with the duke of Argyll,[3] and also with the lord president, Duncan Forbes of Culloden,[4] the two ablest and most efficient supporters of the dynasty in that country. When Cope tardily heard of the Pretender's landing, instead of following the late duke of Argyll's example in 1715, by concentrating his small force at Stirling to protect the Lowlands, he took most of his troops towards Fort Augustus; then, finding Charles Edward strongly posted in his way, went off to Inverness, leaving the rebels free to reach Perth and with a clear road to Edinburgh. When at last he had shipped his troops from Aberdeen back to Dunbar he found the capital already in possession of the rebels.

In his march eastwards from Glenfinnan Charles Edward's

---

[1] On Louis XV's protest against the use of these Dutch troops, who had submitted on terms at Tournai, they were later replaced by 6,000 Hessians hired by the Dutch.

[2] See *Notes and Queries*, cxcii. 169.

[3] Archibald, 3rd duke of Argyll, 1682–1761, succeeded John the 2nd duke in 1743.

[4] Duncan Forbes, lord president of the court of session. See on him and on the 3rd duke of Argyll, Chap. X below, *passim*.

ranks were increased by reinforcements from Stewarts of Appin, Macdonalds of Glengarry and Glencoe, Frasers, and others; and by the time he reached Perth his host was more than doubled. By this time he had been joined by three men who became his chief Scottish advisers,[1] Murray of Broughton, his secretary, who later turned king's evidence, Drummond, titular duke of Perth, and Lord George Murray, a wise but unaccommodating counsellor. At Perth he proclaimed his father king and himself guardian of the realm, and, to provide money for his Highlanders' pay, instituted the system of levying tribute from the cities he captured. He entered Edinburgh on 17 September, having dispersed some dragoons and the town guard on the previous day at the 'Canter o' Coltbrigg', and, though unable to capture the castle, held court at Holyrood and had the whole city at his disposal. On 21 September he gave Cope and his troops returned from Aberdeen their final quietus at the battle of Prestonpans, which lasted little more than five minutes. This victory brought Charles Edward many new recruits, and by the end of October he had a force of 4,500 infantry and 400 horse. With this force he started for the invasion of England against the advice of some of his wisest counsellors.

Since Marshal Wade[2] was reported to be at Newcastle with an army of 18,000, the western route, as in the '15, was chosen. On 17 November the city of Carlisle, unable to get help from Wade, who was snow-bound at Hexham, surrendered to Charles Edward. But so far hardly any English Jacobites had come in, nor was there any sign of the hoped-for diversion from France; Cumberland, too, with another army was reported to be at Lichfield; so Lord George Murray and others strongly urged a return to Scotland, where there was some chance of success, rather than persistence in a hopeless adventure in England. But the prince, bent on reaching London, ordered the march to be continued through Preston, with its unhappy memories of 1648 and 1715, Manchester and Macclesfield, tribute being exacted from the towns, but hardly any recruits coming to swell the ranks of the invaders which were rather shrinking from desertion. On 4 December the Highland host reached Derby;

---

[1] The Scotsmen, however, complained that he was too much influenced by some of his Irish followers from the Continent.

[2] George Wade, 1673–1748, one of Stanhope's officers in Spain, road-maker in the Highlands (see below, p. 281). Field-marshal and commander-in-chief in Flanders Dec. 1743 to Oct. 1744; resigned command Mar. 1745.

but here ended this ill-judged adventure into England. With no prospect of English support and with Cumberland dogging their footsteps, Charles Edward's officers refused to follow him farther, so on 6 December—Black Friday both for the Scottish host and also for the Londoners panic-stricken at its proximity —he began the retreat. The Highlanders, orderly on the march south, now indulged their predatory instincts and left hateful memories of their cause behind them; but, thanks to Murray's leadership, they crossed the border without serious interference from Cumberland or Wade.[1]

In Scotland the prospects still seemed bright. Dumfries in the Lowlands and Glasgow were at the rebels' mercy and had to provide large sums for the prince's military chest. In the north the Jacobites had captured Aberdeen in September and held it for five months; Lord John Drummond had brought 800 men from France with some artillery and engineers in November; and, in spite of Duncan Forbes's success in gathering some loyal clans to the king's standard, by 1746 the rebel forces in the north had been increased by 4,000 more recruits from the Jacobite clans. Early in January Charles Edward united with these reinforcements, captured the town of Stirling and besieged its castle. But although he defeated at Falkirk in less than half an hour a relieving force under the incompetent General Hawley he failed to reduce Stirling Castle, stoutly defended by the gallant veteran Blakeney. Withdrawing northwards he took Inverness and forced Duncan Forbes and its governor Loudoun to wander about the Highlands and Islands as fugitives. During March he captured Fort Augustus and some thirty other guard-houses in the north. But here the tide turned.

On 2 February, the day after Charles Edward had crossed the Forth on his way north, Cumberland had arrived at Stirling, and thence moved northwards by slow stages. Cumberland reoccupied Aberdeen on 27 February, but waited there over a month, securing his supplies and protected by cruisers on the coast that captured a sloop with 12,000 guineas for Charles Edward and stopped a French fleet from disembarking the reinforcements of men and material it was bringing from France. By 15 April[2] he had reached Nairn and found the rebels, ill-

[1] Interesting letters about the rebels' march to Derby and back are printed in *Hist. MSS. Comm.* XIII. vi. 160–78. On the organization of loyal forces, see C. T. Atkinson, *Army Hist. Journ.* xxii. 292.

[2] He arrived on 14 Apr.

supplied with money and food and divided by intestine quarrels, encamped on the open moor of Culloden, instead of a much more protected position near at hand, strongly urged by Murray. A night attack led by Murray on Cumberland's camp was a complete fiasco, and next day Cumberland's army, 9,000 strong and in good condition, appeared to deliver battle to Charles Edward's 5,000 men, half-starving and exhausted by the night march. After a galling artillery fire from Cumberland's artillery the rebels' right wing made a furious charge in which they were mown down by the Englishmen's deadly fire: the left wing, to which the Macdonalds, who since Bannockburn had claimed the place of honour on the right, had been assigned, showed no stomach for the fight, and Cumberland soon completed the victory by cavalry charges on either flank, which sent most of the Highlanders fleeing to the gates of Inverness; one small detachment, however, proudly marched off with colours flying and bagpipes skirling southwards to the comparative safety of Ruthven in Badenoch. In this decisive battle the Highlanders lost 1,000 slain and 1,000 taken prisoner, Cumberland only 310 killed and wounded.

But Cumberland did not feel his work ended with this decisive victory. For three more months he remained in Scotland earning his nickname 'The Butcher' by his savage measures against the fugitives who had taken up arms for the Stuarts. They were pursued ruthlessly into the fastnesses where they had taken refuge, often summarily executed and their homes destroyed.[1] Some eighty of the prisoners were sent to trial and suffered the extreme penalty, among them Lords Kilmarnock and Balmerino.[2] Lord Lovat, executed in April 1747, was a final victim. He was betrayed by Murray of Broughton, and was indeed a double-dyed traitor, for he had always professed allegiance to the government, but had secretly encouraged his clan to take up arms against it.[3] Charles Edward himself, in spite of every effort made by the soldiers sent to hunt him down, escaped to France after five months' wanderings as a fugitive, often starving, in the western islands and mainland. It says

[1] See *The Lyon in Mourning* (Scottish Hist. Soc. xx–xxii) for the contemporary Jacobite view of the atrocities committed by Cumberland's soldiers after Culloden. But these accounts must be received with caution: some are obviously exaggerated.　　　　[2] Lord Cromarty, a third, was reprieved.

[3] The more important measures taken to bring Scotland more into line with England are dealt with in Chap. X.

much for the romantic devotion he had been able to inspire in the Highlanders that, though there was a reward of £30,000 offered for his capture, not a single man or woman of those, mostly poor fishermen and crofters on the edge of starvation, whom he met ever dreamed of betraying him; most indeed, such as the heroic Flora Macdonald, willingly risked their fortunes and their lives in his cause.[1] The most surprising features, indeed, of the '45 are the length of time it lasted and its long-continued success in Scotland. The prince himself, though possessed of a winning charm which appealed to the romantic Scots, great personal courage, and a conviction of his ultimate success, was no judge of character or of strategy. Towards the end he antagonized his ablest followers by relying chiefly on the advice of the second-rate Irishmen who accompanied him, in preference to that of Lord George Murray, his wisest and most capable officer, and of other Scotsmen. They, for example, advised him against the ill-starred expedition to England and the weak tactical position he insisted on taking at Culloden. What success he had was due largely to the fact that Wade's work in opening up the Highlands[2] was only half done, to the independence from central control of the Scottish clans, to the bad state of the army under such commanders as Cope and Hawley, and to its small numbers at home, and above all to the romantic attachment in the Highlands to their own exiled line of kings. But as soon as resolute measures had been taken by the dispatch of Cumberland, with the help of Ligonier, and a well-disciplined force, the collapse of the rebellion was assured.[3]

Before the rebellion was over there had been a ministerial crisis in England the outcome of which was finally to establish the Broadbottom administration. Since Granville's resignation

[1] See W. B. Blaikie, *Itinerary of Prince Charles Edward Stuart* (Scottish Hist. Soc. vol. xxiii), for his wanderings in Scotland and England from his first landing till his rescue by the French man-of-war *L'Heureux* on 19 Sept. (O.S.) 1746. A moving though not entirely accurate account of his five months as a fugitive is given by the Jesuit Cordara's *Commentary* (Scottish Hist. Soc. 3rd series, vol. ix). A. and H. Tayler have published, in their *1745 and After*, 1938, the *Narrative* of J. W. O'Sullivan from the Stuart Papers at Windsor. O'Sullivan was one of the 'Seven Men' and accompanied Prince Charles throughout his expedition.

[2] See below, p. 281.

[3] Ligonier was completely confident that the rebels 'must infallibly be destroyed' as early as 28 Nov. and wrote on that day from Lichfield, 'Advise all your friends to buy stocks'. See Whitworth, *Ligonier*, pp. 111–12 quoting *Hist. MSS.Comm.*x.i.287.

in November 1744[1] the ministry had been exposed to the king's unconcealed hostility. In May 1745 George left for Hanover, in spite of the remonstrances of his ministers, and even on his return at the end of August under the shadow of the Pretender's landing in Scotland his hostility was unabated.[2] The source of this friction was the king's reluctance to accept the resignation of Granville as final, coupled with his ministers' belief that Granville's influence at court was denying them the royal favour.[3] In this situation the Pelhams resolved in October to gain additional strength by bringing in Pitt. At first Pitt laid down unacceptable terms; but in January 1746 he expressed his readiness to join the ministry as secretary at war unconditionally, realizing that the Pelhams were in substantial agreement with him on continental policy since they aimed to make the Dutch take their proper share in defending their own country.[4] It only remained to win over the king. During the critical weeks of the Pretender's advance into England he had behaved reasonably towards his ministers. But as the Pretender retreated he relapsed into his earlier ways. He consented, unwillingly, to limit the supplies asked for in the king's speech for the continental war 'according to the circumstances of my own dominions', but when the admission of Pitt to the post of secretary at war was proposed he was adamant in his refusal.

Pitt at once abandoned his personal claim for that office, but both the king and his ministers were now resolved to bring their long-submerged conflict to an issue. George summoned Bath on 6 February and discussed the formation of an alternative administration. The Pelhams, on their side, decided to force the king's hand before he could act and on 9 February, in conclave with Hardwicke and Harrington, they agreed to resign *en bloc* immediately. The moment was well chosen. They had come to terms with Pitt and they felt sure of their own following.

[1] See above, p. 249.
[2] For examples of George II's conduct during 1745 see Yorke, *Hardwicke*, i. 384–5, 454.
[3] [To what extent Granville encouraged the king's resistance towards his ministers is not clear. Owen accepts the evidence of one of Horace Walpole's letters that Granville instigated George's conduct. However that may be, the Pelhams' firm conviction that this was the case meant that, in Owen's words, they were 'haunted by the political shadow of the man whose fall they had encompassed'. See Owen, op. cit., p. 268. C.H.S.]
[4] The Dutch had refused to declare war against France or to contribute their fair quota of men and money for the allied army. For Pitt's manœuvres see Owen, pp. 284–93.

So, if the king was to form an alternative ministry he could resort only to the tories and the following of the prince of Wales to buttress the handful who supported Bath and Granville. These were desperate and humiliating steps which George II could never bring himself to take, least of all during a Jacobite rebellion.[1] Accordingly, when on 10 and 11 February the ministers, headed by Harrington, flocked to St. James's to resign their seats, their white staves, their golden keys, or their commissions, the king was helpless. For a moment he resisted. Bath and Granville were given respectively the treasury and the secretaryship of state on 10 February, but a couple of days later, unable to find more than two other colleagues, had to resign their offices into the hands of their predecessors. So the Pelhams, now able to dictate their own terms, insisted on the exclusion of Bath and Granville from the closet, on the king's full confidence for themselves, and on office for Pitt, but, out of deference to the royal prejudice, not as secretary at war, which involved personal attendance on the king.[2] In the end, the king could not govern without the Pelhams, but it is important to remember the extent of his power, which could postpone this solution for more than a year, as well as its limitations which forced him ultimately to accept it.[3]

Meanwhile the continental war was dragging on, to all appearance aimlessly. In 1746 Saxe, after capturing Brussels and Antwerp, had made himself master of the whole of the Austrian Netherlands: owing to the rebellion, the English contingent under Ligonier,[4] a dashing cavalry leader, was small,

[1] [This was the concealed strength of the Pelhams' position at a time when the rebellion was still active. As Glover put it, 'the defeat at Falkirk furnished occasion to the Pelhams of demonstrating their . . . power to the king'. See *Memoirs by a Celebrated Literary and Political Character*, 1814, p. 40. Granville made the same point after the event when he claimed that the Pelhams had 'done a thing not known before in any country, deserting the King . . . in a dangerous crisis'. See Yorke, *Hardwicke*, i. 507, quoted by Basil Williams, *Carteret and Newcastle*, p. 174. See also H. Walpole to Horace Mann, 14 Feb. 1746. C.H.S.]

[2] Pitt was first made vice-treasurer of Ireland, but a few months later obtained the paymastership. For the memorandum of the Pelhams' terms to the king see Yorke, i. 428.

[3] [Owen, who gives a detailed analysis of the events of 1744–6 in his chap. vii, argues that the king's 'unhappy position was entirely of his own making' and that 'the initiative was always in his hands'. Owen, p. 299. For another interpretation emphasizing the personal weakness of George II and the aggressiveness of the Pelhams see R. Pares, *George III and the Politicians*, pp. 95–97. C.H.S.]

[4] John Ligonier, 1680–1770, of Huguenot descent, fought under Marlborough, also at Dettingen and Fontenoy; lieutenant-general of ordnance, 1748–57;

but, though defeated in October at Roucoux near Liège, did credit to itself and its commander. Next year the French invaded Holland, and the Dutch, at last stirred to some action by the national danger, replaced the supine republican government by George II's son-in-law William IV of Orange-Nassau as hereditary stadtholder;[1] but he was not a William III and could not inspire much martial ardour into the Dutch troops, who in September gave up their great border-fortress, Bergen-op-Zoom. Meanwhile, the allied army, again under Cumberland and increased to over 100,000, was hardly more successful than in 1745. It is true it averted the fall of Maestricht, but in the battle of Laffeldt in July it was defeated and only saved from complete rout by two magnificent cavalry charges by Ligonier, who was taken prisoner leading the second of these. Cumberland indeed, though a good organizer of the army in peace-time, and a dogged and gallant fighter, showed no special qualifications as a commander in the field. At Culloden he had an easy task against an inferior and dispirited host, but in Flanders, pitted against the most brilliant general of the day, both at Fontenoy and at Laffeldt, he missed victories within his grasp by faulty dispositions and by not making the best use of his available forces.

Even in 1745, however, one gleam of success had pierced the general gloom, but not thanks to any initiative of the Pelham administration. Shirley,[2] the energetic governor of Massachusetts, organized and equipped a force of New Englanders under the command of a colonial, Pepperell, which, with the aid of a royal squadron under commodore Warren, captured the French fortress of Louisburg, and with it Cape Breton island.[3] This was an achievement of which the colonials were justly

commander-in-chief, 1757–66; master general of ordnance, 1759–63; promoted field-marshal and granted an Irish peerage, 1757; raised to an English earldom, 1766. For an excellent account of his career see R. Whitworth, *Field Marshal Lord Ligonier*, Oxford, 1958.

[1] William III's death was followed by a 'stadtholderless régime' in the five provinces of which he had been stadtholder and captain-general; in the two remaining provinces the stadtholderate was in another branch of the Orange family, to which belonged William IV, 1711–51, who had married Anne, the princess royal of England, in 1734. Hervey has much to say about the ceremonial at this marriage.

[2] William Shirley, 1694–1771. He was afterwards governor of the Bahamas.

[3] Sir William Pepperell, 1696–1759. According to Charles Yorke he spent £20,000 of his own money on the expedition. The New Englanders, 'of the true Oliverian strain', much to the disgust of the sailors, insisted on prayer before they made the successful attack. Yorke, *Hardwicke*, i. 436.

proud, for Louisburg not only commanded the entrance to the St. Lawrence, but also was a menace to the English and colonial fishermen off Newfoundland. Pitt, Bedford, and others in England, who foresaw the coming struggle with France for North America, were equally enthusiastic, and urged an expedition for the following year to capture Quebec, whereas Pelham regretted the capture of Louisburg 'as a stumbling-block to all negotiation' for peace.[1] Next year Bedford, with Pitt's enthusiastic support, made ready an expedition to complete the conquest of Canada, but its dispatch was delayed till too late in the season[2] and then, 'purely to save appearances, that the vast charges of our naval armament this year may not seem to have been flung away', was sent off on an ill-prepared and futile expedition to l'Orient.[3] Unfortunately, too, against the success at Louisburg had to be set off the capture of Madras by La Bourdonnais in September 1746.

By this time, however, the fortunes of the allies were once more on the mend. In 1745 the harassed emperor died and Maria Theresa made the peace of Füssen with his son, the new elector of Bavaria: she also secured the election of her husband Francis of Lorraine as emperor, made an alliance with Saxony, drove Frederic out of Bohemia; and finally, by the treaty of Dresden in December, Frederic made his peace with her, securing his conquest of Silesia but definitely retiring from the war. In Italy, too, whereas in 1745 the Gallispans had been carrying all before them, capturing Milan and overrunning eastern Piedmont, so that at the beginning of 1746 Charles Emmanuel was on the point of going over to France, the arrival shortly afterwards of 30,000 Austrian troops, set free again by the treaty of Dresden, induced him to change his mind. He and the Austrians then cleared north Italy of the Gallispans and even invaded Provence. At sea, too, by 1747 the new spirit and the new men in the British navy began to show their effect.

In the spring of 1747 news came to the admiralty of intense activity in the French and Spanish ports and dockyards. Fleets were being made ready to convoy the trade to the East and

---

[1] Coxe, *Pelham*, i. 284.

[2] This delay was not wholly the fault of the ministry. Bad weather prevented the expedition from sailing when it was ready in June and then the escape of the French fleet from Rochefort finally stopped it. See Richmond, iii. 23–25.

[3] Coxe, *Memoirs of Lord Walpole*, ii. 159; see also *Bedford Correspondence*, i. 64–69, 194–6, and *Chatham*, i. 163–4.

West Indies; an expedition was being fitted out to attempt the recapture of Louisburg and to defend Canada against an expected attack from England; and relief was to be sent to the French garrison of Pondichery threatened with blockade by Commodore Griffin. The new spirit at the board of admiralty was shown by the prompt dispatch in April of Anson, himself a member of the board, with an overwhelming fleet to watch the French and Spanish ports and destroy the enemies' fleets as they came out. After a month spent in cruising about the Bay of Biscay, looking into the enemies' ports and constantly exercising his fleet in battle formations and manœuvres, on 3 May Anson sighted de la Jonquière's fleet coming out with convoys to Canada and the East Indies. He at once ordered a chase, which was carried out in a different spirit from that displayed in the inconclusive engagement off Hyères in 1744; by dark all the French men-of-war had been captured and many prizes taken from the convoy for America; and only a small detachment of the squadron destined for India reached Pondichery. On 20 June Captain Fox, with a detachment of eight ships, fell in with the West Indian convoy, escorted by three men-of-war, and captured forty-eight of them.[1] Anson meanwhile had returned to the board of admiralty, and his gallant second-in-command, Warren, was laid up with scurvy; so Hawke, though the youngest of the rear-admirals, got his chance of carrying on the vigil. For the French were feverishly equipping another fleet to make up for their losses. After another three months' watchful cruising, on 14 October Hawke sighted a large convoy of West Indiamen being escorted by a fleet under Létanduère. Another general chase followed, and after a battle lasting from midday till dark, all but two of the French men-of-war had surrendered. The convoy escaped, but, thanks to a timely message from Hawke, Pocock with his West Indian squadron gathered in forty of them as prizes. As a result of this succession of victories the enemy's fleets had been driven off the seas and their colonies exposed to our attacks, while France herself, already suffering from a disastrous harvest, was reduced to the lowest straits financially by the destruction of her commerce.[2]

[1] The prize money from these 48 captures amounted to £294,486. See Richmond, iii. 98, n. 1.
[2] See Richmond, l.c. iii. 78–115, for a full account of Anson's and Hawke's victories in 1747.

Long before 1747 most of the combatants were heartily tired of the war and would have welcomed peace.[1] None indeed were as fortunate or as cynical as Frederic II, who came in or out of the war just as it suited his personal convenience, without troubling as to the effect of his actions on his temporary allies. But as early as 1744 the Dutch, though never officially belligerents, and dragged unwillingly into the turmoil, had made peace proposals to the French. These got no response that year, but in 1745 d'Argenson, the French minister, hoping to detach the Dutch from their alliance with England, took up their proposals. Then in 1746 he put forward first his own 'Idées sur la Paix', and subsequently when these had been rejected by the Dutch under English pressure, a more reasonable project which was submitted to a triangular conference at Breda between English, French, and Dutch envoys, England insisting, however, that the other belligerents should be informed of the proceedings.[2] But when the discussions opened in October, the chief difficulties appeared to be not so much between the principal adversaries themselves, as between those nominally in alliance with one another. The Dutch, for example, cared nothing for England's interest in retaining Cape Breton or for her trade grievances against Spain, but only about liberating the Low Countries and their own soil from the French invader; the uneasy alliance between Maria Theresa and Charles Emmanuel provoked more bitterness than hearty co-operation between them, the former being chiefly anxious to conquer Naples from Don Carlos, the latter only concerned in securing the north Italian gains promised him at Maria Theresa's expense by the treaty of Worms; even the Family Alliance between France and Spain was losing its first cordiality since the death of Philip V in July 1746, and the chief reason why his successor Ferdinand still insisted on a provision in Italy for his half-brother Don Philip seems to have been a fear lest he should return to Spain to cabal with Ferdinand's formidable stepmother. Apart from the Dutch, the French and the English had most interest in obtaining an early peace. France, in

[1] The most exhaustive English account of the various negotiations for peace between 1744 and 1748 is in Lodge's *Studies in Eighteenth Century Diplomacy*, pp. 80–411.
[2] England's participation in the Breda conference was not wholly sincere. Newcastle hoped to secure a separate peace with Spain while spinning out the negotiations with France. See Lodge, l.c., pp. 172–214.

occupation of the Low Countries and of some Dutch territory, had no territorial ambition to satisfy and was retaining those conquests only as a pawn in negotiation; on the other hand, especially after England's naval victories of 1747, her financial and economic position was almost desperate, with her rich Newfoundland fisheries at a standstill since the loss of Louisburg, and her trade at the mercy of the victorious English fleets; whereas England's import and export trade had actually increased progressively during the war.[1] England, though at the end victorious at sea, had been constantly unfortunate on land, and even her capture of Louisburg was counterbalanced by the loss of Madras; rich too as she was, she was beginning to groan under the burden of subsidies to the Dutch, Hessians, Austrians, Saxons, Hanoverians, Russians, and Sardinians in her pay, amounting by 1748 to what seemed the vast sum of £1,750,000; nor had she a ministry fitted to carry on a war, with its acute division between those in favour of an immediate peace, such as Bedford and Pelham himself, and a more warlike section led by Newcastle, who was reluctant to cut his losses and hoped constantly for a change of fortune in the war on land.

Partly owing to the discordant views in her own ministry and to the almost irreconcilable views of her allies, but chiefly owing to the delusive appearance of strength gained by France through her land victories, England had to submit to the almost humiliating terms finally settled at Aix-la-Chapelle, whither the conference of Breda had been transferred,[2] in October 1748. She had, much to the indignation of its New England conquerors, to give up Louisburg in exchange for Madras and even to send two peers to France as hostages for its surrender; the sea-defences of Dunkirk were indeed to be razed, but without any supervision by English commissioners, while its land-defences were to be left standing; France once more obliged herself, as she had done before, to recognize the Hanoverian succession and repudiate the Pretender; but nothing was settled about the disputed possession of the West Indian islands, St. Vincent, St. Lucia, and Tobago, or of frontier dis-

[1] See C. E. Fayle on 'Deflection of Strategy by Commerce', in *Journal of R.U. Service Inst.* lxviii (1923), 281–90.

[2] The Breda conference ceased to meet in Mar. 1747 and remained in a state of suspended animation until it reassembled at Aix twelve months later. See Lodge, pp. 235, 253.

putes in North America; nor were the disputes in India between the French and English East India Companies even temporarily arrested. With Spain the original cause of dispute about the right of search by *guarda-costas* was not mentioned in the treaty, while the South Sea Company's annual ship and Asiento were merely renewed for four years;[1] on the other hand Spain obtained for Don Philip Parma and Piacenza as an independent state, to prevent which England had been at the expense of annual fleets to the Mediterranean and of onerous subsidies to Maria Theresa and Charles Emmanuel. The only ally of England to be satisfied was Holland by the recovery of her own territory, and the evacuation of the Low Countries by France. Charles Emmanuel got back Savoy and Nice from France and obtained most of the territory promised him by Maria Theresa at Worms, but had a grievance in not getting Finale. But the ally most dissatisfied was Maria Theresa, since Silesia and Glatz were once more guaranteed to Frederic II, the Barrier fortresses in her own Low Countries were handed over to the Dutch, who had already proved their inability to defend them, and her position in Italy was seriously weakened by the territory conceded to Don Philip and Charles Emmanuel. As it proved, almost the only effective results of the war and the peace were the settlement of Italy for nearly half a century and the possession of Silesia and Glatz by Prussia.

Bête comme la Paix was the catchword in Paris after the peace of Aix-la-Chapelle. To many of the nations engaged in it the war itself must have seemed equally *bête*; and it has always proved a stumbling-block to historians to give a clear account of its kaleidoscopic phases and of the motives of those engaged in it. To Carlyle, for example, it was merely 'an unintelligible, huge English-and-Foreign Delirium', with its disjointed campaigns in Italy, Silesia, Bohemia, Bavaria, on the Rhine and in the Low Countries, and overseas in India, the West Indies, and North America.

Primarily the war was 'unintelligible' at the time, and is still more so to us to-day, because it was largely fought on sham issues: the dynastic rights of kings and princes, as illustrated by

---

[1] For £100,000 down and the renewal of the special trading privileges granted to England in the treaty of 1667, the Asiento and annual ship were finally surrendered by a further treaty in 1750. See McLachlan, l.c., p. 139.

that gigantic fraud, the Pragmatic Sanction—whereas the real issues, to which most of the statesmen were blind, were concerned with the larger interests of the peoples. Two rulers alone dimly perceived the real issues: Frederic the Great, who, besides his personal interests for Prussia, aimed above all at freeing Germany from foreign tutelage, French, English, or even Austrian; and Charles Emmanuel of Savoy, whose main object was to free Italy from foreign domination and extend his own, Italian, rule over more of the peninsula. None of our own ministers during this war perceived that the real issue in our struggle with France and Spain was not for European but for world expansion, in the interests of our growing trade and adventurous spirit; the rulers of France were equally purblind in confining their attention to Europe, where they already had all they needed for their own security. Happily for us, by the next war, we had found in Pitt a statesman with a clear vision for realities and demonic power in inspiring his people to attain them.

Another cause of confusion is that during the first half of the war nations nominally at peace with one another were, under various subterfuges, fighting and invading one another's territories. France and England, France and Maria Theresa did not declare war against one another till 1744, yet before that the French had been invading Habsburg territory not as principals but as auxiliaries of Bavaria, and similarly France and England met at Dettingen and in the naval battle of Hyères while still nominally at peace with one another. Throughout the war, too, the Dutch though fighting the French for four years and actually invaded by them during two years, resolutely refused to consider themselves at war with France.[1]

Moreover of all the combatants, England, Holland, Russia, Bavaria, Saxony, Poland, France, Savoy, Maria Theresa, Prussia, and Spain, the last four only had clear-cut objectives, and even of these four Prussia and Savoy add to the confusion by uncertainty as to the side on which they should fight to attain these objectives. Maria Theresa and Spain indeed were consistent in their objects and their choice of allies.

[1] An interesting instance of the lax ideas about hostilities then prevalent is the fact that until 1747 it was the practice for French ships to be insured in England against loss in war-time by capture or sinking even by English ships. In that year an act was passed to stop the practice in spite of the opposition of the attorney- and solicitor-general: see Campbell, *Lives of Chief Justices*, ii. 247, 365.

The former's aim was simple enough, to preserve the whole Habsburg inheritance and fight any power that put forward claims to it: for help she clung to the maritime powers, England and Holland, to Russia and to Savoy, if that wily prince's help could be bought at a reasonable price. Apart from her quarrel with England, Spain's object was to secure an apanage in Italy for the Infant Don Philip, and for that object her one certain ally was France.

Frederic of Prussia and Charles Emmanuel III of Savoy had equally definite objects but less certainty as to methods. The former had made up his mind to obtain at least Silesia from Maria Theresa and to break the Habsburg domination in Germany, so that he could stand out himself as the defender of German liberties and prevent any non-German power, French, English, or Russian, from interfering in German concerns. Frederic's first object was not entirely compatible with his second, since he did not at first feel himself strong enough to overcome Maria Theresa without the aid of her secular enemy, France. He therefore encouraged France to make a diversion in Germany, nominally as the ally of the Bavarian emperor, really to help himself against the Austrians. As often, however, as he thought he had gained his own personal objects, he left France in the lurch and made it abundantly plain that the French should not be allowed to make any permanent gains in Germany. The second of Frederic's objects, to teach Germany to be self-sufficient under his guidance, was indeed quite a new idea in European politics, at any rate since the days of Wallenstein, and was so little understood by his contemporaries that it alone caused a good deal of confusion in the grouping of the powers. France always regarded Frederic simply as a potential ally against the house of Austria, while England as inevitably aimed at placing him among her own allies, notably against France. As to Charles Emmanuel of Savoy, of whom Gibbon said that 'after the incomparable Frederic, he held the second rank . . . among the kings of Europe',[1] true to the traditions of his race, he was only concerned in plucking more leaves of the

---

[1] [Professor Williams omitted Gibbon's qualification '*proximus longo tamen intervallo*' and has perhaps raised Charles Emmanuel higher in the scale than he deserves—at least so far as his aim to free Italy from foreign domination is concerned. As Professor Mark Thomson has observed, Charles Emmanuel's 'interest was to maintain a balance of power in Italy between Bourbon and Habsburg'. See *New Cambridge Modern History*, vii. 425. C.H.S.]

Italian artichoke. The question was, who would get him. True he had been with the Bourbons in the previous war, but he was quite willing to change sides for value received. The Bourbons offered him Maria Theresa's Milanese, for which he and his ancestors had long been hankering, but it was not only still to be won, but the proleptic gift was encumbered with the necessity of having a Spaniard as his near neighbour in Parma. So he finally accepted the less spectacular, but immediate, gains of territory offered, on Carteret's prompting, by Maria Theresa.

Of all the powers France, for her own honour, and even in her own interests, might well have been expected to stand out of the continental fray. Only two years before Frederic made his sudden swoop on Silesia France had guaranteed the Pragmatic Sanction for value received, and, though it might have been too much to expect her to fight for her old enemy, yet to support those out to plunder the queen's inheritance was as cynical as Frederic's conduct. Apart from this, it was not to France's interest to take part in another struggle against the Habsburgs. With Lorraine she had obtained the utmost she had fought for in her secular struggle with that family, and there was hardly anything to be gained by going on fighting, as Louis XIV had realized twenty-five years earlier; besides, if any further weakening of the Habsburgs was needed, the Turks had done their share in 1739. To allow Germany and the Habsburgs to stew in their own juice was all the more to France's interest in 1740, since it was fairly obvious that a struggle, needing all her own energies, was impending with England. There were constantly growing causes of dispute between the two countries about the West Indies, the frontiers in America, and interests in India, while France's close connexion with Spain made a colonial and maritime war with England almost inevitable. But at this crisis, as Émile Bourgeois put it, 'France consulted her traditions rather than her interests'. Nor was this shady transaction successful. Even the Bavarian emperor, in whose support France lavished men and treasure to no purpose, realized how unpopular her support was in the empire and was ready to throw her over. Frederic himself soon showed that he had no intention of crushing the Austrians to put France in their place as the arbiter of Germany; but it took France long to realize this, right up, in fact, to the eve of the Seven Years war.

England had no hesitation in honouring her obligation to guarantee the Pragmatic Sanction, an obligation consonant with her general policy since 1689. But it was not till Carteret took office in 1742 that England took vigorous action in support of the queen, partly no doubt because he thought it the best method of fighting France, always to him the great enemy. Nevertheless, he made three serious mistakes. First, he devoted his whole attention to the continental war, thinking that the best way of vanquishing France was to unite all Germany on the queen's side and so defeat France on land. He failed to grasp that the decisive combat with France, now being inaugurated, was for something much more than a European dispute, in fact for an almost world-wide empire, and that England's true part in the war, and even the best way of helping the Austrians, was to keep France in alarm about her oversea possessions rather than to try to fight her on land in Europe, where she was at her strongest and we at our weakest. His second mistake was even more fatal to his limited plan. He never fully realized that Maria Theresa regarded Frederic, not France, as her chief enemy and was more concerned about recovering Silesia or obtaining a slice of Bavaria than about playing England's game against the Bourbons. Thirdly, he failed to realize that in Frederic a new portent had arisen in German politics, a German ruler not only keen on his own aggrandizement, but determined to let no extraneous power—whether France, the Habsburgs, or England—give the law to Germany. Carteret was indeed right in picking out Frederic as the most useful ally England could have in Germany, and his negotiation of the treaty of Berlin took Frederic away from France at a critical period of the war; but even he had not realized that Frederic was no longer a mere German princeling to be fitted, as occasion served, into the plans of great princes. He needlessly antagonized him by his pragmatic army and still more by neglecting to take him into his confidence in the negotiations of Hanau and ignoring him in the treaty of Worms. By these blunders at a critical moment he lost him.

After the formal declarations of war between France and England and France and Maria Theresa in the spring of 1744, the issues were clearer. France carried all before her in the Low Countries, partly owing to the diversion she caused by aiding the Young Pretender's designs on England. On the other hand England, as generally happened after a war had been proceeding for some time, recovered her naval supremacy, which helped her to secure Louisburg in America, but in spite of which she lost Madras. Frederic, having once more secured Silesia,[1] retired from the contest to digest his gains. The two other beneficiaries among the combatants were Savoy, who got part of what had been promised her by the treaty of Worms, and Spain, who secured Parma and Piacenza for Don Philip: a settlement which gave Italy peace for nearly fifty years until Napoleon appeared on the scene. But for the two real protagonists, France and England, the war ended in a stalemate with the certain prospect of its renewal in the near future. Except for Frederic and Italy both war and peace had indeed been *bête*.[2]

[1] Frederic indeed had to fight for Silesia once more in the Seven Years war, to which Carlyle (*Frederick the Great*, Bk. XVII, Ch. 1) gives the alternative name Third Silesian war.

[2] [Professor Williams has put forward in the preceding pages an interpretation of Frederic the Great's aims and motives which is highly individual. Other learned men have taken a less idealistic view and have questioned the sincerity of Frederic's professions of German patriotism. On all this see Lodge, op. cit., pp. 7, 26, and 35; P. Gaxotte, *Frederick II* (translation 1941), p. 237; G. P. Gooch, *Frederick the Great* (1947), p. 23; and V. Valentin, 'Some Interpretations of Frederick the Great', in *History*, n.s. xix (1934), 115–23. C.H.S.]

X

SCOTLAND[1] AND IRELAND

IN spite of the Union which had nominally made one British nation of the English and Scots, in spite too of the closer relations thus brought about between the two races, the differences are still marked enough during this period to justify separate treatment of certain aspects of Scottish history. A gradual diminution of misunderstandings is indeed apparent by the end of George II's reign; they might well have disappeared altogether had they not been revived by Bute's unfortunate incursion into politics at the beginning of George III's. After this set-back it required nearly half a century more of closer co-operation in war and peace before the Scotsman's sense of grievance against England and the Englishman's somewhat contemptuous attitude towards his northern fellow citizens had practically disappeared.

The Union, though providing a uniform legislative and economic system for the whole island, had still left some important differences, in a separate legal system and a separate church establishment for Scotland, differences not only a *sine qua non* for Union but also among the chief reasons for its success. On the other hand, the actual working of Scotland's representative system failed during the eighteenth century to give her the influence in parliament to which she was entitled; while the cleavage between Lowlands and Highlands, economically and even administratively, was, until after the '45, a source of weakness as much to Scotland as to the United Kingdom.

Bad as England's electoral system then was, Scotland's was much worse. In England there was at least a democratic element in the county voters with their very low qualification of a 40s. freehold, and even in some of the boroughs popular opinion could express itself. On the other hand, in all the Scottish counties even as late as 1790 there were

---

[1] The Rebellions of 1715 and 1745, affecting as they did the whole kingdom, are described in Chaps. VI and IX.

only 2,655 voters, half of them with a genuine freehold qualification,[1] the other half simply faggot voters created by the landowners; in the burghs the members were elected by the self-appointed burgh councils, while Edinburgh alone was entitled to a member for itself, the other burghs being grouped by four or five together for each member[2]—a system which enabled the government to secure with very little expense members favourable to itself. The election of the sixteen representative peers was almost as great a farce. A list of the sixteen peers acceptable to the government would be sent down for the election at Holyrood, and almost invariably, by dint of promises or even more forcible means, the list was accepted.[3] Thus in each house there was normally a docile group of Scots members prepared to vote for the government; only on the rare occasions when there was some special Scottish grievance to air did they assert their independence.[4]

For the administration of Scottish business a third secretary of state was at first created; but in times of national crisis involving the whole island this division of responsibility with the two original secretaries proved irksome and confusing. During the '15 the duke of Montrose was dismissed and his duties taken over by Stanhope and Townshend. In 1719, when order was re-established, the duke of Roxburgh was appointed to the post, but, owing to the independent line he took on the malt tax, he was dismissed by Walpole in 1725 and no successor appointed till in 1742 Carteret revived the office for Tweeddale.[5] He resigned just before Pelham formed his second ministry during Charles Edward's rising; and thereafter the office remained in

[1] This qualification was theoretically a 40s. freehold as in England. But a Scottish act of 1681 had laid down that such freeholds should be 'of old extent', i.e. that they should allow for the decline in the value of money since the franchise was established. In consequence, by 1793, 'the unit of land rated for election purposes at 40s. was computed at from £70 to £130 sterling'. See Mathieson, *Awakening of Scotland*, pp. 17–18.

[2] This was done at the time of the Union when the representation of the Scottish burghs was reduced from 66 to 15. Mathieson, p. 21.

[3] In 1734 an unsuccessful attempt was made by the opposition in the house of lords to call for a new election on the grounds of bribery and a display of armed force for securing the government's list. See *P.H.* xv. 759. In 1741 some opposition peers were in fact elected.

[4] For the Scottish electoral system, see Mathieson, op. cit., pp. 17–23.

[5] Lord Selkirk was not, as has been sometimes stated, appointed to the post in 1731: see Thomson, *Secretaries of State*, p. 36. See also above, p. 33, n 2. Roxburgh's dismissal was part of Walpole's attack on Carteret's supporters in the cabinet. See above, p. 203.

abeyance for over a century until Gladstone revived it in 1885. When there was no secretary for Scotland, the English secretaries relied for the routine business of the country and for the support of their Scottish measures in the commons on the lord advocate, and were fortunate in having as such Duncan Forbes of Culloden from 1725 to 1737 and William Grant of Preston Grange from 1746 to 1754, both whole-hearted supporters of the Union, both also vigorous in their defence of Scotland's interests even against the ministries they served so well. Still more than on their official advisers, ministers relied on the influence of the two great Campbell brothers John, duke of Argyll, and Archibald, earl of Islay.[1] They were the leaders of the so-called 'Argathelian' party as opposed to the 'Squadrone', a survival from Scotland's last parliament. Both parties were true to the Union, but the Squadrone was more keenly on the watch against encroachments on Scottish rights, while the Campbells, especially Islay, were the mainstay of the government's policy in Scotland and the chief dispensers of Scottish patronage. But the differences between the two parties were only skin-deep and largely personal: both Roxburgh and Tweeddale, Scottish secretaries in turn, belonged to the Squadrone, while several of the original Argathelians, such as Montrose, Stair, and Marchmont, opposed Walpole's excise in 1733.

Scotland's legal system, so jealously preserved at the Union, differed from that of England, since it was based, not on the common law, but on the Roman law. The court of session, the supreme tribunal in civil cases, was presided over by the lord president, while the lord justice clerk usually presided over the high court of justiciary which dealt with crime. Trial by jury had since 1532 become obsolete in civil cases, so that in the court of session the judges decided both on law and fact: nobody indeed in Europe, according to Lord Cornbury writing to Duncan Forbes, exercised more real power than the lord president, since he was 'intrusted with the property of Scotland'.[2] At any rate the efficiency of the court of session depended largely on him. By 1737 Sir Hew Dalrymple had held that office for nearly forty years, and, though said to have been of

[1] Archibald succeeded his brother John as duke of Argyll in 1743, but before that had superseded him in the confidence of the ministry. John was touchy, quarrelsome, and difficult to work with, and during Walpole's last few years in office was in active opposition to him.

[2] See *Culloden Papers*, 1815, p. 147, Cornbury to Forbes 18 Apr. 1738.

'great private worth and amiable manners',[1] had allowed
arrears in the court's business to accumulate, some cases having
been pending for as long as twenty years. His successor Duncan
Forbes of Culloden, one of the ablest and most public-spirited
Scotsmen of his day,[2] introduced sweeping reforms. By insisting
on a proper rota of service for the judges and ruling that no
cause should be left undecided for more than four years at most
in the Parliament House he soon cleared off arrears. He put
an end to the chicanery of rascally agents in the courts; and he
rescued the Scottish records from the damp, dirt, and rats which
for nearly forty years since the Union had been destroying
them by securing the appointment of Lord Lothian as a lord
register willing to treat his functions as something more than a
sinecure. His own judgements, clear and decisive, deserved the
praise of his friend the English chancellor, Hardwicke, who
commented on the 'different degree of weight and credit with
which your decrees come now before the House [of lords on
appeal] from what they did a few years ago'. Fortunately, too,
both these great judges were agreed in thinking that the legal
systems of England and Scotland should be assimilated, as far as
was compatible with their national characteristics and traditions.[3] Lord Kames, another notable Scottish judge, would have
gone even further and in his active correspondence with Hardwicke went so far as to suggest that the English common law and
equity branches should be merged into one system; this, however, was an innovation which neither Hardwicke nor Blackstone was inclined to entertain.[4] Unfortunately Kames, not
content with his legal work, wrote extensively on other topics
which he understood less well, and provoked Johnson to tell
Boswell he might 'keep him' in Scotland. On the other hand,
by his practical encouragement of Scottish agriculture and
manufactures he rendered some service to his country.

In 1714, indeed, Scotland was still far behind the sister-
kingdom in population, agriculture, industries, and the general
amenities of life. Edinburgh, the largest city, had only about
36,000 inhabitants, Glasgow no more than 12,000–13,000; no

---

[1] A. F. Tytler of Woodhouselee, *Memoirs of Henry Home of Kames*, 3 vols., 1814,
i. 42–43.
[2] See above, pp. 253, 273, and below, pp. 281–3.
[3] See *Culloden Papers*, pp. xxiv–xliv, and 158. Hardwicke to Forbes, 5 Apr.
1740.
[4] Tytler, op. cit. i. 294–356. See also above, p. 66.

other towns in the country had as many as 7,000; while the total population of all Scotland barely exceeded 1,000,000.[1] In the Lowlands, the more progressive part of the country, the prevailing 'run-rig' system on arable farms, whereby each tenant had 'rigs' (ridges), often widely separated, to cultivate, was irksome and wasteful, all the more as the instruments of tillage were hopelessly antiquated and inadequate. The pasture-lands, capable, as experience has proved, of great development, were poor for want of manure and the artificial grasses already introduced into England. From 1696 to 1703 there had been seven disastrous years of famine, followed by another terrible year in 1709, years of actual starvation which had helped to depopulate the country from deaths or the emigration of survivors; even as late as 1740 and 1760 there were serious dearths. However, already in 1723 the Honourable the Society of Improvers in the Knowledge of Agriculture, started by prominent landowners such as Stair, Islay, John Dalrymple, Cathcart, and Hope of Rankeillor, was spreading the knowledge of better methods of clearing the land, planting artificial grasses, and the use of Tull's drill, root-crops, and manures. The 'run-rig' system was being gradually superseded by long leases over compact farms, and the advantages of tree-planting made known by Clerk of Penicuik and by the Edinburgh Society for Encouraging Arts, Sciences and Agriculture founded in 1735. Already by 1730 improvements had been started in Ayrshire which were to make it the great dairy country it has become.[2]

But the chief benefit which came immediately from the Union was the privilege of trading on equal terms with England and her colonies, a privilege which was the making of Glasgow. In 1692 the total tonnage of shipping in the whole of Scotland was only 10,000, whereof Glasgow had no more than 1,182 tons with 15 ships. Directly after the Union Glasgow, as the nearest port to the American colonies, saw her opportunity and began chartering ships from Whitehaven to carry goods to Virginia and Maryland and bring back tobacco; in 1718 the first Glasgow-built and owned vessel crossed the Atlantic. On complaints of fraudulent methods by the Glasgow merchants from their chief English

[1] P. Hume Brown, *History of Scotland*, iii. 45, 254; Graham, *Social Life in Scotland*, ii. 242, 270.
[2] Graham, l.c., chap. v; H. Hamilton, *Industrial Revolution in Scotland*, p. 5 and chap. ii. The good effects of these improvements were not widely felt until well after the end of this period.

rivals at Bristol, Liverpool, and Whitehaven there was in 1723 a temporary set-back in the trade, but within twelve years Glasgow was again forging ahead with 67 ships of 5,600 tons, which by 1783 had increased to 386 of 22,896 tons. Glasgow's total import of tobacco from America rose from 4,192,576 lb. in 1724 to 47,268,873 lb., besides 6½ million lb. of sugar and 826,741 gallons of rum, by 1771. In fact, on the eve of the American war Glasgow had deprived Bristol and Liverpool of the lion's share of the tobacco trade, while her 'tobacco lords' living in palatial mansions, with gorgeous lackeys 'frisking across their barricaded courts',[1] were among the most prosperous merchants of the kingdom; as a result of this prosperity by 1785 the general population of the city had been nearly quadrupled since 1708.[2]

Besides agriculture Scotland's main industries before the Union had been the fisheries, linen, and woollens. The fishing grounds off the Scottish coast were rich enough, but were freely poached on by English and Dutch fleets, with which the few Scottish fishing-boats could not effectively compete. The Scottish linen and woollen goods required by the Glasgow merchants to exchange for American tobacco were rough and of poor quality and could not compete with the English or Irish products. Provision, however, had been made in the Act of Union and in an act of 1718 for the encouragement of such industries. By these measures £28,000 had been set aside[3] to stimulate Scottish fisheries and manufactures, particularly that of coarse wool. In addition, any surplus over £20,000 from the malt tax to be raised in Scotland in 1725 was to be reserved for the same purposes. Till 1727 these sums had been accumulating unspent, when a board of trustees for manufactures was established to distribute the fund; the board's first programme provided for the payment of annual grants of £2,650 each to the herring fishery and linen trade and £750 to the woollen industry. For the linen industry French weavers were brought over from Picardy,[4]

---

[1] Mathieson, op. cit., p. 244; Graham, l.c. i. 143.

[2] For these figures see H. Hamilton, l.c., pp. 3–5.

[3] Article XV of the Act of Union ordered £2,000 per annum for seven years to be put on one side for the encouragement of the coarse woollen industry; the act of 1718 secured another £2,000 per annum for seven years for the encouragement of fisheries and manufactures in general. See Hamilton, l.c., p. 78, and Mathieson, *Scotland and the Union*, p. 346.

[4] Ten weavers with their families were settled in Edinburgh in a quarter still named Picardy Place.

and skilled 'hecklers' from Flanders; flax-growing was encouraged
and suitable bleaching grounds provided: Roebuck's vitriol
factory at Prestonpans,[1] established in 1749, eventually produced
a cheaper and more effective means of bleaching than the sour
milk hitherto used. The trustees in 1751 were given further
powers for maintaining a high quality in the linen sold, and
two years later they were assigned funds from the forfeited
estates after the '45 for encouraging the industry in the Highlands; while the British Linen Company, founded about the
same time, helped the poorer workers by selling them yarn on
credit and buying back the finished article. In fact, between
1728 and 1760 not only had the quality of the linen sold greatly
improved but the output, in the latter year valued at over
£500,000, had increased nearly sixfold. By the end of George
II's reign, too, the woollens of the Lowlands, the tartans,
serges, blankets, and stockings of the Highlands, and the
carpets of Kilmarnock had attained a more than local fame.
The only industry which, in spite of all efforts, seemed unable to
revive was fishing. In 1729 the royal burghs, which claimed the
exclusive privilege of fishing, formed a company to finance
the trade with a capital of £2,200,000 Scots.[2] In 1750 a bill was
introduced into parliament by General Oglethorpe to provide
bounties for the herring fishery not only from Scottish but also
English ports such as Lowestoft and Southwold. In the debate
in the lords Lord Granville took occasion to pay a notable
tribute to Scottish herrings, in his opinion the 'most exquisite
both for taste and flavour . . . yet they were despised by the
country people; even my own servants could hardly be induced
to taste them . . . but if herrings should once come to be frequently served up at the tables of the great, they would soon
come to be coveted by the poor and would be as cheap and as
wholesome a food as any they now use'. But his pleading fell on
deaf ears. In vain had Admiral Vernon gone to Holland to
investigate the Dutchman's better method of curing herrings;
in vain the prince of Wales accepted the governorship of the
Free British Fishery Company established under the act with
power to raise £500,000 at 3 per cent. to be granted out of
the customs for bounties of 30s. per ton to fishing vessels. For

[1] See below, pp. 285 and 387.
[2] The Scots pound was worth about 1s. 8d. in English money. Graham, l.c.
i. 85.

in 1761 it appeared that, whereas the Dutch had 152 ships fishing off the coast of Scotland, the Scots themselves had only 17.[1]

On the whole the Lowlands, during the first fifty years of the Union, were gradually increasing in prosperity. But they still had their grievances, the most serious being the system of customs and excise collections, far more drastic than that to which they had been used in the easier days of their own régime. These grievances led to two ugly incidents. In 1713 a malt tax had been imposed on the United Kingdom, which the Scots complained of as violating a clause in the Act of Union: but in practice the tax had not been collected in Scotland. Then in 1724 Walpole, partly to placate the English brewers, who complained of the unfair competition from Scotland's cheaper beer, imposed a uniform tax of 6d. on every barrel of beer: this in turn aroused an outcry throughout Scotland, as it increased the price of their beloved 'twopenny ale'. So as a compromise in 1725 Walpole reverted to the 6d. a bushel tax on malt for England but of only 3d. for Scotland. But even this moderate tax provoked serious trouble in both Glasgow and Edinburgh. In Glasgow the lord advocate had to call in General Wade and his soldiers to quell the riotous mobs; in Edinburgh the brewers flatly refused to brew any beer till the tax was repealed, but here too Forbes, with the help of Islay, persuaded the court of session to declare such a strike illegal and the brewers to return to their brewing.[2] The Porteous Riots in Edinburgh of 1736 were even more serious. Two smugglers, Wilson and Robertson, were arrested for robbing a collector of customs, an official as much detested as his assailants' occupation was admired throughout Scotland. Robertson was able to escape but Wilson was duly hanged for his offence: on his execution, however, the mob became so violent that Porteous, captain of the Town Guard, ordered his men to fire. Tried by Edinburgh judges for murder, Porteous was sentenced to death, but respited by Queen Caroline, at the time guardian of the realm. The Edinburgh populace, however, was determined he should suffer the penalty, which was duly carried out on the day originally appointed by

---

[1] *Parl. Hist.* xiv. 762–4, 774; Hume Brown, *Hist. of Scotland*, iii. 252–3. Oglethorpe's act was 23 Geo. II, c. 24.

[2] Roxburgh's lukewarmness on the malt tax was the occasion of his dismissal from the Scottish secretaryship in 1725. See above pp. 203 and 272.

a perfectly orderly crowd, without any interference by the magistrates. Such an outrage could not be ignored by the government. Islay, Forbes, and the solicitor-general were sent to conduct an inquiry in Edinburgh but were faced by a conspiracy of silence. Then acts were passed, one requiring all ministers publicly to invite their congregations to discover Porteous's murderers, and another fining Edinburgh £2,000 and deposing the lord provost from office: the removal of one of the city gates and other severe indignities would have been imposed on the city had it not been for the stand taken against them by Forbes and other Scottish government supporters.[1]

In spite of such occasional ebullitions the south of Scotland was, by the middle of the century, well reconciled to the Union, under which it was prospering. It was far otherwise with the Highlands. North of Stirling the country was almost as much a *terra incognita* to the Lowlander as to the Englishman. Rugged mountain paths were the only means of penetrating these fastnesses of patriarchal chiefs who were untroubled by the king's laws and administered their own justice. Their clansmen were bound to them not merely as tenants but for the duty of military service. The clans themselves were divided by feuds personal and political which made raids and forays almost endemic. Fortunately for the government the strongest of the Highland clans, Argyll's Campbells, was on its side.[2] The Highlands, too, were a poor country, dependent chiefly on cattle-raising, but so overstocked and with such bad pastures that the cattle surviving the winters or neighbours' raids were of little value till they had been sent down from the great cattle-marts at Crieff and Falkirk to be fattened on the rich pastures of Norfolk.[3] The Highlanders, however, knew how to supplement their own poor cattle by raids on their Lowland neighbours. As late as 1747 the annual losses of the Lowlands from Highland raids or 'creaghs' was computed at no less than £37,000, made up as on the following page.

[1] All but one of the forty-five Scottish members in this instance voted against the government, Mathieson, *Awakening of Scotland*, p. 22.
[2] A lively account of the clan system is given in Smollett's *Humphrey Clinker* (Letter from Matt. Bramble to Dr. Lewis of 6 Sept.).
[3] In 1723, 30,000 head of cattle were sold at Crieff fair to English dealers for an average of a guinea apiece. Hume Brown, iii. 255, and Hamilton, l.c., p. 62.

						£
Cattle lifted	.	.	.	.	. valued at	5,000
Blackmail to avoid cattle-lifting .			.	.	,, ,,	5,000
Cost of attempting to recover lifted cattle					,, ,,	2,000
Expenses of guarding against thefts			.		,, ,,	10,000
Loss from understocking for fear of plun-						
dering	.	.	.	.	. ,, ,,	15,000

£37,000[1]

Some idea of the lawless state of the Highlands may be gained from the exploits of the most notable of these freebooters, Robert MacGregor or Campbell, known as Rob Roy, who did business by levying ransom from those he protected, chiefly against his own freebooting and cattle-lifting raids. He was no obscure bandit, but acting chief of the Macgregor clan, an ally at times of the dukes of Montrose and Atholl, though that did not prevent his occasional raids on their territories, and always apparently on good terms with the great Campbell, John, duke of Argyll. In the '15 he was nominally on the Pretender's side, but appears to have taken no active part beyond forays for his own profit; he was present at Glenshiel in 1719, but captured in 1722, sent to Newgate and condemned to the Barbados, but pardoned on the eve of sailing. After that he was content with one duel arising from a dispute with the MacLarens and died in his bed in 1734. His son Robert was a pale echo of his father; he continued the feud with the MacLarens, murdering one of them, then enlisted in the 42nd Regiment for a period, and, after his discharge, was finally hanged for his part, with two of his brothers, in abducting and forcibly marrying a rich young widow.

After the '15 the government had made some attempt to break down the barriers imposed by nature and their own disposition on the Highlanders, whereby the north of Scotland was kept apart, not only from England, but also from the Lowlands. But Scottish national feeling obstructed their efforts. The commission appointed to distribute the proceeds of the 1715 rebels' forfeited estates, though realizing £84,043 from sales, secured a net gain of only £1,107 for the benefit of Scotland, owing to the vast expenses incurred in the ill-disposed

---

[1] Hume Brown, iii, 261; Hamilton, l.c., p. 63.

court of session. The act for disarming the Highland clans proved almost a dead letter until in 1725 it was re-enacted and its execution put in the capable hands of Duncan Forbes and General Wade. They realized that nothing would be so effective for its success and for opening up the Highlands as road-construction. Wade raised four, then six companies of Highlanders, the officers being all taken from whig clans, allowed them to wear tartan kilts, and set them to work road-making. In 1739 the companies were raised to ten and formed into the Black Watch, a regiment which fought at Fontenoy.[1] Wade effectively disarmed some of the loyal clans, but the others, while surrendering their old and useless weapons, took care to retain those likely to serve them in another rising. This road-making, however, was most valuable. Between 1726 and 1737 Wade and his Highlanders constructed 259 miles of road and 40 bridges in the heart of the Highlands, from Perth and Stirling over the Grampians to Inverness and thence to Fort Augustus and Fort William.[2] Unfortunately when the '45 was sprung upon the government, most of the thirty or more forts built by Wade to protect the new roads were either empty or inadequately manned, so that the rebels at first profited more from the better communications than the royal troops; and Fort William alone, under the command of Captain Caroline Scott, offered a gallant and successful resistance to the large force of rebels assembled to capture it.[3]

After the second rebellion the government tackled the condition of the Highlands in earnest and to some purpose. Duncan Forbes, as lord president and as laird of Culloden, a man of great influence in the Highlands, had done valiant work, ill-requited by the government, watching suspects such as Lord Lovat and stimulating the activities of loyal clans. William Grant of Prestongrange, appointed lord advocate in 1746, was an equally wise and zealous supporter of reform. It is to their credit, too, that both incurred Cumberland's hostility by their

[1] In the same year a sergeant and a private, kilts and all, were sent to London where they were inspected by George II, who seems to have been much taken with their appearance. See Fortescue, *British Army*, ii. 50.

[2] Details of the roads and bridges, especially the five-arched Tay bridge, are given in C. Dalton, *George I's Army*, ii. 15–16; see also Salmond, *Wade in Scotland*, who calculates (p. 113) that Wade built 240 miles of road and 30 bridges.

[3] Fort Ruthven near Kingussie bravely withstood one attack, but later was overwhelmed. Both Fort George and Fort Augustus were tamely surrendered. See C. L. Kingsford in *English Historical Review*, xxxvii. 361–82.

opposition to savage repression.[1] Among the preventive or punitive measures passed after the rebellion were the forfeiture to the Crown of the estates of the principal rebels, Lovat, the duke of Perth, Cameron of Lochiel, &c.,[2] and acts compelling the episcopalian clergy, mostly Jacobites, to take the oath of allegiance and to pray in church for the king, and forbidding the wearing of the kilt and tartans or the bearing of arms, 'the most important medicine', according to Duncan Forbes, for Highland disaffection.[3] But the root of the troubles was thought to lie in the two powers of the chiefs: (i) hereditary jurisdiction in courts of their own, independent of the king's law; (ii) ward-holding, or the right of claiming military service as a condition of tenancy, whereby it was estimated that great chiefs such as Argyll, Atholl, Sutherland, and Breadalbane could lead into the field independent forces of 3,000, 3,000, 2,000, and 1,000 clansmen respectively.[4] Quite apart from the danger of such powers in times of civil strife, they were quite incompatible, as Hardwicke argued, in introducing the measure of the abolition of heritable jurisdictions, with a uniform law and source of authority for the whole United Kingdom. By two acts passed in May and June 1747 these two privileges were finally abolished, the one substituting royal sheriffs and circuits of the king's judges for the old feudal jurisdictions—a reform in existence in England since the middle ages—the other depriving disloyal chieftains of their power to levy private armies against the king. But as an accompaniment to these stern measures the government, largely on the lord advocate's advice, showed a wise generosity in admitting the principle of compensation to chiefs who gave up

[1] Forbes, for protesting against the slaughter of rebels who had taken refuge in the courtyard of his own house at Culloden, was described by Cumberland as 'that old woman who talked to me about humanity'. This story is discredited by Mr. Kingsford, l.c. in previous note; but at any rate Forbes's great services and expenses for the government were not recognized or requited.

[2] The forfeited estates were restored to their original owners in 1784. Hume Brown, l.c. iii. 337, 352.

[3] *Culloden Papers*, pp. 288–9. Forbes continued 'the Bill for altering the Highland dress . . . without disarming, signifies not one halfpenny'.

[4] Hamilton, l.c., pp. 30–31. It is interesting to note that several of the Scottish prisoners pleaded at their trial after the '45 that they were bound to obey the behests of their superior lords and fight on the side they were so bidden. See *State Trials*, xviii. 391–4. [In fact few of the Highland chiefs possessed any right of jurisdiction and both these measures 'originated in a misreading of the rebellion'. Their importance lay in their more general significance as advanced by Hardwicke. See Mathieson, *Scotland and the Union*, pp. 373–7. C.H.S.]

their heritable jurisdictions, and in allowing their claims to be brought before the Scottish court of session. The total amount claimed was £602,127; the total allowed £152,237.[1] In 1749 parliament also voted, on the lord advocate's proposal, a grant of £10,000 to recoup Glasgow for the tribute exacted from the city by Charles Edward and for her loyalty in raising two regiments against him: on the other hand Lord Provost Stewart of Edinburgh was sent to trial for neglect and misbehaviour, but was acquitted, by a perhaps partial jury of his fellow citizens.[2]

Lord Adocate Grant was also responsible for the wisest measure of conciliation taken by the government—to devote the proceeds of the forfeited estates to 'civilizing the inhabitants upon the said estates and other parts of the Highlands and Islands of Scotland, the promoting amongst them the Protestant religion, good government, industry and manufactures and the principles of duty and loyalty to his Majesty', or, as it was put more cynically by a contemporary, 'Feed the clans and they will obey; starve them and they must rebel'. It took, of course, some time to exorcise the old clan jealousies and establish complete law and order in the Highlands. The Appin murder of a Campbell by Alan Breck Stewart in 1752 and the trial of Alan's brother as an accomplice by a packed tribunal of Campbells presided over by Argyll himself were ugly symptoms of the vindictive clan spirit still remaining.[3] But such instances became rarer and rarer; and less than fifteen years after the '45 Pitt was able to call rebel Highlanders from their mountain glens to help conquer Canada for the United Kingdom. At any rate from this time onwards the Highlands as a whole began to share in some of the prosperity and enlightenment which had already come in some degree to the Lowlands since the Union. Their woollen and linen industries were fostered by judicious grants;[4] improvements were made in farming and tree-planting by rich Lowlanders who had leased some of the forfeited estates and by tenants who were given longer leases than in the past; the good work, too, begun by Wade was greatly extended as a result of

[1] The duke of Argyll was the only chief whose allowance of £22,000 approached his claim for £25,000. The duke of Gordon claimed £22,000 but got only £5,000.
[2] On these preventive measures see Hume Brown, iii. 329–30, and especially Mathieson, *Scotland and the Union*, pp. 369–81.
[3] Stevenson's *Kidnapped* is based on these incidents. There is still some doubt whether Stewart fired the shot.
[4] The attempt to establish a linen industry in the Highlands was not successful except in Inverness and Perthshire, Hamilton, l.c., p. 90.

the further military building whereby some 800 more miles of roads and 1,000 bridges were constructed to open up the country.[1]

But the most beneficial result of the remedial measures taken after the '45 was the impetus given to education in the Highlands. Scotland had long been ahead of England in educational facilities: her universities, at any rate Edinburgh and Glasgow, were far more alive than Oxford and Cambridge in this century; and ever since Knox's time, in theory at least, the Scottish church was responsible for the elementary education of all children of whatever degree, though in fact this responsibility had hardly penetrated beyond the Lowlands, owing to the poverty, the clannishness, and the inaccessibility of large parts of the Highlands. Already, however, in 1709 a patent had been obtained from the Crown for a Scottish branch of the S.P.C.K., the main object of which was to establish schools in the Highlands. Unlike the English branch, the Scottish S.P.C.K. made itself entirely responsible for the finance and management of the schools it established and by careful finance and very small salaries to the schoolmasters[2] had by 1758 established 176 elementary schools in the Highlands; but it was not so successful in the technical schools it was empowered to start by its second patent in 1738. On the other hand the government itself, from the proceeds of the forfeited estates, established after the '45 several schools for combining literary and industrial instruction in the Highlands, some of which were successful. By its elementary schools, however, the society had a very large part in bringing the Highlands into closer relationship with the Lowlands and England. It never tried to compete with schools already established by the church, but set them up in districts hitherto inaccessible to any teaching,[3] and in sparsely populated districts initiated 'ambulatory' schools to secure the greatest number of pupils from the scattered crofts and bothies. In pursuance of its policy of unifying Highlands and Lowlands

[1] See above, p. 104, n. 1. After 1745 roads in the Lowlands also were extended; this was a consequence of the Turnpike Acts of 1751 and subsequent years. See Hamilton, l.c., pp. 227–9.

[2] The average salary of the Society's schoolmasters at the end of the century was no more than £12 per annum. Ordinary parish schoolmasters not employed by the Society averaged £10 per annum. See Graham, l.c. ii. 166, and M. G. Jones, *Charity School Movement*, p. 191.

[3] The Society refused to help where parishes had made no effort of their own. Its purpose was to set up 'assistant' schools, not to relieve indifferent or hostile heritors from their legal obligations to support the parish schools. See Jones, p. 183.

Erse was excluded from the schools, the teaching being only in English: and it was largely owing to the influence of these schools that in 1773 Dr. Johnson noted that 'there was perhaps never any change of national manners so quick, so great and so general, as that which has operated in the *Highlands*, by the last conquest and the subsequent laws. . . . Schools are erected in which *English* only is taught.'[1]

The suppression of the '45 rebellion and the wise measures of appeasement which ensued completed the good work of the Union for Scotland no less than for England. David Masson indeed declared that the half-century that followed was 'the period of Scotland's most energetic, peculiar and most various life'. We have already seen how the Lowlands had profited from their closer connexion with England; the sense of peace and stability that came with the pacification and opening up of the north completed the good work. By the end of George II's reign Scotland was already establishing a lead in important industrial enterprises, such as Roebuck's vitriol factory at Prestonpans, the Carron ironworks just founded, and the Glasgow trade with America, while James Watt was on the eve of his great discoveries which were to revolutionize the steam-engine, and Scottish farmers were no longer lagging behind their English teachers. This growing prosperity was also encouraging the more gracious amenities of civilization. There is indeed a great deal of truth in Voltaire's quizzical remark: 'It is an admirable result of the progress of the human spirit that at the present time it is from Scotland we receive rules of taste in all the arts—from the epic poem to gardening.'[2]

The Presbyterian church, always one of the most important elements in the social organization of Scotland, at the beginning of the eighteenth century still retained much of the dour intolerance which had provoked Oliver Cromwell's scathing retort;[3] but, as the century advanced, it became more mellowed and humanistic. Patronage in the appointment of ministers, which

---

[1] *Journey to Western Islands of Scotland*, quoted by M. G. Jones, l.c., pp. 166–214. Johnson, however, protested strongly against the refusal of the S.P.C.K. to countenance a translation of the Bible into Erse for the benefit of those who could not read English. See his letters of 1766 and 1767 in Boswell. [In fact the prohibition against teaching in Erse was rescinded in 1766. Jones, p. 195. C.H.S.]

[2] Quoted by Hume Brown, iii. 371.

[3] For a picture of the Scottish church in its most intolerant stage see Buckle, *History of Civilization*, vol. ii, chap. v; see also Graham, vol. ii, chap. viii.

had been abolished in 1690, had been restored by the tory parliament in 1712. In the early days of whig rule after 1714 it was little enforced; but by the middle of the century patrons were coming into their rights, and their tendency was to appoint ministers of more enlightened views.[1] Congregations still claimed the right to 'call' (or reject) the patrons' nominees, but an increasing majority in the general assembly had by the middle of the century reduced this right to a mere form. Several secessions, of which the church of Scotland has been so prolific, occurred as a result; but in general the 'moderates', such as Alexander Carlyle and Principal Robertson, the historian, moulded the establishment to a wider toleration. The older prejudices, however, died hard. A theatre established in Edinburgh by Allan Ramsay in 1736 was naturally frowned on then;[2] it is more surprising to find that as late as 1757 the Rev. John Home was not only denounced by the Edinburgh and other presbyteries for producing there his innocuous tragedy *Douglas*, but even forced to resign his charge.[3] Nevertheless the leaders of the church had become less intolerant, especially between 1750 and 1770, when the assembly, guided mainly by Robertson, was at the height of its reputation and could boast, it was asserted, 'of some of the best speaking in Britain, the House of Commons scarcely excepted'. Throughout, too, the Scottish clergy never sank to the level of many in England, being generally respected and fairly educated.

This 'moderatism' in high ecclesiastical quarters helped to encourage the literary revival in Scotland, illustrated by such great names at Hutcheson, the poet Allan Ramsay, Hume, Adam Smith, and many others. Edinburgh was indeed fast becoming one of the most enlightened cities in the kingdom. Clubs such as the 'Rankenian Club' founded in 1716, the 'Philosophical Society' of 1739, still more the 'Select Society' of 1754, each in turn became a focus of light and liberalism with members such as Colin MacLaurin, Robertson, Hume, Cullen, Adam Smith,

[1] Of the 944 benefices in the Scottish church the patronage of 876 rested with the Crown, the nobility, and the gentry, generally less bigoted than many of the congregations. See Mathieson, *The Awakening of Scotland*, pp. 145 sqq., for a full account of these ecclesiastical disputes.

[2] This theatre was closed after only six months. At the same time another theatre, established in 1733, was closed. Mathieson, op. cit., p. 159.

[3] The play was produced in Dec. 1756. Home resigned 'without any mark of censure' in June 1757. See Mathieson, pp. 161–3.

Wedderburn, Home, Alexander 'Jupiter' Carlyle, John, Robert, and James Adam, Lord Hailes, Lord Kames, and Lord Monboddo on its roll.[1] The universities too of Glasgow and Edinburgh, with such teachers as the philosophers Hutcheson and Reid, the scientists Cullen, Black, and James Hutton, and Alexander Monro primus as an organizer, were, as we have seen, the best in the United Kingdom.[2]

In a word Scotland owed her revival and above all the security needed for the full exercise of her great talents for business, industry, and culture to her association with England at the Union; but she was already beginning to repay this blessing with interest.[3]

The history of Ireland during this period stands in striking contrast to that of Scotland, and is one to which England can look back only with shame. No doubt there have been times of more brutal repression and confiscation, but at least in the reign of Elizabeth or the seventeenth century, for example, there was the excuse that Ireland was in rebellion and that if the connexion between the two kingdoms was to be maintained, she had to be subdued. But between 1714 and 1760 there was no such reason. Ireland had no thought of rebellion: on the contrary she was submissive, even cowed. During the risings of 1715 and 1745 she was the only part of the two islands that gave no cause for anxiety. No more favourable opportunity had ever occurred for binding the Irish nation to us by the ties of self-interest, by promoting her industries and general well-being, and removing at least the harsher aspect of her religious grievances. On the contrary the penal laws against the Roman catholics, an overwhelming majority of the population, even though generally modified in practice, were never more savage; industries of the country in any way competing with those of England were ruthlessly suppressed; the most lucrative civil and ecclesiastical posts were chiefly reserved for English nominees, and the impoverished country's swollen pension list largely used for the benefit of English or German pensioners. As Chatham once

[1] For an account of these clubs see Tytler, i. 241–58 and iii. 75–77.
[2] For fuller details of the scientific, artistic, and literary revival in Scotland see Chaps. XIV, XV, and XVI.
[3] I am deeply indebted, for criticisms on this section, to Dr. Meikle and Dr. Law Mathieson. Dr. Mathieson's kind suggestions to me were, I believe, the last piece of work he undertook before his sudden and deeply regretted death. (Note of 1939).

said: 'England . . . profits by draining Ireland of the vast incomes spent here from that country.'[1] By such a policy England was antagonizing, not only the down-trodden Roman catholic majority, but also Ireland's ruling minority of protestants, nearly all of English or Scottish stock, and virtually preparing the way for an alliance between them against herself. In fact, even in this, one of the darkest periods of Irish suppression, the smouldering fires of resentment, stirred by the genius of a Swift, flared up throughout the country in one victorious blaze that for the moment carried all before it—but for the moment only.

On the principle of *divide et impera* Ireland should have been a country easy to govern; for the population was sharply divided into three sections having little in common: native Irish, Ulster presbyterians, and the Anglo-Irish ruling caste. Self-preservation against the Irish Roman catholics, who were five-sixths of the population,[2] was the motive of the penal laws, with which indeed the minority in Ireland heartily sympathized. By these laws the native Irish were little better than pariahs, with no voice in the government, and at times with scarcely even the means of livelihood. An essentially agricultural and pastoral people, they had been deprived of most of their lands in the seventeenth century,[3] and, being legally unable, as Arthur Young says, to 'buy land, take a mortgage, or even sign down the rent of a lease' for more than thirty-one years, were at the mercy of harsh middlemen and liable to be turned out at any moment from their humble tenancies. A premium on apostasy was enacted by a law of Anne, whereby the protestant children of a Roman catholic landowner inherited the bulk of his estate, and the Roman catholic heir of a protestant was similarly penalized. Similar handicaps impeded those who turned to other trades. In 1728, by means of Archbishop Boulter,[4] the Irish catholics were deprived of their last shreds of self-expression, the practice of the legal profession, and the parliamentary franchise. 'Little

---

[1] *Chatham Correspondence*, iv. 300 (24 Oct. 1773).

[2] *Letters . . . (of) Hugh Boulter, Lord Primate of All Ireland 1724–38*, 2 vols., Oxford, 1769, i. 210 sqq.

[3] W. F. Butler, *Confiscation in Irish History*, p. 237, following Arthur Young's view, estimates that at the beginning of the eighteenth century the Roman catholics did not own more than one-twentieth of the soil.

[4] Boulter, l.c. i. 226–31. Hugh Boulter, 1672–1742, promoted to the Irish primacy 1724 from the bishopric of Bristol and the deanery of Christ Church, Oxford.

better than hewers of wood and drawers of water . . . out of all capacity of doing any mischief, if they were ever so well inclined', says Swift of these unfortunate people;[1] and Lord Chancellor Bowes is said, in 1759, to have declared that 'the laws did not presume an Irish Papist to exist in the kingdom, where they were only supposed to breathe through the connivance of Government'.[2] One only consolation remained to them, which nothing would induce them to give up, their Roman catholic religion. Their religious services were not actually suppressed, but their priests had to be registered and to give security, while their bishops were banned and also their monks and nuns: in fact, as the saintly Archbishop King sorrowfully admitted, 'If we should measure our temper by our laws, I think we are little short of the Inquisition'.[3] But in spite of savage legislation it was obviously an impossible task to exterminate the religion of five-sixths of a total population of over 2,000,000. In 1728 Archbishop Boulter declared[4] that, as against only 800 clergy of the established church, there were some 3,000 popish priests, though only 1,080 appear to have been registered; and in a report of 1732 to the Irish house of lords he stated that Ireland contained 892 mass-houses, 51 friaries, and 549 papist schools. By 1751/2, according to another source, no less than 24 popish bishops were exercising their functions. These numbers are the more remarkable when it is remembered that, besides being by law obliged to pay tithes to the Anglican clergy, the miserably poor Irish peasants contributed their pennies to the upkeep of their own priests and bishops as well as for their own schools. In fact, however, except during Jacobite scares, as in 1715 and 1722, the penal laws were to a large extent laxly administered. Even at the height of the '45 Chesterfield refused to interfere with papist chapels, an example which brought no ill consequence to the state and encouraged a growing spirit of tolerance. Nevertheless the repressive laws remained on the statute book for nearly a century longer and could by intolerant juries or

[1] *A Letter concerning the Sacramental Test*, Swift, ii. 17 (Temple Scott edn., 1898), quoted by Lecky, *Ireland*, i. 456.
[2] Quoted by J. C. O'Callaghan, *History of Irish Brigades in Service of France*, 1870, p. 159.
[3] Quoted by M. G. Jones, *Charity Movement in Eighteenth Century*, p. 220.
[4] Boulter, i. 210 and 223; of the 800 established clergy some 600 were incumbents. Lecky, *Ireland*, i. 239, for estimate of population.

magistrates be at any time set in motion against obnoxious persons.[1]

Archbishop Boulter himself, much troubled by the poor results of legislation and proselytism in converting the Roman catholics to protestantism, pinned great faith on the methods of conversion to be obtained by protestant schools. As in England and Scotland, an Irish branch of the S.P.C.K. had been started early in the eighteenth century. Bishop Maule's famous Green Coat Hospital at Cork had been established in 1715, and by 1725 no less than 163 such protestant schools with 3,000 pupils had been opened in Ireland. Then in 1733 Boulter, alarmed at the multiplication of Roman catholic schools, formed the Incorporated Society under the highest patronage for building charity schools primarily 'to convert the poor deluded natives to be good Christians'. To this Society a royal grant of £1,000 per annum was given from 1738 to 1794, and in 1747 the Irish parliament began a system of grants averaging £3,500 annually from 1751 to 1761. The children in these schools, soon dotted all over Ireland, were fed and clothed and, besides religious instruction, were taught farming and trades, in the hope of making them pay their way. But there was no adequate control over the schools, which after the middle of the century were abominably managed, as Howard revealed later, and they became intensely unpopular with the parents, who much preferred the 'hedge schools' run by Roman catholic teachers, whose instruction seems to have been infinitely better.[2]

A deplorable result of these religious disabilities was that for nearly a century Ireland was drained of all the best elements of the Roman catholic community. Pariahs at home, their only hope of vigorous life was in the service of continental rulers. Under the terms of the treaty of Limerick in 1691 some 14,000 of James II's army were actually transported to France by William III to take service in Louis XIV's Irish brigade, which had been established in the previous year. With this accession of strength the brigade could muster some 20,000 men formed into five regiments of infantry[3] and one of cavalry; and, at any

---

[1] For these figures see Lecky, op. cit. i. 267–70. An admirable survey of the penal legislation against Roman catholics is in M. J. Bonn, *Die Englische Kolonisation in Irland*, 2 vols., Berlin, 1906, ii. 169–77.

[2] See Jones, pp. 215–65, and Lecky, *Ireland*, i. 233–8.

[3] Between 1744 and 1762 the strength was increased to six regiments of infantry. For the Irish in foreign service see O'Callaghan, *passim*; Lecky, *England in Eighteenth*

rate till 1748, the losses in the brigade were constantly being made good by recruits from Ireland. Nor was this all: at one time the king of Spain also had five Irish regiments, and in 1736 presented one of them to his son Don Carlos, who had recently acquired the kingdom of Naples, as a better protection than the Neapolitan levies;[1] many Irishmen also found their way to the emperor's and the tsar's armies. According to one estimate, between 1691 and 1745 no less than 450,000 Irish catholics were recruited for the Irish brigade in France alone.[2] In times of war or internal trouble from Jacobites the English government was naturally sensitive about the presence of this Irish brigade on the French coast. Thus in 1722, the year of the Atterbury plot, Carteret sent special thanks to the regent and Dubois for recalling the Irish brigade from Dunkirk.[3] To keep up its strength active recruiting in Ireland by French officers or agents was essential: such recruiting was generally surreptitious, the men enlisted being taken overseas, under the designation of 'Wild Geese', together with contraband wool, by French brandy-smugglers from the ports of Munster and Connaught.[4] Such enlistments were in fact illegal, and in 1726 an Irishman was executed for enlisting men for the service of the Pretender: nevertheless the English government, when Anglo-French relations were friendly, actually allowed Louis XV to send recruiting agents to Ireland, and even welcomed the loss of their papist subjects.[5] How serious the loss was may be seen from the valour of these Irish allies of our enemies in William III's wars, in the war of the Spanish Succession, at Fontenoy, where the Irish brigade snatched a glorious victory from almost certain defeat, and many other battle-fields, not to speak of the great Irish commanders such as Lord Clare, Browne, Lacy, Nugent,

Century, ii. 395–9, and paper on 'Irish Regiments in Service of Spain and Naples' by the Marquis MacSwiney of Mashanaglass in Proc. of R. Irish Academy, xxxvii, § c (1924–7), pp. 158 sqq.

[1] MacSwiney.

[2] O'Callaghan, p. 163; Lecky, England, ii. 262, thinks this estimate perfectly incredible.

[3] Add. MS. 22516, f. 59.

[4] O'Callaghan, p. 162; MacSwiney, l.c.

[5] The opposition, however, was always on the watch against such licences, and owing to an article in the Craftsman in 1730 the government had to withdraw the permission given to French recruiting agents; while in 1738 the Irish parliament was allowed to pass an act imposing the death penalty on any Irishman who enlisted in foreign service. See British Diplomatic Instructions, vi. France, pp. xvi, xxxiv, 206; and Lord King's 'Notes of Domestic . . . Affairs' in his Life of Locke, ii. 115–18.

O'Donnell, the Dillons, Lally Tollendal, Maguire, O'Mahony, O'Reilly, and many others in the Austrian, Russian, French, and Spanish armies, or of statesmen and public men such as Tyrconnel, a French ambassador, Charles Wogan, who rescued Clementina Sobieski for the Old Pretender, and Wall, a chief minister of Spain.

Apart from this crushed majority of Irish Roman catholics, even the Irish protestants were not united or all in possession of equal privileges. The vigorous nonconformist community of Ulster, though allowed freedom of worship and even recognized by the *Regium Donum* raised in 1718 to £2,000 per annum, were excluded by tests from sitting in parliament and, until a Toleration Act was passed in 1719, from civil and military service to the Crown.[1] But they made up for their legal disqualifications by their enterprise and success in business, and in their own Ulster flouted bishops of the established church with all Knox's or Melville's uncompromising spirit. Thus all political power, such as it was in Ireland, was confined to Anglo-Irish members of the established church, who alone could sit in the Irish parliament, and were in possession of nearly all the land. But even this political power was largely an illusion, owing to the restrictions imposed on Ireland by the English ministry and parliament.

The system of government instituted by England was in itself an insult to the Irish people. There were eleven lords lieutenant[2] during this period: four of them at least, Sunderland, Townshend, Carteret, and Harrington, were appointed solely for the reason given by Townshend in writing to the duke of Grafton to excuse his supersession by Carteret: 'I am persuaded that your grace is so well convinced of the necessity . . . of removing Lord Carteret from the employment he was in [secretary of state] and of the impossibility there was of doing it without giving some considerable equivalent that . . . his having the government of Ireland was in a manner unavoidable.'[3] In fact Ireland was often regarded as a convenient shelf for ministers out of favour yet too considerable to be simply

---

[1] Those who held commissions in the militia during the '15 ran the risk of prosecution for so doing and were only protected by resolutions of the Irish house of commons. See Lecky, *Ireland*, i. 434–5.

[2] One of them, the duke of Dorset, held the appointment for two separate periods, 1730–6 and 1750–5.

[3] Coxe, *Walpole*, ii. 295–6.

dismissed. It is not, therefore, surprising that few of these dignitaries took their elevation too seriously. Two of them, Sunderland and Townshend, never took the trouble to go over to Ireland at all; and altogether during the forty-six years of George I and II the aggregate time spent there by the other nine was barely sixteen years. The lord lieutenant was generally expected to hold court in Dublin during the winter months that the Irish parliament was in session, after which he returned to London, leaving lords justices to exercise his functions; but sometimes a whole year passed without a viceregal visit. Of all these eleven holders of the office only two, Carteret and Chesterfield, aroused any enthusiasm in Ireland. Both gained respect by their calm common sense, unruffled courtesy, and strength of purpose in difficult situations, Carteret in the heat of the agitation against Wood's Halfpence, Chesterfield during the '45; and both endeared themselves to the sensitive Dublin public by their wit and charm and their genuine appreciation of the country and its inhabitants. Carteret was also notable for his endeavours to bring some sort of order into the national finances and the army administration,[1] his zeal for the poor, his encouragement of native industries, and his attempts, often thwarted by Boulter and Newcastle, to bestow some of the administrative and ecclesiastical plums on natives of the country, irrespective of their political views. Both houses of parliament voted addresses to him for his 'unwearied application and the exact enquiries you have made into everything that relates to the state of this Kingdom . . . and the affectionate concern you have shown for the welfare of this nation . . . [qualities] which have not rendered your government more acceptable than your candour and humanity have endeared your person':[2] while Swift paid him the highest compliment in his power: 'What the vengeance brought you among us? Get you gone, get you gone; pray God Almighty send us our boobies back again.'[3]

The lords justices who, in the absence of the lord lieutenant, ruled the country, were chosen as far as possible for their docility. The chancellor, one of the two primates, Armagh and

---

[1] Carteret discovered on his arrival that the national accounts were three years in arrear and that the state of the barracks, the equipment of the army, and even the discipline of the officers were very defective. See R.O. Ireland, 63 *passim*, and Add. MS. 9243, ff. 51, 53, 66.

[2] R.O. Ireland, 63, ff. 384, 387.

[3] *Biographia Britannica* (5 vols., 1778–93), iii. 274.

Dublin,[1] and the Speaker of the house of commons were almost invariably appointed lords justices, with or without other colleagues. The chancellor and the archbishop of course owed their appointments to government patronage, and it was not unusual to secure the Speaker's interest by one or more lucrative posts,[2] the one exception being Henry Boyle, the most notable Speaker of this period. Boyle, Speaker from 1733 to 1756, proved himself a match even for Walpole, who called him 'the King of the Irish Commons'. He successfully resisted Walpole's attempt to get supplies voted for twenty-one years ahead, and was equally successful in preventing an internal tax on wool, which would have finally destroyed the Irish industry even for home consumption. Walpole then found it wiser to conciliate him; again, in 1751–3, after Walpole's death, when an attack was made by the English ministers on the Irish commons' power over the Irish purse, Boyle stood up for their rights.[3] Finally, in 1756 he was comparatively tamed by a peerage and a pension. But already Walpole, after his unfortunate experience with three recalcitrant lords justices, Lord Midleton, Archbishop King, and Speaker Conolly, during the Wood's Halfpence agitation, had taken effective steps to secure that at least two lords justices should be faithful mouthpieces of the English government's policy. King of Dublin had been so pro-Irish in this controversy that he was never again appointed a lord justice; and in 1724 Hugh Boulter was sent from the see of Bristol to assume the primacy of all Ireland at Armagh. Thereafter Boulter, till his death in 1742, was always one of the lords justices and became, along with the lord chancellor, the head of the English interest: with him indeed, far more than with Carteret or any other viceroy, rested the dispensation of patronage not only in bishoprics but also in legal appointments to men who, as he himself expressed it, 'would concur with me in promoting His Majesty's Service'.[4] With him originated the system of securing a complaisant house of commons through 'undertakers', i.e. the chief borough-mongers, who agreed to

---

[1] The archbishop of Armagh was primate of *all* Ireland, the archbishop of Dublin, primate of Ireland. There were also two more archbishops, of Cashel and of Tuam.

[2] The Speakers during this period were W. Conolly, Sir R. Gore, Henry Boyle (earl of Shannon), and John Ponsonby.

[3] See *Memoirs of the Boyles*, Dublin, 1754, pp. 227 sqq. [I have not been able to find an edition of 1754 of these *Memoirs*. C.H.S.].

[4] See Boulter, *Letters*, i. 273–4.

support the government through their nominees in the Irish parliament in return for suitable pensions and lucrative offices.[1] Boulter's two successors, Hoadly, brother of the bishop of Winchester, and Stone, brother of Newcastle's secretary, were equally strong in the 'English interest'. Again, the three holders of the Irish chancellorship from 1725 to 1756, West, Wyndham, and Jocelyn, two of whom were appointed from the English bar, could all be relied upon to promote the views of the English ministry. It was only towards the end of this period, when Stone tried to dispense with the undertakers' expensive services, that an effective opposition once more arose under such leaders as Shannon and Malone.

Thus, by the patronage of all important civil and ecclesiastical posts and by the use of so much of the Irish pension list as was not needed for English or German pensioners, the English ministry kept the Irish government well under control. The 'management' of an Irish parliament was comparatively easy, since general elections were infrequent. The house of commons elected on George II's accession lasted for the whole of his reign of thirty-three years: and a majority once secured was fairly stable. Moreover, England had secured an effective stranglehold on independent action by an Irish parliament. Already by Poynings' Law no legislation the heads of which had not been previously sanctioned by the English privy council could be brought before it. A further inroad on its powers was made by an act of the British parliament of 1719,[2] declaring its 'full power and authority to make Laws and Statutes . . . to bind the Kingdom and People of Ireland', and denying to the Irish house of lords any appellate jurisdiction from the Irish courts. In fact, too, the decisions of the Irish law-courts could be over-ruled on a writ of error to the English king's bench.[3] In 1751 the right of dealing with its own finance, a right admitted even for the houses of assembly in the American colonies, was denied to the Irish house of commons when it proposed to dispose of a surplus on its own budget. The English ministers held that any surplus belonged to the Crown, and could not be disposed of

[1] The list given by Froude, l.c. ii. 109, of considerations given to undertakers in 1771 is illuminatory of the system. The Irish house of commons had 300 members: of the 216 borough members 176 were dependent on landlords, 53 peers naming 123 of them in 1750. See Bonn, ii. 192–3; Lecky, *Ireland*, i. 195–7.

[2] 6 Geo. I, c. 5.

[3] See Campbell, *Lives of Lord Chancellors*, iv. 528.

without the king's leave, while the Irish house maintained that, having voted the revenue for specific purposes, any surplus arising therefrom was at their disposition. After prolonged wrangling the English ministry two years later sent instructions for the disposal of the surplus overruling a vote of the Irish commons: but in this case the real victory lay with the Irish house, who resolved that for the future there should be no surplus, and to that end increased the pension list and voted some useful but many wasteful bounties.[1]

More fatal, however, to Ireland's prosperity was the English parliament's control over the whole economic system of Ireland. The country's industries were, like those of the American colonies, subordinated to the supposed industrial interests of England; but in Ireland's case, owing to her proximity, the control could be made far more effective. Any industry which seemed, by its competition, to threaten an English industry was ruthlessly suppressed. Already in the reign of Charles II Ireland was forbidden by English legislation[2] to export her pastoral products—cattle, sheep, butter, cheese, in which lay her chief wealth—either to England or her colonies, lest the English farmers should suffer from the competition; and this restriction was not removed till the middle of the eighteenth century, when English agricultural and pastoral products began no longer to be sufficient for our needs.[3] For the same reason Irish woollen manufactures might not be exported to England or the Continent, a prohibition which did much to depress a promising Irish industry.[4] Even Irish wool was but grudgingly admitted into England, and that only because the English crop hardly sufficed for the English cloth-makers' looms. In compensation the Irish linen and hempen trades, which needed encouragement, were given hopes of bounties; but though the Irish parliament had been granting a small annual bounty of about £7,000 per annum since the beginning of the century, the English parliament waited till 1745, after the terrible famine of 1740–1, before voting the £10,000 per annum bounty for coarse linens only, as not competing with the English linens.

[1] See Lecky, *Ireland*, i. 464–6.
[2] 18 Car. II, c. 2, and 32 Car. II, c. 2.
[3] The restriction on the export of cattle was removed in 1758 by 32 Geo. II, c. 11.
[4] Bonn, ii. 230, thinks that even without the English tariff policy the Irish manufacturers were not expert or capitalized enough to do much harm to English manufacturers. None the less it was felt as a serious grievance by the Irish.

Moreover, the bounty was counterbalanced by import duties on Irish sail-cloth and other finished linens and the exclusion from the colonies of all but the coarser linens, even those for which no colonial goods could be brought back in return.[1] No wonder Swift in 1720 urged the Irish to buy only Irish manufactures, and in 1727 by his *Short View of the State of Ireland* and his *Modest Proposal* in 1729 tried to lash up Irish indignation. Earlier a proposal had been made in England, but happily not carried out, to forbid all fishing on the Irish coasts except by boats made and manned in England.[2]

An inevitable result of these restrictions was a great increase in the smuggling industry, carried on mainly with the Continent, but also with England. So seriously was this illicit traffic regarded by the English government that in 1732 no less than three men-of-war and eight cruisers were sent to patrol the Irish Channel and wage war on the Irish smugglers. An even more unhappy consequence during the first half of the century was the gradual impoverishment of a naturally productive island. Landlords had no interest in encouraging wool-growing which had little prospect of a remunerative outlet; so they made what they could of their land by letting it out cheaply to middlemen, who in turn let out small parcels at rack-rents to Irish cottiers. These small tenants, liable to be turned out at any moment, had little chance in average years of gaining more than a bare subsistence from their labours. In years of famine, such as from 1726 to 1729, and in 1740–1, the sufferings of these poor peasants were terrible. Archbishop Boulter, who, whatever his faults, was generous in his charities and tender-hearted to the suffering Irish, gives a grim picture of this earlier period of famine. Early in 1728 he reports that owing to the dearness of corn in the previous year thousands of families had left their habitations and hundreds perished; now, he adds, many had consumed their potatoes, the sole winter sustenance, two months sooner than usual, and so had little before them also but starvation. Later in the year, he writes that the distress was such that in three years no less than 4,200 Irish cottiers had emigrated to the West Indies, 3,100 of them in the last summer. In 1729 he headed a subscription which bought £3,000 worth of oats and

---

[1] See below, p. 299, n. 1, for details of the linen bounties.
[2] For the Irish linen trade see Lecky, *England in the Eighteenth Century*, ii. 212–13, 333. For the proposal about the fisheries see Lecky, *Ireland*, i. 179.

potatoes in Munster to feed the starving Ulster peasants, but could not get the relief conveyed owing to the tumults in Munster against food leaving that province, and adds that at that very time seven ships with 1,000 emigrants were leaving Belfast.[1] Again during the grievous famine of 1741 he fed thousands of the Dublin poor at his single expense, spending 'no less than £25 a day'.[2] He was also instrumental in obtaining some remission of the English import duties on wool and yarn in 1730, and initiated legislation in 1727–8 to oblige every one owning 100 acres of land to plough at least 5 acres and in 1730 by an annual grant of £4,000 to encourage the draining of bogs and the improvement of low grounds.[3] Even Bishop Nicolson of Derry, a far less humane man than Boulter, observes on a journey—not in a famine year—from Dublin to his diocese: 'Never did I behold, even in Picardy, Westphalia or Scotland, such dismal marks of hunger and want as appeared in the countenances of most of the poor creatures I met with on the road.'[4] The famine of 1740–1 was even worse than the earlier one, in spite of the efforts of Boulter and others to feed the starving peasantry. One estimate gives 400,000 as the tale of those who perished of starvation in those years, another one-fifth of the population. Berkeley reports having heard that 500 had died in one parish 'though in a country . . . not very populous'.[5] The English public, who contributed £100,000 in 1755 to the relief of sufferers from the Lisbon earthquake, hardly stirred a finger to relieve this Irish calamity.

These famine years, however, are the worst recorded in the period. From 1748 onwards the growing need of England for imported food, besides Boulter's legislation, began to give an impetus to the provision trade. Thereafter beef, mutton, butter, and even cereals found their way to the English market, with the result that it began to pay the great landlords to break up their sheep-walks into agricultural holdings and thereby greatly to increase their rents. We hear, for example, of owners like Lords Longford and Enniskillen and Mr. Cooper doubling or even

[1] Boulter, *Letters*, i. 226–7, 261, 279, 287–8.
[2] Quoted by Froude, *English in Ireland*, i. 403.
[3] Boulter, *Letters*, i. 187–8, 201, 220–3, 225–6, 350–1, 357. Carteret heartily approved of the 'Bog Bill', 'our darling' as he called it, writing to Southwell (1671–1730), Add. MS. 38015, ff. 23–25.
[4] See Lecky, *Ireland*, i. 184.
[5] See on these famines ibid., i. 184–8.

quadrupling their rent-rolls within thirty or forty years. The
linen trade, also, confined almost entirely to Ulster, had a spell
of prosperity till 1771, partly, no doubt, owing to the bounties
first given by England in 1743.[1] The peasantry were indeed
the last to benefit from this growing prosperity, but at any rate
dire famines were less frequent and food probably cheaper.[2]
But even so Irish agriculture did not produce half the amount
it might have under a more enlightened system. In contrast
to the few far-seeing landlords such as those mentioned, the
majority shamefully neglected their duties to the land they
owned, partly as absentees who left their property to rascally or
inefficient agents, partly owing to the bad leasehold system due
to the anti-Catholic laws, which left no incentive to the tenants
to do more for their leaseholds than just to gain their own subsistence at the least expense. Miss Edgeworth's *Castle Rackrent*
and *The Absentee* show how prevalent these evils were even at the
beginning of the nineteenth century.

Ireland in her poverty had all the more cause to complain,
since a considerable proportion of her revenue was used for
English purposes. Most of the fat benefices in the Irish church,
bishoprics and deaneries, were given to Englishmen. The Irish
pension-list, though partly used to reward Irish grandees and
politicians for their services to the government, was also a
favourite hen-roost from which to abstract eggs for purely
English or German claimants to royal benefactions. In the list,
for example, of the year 1715, though the duke of Ormonde, an
absentee Irish landlord, figures with the largest pensions amounting to £5,108. 4s. 11¼d. in addition to an annual grant of £3,500
for 'prizage', most of the recipients of pensions above £100
appear to be English: and this was only a beginning in a list
immensely swollen by 1760.[3] Again it was very convenient for
English ministers to have an army establishment in Ireland, not
merely paid for by the Irish exchequer, but also free of the
English commons' jealous criticism of a standing army. Already

[1] The first bounty was enacted in 1742 and became effective in 1743; this was
extended in 1745. See 15 Geo. II, c. 29, and 18 Geo. II, c. 25.

[2] Arthur Young, who first came to Ireland in 1776, notes the improvement since
the '40's.

[3] At the end of George II's reign pensions of £5,000 to the princess of Hesse-
Cassel and of £2,000 to Prince Ferdinand were added to this pension list in spite of
protests from the Irish house of commons. Pitt was always averse to these Irish
pensions for English beneficiaries and was highly indignant with his sister Ann for
accepting one: see *Chatham*, i. 206.

in 1715 Ireland paid £63,950 for the king's Irish civil list and
£439,895 for his military establishment of which three-quarters
went towards the pay and expenses of four regiments of horse,
two of dragoons, and twenty-two of foot, with a company of
footguards thrown in.[1] This army in Ireland was all the more
convenient since its units could be called upon for service elsewhere without becoming a burden to the English taxpayer. In
1745, for example, out of 9,261 troops left in Ireland at the
beginning of the troubles, no less than two regiments were sent
to reinforce the royal troops in Scotland. This was made
possible by the enthusiasm of the Protestant Association, who
raised 65,000 volunteers to defend the country against Jacobites
and persuaded Chesterfield himself to review those who formed
the City of Dublin's Militia.[2]

But patient and uncomplaining under her burdens and
grievances as Ireland generally was during this period, she had
one grand outburst which actually resulted in a national victory
over England. In 1722 a concession was granted by the English
treasury to the duchess of Kendal for the issue of a new copper
coinage in Ireland; she, for a payment of £10,000, sold the
patent to William Wood, 'a hardware dealer', as Swift called
him, who even at that price could reckon on a handsome
profit.[3] The coinage of Ireland, debased and scanty, was
admittedly in need of reinforcement, but the manner in which
the scheme was sprung upon the country and the actual terms
of the patent stirred up the deepest resentment in Ireland.
Neither the Irish parliament nor even the Irish government had
been previously consulted, and for this reason alone parliament,
privy council, and the lords justices themselves were up in arms
against it. Further, the actual terms of the patent, not made
known in Ireland till over a year after it was granted, and when
some of the halfpence had already been delivered, awakened
the gravest apprehensions. Wood was empowered to flood the
country with copper coins to the nominal value of £100,800,[4]

[1] The details of the civil list and of the Irish army establishment for 1715 may
be seen in *Somers Tracts*, i. 300–19, where the figures given are inconsistent with one
another. Those cited above are from the summary on p. 319.
[2] O'Callaghan, p. 413.
[3] When the patent was withdrawn the Treasury reckoned his prospective profits
from it and for coinage rights in America to be worth a pension of £3,000 for twelve
years (£36,000): Swift, vi. 156 (Temple Scott edn., 1903).
[4] Not £108,000 as usually stated, see Add. MS. 9243, ff. 16 sqq.

whereby, it was urged, since the total currency of Ireland was estimated at only £400,000, most of the remaining silver and gold would be driven overseas and the country still further impoverished. Parliament and the lords justices sent solemn representations to London against the concession, on these grounds and also because many of Wood's halfpence already introduced were said to be below the proper standard. But Walpole and the English treasury were obdurate. Sir Isaac Newton, it is true, as master of the Mint, was called on for a report on the coinage and declared it up to the required standard; but apparently Wood had been free to choose the coins sent for assay, whereas coins of different grades had been sent to Ireland. The only concession Walpole would make was to reduce the nominal value of Wood's halfpence from £100,800 to £40,000, a concession which in no way silenced the clamour against them; but on the principle of the king's sole right of ordering a new coinage, which he thought attacked by the Irish agitation, he remained adamant.

Nevertheless he realized that a stronger personality than the duke of Grafton must be sent as viceroy to carry the measure through. The duke, of whom Hervey said that 'the natural cloud of his understanding, thickened by the artificial cloud of his mistaken Court policy, made his meaning always as unintelligible as his conversation was unentertaining', had mismanaged the whole business. In his place Walpole sent over Carteret, the political adversary he had succeeded in turning out of the secretaryship, calculating that this far abler and stronger man would either, to quote Wood's reputed boast, 'pour the coins down the throats of the people', or, if he failed, would no longer be so formidable to himself. Carteret, indeed, had originally opposed Wood's scheme, but as viceroy he was not the man to yield to popular clamour.[1] He arrived, however, just in time to meet an adversary worthy of his steel.

A few days before the new viceroy landed in Ireland Swift had published the fourth of his *Drapier's Letters*, the culmination of a series of attacks against the halfpence, which had stirred up every class of Irishman—rich and poor, townspeople and peasants, Roman catholics, anglicans, and nonconformists— all for the first time united against this last instance of English dictation. In this fourth letter Swift, abandoning all the special

[1] So Newcastle told old Horace Walpole, Add. MS. 9152, f. 135.

pleading of the first three against the coinage, set out 'to refresh and continue that spirit so seasonably raised' throughout Ireland, and uttered the memorable trumpet-call to his countrymen, 'that by the laws of God, of Nature, of Nations, and of your own Country, you are, and ought to be as free a people as your brethren in England'. So outspoken was this letter in its attacks on the English ministry and even in indirect reflections on the king, that Carteret felt he had no alternative but to summon the Irish privy council and issue a proclamation offering a reward of £300 for the discovery of the writer, whose identity was of course known to his friend Carteret and to everybody in Dublin;[1] and an indictment was laid against the printer, Harding. But two grand juries in turn, preferring Swift's *Seasonable Advice to the Grand Jury* to the pressure exercised by Chief Justice Whitshed, refused to find a true bill against the printer; nor was anybody found in this impoverished island to stoop so low as to claim the £300 offered for the author's name.

Carteret himself, who, on coming to Ireland, had declared that 'so long as I have the honour to be Chief Governor here, the peace of the Kingdom shall be kept',[2] within two months of his arrival in October 1724 had fully made up his mind that the patent should be revoked.[3] As long as it lasted, however, he loyally did 'all that can be thought on to obtain upon the Minds of the People, and with great applause. . . . But that shall not do', wrote an Irish correspondent, 'neither Eating and Drinking Civilities, nor good Words shall alter their Minds as to that.'[4] But though his advice was reinforced by Walpole's and Newcastle's own nominees Archbishop Boulter and the new chancellor, West, Walpole remained obdurate for nearly a year in the mistaken belief that opposition to the patent was merely an attempt to get rid of English tutelage altogether. Not till August 1725 was Carteret informed that the patent had been surrendered. Thereupon he obtained dutiful expressions of thanks from both houses to transmit to the king; he even managed to get Archbishop King's unseasonable allusion to

---

[1] Archbishop King refused in the privy council to sign the proclamation. Swift's call to his countrymen is in Swift, vi. 115 (Temple Scott edn., 1903).

[2] Add. MS. 9243, f. 39.

[3] See his considered advice to Newcastle of 16 Dec. 1724, in R.O., S.P. Ireland, 63.

[4] Ibid., 9 Jan. 1724/5.

George I's 'great wisdom' in revoking the patent expunged from the lords' address.[1]

After this resounding success Ireland for another quarter of a century relapsed once more into quiet submission. During the '45, largely owing to Chesterfield's tactful régime, Ireland made not the slightest effort to profit from England's difficulties and remained profoundly peaceful. It was not till the last decade of George II's reign that symptoms appeared of a fresh revolt by the Anglo-Irish minority. The two years' wrangle about the Irish parliament's control over its own surplus[2] started the effective opposition to Archbishop Stone's attempt to rule Ireland independently of the 'undertakers'. A party was successfully formed of the leading Irish families under Kildare and Shannon, with the powerful assistance of the great orator Malone,[3] to carry on the government solely through the Irish 'undertakers', who at least had some Irish interests. But the real continuation of the movement inaugurated by Swift came only with the relaxation of England's hold caused by the American troubles in George III's reign. From that time on the Irish people took more and more as their ultimate goal the ideal expressed first and once for all by Swift: 'By the laws of God, of Nature, of Nations, and of your own Country, you are, and ought to be as free a people as your brethren in England.'

Dark as Irish history was in this period, yet the wit and charm of the Irish temperament and its love of art would not be denied, and 'cheerfulness would keep breaking through'. There was not indeed much scope for cheerfulness among the native Irish in this hungry period, though even among them flourished till 1737 Carolan, said to have been 'the last and greatest' of their wandering bards. The cheerfulness in fact centred chiefly in the capital. Dublin, little more than a dirty, ill-built town when George I came to the throne, had within forty years, according to a writer of 1763,[4] increased in size by a fourth and become a city notable for the beauty of its

[1] The clearest exposition of the main features of the Wood's Halfpence agitation is still to be found in Leslie Stephen's *Swift* (Men of Letters Series). See also introduction to Herbert Davis, *The Drapier's Letters*, Oxford, 1935. Mr. A. Goodwin in the *English Historical Review* for Oct. 1936 has an able discussion of the salient issues.

[2] See above, pp. 295–6.

[3] Anthony Malone, 1700–76.

[4] *The Georgian Society* (1909–13), iii. 1 sqq. This book has an admirably illustrated account of Georgian buildings chiefly in Dublin.

public and private buildings. Many of the narrow, squalid streets had been cleared away or widened into broad thorough-fares. Mean houses had been pulled down, and in their stead had risen stately mansions for the great ones of the land, such as the duke of Leinster, the Lords Moira, Tyrone, and Powers-court, the primate, and the archbishop of Cashel. Bishop Clayton had one of the finest houses on St. Stephen's Green, where Mrs. Clayton gave princely entertainments and whence she took the air in a coach drawn by six Flanders mares in greater state than the viceroy himself. Other less ambitious houses, but apt for the generous hospitality of hosts like the Delanys,[1] appeared in Dublin or its outskirts. Some of the great landowners also built on their country-estates palaces which even the owners of Chatsworth or Canons would hardly have disdained. From this period, too, date the noble Library, Printing House, Dining Hall and West Front of Trinity College, besides other public buildings and hospitals which still remain to the glory of Dublin. Castle (or Cassels), a German settled in Dublin, designed many of these buildings; others were planned by English architects, Keene, Saunderson, Chambers; for it was not till George III's reign that the Irish architect Ivory came to the fore. The taste for other arts was also increas-ing. The young Irish men of fashion, like the English, brought back pictures and articles of virtu from Italy; and Mrs. Delany mentions with special approval the bishop of Derry's gallery of 200 pictures and his portfolios of engravings.

In this setting moved a society which for wit and charm would almost rival that of the Paris salons; and Dublin became specially noted for its theatres and concerts. The Smock Alley Theatre, founded in Charles I's day, was taken over in 1745 by Thomas Sheridan, father of Richard Brinsley; during his two periods of management, ending in 1759, several great Irish actors[2] flourished either at his theatre or at the rival house estab-lished in Crow Street in 1758. In the same period he brought over Garrick, Foote, and Mrs. Bellamy from England and set a high standard for Shakespearian productions. He even trained the unruly Irish playgoers to decent behaviour. Concerts were still more popular than the drama. The great violinist Dubourg

---

[1] Dr. Patrick Delany, a fellow of Trinity, married Mary Granville, niece of Lord Lansdowne, in 1743.

[2] These included Henry Mossop and Spranger Barry among actors, and Peg Woffington among actresses.

conducted the viceroy's band; Thomas Arne gave concerts and produced his opera *Rosamund* in 1743; Handel himself, invited by the viceroy Devonshire, had 500 subscribers for his six concerts in 1741–2, and following these gave the first performance of the *Messiah* in Dublin. Lord Mornington and other aristocratic amateurs did not disdain to perform in public; and a favourite form of charity was a concert given at St. Patrick's or one of the churches, the proceeds going to some hospital or other institution for the poor.[1] Apart from public entertainments a society could not be dull which was able to produce writers and talkers such as Swift, Berkeley, Archbishop King, Parnell, Skelton, Henry Brooke, the Delanys, and the learned Mrs. Grierson,[2] or a viceregal court presided over by a Carteret and his charming first wife or a Chesterfield. Both these viceroys were used to entertain informally at the Castle the wits, scholars, and beauties of Dublin, nor thought it beneath their dignity to eat a piece of mutton at the house of a friend in town.[3] Again Trinity College, which in Anne's reign had been undisciplined and disorderly, was brought to order by Richard Baldwin, provost from 1717 to 1758, and produced, if not a Swift or a Berkeley in this period, at any rate a Burke and a Goldsmith.

In 1723 Lord Molesworth had published his *Considerations for the Promotion of Agriculture*, a treatise praised by Swift, which led in 1731 to the foundation of the Dublin Society 'for the Improvement of Husbandry, Manufactures and other useful Arts'.[4] Like

[1] See C. Maxwell, *Dublin under the Georges*, 1936, pp. 100–4, 185 sqq. For the social life of Dublin in this period Mrs. Delany, *Autobiography and Letters* (2 series in 6 volumes), is a first-hand authority. (There is now a revised edition of Maxwell, *Dublin under the Georges*, 1958.)

[2] Mrs. Grierson, described by Croker in his edition of Boswell as 'very handsome as well as learned', edited several of the classics, including Tacitus, dedicated 'in very elegant Latin' to Carteret. The viceroy in return gave her family the lucrative patent of king's printer in Ireland. Her son made Boswell acquainted with Johnson. It was he who once told Johnson that 'he who dressed a good dinner was a more excellent and a more useful member of society than he who wrote a good poem'. See Boswell under 1770, and Mrs. Piozzi, *Anecdotes of Dr. Johnson*.

[3] Mrs. Lætitia Pilkington, *Memoirs* (1928 edn.), pp. 374–5, gives a description of Carteret coming 'quite unattended' to dinner with Dr. Delany, who, making his old mother do the honours of his table, told Carteret the dinner would be simple, quoting,

> To stomachs cloyed with costly fare
> Simplicity alone was rare:

and Carteret went away delighted with his host's good breeding and good talk.

[4] Chesterfield accepted the presidency in 1745, and the Society obtained a royal charter in 1750. Molesworth himself had died in 1725.

similar societies in England and Scotland it did valuable work in promoting better methods of agriculture and encouraging manufactures and scientific research. Among the chief manufactures besides linen and wool (for domestic consumption and for smugglers), were glass, especially the beautiful 'Waterford' glass, the manufacture of which was not confined to Waterford, silver-plate, of which fine specimens date from this period, coach-building, 'Irish Chippendale' modelled on the English original, and book-binding. The booksellers and printers also did a great trade, largely in pirating English books, since the English copyright did not extend to Ireland. Of these piratical booksellers the most noted was Swift's friend Faulkner, who published the Dublin edition of Swift's works and also, much to the author's disgust, Richardson's novels. The literary taste of Dublin seems to have been good, to judge from a publisher's announcement of 1741 with such items as Swift's, Pope's, and Prior's works, *Pamela*, *The Turkish Spy*, Pascal's works, *The Plain Dealer*, and Cibber's *Apology*.[1] Dublin, too, was better off than Scotland for newspapers, the most important being *Faulkner's Journal* and *Pue's Occurrences*, which, though defective in Irish news, kept their readers abreast of English and continental intelligence. These stirrings of enlightened opinion, at least in the dominant minority, help to explain this minority's efforts, at the time of England's weakness during the American war, to wrest greater liberty for itself, and even, maybe, prepared the way for the later uprising of the native Irish majority.[2]

[1] *The Georgian Society*, l.c., p. 37, n.
[2] I have to thank Miss Constantia Maxwell of Trinity College, Dublin, for several corrections and additions in this section. (Note of 1939.)

XI

THE COLONIES AND INDIA

Not the least of the responsibilities inherited by the Hanoverians in 1714 was a colonial empire rivalling in extent those of England's chief continental competitors, France and Spain. It was an empire, too, that appeared to have elements of permanence and solidarity absent from the French and Spanish possessions. In the course of the century since it was inaugurated, with the exception of the two military establishments at Minorca and Gibraltar, its constituent elements had come to depend not solely on the momentary strength or weakness of the central government, but to develop each its own individuality and a fiercely independent sense of responsibility for its own fortunes. Even in India and West Africa or the bleak tracts of the Hudson Bay Territory the English settlements and trading centres relied normally for their prosperity and security on the quasi-independent companies of merchant adventurers who traded there. In our main settlements in the West Indies or the North American continent each community, even in such minute possessions as the Virgin Islands, had its popular form of government with more or less limited powers of taxation and legislation akin to the model at Westminster.

The chief centre of our colonial activity was in the Western hemisphere. In North America, Newfoundland had been finally ceded to Great Britain by the treaty of Utrecht, but with fishing rights reserved for the French over two-fifths of the coast. South of the St. Lawrence nearly all the eastern sea-board was in English possession. First came Nova Scotia, also ceded at Utrecht, then the New England states of Massachusetts, Connecticut, Rhode Island, and New Hampshire. Sandwiched between them and the old dominion of Virginia were Charles II's acquisitions from the Dutch, New York and New Jersey, Pennsylvania, previously unsettled land beyond the New Jersey border granted by Charles II to the quaker Penn, and Delaware, while south of Virginia lay North and South Carolina. One more colony, Georgia, to the south of the Carolinas, was established in this period. In the West Indies we had the Bermudas, Bahamas, and Jamaica, our most prosperous sugar colony, while Spain had Cuba and Porto Rico and shared San Domingo with the French: of the Leeward and Windward Islands our chief possessions were the Virgin Islands, Barbuda, St. Kitts, Antigua, Montserrat, and Barbados, but the French had the two richest islands, Guadeloupe and Martinique and occupied the so-called neutral islands, Dominica, St. Lucia, St. Vincent, Grenada, and Tobago, while Trinidad was still Spanish. English settlements, too, of lawless log-wood cutters and buccaneers had established themselves in the gulf of Honduras and the Mosquito coast on the Spanish main.

Most of these possessions had originally, as was the case with the beginnings of our empire in Rhodesia and West and East Africa in the nineteenth century, been granted to companies or individuals under charter from the Crown. But from the last quarter of the seventeenth century there had been a tendency for the Crown to resume the charters and substitute complete royal control. In 1714 the Bahamas were the only proprietary colony still left in the West Indies: there also in 1717 the six proprietors, one of whom was Carteret, gave up their rights of civil and military government to the Crown to enable the ex-privateer Woodes Rogers, turned governor, to clear a nest of pirates out of their stronghold in Nassau: in 1733, for a payment of 1,000 guineas each, the proprietors also relinquished their claims to royalties and quit-rents in the Bahamas.[1]

On the continent Pennsylvania, Maryland, and the two Carolinas were still proprietary; and Rhode Island and Connecticut retained their curious privilege of electing their own governors; the new colony of Georgia was also at first committed to a board of trustees. But before the end of George II's reign the Carolinas and Georgia had been resumed by the Crown, in both cases owing to the proved incapacity of the proprietors or trustees. The proprietors of the Carolinas were the heirs of the eight created by Charles II, the only notable one among them being their 'Palatine', or chairman, Lord Carteret, the rest being either infants or nonentities; and their constitution still bore traces of John Locke's fantastic creation.[2] In 1715 the

---

[1] *Acts of Privy Council, Colonial Series*, iii. 370–6. For Rogers see G. E. Manwaring, *The Flower of England's Garland*, pp. 126 sqq.

[2] e.g. Carteret as chairman of the proprietors still bore the title of palatine.

proprietors, through Lord Carteret, wrote to the government expressing their inability to deal with the 'melancholy occasion' of a serious rising of the Yamassee Indians in South Carolina and praying the king to interpose to prevent 'the utter destruction of H.M.'s faithful subjects in those parts'. In 1719, after long delays, the colonists took matters into their own hands and elected a convention which declared South Carolina to be a royal province; and at last in 1720 a royal governor was sent out. But it was not till 1729 that the charter for both Carolinas was surrendered to the Crown on payment of £2,500 to each of the proprietors save Carteret who preferred to retain as 'Palatine' a vast tract demarcated for him in North Carolina, from which he drew quit-rents to the end of his life, and was able to boast that he was 'the only subject who has the honour of being joint Proprietor with the Crown'.[1]

Georgia, the one new colony founded in George II's reign, owed its origin to the philanthropic enterprise of General Oglethorpe, Dr. Johnson's tory friend.[2] Moved by the sufferings of debtors immured in the Fleet and other prisons, he raised subscriptions to pay off the debts of the most deserving and to send them overseas to make a fresh start in America. In June 1732 he overcame Walpole's objections and obtained a royal charter granting to a board of trustees for twenty-one years the unoccupied land south of Carolina, in order to provide for poor families in England and make better provision for the defence of South Carolina against Indian and Spanish raiders from Florida. Oglethorpe and other prominent philanthropists such as Lord Egmont and Thomas Coram became trustees; bishops and the S.P.C.K. interested themselves in the project; between 1732 and 1740 private subscriptions amounting to £18,000, including £600 from the king, were collected and grants amounting to £94,000 voted by parliament; a surgeon, a chaplain, and a secretary gave their services gratis, and large numbers of pious tracts, such as *How to Walk with God, Friendly Admonitions to the Drinkers of Brandy*, besides 1,000 spelling-books, were sent for the benefit of intending settlers. In 1733

---

[1] See B. R. Carroll, *Hist. Collections of S. Carolina*, 2 vols., 1836, i. 200–360; Collins, *Peerage*, 1768, iv. 406–9; *Acts of Privy Council (Colonial)*, iii. 172–7, 267–9; Add. MS. 32693, f. 37. The proprietors received jointly, in addition to their individual payments, a grant of £5,000 to meet sums due to their agents in the colony.

[2] See above, pp. 129, 135–6.

Oglethorpe arrived on the Savannah river with the first batch of 114 emigrants and established settlements there and at Frederica on the Spanish border, and also a fur-trading post at Augusta to the north: by 1740 the new colony had received 1,521 settlers, including some 600 foreign protestants driven out of Salzburg and other persecuting states: and among those who came to evangelize the colonists were John Wesley and Whitefield. In the early years there were frequent collisions with Spanish raiders and some discontent owing to Oglethorpe's paternal regulations forbidding slaves and strong drink and restricting individual plots which were then too small for profitable farming;[1] there was trouble, too, from Indians owing to their disputes with the South Carolina settlers, though Oglethorpe himself, by his fair treatment, was on the best of terms with them. He indeed, in spite of these and other troubles, for long consoled himself with the richness and beauty of the country, and was 'animated rather than daunted', as he told his friend Alderman Heathcote, by his difficulties; but at last in 1743 they proved too much for him and he returned to England, a disappointed man. In 1754 the trustees gave up their charter to the Crown, and a government similar to that of the other colonies was established.[2]

Among these American colonies Newfoundland and Nova Scotia were in a peculiar position. The permanent population of Newfoundland was small—only about 1,000 in the seventeenth century—and it was kept small by the policy of the 'adventurers' owning the summer fishing-fleets, who feared local competition with their industry: until 1729, too, there was no regular government save for the brief authority exercised by the captain of the first ship to touch land for the summer fishing. But in that year a royal governor, in the person of the convoy commander of the fishing fleet, was appointed, and thereafter the restrictions on permanent settlement were relaxed, so that by 1760 the population had increased to 2,400. By that time also a permanent council of settlers, with some administrative and judicial powers, had been established to act

---

[1] The foreign protestants seem to have been restricted to plots of 50 acres each; other grants do not appear to have exceeded 500 acres. See *Hist. MSS. Comm., Egmont Diary*, ii. 126, 274, 278, 438, 450, and 481.

[2] P.R.O. Georgia, 1, 2, 7, 51, give the early history of Georgia. See also *Hist. MSS. Comm., Egmont Diary*, vols. i–iii, and Beer, *British Colonial Policy 1754–65*, p. 13.

during the absence of the governor.[1] The population of Nova Scotia, on its cession in 1713, was almost entirely French, and the Jesuits, notably a certain Father Le Loutre, kept up an active propaganda among them to maintain their French allegiance, a movement encouraged by the Canadian governors, who constantly raised border disputes and claims to a large part of the old province. In 1749, however, the new and energetic president of the board of trade, Halifax,[2] began to strengthen the English position by establishing the fortress named after himself; the following year Fort Lawrence was established on the isthmus of Chignecto only to be countered by the French Fort Beauséjour immediately opposite; finally in 1755 Governor Lawrence took the drastic step of expelling 5,000 of the French colonists, who after untold hardships found an asylum, some in Louisiana, some in the English mainland colonies, and a few back again in Nova Scotia. After that colonists from New England, hitherto deterred by the alien and Roman catholic population, came in to colonize the province anew; and a regular system of colonial government with a legislative assembly elected by the settlers was inaugurated in 1758.[3]

In London the secretary of state for the south was responsible for colonial business, assisted by the board of trade and plantations, an independent committee established *ad hoc* by William III in 1696. Before 1724 the board was an active body, but for the next twenty-four years was allowed to slumber by Newcastle, who neglected colonial business himself and afforded little scope for the board's activities. This inaction was largely due to Walpole's set policy, perfectly congenial to Newcastle's own inclination, of interfering as little as possible with the colonies. But when, in 1748, Halifax, at Bedford's suggestion, was made president of the board, he took its duties seriously. In 1752 he obtained for it the conduct of correspondence directly with the colonies and the control of patronage, and in 1757 enhanced its importance by insisting on a place in the cabinet for himself.[4] Other government departments, the treasury, the

---

[1] See A. B. Keith, *The First British Empire*, pp. 171-2. For population figures see *Cambridge History of British Empire*, i. 264, 385.

[2] George Montagu Dunk, earl of Halifax, 1716-71, afterwards secretary of state. [3] See Keith, p. 169.

[4] See M. A. Thomson, *The Secretaries of State 1681-1782*, 1932, pp. 50-53, for board of trade and Halifax. It was as earl of Halifax, not as president of the board of trade, that he was granted his seat in the cabinet in 1757.

customs, the admiralty, the war office, and the auditor-general, also had representatives in the colonies, with whom they dealt directly.[1]

In the colonies themselves the chief representative of the imperial government was the governor, appointed, as the case might be, by the king, or by the proprietors with his approval.[2] The governor was assisted by a council of about twelve colonists nominated by the Crown:[3] in most colonies this council had triple functions, as a body to advise the governor in his executive functions, as a second legislative chamber, and as a court of equity. But in nearly all the colonies the chief power lay with the assemblies chosen by popular election. This power came mainly from their control of the purse, on which, in most colonies, even the salary of the governor depended.[4] The assemblies of New York, New Jersey, Massachusetts, and New Hampshire were especially difficult in providing supplies for the government, using their financial control as a means of extorting concessions. Thus, though no legislation was valid without the governor's assent, the assemblies sometimes extorted an assent by using the financial weapon. It is true that, even when assented to by the governor, a provincial act might be disallowed on the advice of the privy council in London; but that took time—often some two or three years or more—during which the act was in vigour; and some ingenious assemblies, on notification of disallowance promptly re-enacted the legislation, thereby ensuring for it another long period of legality before another notification of disallowance. In Jamaica, at the beginning of this period, there was a long struggle between the Crown and the assembly, owing to the latter's refusal to vote a fixed revenue for civil and military purposes. Finally the Crown got the better of the assembly by refusing assent to all new acts, and in 1729 obtained a permanent revenue of £8,000 in exchange for the confirmation of the island laws.[5]

[1] See Keith, pp. 277–83.
[2] Rhode Island and Connecticut were exceptional in electing their own governors: see above, p. 308.
[3] Massachusetts was unique in having an elective council of 28 members. Keith, pp. 192–3.
[4] The only governors independent of assemblies for their salaries were those of Virginia, Maryland, Georgia, North Carolina, Nova Scotia, Barbados, Jamaica, and the Leeward Islands, where the Crown had quit-rents, &c., sufficient for the purpose. Keith, p. 202.
[5] *Cambridge History of British Empire*, i. 378.

In general, however, the West Indian islands were less assertive of their independence than the mainland colonies, partly owing to their more enervating climate, partly owing to their greater dependence on the mother country. The climate was not well fitted to an active life for Europeans, with the result that their numbers, if not actually dwindling, increased very slowly: in Barbados, for example, from 12,528 in 1712 to no more than 18,419 in 1762, and in Jamaica from 8,500 to 26,000 in the century up to 1764, while the negro slaves, who did the work, were almost doubled in fifty years in Barbados, and increased in a century from 9,500 to no less than 140,000 in Jamaica.[1] Again, the West Indies were almost entirely dependent, apart from illicit traffic, on the English market for the sale of their sugar, and solely dependent on the British navy for defence against their French and Spanish neighbours. Moreover, many of their principal planters, such as the Beckfords, educated their children and spent a large part of their lives in England, leaving the management of their estates to overseers. Thus they found it easier to secure benefits for themselves— such as the Molasses Act of 1733, the privilege of direct trade with south Europe in 1739, and the defeat of the proposal to raise the tax on imported sugar in 1744[2]—by personal pressure on ministers and the house of commons than by making themselves troublesome to the government in their own islands.

Closely connected with the West Indies, especially during the earlier half of this period, were two of the great English trading companies, the Royal African and the South Sea. It was stated, indeed, in a pamphlet of 1749 that 'our West India and African trades are the most nationally beneficial of any we carry on. . . . The Negroe-Trade . . . may be justly esteemed an inexhaustible Fund of Wealth and Naval Power to this Nation.'[3] The traffic in negro slaves was carried on partly by the Royal African Company, and partly by groups of independent merchants who came to dominate the trade during this period. The slaves were brought from the interior by Arab or native traders and lodged in forts and depots on the Gold Coast

[1] Ibid., p. 380. The climate was probably less of a discouragement to the white settlers than the economic effects of concentrating on sugar as the staple crop. As sugar required large capital the small planter tended to sell and emigrate to the mainland.

[2] Ibid., p. 381.

[3] Quoted ibid., p. 437.

before being shipped in the closely packed and stinking slave-holds for the horrible 'Middle Passage' to the West Indies. These human cargoes were chiefly exported to our sugar colonies, but also under the Company's contract with the South Sea Company, to fulfil its obligation under the Asiento for the supply of slaves, to the Spanish colonies.[1] Between 1730 and 1747 the Royal African Company was granted £10,000 per annum by parliament for the upkeep of the Gold Coast forts necessary for the protection of its interests against French and Dutch competitors in the trade; but in 1750 it was superseded in this task by the newly created 'Company of Merchants Trading to Africa', open for a fee of 40s. to all British subjects, chiefly merchants of London, Bristol, and Liverpool, interested in the traffic; an annual parliamentary vote henceforth provided the new company with funds to maintain the forts. In the later years of Charles II the purchase price of a slave in Africa had been about £3 and the sale price in the West Indies £13–£16,[2] showing a profit which covered the waste of slave life inevitable from the disgraceful conditions of the 'Middle Passage'. An extension of our West African commerce to the gum-trade, monopolized by the French on the Senegal coast, was aimed at by Pitt in his conquests of Fort Louis and Goree in 1758, but his successors retained only Fort Louis (Senegal) at the treaty of Paris.

No country in the past had been more peremptory than Spain in asserting, as all nations then did, the exclusive right of trading with her own colonies; but having no recruiting ground of her own for slaves, she had long been forced to obtain the necessary supply from either France or England. Far more significant of her weakness in the eighteenth century was the concession to the English at Utrecht of an annual ship filled with English goods up to 500 tons burthen,[3] to be disposed of directly at the regular Spanish fairs held for the 'flota' at Vera Cruz in New Spain (Mexico) and for the 'galleons' at Cartagena on the Spanish Main. Harley assigned this concession to the South Sea Com-

---

[1] Later the South Sea Company found it more profitable to buy its slaves in the open market at Jamaica. *Cambridge History of British Empire*, i. 337.

[2] Ibid., p. 444. By 1700 the sale price had risen steeply, and in the 1730's it was a complaint of the Company that interlopers were selling slaves at the unremunerative rate of £28 per head. See G. B. Hertz, *British Imperialism*, p. 15.

[3] Raised to 650 tons by the treaty of 1716; see J. O. McLachlan, *Trade and Peace with Old Spain*, p. 24.

pany, but in fact it provided abundant excuses for dispute between Spain and England and brought small returns.[1] Actual hostilities between the two nations entirely interrupted the traffic for some six years between 1717 and 1732, when the last ship sailed, and in the intervening periods the chicanery and calculated delays in which Spanish officials were adepts were often used to prevent the ships sailing in time for the fairs.[2] The South Sea Company on their side gave cause for complaint. The accounts and dues they were bound by treaty to render to the Spanish court were habitually in arrear; and they seem to have made a practice of sending with the annual ship one or two additional vessels, so-called provision-tenders, from which the ship was reloaded as the original cargo was discharged, 'ce qui fait', as a French observer noted, 'que le vaisseau ne désemplit jamais'.[3] In fact the concession of the Asiento and of the annual ship, especially the latter, regarded at the time of the treaty of Utrecht as a master-stroke of the tory negotiators, proved a constant source of friction between the two nations; and there were few regrets at its abandonment in 1750 for renewed trading privileges with Spain and a lump sum of £100,000.[4] On the other hand, the contraband traffic with the Spanish colonies carried on by smugglers and pirates from England and the English West Indies, in spite of the reprisals of *guarda-costas* and prejudiced Spanish judges, proved far more lucrative: and, though nothing was said in the treaty of Aix-la-Chapelle about the disputed 'right of search' claimed by the Spaniards, little more was heard afterwards of their serious interference with English trade in the West Indies.[5]

---

[1] Adam Smith, *Wealth of Nations*, bk. v, chap. 1, asserts that the *Royal Caroline*, the last ship sent by the South Sea Company, was the only one to make a profit, but this is an exaggeration. The first voyage showed a profit of only 5 per cent., but the next five voyages showed profits of about 100 per cent. each and the *Royal Caroline* even more. The profits for all the seven voyages exceeded 2,000,000 Spanish dollars. McLachlan, l.c., pp. 130–1.

[2] In fact only seven ships reached the fairs: *Royal Prince*, July 1717; *Royal George* delayed, owing to the hostilities of 1718–19, till 1721; the three ships due 1723–5 in fact sailed; the last of these, the *Prince Frederick*, was held up at Vera Cruz from 1726 to 1729; the *Prince William* sailed in 1730; the *Royal Caroline*, the last to sail, in 1732. See McLachlan, l.c., p. 176, which corrects the details in *Cambridge History of British Empire*, i, chap. vi.

[3] Brit. Mus. Add. MS. 32759, ff. 161 sqq.

[4] See p. 265, n. 1.

[5] For a fuller account of the disputes with Spain about trade in the West Indies and the 'right of search' see above, pp. 207–10.

The profound difference between the continental colonists and their brethren in the West Indies was that the former had originally emigrated not so much to acquire wealth as to find a home free from governmental interference with their religious and similar liberties.[1] Thus, especially in New England and Virginia and only to a less extent in the middle and more southerly colonies, any attempt at interference from Westminster or St. James's was looked on with suspicion. During this period indeed all the seeds were being sown for the final separation of George III's reign, which had been foreseen as early as 1656 by Harrington in his *Oceana* when he wrote that 'the Colonys in the Indies, they are yet Babes that cannot live without sucking the breasts of their Mother Cityes, but such as I mistake, if when they com of age they do not wean themselves'.[2] By 1729 it was openly said by a New Englander that he was a 'subject of this Country, not to the King', and again in 1755 Robert Hunter Morris of Pennsylvania declared that people were disaffected 'to his Majesty's Office and Authority, tho' not to his Person or Family'.[3] From the royal office to the personal 'tyrant' of the revolutionary period the step was short.

Three circumstances alone during this period prevented an earlier break-away to independence; first the settled policy of Walpole, *quieta non movere*, continued till 1754 by Pelham and Newcastle; secondly the need of England's protection against France; and thirdly the want of union among the colonists themselves. In theory the colonies were as much the victims of England's trade policy as Ireland. Their natural products suitable for English consumption or manufacture were strictly reserved for the mother country. A royal officer was stationed in America with the duty of inspecting the great American forests, preventing waste by settlers, and encouraging the production of timber, tar, &c., needed for the royal navy. The working of the abundant iron ore in its earlier stages, for export to the English iron-masters to manufacture the finished articles, was encouraged, but—in accordance with a resolution

[1] [As the late Professor Pares pointed out in his review of the first edition of this work (*E.H.R.* lv) this 'pilgrim fathers' theory of the foundation of the American colonies is not accepted by recent workers in the period. C.H.S.]
[2] Quoted by Beer, p. 166; 'the Indies' of course refers to the western hemisphere.
[3] Ibid., p. 168.

of the house of commons in 1719 that 'the erecting of manufactures in the colonies tended to lessen their dependence upon Great Britain'—it was as if the Americans were forbidden, as Chatham later put it hyperbolically, to make 'a lock of wool, or a horseshoe or a hobnail' for themselves.[1] Beaver-skins from America were eagerly sought after by English hatters, but Americans were not allowed to make beaver hats. No doubt there were compensations in the ready market provided by England for tobacco and other American products and in the protection afforded to the colonies by the royal navy and at need by the royal armies. But that was not so obvious to Americans as the fact that they had no voice at all in the matter. In practice, however, Walpole's set policy and Newcastle's lethargy to a large extent took away the sting of the grievance. Walpole, it is true, agreed to the West Indian planters' demand for the Molasses Act of 1733, the chief object of which was to stop the export of French and Dutch sugar competing with theirs to America. Had this act been effective it would have hit the American rum-factories hard, as they needed more and cheaper sugar than our West Indian planters could supply: in fact, however, for over twenty years the act was allowed to be almost a dead letter, as far as the American trade was concerned, till Halifax at the board of trade had begun to take active measures to stop the smuggling.[2] This laxity in control is also illustrated by the unwillingness of the home government to push to an issue their legal rights against recalcitrant assemblies that were tending more and more to ignore the royal authority in matters of legislation and taxation.

Till the end of this period, however, the pressure of the French on almost all sides of the American colonies except the sea was a constant reminder to them of their ultimate dependence on England's military support. As far as numbers went the English colonists had an overwhelming superiority. By 1744 the French population of Canada was only 54,000,[3] whereas

[1] This phrase was used by Pitt in Jan. 1766. He argued that if parliament's power to limit trade was denied by the colonists then he would not permit them to manufacture a lock of wool, &c. See *Chatham*, ii. 191–2.

[2] Beer, pp. 115–16, notes that between 1734 and 1755 only £5,686 was collected in America as duty under the Molasses Act (an average of £259 per annum), whereas in the nine years from 1756 to 1764 £8,016 was collected (£890 per annum).

[3] Williamson, *Short History of British Expansion*, p. 359.

in 1720 the English colonists in America already numbered 339,000 and by 1760 over 1,200,000.[1] But the French had two great compensating advantages, unity and position. In contrast with the haphazard methods of settlement and expansion in the scattered English colonies, the French seigneurs and *habitans* were mostly concentrated under feudal conditions in properties regularly surveyed and defined along the course of the St. Lawrence. The administrative, financial, and spiritual control of the whole community was in the hands of one governor, one intendant, one bishop, as the case might be. Above all the governor could call up for military service the whole male population between the ages of 14 and 70, and had an intelligible policy for defence and expansion. By a series of forts starting from the great lakes along the course of the Ohio and the Mississippi not only was connexion established between Canada and the French settlement at New Orleans on the Gulf of Mexico, but the expansion of the English coast colonies westwards over the Alleghanies was threatened. By advanced posts connecting the St. Lawrence up the Richelieu river with Lake Champlain France was ready to strike a blow at the very heart of the northern and middle colonies, and by her propaganda and a military fort on the border was rendering precarious the English hold on Nova Scotia, while the entrance to the St. Lawrence was defended by the citadel of Louisburg. Against such menaces, without England's help, the English colonies, like 'a Rope of Sand . . . loose and inconnected', as was said in 1754,[2] were comparatively defenceless. Their mutual jealousy was almost more marked than their suspicion of England's interference with their internal concerns. In principle England, except during a European war in which they were involved, expected most of the American colonies to look after their own defence. There were exceptions, it is true: she was ready to help comparatively new colonies or to protect vulnerable strategic positions; independent companies of the royal army were permanently stationed in South Carolina, Georgia, and New York; comparatively large sums were voted to Georgia in its infancy; and between 1750 and 1757 no less than £543,625 was spent by the English government in settling and fortifying Nova

---

[1] *Cambridge History of British Empire*, i. 400–1. In the same period the negro population increased from 96,000 to 299,000.
[2] Quoted by Beer, p. 17.

Scotia.[1] But as a rule the colonies were left to settle their own difficulties with Indian tribes or even French aggressors. This would have been perfectly feasible had it not been for their mutual jealousies. A colony in difficulty usually found little support from its neighbours; and boundary disputes between neighbours were not uncommon. So patent and so dangerous was this disunion that in 1721 and 1754 the board of trade suggested conferences of the colonies for joint action in defence and a common policy with the Indians, and at the 1754 conference Franklin, the delegate of Pennsylvania, actually proposed a definite plan of union for such purposes: but even then, on the eve of the Seven Years war, the jealousies were too acute for co-operation.[2] The only notable achievement of the colonials in their own defence during this period was due to Governor Shirley's enthusiasm in raising a force under Pepperell from his own colony, Massachusetts, with active help from New Hampshire and Connecticut and a few guns from New York for the capture of Louisburg in 1745;[3] though even that would not have been possible without the co-operation of an English squadron under Warren. Pitt alone, by his tactful concessions to colonial feeling[4] and by the contagious enthusiasm of his calls to action in his dispatches to the governors, was the first to obtain willing service from three at least of the most important colonies, Massachusetts, Connecticut, and New York. For the final assault on Canada, some 16,000 troops were raised in the colonies, over half of these coming from Massachusetts and Connecticut.[5] When, however, the immediate menace of France had been removed by the surrender of Canada in 1760, and Pitt's trumpet calls to unity had ceased in 1761, his feeble successors were unable to stir the colonies to take common action against the French left in Louisiana, or even against the serious incursions of Pontiac and his Indians in 1763–4.

More disgraceful even than the backwardness of some colonies to give active support to a war waged chiefly for their own pro-

[1] Ibid., p. 13; Keith, pp. 313–19.
[2] In 1721 and also in 1726 the board of trade suggested a governor-general for centralizing purposes, but nothing came of the suggestion. Keith, p. 314.
[3] See above, pp. 260–1.
[4] The chief concession was that of substantive rank to colonial officers. Previously a 2nd lieutenant in the imperial service took precedence over a colonial colonel. See also G. S. Kimball, *Correspondence of William Pitt*, 2 vols. 1906, *passim*.
[5] Williamson, p. 424.

tection was their eagerness to make profit by trading with the enemy. During the Seven Years war the French colonies, deprived of their fleets' protection, were in urgent need of supplies for which they were only too willing to trade. Passes granted by the French or by their own governors on the pretext of exchange of prisoners enabled colonial ships to trade directly with the French islands; or, when these means failed, the neutral Dutch or Spanish ports proved convenient meeting-places for the traffic. As a result of this 'illegal and most pernicious Trade . . . so utterly subversive of all Law, and so highly repugnant to the Honor, and well-being, of this Kingdom', as Pitt called it,[1] prices of necessaries rose to such an extent that Amherst and other commanders in North America found great difficulty in getting supplies for their own troops. Pennsylvania and Rhode Island seem to have been the chief culprits, but nearly all the continental colonies, and at least one West Indian island, Barbados, appear to have taken some part in the illicit trade.[2]

A serious result of the want of co-operation between the English colonies was the absence of any fixed policy with the Indian tribes in their midst or on their frontiers. The French with their centralized government, a definite policy, a more sympathetic attitude, and the powerful aid of the Jesuit missionaries were on the whole more successful in enlisting native support. With the English colonies there was no uniform system. Each of them claimed control over the tribes in its vicinity and few of them exercised any proper supervision over the traders dealing with the Indians, who to gain temporary advantages unscrupulously cheated or maltreated them; practices which led governors Shirley of Massachusetts and Dinwiddie of Virginia to urge—but all in vain—that traders should be licensed and supervised. There were of course instances of fair treatment by the English, the most notable being Penn's treaty of 1681 with the Indians on Philadelphia Common and its exact observance by the Pennsylvanians thereafter. It was, however, fortunate for us that the Six Nations of Iroquois, occupying a key-position between the English and French settlements near the great lakes and commanding the entrance to the fur-trading districts of the interior, were generally on our side, owing to their alarm at French designs along the Ohio and the Mississippi. One of Halifax's main reasons for promoting the Albany con-

---

[1] Kimball, ii. 320.   [2] Keith, pp. 331–4.

ference of 1754 was to secure some unity of Indian policy among the various colonies. Since, however, the delegates could not agree to this, the English government appointed Sir William Johnson and Edmund Atkin as its own agents in political matters with Indians of the north and south respectively; but commercial matters were still to be dealt with by the separate colonies. During the Seven Years war there was no trouble with the Indians; but in 1763 the grievances against the English colonists led to the serious Pontiac rebellion of all the Indian tribes from Michigan to Mobile, joined in even by the Senecas, one of the Six Nations.

Distance and length of travel account partly for the particularism of the Americans in relation not only to England but also to one another. Six weeks or more was occupied by the journey to England from Boston or New York, while, in the absence of good or in some parts of any roads, communication between the colonies was chiefly dependent on slow coasting vessels.[1] Thus the colonists had no great temptation to cross the Atlantic or even to visit their neighbours, nor is it surprising that travellers like the Rev. A. Burnaby in 1759–60 were chiefly impressed by the differences between the various colonies. The two cities that he found the most cultivated were Philadelphia and Boston. Of the latter he says he found more progress in the arts and sciences than anywhere else in America; but, as with the Swedish traveller Kalm, his special enthusiasm is aroused by Philadelphia, the site of which only eighty years before had been a desert haunted by savage beasts and wild men and now was a city of 3,000 houses with good, well-lighted streets two miles in length with fine wharves and shipping along the river Delaware, a college, the best school of learning in America, and churches of many denominations including a Romish chapel: its population of 18,000–20,000 people was rich and flourishing and the most enterprising on the continent.[2] Much of this enlightenment was of course due to Philadelphia's most distinguished citizen Benjamin Franklin, with his dissemination of popular aphorisms and common-sense philosophy in *Poor Richard's Almanack*, his circulating library, his American

---

[1] In 1758 Forbes, one of Pitt's generals, complained that letters from the coast took three months to reach him; see *Chatham*, i. 335–6.
[2] *Cambridge History of British Empire*, i. 806 sqq.

Philosophical Society, the city hospital he founded, and his Academy for the Education of Youth, all started between 1731 and 1751; while his own scientific researches, especially in electricity, had brought him European fame by the middle of the century, and his activities at the Albany Congress of 1754 and as agent for Pennsylvania in England gave him a commanding position in American and even English politics.

Maryland, Virginia, South Carolina, with their large estates and increasing amount of slave labour, were socially nearer to the West Indian conditions than to their northern neighbours. Though described as haughty and jealous of their liberties, the planters were convivial and good natured, and very hospitable to strangers, as their successors still are. Those of Virginia, established mainly on the James river, lived in beautiful Queen Anne houses with underground tunnels communicating with the slave quarters, and wharves handy for loading the tobacco for the ocean voyage. Tobacco indeed was not only the staple product of the colony but even used as a standard of currency, the pay of the established clergy being fixed at 16,000 lb. of tobacco.[1] They were an enterprising community and among the first to push up to and beyond the Alleghanies in search of new land to exploit. One of these pioneers was Alexander Spotswood, lieutenant-governor from 1710 to 1722, who in 1720 secured for himself a tract of 45,000 acres. South Carolina had much the same conditions but also had, as Virginia had not, a flourishing town, Charleston, as a social centre.

In most of the northern and middle colonies educational facilities were probably at least as good as if not better than in England: in Massachusetts and Connecticut, for example, there was an elementary school for every township of 50 householders and a higher school in those of 100. Harvard in Massachusetts and the College of William and Mary in Virginia dated from the seventeenth century while Yale in Connecticut, Princeton in New Jersey, and Dartmouth in New Hampshire were all in existence by 1769.[2] The press was already becoming a power in some states; and in 1735 Zenger, publisher of the *New York Weekly Journal*, won the right for juries to decide not only on the fact of publication of a statement but also whether it was in fact libellous. This was only four years after an exactly contrary decision in Francklin's case had been upheld at home

---

[1] Keith, p. 223. [2] *Cambridge History of British Empire*, i. 399.

by L.C.J. Raymond and fifty-seven years before the English law was finally decided in the more liberal sense by Fox's Libel Act.[1]

In the early times the religion of the New England colonies was a dour and narrow puritanism; but by the eighteenth century a more tolerant spirit was spreading. Unitarianism was impinging on the straiter sects; Jonathan Edwards himself, though uncompromising in his stern predestinarianism, by his saintly example of self-sacrifice for his opinions, still more by the appeal to the intellect in his writings, helped towards a spirit of greater charity and freer inquiry. The church of England was established in Maryland, Virginia, and the Carolinas, but was hardly a great spiritual force in America. Whitefield indeed declared that most of the Anglican clergy would be rejected for the dissenting ministry.[2] In Anne's reign there was talk, which came to nothing, of appointing a bishop for America; for want of one the bishop of London was charged with a vague control exercised through commissaries, of whom Blair in Virginia is noted as effective. Bishop Gibson from 1723 to 1748 was the only one who took this duty seriously, but even he at that distance could not hope for much control. The one attempt to spiritualize the church of England in America failed. In 1725 Berkeley, then dean of Derry, obtained a royal charter to found a college in Bermuda for training planters' sons as well as candidates for the mission field. His idea was that this college should be a new centre of Christian civilization in America, as an antidote to the materialistic conception of empire then prevalent in England. After obtaining promises of private subscriptions of £5,000 and a vote from parliament of £20,000 for his scheme, he went over to Rhode Island to prepare the ground by conferences with Anglican and dissenting clergy and laymen in America. But Walpole saw to it that the £20,000 voted should never be paid by the treasury, and without it the Bermuda scheme fell to the ground.[3]

With the end of French sovereignty in Canada one great guarantee for the fidelity of the American colonists to the protective mother country had disappeared; and to those who during Pitt's negotiations with France in 1761 and Bute's in 1762

---

[1] *State Trials*, xvii. 626 sqq., for Francklin case, ibid., pp. 675 sqq., for the Zenger case. See too above, p. 61.

[2] Whitefield letters of 1739–40 preserved by S.P.G.

[3] A good deal about the Bermuda scheme is to be found in B. Rand's *Berkeley and Percival Correspondence*, 1914. See too above, p. 91.

urged that Canada should be returned to France and Guadeloupe retained, the restraining influence of French proximity
on the colonists' allegiance was an important consideration. On
the other hand Shirley, one of the ablest of the governors, was
strongly in favour of keeping the French out of Canada, holding
that the mutual jealousy of the various colonies would alone
prevent their uniting to throw off the dominion of Great Britain:
and Franklin was then of the same opinion. Certainly the fierce
isolationism of the colonies up to 1760 was a strong argument
for this view. On the other hand it is apparent to us today,
wiser perhaps after the event, that the overmastering feeling in
the continental colonies was then, and always had been, a
determination to be arbiters of their own fate. This applies not
only to the dour puritans and independents of New England,
but also to the quakers of Pennsylvania, with all their aversion
to 'carnal weapons', the growing business community of New
York, and not least to the aristocratic planter settlements of
Maryland and Virginia, heirs of the English squires' and J.P.s'
tradition of revolt against Stuart autocracy. When, therefore, a
stupid generation of English politicians set themselves to tighten
the bands of discipline, even this particularism gave way, for
the time being, to the need of united resistance, especially when
they found that some of the noblest Englishmen looked on them
as fighting for a constitutional issue common to lovers of freedom whether in Great Britain or in America.

In India this period marks the culmination of the East India
Company's commercial prosperity as well as the beginnings of
its territorial aggrandizement. In 1708 the competition, weakening to both, between the old East India Company and the
New Company, incorporated in 1698, had been finally brought
to an end by their merger in the 'United Company of Merchants
of England Trading to the East Indies'.[1] An act of parliament
passed in 1711 had extended the Company's exclusive trading
rights till 1733; and in 1730, in spite of an attempt by free
merchants to share in the trade, its monopoly was continued
by parliament till 1769, and again in 1744 till 1780.[2] For these

[1] See *Oxford History of England*, x. 354 (2nd edn.). An amicable arrangement had
actually been made in 1702. The difficulties of this competition are illustrated by
the career of Governor Pitt at Madras. See *Chatham*, i. 14–17.
[2] The Company was to have three years of grace up to 1783 if its exclusive rights
were not renewed. See L. S. Sutherland, *East India Company in 18th Century Politics*, p. 30.

privileges the Company had increased its loan to the government and its own capital to £3,200,000, at an interest diminishing gradually from 4 to 3 per cent. by 1757, and in 1744 it had made a further loan to the government of £1,000,000 at the same rate. Its growing prosperity is indicated by the increase of its homeward imports from nearly £500,000 in 1708 to about £1,100,000 in 1748, and of its exports to India from £576,000 to £1,121,000 between 1710 and 1750; while its dividends rose from 5 per cent. in 1708/9 to 10 per cent. from 1711 to 1721, and thereafter fluctuated between 7 and 8 per cent. till 1755, when the war in India had increased its expenses. In the same period the average number of ships employed annually in the trade increased from 11 to 20.[1] Its main imports to England were raw silk, cotton yarn, and undyed calicoes, besides a growing amount of tea from China[2] and of coffee through Surat or directly from Mokha.[3]

By the eighteenth century the Portuguese and Dutch, once holding commanding positions in India, were left with few and unimportant possessions or factories. The chief European rivals now left in India were the French and English companies. On the east or Coromandel coast the French had their headquarters at Pondichery, and other factories at Chandernagore in Bengal and Yanaon and Masulipatam farther south; on the west coast they had trading stations at Surat, Calicut, and Mahé. But in number and importance of factories the English Company came first. It had three presidencies at Bombay, Calcutta (Fort William), and Madras (Fort St. George); and Bombay was the only absolute possession in French or English hands, the other factories being leased from native rulers. In the Bombay presidency there were seven other factories extending from Surat to Tellicheri on the Malabar coast; under Fort St. George on the Coromandel coast were Fort St. David, Cuddalore, and Porto Novo south of Pondichery and Vizagapatam farther north; in the Bengal presidency besides Calcutta on the Hughli the English Company had factories at Balasore on

---

[1] The Company never, during this period, chartered a ship of a tonnage over 499, since they were obliged to send a chaplain on every ship of 500 tons or more.

[2] The rapid increase of the tea-drinking habit in England may be seen from the importation figures for tea of 54,600 lb. in 1706, when the price in England was nearly £1, to 2,325,000 lb. in 1750, when the price had come down to 5s. a lb.

[3] *Cambridge History of India*, v. 108–11. This volume is also published as *Cambridge History of British Empire*, vol. iv.

the coast and others as far inland as Kasimbazar, Dacca, and Patna. The main factories of both English and French, Madras and Pondichery, being on the Coromandel coast, were for nearly four months each year, from October onwards, exposed to the full force of the monsoons. So violent are these monsoons that the fleets of those days had to seek shelter elsewhere during their season. For this purpose the French had acquired Île Bourbon (Réunion) in 1664 and Île de France (Mauritius) in 1721, both in favourable circumstances within a month's sailing; whereas, besides Bombay on the west coast, St. Helena, some months' distance from India, was the nearest port of refuge for the English. The English Company, being a vigorous commercial company independent of government interference, but able in emergencies to rely on help from the navy, had an advantage over the French Company entirely dependent on government support that was apt to fail it in times of stress in Europe. On the other hand the French Company, in the early days of the struggle for domination in India, had an initial advantage in the concentration of power and the direction of policy in the hands of the far-seeing Dupleix, appointed governor of Pondichery in 1741, and with an able military assistant Bussy together with a great naval commander in La Bourdonnais.[1]

In the chaotic condition of India through the depredations of Maratha bands, the weakening of the Great Mogul's central authority, and the rival claims of provincial nawabs and rajahs to secure independent rule, Dupleix found his opportunity to establish and extend French influence in India. Already by 1739, before France and England were at war, La Bourdonnais was planning an attack on the English settlements and was only prevented from carrying out the scheme in 1742 by the decision of the two East India Companies in London and Paris to abstain from hostilities. But after the declaration of war in 1744 Dupleix and La Bourdonnais were able to take the offensive. La Bourdonnais had only one 70-gun man-of-war against the four sent to Madras by the English government, but by arming East Indiamen he collected a superior squadron of ten ships[2] with which in June 1746 he drove off the English squadron and

---

[1] *Cambridge History of India*, v. 102–8, 111–13, and *Cambridge Modern History*, vi. 529 sqq.

[2] La Bourdonnais's ten ships included one small tender which took no part in the action of June 1746. The English squadron totalled six including a small frigate which was not in the line. See Richmond, *The Navy in the War of 1739–48*, iii. 193–4.

in September captured Madras, which had made a poor resistance. In 1748 Boscawen came out with naval reinforcements and with Major Stringer Lawrence,[1] already sent 'to command all the Company's troops' in India, made a vigorous attempt to capture Pondichery; but though La Bourdonnais's fleet had been shattered by a storm,[2] Dupleix forced them to raise the siege just before news of the treaty of Aix-la-Chapelle had reached India.

The peace of 1748 restored Madras to the English, but was far from restoring peace to India. Dupleix now embarked on his great scheme of bringing not only the Carnatic but the whole of the Deccan, or southern India, under French control by means of military aid to puppet native rulers. To carry out this scheme he had an ideal coadjutor in Charles Castelnau de Bussy; for he was a man not only of great military attainments, but endowed with the presence of mind, tact, and patience needed for dealing with eastern princes. At first all went well: in 1749 Dupleix replaced the nawab of the Carnatic, supported by the English, by his own nominee Chanda Sahib in return for a large extension of French territory round Pondichery: in 1750 he solemnly recognized at Pondichery another nominee, Mozaffar Jang, as subadhar of the Deccan, and early in 1751 sent him up to Hyderabad accompanied by Bussy,[3] who was to reorganize his army and make it an instrument of French influence throughout southern India.

But at last the tide began to turn. In September 1750 the English Company had replaced as governor of Fort St. George the feeble Charles Floyer by Thomas Saunders, a man of sterner stuff; in the previous year Stringer Lawrence had secured Devikottai in Tanjore as a counterpoise to the French acquisition of Karikal ten years previously. The superseded nawab of the Carnatic, Mohammad Ali, friendly to the English, had taken refuge in the mountain fastness of Trichinopoly, and had resisted all efforts to dislodge him although by the spring of 1751 he was desperately hard pressed. Then appeared Clive, 'that man not born for a desk, that heaven-born general', as

---

[1] Stringer Lawrence, 1697–1775, called 'the father of the Indian army'.

[2] This was in Oct. 1746. After refitting his ships La Bourdonnais quarrelled with Dupleix and withdrew to the islands. 'Thus the superiority which the French might have used . . . was wasted.' Richmond, l.c. iii. 204.

[3] Mozaffar Jang was killed within a few days of leaving Pondichery. Bussy replaced him with his uncle Salabat Jang.

Pitt acclaimed him. At nineteen he had reached India as a writer in the Company's service, tried to shoot himself, but soon found his true vocation as soldier and statesman. He fought gallantly in the attempt on Pondichery, distinguished himself at Devikottai as a lieutenant under Lawrence, and in the summer of 1751 was given leave to make an attempt on Arcot, the capital of the Carnatic. He captured it and then withstood a siege there against an army of 10,000, and won the victories of Arni and Coveripak against both native and French troops.[1] In 1752, with Lawrence, he defeated Chanda Sahib and restored Mohammad Ali as nawab of the Carnatic. Finally in 1754 the French Company, alarmed at their governor's expensive and ambitious schemes, recalled Dupleix in disgrace; his successor Godeheu recognized Mohammad Ali and made peace with the English in the Carnatic.[2]

Meanwhile dangers were threatening the English in other quarters. Bussy, by his tact and conciliatory methods and by his masterly training, with the aid of a few French troops, of Salabat Jang's army, had established the French as the paramount power at Hyderabad. At the end of 1753 Bussy's well-trained army was rendered independent of native intrigues by the assignment to him personally of the four northern Sarkars of the Deccan, the revenues of which were more than sufficient for its upkeep; and in 1756 Bussy captured four of the English factories in that region, including Vizagapatam. In that year war was again declared between France and England and the truce in India came to an end. The first blow fell in Bengal, where the new subadhar, Siraj-ud-Daula, was inclined to an understanding with the French. Picking a quarrel with the English in June 1756 he captured their factory at Kasimbazar and then attacked Calcutta, garrisoned by some 230 European troops, with an army of 30,000–50,000 men. The governor, Drake, leaving the garrison and the male inhabitants to their fate, embarked with the women and children on a ship which sailed down the river;[3] the rest of the inhabitants made what

---

[1] The siege of Arcot lasted 50 days, Sept.–Nov. 1751. Arni was fought at the end of Nov., after the siege was raised, and Coveripak in Feb. 1752. Fortescue, *History of the British Army*, ii. 205–11.

[2] Dupleix, for all his services, was left by the French Company to languish in poverty after his return. La Bourdonnais was thrown into the Bastille.

[3] [Drake's conduct was feeble but not base. He 'yielded to a momentary panic after freely exposing himself to the enemy's fire'. Williamson, p. 374. C.H.S.]

COMPLETE TRIUMPH OF ENGLISH

fight they could, but, after capitulating to overwhelming numbers, were mostly done to death in the Black Hole of Calcutta.
When the news came to Madras the governor[1] and council, in
spite of the risk in denuding their own forces, fortunately decided to send a force under Clive[2] to be conveyed to the Hughli
by Admiral Watson,[3] who had been sent to Madras two years
before with a squadron and a royal regiment. In January 1757
Clive recaptured Calcutta; in the following June, with his 2,200
Sepoys and 800 Europeans, he defeated Siraj-ud-Daula's army
of 50,000 at Plassey, and in his place established a rival, Mir
Jafar, as the puppet subadhar of Bengal, Behar, and Orissa;
earlier in the same year he had driven the French out of
Chandernagore, their headquarters in Bengal. Two years later,
after an ill-advised attempt by the Dutch at Chinsura to dispute
the English control in Bengal, Clive's second in command Forde[4]
routed their garrison and a small squadron of armed East Indiamen captured their ships in the Hughli; and the Dutch were
compelled to limit their forces in Bengal and restrict their trade
within prescribed limits.[5] In 1760 Clive himself returned to
England. Within three years he had exacted swift retribution
for the Black Hole, had established virtual English rule in the
three north-eastern provinces, and had successfully maintained
the authority of Mir Jafar against internal intrigues and an
invasion from the neighbouring state of Oudh. Before leaving,
however, unhappily for his reputation, he accepted a jagir, or
present of revenues amounting to £27,000 per annum, all the
more questionable a proceeding for a servant of the Company
since this sum was in fact the rent payable by the Company to
the subadhar for their lease of lands south of Calcutta.

But the principal fighting between French and English in
India was still about the Carnatic. There the French and English forces were fairly matched, with a slight superiority at sea
to the French. D'Aché, La Bourdonnais's successor, had his
fleet concentrated off the coast by April 1758; a few months

[1] George Pigot, 1719–77, later Lord Pigot, who had succeeded Saunders in 1755.
[2] It was fortunate that Col. Adlercron, the senior officer on the spot, refused the
command, as he could not secure a large enough share of the prospective plunder,
nor would engage to return when summoned by the council of Madras.
[3] Charles Watson, 1714–57.
[4] Francis Forde, d. 1770.
[5] The Dutch and English governments were of course at peace then; and these
incidents at Chinsura are only another illustration of the loose conception of inter-
national law at this period.

earlier Pocock,[1] who on Watson's death in August 1757 took command of the English fleet, had been reinforced by four ships and a frigate under Steevens. On land the new French general, Lally Tollendal, had brought reinforcements of 2,000 regulars and later received 1,200 more: to supplement the English Company's forces, Pitt in 1757, as soon as he heard of the Black Hole, had arranged for a new regiment to be raised under Draper which reached Madras in September 1758; twelve months later a second regiment reached Madras where it was met by its commander, Eyre Coote.[2] At sea in April and August 1758 Pocock, though unable to prevent the capture of Fort St. David by Lally, more than held his own with an inferior force against D'Aché. Then for over a year the French admiral left Indian waters to refit and revictual at Île de France, Île Bourbon, and the Cape, reappearing only in September 1759, when he was so hammered by Pocock that he left India for good in October. Lally had greater success on land. He captured Fort St. David in June 1758, made raids on the territory of Tanjore, and in December once more closely invested Madras itself. Here the English made a far better defence than in 1746, but were only saved from surrender in the following February, when a detachment from Pocock's fleet appeared and forced Lally to retire. Unfortunately for him, in order to supplement his besieging force, Lally had recalled Bussy and the greater part of his troops from the Deccan, the most promising sphere of French influence, an opportunity immediately seized by Clive, who sent Colonel Forde from Bengal to expel the French from the northern Sarkars. After Forde's victory at Condore in December 1758 and the recapture of Masulipatam in the following April the Nizam ceded that rich territory to the English. By 1760 Colonel Eyre Coote had cleared the Carnatic of the French, defeating Lally and capturing Bussy at Wandewash, recovering Arcot, Karikal, Fort St. David, and Cuddalore; and with Steevens he finally obtained the surrender of Pondichery itself from Lally in January 1761.[3] This was the end of French territorial dominion in India. By the treaty of Paris they

---

[1] Admiral (Sir) George Pocock, 1706–92.

[2] (Sir) Eyre Coote, 1726–83, present at Plassey; commander-in-chief in India 1779–83. For the raising of these regiments see Fortescue, l.c., pp. 442, 463–6.

[3] In 1766 Lally Tollendal himself was beheaded in Paris *pour encourager les autres* for 'betraying' Pondichery. Steevens had succeeded Pocock in command of the fleet in Apr. 1760.

were allowed to keep their trading factories, but no garrisons, and in 1769 the Compagnie des Indes, which had lost 169 million francs of capital since 1725, was abolished.

Clive's conquest of Bengal, Behar, and Orissa and the cession of the revenues of the northern Sarkars produced a revolutionary change in the status and responsibilities of the East India Company, a change hardly appreciated at first, but to cause anxious consideration in the future. Hitherto the Company had been a purely trading concern with no territorial or administrative responsibilities except for the comparatively trivial police and municipal requirements in the small possession of Bombay or the rented areas of Calcutta, Fort St. David, and Madras. But now great provinces and immense land revenues had been added to the Company's charge, with no provision in its charter or experience to guide it. Clive himself seems at first to have been alone in foreseeing the difficulty: writing to Pitt in January 1759, and through his agent Walsh in the following November, he suggested that the Crown rather than the Company should assume these vast new territorial and financial responsibilities. Unfortunately Pitt at the time was too much taken up with the conduct of the war and put aside consideration of the question.[1]

It is true some of the governors of the Company's settlements or factories at Bombay, Madras, and Calcutta, such as Thomas Pitt, Saunders, and Pigot, in his first term of office, and in the previous century Child at Surat and Bombay, were on the whole wise and efficient administrators. But they were rather exceptional; and even some of the best of them, such as Governor Pitt, managed to amass wealth enough to buy seats in parliament and found the family fortunes. The general run of writers and clerks, on the other hand, were almost compelled by the Company's system to devote most of their attention to their own personal enrichment. Their pay from the Company was so small that they had to be allowed to trade on their own account to enable them to live on the luxurious scale universal in the country, and also to take back to England fortunes for an equally wealthy retirement as 'nabobs' in England. Alexander Hamilton, a traveller and trader in the East between 1688 and 1723, gives us some idea of conditions at that time in some of the

[1] See *Chatham*, ii. 29, 30.

Company's settlements. At Calcutta he describes with enthusiasm the commodious houses of the Company's agents and factors, their gardens and their fish-ponds where they and their ladies lived splendidly and pleasantly. Their normal day was taken up with business in the morning, dinner followed by a rest, and in the evening friendly visits with excursions in chaises and palanquins, or by water in budgeroes to the fields and gardens, or else fishing and shooting by the men. To keep up this style they had not only to trade on their own account, but to take heavy bribes from private traders, including natives, in return for lending their names to cover commercial transactions in the Company's preserves. Even outside India, as far afield as Siam or China, Hamilton notes, private traders such as himself found the Company's agents at most of the ports, where they exacted toll for permission to trade with the native merchants and dealers.[1] In Madras, some twenty years later, it was much the same; though there, perhaps owing to the lack of Calcutta's natural amenities, gaming was the principal sport and for stakes so high as to bring down the Company's animadversions. The Company, it is true, tried to put a stop to the enormous bribes or 'presents' exacted by their servants from local merchants, but apparently with little success. At Fort St. David, for example, we hear of presents totalling 52,000 pagodas,[2] and at Fort St. George over 22,000. In 1755 in a letter to the chairman of the Company, Orme, the historian, then on the council of Madras, accuses one of his colleagues, Wynch, of having made £20,000 in the service of the Company, the chaplain at St. David, Palk, of having enlarged his original fortune of £2,000 to £10,000 by his influence with Colonel Lawrence, and Clive himself of having made a profit of no less than £40,000 by victualling the army.[3]

---

[1] 'New Account of the East Indies' in *Pinkerton's Travels*, viii. 410–13. Hamilton was an 'interloper' and so inclined to emphasize the 'tyranny and villainy' of the Company.

[2] The pagoda was then worth about 9s. Hamilton valued it at 8s. 3d. Ibid., p. 521.

[3] H. D. Love, *Vestiges of Old Madras 1640–1800*, 4 vols., 1913, ii. 249, 486. Orme himself was accused by his enemies on the council of having tried to extort baksheesh from the nawab of the Carnatic. Ibid., pp. 513–19. [The amassing of large fortunes by the Company's servants was the exception rather than the rule. For an admirably just assessment of their standards of conduct see Sutherland, *East India Company*, pp. 53–54. See also T. G. P. Spear, *The Nabobs ... in 18th-Century India*, p. 32. 'Before 1750 ... few Company's servants ... acquired fortunes ...' C.H.S.]

Such practices were bad enough when the Company's servants were merely factors or agents in a trading concern; but when, with no better pay and no experience of administration, they were called upon to govern large provinces, their extortions and their incapacity became a crying scandal. It was left first to the Company and finally to the government to find a remedy in the following reign. It was not till 1786 that Fox laid down in noble words the principles on which India should in future be governed—by 'those laws which are to be found in Europe, Africa, and Asia—that are found amongst all mankind—those principles of equity and humanity implanted in our hearts, which have their existence in the feelings of mankind that are capable of judging'.[1]

[1] Speech on the Rohilla charge of 2 June 1786, *P.H.* xxvi. 65.

XII

NEWCASTLE IN SEARCH OF A POLICY

THE Peace of Aix-la-Chapelle was nothing more than a truce, and an ill-kept truce, between England and France, useful only as a breathing-space before the decisive struggle. For the first six of this eight years' truce power in England was monopolized by the brothers Pelham, Henry, the younger, nominally head of the government as first lord of the treasury and also chancellor of the exchequer, being responsible for finance, his elder brother the duke of Newcastle, as a secretary of state, for foreign policy. Henry Pelham, an apt pupil of Walpole in his careful management of the country's finances, had none of his master's power of controlling colleagues and was too apt, against his better judgement, to give in to the ill-digested schemes of his woolly-minded and touchy brother Newcastle. Fortunately, however, except in so far as Newcastle's schemes required futile subsidies to continental princes, Pelham had a free hand in reducing the normal expenditure of the country as well as the national debt charges, so that England, at the outbreak of the Seven Years war, found herself in a comparatively strong position financially.

The budgets of those days were comparatively simple affairs, since the civil government's expenditure was met mainly by the civil list, voted to the sovereign at the beginning of each reign, and thereafter not subject to parliamentary sanction. Except for occasional grants for such purposes as an aid to the plantations, for rebuilding Westminster Bridge, for the loss of horned cattle, for road-making, or to make good interest on the debt, the annual budgets were almost solely concerned, on the supply side, with the upkeep of the army and navy and subsidies to foreign princes, and, on the ways and means side, with the annually voted land-tax, the allocation of the surplus of permanent taxes granted for the civil list, and occasional new taxes, as on wines, beer, &c., or raids on the sinking fund. A war-budget, amounting at the peak in 1747–8 to £9,819,345,

was thought unduly burdensome.[1] As soon as peace was signed
Pelham ruthlessly cut down expenditure, reducing the number
of seamen and marines from 51,550 to 17,000 for 1748–9, and
thereafter to 10,000 and even to 8,000 in 1750–1, but next
year, owing to protests from Pitt and others, he restored it to
10,000: similarly the establishment of the army was brought
down from 50,000 to 18,850, and the subsidies to foreign princes
for troops, &c., from £1,677,639 in 1748 to £30,000 in 1750–1.
By 1750, however, Newcastle was turning again to his policy of
subsidies to foreign princes in pursuit of a visionary combination
against France: so Pelham, though opposed to this policy, had
to burden his three remaining budgets with renewed payments
to German princes. Nevertheless, within four years from the
peace he was balancing the budget at £2,628,356 instead of

[1] Coxe, *Pelham Administration*, gives, from Postlethwayte's *History of the Public
Revenue*, all the budgets during Pelham's administration. Here is the budget,
epitomized, for 1747–8:

Supply	£	*Ways and Means*	£
Navy—40,000 seamen and 11,550 marines, &c., including £1,000,000 towards the discharge of the navy debt . . .	3,640,351	Land-tax of 4s. in £, after deducting £159,727 interest	1,920,272
Army—49,939 men, home and foreign service .	2,693,789	Malt tax, after deducting for interest, &c., £181,756 .	598,243
Charges for 6,172 Hessian, 22,070 Hanoverian, 30,000 Russian, and 4,800 Brunswick troops . . .	942,173	Contributions for purchase of annuities and lottery of £630,000, interest payable by addl. duty of 12d. in £, on tonnage and poundage	6,930,000
Subsidies to Sardinia, Maria Theresa, and Electors of Maintz and Bavaria .	735,466	From the Sinking Fund	1,000,000
Vote of credit . . .	500,000		
For building Westminster Bridge . . .	20,000		
Compensation for proprs. of heritable jurisdictions [Scotland] . . .	152,037		
For loss of horned cattle .	62,000		
For making good deficiencies and interest and other charges . . .	1,073,529		
	9,819,345		
Balance	629,170		
	£10,448,515		£10,448,515

£9,819,345, and was able to reduce the land-tax to 3s. in 1749–50 and even to 2s. by 1752–3.

Besides the great savings he made in the annual budgets Pelham also tackled the growing national debt, always a subject of anxiety in the first half of the eighteenth century. Walpole had already done much in reducing the general rate of interest and something towards consolidating the various loans, but latterly had used his sinking fund, originally instituted to reduce the capital of the debt, mainly to lighten the burden of current taxation, and in 1737 definitely rejected the proposal of Sir John Barnard, the great city authority on finance, for more drastic methods of reduction.[1] In 1739, the last year of peace, the debt had stood at £46 million; by 1749 Pelham was faced with one of over £77 million, an amount then considered dangerously high besides being expensive to manage, as it was divided into some fourteen different stocks at varying rates of interest from 4 per cent., payable on nearly £58 million, to 3½ or 3 per cent. for the rest. Barnard's drastic proposal was to earmark £600,000 a year from the sinking fund in order gradually to pay off the debt altogether; but Pelham, though enlisting his support for his own measures, refused to adopt so dangerous a scheme.[2] His own proposal in 1749 was to offer the holders of stock at 4 per cent. interest at 3½ per cent. till 1757 and thereafter at 3 per cent., with the alternative of having their stock redeemed by means of loans then easily floated at 3 per cent., since the 3 per cent. stock was then being quoted at above par. After some hesitation most of the 4 per cent. stock-holders agreed to these terms, those outstanding being repaid their capital.[3] The holders of 3½ per cent. stock, comparatively small in numbers, were left undisturbed. Thus by 1758, except for the small amount at 3¼ per cent., the interest on the national debt was to be reduced to a uniform 3 per cent. Two years later he simplified and cheapened the debt service still further by amalgamating the fourteen different stocks into five. Already by 1754,

[1] See above, p. 187.
[2] H. Walpole, *Memoirs, George II*, i. 255. The result of such a scheme in war-time might have been the obligation to borrow money at 5 or 6 per cent. to pay off debt at 3 per cent.
[3] By Feb. 1750 holders of nearly £19,000,000 of the 4 per cent. stock were still holding out against Pelham's terms, but most of these hastened to agree when in that year Pelham passed a second act reducing their interest from 4 per cent. to 3½ per cent. in 1755 instead of 1757. See E. L. Hargreaves, *National Debt*, 1930, p. 54.

the year of his death and four years before the full reduction of interest to 3 per cent., the management of the debt had been much simplified and a saving of over £270,000 in interest had been secured.[1]

In other ways Pelham, as far as he was allowed a free hand by his brother, showed himself an enlightened administrator. In spite of the duke's opposition he supported Chesterfield's measure for reforming the calendar in 1751;[2] he spoke warmly for the Jew Naturalization Bill and only consented to its repeal because the duke, who always had a number of agents throughout the country keeping their hands on the pulse of the public, was alarmed at the agitation against it in view of the forthcoming general election.[3] He favoured various schemes for the development of trade and industry, such as the exportation of wool from Ireland, hitherto prohibited, and of other raw materials, and especially Oglethorpe's bill to encourage, by a bonus to fishing vessels and grants in aid of a fishery company with the prince of Wales as governor, the national fisheries against Dutch competition.[4]

Pelham was little troubled by opposition in parliament, partly owing to his own conciliatory methods, partly because he had taken care to have the most effective politicians on the government benches. Pitt, potentially the most dangerous critic in the commons, had little fault to find with his policy and gave a general support to his measures. The only serious protest he made during this period was in 1751 against Pelham's reduction of the seamen voted for the navy to 8,000, a protest which bore fruit in restoring the normal 10,000 in the following years. Otherwise Pitt was content to bide his time in the subordinate office of paymaster, where he found scope for some much needed reforms. The salary and legitimate allowances to the paymaster were in themselves considerable, amounting to some £4,000 per annum. But this sum was as nothing compared with the

---

[1] For Pelham's debt operations see Coxe, *Pelham*, ii. 45, 77–79, 89–93, 221–2, 300; *P.H.* xiv. 576–7, 591–2, 619–21. The annual saving in interest rose to £350,101 between 1755 and 1757 and after 1757 to £544,134. See Hargreaves, l.c., p. 55. The consolidation of the different stocks produced one each for the 3 per cent., 3½ per cent., Bank, Old South Sea, and New South Sea annuities. See Coxe, *Pelham*, ii. 221–2.

[2] See below, p. 381.

[3] See above, p. 73–74.

[4] *P.H.* xiv. 762–4; Coxe, l.c., pp. 75, 106, 187, 223. The Fisheries Bill hardly answered the enthusiastic expectations which it aroused. See above, pp. 277–8.

perquisites it had become the custom of previous paymasters to exact for themselves. In the first place they demanded a commission of ¼ per cent. on all subsidies paid to foreign princes, a fruitful source of gain in years when these subsidies amounted to as much as £1,000,000, or even over £1,500,000 as in 1748. Besides that they made handsome profits from the pay of the soldiers, for in those days the treasury paid over to the pay-master at the beginning of the year the total sum voted for the army for that year, and it was their custom to invest in their own name these army balances, drawing the interest for their private accounts until the soldiers' pay became due six months or even a year later. By such methods many of these paymasters, espe-cially in war-time, had acquired immense wealth. The duke of Chandos, paymaster from 1705 to 1713, was said to have built his vast and magnificent palace at Canons from such irregular profits, and after Pitt's time, when these methods were revived, Henry Fox established the family fortunes thereby. But Pitt set his face against such practices, refusing to accept 'the great and the invidious profits of the Pay Office', as Burke called them. He lodged all his unexpended balances in the Bank of England and took no interest for himself from them: nor would he accept the customary percentage from subsidies paid out to foreign princes, much to the astonishment of the Sardinian minister and of his sovereign at such quixotic abnega-tion. By this example of a high standard of public duty in his own case, he was in a stronger position for reforming such abuses as he found in irregular returns from commanding officers or wasteful expenditure in the regiments. He also much alleviated the lot of the poor Chelsea out-pensioners, by paying them their allowances regularly and prohibiting the exorbitant commis-sions exacted in the past by unscrupulous agents who traded on their needs.[1]

Pelham's task was considerably lightened in 1751 by the death of Frederick, prince of Wales, who might have become a formidable prop for the opposition of disappointed office-seekers. Ever since he had been brought over to London from Hanover in December 1728 he had been a source of trouble to his father and still more to his mother. It was largely their own fault; for, as has been the case with others of that family, they were desperately afraid of their first-born gaining popularity at their

---

[1] For Pitt's reforms in the pay office in more detail see *Chatham*, i. 151–7.

own expense. For a long time they tried to keep him in leading-strings and restricted his allowance to £50,000, though George II had been granted an extra £100,000 for his civil list on the tacit understanding that the prince of Wales should be allowed that amount. Being neglected and despised by his father and mother,[1] he rather naturally found his friends in opposition circles, where he was used as a stalking-horse for attacks on ministers or even his parents. There was some justification for the motion made on his behalf in 1737 for an increase of his allowance; but nothing can excuse the risky and insulting journey he took his wife in the agonies of labour in that year from Hampton Court to St. James's to prevent the delivery of his first-born under his parents' roof.[2] For this insult he was naturally forbidden the court; and the establishments he set up in Leicester Square and Carlton Gardens became the avowed rendezvous of the opposition. Five years after his mother's death and on the eve of his own resignation Walpole persuaded the king to make it up with his son and offer him the additional £50,000 a year. To this offer, brought to him by the bishop of Oxford, the prince replied that he would accept nothing while Walpole remained in office, a reply which so infuriated the king that 'flinging off his wig' and 'meeting the Duke of Newcastle and, not seeing him through the blindness of his rage, he flung him down'.[3] Later, however, after Walpole's resignation and when many of his political friends were in office, the prince accepted his father's renewed offer of the additional £50,000 and was admitted to pay his duty at court.[4] But though Frederick showed a becoming spirit during the '45 the reconciliation was only skin-deep, and in his last year he was trying to form a party composed of such dregs of the opposition as Dodington, Potter, and the second Lord Egmont. In 1750 he was even planning his first ministry and drafts of his own speeches and political programme in anticipation of his father's death.[5]

[1] Their animus, and especially the queen's, against him is described with vitriolic fervour by Hervey, who undoubtedly, for his own purposes, stimulated their animosity.   [2] See above, p. 204.

[3] Egmont commented on this story of George II's tantrums, 'this I believe is an idle report, but you see how ready people are to make stories of the King'.

[4] For the stages of this negotiation see *Hist. MSS. Comm., Egmont Diary*, iii. 238–40, 263–4.

[5] In the *Bedford Correspondence*, i. 320–2, appears a programme of reforms first promised by Frederick in 1747 to the party supporting him. For the plan of his first ministry on his accession to the throne see the quotations from the MS. Diary

The prince undoubtedly had merits for which the consensus of contemporary diarists and letter-writers has not given him credit. In the first place he was the first of the Hanoverian line to identify himself exclusively with English interests as opposed to the Hanoverian predilections of his father and grandfather, and he left this spirit as a legacy to his own son, who began his reign by declaring 'I glory in the name of Britain'. He also took or at least affected to take a far greater interest in the arts, painting, and literature, than George I and II even pretended to do. Though his taste in literature was rather indiscriminating, he did good service in bringing out of their hiding-places some of the artistic treasures forgotten in the royal palaces. But he gave no evidence of statesmanship, and left as a legacy to his son the pretentious political ideas expounded by Bolingbroke in *The Patriot King*.[1]

The death of the prince of Wales did not entirely break up his party, for opposing interests in the royal family appeared afresh on the Regency Bill of 1751, required to meet the case of George III succeeding during his minority. The ministry's proposal was that the princess of Wales should be regent in that case, but assisted by a council presided over by the duke of Cumberland, who was not popular at Leicester House.[2] The Cumberland faction, headed by Henry Fox, was for giving larger powers to the duke and his council, but was resisted by Pitt and others who feared a military domination and had never given up friendly relations with the prince's court. Two years later the education of the young prince became the subject of inquiry by the cabinet and of acrimonious debate in parliament owing to the charge absurdly made against his preceptor Andrew Stone, formerly Newcastle's faithful secretary, as well as against the bishop of Gloucester and William Murray, the solicitor-

of the second Lord Egmont (hitherto unpublished) in Williams, *Chatham*, ii. 59. The second Lord was very inferior to the first Lord Egmont (whose *Diary* has been published by Hist. MSS. Comm.), a notable philanthropist and politician, patron of Wesley and Whitefield. The first Lord's dates are 1683–1748, the second Lord's 1711–70.

[1] An interesting, though not convincing, attempt to rehabilitate the prince has been made by Sir George Young in his *Poor Fred*, 1937. An illuminating analysis of the relations between the Hanoverian kings and their heirs is given in the Introduction to R. Sedgwick's *Letters from George III to Lord Bute*, where the question of the influence of Bolingbroke on George III is discussed.

[2] The unpopularity of Cumberland was widespread. When the prince of Wales died the street song was 'Oh! that it was but his brother! Oh! that it was but the butcher!' Coxe, *Pelham*, ii. 169.

general, for having in their youth drunk the Pretender's health. The king himself made the most sensible comment on the matter: 'It is of very little importance to me what the parties accused may have said, or done, or thought, while they were little more than boys.'[1] But absurd as the charge of Jacobitism was, through the influence of the princess herself and of Lord Bute, who was in high favour with her, the young prince became imbued with a highly authoritarian conception of his functions.[2]

But Pelham's chief trouble during his ministry was with his own brother. Newcastle, an essentially weak man, without clear conceptions of his own, resented any signs of superiority in colleagues abler and clearer in purpose than himself. Unable to dominate by force of character, he would undermine such rivals by secret intrigues until finally he was left with docile nonentities content to bow down to him. During the early stages of the recent peace negotiations, which properly belonged to the northern department of his co-secretary Harrington, he kept up a secret correspondence with Sandwich, the envoy in Holland, giving him instructions contrary to the policy of Harrington and of Pelham himself.[3] Harrington was in a weak position, as he had incurred George II's vindictive hostility by being the first minister to deliver up his seals in February 1746,[4] so on discovering Newcastle's intrigues in November he had no alternative but to resign once more. To succeed him Newcastle pitched upon Chesterfield, under the fantastic delusion that he would find an obedient henchman in that cynical and accomplished statesman.[5] But Chesterfield was even less

[1] Horace Walpole revels in the scandal: *Memoirs of George II*, i. 298 sqq. See also above, p. 37. The source of this accusation was Fawcett, the recorder of Newcastle. For a detailed discussion of the incident see R. Sedgwick, *Letters from George III to Earl Bute*, pp. xxxi–xxxvii. See also Coxe, *Pelham*, ii. 254–6.

[2] Mr. Sedgwick argues cogently against this view of George III's education. See Sedgwick, l.c., p. lvi. For a criticism of his argument see R. Pares in *E.H.R.*, lv, pp. 475–9.

[3] Pelham's abject complaint of such conduct to Newcastle's secretary Andrew Stone is quoted in Lodge, *Studies in Eighteenth Century Diplomacy*, p. 186.

[4] See above, p. 259.

[5] [Newcastle's choice of Chesterfield was based on a realistic appreciation of the existing political situation as well as on his fantastic hopes for the future. Both he and his brother feared lest the king should try to use Harrington's resignation as a means of restoring Granville and they saw in Chesterfield an insurance against this. Furthermore, Chesterfield had assured Newcastle that 'now that the die of war was cast' he was in favour of its vigorous prosecution. Finally, Chesterfield's part in helping to create the Broad Bottom ministry had ensured his and his brother's gratitude. See Coxe, *Pelham*, i. 342, 346; Yorke, *Hardwicke*, i. 630, 637; *Marchmont*

inclined than Harrington to act the mere 'commis', as he told his friend Dayrolles, to forward Newcastle's instructions, so he too resigned in February 1748. As his successor Newcastle wanted Sandwich, then high in his favour; but the king had taken a juster measure of that young man and chose the duke of Bedford, a greater whig magnate than Newcastle himself, and a man dangerous to quarrel with.[1] Newcastle of course interfered with Bedford's department, but Bedford, then more interested in cricket than in wrangles with his colleague, simply responded by 'an obstinate silence'.[2] This silence provoked Newcastle even more than complaints; and during his sojourn in Hanover with the king in 1750 he filled reams of paper to his brother or the chancellor demanding Bedford's dismissal, 'perpetually fretting your friends', as Pelham frankly told him, 'with unjust suspicions of them, or tiring of them with continued communications upon what does not always appear very material'.[3] It was not indeed till June 1751 that Newcastle was able to get rid of Bedford, and then only by the subterfuge of persuading the king to dismiss Sandwich from the admiralty, whereupon Bedford, indignant at this treatment of his adherent, gave in his own resignation.[4] The choice of a successor had long been debated between the brothers, Newcastle suggesting Robinson, Waldegrave, and Holderness, who had been

Papers, i. 185. Professor Williams later accepted this interpretation of Newcastle's action. See Basil Williams, *Carteret and Newcastle*, pp. 185–6. C.H.S.]

[1] Newcastle then took over the northern department, leaving the southern to Bedford. [Both Pelham and Hardwicke were opposed to the promotion of Sandwich and so the more ready to accept Bedford. Hardwicke thought the chief argument in favour of Bedford was 'his dignity and weight from his property'. Newcastle acquiesced because, as Fox put it, he hoped Bedford would be 'a shoeing horn to Lord Sandwich'. See Coxe, *Pelham*, i. 389–90; Yorke, *Hardwicke*, i. 630. C.H.S.]

[2] Coxe, *Pelham*, ii. 129. Bedford was exasperatingly idle. Pelham expressed surprise at his 'total neglect of business', the consequence, he thought, of 'jollity, boyishness and vanity'. See ibid., pp. 365, 377.

[3] Ibid., p. 366. The whole dreary correspondence is to be found in that volume, pp. 336–402. See also ibid., pp. 108–12. Among the duke's other grievances was that Cumberland and the Princess Amelia had left him out of their parties and deserted him for Bedford.

[4] [Newcastle had badgered his brother into asking for Bedford's dismissal on the king's return from Hanover at the end of 1750. George had then refused, as he did again early in 1751 when Newcastle made a direct approach. But the death of the prince of Wales, by temporarily destroying the opposition and so reducing the danger of alienating Bedford, encouraged Pelham to try again. Even then George refused to dismiss Bedford, though agreeable to the removal of Sandwich. See ibid., pp. 136, 163, 188–9. C.H.S.]

ambassadors in Vienna, Paris, and The Hague respectively. The king eventually chose Holderness, and at last Newcastle found a colleague to his liking, describing him as 'good-natured so you may tell him his faults and he will mend them', and also as having 'no pride about him though a d'Arcy'. At the same time, although Pelham was reluctant to do this, Granville was made president of the council.[1] In this one instance Newcastle's judgement proved the better of the two. Granville had by this time lost all ambition and much of his old fire, at any rate before he had *eu sa bouteille*. At such times he was still apt to blurt out home truths, as on an occasion mentioned by Newcastle, when 'My Lord President had dined and talked very unguardedly. . . . I was frightened the whole time.' For the rest he was in need of his £5,000 a year and wanted to live in peace with ministers and enjoy the king's affection. In his office duties indeed he showed his old power of dispatch, clearing off, it is said, in two years more business than was formerly done in ten, and more than the ordinary law-courts did in thirty years. But in the cabinet or to ministers singly he would give his shrewd, pithily expressed opinions only when asked, and even then professed to leave all to Newcastle's 'better judgement'! 'Enfin', he is summed up by a foreign observer at this period, 'il ne veut plus de bruit ni de noise, et il donne beaucoup de poids dans la chambre haute.'[2]

Newcastle thus for the first six years after the war had almost complete control of foreign policy, and a sad mess he made of it. He realized indeed, as everybody else in Europe, that the peace was nothing more than a truce—with England, France, Frederic of Prussia, and Maria Theresa all either with grievances or fears for the future. But what he could not conceive was that the combatants might well be ranged on different sides to those

---

[1] [Granville's recall had been a matter of contention between the Pelhams for more than a year. During 1750 Newcastle had first suggested him as secretary of state when he had been considering becoming lord president himself. Later, he had urged his claims as lord president. Pelham opposed both suggestions and for a time placed an absolute veto on Granville which Newcastle accepted. The changed political circumstances in 1751 persuaded Pelham to give way, but even as late as Sept. 1752 he thought Granville had 'as much vanity and ambition as he ever had'. See Coxe, *Pelham*, ii. 355, 388, 391, 396–8; Yorke, *Hardwicke*, ii. 35, 104. C.H.S.]

[2] A remarkable picture of the changed Granville by W. Bentinck in 1753 is to be found in *Archives . . . de la Maison d'Orange Nassau*, 4e série, 4 vols., ii. 283–5, a picture fully confirmed by Granville's correspondence at this period in the Newcastle MSS. at the British Museum.

they held in the last war, and, though paying lip-service to the need of a strong navy, he still acted as though the issue between this country and France would be decided on European battle-fields.[1] He was confirmed in these narrow views by his close association with George II as minister in attendance at Hanover in 1748, 1750, and 1752. Here he imbibed all the king's anti-Prussian prejudices and refused Frederic's offer of alliance in 1748,[2] and, like his master, failed to plumb Vienna's deep dissatisfaction at the results of the last war. While the new Austrian minister, Kaunitz, was gradually leading Maria Theresa towards the *renversement des alliances*, Newcastle had conceived the absurd scheme of procuring the election of Maria Theresa's son as king of the Romans to avoid disturbance in the Empire on the death of her husband the Emperor Francis, telling the king that 'he had made an Emperor' and 'if he could make a King of the Romans too, it would be the greatest honour to him in the world'; to which the king complacently replied: 'and that of my own proposing, without being asked'. But the electors were venal and required subsidies. A modest beginning was made with a contribution to the subsidy for Cologne undertaken by Hanover and Holland. But much more was needed to secure what Newcastle called 'the great system, the great object of my life, in foreign affairs'.[3] Cologne began asking for more, Bavaria, the elector palatine, and Saxony had also to be bribed and the only source of supply left was England. Pelham, supported by Hardwicke, was against the whole scheme but eventually yielded so far as to agree to a subsidy of £30,000 for Bavaria only payable in 1751; for the next year he was weak enough to give in to his brother's demand for £32,000 for Saxony.[4]

---

[1] See in Yorke, *Hardwicke*, ii. 9, an abstract of Newcastle's letter of 6/17 Nov. 1748.

[2] Lodge, *Great Britain and Prussia*, pp. 66, 76.

[3] Coxe, *Pelham*, ii. 121, 340. For a full discussion of the scheme see D. B. Horn in *E.H.R.* xlii. 361–70. The treaty between Cologne, Holland, and Hanover was signed at Neuhaus in Feb. 1750. It was repudiated in Apr. 1751. The total subsidy was fixed at £40,000; the English contribution, to be paid through the king in his electoral capacity, was £10,000. Pelham never expected much of this manœuvre, writing in July 1750, 'I am unwilling to run the civil list more and more in debt for nothing but moonshine'. See Coxe, *Pelham*, ii. 120, 350, 398. See also D. B. Horn, *Sir C. Hanbury Williams and European Diplomacy*, p. 75.

[4] The subsidy treaties with Bavaria and Saxony were completed in Sept. 1750 and Nov. 1751. By the one Bavaria was promised £40,000 per annum for six years, Austria and Holland paying £10,000 each and England £20,000. But for the first year England paid £30,000, apparently bearing the Austrian share in addition to her own. By the second Saxony was promised £48,000 per annum for four years,

Even then Newcastle was not satisfied, and in October 1752 he negotiated a treaty with the elector palatine by which England would have paid more than £45,000 to secure his vote. Fortunately, Austria refused to co-operate, so the treaty was nullified.[1] In any case Frederic II, in self-righteous indignation, denounced these attempts to tamper with the purity of imperial elections; the Austrians themselves contemptuously rejected the scheme as an impertinent interference;[2] and even George II got tired of 'the great system . . . [which was] to bring him the greatest honour in the world'.

'Now I shall have no more peace', said George II on the news of Pelham's death on 6 March 1754. He was right in that, for though Pelham was not a strong minister, allowing himself too often to be talked over by Newcastle, he had a soothing influence on politics, and since 1746 had carried on the government with far less friction than abler predecessors, such as Stanhope and Walpole.[3] With Newcastle grief-stricken and unfit for business the king, who was reluctant to select a successor on his own, turned to Hardwicke for help and referred the matter through him to the cabinet. Hardwicke, although surprised by this abdication of royal power,[4] used the opportunity to forward the claims of Newcastle, who was duly made first lord of the treasury. But the difficult question remained, who was to replace Pelham as the ministry's chief representative in the commons? Newcastle's dilemma was twofold, for he wanted a man in the first place willing to subordinate his

Holland paying £16,000 and England £32,000. It was of the first that Pelham wrote 'I yielded, but not from a conviction that the thing was right'. See Coxe, *Pelham*, ii. 120, 151, 196, 350, 379.

[1] See ibid., pp. 231–2.

[2] Joseph (II) was actually elected king of the Romans in 1764, unanimously, and without any bribery of the electors. D. B. Horn, *Sir C. Hanbury Williams and European Diplomacy*, Part I, deals with the Saxon negotiations.

[3] [It is arguable that Henry Pelham exercised a more dominating influence in politics than Professor Williams, as the biographer and champion of Pitt, was prepared to allow. Certainly it required more than the mere capacity to 'soothe' on his part to secure the acceptance by Pitt and Henry Fox of his leadership over several years. The acquiescence of these powerful and ambitious men in his predominance suggests that he had positive qualities as a politician, if not as a statesman, which have been insufficiently considered. In this context see Dodington, *Diary*, under 27 Nov. 1752, for Henry Fox's acceptance of Pelham's position and his determination 'if accidents should happen . . . to be next'. C.H.S.]

[4] Hardwicke's surprise was expressed in his well-known expostulation to Pitt, 'to poll in a Cabinet Council for his first minister, which should only be decided in his closet, I could by no means digest'. See Yorke, *Hardwicke*, ii. 211.

ideas to his own cloudy understanding, and secondly one who not only carried weight himself but also brought an important following in support of the government. In the house of commons three men stood out as possible leaders, William Murray, Henry Fox, and William Pitt. Murray was an able and persuasive speaker, but his heart was not really so much in politics as in the law, where he aspired to be lord chief justice, so that he was content to be promoted from solicitor- to attorney-general. Fox, perhaps the ablest debater in the house, as he had recently shown in his devastating attacks on Lord Chancellor Hardwicke for his Marriage Bill,[1] could put a case as well as any man and was important politically as representing the interests of the duke of Cumberland and the army, and thereby *persona grata* to the king. But of the three Pitt was far the greatest, a man with vision and initiative, and endowed with a demonic force of oratory to persuade coupled with capacity to carry through an undertaking. On the other hand, he was still disliked by the king[2] and though he brought with him a small group of Grenvilles and Lyttelton who were in favour at Leicester House, that could not be called an important following; moreover, except for the coolness and courage he displayed during the '45 and the stand he had taken for the navy in 1751, he had made no great mark in debate since 1746, confining himself chiefly to the removal of abuses in his pay office. Newcastle therefore, thinking that Pitt could be the more safely ignored, offered the post of secretary of state with the leadership of the house to Fox, but with the proviso that he himself should retain the 'management' of the commons. Fox, on the ground that in that case 'he should not know how to talk to members of Parliament, when some might have received *gratifications*, others not', refused the offer; whereupon Newcastle appointed Sir Thomas Robinson,[3] a dull, long-winded diplomat, almost a

---

[1] See above, pp. 136–7.

[2] [This was a genuine barrier to his advancement. George made it plain to Hard-wicke that he did not want Pitt. The removal of these 'obstacles in the closet' was, Lyttelton later noted, 'a work of much more difficulty than Pitt's impatience would believe'. See Yorke, *Hardwicke*, ii. 193, 206. C.H.S.]

[3] 1695–1770; envoy plenipotentiary at Vienna 1730–48, created Lord Grantham 1761. [Robinson's failings were parliamentary; he was well equipped to handle the business of his department. Newcastle would have preferred him to Holderness in 1751. He had a genuine admiration for his knowledge and experience 'as one who has been concerned, and principally, in all the great foreign transactions of Europe'. See Coxe, *Pelham*, ii. 397. C.H.S.]

stranger to the house of commons, but entirely subservient to himself. Legge,[1] a friend of Pitt's and a good financier, succeeded to Pelham's other office as chancellor of the exchequer. It was a sorry cabinet to undertake the responsibility of conducting a great war, without a man in it fitted to take the direction of affairs. Hardwicke was a prudent adviser in matters of domestic policy and a comforting receptacle for Newcastle's grievances, Anson a great first lord of the admiralty but a subordinate minister, Granville the only one with a comprehensive grasp of foreign policy but no longer with the power or wish to take responsibility, and Newcastle himself without a clear idea in his head save for the maintenance of his own supremacy; the rest mere dummies. And already in fact, if not avowedly, war had begun.

The peace of Aix-la-Chapelle had indeed proved barely a truce. In India it had not proved even a truce for the two East India Companies. The Frenchmen Dupleix and Bussy had already formed their ambitious plan of bringing the Carnatic and the Deccan under French control, and in 1751 and 1752 Clive and Stringer Lawrence at Arcot and Trichinopoly had successfully inaugurated the English company's resistance to this scheme.[2] There were disputes with France as to the occupation of the so-called 'neutral' West Indian islands,[3] and even in Europe as to the fortifications of Dunkirk. But in America the clash of interests was sharpest. In anticipation of a renewed war Louisburg, restored by the treaty to the French, was being strengthened, and on the English side Halifax, founded in 1749, was being fortified as a counterpoise. The French Canadians had built a fort at Beauséjour within the borders of Nova Scotia and were carrying on an active propaganda with the population of that colony, mostly French by origin, until in 1755 5,000 of them were drastically expelled by Governor Lawrence.[4] Both French and English were strengthening their defences on Lakes Ontario and Champlain, as the most likely points of attack on either side. The French too were actively pursuing their policy of linking up Canada and Louisiana by a chain of forts along the Ohio and the Mississippi, which would effectively bar attempts of English colonists to expand westwards of the Alleghany Mountains. The first actual clash

---

[1] Hon. H. B. Legge 1708–64.
[2] See above, pp. 327 sqq.
[3] See above, p. 308.
[4] See above, p. 311.

occurred in May 1754 on the borders of Virginia, when Colonel Washington overpowered a small French detachment advancing from Fort Duquesne on the Ohio, but was himself forced to surrender to a larger force sent to avenge this defeat.

Such provocations could hardly be ignored, but the cabinet could not make up its mind on any definite policy. Halifax at the board of trade[1] was for vigorous action on all fronts in America, Granville for raising men among the colonists, Cumberland for sending out two regiments from Ireland, a course decided upon by the cabinet, then countermanded by Newcastle, who in his dilemma consulted Pitt and was told that every vigorous action should be adopted. But it was not till the end of October that Fox as secretary at war took the matter into his own hands and ordered the regiments to be transported to America under the command of General Braddock;[2] at the same time orders were sent for raising men in America. When the session opened in November Fox and Pitt for the first and last time found themselves allies in a common grievance at their supersession by an incompetent leader such as Robinson, and had a rousing time belabouring him and the other government spokesman Murray. Before a fortnight of the session had passed Newcastle had been forced to the conclusion that at least one of these two persistent critics must be muzzled. He would have preferred Pitt, but there was one great objection. Pitt would be sure to demand a decisive voice on policy, and this he was not prepared to allow. Accordingly in December 1754, while still continuing his negotiations with Pitt, he secured Fox by the offer of a place in the outer cabinet but without the secretaryship.[3] In the following September, however, he raised Fox to the inner cabinet, making him secretary and leader of the house in place of Robinson. Two considerations brought him to do this; first, the approach of another parliamentary session and his knowledge of Robinson's utter incompetence to manage this, and, secondly, Pitt's growing demands, expressed in the

---

[1] This was not yet a cabinet post.

[2] General Edward Braddock, 1695–1755, had served in the expedition to l'Orient of 1746; see above, p. 261.

[3] [Newcastle's decision in Dec. 1754 to settle with Fox in preference to Pitt, who had not yet put forward his full claims to decide policy, was prompted by his belief that Fox would be the more acceptable at court and the more useful in the ministry. As Waldegrave said, Fox was thought 'more practicable, less disagreeable to the king and more a man of business'. See Ilchester, *Henry Fox*, i. 231. C.H.S.]

renewed negotiations of the summer, for a complete change of policy and full responsibility for the conduct of business. This junction of Newcastle and Fox inspired Pitt to his famous Rhône and Saône speech of November 1755.[1]

The year 1755 had not been a happy one for England. Beauséjour indeed had been captured from the French in June, though solely through the exertions of the New England militia. But in July Braddock, a barrack-square general without the slightest conception of American conditions of warfare, led his force into an ambush on the Monongahela, where French troops with their Indian allies shot him down as well as most of his men. At sea Boscawen had been sent out in April with a squadron to intercept the French fleet under de la Motte with reinforcements for Canada, but without clear instructions as to how he should act if he met the French fleet before war had been declared. Unfortunately he only captured two French ships, the *Alcide* and the *Lys*, without doing any damage to the rest of their fleet which had disappeared, so that this dubious act of war, while putting us in the wrong, gave us no material advantage. Nor could Newcastle make up his mind what instructions to give to Hawke, sent out in July with a strong squadron to watch Brest. At first he was for giving him no definite instructions, so that if Hawke made a mistake ministers could not be blamed; then he was to be ordered to attack commerce, 'vexing your neighbours for a little muck', as Granville put it; but finally Newcastle told him he was to confine himself to attacking ships of the line, comforting himself with the reflection that 'ships of the line will probably keep out of his way'.[2] From July to December Hawke was cruising on the watch round Brest, but then, owing to the foulness of his ships, was obliged to return to Plymouth, just before de la Motte's fleet slipped into Brest.[3]

There is this excuse for Newcastle's hesitations about orders to the fleets, that he was anxious not to be finally committed to war with France till he had completed his continental alliances. His idea, so far as he had it clear in his own mind, seems to have

---

[1] For the Newcastle–Fox–Pitt negotiations of 1754–6 see Ilchester, op. cit., chaps. x, xi, xiii, xvii; *Chatham*, i. 218–37, 249–86; and Yorke, *Hardwicke*, ii. 187–339. See also p. 39, above.

[2] These orders were soon extended to cover all warships, privateers, and merchantmen. See J. Corbett, *England in Seven Years War*, i. 70.

[3] For an account of these naval operations see Corbett, l.c., i. 44–73. See also Yorke, *Hardwicke*, ii. 258, 283.

been to make so strong a system of continental alliances against France that, unable to move in Europe, she would be obliged to confine herself to the overseas struggle, where she would be at a disadvantage owing to England's great superiority at sea. But he unfortunately did not realize that the sheet-anchor of his scheme, the 'Old System' of alliance with the Austrians and the Dutch, was no longer feasible. The Dutch, as they had clearly shown in the last war, had lost the power, almost the desire, to defend even their own territory and were determined to avoid any entangling alliance with England. The Austrians were bellicose enough, but Frederic of Prussia, and no longer France, was to them the main enemy, while their disputes with the Dutch about the Barrier fortresses and trade privileges in the Low Countries should have shown Newcastle that any close union between the two was impossible. Newcastle's first continental scheme of subsidizing the electors to vote for a king of the Romans had, as we have seen, failed utterly, but he and the king, undeterred by that rebuff, were now attempting to bolster up the Old System by fresh alliances and subsidies. The king was naturally concerned about the safety of Hanover, endangered by the French in the last war, and Newcastle supported him in the attempt to find security for it. The most obvious safeguard for the electorate was Frederic of Prussia, who in 1748 had been willing to come to terms but had met with a rebuff, repaid with interest by an ostentatious anti-English and anti-Hanoverian policy. So almost to the outbreak of war, besides the Old System, Newcastle and the king were busied in finding further pledges of security for the electorate, the business being left mainly in the hands of George II and Holderness in Hanover during 1755, since Newcastle could not leave England. Bavaria and Saxony had already been gained by 1752; the right to call for 6,000 Hessian troops was secured by another subsidy in 1755 and in September of the same year a treaty with Russia was negotiated by Hanbury Williams. By this treaty the Tsaritsa Elizabeth agreed to keep 55,000 men on the Livonian frontier and 40–50 galleys on the coast, to be set in motion in case England or any of her allies, notably Hanover, were attacked: in consideration of this engagement the tsaritsa was to receive £100,000 per annum during peace, and £500,000 per annum in war-time, as soon as her troops and galleys started.[1]

[1] Martens, *Recueil des Traités . . . Russie*, ix (x), 175 sqq.

This treaty, though never put into operation, was so revolutionary as in fact to become the mainspring of the so-called *renversement des alliances*. Russia was Frederic II's special bugbear, and the prospect of 55,000 Russians marching into his own territory caused him to make a sudden volte-face and welcome suggestions already made by England for a mutual guarantee of each other's dominions. On 16 January 1756, therefore, he agreed to the Convention of Westminster embodying this guarantee and a promise jointly to resist the entry of foreign armies into Germany. France, thereby deprived of her one serious ally in Germany, was thus led on 1 May to agree to the alliance with the empress, long desired by Kaunitz, by the first treaty of Versailles.[1] Newcastle seems to have believed that his treaty with Russia, envisaging the entry of Russians into Germany, was compatible with the Convention of Westminster promising joint resistance to such an invasion, but was soon undeceived by Russia making common cause with the allies of Versailles.[2] A more serious objection to all this treaty-making in the eyes of Pitt, supported by a growing feeling in the country, was that it was chiefly directed according to the meridian of Hanover. As Pitt admitted in one of his talks with Hardwicke, the English people could not allow their king to suffer the loss of his electorate in a quarrel chiefly England's concern, and he would be quite prepared to indemnify the king up to £5 millions for any damage incurred by the electorate from Prussian or French soldiers; but it would be as reasonable, he said, to concentrate all the efforts of a campaign on defending Jamaica as on Hanover.

Indeed, for all Newcastle's elaborate alliances the preliminary phases of the war[3] were among the gloomiest in our history. Braddock's defeat and the fleet's inconclusive, yet highly provocative, actions in 1755 were followed by a serious threat of invasion by France in 1756,[4] which threw the ministry into a panic about the defenceless state of the country. Pitt and George Townshend had in May 1756 got a bill for establishing a

---

[1] [This French decision was made more to avenge her humiliation at the hands of Prussia than from fear of the Anglo-Prussian convention. C.H.S.]

[2] See Horn, op. cit., pp. 178–253, for a good account of the negotiations for the Russian treaty and its results.

[3] War was not actually declared by England till news had come of the French landing in Minorca in May 1756.

[4] For the French project of invasion planned by Belleisle see Corbett, l.c., i. 88–95.

national militia for defence passed in the commons, but Hard-wicke had secured its rejection by the lords. So the country was reduced to the ignominy of having hired troops of Hesse and Hanover brought over to guard our soil. The final blow was the loss of Minorca.[1] In February Newcastle had been warned of a meditated attack on it, but it was not till April that a squadron of ten ships was sent out to relieve it under the com-mand of Admiral Byng, already well known to the admiralty for his hesitancy and want of initiative. Byng took a month to reach Gibraltar, where he heard that Richelieu, with a French army escorted by La Galissonière's fleet, had invested Minorca a fortnight before; and even then he waited six days before going to meet the French fleet. After an indecisive encounter Byng returned to Gibraltar and took no further steps to relieve the garrison which, under the gallant old General Blakeney, did not surrender till 28 June after seventy days' siege. The loss of Minorca was the culmination to a series of disasters which aroused public indignation to fever-heat, not only against Byng but ministers themselves. Newcastle, alarmed at reports from all over the country, wrote to Hardwicke urging that Anson should order 'the immediate trial and condemnation of Byng'. By a recent change in the Articles of War the court martial that tried him in February 1757 had no alternative but to sentence him to death, but strongly recommended him to mercy. Pitt, by that time secretary of state, vehemently supported the plea and in the excited state of the country lost some popularity thereby. But the king was adamant, and in March Byng was shot on the quarter-deck of the *Monarque, pour encourager les autres*.[2]

So by the summer of 1756 even Newcastle, panic-stricken lest his own head too should be demanded by an indignant people, was beginning to see that the power he had held so long and cherished so dearly was beginning to slip away from him. Almost from its formation his ministry had been reeling under accu-mulated blows. Pitt had been dismissed from the paymaster-ship after his Rhône and Saône speech in November 1755, and with him had gone Legge from the exchequer for refusing to pay the Hessian subsidy not yet voted by the house. Pitt, then a

[1] For the state of the garrison there see above, p. 216.
[2] For an admirable discussion of the Minorca incident and the Byng trial see Corbett, l.c., i. 96–138.

free man, had felt no further scruples in attacking the fumbling and disastrous policy of Newcastle and his myrmidons, 'Xerxes's troops' he called them.[1] Fox avoided another duel with him; Hume Campbell,[2] to earn a recent increase in salary from £600 to £2,000, had tried a fall with him, but retired in terror at the lashing he received; Murray was silenced by a look. Pitt's example had stirred his friends Legge, George Grenville, George and Charles Townshend, and even Lord George Sackville to heights of patriotic fervour and eloquence. Nor was the news from abroad bringing any comfort. Another fort in America, Oswego, had fallen to the French; while Frederic's dash into Saxony on 29 August had precipitated the continental war, for which Newcastle had been preparing for eight years but was still unready. After blow upon blow shattering and scattering Newcastle's system of continental subsidies and hesitating measures, at home Murray insisted on leaving the government bench to take up the chief justiceship of the king's bench, which he claimed of right, and—the *coup de grâce*—Fox resigned in October. Newcastle then at last had to go cap in hand to Pitt.

[1] This phrase was Charles Townshend's but inspired by an earlier allusion of Pitt. See *Chatham*, i. 274.

[2] Hon. Alexander Hume Campbell, 1708–60, once an ally of Pitt and the patriots, was then chancellor of the duchy of Lancaster. The salary of this office had been raised in Sept. 1755 to persuade him to accept it.

XIII

THE GREAT COMMONER

PITT was in no mood to accept the proposal made to him by Newcastle in October 1756 to join his ministry and help him out of his difficulties. He had no means of approaching the king directly, so he availed himself of the only method of communicating with him, through Lady Yarmouth, the king's mistress. Amalie Wallmoden[1] had first attracted George II's attention during his sojourn at Hanover in 1735. After Queen Caroline's death she lived openly with him—'Non, j'aurai des maîtresses', George had replied to the queen's dying suggestion that he should marry again[2]—and was created countess of Yarmouth in 1740. She appears to have been a sensible body and to have taken little part in politics beyond transmitting to the king views confided to her by politicians. To her Pitt explained that he would neither work with Newcastle nor be responsible for his measures. The king grumbled, but the voice of the people called for Pitt, whose championship of their cause and interests in the house was earning him the proud title of The Great Commoner. So a month later, 15 November, Pitt's own ministry was formed, with himself as secretary for the south, the duke of Devonshire[3] in Newcastle's place as first lord of the treasury, and Pitt's brother-in-law Temple at the admiralty. Of Newcastle's chief ministers only two were retained, Holderness who continued as secretary for the north and Granville who remained as lord president, proving 'a new and potent ally [owing to his] personal weight in the cabinet', and acting as a conciliatory

---

[1] 1704–65. Her maiden name was von Wendt; she was divorced from her husband in 1739. She was the niece of George I's mistress, Lady Darlington, and the great-niece of his father's mistress the elder countess von Platen. Her grandmother, sister to the elder Platen, had been an early mistress of George I. She was thus bred to her task.

[2] 'Ah, Mon Dieu! cela n'empêche pas' was the queen's rejoinder to this celebrated remark.

[3] [This was the fourth duke who had succeeded in Dec. 1755. He was a personal friend of Fox and acceptable to Cumberland. For these reasons the king pressed him to take the treasury. So even though Pitt could drive Newcastle, the king's chosen minister, from office he could not dictate his replacement. See Dodington, *Diary*, p. 391. C.H.S.]

element between Pitt and the king.[1] Nevertheless the ministry was short-lived. Formed against the king's wish, denied his confidence in the closet and any sign of his favour in public, it had no solid basis, either at court or in the commons.[2] Pitt himself had lost some ground by the stand he made against Byng's execution[3] and had not yet had time to organize victories. On 6 April 1757 the king curtly ordered him to return the seals, because Cumberland refused, while Pitt was in power, to take up his command in Germany. It was easy for the king to dismiss Pitt, but not so easy to form a ministry without him, particularly as he was now sustained by a sweep of popular sentiment. For nearly three months the country, engaged in a crucial struggle with France, was left with a sketchy ministry of caretakers, until finally, on 29 June, the solution was found in a junction of Pitt with Newcastle. The essence of this settlement was compromise; each of the contestants gave way sufficiently to allow a lasting arrangement. In agreeing to work with Newcastle as first lord of the treasury, Pitt gave up his 'visionary notions' of single rule; Newcastle, for his part, at last accepted Pitt's dominant position in the cabinet and the commons; finally, Fox, the third force in the ministerial battle, withdrew from the major struggle and accepted the subordinate post of paymaster.[4] The king alone yielded all and gained nothing. As Fox perceptively observed, Newcastle, Pitt, and Leicester House[5] had joined

[1] *Memoirs of a Celebrated Literary and Political Character* [R. Glover], pp. 101–4. According to Glover it was due to Granville that Pitt was persuaded not to make a clean sweep of the treasury board, and again to him that the king withdrew his demand that Pitt should move an address of thanks to himself for bringing the electoral troops to England.

[2] [Pitt's position in the commons was unusual. He hoped to govern with the support of the independent voters alone, particularly the country gentlemen. In these circumstances the regular ministerial body in the commons, which was essential to the steady conduct of business, held back from supporting the ministry, more particularly as Pitt lacked the king's favour. At the same time the majority of the 'old corps' of whigs stayed loyal to Newcastle. The peculiar circumstances of this period misled Newcastle into thinking that his followers were more loyal than they were. In the new reign he was disillusioned. See Yorke, *Hardwicke*, ii. 377, 394; and cf. above, p. 205, n. 1. See also *Oxford History of England*, xii. 89–90, and Namier, *England in the Age of the American Revolution*, p. 374. C.H.S.]

[3] See above, p. 352.

[4] In October 1756 Pitt had made it a condition that he would not serve with Fox 'in any ministerial place' though he could have 'a lucrative one'. See Yorke, *Hardwicke*, ii. 333.

[5] [Pitt's alliance with Leicester House, as Sedgwick shows, 'transformed the whole political situation'. It gave the new ministry the appearance of support from both courts; Bute, acting for the young prince of Wales, had joined Pitt and

to make him prisoner. George was aware of his predicament and resented it; but he was old, tired, and anxious for quiet, so he reluctantly acquiesced although 'much disturbed at the disagreeable situation that he found himself in'.[1]

Pitt from the outset took the people into his confidence. He had been blamed for his open attacks on the shortcomings of the ministry at a time of national danger, but, as he once told the house of lords, 'I despise the little policy of concealments, you ought to know the whole of your situation';[2] and, as a minister, he never deviated from this principle. When, for example, he heard of Abercromby's disaster at Ticonderoga in 1758, he at once 'laid the whole detail open to the inspection of the nation at large, and by so doing he ensured that confidence which a contrary conduct would have certainly deprived him of';[3] and he was equally frank about Murray's reverse at St. Foy on the Plains of Abraham in 1760. Accordingly, at the outset of his first ministry, the first task he had set himself was to compose a king's speech 'captivating the people' by its frank statement of difficulties to be met and a clear exposition of the calls he proposed to make on their patriotism. He had then sent back to Germany the Hanoverians and Hessians brought over by Newcastle; and by passing the Militia Bill, rejected in the previous year,[4] gave Englishmen the means of defending their own country. Among the new regiments he raised for the regular army he included two to be drawn from Highland clans actually in revolt against the king eleven years before.[5] As he said in a

Newcastle in allotting places in the administration which was thus launched without any risk of immediate opposition from that quarter. As Hardwicke pointed out, it was important for any solid plan to 'unite the whole Royal Family and bring *the succession* to support and give quiet to *the possession*'. See Yorke, *Hardwicke*, ii. 392, and Sedgwick, l.c.; see above p. 340, n. 1. C.H.S.]

[1] [The king particularly resented the resignation of Holderness and the threat of further resignations at court designed to force his hand in the manner of 1746. See Yorke, *Hardwicke*, ii. 399, 401, 403; Walpole, *Memoirs of George II*, ii. 220–1, 223. For a discussion of the significance of these threatened resignations see Pares, *George III and the Politicians*. For further details of this long ministerial interregnum see Yorke, ii, chap. xxv, particularly pp. 388, 391–2, 401, 403–4; Williams, *Chatham*, i. 317–25; Ilchester, *Fox*, ii. 33–67; Dodington, *Diary*; Waldegrave, *Memoirs*; and H. Walpole, op. cit. C.H.S.]   [2] *P.H.* xvi. 1099 (22 Nov. 1770).

[3] Quoted from a speech of Shelburne in 1776. See *Chatham*, ii. 273, and also ii. 18.

[4] See above, pp. 351–2. The second Militia Bill was passed by the commons during Pitt's first ministry but did not pass the lords until June 1757.

[5] Wade had already raised a Highland regiment but only from loyal clans. See above, p. 281.

later speech:[1] 'I sought for merit wherever it was to be found. . . . I found it in the mountains of the north. I called it forth . . . an hardy and intrepid race of men . . . who . . . had gone nigh to have overturned the State [in 1745–6] . . . they served with fidelity as they fought with valour, and conquered for you in every part of the world.' It was in the same spirit that he approached the American colonists. They were sore at the return to France of Louisburg, their own conquest, in 1748; they resented the contemptuous way their officers were treated by the regulars from England: Colonel Washington, for example, would have had to take orders from a lieutenant in the regular army who happened to be brigaded with him, and the fact that they were kept in the dark as to English plans affecting their own country. Pitt altered all that. By circular letters to the governors he informed the king's 'good subjects and colonies of North America' of his resolution to act vigorously in their interests against the French, urged them to raise troops, and later saw that they had generous grants for the purpose.[2] In December 1757 he sent out a warrant ordering that American officers should in future take rank with the regulars according to the date of their commissions. Nor did he even in war-time make military exigencies an excuse for curtailing the liberty of the subject. When Lord Mansfield refused a writ of habeas corpus to a man illegally pressed for the army, he got his attorney-general, Pratt,[3] to bring in an amending bill to remove such doubts, and implored Newcastle to get it through the house of lords so as 'not to throw away all the confidence, goodwill and national concord which at present attend his Majesty's service'.[4]

In his war-plans relating to Germany he seemed to lay himself open to the charge of inconsistency, for he had always condemned continental entanglements which appeared to be chiefly for the benefit of Hanover. But now circumstances were altered. In the first place, even had he so wished, he could not repudiate the recent Convention of Westminster for mutual

[1] *P.H.* xvi. 98 (14 Jan. 1766).

[2] Levy money, &c., paid to the American colonies by the mother country between 1756 and 1763 appears to have amounted to £1,275,759, about two-fifths of their expenses. See *Chatham*, ii. 180, and Beer, *British Colonial Policy*, pp. 53–58.

[3] Sir Charles Pratt, 1714–94; afterwards chief justice (C.P.) and lord chancellor, Earl Camden.

[4] In spite of this appeal the bill, carried with ease in the commons, by the efforts of the lawyers was stifled in the lords.

protection with Frederic. And he had no such intention. For with French and Austrians and soon Russians arrayed against our only ally Frederic, Pitt saw that without our help he would soon be crushed and leave France free to devote her undivided attention to fighting us in America and the East. To help Frederic was no longer a mere Hanoverian side-show, but a necessity both for our honour and our security; as he later said, hyperbolically, 'America had been conquered in Germany'.[1] Accordingly in February 1757 he had proposed and gained the full approval of the house for the dispatch of an army of Hanoverians and Hessians, the former paid by Hanover, with Cumberland in command, to guard the banks of the Weser against any attack by the French on Hanover or Frederic's flank. But, as always, England's maritime supremacy was his chief concern. In 1751 he had protested successfully against Pelham's reduction of men for the navy:[2] again in a speech of 1755 he had urged England, instead of trusting to foreign mercenaries, like Athens, 'to put herself on board her fleet'.[3] In his first session as minister he got supply voted for no less than 55,000 sailors, and he called on the admiralty for a return of available ships and a statement of their needs 'for the total stagnation and extirpation of the French trade upon the seas and the general protection of that of Great Britain'. It appeared that in April 1756 the admiralty had only 134 men-of-war and frigates available, but required over 200 to satisfy Pitt's requirements, a number actually exceeded by 1760.[4]

The success of the Seven Years war was almost entirely due to Pitt's torrential energy, to his far-seeing preparations, to his wise choice of commanders on land and sea,[5] and still wiser trust in them when they were chosen, and above all to his strategic insight into the crucial objects of his world-wide campaigns. Like Marlborough he did not confine himself to one field of operations. His object was to take the initiative in every quarter of the globe and prevent the French from concentrating their

[1] This was on 13 Nov. 1761; see H. Walpole, *Memoirs of George III*, i. 76.
[2] See above, p. 337.
[3] H. Walpole, quoted by Rosebery, *Chatham, Early Life*, p. 437.
[4] See tables in Clowes, l.c. iii. 7, 8; and references in *Chatham*, i. 295–6.
[5] [Not all authorities agree on this point. Corbett's view was that 'no great war minister ever appointed so many bad ones'. Ligonier's recent biographer thinks that Pitt's choice was often influenced by his commander-in-chief. See Corbett, l.c. i. 376, and Whitworth, l.c., p. 201. C.H.S.]

efforts on any one field of action, bewildering them by lightning strokes and so leading them to dissipate their forces without knowing where he would attack them next. America and India were his main objectives, but he always kept material in hand to occupy the enemy's attention elsewhere. Frederic in Germany proved his best instrument for keeping large French armies employed and so diverting their energies and resources from the maintenance of a fleet comparable to that of England. By his expeditionary force in Germany he materially helped Frederic to maintain himself against the French, Russian, and Austrian forces encircling him. By his raids on the French coast, ridiculed by the English quidnuncs who did not understand their underlying object, he distracted the French headquarters and caused them to withdraw troops from the campaign against Frederic, who warmly encouraged these diversions. By his bolt from the blue on the French stations in West Africa and his successful *coup de main* on Guadeloupe and Maria Galante, very differently managed from the futile attacks on the West Indies in 1741, he not only gained valuable counters for a favourable settlement at the peace, but kept up a serious drain on the enemy's resources. More than all he showed his mastery in his use of the fleet, both to co-operate with the land forces in Canada and India, and also in purely naval actions such as Boscawen's and Hawke's great victories at Lagos and Quiberon Bay in 1759, which once for all stopped Choiseul's plans for the invasion of England.

In his first year as minister, when everything was still to do in preparing plans, getting rid of much dead wood, and choosing his instruments, Pitt had no successes to record. The fleet under Holburne, designed during his first ministry to attack Louisburg in May, had not reached American waters when he returned to office in June 1757;[1] his proposed expedition against the French settlements in West Africa had been dropped; on 29 June, the very day he resumed the seals, news came of Frederic's crushing defeat at Kolin; and about the same time that of the Black Hole of Calcutta. On 8 September Cumberland, in command of the expeditionary force to support Frederic and defend Hanover, driven into a corner by Richelieu, the victor

---

[1] Holburne had sailed from Cork early in May and arrived at Halifax on 9 July. See Corbett, l.c. i. 160, 169.

of Minorca, signed the Convention of Klosterseven, leaving
Hanover at the mercy of the French and Frederic's western
flank fully exposed. In one respect, however, this was a blessing
in disguise; for the king, furious with his son, not only recalled
him from Germany, but also dismissed him from his post as
captain-general, and appointed Pitt's nominee, the gallant
Ligonier, as commander-in-chief at home. To Cumberland
himself, who had been his political adversary and was chiefly
responsible for his dismissal in April, Pitt showed magnanimity.
For, when the king growled out that he had given his son no
orders to conclude the convention, Pitt replied, 'But full powers,
Sir, very full powers.' There were other reverses too. The first
of Pitt's raids against the coast of France, though well supported by the escorting squadron under Hawke, failed miserably
in September in the land attack on Rochefort under the ailing
General Mordaunt, chosen by the king in preference to Pitt's
nominee, young Conway.[1] Lord Loudoun, the commander-in-
chief in America, having learned of the size of the French
squadron in Louisburg, agreed with Holburne that there was
'no probability of succeeding' in an attack and gave up the
attempt early in August.[2] In September, too, came news that
Fort William Henry on Lake George had been captured by
Montcalm in August, for want of relief from an English garrison
only six hours' distance away.

But at last in November 1757 came the turn of the tide with
Frederic's glorious victory over Soubise and the flower of the
French army at Rossbach, followed a month later by his victory
over the Austrians at Leuthen. Frederic at once became the 'Protestant Hero', and his head swung as a sign on countless English
inns; above all Pitt felt free to enlarge his plans. The army of
observation to protect Frederic's flank was reconstituted and
stiffened with English troops, and Pitt found an ideal successor to Cumberland as its commander in Prince Ferdinand of
Brunswick, seconded from Frederic's army. Within a month of
assuming the command Ferdinand had driven Richelieu's army
away from Hanover back almost to the Weser; by April 1758
the French had withdrawn across the Rhine; and in June he

---

[1] [Horace Walpole is the authority for this tale. But it appears from a letter
of Ligonier to Pitt of 9 July that the king was 'extremely pleased with the
project and had agreed commanders'. See Whitworth, *Ligonier*, p. 221. C.H.S.]

[2] Loudoun's decision has been much criticized; but Corbett judged him to have
been 'more than justified'. See Corbett, l.c. i. 171–2.

beat them at the battles of Rheinberg and Crefeld. Already
in April Pitt, now entirely converted to the need of a diversion
in Germany, had made a new treaty with Frederic, giving
him a subsidy of £670,000[1] and engaging him to even closer
co-operation for the common object of defeating France.

Even more important was the freedom Pitt had now secured
to choose his own generals and admirals for England's colonial
campaigns. In America Loudoun and Holburne, the un-
adventurous general and admiral who had failed at Louisburg,
were replaced by Amherst, a colonel of forty, and Boscawen,
and with them went Colonel Wolfe, just turned thirty. To
prevent French fleets with reinforcements reaching Canada,
Osborn and Saunders[2] were instructed to watch de la Clue and
Duquesne in the Mediterranean; in March they captured the
80-gun *Foudroyant*, with Duquesne on board, and the *Orphée*, and
bottled up de la Clue in Cartagena; while Hawke in the Bay
drove the Rochefort fleet back to port in April. By 26 July
Louisburg, the 'Gibraltar of the West', had been captured for
good, and the French squadron in the harbour destroyed.[3]
Pitt's hope, indeed, had been that the capture of Louisburg
would be followed in the same year by that of Quebec itself, his
idea being that, while the French were preoccupied with the
siege of Louisburg, Abercromby, the commander-in-chief in
America, should make his way down the Richelieu river to the
St. Lawrence and capture Quebec. But Abercromby, 'Mrs.
Nabbycromby' as the colonials called him, in spite of his
15,000 men against Montcalm's 4,000, was of the old oodentaiy
ochool. Lord Howe, his second in command, another of Pitt's
young men in the thirties, and of the same kidney as Wolfe,
was killed by a stray shot in the advance to the French fort
Ticonderoga on Lake Champlain; and on 8 July, during the
whole summer day, while Abercromby stayed behind at the
base, his gallant men, including some of Pitt's Highlanders,
were shot down attacking an impenetrable stockade, built by

---

[1] The sum named in the treaty was four million thalers or German crowns.
The treaty was for one year only but was renewed three times: in Dec. 1758, Nov.
1759, and Dec. 1760.

[2] Saunders had been left in the Mediterranean by Hawke with a small squadron
at the end of 1756. In May 1757 he was reinforced by Osborn who then assumed
command. De la Clue was blockaded in Cartagena from Nov. 1757 to Mar. 1758.
In Apr. he slipped back to Toulon. Corbett, l.c. i. 138, 159, 238, 260.

[3] The French capitulated on 26 July; the English took possession the next day.

the French to defend the position. After this reverse Abercromby for the rest of the season remained idle in camp until recalled by Pitt. Nevertheless two more of the men picked out for service by Pitt did good work in Canada. Bradstreet, a colonel of militia from Maine, captured forts Frontenac and Oswego on Lake Ontario; and the veteran Forbes, though a dying man, climbed mountains and hewed a way through dense forests till he reached Fort Duquesne, the immediate cause of the war, captured it and renamed it Fort Pitt, now the spot where roar the great foundries of Pittsburg.

The year 1758 was also marked by more of Pitt's eccentric expeditions. The first was made at Frederic's special request to Pitt that, even if he could not spare a squadron for the Baltic to overawe Russia,[1] he should at least safeguard for him a base on the North Sea. Accordingly, early in February, as soon as the ice was broken, Commodore Holmes was sent with a squadron[2] to the Ems and expelled the French from Emden, which was garrisoned the next month by an English regiment and proved a convenient base both for Frederic and Prince Ferdinand. Three more raiding expeditions were sent under Howe, another young commodore who succeeded to the title of his soldier brother, to look into St. Malo and Cherbourg and do what damage they could. Howe did his part well enough; but unfortunately the military commanders available, the duke of Marlborough with Lord George Sackville as his second in command in the first raid, and in the other two General Bligh, a veteran of 73, had no heart in the adventures, which were ridiculed by the high society frequented by Horace Walpole.[3] In the first expedition all the shipping and stores in St. Malo were burned, but the landing force re-embarked, perhaps over-hastily, on the rumoured approach of French troops; in the second Cherbourg was actually captured and then relinquished; in the third, again at St. Malo, the Guards lost heavily in a hasty retreat. Some

[1] Frederic several times pressed for this diversion, but Pitt, with all the duties of the fleet in American and Indian waters, the Bay of Biscay, and the Mediterranean, was not able to satisfy Frederic in this particular.

[2] Holmes's force consisted of two frigates, a bomb ketch, and an armed cutter. One frigate was soon sent home, after grounding in the Ems, and Emden was captured with the remainder. See Corbett, i. 248–9.

[3] An incident much appreciated by Horace Walpole was the duc d'Aiguillon's return, 'politely to mark contempt', of Marlborough's spoons left behind on his precipitate re-embarkation from St. Malo. 'The French learned', he adds, 'that they were not to be conquered by every duke of Marlborough.'

damage, however, had been done to both ports, which, according to Pitt, might have been retained had not the soldiers 'made a present of them to the French'. But even so these raids succeeded in Pitt's object of distracting the French staff and diverting their troops from more vital centres in Germany and America.[1] Two, however, of his diversions, against the French settlements in West Africa, were materially, as well as strategically, most successful. Both beautifully planned by Pitt and admirably carried out, the first under Captain Marsh and Major Mason, the second under Commodore Keppel, another of Pitt's boys in the thirties, resulted in the capture of all the French factories on that coast, including Goree and Senegal.[2]

1759 was the *annus mirabilis*, when Horace Walpole complained that the church bells were worn threadbare with ringing for victories, and wrote with unwonted sincerity to the great organizer of these victories 'to congratulate you on the lustre you have thrown on this country. . . . Sir, do not take this for flattery: there is nothing in your power to give that I would accept; nay there is nothing I could envy, but what I believe you would scarce offer me—your glory.'[3] The victories of this year were all the more remarkable since at last Pitt had to meet in Choiseul, the new minister in France, an adversary almost worthy of his steel. Choiseul, indeed, might have given Pitt more serious trouble had he been in power since 1756: as it was, he did much to make better use of his country's resources and to revive the gallant spirit of France. But by this time Pitt had shed most of his shackles, including the old incapables, and in every quarter of the globe had young men after his own heart gaily carrying out his projects. From such he got the best work by the contagious enthusiasm with which he inspired them and the confidence he gave them. 'No man', Barré said in his funeral oration, 'ever entered the Earl's closet who did not feel himself, if possible, braver at his return than when he went in'; and Pitt's own maxim, applied to Wolfe, was that 'in order to render any general completely responsible for his conduct he should be made, as far as possible, inexcusable if he should fail; and that

[1] For a clear statement of the value of these despised raids in confusing the enemy see Corbett, l.c. i. 302–4. See also *Chatham*, i. 359–62.

[2] See *Chatham*, i. 300, 362–4, and Clowes, *Royal Navy*, iii. 187.

[3] H. Walpole, *Letters* (ed. Toynbee), no. 664. Pitt's elaborate letter of thanks is given in *Supplement*, vol. iii, no. 72, of the same work.

consequently whatever an officer entrusted with a service of confidence requests should be complied with'.[1]

The first success of the year was the capture in May of Guadeloupe, a rendezvous of French privateers, followed by that of Marie Galante in June.[2] In Germany Frederic was still being hard pressed by Russians and Austrians, and in 1758 had barely saved Berlin by the costly battle of Zorndorf, while in August 1759 he suffered the crushing defeat of Kunersdorf. Ferdinand of Brunswick, too, in the early part of the year had been driven out of Hesse by the French and right up to the borders of Hanover. But on 1 August, by the brilliant victory of Minden with 42,000 men against 54,000[3] of Contades, he recovered all the ground lost since the previous year and thereby probably saved Frederic from destruction after his defeat at Kundersdorf a few days later. The brunt of the fighting at Minden was borne by six English infantry regiments, that still bear 'Minden' on their colours, but the English cavalry, owing to Lord George Sackville's disobedience to an order to advance, took no effective part in the victory. It is characteristic of Pitt that, though previously a friend and political ally of Sackville's, he ordered the sentence of the court martial declaring him unfit to serve the king in any capacity to be read out at the head of every British regiment, so 'that officers [may be] convinced that neither high birth nor great employment can shelter offences of such a nature'.[4] It is characteristic of the change of spirit in the services that Lestock had been honourably acquitted in 1746[5] for much the same offence as that for which Sackville was condemned in 1759.

---

[1] The king had objected to Carleton (1724–1808), whom Wolfe wanted on his staff, but yielded to Pitt's representation. See *Chatham*, i. 397; Whitworth, *Ligonier*, p. 280.

[2] The expedition had been intended to capture Martinique but on being checked there in Jan. had attacked Guadeloupe as an alternative objective, which was consistent with its main purpose of securing a pledge for the return of Minorca. See Corbett, l.c. i. 377–9, and *Chatham*, ii. 2.

[3] These are the figures given in *Chatham*, ii. 3. Fortescue, *History of the British Army*, ii. 496, says 41,000 against 51,000. Carlyle in *Frederick the Great*, bk. xix, chap. iii, says 36,000 against 51,400. C. T. Atkinson, *History of Germany*, p. 269, says the allies' inferiority was at least 12,000.

[4] It appears that these orders were written by Ligonier, not Pitt. See Whitworth, l.c., p. 323.

[5] See above, p. 248. Lord George Sackville, under the name of Lord George Germain, was unfortunately allowed once more to 'serve the king'. He was probably not a coward, but was 'disobliged' with Prince Ferdinand.

The crowning mercies of this great year came last. Saunders and Wolfe had arrived at the Île d'Orléans below Quebec at the end of June, and then for over two months gave one of the happiest examples of perfect unison in amphibious operations by army and fleet, each helping the other to find good landing-places and points of attack and supporting one another loyally in the joint assault on the enemy's lines below the St. Charles river. It was no easy task even to approach the great citadel so strongly placed and defended by such men as Montcalm, Lévis, and Bougainville; and it was only after feints of attack above Quebec and exploration of the banks by Wolfe and the seamen that the narrow, barely defended path up to the Heights of Abraham was at last discovered and his men brought up secretly by Wolfe on 13 September.[1] On that day the fate of Canada was settled and Wolfe himself died happy at the moment of victory, murmuring, 'Now God be praised, I will die in peace.'

Meanwhile, throughout the year Choiseul had been building ships and flat-bottomed boats and collecting troops for his great coup, the invasion of England itself. But Pitt, well served by his intelligence,[2] was ready for him. In June he called out the militia which, although it still provoked some local disturbances, had a widespread moral effect, uniting all classes in defence of their country;[3] at the same time he had reserve regiments of regulars encamped in the Isle of Wight and elsewhere on the south coast. In July Rodney, just promoted rear-admiral, bombarded the flat-bottomed boats assembled in Havre, while Commodore Boys blockaded Dunkirk. In April, Boscawen had been sent to reinforce Brodrick in the Mediterranean to watch Toulon and Cadiz, while in May Hawke had sailed for the Bay of Biscay. In August de la Clue once more ventured out of Toulon but was promptly pursued by Boscawen and Brodrick who, at Lagos, captured or drove ashore most of his ships. Finally, in November, when Conflans' great fleet of twenty-six ships[4] sallied forth from Brest to escort across to England the

[1] Quebec surrendered on 18 Sept. before Lévis, who had been sent to Montreal early in Aug., could bring relief. *Chatham*, ii. 12, and Corbett, l.c. i. 445, 472.

[2] Pitt's information was not always as reliable as that of Newcastle. The intercepted dispatch from Choiseul to the French ambassador at Stockholm which revealed the full scope of his invasion plan was obtained by Newcastle. See Corbett, ii. 14–15, 17–18, 23.

[3] For reports illustrating the good effect of this embodiment of the militia see *Chatham*, i. 405–6.

[4] Twenty-one were ships of the line and five were frigates.

French troops gathered at Quiberon, Hawke with the swiftness of a bird of prey was upon them and drove the French fleet head-long into Quiberon Bay, where they were caught as in a trap. The French admiral's ship was burned, his rear-admiral's taken, four others destroyed, and as many more hopelessly stranded on the mud. It is characteristic of the new spirit in the navy that Saunders, on his way back from Quebec, hearing of Hawke's engagement 'made the best of his way in quest of him', though he arrived too late to take part in the victory. Thereafter there was no further talk of a French invasion, and for the rest of the war the French navy was no longer in a position to take effective action.[1]

The conflict in India between the French and English East India Companies was not, except for the maintenance of sea communications and coast defence, the home government's immediate concern.[2] But Pitt, by family tradition deeply interested in India, where, he once said, 'I had garnered up my heart, where our strength lay, and our happiest resources presented themselves',[3] watched the struggle eagerly and was always ready to help the Company in difficulties. After Plassey he paid a notable tribute in the house of commons to Admiral Watson and his successor Pocock, and especially to Clive, with whom thereafter he kept in close touch. Early in 1759, after the capture by the French of Fort St. David in June 1758, a prelude to the investment of Madras itself in the following December, Pitt, anticipating an appeal from Clive, had already sanctioned the raising of a new regiment in England for service in India,[4] and three months later granted an annual subsidy of £20,000 to the Company for the rest of the war. In 1760, when released by the victories of 1759 from some of his anxiety at home, he sent out further reinforcements to India, and even contemplated an expedition to capture Île de France (Mauritius), the chief French port of refuge for their Indian squadrons.[5] In fact, as the chairman of the East India Company said of him in 1761,

[1] To Quiberon has been attributed the final destruction of Jacobite hopes. See A. and H. Tayler, *1745 and After*. For an account of the battle see Corbett, ii. 63–69.
[2] The main lines of the war in India have been indicated in chap. xi, pp. 324 sqq.
[3] *Chatham Correspondence*, iv. 331.
[4] This regiment arrived in Madras between July and Oct. 1759, when Eyre Coote took command of it. See above, p. 330.
[5] See references in *Chatham*, ii. 27–28.

they owed not only 'their present glorious situation, but their very existence to his generous protection'.

On 25 October 1760 the old king, George II, died. A choleric, obstinate little man with violent prejudices and a great sense of his own importance, for the first ten years of his reign he was entirely swayed by Walpole and his wise queen, Caroline, who took care to veil her influence by persuading him that her own suggestions were originated by himself.[1] During the following decade he showed greater political independence, particularly while Granville was in office or advising him 'behind the curtain'. But this ended in 1746[2] and thereafter he relied on Walpole's solid but unimaginative pupil Pelham. For the last six years of his reign he was bewildered by the intrigues and incompetence of Newcastle and still more by the masterful assuredness of Pitt. But, though vastly preferring his *gemütlich* little electorate, where he had no worries and everybody was deferential, he was a good constitutional king in always recognizing, after much preliminary blustering, his own limitations and the necessity of acceptin the advice of ministers supported by 'that d——d House of Commons'. Even Pitt, whom he had long kept out of office, came to recognize that the 'good old king . . . possessed justice, truth and sincerity in an eminent degree; so that . . . it was possible for you to know if he liked you or disliked you'.[3]

The new king, George III, in his first public act showed his anxiety for peace and his antagonism to Pitt's bellicose humour. In his declaration to the privy council on his accession he spoke of 'this bloody and expensive war', softened down, it is true, on Pitt's demand, in the published version, to 'expensive but just and necessary war'.[4] In the following March he appointed his equally pacific groom of the stole, Lord Bute, as secretary in

[1] See above, p. 203. [2] See above, pp. 257–9.
[3] Contemporary appreciations of George II are to be found in H. Walpole, *Memoirs . . . of George II*, iii. 301–9; Waldegrave, *Memoirs*, pp. 4–7; Chesterfield, *Character of George II* (in printed works); and, for the absurd side of him, Hervey, *Memoirs, passim*. Pitt's comment was made when he was anxious to contrast George II favourably with George III. See *Chatham*, ii. 58, 270, and *P.H.* xvi. 849 (14 Mar. 1770).
[4] For the ferocious antagonism at this time of George III and his favourite towards Pitt see R. Sedgwick, l.c. Pitt's alliance with Leicester House (see above, p. 355, n. 5) had broken down by the end of 1758; the breach was widened during 1759 by his lofty disregard of Bute and his severity towards Sackville. See *Chatham*, ii. 63–64.

place of Holderness. A few days later the Russian ambassador Galitzin proposed a negotiation for peace on behalf of France and her allies. Pitt agreed to treat, but without ceasing hostilities meanwhile, for he wished to have counters in hand with which to bargain for his less fortunate ally Frederic II; for throughout he was determined that Frederic should not be a loser by the war, even if England had to sacrifice some of her conquests to recover for Frederic Wesel and his other lost territories. Already in 1760 the whole of Canada had been surrendered by the French on Amherst's capture of Montreal on 8 September and in June 1761 Dominica was taken. Pitt also had his plans prepared for the capture of Martinique, Grenada, and St. Lucia, which fell early in 1762, after his resignation. On the very eve of the negotiations Commodore Keppel and Brigadier Hodgson had been sent to capture Belle Île, near the scene of Hawke's great victory at Quiberon, and this they succeeded in doing on 8 June, so that Pitt actually had a portion of France itself to throw into the scale.

The peace negotiations of 1761 were conducted by Pitt and Choiseul through agents sent to Paris and London respectively. Choiseul sent over to London a certain F. de Bussy, an official in the French foreign office, who during the 1730's used to receive large sums from our secret service fund for revealing secrets, mostly *de Polichinelle*, to Newcastle;[1] Pitt's representative in Paris was Hans Stanley. Choiseul sent to Pitt a *petite feuille* with his proposals, which were: (1) France to return Minorca in exchange for Guadeloupe, Marie Galante, and Goree; (2) France to give up Canada with its southern and western limits fixed at Niagara, but to retain Île Royale (Cape Breton) and her former share of the Newfoundland fisheries; (3) France to restore all conquests made in Germany at the expense of England's allies and specifically the fortress of Wesel in Frederic's Rhenish province.[2] In England there was some controversy as to whether Canada or Guadeloupe should be retained. William Beckford,[3] an ally of Pitt and representing the sugar interests

[1] For further details of de Bussy's activities see Basil Williams, 'Foreign Office of the Georges' in *Blackwood's Magazine* for Jan. 1907.

[2] The promise in respect of Wesel was verbal only and was later repudiated by Choiseul. See below, p. 369, and *Chatham*, ii. 91–92, 94.

[3] William Beckford, 1709–70, M.P. for the City, 1754–70, lord mayor in 1761, 1762–3, and 1769–70, and a supporter of John Wilkes. [For Pitt's connexions with the City at this time see Miss L. S. Sutherland's Raleigh Lecture in *Proc. of Brit. Acad.* vol. xlvi (1960). C.H.S.]

of Jamaica, was all for giving up Guadeloupe, lest the large sugar-production of that island should interfere with the profits of the Jamaica planters. On the other side were those attracted by the prospective wealth to be derived from Guadeloupe, who also advanced the argument that, if we retained Canada, the American colonists, once the French danger on their border was removed, might become too independent and even secede. Pitt himself, however, had no such apprehensions; he was for retaining Canada, partly to clear away the French danger, partly as a colony better fitted for English settlers by its climate than a West Indian island, as well as for its openings for mutual trade between England and America. Indeed he was not prepared to leave any opening for the French in North America. He rejected Choiseul's proposals to limit the Canadian boundary at Niagara and for the return of Cape Breton. He was even opposed to allowing the French to retain their fishing rights on the Newfoundland Banks, regarding these fisheries, apart from their trade-value, as the best recruiting-ground for the British navy. In this respect, however, the cabinet was against him; and he had to yield on that point and also to allow the French fishermen the tiny island of St. Pierre in the St. Lawrence as a drying-ground for their fish and nets. But at this stage Choiseul began to show himself recalcitrant. He withdrew his offer to restore the conquests made at Frederic's expense and began to make other difficulties. This seemed all the more surprising since Pitt's hands were being strengthened at this very time by the news in July of the capture of Dominica and of Pondichery, as well as of another victory by Prince Ferdinand at Vellinghausen over two marshals of France. But the fact was that Choiseul had then almost concluded a secret treaty with Spain from which he had great hopes of retrieving his position.[1] King Ferdinand of Spain, friendly to England, had died in 1759 and been succeeded by his half-brother Don Carlos, the king of Naples. The new king was concerned to protect the Spanish empire against England and, like his mother before him, to maintain the Spanish princes in Italy against Austria. He looked to a French alliance to achieve these objects and so was ready to receive Choiseul's overtures.[2] In anticipation of this alliance

[1] The treaty was actually signed 15 Aug. 1761.
[2] For a discussion of Charles III's motives in making the family compact see Z. Rashed, *The Peace of Paris*, pp. 33–44.

Choiseul, in an ultimatum of 13 July, repudiated many of the concessions he had hitherto made, and coolly included in his dispatch a demand that England should also satisfy various Spanish grievances. Pitt haughtily replied that it was not England's habit to discuss the grievances of an ally, as Spain then nominally was, with an enemy; and, though Bussy and Stanley were not recalled till the middle of September, it was obvious that further negotiations would be fruitless.

Apart from Choiseul's provocative advocacy of Spain's grievances, Pitt had full information of the Franco-Spanish treaty of 15 August from intercepted letters of the Spanish ambassador; and he may even have seen a copy of the treaty itself. At any rate he was convinced that sooner or later England would have to fight Spain as well as France. On 18 September he proposed to the cabinet to declare war on Spain forthwith, before she was ready with her treasure-galleons safely in harbour; and, when the cabinet rejected his advice, followed it up with a memorandum to the king. The cabinet, on the king's order, met twice more to consider this memorandum; but Pitt found no support for his view except from his unpopular brother-in-law Temple. At the last meeting, on 2 October, Pitt once more gave his reasons for immediate war, but found the cabinet against him still. Thereupon, as the cabinet minute runs, he declared that he had been 'called . . . by his sovereign and . . . in some degree by the voice of the people, to assist the state when others had abdicated the service of it. . . . That this being his case, nobody could be surprised that he could go on no longer and . . . that he would be responsible for nothing but what he directed.' On this Granville, after a compliment to his services, dryly commented: 'that the point Mr. Pitt went upon was too much, unless he claimed infallibility: that . . . the king might take a foreign measure with his secretary of state only; but that if the king referred the matter to his council, the opinion of the majority of the council was the measure'. Three days later Pitt gave up the seals of office. Unfortunately for his own popularity, he accepted a pension of £3,000 for himself and the barony of Chatham for his wife.[1]

---

[1] [For the minutes of this meeting taken by Newcastle and Hardwicke see *E.H.R.* xxi. 130-2, 329-30, and Yorke, *Hardwicke*, iii. 277-80. Hardwicke's note included Pitt's famous claim 'I will be *responsible* for nothing that I do not *direct*'. The more highly coloured version, generally attributed to Burke, which was accepted by

Within three months Pitt was proved right. The treasure-galleons had arrived, and Spain contemptuously rejected the English ministers' complaints of unfriendly action; so on 4 January 1762 war was declared by England. It was a brief but successful war, mainly owing to the plans already prepared by Pitt. Besides the conquest of the French islands, Martinique, Grenada, St. Vincent, and St. Lucia by Rodney and Monckton early in 1762, within ten months Havana in the West Indies and Manila in the Philippines were captured from Spain. But owing to the neglect of Pitt's advice to reinforce the North American station, the French actually captured St. John's, Newfoundland. Then, on the plea that support was needed for our ally Portugal against a Spanish invasion, the expenses of Prince Ferdinand's army were cut down by Bute, the subsidy to Frederic was suspended,[1] and even the treaty of alliance with him not renewed. Fortunately, by the death of his implacable enemy the Tsaritsa Elizabeth in January 1762 and the accession of his fanatical admirer Peter III, Frederic was relieved of any further danger from Russia.

By May 1762 Bute had become supreme in the king's councils. The poor old duke of Newcastle, who had stood up manfully for honouring our obligations to Frederic,[2] was finding himself edged out of all power, and even over-ruled in his own department, the treasury, which finally led him on 7 May to offer the king his resignation; this was accepted, but he remained in office until the end of the session. Then at last on 26 May he resigned from the king's service, in which he had held the 'labouring oar', as he regarded it, for over forty years. Bute then became first lord of the treasury and so ostensibly, as well as in reality, chief adviser to the king, and the dispenser of all patronage and of all pensions and grants from the civil list. He had already initiated peace negotiations with Choiseul through the extraordinary agency of the Sardinian ambassadors, Viry in London and de Solar in Paris, who acted as intermediaries for communicating to the French and English

Professor Williams, is in the *Annual Register* for 1761. See above, p. 17, n. 1, and *Chatham*, ii. 114 n. C.H.S.]

[1] Bute refused to renew the subsidy treaty, which had expired in Dec. 1761, but offered in its place an equivalent parliamentary grant subject to conditions which Frederic repudiated. See Lodge, *Great Britain and Prussia*, p. 119.

[2] For Newcastle's ambivalent attitude towards the war in Germany see Namier, *American Revolution*, pp. 353–80.

ministries the proposals from either side. The negotiations were completed by the duke of Bedford, who had been sent to Paris in September, and on 3 November 1762 he signed the Preliminary Articles at Fontainebleau with Choiseul and the Spanish ambassador Grimaldi. By these Preliminaries Great Britain was confirmed in the possession of her conquests, Canada and Cape Breton, St. Vincent, Tobago, Dominica, Grenada, and the Grenadines in the western hemisphere, and of Senegal in Africa: she recovered Minorca in exchange for Belle Île, and once more the fortifications of Dunkirk were to be demolished;[1] in India France was restricted to her original trading factories, as held at the beginning of 1749 before Dupleix began his military conquests, and agreed to keep no troops there, while Great Britain retained all Clive's conquests in Bengal and was left the dominant European power throughout the peninsula. On the other hand, Goree in Africa, Guadeloupe, Martinique, Marie Galante, and St. Lucia in the West Indies were given back to France, her fishing rights in Newfoundland restored, and Miquelon as well as St. Pierre granted her as drying-grounds in the St. Lawrence. From Spain Great Britain gained Florida in exchange for Havana, but restored Manila without an equivalent[2] because the news of its capture did not reach Europe until after the Preliminaries had been signed. But, to Bute's lasting disgrace, Frederic's interests were almost entirely neglected by 'perfide Albion'.[3]

Before being reduced to a formal treaty the Preliminaries had to be submitted to parliament for sanctioning the return to France of territory conquered by our arms. To secure consent

[1] The French did not agree to the complete demolition of the Dunkirk fortifications until the final treaty was drafted; in the Preliminaries they had bargained for the partial demolition laid down at Aix-la-Chapelle.

[2] The so-called 'Manila ransom' was promised by the local authorities as the price of saving the town from being sacked; the Spanish government repudiated this. See V. T. Harlow, *The Founding of the Second British Empire*, i. 76.

[3] [In fact Prussian interests were guarded by a separate convention negotiated after the preliminary treaty was debated in parliament. See Corbett, l.c. ii. 364–5. Professor Williams takes here and in the following paragraphs the most extreme view of England's 'desertion' of Prussia, for which he had the weighty authority of Lodge, *Great Britain and Prussia*, pp. 113–38. But W. L. Dorn has since demonstrated, in his article 'Frederic the Great and Lord Bute' in *Journal of Modern History*, i. 529–60, that 'the extreme charge of treachery and perfidy made against Bute [is] wanting in authentic evidence'. Nevertheless, as Professor Williams shows, Frederic's lasting resentment of this 'desertion', as he genuinely believed it to be, contributed to England's diplomatic isolation for a generation. See also Frank Spencer in *History*, n.s. xli. 100–12. C.H.S.]

for a treaty whereby the country, in spite of further successes, gave more favourable terms to France than Pitt would have exacted in 1761 was less difficult than would appear at first sight. The idea of peace was popular; opposition was directed against Bute personally; as Fox observed, it was 'against the man not the measure'. Furthermore, in spite of his unpopularity, Bute's position as first lord of the treasury chosen and supported by the king secured for him the obedience of many politicians who, for much the same reason, had long supported Newcastle. Finally, in October 1762, Bute further strengthened himself by obtaining the king's reluctant consent to the appointment of the unscrupulous Fox as his 'Minister in the House of Commons'. By the time parliament met at the end of November the opposition had been undermined in both houses.[1] Pitt came from a sick-bed to criticize the Preliminaries for the concessions to France on the Newfoundland fisheries, for the return of 'all the valuable West India Islands', whereby we had 'given to her the means of recovering her prodigious losses and of becoming once more formidable to us at sea', and above all for the desertion of Frederic, 'the most magnanimous ally this country ever had', as contrasted with his own 'perseverance in the German war and . . . our observing good faith towards our Protestant allies on the Continent'.[2] There indeed he put his finger on the chief blot in the treaty. This desertion was never forgotten or forgiven by Frederic, who thereafter manifested a special animus against England; nor indeed was it forgotten by later generations of his countrymen, down even to the time of Bismarck, who took note of the probability that but for Frederic's victories his cause 'would have been abandoned by England even earlier than it actually was'.[3] But Pitt made little impression; he had refused to concert beforehand with Newcastle and did not even take part in the division when the Preliminaries were passed by 319 votes to 65. On 10 February 1763 the Treaty of Paris,[4] formally embodying these Preliminaries, was signed.

[1] [Many historians have accepted Horace Walpole's allegation that Fox made extensive use of bribery to ensure that the peace was approved in the commons. Sir Lewis Namier has shown this to be without foundation. In any case, Fox did not need to use bribery when his opponents were divided, unable to agree on a positive line of action, and, in many cases, anxious to come to terms with the new political order. See Namier, *Structure of Politics* (2nd edn.), pp. 181–4, and *American Revolution*, pp. 417–85. C.H.S.]   [2] *P.H.* xv. 1265–70 (9 Dec. 1762).

[3] Bismarck, *Reminiscences* (trans. A. J. Butler), ii. 252–3.

[4] For the full text see Rashed, l.c., appendix.

It did no credit to the English nation that three times within fifty years her statesmen made her unfaithful to solemn engagements. The desertion of Prince Eugene by Ormonde at Denain in 1712, on Bolingbroke's restraining orders, followed by the abandonment of the Catalans in the treaty of Utrecht, was the first signal instance. For these laches the country justly suffered by being left without a real friend in Europe, until Stanhope by his bold and straightforward diplomacy restored confidence in our integrity. Again Walpole, by refusing, during the War of the Polish Succession, to honour his guarantee to the emperor of the Austrian possessions, made only three years previously for value received,[1] alienated our chief ally in Europe and left us friendless when our own next war began in 1739. Indeed, it was partly the people's sense of national humiliation that drove Walpole into that futile war with Spain. Lastly, in 1763, Bute, by his separate peace and his desertion of Frederic,[2] created in the German nation a distrust of us which lasted for over a century, and once more left us friendless when, barely more than ten years later, we had to fight for our empire. As history shows, a temporary relief from difficulties may be gained by such repudiations of engagements, explicit or implied, but they are always followed in the end by a just nemesis.

For the time being, indeed, we appeared in 1763 at the peak of glory. The great gains of the Seven Years war secured by the treaty of Paris were the addition of a vast territory in America, destined within less than a quarter of a century to be our only possession on that continent, and free scope for the development and administration of what became our great eastern dependency. On the other hand it left, contrary to Pitt's original intentions, an open sore with France in the Newfoundland fisheries. By this treaty, the French fishermen were entitled not only to fish on the Newfoundland Banks from Cape Bonavista on the east round the north to Point Riche on the west,[3] but also to dry their fish and nets on land. This proviso led to extravagant claims of an exclusive right to landing and drying-grounds, the cause of disputes for a century and a half with the local fishermen, whose lobster-canning factories there were

---

[1] Walpole's cynical defence to the queen will be remembered: 'Madam, there are 50,000 men slain this year in Europe and not one Englishman.'

[2] See above, p. 372, n. 3.

[3] By the treaty of 1783 the French gave up their rights between Cape Bonavista and Point Riche.

actually destroyed by the French. It was not till 1904 that the French finally gave up their landing rights, reserving only the fishing on the Banks. Besides such disputes, which Pitt foresaw in his refusal to entertain Choiseul's claim to any fishing rights in America, this treaty left, as any treaty, after a war so calamitous to the French, might have, an intense desire for *revanche* in their able and public-spirited statesmen Choiseul and Vergennes. This desire the folly and incompetence of Pitt's successors enabled them largely to satisfy in 1783. But whatever may have been the results of the peace, the conduct of the war by Pitt is a standing and almost unique example in our annals of well-planned schemes brought to fruition by a statesman able to survey the whole field of operations and to make the fullest use of the nation's resources. By his eloquence in action no less than in words, by his sympathetic understanding of the people in this country and in America, by his own untiring labours, and by that magnetic personal touch whereby 'no man ever entered [his] closet who did not feel himself, if possible, braver at his return than when he went in'—by qualities such as these he was able to make the nation do its utmost in its own cause.

'Walpole was a minister given by the King to the people:— Pitt was a minister given by the people to the King.'[1] The flash of this epigram lights up the whole matter. Even more far-reaching than the Great Commoner's achievements in winning an empire was the silent revolution accomplished by his attainment of the chief office in the state. Up to the time of the Rebellion ministers were chosen by the king to carry out his own policy; since then they had indeed been dependent on the support of parliament but were still chosen by the king from those most likely from their political associations in parliament to be able to carry out his measures. In 1756 for the first time in our history a man was called to supreme power by the voice of the people, expressed, not as represented in parliament, but in the fact that 'the eyes of an afflicted, despairing nation were now lifted up to a private gentleman of a slender fortune, wanting the parade of birth or title, of no family alliance but by his marriage with Lord Temple's sister, and even confined to a narrow circle of friends and acquaintance. Under these

[1] Boswell's *Johnson* under year 1772.

circumstances Pitt was considered as the only saviour of England.'[1] Again, when he was summarily dismissed by the king from his first ministry in April 1757 the solid middle-class of England, Scotland, and Ireland, having no better means of expressing their sentiments, 'rained gold boxes' upon him with the freedom of the City of London and of no less than eighteen other principal cities in the United Kingdom as a token of support transcending that of an unrepresentative parliament. Lord Waldegrave himself, charged by the king to form an alternative ministry, gave up the task as hopeless, since 'the popular cry without doors was violent in favor of Mr. Pitt'.[2]

Of Stanhope, Walpole, Pelham, and Newcastle, the other chief ministers of George I and II, two at least were indeed supremely fit to rule; they were all chosen and remained in office because they pleased the king and were good managers of parliament; but it can safely be asserted that not one of them aroused any general enthusiasm in the country. Pitt, forced by popular opinion on the king and the ruling cliques in parliament, opened the way to a more democratic choice of our rulers; by his stirring appeals to the people of the United Kingdom and America, by the prompt and frank intelligence he gave them of reverses, as well as victories, he taught them to regard government not as a mere preserve of a limited class, but as the concern of the whole community. He had therefore every right to claim that he had been 'called by his sovereign and by the voice of the people to assist the state, . . . [and] that he would be responsible for nothing but what he directed'.[3] It is true that the precedent of his case was not immediately followed: it needs a Pitt to continue as well as to inaugurate such a change. But, Chatham himself in later life and his son after him put their fingers on the corrupt and defective electoral system as the chief source of our domestic and American troubles; and they both proposed reforms that might have gone some way to make parliament more truly representative of the voice of the people. Pitt for the United Kingdom and the colonies, no less than Swift for

---

[1] *Memoirs by a Celebrated Literary and Political Character*. [Richard Glover], 1814, pp. 84–85. [The suggestion that Pitt owed nothing to his family alliance is misleading. His connexion was with the Grenvilles, 'the most troublesome oligarchical faction in English politics' as Professor Pares once called them. See *E.H.R.* lv. 138. For the sources of Pitt's power see above p. 355, notes 2 and 5 and p. 368, n. 3. C.H.S.]

[2] Waldegrave, *Memoirs*, pp. 129–30.   [3] See above, p. 370.

Ireland, blazed the trail for democratic government in substitution for control by privileged interests. His proud title, the Great Commoner, signified even at the time something greater than his domination over the house of commons—his power of representing the voice of the whole British people.

XIV

SCIENCE AND HISTORICAL RESEARCH

'Newton ... determined the course of western thought, research, and practice to an extent that nobody before or since his time can touch. ... Before Newton there existed no self-contained system of physical causality ... capable of representing any of the deeper features of the empirical world.'[1] By the end of the seventeenth century Newton had indeed given the world most of the great thoughts and their exact proofs which justify this tribute from his successor Einstein; but for over a quarter of the eighteenth he was still there to watch over the development of his theories and inspire those carrying on his tradition. Voltaire, present at his funeral in Westminster Abbey in 1727, was deeply stirred by the honour done to him by the greatest in the land, who buried him as they would 'a King and Benefactor of his people', contrasting the sway he held in England with the persecution he would have suffered in France, the imprisonment in Rome, or the *auto-da-fé* in Portugal.[2] Small wonder that the eighteenth century not only in England but also abroad became remarkable for the progress of scientific thought and even more for the practical uses to which this increasing comprehension of the universe could be put. In mathematics, astronomy, physics, botany, chemistry, and medicine Newton's lead in patiently prolonged investigation of facts and fearless deductions from the facts thus ascertained was bringing home to the world the interdependence of all these sciences in a far more effective way than Descartes's attempt to explain all nature by one brilliant hypothesis. Notable also during this century were the practical uses to which this increasing comprehension of the universe was being put.

[1] L. Einstein, *The World as I see it*, 1935, pp. 146–7.
[2] *Lettres Philosophiques* and *Dictionnaire Philosophique*. Voltaire, no doubt, in these passages was thinking especially of Newton's heretical opinions on religion. In fact the edition of the *Principia* published in 1732 with a commentary by Fathers Le Sueur and Jacquieu of the Propaganda in Rome is still the best, so I gather from Professor Whittaker. [Note of 1939.]

In almost every branch of science developments were taking place which materially contributed to the service of human needs.

Newton's influence is specially notable in the two allied sciences of mathematics and astronomy. In 1704 he had published the first edition of his *Opticks* with an appendix on the fluxional (or infinitesimal) calculus, to the discovery of which Leibniz claimed prior rights. Hence arose a bitter controversy, lasting till 1724, in which most of the mathematicians of this country, Newton's friends and disciples, took part on his side. Prominent among these were the astronomer Halley and the mathematician Abraham de Moivre, both of whom—the former by his *Breslau Table of Mortality*, the latter by his *Doctrine of Chances* and *Annuities upon Lives*—may claim to have founded the practical science of life-contingencies and been the progenitors of such great institutions as the Equitable or the Scottish Widows. The precocious Scots mathematician Colin Mac-Laurin, a professor in his subject at the age of nineteen and F.R.S. two years later, was second only to Newton in developing the theory of the fluxional calculus in his *Geometrica Organica* and *Treatise of Fluxions*, the latter described by Lagrange as 'le chef-d'œuvre de géométrie qu'on peut comparer à tout ce qu'Archimède nous a laissé de plus beau et de plus ingénieux'. Another brilliant Scotsman, James Stirling, also an intimate friend of Newton, and a correspondent of the great Swiss mathematicians Euler and Bernoulli, developed Newtonian mathematics, especially in upholding his master's correct view that the earth is flatter at the poles than at the equator. Both these Scots mathematicians were as able in practical life as in theory. MacLaurin died of dropsy in 1746 as a result of his exertions in organizing the defence of Edinburgh in the '45; while Stirling proved most successful as manager of Leadhill Mines and in developing the port of Glasgow.[1] Another mathematician, Brook Taylor, solved the problem of the centre of oscillation, and enunciated the formula called 'Taylor's theorem' on the functions of a single variable to an infinite series; he also published in 1715 and 1719 two learned treatises on the mathematics of *Linear Perspective*, too abstruse for most artists' comprehension, but the basis for more popular expositions by J. J. Kirby in 1754 and D. Fournier in 1761.

[1] See C. Tweedie, *James Stirling*, 1922.

John Flamsteed, the first astronomer royal in 1675, by his observations of the stars had been helpful to Newton when writing the *Principia*; but later the two had quarrelled owing to Flamsteed's delay in publishing his calculations at Greenwich. His successor in 1721, Edmund Halley, who in 1686 had published the *Principia* at his own expense, predicted and observed the total eclipse of the sun in 1715, but is best known for his accurate forecast of the return of 'Halley's Comet' in 1758. He also spent a year in St. Helena mapping out the southern stellar hemisphere, and, as Anson found in his circumnavigation of the globe, did valuable work for navigators by his chart of the compass variations and corrections in the maps of coasts and islands in the southern seas.[1] Partly, however, owing to the government's stinginess in providing the necessary instruments, he was less successful in his practical duties at Greenwich. James Bradley, astronomer royal from 1742 to 1762, has been called 'the founder of modern observational astronomy'. Working on suggestions from Newtonian theories he calculated the time of propagation of light from the sun to the earth at 8 m. 13 sec.; in 1729 he enunciated the important law, described by Whewell as 'the greatest astronomical discovery of the . . . century',[2] of the 'constant of aberration', i.e. that the progressive transmission of light combined with the advance of the earth in its orbit causes an annual shifting, by an amount depending on the ratio of the two velocities, of the direction in which the heavenly bodies are seen; and in 1748 he published his discovery of the 'nutation' of the earth's axis, a discovery which, with that of 'aberration', 'assure him the most distinguished place among astronomers after Hipparchus and Kepler'.[3] On the practical side he greatly improved the instruments at Greenwich by his persistence in securing a grant of £1,000 for that purpose.[4] Bradley's calculations also were of

---

[1] See *A Voyage round the World . . . by George Anson, Esq.*, compiled by Richard Walter, bk. i, chap. 9. [But Anson found Halley's chart of the south coast of America defective.]

[2] W. Whewell, *History of the Inductive Sciences* (1857), ii. 200.

[3] Ibid., p. 202, quoting Delambre, p. 420.

[4] The astronomer royal's salary was then only £100. To supplement this Pelham in 1752 offered Bradley, who was in holy orders, the Crown living of Greenwich, and on Bradley's refusal of it from conscientious motives, increased the salary to £350. He would, it is said, have made it larger had not Bradley objected that, if the salary were too high, the post of astronomer royal might no longer go to an astronomer. J. B. Delambre, *Histoire de l'astronomie au 18ᵉ siècle*, 1827, p. 421.

material assistance to his fellow astronomer the second Lord Macclesfield in his successful efforts in 1751 to harmonize the English calendar with the continental Gregorian system. The bill, introduced in a luminous speech by Chesterfield, and supported by a learned disquisition from Macclesfield, passed without difficulty in parliament, but aroused much antagonism outside. In order to adjust the old and the new calendars eleven days of September 1752 had been obliterated, and for some time the most popular cry in the country was 'give us back our eleven days'.

Greenwich, then the chief English centre for astronomical observations, was intended primarily for the practical uses of navigation. On the nautical side of its work Greenwich was supplemented by the board of longitude, commissioners established in 1714 with power to grant rewards up to £20,000 'for the discovery of Longitude at Sea'. During its existence of 114 years the board expended £101,000 on this and cognate purposes. Its first contribution to navigation seems to have been a grant for a successful survey of all the coasts and head-lands of Great Britain, suggested by William Whiston, a some-what cranky theologian and mathematician. It also did valuable work in encouraging the invention of chronometers free from errors for calculating longitudes. John Harrison, by his inven-tion of a self-compensating mechanism and by his discovery of the 'gridiron pendulum'—a bob suspended by parallel rods alternately steel and brass, so that the downward expansion of the steel rods from a change of temperature was compensated by the upward expansion of the brass rods—was enabled to make successful observations of longitudes.[1] Meanwhile the lunar observations at Greenwich and Bradley's discoveries of 'aberration' and 'nutation' enabled the German mathematician Tobias Mayer in 1753 to produce lunar and solar tables so correct that they were bought by the British government and made the basis for the admirably exact *Nautical Almanac*, first published in 1766. Another name for which mariners should ever give praise is that of the engineer John Smeaton, elected to the Royal Society for his work on the mariner's compass and on pulleys. For, besides that, he was not only a

[1] Harrison had to wait unduly long for the promised rewards owing to the opposi-tion of the astronomer Maskelyne, who preferred stellar observation to the chrono-meter method.

notable bridge-builder and designer of the Forth–Clyde canal, but he was also given the task of rebuilding the Eddystone light-house. The first had been destroyed by the great storm of 1703, the second burnt down in 1755. Smeaton finished his lighthouse by 1759, and so magnificently had he planned and executed it in every detail that it lasted till 1877, and then had to be re-placed, not for any defect in the building, but only because the rock on which it stood was being undermined.

With the progress of astronomy and the needs of navigation more perfect instruments were required. Newton himself made the first reflecting telescope,[1] but despaired of contriving a re-fracting telescope that would eliminate the bending of the rays of light. This was left to John Dollond, a silk-weaver inspired by his son Peter to help him in instrument-making. In 1758, nearly a century after Newton's attempt, he produced his first achro-matic and refracting telescope.[2] Other notable instrument-makers were George Graham, F.R.S., James Short, who first gave to the speculum of the telescope a true parabolic figure, John Hadley, the inventor of the reflecting quadrant, which Captain Campbell, by extending the arc of the instrument from 45 to 60 degrees, in 1757 improved into the now familiar sextant. During this period, indeed, English instrument- and clock-makers were famous throughout Europe.

The father of the modern science of electricity was the English-man William Gilbert, who in 1600 had published his researches in magnetism and electricity, and invented the name electricity from the Greek ἤλεκτρον (amber).[3] Newton in the seventeenth century had proved, from the characteristically empiric ob-servation that a substance emitting electricity lost no weight, that electricity, like heat, was not an element in itself but simply a condition producible in bodies. But the eighteenth century witnessed the greatest advance yet made in the science, an advance due largely to the happy spirit of co-operation between English and foreign scientists. The Englishman Francis Hauks-bee in 1709 had observed the electric force of repulsion as well as attraction, and about 1729 Stephen Gray discovered that certain substances, such as pack-threads, had the property of

[1] A German Jesuit, who knew of him only by this telescope, described him as 'artifex quidam nomine Newton'. Voltaire, *Dictionnaire Philosophique*.
[2] Chester Moor Hall had made one in 1733 but had kept it and the secret to himself.
[3] See vol. viii in this series, pp. 307–8 (2nd edn.)

'conducting' electricity from an electrified body to another unelectrified, whereas others, such as silk threads, had not that power; and so established the distinction between 'electrics'[1] *per se* (non-conductors) and 'conductors' of electricity (non-electrics). This discovery was, with Gray's hearty co-operation, developed by the Frenchman Dufay, who in 1733 distinguished between two kinds of electricity, 'vitreous' (glass, rock-crystal, hair, wool, &c.) and 'resinous' (amber, copal, silk, paper, &c.), and showed that electrified vitreous bodies repelled other vitreous bodies while attracting resinous bodies and vice versa. In 1745 the Dutchman Musschenbroek, observing that electrics lost electricity in the open air, invented the Leyden Jar, a container made of a non-conductor, such as glass, coated with a conductor and filled with water, wherein the electric charge, admitted through a metal nail inserted into the cork of the jar, could be preserved without dissipation. This invention was improved by Sir William Watson, assisted by John Smeaton, who devised the Leyden Jar as we know it by coating the glass vessel inside and outside with tin-foil. Watson also organized the interesting experiments conducted by the Royal Society in 1747–8, whereby it was proved that an electric discharge conducted on a circuit from Westminster Bridge by Highbury and Shooter's Hill could be conveyed instantaneously for a distance of 12,276 feet. A similar but more amusing experiment was made by the Abbé Nollet before Louis XV and his court. He arranged a party of Carthusian friars in a line a mile long and connected each friar with his neighbours by wires; he then discharged electricity along the wires, whereupon all the friars leapt simultaneously into the air. Watson also exhibited the wonders of electricity to George III, when prince of Wales, the duke of Cumberland, and their courtiers.

But the scientist who more than any other brought home to the people the wonders of this new science and turned it to practical uses was Benjamin Franklin, that self-taught genius in America. A certain Dr. Spence came over to Boston in 1746 and gave some crude demonstrations of electrical phenomena, whereby Franklin's interest in the subject was aroused. Shortly afterwards he obtained from a member of the Royal Society a Leyden Jar for his public library at Philadelphia. His first

---

[1] This nomenclature was adopted by Gray's contemporary John Desaguliers (1683–1744).

important discovery was that the inner tin-foil of the jar being electrified positively, its outer tin-foil was electrically negative, and that when the inner and outer surfaces were connected together an electric spark and shock were produced by the restoration of an electrical equilibrium between the two, a demonstration which indicated the way to the use of electricity as a motive force, as later discovered by Galvani and Volta. Even more arresting at the time was Franklin's demonstration of the identity of thunder and lightning with the shock and spark of electricity. This identity had been surmised by earlier investigators, but it was left to him to prove it by his famous kite experiment. This experiment had an immediate practical result in his invention of the lightning conductor as a protection to buildings, an invention adopted by George III for his own palace. These discoveries of Franklin brought him sudden fame. The Royal Society, which had at first looked coldly on his claims, awarded him the Copley Medal and elected him a member, and his European reputation brought him admission to most foreign academies. By the end of George II's reign indeed the ground was prepared for the further discoveries, not only of Galvani and Volta, but also of Davy, Faraday, and others who made possible the all-pervasive employment of electricity for the common uses of life.[1]

Stephen Hales, who was born in Charles II's reign and lived to see George III on the throne, was a characteristic product of the Newtonian age. A simple, innocent, kindly man of encyclopaedic interests, parish priest, man of affairs (he was trustee for Georgia and a founder of the Society of Arts), pamphleteer against dram-drinking, the ingenious inventor of ventilators and of methods for distilling water and preserving meat on sea voyages, a friend of Pope and of Frederick, prince of Wales, he was also an enthusiastic investigator of almost all branches of natural phenomena. In physiology, by a celebrated experiment on the carotid artery of a horse, he discovered the phenomenon of arterial pressure, a discovery perhaps second only in importance to Harvey's of the circulation of the blood. But his main

[1] Among the clearest expositions, to a layman, of electrical history appear to me to be, first the section on electricity in Whewell's *History of the Inductive Sciences* (1857), then those produced by two successive Professors of Mathematics at Edinburgh, George Chrystal in his article on *Electricity* in the 9th edition of the *Encyclopaedia Britannica*, and Professor Whittaker's *History of Theories of Æther and Electricity*, 1910. [Note of 1939.]

interest was in the study of plant physiology, especially in experiments on the gaseous nutrition of plants. In his *Vegetable Staticks* he deals with the pressure of the sap and attempts an analysis of the 'Air . . . wrought into the composition of animal, vegetable, and mineral Substances and . . . how readily it resumes its former elastick state, when in the dissolution of those Substances it is disingaged from them'; he even constructed a remarkable apparatus for measuring this 'air' when set free by heat. By these experiments he was thus on the track of the discoveries made after him relating to carbon-dioxide by Black, of nitrogen by Rutherford, of hydrogen by Cavendish, and of oxygen by Scheele, Priestley, and Lavoisier. Boyle's researches in the seventeenth century had already shown a marked advance by the mode in which he collected gases and worked with them; yet neither he nor his contemporaries felt quite sure whether carbon-dioxide and hydrogen, the characteristic properties of which they knew, differed materially from atmospheric air. Nor did Hales—though, as Priestley said, 'nitrous air obtruded itself upon Dr. Hales'—entirely abandon the erroneous idea that gases were ordinary air with various admixtures. To Black is due the merit of proving the separate nature of carbon-dioxide by showing its 'fixation' by 'caustic alkalis'.

Of Joseph Black, the founder of 'pneumatic chemistry', Sir William Ramsay writes, 'few can be said to have made such a lasting impression on science . . . by his fundamental experiments on chemical combination and on heat'.[1] Black was trained at Glasgow under the great teacher William Cullen, who in 1744 established the medical school there on a sound basis and was notable for the importance he attached to chemistry as a liberal science, and also as the first to illustrate his lectures by clinical instruction in the hospital ward. The thesis by which Black made his name, *De Humore Acido a Cibis Orto, et Magnesia Alba*, was offered in 1754, when he was only twenty-six, for the degree of M.D. at Edinburgh.[2] At that time the phenomena of combustion were generally explained by the theory propounded by the German Stahl that all combustible substances contained a fire element, to which he gave the name of 'phlogiston'. By this

---

[1] *Life and Letters of Joseph Black*, 1918, p. 144.

[2] Black is said to have chosen his subject to expose the absurdity of Mrs. Joanna Stevens's quack remedy for the stone, composed of egg-shells, snails, soap, and other nastiness. Walpole procured a grant of £5,000 for Joanna for making known her remedy. Ibid., p. 22.

theory the phlogiston present in metal, for example, was, in the process of reducing the metal by fire into a calx or ash, expelled into the air. The difficulty of this theory, not seen at a time when the idea of quantitative chemistry had not emerged, is that the 'dephlogisticated' metal or calx, instead of losing weight, is actually heavier than the metal said to contain phlogiston. The chief importance of Black's thesis is that, though he did not actually abandon the theory of phlogiston at first, as he did later after hearing of Lavoisier's experiments continuing his own, he gave it the first death-blow by his insistence on the quantitative method and the use of the balance in all experiments. His main experiment was made in the conversion of chalk into lime by burning, resulting in the discovery that the loss in weight in the quicklime was nearly 60 per cent. Since the water condensed in the process was proved to be almost negligible, he concluded that the loss in weight must be due to the escape during combustion of the air fixed in the chalk. To this air or gas he gave the name of 'fixed air', later known as carbon-dioxide (CO_2), and in his lectures of 1757 he had already noted the characteristics of this gas in respiration, fermentation, and combustion.[1] When, some twenty years later, Lavoisier wrote to Black telling him of his own experiments on respiration, he added, with Gallic courtesy, 'il est bien juste que vous soyez un des premiers informés des progrès qui se font dans une carrière que vous avez ouverte, et dans laquelle nous nous regardons comme vos disciples'.[2] In his thesis Black had also shown that the effervescing effect of acids on limestone, carbonates, magnesia alba, and other mild alkalis was another indication of the release of 'fixed air' contained in those substances, thus providing, as was said, 'a ready way of assaying limestone or marl to ascertain its purity or its value to the husbandman in particular, who would employ it to improve his soil'. Later he conducted a series of delicate experiments to ascertain the relative times taken in raising the temperature of water and in thawing ice under a uniform heat, laying stress on the large quantity of heat absorbed in melting a solid or evaporating a liquid. From these experiments he evolved the conception of heat rendered latent or absorbed in the process of changing the physical state of a substance without rise of temperature, and contrasted it with

[1] See T. M. Lowry, *Historical Introduction to Chemistry*, 1915, p. 385, n.
[2] Adam Ferguson, *Minutes of Life . . . of Joseph Black*, 1801.

the specific heat required to raise the temperature of a unit mass of substance by one degree. He was always, too, alert to the practical applications of his discoveries. He advised the Linen Board to discourage the use of lime in bleaching owing to its caustic properties, and took a deep interest in Roebuck's sulphuric acid factory at Prestonpans. As a result of a paper by Cavendish on hydrogen gas he was perhaps the first to demonstrate, in his own house, the possibilities of aeronautics by a membrane filled with hydrogen, twelve years before the first balloon so filled was launched in Paris.[1] His discovery of the latent heat of steam enabled Watt, in whose experiments he took the deepest interest, to revolutionize the system of condensers. His closest friend in Edinburgh was James Hutton, also a chemist, who started a sal-ammoniac factory, but is better known as the geologist who originated the modern theory of the formation of the earth's crust, a theory which Black's own researches supported.

A notable development in this period is the establishment of factories for producing sulphuric acid, the first chemical product to be manufactured on a commercial basis. In the seventeenth century Glauber had prepared, from the reaction of sulphuric acid (oil of vitriol) on sea salt, a 'salt' named after him, the popularity of which as an aperient had created a demand from pharmacists for sulphuric acid. It was also much in use by Birmingham metal-refiners. But its production from a mixture of nitre (saltpetre) and sulphur, chemically treated, was a long and expensive process until Joshua Ward, a quack doctor,[2] with the assistance of John White, who probably contributed the scientific knowledge, established in 1736 a factory for its manufacture at Twickenham. His process involved the use of glass globes with a capacity of 40–50 gallons, which were expensive to make and liable to break; but even so he sold the acid per lb. at its previous price per oz. (viz. 1s. 6d. to 2s. 6d.). In 1746 John Roebuck,[3] M.D. of Edinburgh but more interested in chemistry and commercial ventures than in medicine, set up a factory at Birmingham, and, by using lead instead of glass containers, was able by 1767 to sell the acid for 4½d. a lb. In 1749 he had established a larger factory at Prestonpans, which soon became the principal factory in Great Britain. In 1799 the price was down to 2¼*d.* a lb., and by 1820 there were 23 factories in England alone. With this increased and cheaper production of sulphuric acid, new industrial uses for it were constantly being discovered—for bleaching, agricultural manures, &c. The chemist Liebig indeed declared that, 'We may judge with accuracy the commercial prosperity of a country from the amount of sulphuric acid it consumes.'[1]

In the science of botany England produced during this period one great pioneer, Stephen Hales, the author of *Vegetable Staticks* already alluded to,[2] a work which earned him the title of 'father of vegetable physiology'. Otherwise the English botanists were chiefly concerned with the useful business of collecting and propagating plants. Gerard's *Herbal,* as edited by Thomas Johnson in 1633, was still the principal vade-mecum of these enthusiastic plant-lovers, collectors, and gardeners, then, as now, abundant in this country. Among the best known of them were the two Sherards, James, famous for his garden at Eltham, and William, who endowed a chair of botany at Oxford. The first holder of this chair was John James Dillenius, a German by origin, who produced two notable works, the *Hortus Elthamensis* in 1732 and the *Historia Muscorum* in 1741. Dr. Richard Pulteney, a kinsman of Lord Bath, and a botanist of the same type, produced in 1790 *Historical and Biographical Sketches of the Progress of Botany in England.* Another famous botanist in his day was Sir Hans Sloane, who also collected butterflies, but he is chiefly remembered for his gift, as lord of the manor of Chelsea, to the Apothecaries of their Physic garden still flourishing on the banks of the Thames. One of the conditions of the gift was that the Society should proceed from it on an annual 'herborizing' expedition; and there were also five other such 'herborizing' expeditions for the apprentices of the Society. This garden induced many foreign botanists to come over to England, among them G. D. Ehret, a protégé of Linnaeus, and the illustrator of *Plantae Selectae,* 1750–73, and *Plantae et Papiliones Selectae,* 1748–59. It was also one of the attractions which brought the great Linnaeus to England in 1736, and in 1748 his pupil Peter Kalm, whose *Account*

[1] For this paragraph on sulphuric acid I am much indebted to Professor Hogben's *Inaugural Lecture* at Aberdeen, 1937, and to Mr. H. W. Dickinson's article on *History of Vitriol Making in England* (Newcomen Society, *Transactions,* xviii. 43–66) and for friendly hints they have given me. [Note of 1939.]

[2] See above, pp. 384–5.

of his Visit to England has many interesting botanical observations on the country; and they were both able to take away from it many specimens unprocurable elsewhere. But though Dillenius at Oxford came to recognize Linnaeus's importance, the great Swede was treated with scant attention by Sir Hans Sloane, then the great pundit; and it was not till about 1760 that the Linnaean system of nomenclature became generally adopted in England.[1]

From poor beginnings this age shows a remarkable advance in both the theory and practice of medicine and surgery. In Queen Anne's reign there had been little opportunity for medical training in Great Britain. It was not till 1705 that anatomy began to be taught systematically at Edinburgh, at Cambridge two years later, in 1718 at Glasgow, and at Oxford not till 1750. A chair of clinical medicine was established at Edinburgh in 1741, but at Oxford there was none until 1780.[2] The best medical instruction was still to be found abroad, under such teachers as Boerhave and Albinus at Leyden, and Albrecht von Haller, appointed by George II in 1736 to his new university at Göttingen. Many of the best-known practitioners, when George I came to the throne, had been trained abroad, Mead and Pringle at Leyden, Sloane at Paris and Montpellier, James Douglas at Rheims. Surgeons were still regarded as distinctly inferior to physicians, and were lumped with barbers until, in 1745, the Company of Barber Surgeons was dissolved and the surgeons given a company of their own.[3] But even so in 1757, much to the indignation of the profession, a majority of judges in the common pleas decided that 'a surgeon is an *inferior tradesman*' within the meaning of an act of William and Mary.[4]

---

[1] The best account of English botany at this time is in J. Reynolds Green, *History of Botany in United Kingdom*, 1914: see also, for Hales, J. V. Sachs, *History of Botany, 1530–1860*, trans. by H. E. F. Garnsey, Oxford, 1891; F. D. Drewitt, *Romance of the Apothecaries' Garden*, 1924, gives some interesting details.

[2] There was, indeed, a lectureship in anatomy established at Oxford in 1623, with a salary of £25; and some rather fitful work on the subject was done during the seventeenth and early eighteenth centuries, but nothing systematic till, in 1750, Dr. Lee founded a readership in the subject at Christ Church, and left £100 per annum to pay the reader, with £40 per annum for anatomical specimens and funds for building an anatomical school. See F. H. Garrison, *Introduction to History of Medicine* (1913), pp. 330–1; and R. T. Gunther, *Early Science in Oxford* (1925), iii. 87, 114–15.

[3] Smollett, in *Roderick Random*, gives an insight into the slight qualifications required for a surgeon in the navy.

[4] Campbell, *Lives of Chief Justices*, ii. 276.

The apothecaries, luckier than the surgeons, had broken away from the grocers and been incorporated in 1617: though without medical training, except in the composition of drugs, they were often called in to treat cases by those unable to afford the physicians' high fees. Quacks abounded and reaped a rich harvest. William Read, originally a tailor, professed to cure blindness, and had been oculist to Queen Anne and knighted, and he associated with Swift and his friends: the Chevalier Taylor, who also had a cure for blindness, Dr. Johnson described as 'an instance how far impudence could carry ignorance': Joshua Ward, besides being the first manufacturer of sulphuric acid,[1] amassed a fortune by his 'drop and pill' composed of antimony, and was patronized by Chesterfield, Horace Walpole, and George II, who gave him a room in Whitehall as a reward for reducing his dislocated thumb.[2] Even women such as Joanna Stevens with her cure for the stone and the bonesetter Mrs. Mapp (Crazy Sally) made fortunes from a gullible public. On the other hand, medical men have rarely enjoyed so high a position socially as at the beginning of George I's reign. Prominent among the friends of Pope and his aristocratic circle were the physicians Garth, Arbuthnot, Sloane, Mead, John Freind, and even the surgeons Cheselden and Douglas. 'I'll do what Mead and Cheselden advise', sang Pope and addressed an *Epistle* to Arbuthnot. Their fees were enormous for those days, Sloane, Mead, Radcliffe, and Fothergill each receiving some £5,000–6,000 per annum; and they were equally generous in their expenditure, often charging nothing to the poor, and spending their money royally, Radcliffe on his benefactions to Oxford, and, as Pope says,

Books for Mead and butterflies for Sloane.

Sloane, too, even received a baronetcy, then unheard of for a doctor. It is also worth noting that at the time of George I's accession at least eleven members of the medical profession were fellows of the Royal Society.

Few of Pope's doctor friends were eminent for any advance they made in their science. The only exception, perhaps, was William Cheselden, great as surgeon and anatomist and with a European reputation for his 'lateral operation for the stone',

[1] See above, p. 387.
[2] A statue by Agostini Carlini of this prosperous quack still holds a place of honour in the Hall of the Royal Society of Arts.

a new method which he could perform almost painlessly in 54 seconds, and also for his publications on human anatomy and the *Osteographia*, illustrated by himself. For he had great gifts as a designer and made the plans for the first Putney Bridge. But, apart from these fashionable practitioners, under the inspiration of such men as Hales and Black, Cullen and James Jurin, the friend of Newton and a notable physiologist, great advances were made in medical science and training. Already by 1720 Edinburgh was beginning to provide medical instruction to rival that of Leyden. In that year Alexander Monro *primus*, trained in London, Paris, and Leyden, was made professor of anatomy at the age of twenty-three and virtually founded the Edinburgh school, which, at first with the co-operation of such men as Cullen and Black, was carried on successively by himself, his son, and grandson, Alexander *secundus* and *tertius*, till 1846. Between 1720 and 1749 *primus's* students had increased from 57 to 182; and by 1790 no less than 12,800 medical students had been trained by himself and *secundus*.[1] Foremost among the pupils of the Glasgow medical school was William Hunter, who came up to London in 1741 to learn dissection from Douglas and midwifery from Smellie, the friend of Cullen and Smollett, and one of the first scientifically trained men to supersede the ignorant women hitherto practising the art. Then setting up for himself as a lecturer on surgical operations to navy surgeons, William Hunter sent for his brother John to learn dissection and help him with his practical class. Soon William left most of the lecturing to John, devoting himself to his practice in midwifery and to his great treatise on the *Human Gravid Uterus*. John was also learning surgery from Cheselden and the famous Percival Pott; and, as a staff surgeon between 1760 and 1762, at Belle Île and in Portugal, gained valuable experience in gunshot wounds. On his return he began his study of comparative anatomy with the help of his collection of animals at Earls Court. It is not indeed so much for his practical surgery, great as that was,[2] that he is memorable, as for his deep and minute studies in comparative anatomy, whereby surgery ceased to be regarded 'as a mere technical mode of treatment, and . . . [became] a branch of scientific

[1] Garrison, pp. 259–60.
[2] His most notable surgical advance, made in 1786, was in tying the artery *above* an aneurism, whereby thousands of limbs and lives are said to have been saved.

medicine, firmly grounded in physiology and pathology'.[1] His four great books on *Human Teeth*, on *Venereal Disease*, on *Animal Economy*, and on *Gunshot Wounds*, his famous pupils such as Astley Cooper, Abernethy, and Jenner, and his great collection of anatomical specimens now at the College of Surgeons serve as a record of his eminence and of the great advance made by medical science largely through him.

In other ways besides medical education the period was progressive. When Lady Mary Wortley Montagu returned from Constantinople in 1718 a convinced believer in inoculation for smallpox, she not only had her own children inoculated, but persuaded the royal family and some of the leading doctors of its efficacy against a disease till then almost endemic in England. It was an age, too, that witnessed a notable increase in hospitals, especially in London. In 1714 St. Bartholomew's and St. Thomas's were the only two hospitals there: by 1760 Guy's, St. George's, and the Wesminster, London, and Middlesex hospitals had been opened, besides three lying-in hospitals and one for smallpox. In the provinces and Scotland and Ireland there appears to have been only one hospital before 1714, at York; by 1760 there were twenty. This multiplication of hospitals was especially valuable for the increasing clinical instruction of practitioners, though for patients the sanitation in most of them left much to be desired. For the unfortunate insane Bedlam, founded in 1547, was a horror and a show place, but a more kindly system was adopted in the hospital of St. Luke's, opened in 1751.[2]

Among those most in need of more efficient medical and sanitary precautions were the soldiers and sailors, especially the latter, who, owing to their cramped quarters and abominable food, were a prey to scurvy and other diseases. At sea, during the wars of 1739–48, more men died of scurvy than in battle, and 75 per cent. of Anson's crews perished during his famous circumnavigation of the world. Two Scotsmen, John Pringle, a student at Leyden and later a physician and professor of pneumatics at Edinburgh, and James Lind almost simultaneously began studying the ailments of soldiers and sailors respec-

---

[1] Garrison, p. 274.
[2] See Garrison, pp. 331–2; Defoe, *Tour*, i. 367–72. Garrison's remark that hospital nursing and sanitation had sunk 'to the lowest level in the history of medicine' is probably exaggerated.

tively. Lind saw the worst of naval conditions when serving as a surgeon between 1739 and 1746 in the Channel, the Mediterranean, the West Indies, and off the Coast of Guinea; and in 1754 he published his *Treatise on the Scurvy*, suggesting green food, fresh fruit, and lemon juice as effective preventives; but it was not till 1795 that the admiralty ordered rations of lemon juice to be served at sea.[1] Later he published an *Essay . . . [for] preserving the Health of Seamen*, full of wise suggestions, some of which he was able to carry out as physician to the Haslar Hospital from 1758. Pringle's work was even more remarkable. From 1742 to 1748 he was attached to Stair's and Cumberland's armies in Germany, Flanders, and at Culloden, where he did much to improve the sanitary condition of field hospitals and the care of the wounded. In his *Observations on the Diseases of the Army*, published in 1752, he expounded modern views on the sanitation and ventilation of hospitals and the results of his experiments on septic and antiseptic substances in relation to wounds, views that gave him a European reputation. To him also we owe, from a suggestion he made to Stair and Noailles, the opposing generals in Germany, the permanent neutrality of hospitals in war.[2]

Scholarship and historical research were especially vigorous, as we have seen,[3] in the last part of the seventeenth century: in fact the seventy years after 1660 have been called the 'golden age of English medieval scholarship'; and Bentley is now recognized as one of the giants of classical scholarship. But with the eighteenth century came a change. In classical scholarship between 1714 and 1760 hardly a name deserves remembrance. Bentley indeed still survived well into the reign of George II, but was now mainly absorbed in his quarrels with the fellows of Trinity and the bishop of Ely. Middleton's *Life of Cicero*, in two volumes, is to a large extent plagiarized from Bellenden and is chiefly remembered by a scornful distich in the *Dunciad*;

[1] It is characteristic of Pitt's comprehensive care for details that he insisted on the admiralty providing fishing seynes 'to catch fish for the refreshment of the men' and also spruce beer, as an antiscorbutic, on all the ships he sent to America during the Seven Years War. He may not have heard of Lind, but probably had talked to Pringle, as both were fellows of the Royal Society. See *Chatham*, i. 297.

[2] Pringle was elected a fellow of the Royal Society on his return from Flanders in 1745 and became its president in 1772; his name is one of those recorded on the front of the new University College Hospital buildings.

[3] See vol. x in this series, pp. 377–85 (2nd edn.).

and Wood's learned *Essay on Homer* lives only from a reference
to Carteret in the preface. Not that a fair acquaintance with
the classics was at a discount in polite society. In the house of
commons Latin tags could be quoted and allusions understood:
and in the lords Carteret, a real scholar as Swift testified, could
make effective points with a phrase from Tacitus or an example
from Scipio's strategic methods; and on his death-bed could
roll out part of Sarpedon's great speech in the twelfth Iliad.

On the other hand antiquarianism was much in the mode.
At its best manifested in the scholarly study of relics of the past
and editions of old records and chronicles, but too often less
usefully in haphazard collections of unconnected facts and fantastic theories, it had been a favourite pastime in England since
Elizabeth's day. In that reign a Society of Antiquaries had been
formed with Stowe, Cotton, Raleigh among its members, but
had been suppressed by James I, who 'misliked' it as likely to
meddle with affairs of state and religion. Nevertheless in the
seventeenth century Selden, Ashmole, Wood, and Rymer had
carried on its tradition, and the Society was revived in 1718,
and later obtained a charter from George II.

The eighteenth century is indeed notable for the number of
antiquarians, a few of the best, but most of the dilettante type.
The scholars who in the seventeenth century did such great
work in reviving the knowledge of Anglo-Saxon and medieval
documents were largely inspired by the desire to find confirmation for their own views or condemnation for their opponents'
in the legal, constitutional, and doctrinal views of Anglo-Saxon
or Norman writers and lawgivers. In the following century
such controversies were less acute; and the taste of the age is
reflected in Bolingbroke's dictum that 'to be entirely ignorant
about the ages that precede this era would be shameful. Nay
some indulgence may be had to a temperate curiosity in the
review of them. But to be learned about them is a ridiculous
affectation in any man who means to be useful to the present
age.'[1] Some, indeed, of the great medievalist scholars such as
Wanley, Madox, Bishops Gibson and Tanner still survived,
but most of their work in that line had already been published.
The only three survivors who produced important work were
Francis Wise, the editor of Asser's *Annals of Alfred* (1722),
David Wilkins, whose great *Concilia* was published in 1737, and

[1] Bolingbroke, *Letters on History*, vi.

Thomas Hearne, the ferocious non-juror, whose 145 manuscript volumes of gossiping diaries illuminate the seamy side of Oxford politics and jealousies. Besides these entertaining diaries Hearne's chief services to learning were his publication of Leland's *Itinerary* and *Collectanea* and his editions of the English chroniclers, unique until the Rolls series was begun in the last century, and still in some cases the only editions in print. J. Horsly, A. Gordon, and F. Drake made useful antiquarian researches.[1] William Stukeley, an indefatigable traveller in search of 'the Antiquities and remarkable Curiosities in Nature and Art', did good service in calling attention to the Roman Wall, Stonehenge, and Avebury; but being, as his friend Warburton said, a strange compound of 'simplicity, drollery, absurdity, ingenuity, superstition, and antiquarianism', he was often wrong in his deductions and made fantastic errors in his readings of medals, coins, inscriptions, and plans of Roman camps. A host of other antiquarians, too numerous to specify, indulged in these 'archaeological rides', which often became agreeable jaunts, such as those of the two cronies, Samuel Gale and Andrew Ducarel, which always concluded at a comfortable inn, where Ducarel wrote up his notes, while Gale placidly smoked his pipe.[2]

In 1728 Ephraim Chambers published his *Cyclopaedia or Universal Dictionary of Arts and Sciences* in 2 volumes, one of the first attempts in English at a comprehensive survey of human knowledge for the general public. Later, in his *Considerations*, he planned a radical revision, but abandoned this in 1738 with the issue of his second edition. The *Cyclopaedia*, which reached a fifth edition by 1746, contains clear, concise articles illustrated by excellent plates on such subjects as anatomy, architecture, fortifications, &c. On the strength of this work Chambers was made an F.R.S.; Johnson expressed his debt to the *Considerations* in forming his style; and a French translation of the *Cyclopaedia* is said to have suggested to d'Alembert and Diderot their great *Encyclopédie*. Other collectors of the most miscellaneous information were James Granger, whose name gave a new

[1] See vol. i of this series, pp. 466–7, 474.
[2] Ducarel once nearly 'talked Horace Walpole to death', and perhaps for this reason, or because his *Historic Doubts on Richard III* had been attacked with 'old Women's logic' by the Society of Antiquaries, Walpole resigned his membership, 'leaving them in peace' to discuss such things as 'Whittington and his Cat'. *Letters*, 7 Feb. 1762, 11 June 1771, 8 Jan. 1773.

verb to the language, John Anstis, Garter King, who specialized in heraldic and antiquarian lore,[1] and those marvels of industry in amassing out-of-the-way and interesting but undigested facts, the Rev. William Cole, the 'temperately curious' friend of Horace Walpole,[2] and that delightful, indefatigable searcher after recondite allusions and literary curiosities, William Oldys, a man after Isaac Disraeli's own heart, who wrote the delicious verses on the

> Busy, curious, thirsty fly,

was rescued from the Fleet prison by the duke of Norfolk to become Norroy king at arms, and was so drunk with beer, his favourite tipple, at the Princess Caroline's funeral that her coronet, which he was carrying on a cushion, was titubating as much as himself.[3]

Two great institutions served during this and later periods to establish continuity in science and learning and to provide material for further investigation. The first was the Royal Society, which, especially under Newton's presidency, kept well before it the objects for which it was founded. Here all the chief discoveries and theories in science were put forward and discussed, and to its fellowship were elected not only those who advanced pure science, but also, for want of a British or Royal Academy at the time, those such as the two Lords Oxford, Elihu Yale, Lord Burlington, Thornhill and Reynolds, Stukeley, Archbishop King, and Samuel Clarke who were distinguished in art, scholarship, or theology. Some no doubt were elected for purely social or political reasons, such as Newcastle, Lyttelton, Chesterfield, Horace Walpole, Pitt, and even Wilkes. On the other hand, it was a great merit of the Society that it kept abreast of foreign learning and research by electing all the great foreigners such as Maupertuis, Montesquieu, Voltaire, Boerhave, Buffon, Linnaeus, Réaumur, and many others.

The British Museum, even more important for the advance-

[1] It was to his son, also Garter King, that Chesterfield said, 'You foolish man, you don't know your own foolish business'.
[2] The letters exchanged between Cole and Horace Walpole have been brought together in the first two volumes of Mr. W. S. Lewis's edition of the Walpole correspondence. [Note of 1939.]
[3] A belated instance of the *olla podrida* published by some of these collectors of insignificant facts occurs in a magnificent folio (*penes me*) on the *Museum Britannicum*, 1791, where the index contains this item: 'Queen, Progression of the Chicken in a Hen's Egg, painted by the Author, in the possession of Our Most Gracious.'

ment of learning, was founded in this period. In 1753 Sir Hans Sloane left to the nation his library of 50,000 books and 3,516 manuscripts together with his collection of curiosities, the whole said to have cost him £50,000, for a payment of £20,000 to his heirs. In the same year the widow of the second Lord Oxford offered to the government for £10,000 all that was left of the magnificent library formed by her husband and the first lord. She had already, in 1742, sold the 50,000 printed books, 350,000 pamphlets, and 41,000 prints,[1] but fortunately not before Oldys had compiled the *Harleian Miscellany* with its preface by Dr. Johnson; but there still remained for the nation 7,639 volumes of manuscripts and 14,236 original Rolls. In 1753 Pelham, then first lord of the treasury and an enlightened patron of learning,[2] welcomed these offers and raised by a lottery the amount required for the purchase of these collections as well as of Montagu House wherein to house them. To this nucleus was added the great Cottonian Library formed by Sir Robert Cotton in the seventeenth century and already purchased by the nation for £4,500 in 1707. Unfortunately Ashburnham House, where it was stored, was burned in 1731, and with it some 200 of the 958 priceless manuscripts were destroyed either entirely or partially.[3] In 1757 George II presented 10,000 volumes and 1,800 manuscripts collected by the kings of England, and above all gave the British Museum the inestimable privilege of obtaining a free copy of every book entered at Stationers' Hall.[4] This great collection of books, curiosities, works of art, and scientific specimens thus became the nucleus of that immeasurably great collection which now illustrates the phenomena of the universe and the activities of man more completely perhaps than any other single institution in the world.[5]

[1] For all this she obtained only £13,000, less than the cost of the bindings.

[2] In the previous year Pelham had already conferred a great boon on historians and constitutional lawyers by granting £5,000 to Nicholas Hardinge, late clerk to the house of commons, for printing the journals of the house. See Coxe, *Pelham*, ii. 221.

[3] All but two of the existing manuscripts of the Anglo-Saxon Chronicle come from the Cottonian Library: three charred leaves of another still remain, but happily this manuscript had previously been printed by Wheloc. After the fire, till its transference to Montagu House, the Cottonian collection was housed in the dormitory of Westminster school.

[4] The Bodleian had already been granted this privilege. See vol. ix in this series. p. 353 (2nd edn.).

[5] Besides those already mentioned, I am deeply indebted for help and criticism in this chapter to Professor Whittaker, Mr. Kenneth Swan, K.C., Dr. Charles Dorée, and especially the late Professor Barger. [Note of 1939.]

XV

THE ARTS[1]

SINCE the Conquest England has never failed in maintaining a native and very noble architecture of her own, exemplified first in the great religious edifices of the middle ages and, after the Reformation, by the stately or homely houses of the Elizabethan and Jacobean periods. Our music, too, though never attaining the gaunt magnificence of a Bach, the sheer beauty of a Mozart, or Beethoven's sublimity, has always, it may be claimed, from the remote times when Theodore of Tarsus first brought church music to Northumbria, possessed a fresh and individual beauty of its own. It has not been the same with the arts of painting and sculpture. In the middle ages, indeed, our artists were famous throughout Europe for the beauty of their illuminations and illustrations to manuscripts and for their mural decorations. Our sculptors, mostly anonymous, produced such glorious work in our cathedrals and churches as the large figure-work at Wells and Lincoln, a host of noble tombs such as that of the Black Prince at Canterbury, William Torel's Henry III and Eleanor in the fourteenth century, or William Austen's Beauchamp at Warwick in the fifteenth, besides a wealth of small sculptures in stone and the wood-carving of misericords. But after that the line of our English sculptors and artists seems to wear very thin. Torrigiano had to be brought from Italy by Henry VII to decorate his chapel at Westminster, and 'Charles I', almost the only really noble statue in the streets of London,[2] was the work of a passing Frenchman, Le Sueur. There are, indeed, still many fine sepulchral monuments of the seventeenth century to be found in the length and breadth of the land, but very few of these are by purely English sculptors, being mostly the products of a notable school founded at Southwark by a Rotterdam family of Jannsens, later Englished into Johnson. In painting, between the fifteenth and eighteenth

---

[1] For suggestions and criticisms on this chapter I am especially grateful to Mr. D. S. McColl. [Note of 1939.]

[2] 'James II' in Roman armour, another fine statue, has been moved from Whitehall and is now in Trafalgar Square.

centuries, the only truly English school of which we can boast was that of our miniature painters. There we were supreme, notably in the case of that 'prince of limners', Samuel Cooper, employed by both Oliver Cromwell and Charles II. Two other painters, Sir Nathaniel Bacon and William Dobson, notable for his 'Endymion Porter' and 'Old Stone and his Son', were good, but hardly of European consequence. All our best-known portraits of that period are the work of foreigners, Holbein, Antonio Moro, Vandyck, and Lely, or their English imitators.

At the beginning of the Hanoverian era these arts still showed the same characteristics. Architecture was strong, with Inigo Jones still a living memory to some of his contemporaries; while the great Sir Christopher was still working and survived George I's accession by nine years, and Vanbrugh, 'a poet as well as an architect', as Reynolds was careful to remind his students, lived to within a year of George II's reign: and these three great men had pupils living to carry on their traditions. In music the seventeenth century had been made glorious by Lawes, Blow, Orlando Gibbons, Byrd, and, the greatest of all, Purcell; and Mr. Pepys bears witness to the widespread musical taste that later encouraged Handel to settle here for life in 1712. But in painting we were barren indeed. The only native pictures to find appreciation or a ready sale were formal portraits; for, as Hogarth sourly observed to Bute many years later, it is impossible for us to vie 'with . . . Italian and Gothic theatres of art. . . . We are a commercial people, and can purchase their curiosities. . . . In England vanity is united with (selfishness). Portrait painting therefore ever has and ever will succeed better in this country than in any other.'[1] The German, Godfrey Kneller, soon to become a baronet and painter to the king, had inherited the gradually diminishing mantle handed down from Vandyck through Lely, and was the pontiff of this fashionable portraiture, which aimed at giving the sitters the looks they were supposed to like rather than those they possessed. He was acclaimed by patrons and pupils as the last word in British portrait-painting, only fitting, so it seemed, for an artist who had painted ten reigning sovereigns and all the most important people of his day. J. Ellys, one of his pupils, when he first saw Reynolds's portraits, criticized them as not

[1] Quoted in R. and S. Redgrave, *A Century of Painters of the English School*, 2 vols., 1866, i. 5.

enough like Kneller's—for 'Shakespeare in poetry, Kneller in painting, damme!'—while Pope's epitaph on him declared that

> Living, great Nature fear'd he might outvie
> Her works; and dying, fears herself might die.

None the less, in spite of such exaggerated praise and of much bad and perfunctory work to his discredit, he was in many ways serviceable to English painting, and at his best reached a high level as an artist. In some of his portraits, such as those of Matthew Prior at Cambridge and his admirals at Greenwich, he showed himself 'a great and original executant'. Moreover, he was a generous helper of young artists, not least by founding the first academy for their training in England.[1]

After his death in 1723 his pupils, Richardson and Jervas, succeeded to his pontificate and his conceit, illustrated by Jervas's complacent remark after finishing a copy of Titian: 'Poor little Tit! how he would stare!', and by Prior's advice to Richardson, then contemplating a History of Art, to entitle it 'The History of Myself and My Son Jonathan with a word or two about Raphael and Michael Angelo by the way'. But, barring his overweening conceit, Richardson was for heads not a bad artist; Horace Walpole calls him 'one of the best English painters of a head that had appeared in this country . . . yet . . . he drew nothing well below the head'.[2] For in those days most of the fashionable portrait-painters were too busy or incapable to paint anything but the faces, leaving hands, shoulders, drapery, and background either to specialists in those provinces or to one 'drapery man', chief of whom was Vanaken, paid 800 guineas a year by two rival painters to work exclusively for them. Artists had hardly any proper means of training in those days, unless it were to be apprenticed to some eminent artist, but that meant little but acquiring the 'mystery' of preparing canvases and mixing paints or possibly painting in the drapery for the artist's portraits. Thus Richardson learned his art from Kneller and in turn taught Hudson, who was chiefly notable for having had Reynolds as his apprentice when he first came up from Devonshire.

---

[1] See Collins Baker, *British Painting*, 1933, pp. 57–58, and 62.
[2] *Anecdotes of Painting*, iv. 15.

Sculpture was hardly in better case: no Englishman at the time claimed the title of sculptor. What sculptures were needed for tombs or monuments of the living were generally designed by architects such as Wren, Gibbs, or Kent, and left to stone-masons for the actual hewing. Nor, to Horace Walpole's eye, did the reign of the first Hanoverian show much promise of improvement. 'No reign,' he said of it, 'since the arts have been in any esteem, produced fewer works that will deserve the attention of posterity.'

But this is unjust, for much of the preparation and some even of the works which were to make our period one of the most prolific in the development of the three sister arts of painting, sculpture, and architecture in this country were already being accomplished by the end of George I's reign. The full flower was not apparent till the beginning of George III's reign, but it owed its glory hardly less to the beginning in George I's time than to the progress in George II's. Sir James Thornhill, a con-temporary of Kneller and father-in-law of Hogarth, is notable not only for some good portraits, but chiefly for his decorations at Greenwich, on the dome of St. Paul's, and in many of the great houses such as Blenheim.[1] But how wonderful was the change that had come about by 1760 will be evident when we remember that by that time Hogarth had all but run his course; Gainsborough and Reynolds had produced some of their most glorious pictures; Romney was painting heads at two guineas each in the north of England; Copley was sending over his Boston portraits to London. In these years, too, the great school of English landscape painters was beginning with Samuel Scott, Stubbs, Wootton, Richard Wilson, Gainsborough himself, Paul Sandby, and Alexander Cozens, leading up through J. R. Cozens and the masterly Crome to the great quartet Cotman, Girtin, Constable, and Turner who, by the beginning of the nineteenth century, were making English landscape artists the dominant school in Europe. In sculpture the Flemings, Scheemakers and Rysbrack, and the Frenchman Roubiliac had settled here, the first two in George I's reign, Roubiliac early in George II's, and had so completely identi-fied themselves with English conditions that they formed the

---

[1] Walpole, *Anecdotes*, iv. 21, states that Thornhill received only 40s. per square yard for his work on the cupola of St. Paul's; but Collins Baker, l.c., p. 66, states that the total sum he received for it was no less than £19,375.

English taste for statuary such as those of Newton and Daniel Lock at Trinity, Cambridge, and of Swift at Trinity College, Dublin, hewing as well as desigining their own works and living to see such respectable English followers as Joseph Wilton, Thomas Banks, and John Bacon. For the first seven years of George I's reign, too, Grinling Gibbons was still carrying on his glorious craft as a statuary, and still more as a wood-carver and artist in monumental script. After his death his large band of pupils and assistants carried on his tradition, the most notable being Francis Bird, sculptor of the Busby monument in Westminster Abbey, besides many others less known for their work in remote country churches.[1] In architecture, besides Vanbrugh, the relic of an older generation, Hawksmoor had carried on Wren's tradition, James Gibbs had added new glories to Oxford and Cambridge, Burlington had introduced the Palladian style, while with the Woods, father and son, who had used Bath's unique natural position for one of the most splendid examples of town-planning, and the Adam brothers, already beginning their work, a new form of domestic architecture was being developed, exquisitely fitted to the requirements of a more prosperous and exacting middle class, both in the growing towns and in the country, no less than to the more luxurious demands of a rich aristocracy.

What were the reasons for this sudden birth of a genuine English school of painting and sculpture, and the undiminished vigour of our native architecture? The political and social condition of England no doubt largely accounts for these phenomena. The victories of Queen Anne's reign, after a century of unrest and dissension at home and weakness abroad, had awakened the pride of Englishmen in themselves and stimulated the expression of this pride not only in literature, but also in the arts. The prosperity that resulted from security at home and from Walpole's peaceful development of the country's resources and foreign trade had perhaps even more to do with the particular forms this manifestation took. For with all its splendour there was little evidence during this period, except in the works of Hogarth, the greatest artist of them all, of that divine discontent, of that search for the ideal which characterize

---

[1] In Okehampton church, for example, the panel with the royal arms and several beautiful monuments and mural inscriptions are by one of these pupils, Michael Chuke (1679–1742), who also did work at Stowe.

the greatest art and the greatest literature and are generally incompatible with too great comfort. The great nobles, the country gentry, and the prosperous merchants, who formed the Venetian oligarchy controlling most of the power and wealth, called in artists, as had done their predecessors at Venice, to represent their features on canvas or in stone, to build and adorn great houses and palaces worthy of their magnificence; we hear, for example, of Sir Robert Walpole spending £100,000 on his collection of pictures, typical of the vast sums spent by those even better endowed with wealth. And to some extent their example was followed by the comfortable middle classes. Taste, too, was being developed by foreign travel, more easy than during the troubled times at home and abroad of the preceding century. During the comparative peace from 1713 to 1739 it became the fashion for young men of family to go abroad, especially to France and Italy, and, armed with the painter Richardson's textbooks on *The Theory of Painting* (1715), or *Criticism* (1719), and his guide-book to foreign art treasures (1722), to acquire some standards of taste. Some of them also published accounts of their travels illustrated by the sketches of 'topographic' artists they had taken in their train, and helped thereby to develop the art of some of our early landscape painters such as Richard Wilson and, later, J. R. Cozens. Nor did the leisurely wars of 1739 to 1748, or even the more bitterly contested Seven Years war, seriously interfere with this practice. Sometimes, it is true, difficulties might arise, such as Hogarth's arrest at Calais in 1748, or the engraver Major's incarceration in the Bastille in 1746; but such difficulties were soon adjusted, for governments in those days were not severe on the non-combatants of even an enemy nation.

The most notable of those travellers was Pope's friend, Lord Burlington, who as a lad at the beginning of George I's reign made a long sojourn in Italy, where he became so enamoured of Palladian architecture that on his return to England he formed a school of young architects to design and carry out buildings in that style. Though he got credit at the time for himself designing and carrying out some of these, notably Burlington House, his own villa at Chiswick, and the dormitory at Westminster school, he does not appear to have done much more than suggest the general ideas and leave the work to be carried out by such protégés as Kent, Colin Campbell, Isaac

Ware, and Flitcroft.[1] Later, after the rediscovery of Hercu-
laneum in 1719 and of Pompeii in 1748, connoisseurs were
attracted by more purely classical art: in 1749 Lord Charlemont
travelled to Greece as well as to Italy, and in Italy made the
acquaintance of Piranesi who dedicated his engravings to
him: shortly afterwards James (Athenian) Stuart extended his
archaeological and artistic researches beyond Greece to Asia
Minor. Horace Walpole and many other art-loving Englishmen
were almost as much at home in Paris as in London. Besides the
patrons, the artists either scraped means for themselves or were
helped by some of these patrons to study the great masters in
Italy. In fact, the Dilettanti Society, founded in 1734 by some
fifty peers or peers' sons who had been on the Grand Tour,
made it one of their objects to help promising artists to travel
abroad. The Scottish artist Allan Ramsay[2] went to Italy for
two years in 1736, Stubbs in 1754; Richard Wilson's journey
thither in 1749 proved the turning-point in his career, for at
Venice he was persuaded by Zuccarelli to give up portraits and
devote himself to landscape; Reynolds's memorable three years,
1750–2, in Italy were facilitated for him by his Devonshire
friend Commodore Keppel. Two of the greatest artists of the
period, however, Hogarth and Gainsborough, were almost the
exception in never having gone abroad to study in their youth;
but as Reynolds said of the latter—and the judgement is equally
applicable to Hogarth:

the style and department of art which Gainsborough chose, and
in which he so much excelled, did not require that he should go out
of his own country for the objects of his study; they were everywhere
about him; he found them in the streets, and in the fields. . . . In such
subjects . . . the want [of the study of the great masters] is supplied,
and more than supplied, by natural sagacity, and a minute observation of particular nature.[3]

Apart from such opportunities for studying the great foreign
masters and the perfunctory apprenticeship to popular painters,
already described, the means of instruction available for young

[1] See Reginald Blomfield, *History of Renaissance Architecture in England*, 1897, ii.
223 ff., and H. M. Colvin, *Biographical Dictionary*, pp. 86–88.
[2] The room devoted entirely to Allan Ramsay's paintings in the 1939 Exhibition
of Scottish Art at Burlington House was a revelation to many of this artist's great
charm.
[3] Sir Joshua Reynolds, *Discourses*, xiv.

artists were meagre. It is true that as early as 1711 Kneller had
founded an Academy of Art, succeeded by the better-known
New Academy in St. Martin's Lane chiefly associated with
Hogarth who remodelled it in 1735 and also portrayed it. But
those academies only supplied to the subscribers casts and nude
models, at first male and later, in spite of the prudes, female
also. There was no attempt to provide formal instruction in
drawing or painting, perhaps for the reason given by Hogarth's
friend Rouquet, who declared that this want of guidance was
'admirably adapted to the genius of the English; . . . each is his
own master, there is no dependence; . . . [for] every true-born
Englishman is a sworn enemy to all such subordination, except
he finds it strongly to his interest'.[1] They served, however, a useful
purpose, apart from material for study, in bringing together
young and more experienced artists, who no doubt compared
notes and criticized one another. At any rate, Reynolds, on his
return from Italy, and Gainsborough, when he came up to
London from Sudbury at the age of fourteen, were glad enough
to use the St. Martin's Lane Academy for working at models.
Again, since there was no public exhibition of pictures, old or
new, it was difficult for young artists to study the artistic
treasures already in the country or to make their own efforts
known to discerning patrons. Visitors were sometimes admitted
to the great private galleries, but the vails expected by the
lackeys who showed visitors round made entry prohibitive
except for the well-to-do, and even at public auctions of pictures,
intended for rich connoisseurs, the down-at-heel artists were
not admitted. A few public-spirited collectors, indeed, such as
Dr. Mead, Dr. Sloane, and Thomas Hollis, welcomed all who
wished to view their pictures and busts, and were generous
patrons to young artists of merit: and a few tavern-keepers, as is
not uncommon in Paris today, found it to their advantage to
allow artists to exhibit their wares for sale on their premises.

There was, indeed, no lack of purchasers during this period;
but their custom was apt to go to the very limited number of
fashionable portrait-painters for flattering likeness of their
features, to a few well-known foreign artists, and to the dealers
in old masters or classical sculpture, genuine or faked. Unfortunately the patrons were not always good judges of the old
masters they bought, as is illustrated by the story told of Hogarth

[1] Quoted in Redgrave, i. 66.

and Benjamin Wilson taking in 'the greatest or top virtuosi in London' by fictitious Rembrandt etchings of Wilson's fabrication; and it may be suspected that the busts Sir Robert Walpole ordered 'by the dozen' to adorn his new palace at Houghton were not all of the best quality. Neither George I nor George II, whose patronage of art was treated with more respect than that of their royal successors, was always happy in his choice of painters, such as Jervas, and William Kent, after Kneller successively appointed principal painter to his majesty, and of others rewarded in one case by the office of keeper of the royal beasts at the Tower, in another by that of painter to the board of ordnance, which in war-time brought him the handsome income of £4,000. It was Kent the royal painter who ignominiously hustled Hogarth out of the Chapel Royal when he had come to sketch a royal wedding, an incongruous subject which might, however, have resulted in a picture as charming and delightfully humorous as Turner's two sketches of court ceremonial when he accompanied George IV to Edinburgh. Hogarth also came into trouble with George II in person by venturing to burlesque his Guards in the *March to Finchley*. 'Take his trumpery out of my sight' was the angry monarch's verdict on it. On the other hand, to judge from Vertue's account of him, Frederick, prince of Wales, like his mother Queen Caroline, was a discerning critic of the many valuable but almost forgotten pictures in the royal palaces. This growing taste for pictures induced large numbers of foreign artists to cross the Channel and compete for the connoisseurs' favours. Watteau came for a short time about 1720; Canaletto was in England off and on between 1746 and 1755, and painted for ducal and other patrons those pictures of Westminster and London, the Thames and country seats, memorable not only for their beauty but as monuments of a vanished past: indeed his style was so popular that he had to compete against English forgeries of his own pictures. Other foreign visitors were the Swede Michael Dahl, the Frenchmen Goupy, who taught George III as a boy to draw, Gravelot the engraver, and Jean Baptist Vanloo, besides the Italians Cipriani, Zuccarelli, and Casali, and the German enameller Zincke. This invasion was all to the good for English art, in introducing new methods and new ideas; and there soon grew up a painters' quarter about Soho and Covent Garden, where artists forgathered to discuss their art among themselves or with such neighbours as Dr. Johnson, Garrick, Burke, and Goldsmith. There they found an escape from the stodgy atmosphere of 'Kneller in art, damme', and welcomed new theories or experiments in undreamed of fields. Disquisitions on the painter's art began to appear which bettered Richardson's crude *Theory of Painting* of 1715. Vertue the engraver, who died in 1756, had during a long career compiled notes on the lives and criticisms on the work of all his artist contemporaries which Horace Walpole used as a basis for his *Anecdotes of Painting*, published 1762–71. In 1748 the *Art of Painting* appeared anonymously, with information about painters' tools and materials and a list of some sixty 'eminent masters' then living, which shows some discernment by including Gainsborough and Reynolds, then aged only 21 and 25 respectively. Five years later Hogarth himself followed with his *Analysis of Beauty*, which, in spite of the forced attempts to relate all beauty in art to his mysterious 'waving line of beauty', contains, as one would expect, many robust and suggestive observations, such as those on Wren's architecture, the need for anatomical study, the heresy that colours improve with age. Allan Ramsay, under the name of *Investigator*, controverted his theories; and in 1757 Burke stimulated further thought on the objects of art by his essay *On the Sublime and Beautiful*, leading the way to Reynolds's great series of *Discourses*, which, though not begun till 1769, are an expression of what Reynolds and his friends had been learning or discussing on the principles of art and training of art students during this prolific period.

Long before George II's death the great need felt by artists was for a real academy of arts on the continental model, which would have the twofold function of giving instruction to art students and holding annual exhibitions for the display of new pictures and works of art, besides constituting a meeting-place for artists to discuss their own interests. The last object had been partially attained by Vandyck's Society of the Virtuosi of St. Luke, the members of which met periodically to dine at a tavern—with a strict rule against cursing and swearing—and to raffle for pictures; but this club of artists appears to have come to an end about 1744. The Society for the Encouragement of Arts, Manufacture, and Commerce, founded in 1754, though devoting most of its energies and income to fostering mechanical inventions, offered annual premiums for competitions by young artists, and also exhibited their productions. But the most important exhibition of contemporary art derived its origin from the accident of Hogarth in 1740 presenting to the Foundling Hospital his portrait of its founder, Captain Coram. Other artists, Hayman, Joseph Highmore, Edward Haytley, Richard Wilson, and later Gainsborough followed his example by presenting pictures of their own to adorn the court room of that institution;[1] and the public began to flock thither to see the pictures. This only whetted the appetite of artists and public for more comprehensive exhibitions. Attempts were made by the Dilettanti Society, representing the patrons of art and the principal artists, who met at an annual dinner in the Foundling Hospital—under the presidency of John Wilkes, of all people, as treasurer of the hospital—to arrive at some agreement for an annual display of pictures by living artists. These negotiations fell through, since the patrons wanted to manage the show entirely and even choose the pictures. But finally the artists, in the last year of George II, persuaded the Society of Arts to hold an exhibition at their rooms in the Strand, to which pictures were sent by Cosway, Hayman, Richard Wilson, and Paul Sandby, several busts by Roubiliac and four portraits by Reynolds, while the need for such an exhibition was further testified by an attendance of 6,582 of the general public. In succeeding years some differences between the artists and the Society of Arts led to two rival exhibitions until finally in 1768 the Royal Academy of Arts was instituted under the patronage of George III to promote annual exhibitions of pictures, to give the most eminent artists a definite status, and to provide for the systematic instruction of art students, at whose prize-givings the first president, Sir Joshua Reynolds, gave his fifteen memorable *Discourses* between 1769 and 1790.

In the list of the first forty R.A.s the names of only three sculptors are to be found, Wilton, Carlini, and Nollekens. By 1773, when this list had been completed, the three most illustrious sculptors of George I's and George II's reigns, Roubiliac, Rysbrack, and Scheemakers, were dead. They had done much to revivify English sculpture, not least, perhaps, by their example

---

[1] When the Foundlings migrated to Berkhampstead in 1926, and the old Hospital was demolished, the wall panels, pictures, and the ceiling by Wilton of the old court room were carefully preserved, and are now to be seen in all their original splendour in the court room of the new offices in Brunswick Square. [Note of 1939.]

of hewing out their own designs, instead of leaving that part of their craft to stone-masons. Of the three Roubiliac is beyond dispute the greatest. Unhampered as a rule by the tradition of absurd classical costumes to indicate warriors or statesmen,[1] he concentrated on a keen observation of the individual characteristics he had to portray. He was not content, for example, with the likeness in the great statue of Newton until he had taken note of the philosopher's death-mask. It is true that in some of his most ambitious monuments, such as those of the duchess of Montagu at Warkton and of Lady Elizabeth Nightingale in Westminster Abbey, the allegories and florid details have become tasteless to our eyes, and unfortunately such achievements became a precedent for worse excesses in some of his successors' work. But he will be chiefly remembered for his noble busts and statues already mentioned, the clean and direct work of which has never entirely disappeared from the better traditions of our sculpture.

Thus within the bare fifty years covered by our period artists, from being an obscure and struggling confraternity dependent on patrons often too ignorant to distinguish between the pretensions of a Kneller or a Jervas and the genius of a Hogarth, had obtained a status of their own and a consideration hitherto undreamed of from the community. As an illustration of the earlier relation between patron and artist a typical story is told about the proud duke of Somerset and his namesake, James Seymour, one of those painters sought after by owners of famous racehorses to be drawn to the life 'with a jockey clapped on his back'. The duke once addressed him in condescending banter as 'cousin Seymour', to which Seymour presumptuously replied that they were no doubt of the same race: for this impertinence he was summarily packed off, but the duke, unable to find a better horse-painter, recalled him to paint his stud: 'My lord,' answered Seymour, 'I will now prove I am of your Grace's family, for I won't come.' When Reynolds had become president of the Academy even a proud duke would hardly have treated an artist with such insolence.

English artists had indeed made a new position for themselves by the end of our period. No longer were they content to shelter under the name of a Lely or a Kneller as ghosts or 'drapery men', when they could produce a Joseph Highmore or a Devis,

---

[1] Not, however, in the case of Argyll's monument in Westminster Abbey.

not to speak of the acclimatized German Zoffany, for portraits and conversation-pieces, a Gainsborough, George Lambert, Samuel Scott, Richard Wilson, Sandby, Stubbs, and Wootton as landscape and animal painters,[1] a Reynolds, Gainsborough, Cotes, Romney, Copley, Wright of Derby for portraits, and greatest of all, Hogarth. He is in a class by himself, the most characteristically English of them all, who, as he said of himself, 'grew so profane as to admire *nature* beyond the finest productions of art', and declared that his *Gin Lane* contained better morality and art than all the allegorical gods and goddesses. A man of humble origin, for seven years apprentice to an engraver and silversmith, he was essentially of the people, mixing daily with tradesmen, journeymen, soldiers, draymen, and even drunkards, criminals, and harlots, observing them no less closely than the well-dressed patrons whose contempt he reciprocated. With his superb gift of draughtsmanship and his incorruptible sincerity as an artist, his drawings and pictures not only give us the truest view of the crime and misery underlying all the polished elegance which alone occupied society diarists such as Horace Walpole, but, except when he essayed 'historical pieces' such as *Sigismunda*, are the greatest graphic works of this period. To him, perhaps even more than to the courtly Sir Joshua, great too as he was, art in England owes the beginning of the consideration which comes to an art not only beautiful but formidable.

Though the moderns have not made many additions to the art of building, with respect to mere beauty or ornament, yet it must be confess'd [writes Hogarth in his *Analysis of Beauty*] they have carried simplicity, convenience, and neatness of workmanship to a very great degree of perfection, particularly in England; where plain good sense hath prefer'd these more necessary parts of beauty, which everybody can understand, to that richness of taste which is so much to be seen in other countries, and so often substituted in their room.

No better statement could be made of the main characteristics

---

[1] To get a comprehensive idea of our landscape painters Colonel Maurice Grant's *Old English Landscape Painters*, 3 vols. [revised edn. 1959], is invaluable. Collins Baker, l.c., p. 37, justly speaks of the English school, of which this period sees the beginnings, as 'supreme in the use of water-colour'. Kenneth Clark, *On the Painting of English Landscape* (Proceedings of British Academy, vol. xxi), is also suggestive.

of our very typical architecture during this period. It was the age in which England found its best expression in a dignified and appropriate form of building for moderate-sized homes in town and country, relying for its beauty simply on exquisite proportions and good craftsmanship, and particularly adapted in towns for the harmonious planning of streets, crescents, and squares. London itself was being gradually rebuilt much as we, or at any rate our fathers, found it. For, as the poet Bramston sang in 1729,

> Where's Troy, and where's the Maypole in the Strand?
> Pease, cabbages and turnips once grew where
> Now stands New Bond Street and a newer Square;
> Such piles of buildings now rise up and down,
> London itself seems going out of Town.
> Our Fathers crossed from Fulham in a Wherry,
> Their sons enjoy a Bridge at Putney Ferry.

Typical examples of the earliest stage of the characteristic eighteenth-century town and village houses are Cheyne Row in Chelsea, Church Row in Hampstead, and other such Rows, built, at any rate the first, towards the end of Queen Anne's reign; and stately mansions showing direct traces of the style adopted by Inigo Jones, or one of his school, may be seen in the Marquess of Hertford's house (now part of the College) at Marlborough and by Sir Christopher Wren in Kensington Palace. The same care for exact and harmonious treatment of elevation, the placing and scale of windows and doors or the pitch of roofs, and the same absence of superfluous ornament to distract the eye from a pure symmetry are to be found in all the most characteristic streets of London, Bath, and other towns, as well as in countless farm-houses, parsonages, and squires' houses of the country-side built during the first three-quarters of the eighteenth century. Most of the houses were put up either by unknown architects or by local builders who followed the prevailing fashion; but even the greatest domestic architects, such as the Woods of Bath or later the Adam brothers, were only more exquisite workers in that sober style. The architects who specially devoted themselves to public buildings or the more ambitious mansions required by the great nobles still preserved, as a rule, a restrained dignity in their designs. The Palladian style of Burlington and his followers toned in with homelier surroundings. James Gibbs's Senate House, and Fellows' Buildings at King's were worthy of the finest site in Cambridge, his St. Martin-in-the-Fields and St. Mary-le-Strand[1] dignify their famous positions in London; and in Oxford the Radcliffe Camera, one of the three great domes of the world, was erected by him between 1737 and 1749 although he probably owed the idea to Wren's pupil, Hawksmoor. Hawksmoor himself was responsible for the Clarendon Building and the Codrington Library at All Souls, as well as for Christ Church, Spitalfields, and St. George's, Bloomsbury, in London. To this period also belong Kent's Treasury Chambers and the Horse-Guards and the Admiralty screen of Adam in Whitehall; Jacobsen's Foundling Hospital; George Dance's Mansion House; Isaac Ware's Chesterfield house (demolished in 1937); Taylor's Ely House (built about 1772); Lichfield House in St. James's Square, Lord Spencer's and Lord Portman's mansions by James Stuart; and John James's St. George's, Hanover Square. In the country Vanbrugh's Blenheim was completed; the duke of Chandos's Palladian palace at Canons rose from the ground, to the wonder and delight even of such matter-of-fact creatures as Defoe, only to be razed to the ground again within thirty years; others such as Houghton, Holkham, Wrest, Castle Howard, and Studley Royal remain as monuments to their owner's wealth and princely estate. The elder John Wood made his great plan for the north-west quarter of Bath; and, helped later by his son, built Prior Park, Queen Square, Royal Crescent, and the Circus where Chatham, Clive, and Gainsborough deigned to take houses. The Adam brothers, Robert and James, were just beginning to crown the characteristic domestic architecture of the century by the concord of their internal and external decorations and adjustments, harmonizing unostentatiously with the symmetry of the main design.

Together with this new attention to restraint and simplicity in domestic architecture came a corresponding care for the accessories of a house, especially its furniture and the gardens. Chippendale's *Gentleman and Cabinet Maker's Directory* of 1754 and his own and less-known cabinet-makers' craft confirmed the desire for simply designed and perfectly fashioned furniture in

---

[1] Gibbs also added the fine belfry and spire to St. Mary's sister-church, St. Clement's Danes.

harmony with the well-proportioned rooms, furniture such as we see depicted in genre pictures by Hogarth, Highmore, Arthur Devis, Hayman, and Zoffany. Robert Adam designed furniture in keeping with his houses, just as Kent, at an earlier period, produced furniture more suited to his heavier style. Kent indeed dabbled in all the arts, for, besides designing houses and furniture and painting pictures, he devised a most beautiful barge for the prince of Wales, still to be seen at South Kensington. He was also one of the first of those landscape gardeners who became so prominent in the century. At first the fashion was all for the formal beds and parterres with straight vistas of water, regular alleys of trees, and trim-clipped box-edging introduced by William III from Holland. In this style the palace gardens of Kensington with its Serpentine were laid out by Charles Bridgman, between 1730 and 1733, as were the grounds of Stanhope's Chevening about 1722. But whereas regularity and exact proportions still remained the norm for houses and furniture, a taste grew up for a more romantic and irregular form of landscape gardening with sudden changes of scene to ravish and surprise the beholders of temples, cascades, groves, and statues in unexpected corners, such as Kent planned for the grounds of Pelham's villa at Esher. One of the most perfect examples, probably, of the new style was the park at Stowe, begun by Cobham and improved by Cobham's heir, Lord Temple, helped by Pitt, Lyttelton, and other 'Patriot' friends, with its ingeniously disposed masses of trees and its temples dedicated to friendship, oratory, and such-like and peopled by bustos of relations and other notable examples of the consecrated quality. On a smaller scale, but in exaggerated style, the poet Shenstone's miniature grounds at the Leasowes excited the kindly ridicule of his great neighbours the Lytteltons and the patronizing tolerance of Dr. Johnson. Kent's greater successor as landscape gardener was Lancelot Brown, whose masterful 'capability' is well indicated in his portrait by Dance: he had something of that 'prophetic eye of taste', needed in Pitt's estimation for artificially creating the tumbled landscape, streams, and massive groves out of unpromising natural surroundings. The Great Commoner, indeed, threw himself into the pastime with characteristic zest, grouping the landscape and erecting temples in the grounds of his temporary abode at Enfield Chace, and with imperious haste supervising the work of his gardeners and workmen by torch-light in the park of his more permanent home at Hayes.[1]

How much more widespread the taste for beautiful things was becoming may be seen in the development of other minor arts, more accessible to purchasers of average means. For those who could not afford a picture by Reynolds or Gainsborough the skill of Strange and Woollett in line-engraving, of McArdell and Valentine Green in mezzotint provided notable reproductions. Even the cheapest caricatures, such as Boitard's *Imports to Great Britain from France*, sold at 6*d*. a copy, with, incidentally, a wonderful representation of the Port of London, or a caricature called *Shabear's Administration*, with a masterly sketch of Pitt in a few strokes, are pure works of art in place of the gross and ugly flying sheets and woodcuts at the beginning of the century. There is, too, a revival of beautiful printing, led by Baskerville of Birmingham and Foulis of Glasgow.[2] The inscriptions on monuments and houses and shop signs are a delight to the eye; and handwriting, which in the seventeenth century was as a rule untidy and difficult to decipher, becomes, with exceptions such as Newcastle's, pleasant and easy to read. It was the age also of beautiful china, such as came from the Chelsea, Bow, Derby, and Worcester factories, all started in the first half of the century, and it saw the beginning of Wedgwood's[3] craft, later helped by Flaxman, in Staffordshire pottery.

English music of this period is dominated by the great figure of George Frederick Handel, one of the supreme musicians of the world. A German from Saxony by origin, he first came to England at the age of twenty-five in 1710, and, after one more brief sojourn in Hanover, where he had been made *Kapellmeister* by the Elector George Lewis, finally settled here in 1712, and fourteen years later became naturalized as an Englishman. Both George I and George II, whatever may have been their shortcomings in appreciation of the other arts, had enough

[1] For criticisms of the good and bad styles of landscape gardening see Pope, *Moral Essays*, iv. 39–126; Johnson, *Lives of the Poets*, s.v. 'Shenstone'.

[2] A magnificent production of the Foulis press was shown at the 1939 Exhibition of Scottish Art at Burlington House. It is a folio edition in four volumes of Homer's works, originally presented by Glasgow University to the elder Pitt, inherited by his son William, and later successively in the possession of three other prime ministers, Peel, Rosebery, and Ramsay Macdonald, the last of whom bequeathed it to the Scottish National Library.

[3] Josiah Wedgwood (1730–95) opened his own Burslem pottery-works in 1759, but he had been working and experimenting since 1739. See above, p. 120.

music in their composition to recognize Handel's greatness. George I seems readily to have forgiven his desertion of the post of *Kapellmeister* at Hanover; attended his operas assiduously and increased his pension of £200 granted by Queen Anne: and it was for a river-fête organized for George I in 1717 that Handel composed his famous *Water Music*.[1] For George II's coronation Handel composed his noble anthem *Zadok the Priest*; and when the opposition clique thronged to the other opera house in support of his rival Buononcini, the king still patronized Handel's operas at the half-empty Haymarket, whence Chesterfield withdrew as 'unwilling to disturb the King at his privacies'. But in 1736 Handel was tactless enough to compose a wedding anthem for the king's hated son Frederick, prince of Wales, and, without conciliating the opposition, lost the king's favour until it was finally restored by the magnificent *Dettingen Te Deum* of 1743 —revived at the Worcester Festival in 1935 in fitting celebration of George II's great-great-great-great-grandson's jubilee—followed by *Judas Maccabaeus* and the Aix-la-Chapelle *Firework Music*. Best known at first for his operas, notably *Rinaldo*, *Teseo*, *Radamisto*, and *Acis and Galatea*, by this time Handel had lost control of the Haymarket and never wrote an opera after 1740. Already, however, as early as 1720, he had produced for the duke of Chandos at Canons, *Esther*, the first of those oratorios on which his fame chiefly rests. When advertised for public performance in London in 1732 it was stopped by Bishop Gibson, but in the following year not only *Esther* but also *Deborah* and *Athaliah* were triumphantly acclaimed at Oxford, though *Saul* and *Israel in Egypt* were a failure in 1739. In disgust Handel took his *Messiah* for its first performance in 1742 to Dublin, as Pope records:

> Strong in new arms, lo giant Handel stands,
> Like bold Briareus, with a hundred hands;
> To stir, to rouse, to shake the soul he comes,
> And Jove's own thunders follow Mars's drums.
> Arrest him, Empress, or you sleep no more—
> She heard, and drove him to th' Hibernian shore.[2]

---

[1] The story, originated by Handel's first biographer, John Mainwaring, in 1768, that the *Water Music* was composed in 1715 and offered as a peace-offering to George I for deserting Hanover in 1712, seems to have been disproved by Professor W. Michael in articles published in *Zeitschrift für Musikgeschichte* of Aug.–Sept. 1922, and in the *Musical Courier* of 14 Apr. 1934. He draws his information chiefly from reports of the Prussian envoy, F. Bonet, of 19–30 July 1717.

[2] *Dunciad*, iv. 65–70.

Here it was acclaimed with enthusiasm; and on its first hearing in London in 1743 the king himself set the example, ever thereafter followed, of rising in his seat as the first strains of the glorious 'Hallelujah Chorus' burst upon the awed assemblage. Handel himself made it a practice from 1750 annually to conduct this great oratorio at the Foundling Hospital, which in other ways benefited from his, as well as Hogarth's and other artists', munificence.[1] After finishing his last oratorio, *Jephthah*, in 1751, he went blind, but, undefeated, still would play publicly on the organ almost to his death in 1759. No native Englishman has hitherto produced such magnificent music as Handel, but it may be said that, in spite of all his quarrels and difficulties, he found England the country most congenial and attuned to his particular genius. The English in their turn have taken him to their hearts. As early as 1738 the whole of London flocked to Vauxhall to admire his statue by the then unknown sculptor Roubiliac, who thereby gained his passport to fame. England has made it her pride and her delight to produce his oratorios more perfectly and more frequently than anywhere else; and they, with many of his operatic arias and anthems and such songs as the *Harmonious Blacksmith*, are still, after two centuries, better known here and more widely appreciated than any of the other great composers' works.

Even before Handel entirely abandoned opera, this form of music was falling into decay. Farinelli himself, that marvellous soprano, could hardly revive it; and in 1737 he quitted our shores in order to soothe the melancholy of two successive kings of Spain by singing to them the same four songs nightly. High and low, tired of the artificiality and display of bravura even in the best operas of the time, welcomed the pointed and intelligible plot and rough talk of Gay's *Beggar's Opera* with the jolly music provided for it by Pepusch; but unfortunately Gay was too pointed in his allusions to please the government, and a stringent censorship was established to prevent any more such impertinences. Music, however, with or without politics, was a need of the times. Great nobles such as the duke of Chandos had their private orchestras with men even of Handel's calibre to conduct and write music for them: the nobility generally

---

[1] Handel not only presented to the Foundling Hospital its organ, but also bequeathed to it 'a fair copy of the score and all the parts of my Oratorio called Messiah'.

patronized the Academy of Ancient Music, which lasted from 1710 to 1792 and was also favoured by Handel; and just at the end of our period they established the Noblemen's and Gentlemen's Catch Club to foster the characteristically English taste for glees, canons, and catches. Evidence of the more widespread love of music appears in the prominence given to concerts and musical burlettas at such popular places of entertainment as Marylebone Gardens, Ranelagh, and Vauxhall. The Swiss Heidegger, Fielding's 'Count Ugly', associated with Handel in the management of the Haymarket in the heyday of its operatic glory and with the Academy of Ancient Music, turned his great gifts as an impresario to the new form of entertainment. That the standard of music in these places was high may be judged from Burney being the organist at Ranelagh, the production of a Pergolesi opera at Marylebone, while at Vauxhall Arne conducted the orchestra and brought with him his wife and other famous singers; and Handel himself gave a performance there of his *Firework Music*. To Arne, the composer, in 1740, of *Rule Britannia* and *God Save the King*, after Handel, we owe the best of our music in this century, notably such songs as 'Where the bee sucks' and 'Blow, blow thou winter wind'; to this period also belong William Boyce's 'Heart of Oak' and, somewhat later, Charles Dibdin's 'Tom Bowling'; all these are among the most typical examples we possess of lovable, homely English sentiment, robust patriotism, and love of the sea. In church music William Croft, composer of the lovely burial service first performed at Marlborough's funeral in 1722, and in the direct succession from Purcell and Blow, survived till 1727. During this period, too, the great *Corpus* of our Cathedral Music was being compiled by Maurice Greene, composer of two of our finest anthems and of the music to Pope's *Ode to St. Cecilia*, and William Boyce, who added to it such notable anthems as Greene's 'Lord, let me know mine end' and 'Lord, how long wilt Thou be angry', and his own 'By the waters of Babylon' and 'O praise our God, ye people'. James Nares, another composer of fine anthems, also wrote some beautiful music for the harpsichord. Burney, too, was at work on his *History of Music*, which he began when he was organist at King's Lynn in the fifties. Newcastle in Charles Avison and Ipswich in Joseph Gibbs also had their own notable composers and musicians. The century is likewise memorable for the initiation in 1724 of the Three Choirs (Gloucester, Worcester, and Hereford) Festival, which has since then never missed a year; Boyce from 1737 was appointed its conductor and under his auspices the *Messiah* was produced at Hereford in 1759. So far had the love of music penetrated into the provinces that even the hard-drinking old tory foxhunter, Squire Western, allowed Sophia, it will be remembered, to have her harpsichord and, when he was feeling lethargic and amiably sentimental after dinner, himself took pleasure in her playing; and at the tea-party where Squire Thornhill first cast his lascivious eye on Olivia, the Vicar's daughters sang a favourite song of Dryden's to the guitar, which even Mr. Thornhill was able to play, though 'very indifferently'.

XVI

LITERATURE[1]

I N the literature of the first two Georges' reigns Shakespeare's 'native wood-notes wild' were little heard, nor Milton's solemn organ-tones. Gone too was the orgy of crude or witty indecency that had celebrated release from the sour puritanism of the mid-seventeenth century. As it were in a night, Jeremy Collier's *Short View of the Immorality and Profaneness of the English State*, of 1698, had cleansed the stage, making it very dull; and indeed to some extent it had purified general literature.

Shakespeare's greatness was indeed admitted by all the chief critics, Addison, Pope, Johnson; his works were edited by Pope, Theobald, Hanmer, and Warburton, and above all by Johnson in 1765; and his plays were being acted by Garrick. But he was generally criticized for not conforming to the rigid classical rules of unity in time, place, and sentiment, faults barbarously corrected by Garrick in his acting versions. Even Johnson in his great edition, though ready to admit that he was 'above all writers . . . the poet of nature', and that his dramas were the 'mirror of life', reserved most of his praise for the comedies and complained that there was 'always something wanting' in his tragedies, which often resulted in 'tumour, meanness, tediousness and obscurity'. Milton's *Paradise Lost*, largely no doubt owing to the attention paid to it in the *Spectator*, was more generally accepted as the model, materially if not in spirit, for most of the blank verse poets of the age.[2]

It was an age with literary standards already established in the coffee-houses of Anne's Augustan Age. At Wills's Dryden, till his death in 1700, had laid down the law to Addison, Prior, Steele; and there Pope, a boy of twelve already lisping in numbers, was brought to gaze upon him. Addison then, first at Wills's and later at Button's, assumed Dryden's mantle as

[1] For this chapter I owe much to the criticisms of Dr. A. Melville Clark. [Note of 1939.]
[2] See D. Nichol Smith, *18th Century Essays on Shakespeare*, 1903, and A. Ralli, *Shakespearean Criticism*, 1932.

the arbiter of taste. Dryden had handed down to his successors
a simple, direct, nervous language, but they had inherited little
of the vehement, boisterous energy of his thought. It was an
age in literature disturbed by few doubts and chiefly concerned
in expressing the comfortable complacency of the middle and
upper classes, an age fitly introduced, in a volume of eighteenth-
century verse, by the poem of Pomfret, whose sole preoccupation is

> That Life might be more Comfortable yet
>
> .   .   .   .
>
> Thus I'd in Pleasure, Ease, and Plenty live.
> And as I near approach'd the Verge of Life,
> Some kind Relation, (for I'd have no Wife)[1]
> Shou'd take upon him all my Worldly Care.

Johnson, nearly eighty years after the publication of this poem,
declared that 'perhaps no composition in our language has been
oftener perused'.[2]

As inheritors of the Augustan Age, the poets and literary men
of the next two reigns succeeded to a position rarely equalled in
importance, not only in the political world, but also in society.
They no longer depended almost solely on the goodwill of a
few rich patrons or on the pittances offered to all but the most
popular writers by speculative booksellers. Thanks to the talk
in the coffee-houses, talk which begat the famous twin journals,
the *Tatler* and *Spectator*, a wider public was being educated to a
taste in good literature. The increasing value of public opinion
as a support to the government had opened another avenue to
writers. Godolphin, Harley, and Bolingbroke had not only enlisted the ablest writers to state the arguments for their side
in politics, but even took them into their counsels. Defoe had
been used to promote the Union, Swift, besides writing his
great pamphlet on *The Conduct of the Allies*, was often present
at informal ministerial meetings at Harley's house, Prior went

---

[1] Pomfret, a clergyman, was denied a rich benefice he sought from the bishop
of London, as he had intimated in this poem his choice
            'Near some Obliging, Modest Fair to live',
without marrying her.

[2] Other examples of such complacent ideals of home-comforts could be quoted
from the works of Green, Shenstone, Byrom, Cunningham, and notably Thomson.
Almost as prominent are the boastful assertions of England's greatness, again in
Thomson, in Dyer, and many other poets. In this age, too, it may be noted, *Rule
Britannia* was written.

as ambassador to Paris, Addison became a secretary of state, and Steele had the distinction of being expelled from the house of commons for a political pamphlet. Harley himself belonged to the Scriblerus Club with Pope, Gay, Congreve, and Swift; and, besides St. John and several tory peers, Swift, Prior, and the literary doctors, Freind and Arbuthnot, instituted the Brothers' Club to advise on ministerial patronage to men of letters. With the Hanoverians and Walpole such ministerial patronage of great writers ceased. As Pope said, 'Verse, alas, Your Majesty disdains'. Colly Cibber, a player, was made poet laureate in 1730:[1] Walpole, it is true, consulted Swift on Ireland in 1725, but did not take his advice; still, as Pope records, Walpole could

> in his happier hour
> Of social pleasure, ill-exchanged for power; . . .
> Smile without art and win without a bribe.[2]

But the neglect of literature by court and ministers was more than compensated for by the welcome given to it by the opposition. Caroline, as princess of Wales, graciously received Swift and promised him some medals, which, however, as queen she forgot to send him. Frederick, prince of Wales, visited Pope at Twickenham, and patronized the wits and poets gathered by Bolingbroke into the ranks of the opposition, such as Gay, Thomson, and such lesser fry as Mallet and 'Leonidas' Glover. Apart from politics the great writers were welcomed, without a hint of patronage, by such leaders of society as the duke and duchess of Queensberry, Lord Harcourt, Lord Burlington, Craggs, a secretary of state, and not least Lord Bathurst. Sterne relates how Bathurst, when nearing eighty, came up to him at the princess of Wales's court and introduced himself with these words of old-world courtesy:

I want to know you, Mr. Sterne; but it is fit you should know, also, who it is that wishes the pleasure. You have heard . . . of old Lord Bathurst, of whom your Popes and Swifts have sung and spoken so

---

[1] The aptness of the appointment was recorded by Dr. Johnson in his epigram:
> Augustus still survives in Maro's strain
> And Spenser's verse prolongs Eliza's reign;
> Great George's acts let tuneful Cibber sing;
> For Nature formed the Poet for the King.

[2] *Epilogue to Satires*, i. 29–30, and 32.

much; I have lived my life with geniuses of that cast; but have survived them; and, despairing ever to find their equals, it is some years since I have closed my accounts, and shut up my books, with thoughts of never opening them again; but you have kindled a desire in me of opening them once more before I die; which I now do; so go home and dine with me.[1]

The more general growth of a taste for literature is also notable. Indications of this are the increase of newspapers, of which by 1724 there were sixteen in London alone, and the growing popularity of such magazines as the *Gentleman's* and its rival the *London Magazine*, containing, besides parliamentary debates, poems and literary criticisms, Johnson's *Rambler*, Smollett's *Critical Review*, and Newbery's *Universal Chronicle*, in which the *Idler* appeared. Scotland started a magazine of its own in 1739 and Newcastle in 1747. The *Craftsman* is said at times to have had a circulation of 10,000–12,000 over its first ten years of existence. There was also a ready sale for books such as *Robinson Crusoe*, *Gulliver's Travels*, Pope's *Homer* and *Dunciad*, Gay's *Polly* and *Fables*, and especially for Richardson's, Fielding's, and Smollett's novels; with correspondingly large rewards for the authors. Pope had £4,000 subscribed for his *Homer* before publication, thus giving him independence for life; Fielding was paid £600 for *Tom Jones* and £1,000 for *Amelia*. No doubt Grub Street hacks were still unmercifully sweated by the publishers, and even authors like Savage, and Johnson himself, before he had made his name, experienced the bitterness expressed in his couplet,

> There mark what ills the scholar's life assail,
> Toil, envy, want, the patron, and the jail.[2]

But that has been the fate of budding or feckless authors in all ages. Apart, too, from those who bought new books, the circle of readers was even increased, on the appearance of *Pamela*, by Fancourt, an enterprising bookseller, who started the idea of circulating libraries at a guinea subscription. This idea soon caught on: Smollett's Lydia Melford, for example, writes from Bath of the 'booksellers' shops which are charming places of

[1] Sterne, *Works* (1794), vi. 164–5 (letter to Eliza, undated).
[2] *Vanity of Human Wishes*, ll. 159–60.

resort, where we read novels, plays, pamphlets and newspapers, for so small a subscription as a crown a quarter'.[1]

Pope's poetry, wrote Leslie Stephen, 'is the essence of the first half of the eighteenth century. What was spontaneous in him became conventional and artificial in his successors.' But spontaneous as it may have been in his case, it is not the spontaneity of a great thinker, of a man with a vision or of one with a message to give to his generation.

> What oft was thought, but ne'er so well expressed,

is in fact the best description of Pope's own poetry. Exquisite polish, pithy expression, and almost faultless versification are what entranced his contemporaries and can still give us the enjoyment of his virtuosity. The *Rape of the Lock*, one of his earlier pieces, has perhaps never been excelled as an exercise in dainty mock-heroics. In his more solemn poems, the *Essay on Criticism* or the *Essay on Man*, the polished terseness of isolated lines or couplets has given them such universal currency that they have become embedded in the language, their author almost forgotten,—lines such as,

> A little learning is a dangerous thing;
> For fools rush in where angels fear to tread;
> Hope springs eternal in the human breast;

one could reel off dozens. But as for the matter of these ambitious attempts in high philosophy or deep criticism, it is almost as commonplace as such lines have become from frequent usage. As Dr. Johnson unkindly says of the *Essay on Man*, 'never were penury of knowledge and vulgarity of sentiment so happily disguised . . . [by] the dazzling splendour of imagery and the seductive powers of eloquence'. The *Dunciad* has by some been acclaimed as great and has undoubtedly some fine passages; but, though its apparent object—to abolish the reign of dullness under the pedants and Colley Cibbers of the day—was meritorious enough, it is so overladen with denunciations of forgotten bores, and especially Pope's personal enemies, that its interest to-day is slight. He is perhaps the last of the great poets we in this age should have chosen to translate Homer; but

---

[1] *Humphrey Clinker* (letter of 6 April). See also A. S. Collins, 'The Growth of the Reading Public in 18th Century' in *Review of English Studies*, 1926.

there he does occasionally give a touch of the original spirit, as when Briseis

> Pass'd silent, as the heralds held her hand,
> And oft looked back, slow-moving o'er the strand.[1]

But where Pope touches greatness is in his *Moral Essays* and *Satires*. Nobody perhaps has excelled him in capacity to fix for ever the traits of a character that he admired, or, as more often happened, hated. His duchess of Marlborough, Atossa, his Lord Hervey, Sporus, are preserved like flies in amber in his terse and vitriolic couplets; his verses on St. John, on Peterborough, or on Craggs are a monument to his rare but whole-hearted friendships; even the famous lines on Addison (Atticus), in spite of the venom of the first twenty, are redeemed by the last superb couplet,

> Who but must laugh, if such a man there be,
> Who would not weep, if Atticus were he!

Deep emotion of universal appeal is what one chiefly misses in Pope and his school, such emotion being replaced by personal likes and dislikes, characteristic of the complacent and comfortable society for which he wrote. Compare, for example, as denunciations Pope's

> Sporus! that mere white curd of ass's milk,
>
> .   .   .   .
>
> Amphibious thing! that acting either part,
> The trifling head, or the corrupted heart,
> Fop at the toilet, flatterer at the board,
> Now trips a lady, and now struts a lord.

with Shelley's tremendous lines beginning

> I met Murder on the way—
> He had a mask like Castlereagh—

In Pope's attack one is always conscious of the poet's *spretae injuria formae* as the main motive: Shelley did not even know Castlereagh; but he was expressing a generous emotion of hatred against a man whom he regarded as the oppressor of the poor and downtrodden at home, as the supprter of tyranny abroad.[2]

[1] *Iliad*, i. 348.
[2] For another view of Pope's poetry see Edith Sitwell, *Alexander Pope* (1930), and especially the excellent appendix on Pope's versification.

The worst of Pope was that he influenced nearly a generation of poets to imitate measures and diction and trite ideas, intolerable unless expressed with Pope's own perfection. There are, it is true, charming occasional pieces, some, such as Prior's and Lady Winchilsea's, inspired before Pope had attained his pontificate. Later, too, Gay, Parnell, Dyer, author of *Grongar Hill*, Byrom with his lovely *Pastoral*, Henry Carey with *Sally in our Alley*, have something fresh and spontaneous to say, and Savage's *saeva indignatio* can still stir us. As might be expected, too, it was an age when clever society verses and satires such as Hanbury Williams's flourished. Scotland also gave us some haunting melodies, Allan Ramsay's *My Peggy is a Young Thing*, Hamilton's *Braes of Yarrow*, Jean Elliot's *Flowers of the Forest*, and Carolina Nairne's *Will ye no come back again?*; Watts and the Wesleys gave us some of our noblest hymns. But many of the best-known poets of the time, such as Blair, Akenside, Young, are now, justly, little more than names to us.

Nevertheless, as in the industrial world the way was being cleared in this first half of the century for the industrial outburst in the second half, so too was beginning to appear a new race of poets, untrammelled by worn conventions and with a fresher outlook on nature and man, forerunners of such as Keats, Shelley, Wordsworth, Blake. This revolt against stale conventions is actually expressed in the last year of George II's reign in Robert Lloyd's lines:

> Had Shakespeare crept by modern rules,
> We'd lost his Witches, Fairies, Fools;
> Instead of all that wild creation,
> He'd formed a regular plantation,
> A garden trim, and all enclosed,
> In nicest sympathy disposed.
>
> .   .   .   .
>
> When Shakespeare leads the mind a dance
>
> .   .   .   .
>
> Talk not to me of time and place;
>
> .   .   .   .
>
> Whether the drama's here or there,
> 'Tis nature, Shakespeare everywhere.

Thomson, though he could not rid himself entirely of such stilted stuff as 'O, Sophonisba, Sophonisba, O', or 'Hail mildly pleasing solitude', was beginning to look at nature afresh and sing in simple language of what he saw, as in the lines,

> Thro' the hush'd Air the whitening Shower descends
> At first thin-wavering . . .

Collins, though still encumbered by some of the frippery of the conventional Muse, showed in his odes *On the Death of Thomson*, *To Evening*, and *To Simplicity*, and the *Dirge in Cymbeline* that he could burst the shackles, while his ode on *Popular Superstitions in the Highlands*, with all its occasional harshness, was opening the way to a fruitful field for song. Smart, like Collins, perhaps because the struggle for self-expression was then so hard, became deranged in mind, but not so as to prevent his writing his lovely *Spring* and the tremendous *Song to David*. Lastly Gray, who showed in his *Ode on the Death of a Favourite Cat* that he could almost rival Pope in an exquisite triviality, broke new ground by his *Bard* and *Progress of Poesy*, and above all by his great *Elegy*, now deeply embedded in our language.

Swift stands apart from the other writers of the age. He alone may be called a genius—a tortured genius—supremely effective for the public causes he made his own, frustrated and embittered by the failure of his personal ambitions. By his *Conduct of the Allies* he brought to an end a war that had become futile, and was largely responsible for the peace; by his *Drapier's Letters* he routed England hip and thigh in her attempt to impose an unwanted coinage on Ireland, and was the first to voice, in words that could be heard and understood, the grievances of that much oppressed country. He wrote two of the greatest satires in the language, the *Tale of a Tub* and *Gulliver's Travels*, the latter all the more effective as a satire for its 'grave verisimilitude'.[1] These two works are enough to account for the failure of his personal ambitions, for his banishment from the London he loved to an Irish deanery, instead of the English bishopric to which he felt himself entitled. He himself, indeed, confessed to Pope that 'the chief end I propose to myself in all my labours is to vex the world rather than divert it. . . . I have ever hated all nations, professions, and communities, and all my love is towards individuals';[2] and the world is apt to avenge itself on those who vex it. His verse, rugged and impetuous, has the same

---

[1] A phrase borrowed from Mr. R. Quintana's *The Mind and Art of Jonathan Swift* (1936). For a definitive edition of his poetry see Harold Williams, *The Poems of Jonathan Swift*, 3 vols. (1958).   [2] To Pope, 29 Sept. 1725.

characteristic as his prose, enormous vigour. No greater contrast can be imagined than between his satire and Pope's:
where Pope is sly and malicious, Swift bludgeons and annihi-
lates: for as he says,

> Scorn torments them more than Spight.[1]

But even Swift had his rare moments of tenderness: witness his
birthday poems and *Journal to Stella* and passages in his two
great poems, *Cadenus and Vanessa* and the *Death of Dr. Swift*.

From the very outset of the eighteenth century, under the
influence of that band of working journalists, Defoe, Addison,
Steele, and Swift,[2] English prose, unlike English poetry, was
adapting itself to the practical common-sense needs of a business
community. The immense vogue of our two first great English
novels, *Robinson Crusoe* and *Gulliver's Travels*, had a good deal
to do with this: for both tales were put into the mouths of
simple members of the middle class, who used direct plain
English. The three successors of Defoe and Swift, Richardson,
Fielding, and Smollett, had before 1760 established the novel
as the most popular form of literature in England, and even
abroad in the case of Richardson, mainly for their power of
giving a true picture of English life and sentiment through the
medium of an exciting story. All three can hold us to-day, even
Richardson, in whose case skipping is venial and not fatal to
the appreciation of his long-winded courtships and seductions
and his immaculate sentiment.[3] Not the least of Smollett's and
Fielding's merits is that they lead you through the English or
Scottish country-side or the prisons, spunging-houses, and
lodgings of London, as if it were a newly discovered land, and
introduce to you the queer, angular, prejudiced Matt. Bramble,
Commodore Trunnion, and the like bred in this strange land,
and above all to such immortals as Squire Western, 'swine-
feeding' Parson Trulliber, and his counterpart the noble Parson

---

[1] *Epistle to a Lady*, l. 146.
[2] The post-Restoration writers, such as Dryden and Bunyan, had, of course,
already set the model of clear, straightforward English prose.
[3] Skipping in Richardson's case is made easy by the author's convenient habit
of giving short summaries of each chapter. Dr. Johnson did not, as we know, take
even so favourable a view of Richardson's stories. 'Why, Sir,' he said to Boswell in
1772, 'if you were to read Richardson for the story, your impatience would be so
much fretted that you would hang yourself. But you must read him for the sentiment.'

Adams. Of the many other novelists who followed in their wake none in this period need be recalled except Laurence Sterne, the leering, insinuating prebendary of York, with his furtive hints and innuendoes. True, he was a nasty fellow, but also what a consummate artist! Who but he, from the untidy, inconsequent, and jumbled narrative of *Tristram Shandy*, could have produced such living, rounded figures as Mr. Walter Shandy, the Widow Wadman, Corporal Trim, and my Uncle Toby?[1]

While the poets and novelists were busy publishing their views on life in general, hardly an age has been so rich in letter- and memoir-writers, eager to fix the actually passing scene for the benefit of posterity. No doubt many of these private journals such as Egmont's, Marchmont's, or even Dodington's, now perhaps not the least valuable to the historian, were originally intended solely to refresh their authors' own memories. But diarists and letter-writers such as Lord Hervey and Horace Walpole took a malicious pleasure in chronicling the talk of the town, the court, or the political world, so as to ensure that their own particular prejudices should have the fullest weight with future generations. Horace Walpole with this end in view wrote his letters to that dreary diplomat Horace Mann at Florence, and enjoined on him to preserve them; and in his will he left elaborate directions for the ultimate publication of his *Memoirs*. Hervey's intentions are equally obvious, for he saw to it that his *Memoirs* should be carefully preserved until such time as their astonishing frankness might with safety be divulged. They were certainly justified in their dispositions, for their Memoirs and Letters have been quarried by all historians of the political and social life of England during the fifty years after 1730; and, as both authors on the whole agree in their likes and dislikes, their testimony has in the main fixed the views of posterity. The reputations of Frederick, prince of Wales, and of the duke of Newcastle, for example, have suffered ever since from the ridicule cast upon them by both these diarists—in their case, it must be admitted, justly. It may also be said that many a young man has been stimulated, after dipping into Walpole and Hervey, to pursue the study of a century introduced to them in such fascinating guise. Besides the professed writers of Memoirs and Letters concerned with politics, many in this

[1] Though *Tristram Shandy* was not completed till 1767, the first two volumes appeared in 1759; they were dedicated to Pitt of all people.

century cultivated the art of letter-writing for itself. Chester-field's letters are valuable as reflecting the cynicism of a fashion-able, witty, and highly gifted nobleman, especially on the congenial topic of a cherished son's worldly education. Lady Mary Wortley Montagu, though a blue-stocking, wrote delightful letters on her travels, her friends in society, her enemies such as Pope, and the new novels she passed judgement on as soon as they appeared. From Pope's and Swift's pungent corre-spondence and Gray's more academic epistles illumination is shed on the literary world of these fifty years. Gray's letters are also remarkable for their descriptions of natural scenery: he was perhaps the first of the moderns to rejoice in the grandeur and beauty of the Alps, the Lake District, and the Highlands.

Among all the writers of the age David Hume had so wide a range of worldly and intellectual interests that he is in a class by himself.[1] Philosopher, economist, historian, librarian, judge-advocate, and secretary of embassy, darling of the Paris salons, it is hardly surprising that he incurred Dr. Johnson's wrath for vanity no less than infidelity, a wrath not even appeased by his staunch tory principles: 'Sir,' said the sage, 'he was a Tory by chance.' His philosophy is contained first in his youthful *Treatise of Human Nature* of 1739, superseded by his more mature *Enquiry concerning Human Understanding* (1748) and *Principles of Morals* (1751) and the *Natural History of Religion* (1757). His theory of causation, the most revolutionary of his doctrines, struck at the root of all religion, whether revealed or the result of deduction, as in the case of the Deists; and in fact made all knowledge empirical. To him cause and effect were but names for conjoined phenomena.

We know, that, in fact, heat is a constant attendant of flame; but what is the connexion between them, we have no room so much as to conjecture or imagine. . . . Experience only teaches us, how one event constantly follows another; without instructing us in the secret connexion, which binds them together, and renders them inseparable. . . . But there is nothing in a number of instances, different from every single instance, which is supposed to be exactly similar; except only, that after a repetition of similar instances, the mind is carried by habit, upon the appearance of one event, to expect its usual attendant. . . . This connexion, therefore, which we

[1] For Hume's views about religion see above, p. 85.

feel in the mind . . . is the sentiment or impression from which we form the idea of power or necessary connexion. Nothing farther is in the case.

Nor will he allow any short cut to knowledge of causes by the postulate of a Deity: 'We have no idea of the Supreme Being but what we learn by reflection on our own faculties.'[1] Hume was of course abused as an atheist, but no satisfactory answer was then found to his arguments, expressed in the limpid clarity of his beautiful style; with the result that constructive theories based on the fundamental causes of events or phenomena were to a large extent abandoned thereafter in eighteenth-century England.

On the other hand Hume himself set the example in his other writings of so sane an empirical examination of facts that he proved a pioneer in both history and economics. In the latter branch he anticipated many of his great disciple, Adam Smith's, views, especially in his notable chapter on the *Balance of Trade*. In his Histories of Great Britain and of England too, though not based on a critical study of original materials, he has, as Carlyle expressed it, the 'methodising, comprehensive eye' essential for the historian, and 'something of an Epic clearness and method, as in his delineation of the Commonwealth Wars'.[2] Hume is also memorable as the last great continuator of that clear, simple, transparently honest English prose introduced at the opening of the century: in his hands it becomes the perfect instrument of a sincere and luminous mind

It is only fitting that this section on literature should conclude with Hume's great antagonist, Dr. Johnson, a link between the two halves of the century, which he bestrides like a Colossus. By the end of George II's reign Johnson had already published nearly all on which his literary fame rests,[3] except the *Journey to the Western Isles of Scotland*, his edition of Shakespeare, and the *Lives of the Poets*, but had not yet found the great trumpeter of his social and conversational fame, Boswell, who met him first in

---

[1] These quotations all come from § VII of the *Enquiry concerning Human Understanding. Of the Idea of Necessary Connexion.*

[2] *Miscellaneous Essays;—Boswell's Life of Johnson.*

[3] It will be remembered that in Feb. 1767, when George III asked him if he was then writing anything, Johnson said he thought he had already done his part as a writer: 'I should have thought so too', said the king, 'if you had not written so well'; and that the king's wish that he should execute 'the literary biography of this country' may have been the stimulus needed for the *Lives of the Poets.*

1763. Johnson, indeed, is the greatest literary character of the century, not for what he wrote so much as for what he was. His sturdy toryism, expressed with provocative and uncompromising vigour, was a tonic reminder that whig doctrines need no longer, with the removal of the Jacobite danger, be the sole passport to respectability, patronage, and office, and that tory principles, untainted as his were with serious Jacobitism,[1] still had a value as an antidote to the flaccid whiggism of the Dodingtons and time-servers of the age. His courage, his vast industry, his violent prejudices, his thunderous exposures of pretence or affectation, his rollicking Olympian humour, and withal his deep and abiding tenderness were already giving him that magisterial place in the world of letters which in the next reign became sway undisputed. So great was his influence that he was already diverting the limpid stream of English prose, seen at its best in Hume, back to the more involved and turbid channel of the seventeenth century, where it rolls with ponderous profundity through Gibbon's six majestic tomes.

Besides pamphlets Johnson's chief productions before 1760 were the parliamentary speeches he wrote for the *Gentleman's Magazine*, *London*, *The Vanity of Human Wishes*, the *Rambler*, the *Idler*, *Rasselas*, and the *Dictionary*. The speeches are eloquent versions of what members may have said in debate; *The Vanity of Human Wishes* abounds in magnificently turned epigrams worthy of Pope, such as:

> To point a Moral or adorn a Tale;

> If Dreams yet flatter, once again attend,
> Hear Lydiat's Life, and Galileo's End;

> Superfluous lags the Vet'ran on the Stage
> Till pitying Nature signs the last Release,
> And bids afflicted Worth retire to Peace.

The Rambler, with its obvious and ponderously expressed sentiments, is, it must be confessed, dull reading: but *Rasselas*, in its quiet and sad tranquillity, though without the verve and caustic wit of its exact contemporary *Candide*, can still be read with pleasure. And above all there is the *Dictionary*.

---

[1] Johnson, though ready to shelter a Jacobite friend after the '45, was obviously never a serious Jacobite, thought James II impossible as a king, and easily yielded to the blandishment of George III's courtesy.

The great *Dictionary*, a task such as the forty immortals of
the French Academy had taken nearly a century to complete,
Johnson accomplished in seven years, unaided save for the
assistance of six copyists. He had few forerunners to show him
the way. The first English dictionary was a small book by
Cockeram in 1623; two more, by Blount and Edward Phillips,
followed in 1656 and 1658. In 1721 Nathaniel Bailey produced
a far more comprehensive work, which immediately became
popular, passed through many editions, and is said to have been
read through twice by the Great Commoner. Johnson himself
used an interleaved copy of it for his notes and additions. But
none of these gave more than short definitions of words, with
no quotations to illustrate their meanings. Johnson's original
idea for his dictionary was that it should stereotype the language
as a standard for literature, in his belief, shared by Pope and
others, that English had then attained its highest perfection:
but he soon gave up that idea, finding, as he went on, that 'to
enchain syllables, and to lash the wind, are equally the undertakings of pride, unwilling to measure its desires by its strength'.
Later in his preface he speaks of 'language as yet living', and
condescends to define terms used by commerce, which 'depraves
the manners and corrupts the language'. Starting, after this
characteristic preface, with a *History of the English Language* and
a *Grammar of the English Tongue*, Johnson carries out his scheme
of explaining the meaning of words, not only by his pithy and
at times caustic definitions, but by quotations illustrating their
various uses, rarely, however, quoting any author subsequent
to the Restoration. His dictionary cannot claim to be founded
on a scientific and exhaustive basis, such as is the *Oxford English
Dictionary*, but at least it set its readers on the track of more
exact lexicography. Moreover it is, what perhaps no other
dictionary has ever been, a mirror of the author's robust prejudices and devastating wit, as in the famous definitions of
pension and *pensioner*, *oats* and *lexicographer*.[1] But apart from these
famous definitions nobody now sets great store by the *Dictionary*.
Of all Johnson's works the most lasting, in spite of his depre-

---

[1] It is interesting to compare an edition of Bailey's *Dictionary* of 1730, and one of
1764, nine years later than Johnson's. The 1730 edition has no preface, no *History*
or *Grammar of the English Language*, nor any illustrative quotations in the text. In
1764 all these features, obviously based on Johnson, appear; and the editor, Dr. J.
Nicol Scott, even ventures, but flatly and without the wit, to reproduce something
reminiscent of Johnson's most famous definitions.

ciations of what seem to us today among the most beautiful of Milton's poems, is *The Lives of the Poets*. Though published as a whole in 1779–81, one of the most elaborate and characteristic, the life of his friend Savage, had already appeared in 1744. Of this life the last paragraph sums up much of Johnson's brave philosophy, characteristic of much that is best in the age:

This relation will not be wholly without its use if those who languish under any part of his sufferings shall be enabled to fortify their patience by reflecting that they feel only those afflictions from which the abilities of Savage did not exempt him; or those who, in confidence of superior capacities or attainments, disregard the common maxims of life, shall be reminded that nothing will supply the want of prudence, and that negligence and irregularity long continued will make knowledge useless, wit ridiculous, and genius contemptible.

BIBLIOGRAPHY

[In the revision of this Bibliography titles of books published down to the end of 1959 have been included, but as it was strongly marked by Professor Williams's individuality and closely related to the preceding text, it has been thought right to preserve its general lines. Square brackets indicate places where more is added than mere notices of books.]

GENERAL

BIBLIOGRAPHIES, WORKS OF REFERENCE, AND GUIDES TO MANUSCRIPT SOURCES. For books the most useful bibliography is the *Bibliography of British History, the Eighteenth Century, 1714–89*, ed. by S. Pargellis and D. J. Medley, 1951. An alternative is to be found in the four instalments of the *Subject Index of the London Library*, published in 1909, 1923, 1938, and 1955; the *Author Catalogues of the London Library* published in 1912, 1920, and 1929 are also essential.[1] The *British Museum Catalogue of Printed Books*, together with G. K. Fortescue's *Subject Index*, are naturally more exhaustive but not so easily accessible. For economic subjects H. Higgs, *Economic Bibliography*, 1935, based mainly on H. S. Foxwell's magnificent collections of economic literature, should be consulted.

Many libraries have large collections of the numerous pamphlets published in this period, among others McGill University Library with its fine Redpath collection of pamphlets, mostly of the eighteenth century. Among the best guides to the pamphlet literature in this country are the British Museum, which has a bound series of Political Tracts, and London Library catalogues. The separate issues of the *Craftsman*, really political pamphlets against Walpole, were published in a collected edition in 14 volumes in 1737.

In the bibliography of my *William Pitt, Earl of Chatham*, ii. 367–8, will be found a list of the chief pamphlets relating to him; reference too should be made to R. Watts's *Bibliotheca Britannica*,

---

[1] When I left Marlborough a parting advice of the Master, the Rev. G. C. Bell, was to become a life-member of that great institution the London Library. I did so and have never regretted it.

1824. There are some useful short bibliographies on various aspects of English life at the end of each chapter in *Johnson's England*, 2 vols., 1933.

For manuscripts in the Public Record Office, both foreign and domestic, M. S. Giuseppi's *Guide to Manuscripts preserved in the Public Record Office*, 2 vols., 1923–4, is useful, but to ascertain its wealth of documents it is necessary to consult the catalogues, chiefly in manuscript, kept in the Office, and still better the officials there, ever ready to assist students. In the manuscript room of the British Museum, where the accumulation of documents is not so vast, there are admirable printed catalogues and indices, whereby it is easy to find one's way to its treasures. C. M. Andrews, *Guide to Materials for American History in Public Record Office*, 2 vols., 1912–14, and C. M. Andrews and F. G. Davenport, *Guide . . . in British Museum, London Archives and Libraries of Oxford and Cambridge*, 1908, both published by the Carnegie Institution at Washington, are invaluable, as the plan of the series embraces a wide view of its province.

The French government have published an admirable *Inventaire sommaire des archives . . . des affaires étrangères* I, *Allemagne, Angleterre, &c.*, 1903, which gives the student a complete conspectus of all diplomatic papers at the Quai d'Orsay relating to England between A.D. 1200 and 1827. Such a work greatly facilitates research there, not only with regard to our foreign policy but also for reports of our domestic affairs, and notably of debates in parliament in this period. It were much to be wished that our Record Office would publish such handy guides to its treasures both for foreign and domestic documents in its archives. In the Hanover archives is an important collection entitled 'Correspondance particulière de . . . St. Saphorin avec les autres Ministres du Roi' (among others Carteret), which has been used by Professor Michael and others.

On many subjects the *Encyclopaedia Britannica*, especially the 10th (1902–3) and 11th (1910–12) editions, has admirable articles, and for persons the *Dictionary of National Biography* is invaluable, not least for this period, which especially interested the first editor, Leslie Stephen: the *Concise Dictionary of National Biography* in one volume containing brief epitomes with dates of the articles in the main work is almost indispensable as a book of reference to the historian. For all dating and for lists of the holders of the most important civil and ecclesiastical offices the Royal Historical Society's *Handbook of British Chronology*,' ed. Sir Maurice Powicke, 1939, is indispensable. Haydn's *Book of Dignities*, 1910, &c., based partly on R. Beatson's *Political Index*, 3 vols., 1806, is very useful, but sometimes requires checking. Of contemporary publications the *London Gazette* gave the official news, the *Gentleman's Magazine* and the *London Magazine* made a special feature of parliamentary debates; J. Chamberlayne's *Magnae Britanniae Notitia*, published biennially from 1708 to 1755, is a sort of *Whitaker's Almanac*, with useful lists of state officials, university dignitaries, &c., and, among other items, of all the charity schools in England; Guy Miège's *Present State of Great Britain and Ireland*, 1691–1758, is a somewhat similar production. The Sun Fire Office issued to its clients between 1714 and 1738 an *Historical Register* in three monthly parts, so as to provide reports of 'more solid and lasting use'. The *Annual Register* itself begins in 1758.

The new edition of G. E. C.[okayne], *The Complete Peerage*, edited by the Hon. Vicary Gibbs, 1910–59, supersedes the original edition by G. E. C. in 8 vols., 1887–98, and is especially valuable for its frank exposure of mistaken claims, its historical accuracy, and its numerous items of out-of-the-way information. G. E. C. also published *The Complete Baronetage*, 16 vols., 1900–9; and W. A. Shaw's *The Knights of England*, 2 vols., 1906, is authoritative. A. Collins, *Peerage of England*, 9 vols., 1812, is also useful.

For dates of events a useful compendium is A. E. Stamp's *Methods of Chronology*, Historical Association, 1933. J. P. Migne, *Dictionnaire*, S. 2, xlix, *L'Art de vérifier les dates*, 1844–66, is an abbreviated form of the longer work with the same title.

The *English Historical Review*, *History*, and the *American Historical Review* are the chief periodicals on our subject: the *Cambridge Historical Journal*, since 1958 entitled *Historical Journal*, also has useful articles. The *Transactions of the Royal Historical Society* and the Society's separate publications in the *Camden Series* are of great value.

An understanding of the personalities of this period is much helped by visits to the National Portrait Gallery, which is particularly rich in eighteenth-century portraits, and to the National Gallery, where some of the best, artistically, are preserved. It is true the full-bottomed wigs, worn by nearly all the men, give a certain sameness in appearance to many of the portraits; but even so a Pitt, a Walpole, a Chesterfield, a Stanhope, and a Pulteney retain a distinct individuality on the canvas; and the same is true of Hone's portrait of Wesley and of all those painted by Hogarth.

POLITICAL HISTORY

GENERAL AND DOMESTIC. The fullest history of this period hitherto published is W. E. H. Lecky's *History of England in the Eighteenth Century* (cabinet edition, 7 vols., 1899–1901): it is not based on much research into original authorities, and is in some aspects, e.g. labour movements, defective; but it is valuable as an estimate of institutions and tendencies by a highly cultured and philosophic thinker. Lord Mahon's (5th Earl Stanhope) *History of England 1713–83*, begun in 1836, of which there are many editions, is interesting from its whole-heartedly whig point of view and from the many documents quoted from Jacobite and other archives. A good general account of the period is given in vol. ix of the *Political History of England* (ed. W. Hunt and R. L. Poole) by I. S. Leadam, 1909, which is well documented, and the *New Cambridge Modern History*, vol. viii, 1957, both having useful maps and tables. The *Cambridge Modern History*, vol. vi, 1909, has accounts by various authorities on aspects of the period. Professor Wolfgang Michael's *Englische Geschichte im 18. Jahrhundert*, the first volume of which was published in 1896 and the fourth in 1937, is especially valuable for the light cast on English politics, both domestic and foreign, as a result of Dr. Michael's researches in German, Austrian, and French, as well as English, public and private records, guided, too, as they have been by his remarkable insight into English institutions and traditions of government. Professor Namier has published translations (adapted) of the first two volumes, *The Beginnings of the Hanoverian Dynasty*, 1936–7, and *The Quadruple Alliance*, 1939. Of contemporary historians, Abel Boyer continued his *Political State of Great Britain* till 1740, and N. Tindal his sequel to Rapin till 1763 (see vol. x, 2nd ed., pp. 379 and 425–6). Tobias Smollett brought out a *History of England* down to 1748, and later a continuation of Hume's *History* from the Revolution to 1760. The latter is useful even to-day in conveying the views of a bystander on contemporary events.

[Since the present Bibliography was first written very important additions have been made to our knowledge of this period and that which follows it by English and American historians who have acknowledged the leadership of Sir Lewis Namier and so far taken his methods as their example that they are commonly spoken of as the Namier school. The movement began in 1929 with the publication of his two-volume work *The Structure of Politics at the Accession of George III*. This was a work of rare originality and critical power, in which he transformed the accepted views of electoral practices and parliamentary life by exploiting all the available materials especially from a biographical point of view. The full results of this technique will not be available until the History of Parliament Trust has completed its comprehensive work, and the results so far attained can only be understood by wide reading in reviews and articles. The somewhat disparaging critique of Professor H. Butterfield, *George III and the Historians*, 1957, makes some interesting points but has not detracted from the general confidence in the services of the school. Sir Lewis himself published a revised second edition of the *Structure of Politics* in 1957, and his Romanes Lecture of 1952, *Monarchy and the Party System*, gives the broad results of his researches. Among books closely related to his work are Lucy S. Sutherland, *The East India Company in Eighteenth-Century Politics*, 1952; G. P. Judd, *Members of Parliament, 1734–1852*, 1955; J. B. Owen, *The Rise of the Pelhams*, 1957, which deals with the years 1741–7; W. R. Ward, *Georgian Oxford, University Politics in the Eighteenth Century*, 1958; A. J. Henderson, *London and the National Government, 1721–42*, 1945, and several works mentioned in other sections below. See also above, p. 29, n. 1.]

The period is particularly rich in the manuscript materials available for the historian. First comes the vast correspondence of the duke of Newcastle accessible in the 522 volumes (Add. MSS. 32679–33201) at the British Museum; the Hardwicke Papers (Add. MSS. 35349–36278) supplement Newcastle's; the only Carteret papers still undestroyed, chiefly official, are also at the British Museum (Add. MSS. 22511–22545), as well as the important diplomatic papers of Titley, Robinson, Hyndford, Whitworth, and Mitchell; of the last A. Bisset, in *Memoirs and Papers of Sir A. Mitchell*, 2 vols., 1850, published a selection. There is also a collection of intercepted dispatches, Add. MSS. 32271–88. At the Record Office the principal divisions are *State Papers, Domestic* (*General Series*, Entry Books, Naval, &c.), *State Papers, Foreign* (*Spain, France, &c.*), *War Office, Colonial* and *Admiralty* Records. There also are the *Chatham MSS.*, the first 100 bundles of which contain the elder Pitt's papers, &c., of which only a small number were published in the four volumes of his *Correspondence* (1838–40). In both the British Museum and the Record Office, as well as in private collections, are innumerable letters and documents still unpublished.

Of the printed letters, &c., available there are *Correspondence of 4th Duke of Bedford*, 3 vols., 1843, *Grenville Papers*, 4 vols., 1852, *Memoirs and Correspondence of George, 1st Lord Lyttelton*, 2 vols., 1845, *Private Correspondence of Chesterfield and Newcastle 1744–6*, ed. by Sir R. Lodge, 1930. *Letters of Horace Walpole*: the edition in 16 volumes published 1903–5 by Mrs. P. Toynbee, with *Supplement*, 3 vols., 1926, is the best and most complete, superseding Peter Cunningham's ed. in 9 vols., 1857–9. Another (American) edition by W. S. Lewis and others is arranged according to correspondents and richly annotated. The twenty-ninth volume was published in 1955; these *Letters* are valuable for political, no less than for social and literary information. Mr. R. Sedgwick's *Letters from George III to Lord Bute* (1940) is illuminating on the relations of these two men and their hatred of Pitt. Professor W. T. Copeland's *Correspondence of Edmund Burke*, i. *1744–68*, 1958, contributes little of importance until after 1759. The Royal Commission on Historical Manuscripts has published many collections of letters, &c., chiefly from private repositories. The arrangement of the volumes is somewhat confusing, owing to changes in the system, but in 1935 and 1938 two volumes of a *Guide to the Reports* were published with an index of names occurring in the reports published between 1870 and 1911, which are a great help to the student. In the Commission's 18th and 19th reports will also be found lists of materials for British diplomatic history prepared by Miss Davenport. Among the volumes with information on this period are:[1]

Stuart MSS., vols. i–vii up to Dec. 1718 (1902–23)—on Jacobite activities;

Portland MSS. (*Harley papers*), vols. v–vii (1899, 1901)—on early years of the period;

Polwarth MSS. i (1911), ii (1916), iii (1931)—useful for foreign negotiations in George I's reign;

[1] Dates of publication by Hist. MSS. Comm. are given in brackets.

Egmont Papers, i, 2 parts (1905), ii (1909) } —very valuable on Georgia, Wesleyans, and court affairs;
Diary of 1st Earl of Egmont, 3 vols. (1920–3) }

Fortescue, Dropmore MSS., i (1892)—useful for Pitt family;
xiv. ix with *Trevor, Hare,* and *Onslow MSS.* (1895);
xii. v *Rutland papers* (1897)—useful for Pitt and Lord Granby;
xv. ii *Hodgkin papers* (1897)—useful for Jacobites and the '45;
xv. vi *Carlisle* (1897)—political and court letters;
xiii. vi *Fitzherbert* (1893)—account of the '45; *Delaval,* navy matters;

Report on Various MSS. vi (1909) contains important letters about Bubb Dodington's activities with the prince of Wales, 1748–9, &c., from Miss Eyre Matcham's collection.

Other volumes with points bearing on this period are xi. vii *Leeds MSS.* (1888) on Holdernesse; xiii. vii *Lonsdale* (1893); xiv. i *Rutland* (1894); *Lothian* (1905); *Eglinton* (1883); *Townshend* (1887); *Beaufort* (1891); *Buckinghamshire* (1895); *Du Cane* (1905); there are doubtless many others.

The age is singularly prolific, too, in contemporary memoirs and diaries. Among the memoir-writers Lord Hervey and Horace Walpole are in a class apart. Hervey's *Some Materials towards Memoirs of the Reign of George II,* of which the best edition is that of Romney Sedgwick, 3 vols., 1931, though vitriolic in intention, is to be relied upon for the facts narrated: Horace Walpole's *Memoirs of the Reign of George II,* ed. by Lord Holland, 2nd ed., 3 vols., 1847, is a pleasanter book to read, for he, though quizzical, is never nasty or spiteful; he also has a much wider range of interest, especially in the doings of parliament, of which he gives admirable reports for the eventful ten years 1751–60. *Official Diary of Lt.-Gen. Adam Williamson 1722–47,* R. Hist. S. (Camden S.), 1912, gives interesting details of Jacobite prisoners in the Tower 1722 and 1746 and on its administration; Bubb Dodington's *Diary* (new ed. 1784) is almost unbelievably frank in the author's revelation of his own and his friends' seamy side in the politics of 1749–61. *The Memoirs of a Celebrated Literary Character* [Richard Glover], 1813, are particularly useful for Granville's attempt to form a ministry in 1746 and on Pitt's rise to power. Unlike these, Lady Cowper's *Diary 1714–20,* published 1864, is a plain but still valuable record of court and ministerial intrigues during the first years of George I. *The*

Papers of the Earls of Marchmont, 1685–1750, ed. by Sir G. Rose, 3 vols., 1831, are chiefly important for the diary and letters of the 3rd earl, Hugh (1708–94), between 1733 and 1750, in his relations with Carteret, Bolingbroke, and other opponents of Walpole. The duc de Berwick's *Mémoires*, 1828, are useful for Jacobite activities in France. Lord Waldegrave's *Memoirs from 1754 to 1758*, 1821, deal almost entirely with the ministerial negotiations of 1755–7; J. M. Graham's *Annals . . . of the . . . 1st and 2nd Earls of Stair*, 2 vols., 1865, concern us chiefly for the letters about the '15, the 2nd earl's embassy in Paris, his activities in opposition to Walpole, and his command in Germany in 1743.

Biographies for this period also abound. Sir Winston Churchill's great biography of *Marlborough* unfortunately devotes only 40 pages of vol. iv to the Duke's final years under George I. Archdeacon W. Coxe's *Memoirs . . . of Sir Robert Walpole*, 3 vols., 1798, *Memoirs of Horatio, Lord Walpole*, 2 vols., 1808, *Memoirs . . . of Henry Pelham*, 2 vols., 1829, are most useful for the copious illustrative correspondence. Additional matter will be found in *An Honest Diplomat at the Hague, the Private Letters of Horatio Walpole, 1715–16*, ed. J. J. Murray, 1955; F. S. Oliver, *Endless Adventure, 1710–35*, 3 vols., 1903–5; G. R. Stirling Taylor, *Walpole and his Age*, 1931. Valuable contributions to Walpole's biography have been made by Paul Vaucher's *Robert Walpole et la politique de Fleury 1731–42* and *La Crise du ministère Walpole 1733–4*, 1924; and by C. B. Realey, *The Early Opposition to Sir R. Walpole 1720–27*, 1931, but for the period down to 1722 all previous biographies are superseded by the thorough research of J. H. Plumb, *Sir Robert Walpole, the Making of a Statesman*, 1956. W. Sichel's *Bolingbroke and his Times*, 2 vols., 1901–2, gives the most favourable view of that lost angel. On *Stanhope* there is not much besides my volume of 1932 under that title. Of Chatham there are many biographies: among them [J. Almon] *Anecdotes of Life of W. Pitt, Earl of Chatham*, 3 vols., 1797, with many contemporary touches from Earl Temple and others; Rev. F. S. Thackeray, *History of W. Pitt, Earl of Chatham*, 2 vols., 1827, a dull work but well documented; A. v. Ruville, *William Pitt, Graf v. Chatham*, 3 vols., 1905 (translated by H. J. Chaytor and M. Morrison, 3 vols., 1907), shows immense research but is marred by the author's persistent denigration of his subject; Lord Rosebery's brilliant sketch of *Chatham, Early Life and Connections*, 1910, which unfortunately stops just before Pitt's full genius for statesmanship was revealed; my *William Pitt, Earl of Chatham*, 2 vols., 1913, to which I may be allowed to refer for a fuller bibliography of the subject, and Brian Tunstall's excellent *William Pitt, Earl of Chatham*, 1938. J. D. Griffith Davies, *A King in Toils*, 1938, is a lively and well-informed account of George II and his reign. *Henry Fox, First Lord Holland* is the title of two biographies, one by T. W. Riker, 2 vols., 1911, the other by Lord Ilchester, 2 vols., 1920; of these, both good, the latter has the great advantage of being illustrated by the papers preserved at Holland House. A. Ballantyne, *Lord Carteret*, 1887, has some useful quotations from the records but is not worthy of its brilliant subject, who is better appreciated in N. W. B. Pemberton, *Carteret, the Brilliant Failure of the Eighteenth Century*, 1936. [One of the last published works of Professor Basil Williams himself was a vigorous comparative study of the two statesmen Carteret and Newcastle, 1943.] W. H. Wilkins, *Caroline the Illustrious*, 2 vols., 1901, gives a useful account of a remarkable personality; and Lord Ilchester and Mrs. Langford-Brooke give a well-documented account of a minor politician and witty versifier in their *Life of Sir Charles Hanbury Williams*, 1928. *The Political Life of Viscount Barrington*, 1814, another minor politician, is fraternally recorded by his brother the bishop of Durham. P. C. Yorke's *Life and Correspondence of Philip Yorke, Lord Chancellor Hardwicke*, 3 vols., 1913, makes G. Harris's *Life*, 3 vols., 1847, unnecessary: though excessively laudatory, this book is most valuable for the ample quotations from the chancellor's voluminous correspondence on state no less than on legal affairs. S. Shellabarger, *Lord Chesterfield*, 1935, is perhaps the most satisfactory biography; Chesterfield's *Letters* were reissued by Bonamy Dobrée, 6 vols., 1932. There are a few useful little biographical sketches of the period in the same editor's *From Anne to Victoria*, 1937. The one politician of this period whose life calls for an adequate biography is the duke of Newcastle: there is a vast amount of material for it, and it should prove both instructive and highly amusing if undertaken by a writer equipped with the necessary knowledge and a keen sense of humour.

FOREIGN RELATIONS. Manuscript authorities have already been indicated in the previous section. The Royal Historical Society has published a series of *British Diplomatic Instructions* to our ambassadors in *Sweden, 1689–1727* (1922), and *1727–89*

(1928), *Denmark, 1689–1789* (1926), all three edited by J. F. Chance; and *France, 1689–1721* (1925), *1721–7* (1927), *1727–44* (1930), *1745–89* (1934), edited by L. G. Wickham Legg. Owing to the nature of the English diplomatic instructions, which never gave a comprehensive survey of our relations and points at issue with foreign nations, but dealt only with particular questions as they arose, this series is not so enlightening as the great French collection of *Recueils des instructions données aux Ambassadeurs de France,* since it was the custom of the French foreign ministers to provide each new ambassador with a comprehensive survey of the general policy regarding the country to which he was accredited, as well as instructions on immediate issues. Unfortunately the *Recueil . . . Angleterre* has not advanced beyond 1690: nevertheless the *Recueils* relating to other countries are often very useful as a sidelight on our diplomacy. Still, though the English series for the countries named is more limited in scope and perforce more arbitrary in the choice of documents, it is valuable as a guide to the chief questions at issue with them. The Royal Historical Society has also issued a useful list of *British Diplomatic Representatives 1689–1789* (1932), edited by Dr. D. B. Horn.

For Treaties there are: Rousset, *Recueil d'actes et traités 1713–48,* 21 t., La Haye, 1728–55 (texts only); and, for separate countries, L. Bittner, *Chron. Verzeichnis d. österreichischen Staatsverträge,* vol. i, *1526–1763,* Vienna, 1903, useful for negotiations as well as text; F. de Martens, *Recueil des traités, . . . Russie,* t. ix (x), *. . . avec l'Angleterre, 1710–1801,* St. Petersburg, 1892 (also gives accounts of negotiations); C. O. Paullin, *European Treaties bearing on History of U.S.A.,* vol. iv, *1766–1815,* Washington, 1937. See, too, D. P. Myers, *Manual of Collections of Treaties,* 1922, for other collections.

There is no comprehensive survey of our foreign policy during this period, though it has been described piecemeal in various books. Some of the chapters in *Cambridge Modern History,* vi, help to an understanding of the European background, especially E. Armstrong's on *Spain* and Nisbet Bain's on *Poland, Russia,* and *Sweden.* J. F. Chance's *George I and the Northern War,* 1909, deals with our northern policy between 1709 and 1721, especially in regard to Sweden and Russia, and his *Alliance of Hanover,* 1923, with the events between 1725 and 1727; both are based on research in our own and foreign archives and are a mine of detailed information. E. Armstrong, *Elizabeth Farnese, the Termagant of Spain*, 1892, is a good account of one of the chief causes of European unrest in the first part of this period. My *Stanhope*, 1932, and a series of five articles on the 'Foreign Policy of Walpole', published in the *English Historical Review*, vols. xv and xvi (1900–1), attempt to give an idea of our policy between 1714 and 1730. The story up to 1739 is taken up in M. Vaucher's book already referred to, and also in A. McC. Wilson's *French Foreign Policy . . . of Cardinal Fleury 1726–43*, 1936, which deals largely with Anglo-French relations. Sir Richard Lodge in his *Great Britain and Prussia*, 1923, and *Studies in Eighteenth-Century European Diplomacy 1740–8*, 1930, dealt mainly with the period of the war of the Austrian Succession. Sir E. Satow, *The Silesian Loan and Frederick the Great*, 1914, deals with a thorny question in Anglo-Prussian relations. Our diplomatic history between that and the Seven Years war is bridged by D. B. Horn's *Sir Charles Hanbury Williams and European Diplomacy 1747–58*, 1930, and Lord Ilchester's volume already referred to, while the books already quoted on Chatham are naturally concerned with the beginnings and course of the Seven Years war. On the other hand foreign writers have dealt more exhaustively with the foreign affairs of this period. Émile Bourgeois's *Manuel historique de la politique étrangère*, 1892, is a useful summary, and the following French books all deal with questions affecting our policy: Comte de Baillon, *Lord Walpole et la Cour de France*, 2 vols., 1867; A. Baudrillart, *Philippe V et la Cour de France*, 5 vols., 1890; L. Wiesener, *Le Régent, l'Abbé Dubois et les anglais*, 3 vols., 1891–9; A. Baraudon, *La Maison de Savoie et la Triple Alliance*, 1896; J. Dureng, *Le Duc de Bourbon et les anglais*, n.d.; J. Syveton, *Une Cour et un aventurier au 18e siècle, le baron de Ripperda*, 1896; Duc de Broglie, *Hist. de la politique étrangère de Louis XV, 1741–56*, 10 vols. (under different titles), 1883–95; R. Waddington, *Le Renversement des alliances*, 1896, and *La Guerre de Sept Ans*, 4 vols., 1899, &c., based on French, Prussian, Austrian, and English archives; A. Bourguet, *Études sur la politique étrangère du Duc de Choiseul*, 1907; A. D. Schaefer, *Geschichte des siebenjährigen Krieges*, 2 B., 1867–74, is well documented from the Prussian archives. *Archives de la Maison d'Orange-Nassau* (ed. Groen van Prinsteren), Série IV, vols. i–iv, 1907–13, has some useful letters from Bentinck, &c., 1747–59; *Friedrichs des Grossen politische Correspondenz*, 80 vols.

published, 1879–1937, has many, generally unamiable, criticisms of our policy, and the *Mémoires de Frédéric II*, 2 vols., 1866, ardently defend his own tortuous policy; W. Oncken, *Zeitalter Friedrichs des Grossen*, 2 vols., 1881, is useful on our foreign affairs. For diplomatic relations with Russia the following volumes of the *Imperatorskoe russkoe ist. obshch.*: *Sbornik*, 61, 66, 76, 80, 85, 91, 99, 102–113, contain the correspondence (in English or French) from 1712 to 1750; and *Catherine II, Correspondence with Sir Charles Hanbury Williams* (trans.), 1928, has important information about a later period. A useful book by Dietrich Gerhard, *England und der Aufstieg Russlands*, 1933, and D. K. Reading's excellent *The Anglo-Russian Commercial Treaty of 1734*, 1938, deal with trade relations; and in *Roy. Hist. Soc. Transactions*, 1900, D'Arcy Collier gives *Notes on Diplomatic Correspondence between England and Russia in First Half of Eighteenth Century*, 1900. A study by Stig Jägenskiöld, *Sverige och Europa 1716–18*, 1937, based on Swedish, English, Hanoverian, and French archives, deals with a critical period in our relations with Sweden. W. Coxe, *History of the House of Austria*, 3 vols. (3rd ed.), 1847, and *Memoirs of the Bourbon Kings of Spain*, 5 vols. (2nd ed.), 1815, and above all Carlyle, *Frederick the Great*, 10 vols., 1873, are still useful.

Special points relating to our foreign policy are dealt with in A. W. Ward's books mentioned in the next section. A. de St. Léger, *La Flandre maritime et Dunkerque sous la domination française, 1659–1789*, 1900; M. Huisman, *La Belgique commerciale . . . la Compagnie d'Ostende*, 1902; R. Geikie and I. A. Montgomery, *The Dutch Barrier, 1705–19*, 1930, give useful accounts of those teasing questions. H. W. V. Temperley in *Roy. Hist. Soc. Transactions*, s. iii, vol. iii, discusses 'The Causes of the War of Jenkins' Ear'; and in the same series, vol. ii, Miss K. Hotblack gives a good account, based on documents, of 'The Peace of Paris, 1763'.

LEGAL AND CONSTITUTIONAL

Of the eighteenth-century theory of the constitution the most authoritative exponent is John Locke, *Two Treatises on Government*, 1690; Charles de Secondat baron de Montesquieu, *De l'esprit des lois* (v. ed.), gave it almost unstinted eulogy; Sir R. Filmer's *Patriarcha*, 1680, was a textbook for high Jacobite theory; Bolingbroke's *Dissertation upon Parties*, 1735, and *Idea of a Patriot King*, 1750, &c., had influence on his and the next generation. For a contemporary exposition both of the constitution and of the legal system Sir William Blackstone, *Commentaries on the Laws of England*, 4th ed., 4 vols., 1770, is important; and the most authoritative modern work on both these aspects is Sir William Holdsworth's *History of English Law*, 12 vols., 1922–38 (the last 3 vols. are specially concerned with the eighteenth century, but there are many references to it in other volumes). A. V. Dicey, *Introduction to the Law of the Constitution*, is an admirable exposition of its principles; Sir William Anson's *Law and Custom of the Constitution*, 3rd ed., 2 vols. in 3, 1897–1908, supplemented by Sir M. Gwyer's ed. of vol. i (*Parliament*) and A. Berriedale Keith's ed. of vol. ii (*The Crown*), gives the best view of its practical working. For illustrative documents see *English Historical Documents*, x, *1714–83*, ed. D. B. Horn and Mary Ransome, 1957.

For the somewhat peculiar relations between Great Britain and Hanover see A. W. Ward, *Electress Sophia and Hanoverian Succession*, 2nd ed., 1909, and *Great Britain and Hanover*, 1899; and, for a necessary understanding of the Hanoverian system, E. v. Meier, *Hannoversche Verfassungs- und Verwaltungsgeschichte*, 2 vols., 1898; see also authorities quoted on p. 21, above.

On the working of the central government M. A. Thomson, *The Secretaries of State 1681–1782*, 1932, is useful, and essays comparing 'the Secretaries of State in England and France' and 'the Prime Minister in England and France' during the eighteenth century will be found in *Studies in Anglo-French History, Eighteenth to Twentieth Centuries*, 1935. There is a discussion in *The Times Literary Supplement* of 27 Feb. (review of *The Austrian Succession*), 6, 13, and 20 Mar. 1930 on the use of the expression 'Prime Minister' or 'Premier' in this period. For the development of Cabinet Councils see the references in vol. x, 2nd ed., pp. 435–6 of this series, to which may be added W. Hasbach, *Die Parlamentarische Kabinets-Regierung*, Stuttgart, 1917. W. M. Torrens, *History of Cabinets*, 2 vols., 1894, is mainly a chronicle of cabinet meetings. Hervey, *Memoirs*, iii. 925–41, gives an illuminating account of cabinet members and discussions in 1740; and among the few other extant accounts of cabinet meetings *State Papers, Foreign, Russia, 63* contains a minute of 24 Nov. 1743 with a list of members attending and their voting on the decisions taken about the Treaty of Worms; and accounts of Pitt's last cabinet in 1761, derived from the Newcastle and Hardwicke MSS., are printed on pp. 119 and 327 of *English Historical Review*, xxi, 1906. There are also other jottings of business to be considered at cabinet meetings in Newcastle and Hardwicke papers.

For parliamentary lists see R. Beatson, *Chronological Index . . . of Houses of Parliament*, 3 vols., 1807. For the composition and proceedings of the house of lords see A. S. Turberville, *The House of Lords in the Eighteenth Century*, 1927, and J. E. Thorold Rogers, *Protests of House of Lords*, 3 vols., 1875. For the many strange franchises in the boroughs see T. H. B. Oldfield, *Representative System of Great Britain and Ireland*, 6 vols., 1816, and E. and A. G. Porritt, *Unreformed House of Commons*, 2 vols., 1903–9. W. T. Laprade, *Public Opinion and Politics in Eighteenth-Century England*, 1936, though marred by an over-breezy style, is useful for the extensive quotations from the pamphlet literature of the time. The debates in parliament, which it was a breach of privilege to report, are, as far as they were recorded, most conveniently followed in (W. Cobbett), *Parliamentary History of England*, vols. vii–xv, 1811–13; P. Mantoux, *Comptes rendus des séances du Parlement anglais . . . aux Archives des affaires étrangères*, 1906, gives some useful additions; and L. F. Stock, *Proceedings and Debates of British Parliaments respecting North America*, 5 vols., 1927–41, now reaches 1754 and is valuable; a note on other sources available and as to the authenticity of reports is to be found in my *William Pitt, Earl of Chatham*, ii. 335–7. The *Journals* of both houses began to be published in this period, and the few legislative fruits of their labours are found in *Statutes of the Realm*, 1810–28. The proceedings are also illuminated, as above stated, by H. Walpole's *Memoirs* and *Letters*, and in other collections of letters. Keith Feiling, *The Second Tory Party 1714–1832*, 1938, has some brilliant but too brief pages on the tories from 1714 to 1760.

The system of local government in the eighteenth century is described with characteristic thoroughness and clarity in the first seven volumes of *English Local Government from the Revolution to the Municipal Corporations Acts*, 8 vols., 1924–9 (2nd ed.), by Sidney and Beatrice Webb. Though in origin avowedly propagandist in purpose, especially in regard to the Poor Law Systems, this work is a mine of trustworthy information for the historian of the period. The Austrian writer, Josef Redlich's, *Local Government in England*, ed. by F. Hirst, 2 vols., 1903, is a useful book on the same subject. As guides to the now vast literature on separate localities, such as the *Victoria Histories of the Counties of England* and local publications, A. L. Humphreys, *Handbook to County Bibliography*, 1917, and other handbooks (see vol. x, 2nd ed., p. 439 should be consulted.

LEGAL. Blackstone and Holdsworth have already been noted above. Besides these Lord Campbell's *Lives of the Lord Chancellors*, 8 vols., 1845–69, and *Lives of the Chief Justices*, 3 vols., 1849–57, though occasionally prejudiced and with some inaccuracies, are still valuable. E. Foss, *Judges of England*, 9 vols., 1848–64, is a much slighter and duller book, but supplies some gaps in Campbell. Vols. xv to xix of *Cobbett's State Trials* (W. T. Howell), 1812–13, throw light not only on the legal but also on the social conditions of the time. Yorke's *Hardwicke*, ii. 413–555, gives a comprehensive, though uncritical, survey of that great chancellor's work. Sir J. F. Stephen's *History of the Criminal Law*, 3 vols., 1883, is also useful. W. Herbert, *Antiquities of Inns of Court and Chancery*, 1804, and Thomas Lane, *The Student's Guide through Lincoln's Inn*, 1805, give interesting details about the Inns of Court and legal education, such as it was, in the eighteenth century. A useful survey, 'Law and the Lawyers', by Sir F. D. Mackinnon, is given in *Johnson's England*, 1933, ii. 287–309. For the machinery of law-enforcement see L. Radzinowicz, *History of English Criminal Law and its Administration*, vol. i, 1948, which begins at about 1750.

ECCLESIASTICAL

The system of the church of England during this period is most clearly set forth in Professor Norman Sykes's *Church and State in England in the Eighteenth Century*, 1934, which exposes all the evils and scandals of that Erastian age, but gives full credit to the minority of bishops and clergy who upheld the Christian virtues or theological scholarship: it has an excellent bibliography; the same author's *Edmund Gibson, Bishop of London*, 1926, gives a good account of Walpole's chief clerical adviser until they quarrelled. In addition to an illuminating survey *From Sheldon to Secker, 1660–1768*, 1959, Dr. Sykes has written his most important work, *William Wake, Archbishop of Canterbury, 1657–1737*, 1957, in which for the first time the voluminous Wake papers at Christ Church, Oxford, have been fully used. Folkestone Williams, *Memoirs and Correspondence of Bishop Atter-*

bury, 2 vols., 1869, is a well-documented book by an enthusiastic admirer of the protagonist of High Church views; H. C. Beeching, *Atterbury*, 1909, is a cooler estimate. J. H. Overton and F. Relton's *English Church 1714–1800*, 1906, is more concerned with the doctrinal controversies of the period, of which an enlightening account is given; some interesting details are to be found in J. Wickham Legg's *English Church Life from the Restoration to the Tractarian Movement*, 1914; and C. J. Abbey has an account of *The English Church and its Bishops 1700–1800*, 2 vols., 1887.

Some particulars about the non-jurors may be found in J. H. Overton, *Law, Nonjuror and Mystic*, 1881; in vol. i of Jeremy Collier's *Ecclesiastical History*, 9 vols., 1840–1; and in R. J. Leslie's *Life and Writings of C. Leslie*, 1885.

The three great ecclesiastical writers of the age may best be studied in their own works. W. E. Gladstone in 1896 published a 2-vol. ed. of *Bishop Butler's Works* with a separate volume of *Studies Subsidiary to Butler*: there are, of course, many other editions. The best edition of Berkeley's *Works* is by A. A. Luce and T. E. Jessop, 4 vols., 1948–57. Dr. Luce also wrote his *Life*, 1949. There is an admirable appreciation of him by Professor W. R. Sorley in *Cambridge History of English Literature*, vol. ix; and in the same volume is a good chapter by Dr. Caroline Spurgeon on 'Law and the Mystics'; Law's *Works* were published in 1892 by G. B. Morgan.

Several Georgian bishops wrote autobiographies, two of them included in the volume of *Lives of Dr. Edward Pocock, Dr. Zachary Pearce, Dr. Thos. Newton and Rev. Philip Skelton*, 2 vols., 1816, and *Anecdotes of Richard Watson, Bishop of Landaff, Written by Himself*, 2 vols., 1818.

On the position of the Roman catholics, Charles Butler, *Historical Memoirs of English, Irish and Scottish Catholics from the Reformation to the Present Time*, 4 vols., 1819–21, is still the chief textbook. Hon. Charles Howard, *Historical Anecdotes of . . . Howard Family*, new ed., 1817, and Maude Petre, *Ninth Lord Petre*, S.P.C.K., 1928, have some interesting details about two considerable Roman catholic families, by no means ultramontane in their views; and some useful points about Roman catholic organization and numbers in Great Britain are to be found in Bernard Ward, *The Dawn of the Catholic Revival, 1781–1803*, 2 vols., 1909.

The history of the protestant nonconformists is dealt with in

H. S. Skeats, *History of Free Churches*, 1868; A. H. Drysdale, *History of Presbyterians in England*, 1889, has two short chapters on their decline in this century. For the quakers see John Gough, *History of the People called Quakers*, Dublin, 4 vols., 1790; W. C. Braithwaite, *Second Period of Quakerism*, 1919, deals mostly with the seventeenth century but has some details about the eighteenth. Two prominent dissenters wrote accounts of their own lives, Edmund Calamy (1671–1732), *Historical Account of My Own Life* (ed. J. T. Rutt), 2 vols., 1829–30, and Philip Doddridge, *Correspondence and Diary* (ed. J. D. Humphreys), 5 vols. in 3, 1829–31. A particularly useful book on the intellectual and educational activities of dissenters is Olive M. Griffiths's *Religion and Learning, A Study in English Presbyterian Thought*, 1935. For their political activities from 1732, B. L. Manning, *The Protestant Dissenting Deputies*, 1952, is authoritative.

On the Jews there is a good book by A. M. Hyamson, *History of the Jews in England*, 1908, and a lively and well-documented account of the passing, followed immediately by the repeal, of the Jews Naturalization Act of 1753 in G. B. Hertz, *British Imperialism in the Eighteenth Century*, 1908.

For the methodist movement of Wesley and Whitefield, see *Journal of John Wesley*, ed. N. Curnock, 8 vols., 1909–16, and *Letters of John Wesley*, ed. J. Telford, 8 vols., 1931, and biographies of Wesley by W. H. Hutton, 1927, and J. H. Overton, 1891; between 1921 and 1934 J. S. Simon published seven volumes under various titles on aspects of Wesley's work; for Whitefield see *A Selection of Letters of G. Whitefield*, 3 vols., 1772, and L. Tyerman, *Life of Rev. George Whitefield*, 2 vols., 1876. R. Graves, *The Spiritual Quixote*, 1772, is a novel referring to the Whitefield side of the methodist movement. For the countess of Huntingdon's activities see *Life and Times of Selina, Countess of Huntingdon*, 2 vols., 1840, well documented; Sarah Tytler, *The Countess of Huntingdon and Her Circle*, 1907, is a more popular presentation. Egmont, *Diaries*, has much to say on Wesley, Whitefield, and ecclesiastical matters generally.

For the Bangorian and deistic controversies a good guide is Leslie Stephen, *History of English Thought in the Eighteenth Century*, 3rd ed., 1902. Both, connected with one another, gave rise to a vast pamphlet and book literature. J. M. Creed and J. S. Boys Smith, *Religious Thought in the Eighteenth Century*, 1934, is useful for its summaries and extracts from the most important writers in these religious disputes. Hume's *Essays* for the time being closed the controversy on miracles.

MILITARY

The literature on military subjects for this period is not very extensive. C. M. Clode, *Military Forces of the Crown*, 2 vols., 1869, is useful for its historical exposition of the law on the subject; Charles Dalton, *George I's Army, 1714–27*, 2 vols., 1910–12, gives details, &c., of regiments and composition; Hon. Sir J. W. Fortescue's *History of the British Army*, 8 vols., 1899–1917 (the first 2 vols. end with 1763), though good on formation of regiments and in describing engagements, has some serious gaps, e.g. as to systems of drill, &c., and some strange opinions such as that Chatham 'was not a great war-minister'; contemporary accounts of the Seven Years War are J. Entick, *History of the Late War*, 5 vols., 1763, and [An Officer], *Operations of the Allied Army under Prince Ferdinand*, 1764, with good maps; Captain John Knox, *Historical Journal of Campaigns in N. America . . . 1757–60*, 2 vols., 1769. C. T. Atkinson, in *Royal United Service Inst. Journal*, lxxix, no. 516, 1934, writes on 'British Strategy and Battles in Westphalian Campaigns 1758–62'. Sir D. Dundas, *Principles of Military Movement*, 1788, contains an outline of the British campaigns in Germany, 1757, &c., but is more important for its lessons drawn from German methods of marching, manœuvring, &c. H. Bland, *Treatise on Military Discipline*, 1762, gives the views of the time. E. M. Lloyd, *Review of the History of Infantry*, 1908, gives a useful comparison between English and Prussian methods of drill. Hon. Evan Charteris, *William Augustus, Duke of Cumberland*, 2 vols., 1913, 1925, describes the duke's military reforms and failures in action; F. H. Skrine has an account of *Fontenoy and Great Britain's Share in War of Austrian Succession*, 1906. The best-known life of Wolfe is by Beckles Willson, *Life and Letters of J. Wolfe*, 1909, and Lt.-Col. Wood in the Chronicles of Canada series, published at Toronto, has edited *The Winning of Canada: Chronicle of Wolfe*, 1915, *Logs of the Conquest of Canada*, 1909, and *The Great Fortress, Louisburg 1720–60*, 1916. The two latter refer chiefly to the naval operations.

NAVAL

The National Maritime Museum at Greenwich should be visited by all interested in naval matters for its portraits of naval commanders, models of ships of the royal navy (there is, for example, to be seen there the model of Anson's ship *Centurion*, in his voyage round the world, made in 1748 on Anson's order), pictures of naval battles, examples of early uniforms, &c., valuable for an understanding of naval history. A useful *Bibliography of British Naval History*, 1930, has been published by G. E. Manwaring.

The Navy Records Society has published several volumes of contemporary records dealing with this period (editors' names in parentheses): *History of the Russian Fleet during the Reign of Peter the Great* (Sir Cyprian Bridge), 1895, useful since this fleet was built chiefly under English craftsmen, and when built gave much trouble to Admiral Norris and others; *Fighting Instructions, 1530–1816* (J. S. Corbett), 1905; *Naval Ballads and Songs* (C. H. Firth), 1907; *Papers relating to Loss of Minorca* (H. W. afterwards Sir Herbert Richmond), 1911; *Byng Papers* (W. B. Tunstall), i–iii, 1930–2, published so far; *Barrington Papers*, i, 1937, has interesting details about training of midshipmen. In the Historical Manuscript Commission's publications the *Du Cane MSS.*, 1905 (Sir J. K. Laughton), has details about seamen's dress, rations, &c., and naval operations of 1740–8; and the *Delaval Papers* (xiii. 6) are also useful.

R. Beatson, *Naval and Military Memoirs of Great Britain*, 6 vols., 1804, has statistics of navy, &c., as well as accounts of battles; Sir W. L. Clowes, *The Royal Navy* . . ., 7 vols., 1897–1903, conveys information about constitutions of the fleet, pay, prize money, &c., but unfortunately does not give authorities; the lives of admirals of the period in the *Dictionary of National Biography*, all written by Sir J. K. Laughton, are first rate. On Anson see R. Walter, *A Voyage Round the World in Years 1740–4 by George Anson*, 15 ed., 1780, based on Anson's own notes; Sir John Barrow, *Life of Lord Anson*, 1839; and W. V. Anson, *Life of Lord Anson*, which is rather slight but has some useful extracts from the Hardwicke and Newcastle papers and from the Admiralty Letters at the Record Office. Montagu Burrows, *Life of Edward, Lord Hawke*, 1883, and D. Ford's eulogy of *Admiral Vernon and his Times*, 1907 (with useful documents), deal with two other prominent admirals; Mary E. Matcham, *A Forgotten John Russell*, 1905, relates the interesting life of a sea-captain who was consul at Tetuan, clerk of cheque at Woolwich, consul and then *chargé d'affaires* at Lisbon, and had a varied correspondence with his sea-mates. A. T. Mahan may be said to have revived interest in naval strategy by his *Influence of Sea Power upon History, 1660–1783*, first published in 1889; and Sir Julian Corbett's *England in the Seven Years' War*, 2 vols., 1907, made the issues of that war and Pitt's strategy, helped by his great admirals, clearer than they had ever been before. Admiral Sir Herbert Richmond carried on the good work by his careful study of *The Navy in the War of 1739–48*, 3 vols., 1920; his edition of the *Minorca Papers* (N.R.S.) above mentioned; and his article in the *Royal United Service Institute Journal*, lv, 1911, on 'The Expedition to Sicily, 1718'. His final conclusions on the whole period are given in a few pages of *Statesmen and Sea Power*, 1948; those on the earlier part of it more fully in *The Navy as an Instrument of Policy, 1558–1727*, 1953. Two articles by C. E. Fayle in the *Royal United Service Institute Journal*, lxviii, 1923, on 'Deflection of Strategy by Commerce in Eighteenth Century' and 'Economic Pressure in the War of 1739–48' are useful on this subject, then of growing importance; R. Pares, in *Royal Hist. Soc. Transactions*, s. iv, vol. xx, 1937, throws light on 'The Manning of the Navy in the W. Indies, 1702–63'; and in the *Royal Naval Medical Service Journal*, xx. 3, July 1934, H. C. S. Booth's 'Peeps at the Past' deals with the naval medical service, of which Smollett in *Roderick Random* had such hard things to say. G. E. Manwaring, *The Flower of England's Garland*, 1936, contains some useful information on out of the way subjects such as the dress of the navy, &c.

SCOTLAND

H. W. Meikle, *Brief Biography of Scottish History*, Historical Association, 1937, is a good handy guide to all branches of Scottish history; see also C. S. Terry, *Index to Papers relating to Scotland in Hist. MSS. Comm. Reports, 1908*, and C. S. Terry (and C. Matheson) *Catalogue of Publications . . . relating to Scotland . . . 1780–1827*, 1909 and 1929. P. Hume Brown, *History of Scotland*, vol. iii, 1909, is the best general account. H. T. Buckle, *History of Civilization in England*, first ed., 2 vols., 1857–61, devotes his third volume to Scottish thought, and while denouncing the narrow views of the clergy in the seventeenth century gives full credit to the awakening of the eighteenth; W. L. Mathieson, *Scotland and the Union . . . 1695–1747*, 1905, and *The Awakening of Scotland, 1747–97*, 1911, are first rate for social and religious movements. John Galt's *Annals of the Parish*, 1822, though beginning in 1760, throws much light on social life, &c., of previous decades. G. W. T. Omond, *Lord Advocates of Scotland*, 2 vols., 1883, is useful; H. Hamilton, *Industrial Revolution in Scotland*, 1932; and H. G. Graham, *Social Life in Scotland in the Eighteenth Century*, 2 vols., 1900, are good on their subjects. The *Culloden Papers*, 1815, and G. Menary, *Life and Letters of Duncan Forbes of Culloden, 1685–1747*, 1936, are important for understanding one of the leading Scotsmen of the time. A. F. Tytler (Lord Woodhouselee), *Memoirs of Life and Writing of H. Home of Kames*, 3 vols., 1814, gives interesting particulars of the legal system as well as of the numerous literary and philosophic clubs in Edinburgh. Jacobite risings naturally figure largely in past and recent Scottish books: A. and H. Tayler have written about *1715*: *Story of the Rising*, 1936, *1745 and After*, 1938, and *Jacobites of Aberdeenshire, 1747–9*, 1910, all based on manuscript authorities such as the Stuart Papers. For the *Scottish Historical Society* Dr. Dickson has edited the *Jacobite Attempt of 1719*, 1894, based on Ormonde's letters; 3 volumes of Bishop Forbes, *The Lyon in Mourning* (relating to Prince Charles Edward) were published in 1895 as well as W. B. Blaikie's careful *Itinerary of Prince Charles Edward*; besides other volumes in the *Origins, Prisoners*, &c., of the '45, an event still of deep interest in Scotland. J. B. Salmond, *Wade in Scotland*, 1938, is a useful survey of General Wade's road-making with plans, &c., based partly on Wade manuscripts.

IRELAND

GENERAL. W. E. H. Lecky, *History of Ireland in the Eighteenth Century*, 5 vols., 1892, the chapters relating to Ireland from his *England in the Eighteenth Century*, perhaps the best, published separately; J. A. Froude, *English in Ireland in the Eighteenth Century*, 3 vols., 1881, like all that author's books, should be used with caution. There is a good chapter on 'Ireland' by R. Dunlop in *Cambridge Modern History*, vol. vi, 1909. M. J. Bonn, *Die englische Kolonisation in Irland*, 2 vols., Berlin, 1906, goes thoroughly into the legislation and methods of government affecting the Irish population; W. F. T. Butler, *Confiscation in Irish History*, 1917; Arthur Young, *A Tour in Ireland*, 1780, though made after this period, is useful about the land system and agriculture during the whole century. On Irish grievances in the early part of this period see Swift's *Drapier's Letters* and *Irish Tracts*, ed. H. Davis, 1935 and 1948 respectively. For the end of the period R. B. McDowell, *Irish Public Opinion, 1750–1800*, 1944, is very useful. The periodical *Irish Historical Studies* maintains a high standard.

SPECIAL. On Carteret's important vice-royalty the papers in 'Ireland 63' in the Public Record Office in London are useful, as well as Carteret's own correspondence in the Brit. Mus. Add. MSS. 24137–8, and letters from Ireland to E. Southwell, the secretary of state for Ireland, Add. MSS. 21122–3. On the Wood's Halfpence agitation see J. Swift, *Drapier's Letters* (H. Davis ed.), 1935; A. Goodwin, 'Wood's Halfpence' in *English Historical Review*, Oct. 1936; while R. Quintana, *The Mind and Art of Jonathan Swift*, 1936, deals, *inter alia*, with Swift's Irish views. *Letters Written by Hugh Boulter, 1724–38*, 2 vols., 1769; and William Nicholson, D.D., *Letters, 1683–1726/7* (ed. J. Nichols), 2 vols., 1809, are both, especially Boulter's, important for the early part of this period. J. C. O'Callaghan, *History of the Irish Brigades in the Service of France*, 1870, deals with the famous Irish regiments in France, which are also alluded to in *Diplomatic Instructions, France 1724–44*, Royal Hist. Soc., 1930. Constantia Maxwell, *Dublin under the Georges, 1714–1830*, 1936, is an admirable survey of the capital's industry, commerce, social, literary, and artistic life, education, and also of the buildings; on the last, *The Georgian Society (Eighteenth-century Domestic Architecture in Dublin)*, 5 vols., Dublin, 1909–13, is a well-illustrated description. Mrs. Delany, *Autobiography and Correspondence*, 6 vols., 1861–2, is very useful for the polite life of Dublin; and for the social life in the country districts and the evils of the land system Maria Edgeworth's *Castle Rackrent* and *The Absentee* are valuable. Miss Constantia Maxwell's *Country and Town under the Georges*, 1940, is a companion to her Dublin volume.

THE COLONIES

GENERAL. *Cambridge History of British Empire*, vol. i, 1929, has excellent chapters by various writers; J. A. Williamson, *Short History of British Expansion*, vol. i, 2nd ed., 1930, is useful both for the colonies and India. American historians have studied innumerable aspects of the history of the colonies in our period. L. H. Gipson, *The British Empire before the American Revolution*, vols. i–vii, 1936–49, is a comprehensive survey including the British Isles as well as the overseas possessions. The official papers dealing with the colonies in this period are to be found in volumes of *Acts of the Privy Council, Colonial*, ii and iii, ed. by W. L. Grant and J. Munro, iv by J. Munro, 1910–11; the *Calendars of State Papers, Colonial* for 1714–35, 1928–53, ed. by C. Headlam and then by A. P. Newton, are most useful as far as they go; the *Journals of Board of Trade and Plantations, 1714–63*, 13 vols., are only of use after 1738 for colonial purposes in indicating papers at the Record Office not yet calendared in the previously mentioned series; L. F. Stock, *Proceedings and Debates of British Parliament*, ii and iii (1702–39), 1930, 1938, is a convenient source of information.

ON SPECIAL ASPECTS. A Berriedale Keith, *First British Empire*, 1930, is invaluable for the constitutional relations of the colonies with the Mother Country and one another; O. M. Dickerson, *American Colonial Government, 1696–1765*, 1912, deals with similar subjects; G. L. Beer, *Old Colonial System, 1660–1754*, 1917, and *British Colonial Policy, 1754–65*, 1907, are brilliant expositions of the faults of, and excuses for, English policy. B. R. Carroll, *Historical Collections of S. Carolina*, 2 vols., 1836, has a narrative of events leading to the Crown's resumption of Carolina; besides the *Egmont Papers and Diaries* published by the Historical Manuscripts Commission, the Georgia Papers in the Public Record Office contain interesting details about the foundation and early days of Georgia, 'Georgia 1 and 2' containing the Trustees' Journal, 1732–40, ib. 4, the Journal of the Common Council, besides interesting points ib. 7, 8, 51. On the Seven Years War period see Col. Wood's publication *supra* under MILITARY; F. Parkman, *Half a Century of Conflict*, 2 vols., 1899, and *Montcalm and Wolfe*, 2 vols., 1901, are spirited descriptions of the subject of A. G. Bradley's *Fight with France for North America*, 1900; G. S. Kimball, *W. Pitt's Correspondence with Colonial Governors*, 2 vols., 1906, is very enlightening; and Kate Hotblack discusses generally *Chatham's Colonial Policy*, 1917. Two books by the late Richard Pares, *War and Trade in the West Indies*, 1936, and *Colonial Blockade and Neutral Rights, 1739–63*, 1938, contain a mass of new information and ideas. G. E. Manwaring's essay on 'Woodes Rogers' in *The Flower of England's Garland*, 1936, gives an insight into troubles in the Bahamas; E. C. Martin relates the history of *British West African Settlements, 1750–1821*, 1927; and Sir J. A. Burdon deals with the queer vicissitudes of the Mosquito coast in *Archives of British Honduras*, 3 vols., 1931–5. E. E. Rich, *History of the Hudson's Bay Company*, vol. i, *1670–1763*, 1958, is written from the Company's records and supersedes all previous authorities.

INDIA

The *Cambridge History of India*, vol. v, 1929, deals well with this period, and there is a good chapter by P. E. Roberts on the period 1720–63 in *Cambridge Modern History*, vol. vi, 1909. Older books which have some value are R. Orme, *History of Military Transactions of Great Britain in Indostan from 1745*, 2 vols. in 3, 1763–78, the author of which was an eyewitness of the events; R. Auber, *Rise of British Power in India*, 2 vols., 1857; and Sir William Hunter, *History of British India*, 2 vols., 1900. J. Bruce, *Annals of E.I. Co., 1600–1778*, 3 vols., 1810; H. D. Love, *Vestiges of Old Madras* (Indian Record Society), 3 vols., 1913; and Alexander Hamilton, 'New Account of East Indies', in vol. viii of *Pinkerton's Voyages*, give interesting details of the way of life, trading, &c., of the E.I. Company's servants at this time. For the French side in the contest Prosper Cultru, *Dupleix, ses plans, sa disgrâce*, 1901, is useful; H. Dodwell has written *Dupleix and Clive*, 1920; and there are many Lives of Clive by Sir J. Malcolm, 1836, G. R. Gleig, 1848, Sir G. W. Forrest, 1918, and others. La Bourdonnais's apologia is put in his *Mémoires historiques — publiés par son petit-fils*, 2nd ed., 1828.

ECONOMIC

Though the late H. S. Foxwell fixed the beginning of economic science at the year 1750, nevertheless throughout this century, as in the latter part of the seventeenth, evidence of the growing interest in questions of public revenue and trade appears in the large output of statistical and theoretical treatises on those subjects. Among these may be noted Joshua Gee's *Trade and Navigation of Great Britain*, 4th ed., 1738; James Postlethwayt's *History of Public Revenue 1688–1758*, 1759; and his brother Malachy's *Universal Dictionary of Trade and Commerce*, 1757, and *African Trade the Pillar and Support of British Plantations in America*, 1748; Sir Charles Whitworth, *State of the Trade of Great Britain in its Imports and Exports*, 1776, with elaborate statistics based on 'annual accounts by the proper officers to the House of Commons'; D. Macpherson's *Annals of Commerce*, 4 vols., 1787, a specially useful vade-mecum with information on the South Sea Company, W. Indian trade and colonies, the state of the navy, &c.; Adam Anderson, *Deduction of the Origin of Commerce*, 1764; George Chalmers, *Estimate of Comparative Strength of Great Britain . . . since the Revolution*, 1804; Sir John Sinclair, *History of the Public Revenue*, 3 vols., 1803. Adam Smith's *Wealth of Nations*, the first edition of which appeared in 1776, is important not only for its new economic theory, but also for the historical illustrations from the trade of this period. Exhaustive accounts of the South Sea scheme of 1719 and its resulting Bubbles will be found in Sinclair, l.c. i. 488 sqq., Macpherson, l.c. iii. 77 sqq., as well as in Cobbett's *Parliamentary History*, vii. 628–912. The *Journals of the Commissioners for Trade and Plantations, 1714–63*, 14 vols., 1924–35, has references to general trade matters.

Of later general works on trade and revenue G. N. Clark, *Guide to English Commercial Statistics, 1696–1782*, Royal Historical Society, 1938, is most useful as an indication of sources from which such statistics can be obtained. R. H. I. Palgrave's *Dictionary of Political Economy*, ed. by H. Higgs, 3 vols., 1926, besides the *Bibliography* referred to in the General Section above, is a good guide to the literature. The value of E. Lipson, *Economic History of England*, 3 vols., 1931, and of W. Cunningham, *Growth of English Industry and Commerce*, pt. ii, *Modern Times*, 1917–19, has been commented on in vol. x, pp. 443–4. C. R. Fay, *Great Britain from Adam Smith to the Present Day*, 3rd ed., 1932, is a suggestive survey, pertinent also to this period; Professor T. S. Ashton has written from a strictly economic point of view, *An Economic History of England: the Eighteenth Century*, 1955, and *Economic Fluctuations in England, 1700–1800*, 1959; and Paul Mantoux, *La Révolution industrielle au 18e siècle*, 1906 (revised English translation by M. Vernon, 1935), is a most important volume. J. F. Rees, 'Phases of British Commercial Policy in the Eighteenth Century' in *Economica*, v. 14 (June 1925) is suggestive; C. H. Wilson, *Anglo-Dutch Commerce and Finance in the Eighteenth Century*, 1941, is thorough and original. L. W. Moffit, *England on Eve of Industrial Revolution, 1740–60*, 1925, prepares the way for the full efflorescence in the next period; Sir H. L. Trueman Wood, *Industrial England in the Middle of the Eighteenth Century*, 1910, is a handy popular survey; J. L. and B. Hammond's *Village Labourer 1760–1832*, new ed., 1920, *Town Labourer 1760–1832*, new ed., 1920, and especially *Rise of Modern Industry*,

1926, though dealing mainly with the next, have much of interest for this period; and Sidney and Beatrice Webb's great work on *English Local Government*, already referred to, is full of economic information. Two very good regional studies are W. H. B. Court, *The Rise of the Midland Industries*, 1938, and E. Hughes, *North Country Life in the Eighteenth Century: the North-East, 1700–50*, 1952. S. Dowell, *History of Taxation and Taxes in England*, 4 vols., 1884, is a handy account of the subject; William Kennedy, *English Taxation, 1640–1799*, 1913, a more scientific treatment. The most important of the assessed taxes is the subject of W. R. Ward, *The English Land Tax in the Eighteenth Century*, 1953. E. L. Hargreaves, *The National Debt*, 1930, is useful for its concise statement of debt operations and views on the debt in this period. More specialized aspects of trade and taxation are dealt with in N. A. Brisco's valuable *Economic Policy of Walpole*, 1907, and E. Hughes, *Studies in Administration and Finance*, 1934, which is chiefly about the salt tax. Sir John Clapham's standard *History of the Bank of England*, 2 vols., 1944, was based on the Bank's own records, previously unused.

SPECIAL SUBJECTS—*Population*. In the absence of a census deductions had to be made from insufficient data: James Postlethwayt, *Collection of Bills of Mortality 1657–1758*, 1759, made estimates from this defective source; Dr. Richard Price, *Essay on the Population of England*, 1780, made a more elaborate attempt; for other estimates see above, pp. 123–4.

On the *Poor*: see *John Locke's Report of the Board of Trade (Relief of the Poor) 1697*, 1789; H. Fielding, *Proposal for making Effectual Provision for the Poor*, 1753; J. Hanway, *Letters on the Importance of the Rising Generation*, 2 vols., 1767; Arthur Young, *Tours, passim;* Sir F. M. Eden, *State of Poor*, 3 vols., 1797; Dorothy Marshall, *English Poor in the Eighteenth Century*, 1926, a good, well-informed survey; S. and B. Webb, vii, *English Poor Law*, Part I, 1927, is an exhaustive statement of the poor-law system.

On *Wages*: from Defoe's and especially Arthur Young's *Tours* much information is to be gleaned: note especially Young's *Eastern Tour*, iv. 301–6; Mantoux gives some particulars; and the whole matter has been scientifically examined by E. W. Gilboy in *Wages in Eighteenth-century England*, 1934, and in *Review of Economic Statistics*, xviii (1936).

Agriculture. Arthur Young is here again illuminating on actual conditions (and indeed he and Defoe have much of interest on other industries also). R. E. Prothero (Lord Ernle), *English Farming, Past and Present*, 5th ed., 1936, is the chief modern authority, and H. Levy, *Large and Small Holdings* (trans.), 1914, is important. On the vexed question of *Inclosures* much has been written. *Return* (*H.C.*), *Inclosure Acts*, 1911, gives the statistics; J. L. and B. Hammond, *The Village Labourer* (as above), and W. Hasbach, *History of the English Agricultural Labourer* (trans. by R. Kenyon), 1920, dwell mainly on the evils of Inclosures; Levy, l.c., and A. H. Johnson, *Disappearance of the Small Land-Owner*, 1905, are on the whole favourable to the system; D. G. Barnes, *History of the English Corn Laws*, 1930, takes a balancing view; and E. K. C. Gonner, *Common Land and Inclosure*, 1912, deals most exhaustively with the system and gives a useful survey of causes, methods, and effects and tables of statistics. J. E. Thorold Rogers, *History of Agriculture and Prices in England*, vol. vii, parts i and ii, *1703–93*, 1902, edited by his son, gives not only corn prices for the eighteenth century but also those for coal, metal, and sundry other articles, besides statistics about wages, and prices of East India and Bank of England stocks and consols.

Special Industries. Largely, no doubt, owing to the example and influence of the late Professor Unwin, much research work has recently been done, especially at Manchester, into the conditions of special trades: e.g. A. P. Wadsworth and J. de Lacy Mann, *Cotton Trade and Industrial Lancashire 1600–1780*, 1931; T. S. Ashton, *Iron and Steel in Industrial Revolution*, 1924; T. S. Ashton and J. Sykes, *Coal Industry of the Eighteenth Century*, 1920; J. U. Nef, *Rise of the British Coal Industry*, 2 vols., 1932, which, though dealing with a period immediately preceding ours, is an exhaustive account of the processes, methods of trading, &c., little changed in the eighteenth century; H. Heaton, *Yorkshire Woollen and Worsted Industries*, 1920; H. Hamilton, *English Copper and Brass Industries to 1800*, 1926. T. S. Willan's *River Navigation in England, 1600–1750*, 1936, and *English Coasting Trade 1600–1750*, 1939, deal with subjects hitherto little explored; and from Sir E. Broodbank's *History of the Port of London*, 1921, some items can be gleaned about eighteenth-century docks at Rotherhithe and Liverpool.

SOCIAL LIFE

GENERAL. *Johnson's England*, 2 vols., 1933, has several useful chapters with good short bibliographies on these subjects; T.

Wright, *England under the House of Hanover*, 2 vols., 1848, deals with every aspect of social as well as political life; other general surveys of social life are H. D. Traill and J. S. Mann (eds.), *Social England*, vol. v, 1901–4; A. S. Turberville, *English Men and Manners in the Eighteenth Century*, 1926; W. E. H. Lecky, chapters v and xxi. The London life and business affairs of an aristocratic family are described by Gladys Scott Thomson, *The Russells in Bloomsbury, 1669–1771*, 1940.

CONTEMPORARY LETTER- AND MEMOIR-WRITERS abound, e.g. Chesterfield's *Letters* (B. Dobrée, ed.), 6 vols., 1932; H. Walpole's *Letters* and *Memoirs* (*ut supra*); J. H. Jesse, *George Selwyn and his Contemporaries*, 4 vols., 1882; Lady Mary Wortley Montagu, *Letters and Works*, 2 vols., 1861, and R. Halsband, *Lady Mary Wortley Montagu*, 1956, with some further letters; Mrs. Delany, *Autobiography and Memoirs*, 6 vols., 1861–2; L. Climenson, *Elizabeth Montagu*, 2 vols., 1906, has the correspondence of this rather dull 'Queen of the Blue-Stockings'; *Purefoy Letters, 1735–53* (ed. G. Eland), 2 vols., 1931, gives a picture of a country gentleman's life, social surroundings, travels, &c.; Sir Charles Hanbury Williams, *Works*, 3 vols., 1822, contains the best *vers de société* of the time.

TRAVEL SURVEYS are also abundant, e.g. Defoe and Arthur Young, l.c.; the latter especially being very persistent about the bad state of the roads, the system of which is also described by S. and B. Webb, *The King's Highway*, 1913. Dr. R. Pococke was an indefatigable traveller, even when he became an Irish bishop in 1756, in England, Scotland, Ireland, Switzerland, Palestine, Asia Minor, and Egypt: his travels to the East are in Pinkerton's *Voyages and Travels*, vols. x and xv, his *Travels through England, 1750–7* (ed. for Camden Society by J. J. Cartwright), 2 vols., 1888–9, and his *Tours in Scotland, 1747–60*, Scottish History Society, vol. i, 1886. Jonas Hanway, the philanthropist and introducer of the umbrella, stimulated interest in the Far East by his *Historical Account of British trade over the Caspian with Journal of Travels through Russia into Persia*, 1753. Rather later travels by Rev. W. Shaw to the West of England and of William Bray to Derbyshire and Yorkshire, when travel was much the same as up to 1760, are given in Pinkerton, vol. ii. Intelligent foreigners also came to England and noted their impressions of the country, e.g. the Portuguese Gonzales in 1730 in Pinkerton, ii. 1–171; César De Saussure in *A Foreign*

View of England . . ., 1902; [J. B. le Blanc] *Lettres d'un Français*,
3 vols., La Haye, 1745, is a delightful account of the pleasures
and pains of the foreigner in England, interesting too about
our art, the badness of our roads, highwaymen, &c.; Baron
de Bielfeld, *Lettres familières*, 2 vols., La Haye, 1763, was also
happy in England, but was only five months there; C. P. Moritz,
whose *Travels in England in 1782* are available in separate
editions and also in Pinkerton, vol. ii. For the benefit, or as
a result, of such travellers, map-makers became busy, e.g.
Herman Moll's *Set of 50 . . . Maps of England and Wales with the
Great Roads and . . . Cross Roads* (1724); and J. Owen's *Britannia
Depicta, or Ogilby Improved*, 4th ed., 1730, with its elaborate
layouts of every road in the country. The practice for young
Englishmen of wealth and standing to make the Grand Tour
on the Continent encouraged the production of such books as
T. Smollett's *Travels through France and Italy* (v. eds.), various
guides for the Grand Tour, and no doubt suggested the title
of Sterne's *Sentimental Journey*. C. Maxwell, *English Traveller in
France*, 1932, summarizes some of the tours to that country.

The best idea of the LIFE OF THE TIMES is perhaps derived from
such contemporary novels as Defoe's *Moll Flanders*, Adept
[Charles Johnson]'s *Chrysal, or The Adventures of a Guinea* (4 vols.,
ed. of 1785); and all those of Fielding, Smollett, and Richardson, as supplemented by the pictures of Hogarth, Zoffany, and
other artists and the innumerable caricatures, of which a
learned and entertaining history with illustrative examples is
to be found in M. Dorothy George, *English Political Caricature*,
vol. i, 1959. Other illustrations are in George Paston's *Social
Caricature in the Eighteenth Century*, 1905, and in E. B. Chancellor's
Eighteenth Century in England, 1920. The *Diary of Dudley Ryder*,
1939, is useful for social life of dissenting middle class.

On the actual CONDITIONS OF THE PEOPLE, S. and B. Webb's
volumes already cited and their *History of Liquor Licensing in
England, 1700–1830*, 1903, are most valuable. M. Dorothy George,
London Life in the Eighteenth Century, 1925, is excellent, especially
with regard to the poor. H. Fielding, *Inquiry into late Increase of
Robberies &c.*, 1750, goes into the causes and possible cures for
the bad state of the capital. Many of the books suggested above
in the ECONOMIC section are also useful for the social aspect.

On EDUCATION in the eighteenth century, Locke's *Thoughts
concerning Education*, 1693, and *Of the Conduct of the Understanding*

had great influence; Swift's *Letter to a very young Lady on her Marriage* promoted better female education; Steele's *Spectator* articles were also stimulating. One of the best modern surveys, though brief, is Professor J. W. Adamson's chapter in *Cambridge History of English Literature*, vol. ix, 1912, pp. 381 sqq., with the useful Bibliography at the end of the volume. Cambridge with J. B. Mullinger, *History of the University of Cambridge*, 3 vols., 1873–1911, which, though ending in the seventeenth century, gives the system, and D. A. Winstanley's two volumes on *University of Cambridge in the Eighteenth Century*, 1922, and *Unreformed Cambridge*, 1935, is better served than Oxford with Sir C. E. Mallett's *History of University of Oxford*, 3 vols., 1924–7, and A. D. Godley's *Oxford in the Eighteenth Century*, 1908. J. H. Monk, *Life of Richard Bentley*, 2 vols., 1833, throws light on the Cambridge of his time; Thomas Hearne, in *Reliquiae Hearnianae* (Philip Bliss ed.), 2 vols., 1857, and N. Amhurst, *Terrae Filius*, 1726, give an insight into the seamy side of Oxford. *Thomas Hearne's Collections*, 11 vols., edited for the Oxford Historical Society, give ampler extracts of Hearne's correspondence, diary, &c., than the *Reliquiae*. For English schools see N. Carlisle, *Endowed Grammar Schools in England and Wales*, 2 vols., 1818, with an account of all endowed schools, including Eton, Westminster, Rugby, &c., with dates of founding and some details about methods of education; A. F. Leach, *History of Winchester College*, 1899; H. C. Maxwell Lyte, *History of Eton College*, 4th ed., 1911; J. Sargeaunt, *Annals of Westminster School*, 1898. W. O. Allen and E. McClure, *Two Hundred Years: the History of the S.P.C.K.*, 1898, deals with a powerful educational organ of the time; M. G. Jones, *The Charity School Movement of the Eighteenth Century*, 1938, is a very important book, well documented, on this great movement.

SCIENCE AND HISTORICAL RESEARCH

This section merely gives books that have been found useful for writing Chapter XIV and is obviously anything but exhaustive.

GENERAL. W. Whewell, *History of the Inductive Sciences*, 3 vols., 1837, gives very clear expositions; C. R. Weld, *History of the Royal Society*, 2 vols., 1848; *Record of the Royal Society*, 3rd ed., 1912, which includes a register of fellows; *Philosophical Transactions of Royal Society*; Ephraim Chambers, *Cyclopaedia or Universal*

Dictionary of Arts and Sciences, 2 vols., 6th ed., 1750, gives contemporary views on these subjects; R. T. Gunther, *Early Science in Oxford*, 1925; L. T. Hogben, *Inaugural Lecture at Aberdeen*, 1937, is a brief but enthusiastic eulogy of Scottish contributions to industrial science in the eighteenth century.

ASTRONOMY. J. B. J. Delambre, *Histoire de l'astronomie au 18e siècle*, Paris, 1827; biographies of astronomers in *Dict. Nat. Biog.*

MATHEMATICS. C. Tweedie, *James Stirling*, 1922; W. W. Rouse Ball, *Short Account of History of Mathematics*, 1888, rather sketchy. The *Dict. Nat. Biog.* again very useful with its biographies.

ELECTRICITY. E. T. Whittaker, *History of Theories of Aether and Electricity*, Dublin, 1910; *Encyclopaedia Britannica*, 9th ed., 1902–3, article on 'Electricity' by George Chrystal; Benjamin Franklin, *New Experiments and Observations on Electricity*, 1750.

CHEMISTRY. T. M. Lowry, *Historical Introduction to Chemistry*, 1936, a clear and reliable handbook; Adam Ferguson, *Joseph Black*, 1801; Sir William Ramsay, *Life and Letters of Joseph Black*, 1918; Joseph Black, *Experiments on Magnesia Alba, &c.*, 1756, the thesis from which his fame sprang; George Jardine, 'Account of James Roebuck', *Transactions of Royal Society of Edinburgh*, iv. 6587, 1798.

MEDICAL, &c. F. H. Garrison, *Introduction to History of Medicine*, 1913, is a useful survey of all branches of the subject; J. Hunter, *Essays and Observations on Natural History, Anatomy, &c.* (ed. R. Owen), 2 vols., 1861; G. C. Peachey, *Memoir of Wm. and J. Hunter*, 1924, and Sir Stephen Paget, *John Hunter 1728–93*, 1897, are both good accounts; H. Fox, *Dr. John Fothergill and his Friends*, 1919, gives an interesting account of Fothergill's many-sided activities as doctor, botanist, quaker, and social reformer; James Lind's important reforms for the navy are described in his *Treatise on the Scurvy*, 1754, and *Essay on means of preserving Health of Seamen*, 1757; Sir J. Pringle's for the army in his *Discourse on . . . Improvement for preserving Health of Marines*, 1776. John Arbuthnot, though best known as a wit and political pamphleteer, was also a distinguished physician: to him justice is done by G. A. Aitken, *Life and Works of John Arbuthnot*, 1892, and L. M. Beattie, *John Arbuthnot . . . Scientist*, 1935.

BOTANY. J. Reynolds Green, *History of Botany in the United*

Kingdom till end of Nineteenth Century, 1914, is an excellent survey; the German botanist J. v. Sachs, *History of Botany 1530–1860*, trans. by H. E. F. Garnsey, 1906, gives full credit to S. Hales's important discoveries in botany, which are set forth by himself in his *Vegetable Staticks*, 1727; John J. Dillenius, the first professor of botany at Oxford, produced two notable volumes, *Hortus Elthamensis*, 1732, describing the treasures of his friend James Sherard's garden at Eltham, and *Historia Muscorum*, 1741. Peter Kalm's *Account of his Visit to England in 1748* (trans. by J. Lucas), 1892, deals chiefly with his botanical observations.

Historical Research, &c., is mainly indicated by the principal achievements of scholarship in this period, such as D. Wilkins, *Concilia Magnae Britanniae*, 1737; Thomas Hearne's editions of various *Chronicles*; his *Reliquiae Hearnianae* (ed. Dr. Bliss), 2 vols., 1857, also are useful on this subject; see also *Thomas Hearne's Collections* referred to in Social and Educational section; W. Stukeley, *Itinerarium Curiosum*, 1724, is the best known of the then fashionable antiquarian travels; other useful antiquarian works are John Horsley's *Britannia Romana*, 1732, A. Gordon's *Itinerarium Septentrionale*, 1726, and F. Drake's *Eburacum*, 1736.[1] F. Wise, *Annals of Asser*, 1722, is important especially for its reference to a now lost manuscript of Asser; and the *Harleian Miscellany*, first published in 5 vols. in 1743–5 (a later ed. in 10 vols., 1808–13), was prepared by W. Oldys and has a preface by Dr. Johnson. P. Boyle, *Museum Britannicum*, 1791, has an interesting account of the foundation of the British Museum; R. G. B. Partridge, *History of the Legal Deposit of Books throughout the British Empire*, 1938, is pertinent to this subject. Isaac Disraeli, *Curiosities of Literature* (various eds.) has many stories of such antiquarians of the period as Dr. Thomas Birch, Oldys, Stukeley, Anthony Collins, Des Maiseaux, and Neale, the historian of the puritans.

THE ARTS AND MUSIC

Visits to the National Gallery and the Dulwich Gallery for pictures, to the British Museum Print Department for engravings, caricatures, &c., and to the Victoria and Albert Museum for the decorative arts are the best way of appreciating the art of the period: there are of course similar galleries, &c., available at Edinburgh and some provincial towns. For the architecture

[1] For estimates of these works see vol. i of this series, pp. 466–7, 474.

of the period an inspection of the eighteenth-century churches, public buildings, and houses, alas! a diminishing number, in London, Bath, Edinburgh, and many other towns, besides numerous country houses, is recommended.

The Courtauld Institute in London possesses a valuable collection, not only of books on art, but also of tabulated slips for information about the architects of buildings and artists of various periods, to the use of which others, besides students, are welcomed.

E. B. Chancellor, *The Eighteenth Century in London*, 1920, is specially useful for good reproductions of views of London by Samuel Scott (1710–72) and illustrations of buildings, furniture, &c., of the period. A. E. Richardson, *Georgian England*, has good illustrations of arts, trades, industries, &c.

LITERATURE ON PAINTING. Of *contemporary works*, Horace Walpole, *Anecdotes of Painting and Catalogue of Engravers*, 5 vols., Strawberry Hill, 2nd ed., 1765, is still useful, being based on Vertue's elaborate notes and catalogues; W. Hogarth, *Analysis of Beauty*, 1753, though disputable in theory, is interesting for the author; Sir Joshua Reynolds, *Discourses* (ed. Roger Fry), 1903, of first-rate importance.

LATER WORKS ON PAINTING. W. Thieme and F. Becker, *Allgemeines Lexikon d. bildenden Künstler, &c.*, 12 vols., 1907, &c. (unfinished) is exhaustive as a reference book. R. S. Redgrave, *A Century of Painters of the English School*, 2 vols., 1866; W. T. Whitley, *Artists and their Friends in England, 1700–99*, 2 vols., 1937; C. H. Collins Baker, *British Painting*, 1933, are all especially useful. Col. M. H. Grant, *Old English Landscape Painters, Sixteenth to Nineteenth Centuries*, 3 vols. [revised edn., 1957], is a sumptuously illustrated and well-documented account of its subject. Sir Kenneth Clark's 'Painting of English Landscape', *Proceedings of British Academy*, xxi, 1935, is enlightening.

ON ARCHITECTURE, &c., Sir R. Blomfield's *History of Renaissance Architecture in England, 1500–1800*, 2 vols., 1897, is useful. *An Eighteenth-Century Correspondence* [of Sanderson Miller], ed. by L. Dickins and M. Stanton, 1910, gives interesting particulars about this man's architectural work at Hagley and many other Midland country houses. K. A. Esdaile, *English Monumental Sculpture*, 1937, is a good guide on that subject.

ON GARDENING AND THE DECORATIVE ARTS. Horace Walpole has an article on 'Modern Gardening' in his *Anecdotes of Painting*;

T. Whateley, *Observations on Modern Gardening*, gives particulars of gardens at Esher, Ilam, Wotton, the Leasowes, Hagley, Stowe, &c. There are also books on the *English Garden* by William Mason, 1772; and *Essay on Design in Gardening* by George Mason, 1774. In many of the issues of *Country Life* are to be found accounts by Thomas Tipping, and illustrations of eighteenth-century (and other) country houses and gardens. Thomas Chippendale's magnificent folio, *The Gentleman and Cabinet Maker's Director*, 1754, gives numerous illustrations of his special craft; and O. Brackett, *Thomas Chippendale*, 1924, has an account of his life and work.

The revival of beautiful *printing* may best be seen in the books issued by Robert Foulis of Glasgow and John Baskerville of Birmingham, and also in some issued by the Oxford University Press. Dr. Paget Toynbee has edited in a worthily printed volume Horace Walpole's *Journal of the Printing Office at Strawberry Hill*, 1923.

MUSIC. Sir George Grove compiled the standard *Dictionary of Music and Musicians*, 4th ed. by H. C. Colles, 6 vols., 1940. Charles Burney began writing in this period his *General History of Music*, published in 4 vols., 1776–89; ed. F. Mercer, 2 vols., 1935. The *Oxford History of Music*, vol. iv, by J. A. Fuller Maitland, 1931, and vol. v by Sir Henry Hadow, 1931, is not really so informative as Hadow's chapter on 'Music' in *Johnson's England*; E. Walker, *History of Music in England*, 1924, should also be consulted. A. J. [Earl] Balfour's *Essays and Addresses*, 1893, contains an enthusiastic appreciation of Handel. W. Boyce continued and published the collection of English *Cathedral Music* (3 vols., 1760–78) begun in this period by Maurice Greene.

LITERATURE

Again, it may perhaps be suggested that reading for oneself the books written by eighteenth-century authors is more illuminating than reading books about them.

As a guide-post to the poetry the *Oxford Book of Eighteenth-Century Verse*, 1926, is excellent in its choice of specimens likely to beguile the reader to browse in some of the authors' complete works. Swift, more than any other author of the time, needed a good editor to establish the canon of the text and has found him in Sir Harold Williams's edition of *The Poems of Jonathan*

Swift, 3 vols., 2nd ed., 1938; R. Quintana's *Mind and Art of Swift*, 1936, is also useful as a commentary. W. Elwin [and W. J. Courthope], *Pope's Works*, 10 vols., 1871–89, is the most complete edition; and E. Sitwell, *Alexander Pope*, 1930, is an enthusiastic commentator. Edmund Gosse's edition of *Thomas Gray's Works in Prose and Verse*, 4 vols., 1884, should be supplemented by Thomas Gray, *Correspondence* (ed. P. Toynbee and L. Whibley), 3 vols., Oxford, 1935. For the life of that most charming poet see R. W. Ketton-Cremer, *Thomas Gray, a Biography*, 1955. All the other poets of the time worth remembering and some not memorable, except as illustrating the passing taste, are easily accessible. *The New Foundling Hospital for Wit*, 3 vols., 1768–73, contains satires and *vers de société* by Hanbury Williams, Chesterfield, Potter, Horace Walpole, and other lesser versifiers. On the other hand, Johnson's *Lives of the Poets* is an essential contemporary commentary on the poets of his day and their predecessors.

There are, too, innumerable editions of the great novelists, Defoe, Richardson, Fielding, Smollett, and Sterne. Most of their best works, besides those of some others less known, but still worth reading, such as Horace Walpole's *Castle of Otranto*, and Richard Graves's *Spiritual Quixote*, are conveniently collected in the 50 volumes of *The British Novelists*, 1810, *with an Essay and Prefaces Biographical and Critical* by Mrs. Barbauld.

Of modern commentators Leslie Stephen's *Hours in a Library*, 3 vols., 1879, has much interesting reading. Most of the volumes on eighteenth-century authors in the 'English Men of Letters' series are useful, and in the *Essays and Studies by Members of the English Association* are to be found good appreciations. D. Nichol Smith's *Eighteenth-Century Essays on Shakespeare*, 1903, and A. Ralli's *History of Shakespearian Criticism*, 1932, discuss the standard of Shakespearian criticism in this epoch; and A. S. Collins's *Authorship in the days of Johnson*, 1927, throws light on the booksellers, circulating libraries, and tastes of the public of the day. The *Cambridge History of English Literature*, vols. ix, 1912, and x, 1913, has some admirable criticisms of the writers of the period.

LISTS OF HOLDERS OF
VARIOUS OFFICES

[Based upon R. Beatson, *Political Index of Great Britain and Ireland*, 3 vols., 3rd ed., 1806, Haydn's *Book of Dignities*, table in Thackeray's *History of William Pitt, Earl of Chatham*, and verified as far as possible from V. Gibbs, *Complete Peerage* and *Calendars of Treasury Papers* (Redington), *Calendars of Treasury Books and Papers* (Shaw), and the *Dictionary of National Biography*.]

Archbishops of Canterbury

1694	Thomas Tenison (to 1715).	1747	Thomas Herring.
1716	William Wake.	1757	Matthew Hutton.
1737	John Potter.	1758	Thomas Secker.

Lord Chancellors, Lord Keeper (L.K.), and Commissioners of the Great Seal (C^rs.)

1710	Simon, Lord Harcourt.
Sept. 1714	Lord Cowper.
Apr. 1718	Sir Robert Tracy, J.C.P. / Sir John Pratt, J.K.B. / Sir James Montague, B. of Exch. } C^rs.
May 1718	Lord Macclesfield.
Jan. 1725	Sir Joseph Jekyll, M.R. / Sir Geoffrey Gilbert, B. of Exch. / Sir Robert Raymond, J.K.B. } C^rs.
June 1725	Lord King.
Nov. 1733	Lord Talbot.
Feb. 1737	Lord Hardwicke.
Nov. 1756	Sir John Willes, C.J.C.P. / Sir S. Smythe, B. of Exch. / Sir J. Eardley Wilmot, J.K.B. } C^rs.
June 1757	Sir Robert Henley (Lord Henley 1760), L.K.
Jan. 1761	Lord Henley (later Lord Northington), L.Ch.

Lord Treasurer

Aug.–Oct. 1714   Charles, duke of Shrewsbury (the last).

First Commissioners of the Treasury

Oct. 1714	Earl of Halifax.	Apr. 1721	(Sir) Robert Walpole.
May 1715	Earl of Carlisle.	Feb. 1742	Earl of Wilmington.
Oct. 1715	Robert Walpole.	Aug. 1743	Hon. Henry Pelham.
Apr. 1717	James (Lord) Stanhope.	10–12 Feb. 1746	Earl of Bath.
Mar. 1718	Earl of Sunderland.	Feb. 1746	Hon. Henry Pelham.

First Commissioners of the Treasury (continued)

Mar. 1754	Duke of Newcastle.	June 1757	Earl Waldegrave.
Nov. 1756	William, 4th duke of Devonshire.	June 1757	Duke of Newcastle (to May 1762).

Chancellors of the Exchequer

1714 (till Oct.)	Sir William Wyndham.	April 1754	Hon. Henry Bilson Legge.
Oct. 1714	Sir Richard Onslow.	Nov. 1755	Sir George Lyttelton.
Oct. 1715	Robert Walpole.	Nov. 1756	Hon. H. B. Legge.
Apr. 1717	James (Lord) Stanhope.[1]	Apr. 1757	Lord Mansfield.[2]
Mar. 1718	John Aislabie.	July 1757	Hon. H. B. Legge.
Jan. 1721	Sir John Pratt, C.J.K.B.[2]	Mar. 1761	William, Lord Barrington.
Apr. 1721	(Sir) Robert Walpole.		
Feb. 1742	Samuel Sandys.	May 1762	Sir Francis Dashwood.
Dec. 1743	Hon. Henry Pelham.	Apr. 1763	Hon. George Grenville.

Junior Commissioners of the Treasury

It is unnecessary to give the full lists of these men, often changed, and many entirely forgotten. The most notable among them were:

Oct. 1714–Oct. 1715	Edward Wortley Montagu (husband of Lady Mary).
Oct. 1714–Apr. 1715	Paul Methuen.
Oct. 1715–Feb. 1716	Daniel, Lord Finch (3rd earl of Nottingham and 7th of Winchilsea).
June 1716–Apr. 1717, and June 1720–Mar. 1724	Richard Edgecombe.
Mar. 1724	Hon. Henry Pelham.
Apr. 1724–1741	George Bubb Dodington.
May 1736–Feb. 1742	Thomas Winnington.
Aug. 1743–June 1746	Henry Fox.
Dec. 1744–Mar. 1754	George (Lord) Lyttelton.
June 1746–May 1749	Hon. H. Bilson Legge.
June 1747–Apr. 1754	Hon. George Grenville.
June 1759–July 1765	Frederick, Lord North.

Lords President of the Council

Sept. 1714	Daniel, 2nd earl of Nottingham.	June 1720	Charles, Viscount Townshend.
July 1716	William, 2nd duke of Devonshire.	Apr. 1721	Henry, Lord Carleton.
Apr. 1717	Charles, earl of Sunderland.	Mar. 1725	William, 2nd duke of Devonshire.
Feb. 1719	Evelyn, duke of Kingston.	May 1730	Thomas, Lord Trevor.
		Dec. 1730	Spencer, earl of Wilmington.

[1] In July 1717 Stanhope was created a viscount, the last instance of a chancellor of the exchequer in the house of lords.

[2] During a vacancy in the office of chancellor of the exchequer the lord chief justice of the K.B. took over the seals.

| Feb. 1742 | William, Lord Harring-ton. | Jan. 1745 | Lionel, duke of Dorset. |
| | | June 1751 | John, Earl Granville. |

Lords Privy Seal

1713	William, earl of Dart-mouth.	May 1735	Francis, earl of Godol-phin.
Sept. 1714	Thomas, marquess of Wharton.	Apr. 1740	John, Lord Hervey.
		Feb. 1742	John, Lord Gower.
Aug. 1715	Charles, earl of Sunder-land.	Dec. 1743	George, earl of Chol-mondeley.
Dec. 1716	Evelyn, duke of Kings-ton.	Nov. 1744	John, Lord Gower.
		10–12 Feb. 1746	Henry, earl of Carlisle.
Mar. 1718	Henry, duke of Kent.		
June 1720	Evelyn, duke of Kings-ton.	13 Feb. 1746	John, Lord Gower.
Mar. 1726	Thomas, Lord Trevor.	Jan. 1755	John, duke of Marl-borough.
May 1730	Spencer, earl of Wil-mington.		
		Dec. 1755	John, Earl Gower.
June 1731	William, 3rd duke of Devonshire.	June 1757	Richard, Earl Temple.
		Oct. 1761	John, duke of Bedford.
May 1733	Henry, Viscount Lons-dale.		

Lords Chamberlain

1714	Charles, duke of Shrewsbury.	1724	Charles, duke of Grafton.
1715	Charles, duke of Bolton.	1757	William, 4th duke of Devon-shire.
	[vacant July 1715–Apr. 1717]		
1717	Thomas Pelham-Holles, duke of Newcastle.	1762	George, duke of Marlborough.

Secretaries of State[1]

Southern Department		*Northern Department*	
1713	Henry, Viscount Bol-ingbroke.	1713	William Bromley.
		17 Sept. 1714	Charles, Viscount Townshend.
27 Sept. 1714	James Stanhope.		
12 Dec. 1716	Paul Methuen (act-ing from 22 June 1716).	12 Dec. 1716	James Stanhope.
		15 Apr. 1717	Charles, earl of Sun-derland.
6 Apr. 1717	Joseph Addison.	18 Mar. 1718	James, Viscount (Earl) Stanhope.
16 Mar. 1718	James Craggs.		
4 Mar. 1721	John, Lord Carteret.	10 Feb. 1721	Charles, Viscount Townshend.

[1] It is to be noted that both secretaries dealt with home affairs, and either could take the work of the other department in his colleague's absence. In 1723, when both Carteret and Townshend were with the king in Hanover, Robert Walpole took the work of secretary of state in England.

Secretaries of State (continued)

Southern Department		Northern Department	
6 Apr. 1724	Thomas Pelham-Holles, duke of Newcastle.	27 June 1730	William, Lord Harrington.
		12 Feb. 1742	John, Lord Carteret (Earl Granville).
		27 Nov. 1744	William, earl of Harrington.
10 Feb. 1746	John, Earl Granville.[1]	10 Feb. 1746	John, Earl Granville.
12 Feb. 1746	Thomas Pelham-Holles, duke of Newcastle.	14 Feb. 1746	William, earl of Harrington.
		4 Nov. 1746	Philip, earl of Chesterfield.
13 Feb. 1748	John, duke of Bedford.	13 Feb. 1748	Thomas Pelham-Holles, duke of Newcastle.
18 June 1751	Robert, 4th earl of Holderness.		
23 Mar. 1754	Sir Thomas Robinson.	23 Mar. 1754	Robert, earl of Holderness (resigned 9 June, reappointed 27 June 1757).[2]
14 Nov. 1754	Henry Fox.		
4 Dec. 1756	William Pitt (to 6 Apr. 1757).[3]		
18 June 1757	William Pitt.		
9 Oct. 1761	Charles, earl of Egremont.	25 Mar. 1761	John, earl of Bute.
		29 Mar. 1762	Hon. George Grenville.
		14 Oct. 1762	George, 2nd earl of Halifax.

First Lords of Admiralty

Apr. 1712	Thomas, earl of Strafford.	1748	John, earl of Sandwich.
1714	Edward, earl of Orford.	1751	George, Lord Anson.
1717	James, earl of Berkeley.	1756	Richard, Earl Temple.
1727	George, Viscount Torrington.	1757	(Apr.–July) Daniel, 3rd earl of Nottingham and 7th of Winchilsea.
1733	Sir Charles Wager.		
1742	Daniel, 3rd earl of Nottingham and 7th of Winchilsea.	1757	George, Lord Anson.
1744	John, duke of Bedford.[4]	1762	George, 2nd earl of Halifax.

[1] 10–12 Feb. 1746 Granville was sole secretary of state; see above, p. 259.

[2] From 6 Apr. to 9 June 1757 Holderness appears to have acted as Secretary both for the North and the South. He, however, resigned on 9 June, and for nine days there seems to have been no Secretary of State. Waldegrave, the chief authority for the changes of ministry in 1757, unfortunately gives hardly any dates: these, however, are supplied in H. Walpole's *Letters*.

[3] Pitt had been appointed on 15 Nov. but did not receive the seals until 4 Dec. 1756.

[4] 10–12 Feb. 1746 Nottingham held the office of first lord, see above, p. 259.

First Lords of Trade and Plantations

1714	William, Lord Berkeley of Stratton.	1719	Thomas, earl of Westmorland.
1715	Henry, earl of Suffolk.	1735	Benjamin, Earl Fitzwalter.
1718	Robert, 3rd earl of Holderness.	1737	John, Lord Monson.
		1748	George, 2nd earl of Halifax.
		1761	Samuel, Lord Sandys.

Paymasters-General of the Forces

1713	Thomas Moore and Edward Nicholas.	May 1730	Hon. Henry Pelham.
Sept. 1714	Robert Walpole.	1743	Sir Thomas Winnington.
Oct. 1715	Henry, earl of Lincoln.	May 1746	William Pitt.
June 1720	Robert Walpole.	Nov. 1755	Henry, earl of Darlington. Thomas, Viscount Dupplin.
Apr. 1721	Charles, Lord Cornwallis.		
1722	Hon. Spencer Compton.	June 1757	Henry Fox.

Secretaries at War

1713	Francis Gwyn.	May 1730	Sir William Strickland.
Sept. 1714	William Pulteney.	May 1735	Sir William Yonge.
Apr. 1717	James Craggs, jun.	July 1746	Henry Fox
Mar. 1718	Christopher Wandesford (Lord Castlecomer).	Nov. 1755	William, Lord Barrington.
May 1718	Robert Pringle	Mar. 1761	Hon. Charles Townshend.
Dec. 1718	George Trehy	Nov. 1762	Welbore Ellis.
Apr. 1724	Hon. Henry Pelham.		

Treasurers of the Navy

Oct. 1714	John Aislabie.	Dec. 1744	George Bubb Dodington.
Mar. 1718	Richard Hampden.		
Oct. 1720	Sir George Byng (Viscount Torrington).	May 1749	Hon. Henry Bilson Legge.
Apr. 1724	Hon. Pattee Byng.	Apr. 1754	Hon. George Grenville.
Apr. 1734	Arthur Onslow.	Jan. 1756	George Bubb Dodington (Lord Melcombe).
May 1742	Hon. Thomas Clutterbuck.		
Dec. 1742	Sir Charles Wager.	June 1762	William, Viscount Barrington.
Dec. 1743	Sir John Rushout.		

Chief Justices

King's Bench

1710 Sir Thomas Parker (Lord Macclesfield).
1718 Sir John Pratt.
1725 Sir Robert Raymond (Lord Raymond).
1733 Sir Philip Yorke (Lord Hardwicke).
1737 Sir William Lee.
1754 Sir Dudley Ryder (Lord Ryder).
1756 Lord Mansfield.

Common Pleas

1701 Thomas, Lord Trevor, removed Oct. 1714.
1714 Sir Peter King.
1725 Sir Robert Eyre.
1736 Sir Thomas Reeve.
1737 Sir John Willes.
1762 Sir Charles Pratt (Lord Camden).

Chief Barons of the Exchequer

1714 Sir Samuel Dodd.
1716 Sir Thomas Bury.
1722 Sir James Montague.
1723 Sir Robert Eyre.
1725 Sir Geoffrey Gilbert.
1726 Sir Thomas Pengelly.
1730 Sir James Reynolds.
1738 Sir John Comyns.
1740 Sir Edmund Probyn.
1742 Sir Thomas Parker.

Master of the Rolls[1]

1693 Sir John Trevor.
1717 Sir Joseph Jekyll, M.P.
1738 Hon. John Verney.
1741 William Fortescue.
1750 Sir John Strange, M.P.
1754 Sir Thomas Clarke, M.P.

Attorneys-General

1710 Sir Edward Northey.
1718 Sir Thomas Lechmere.
1720 Sir Robert Raymond (Lord Raymond).
1724 Sir Philip Yorke (Lord Hardwicke).
1734 Sir John Willes.
1737 Sir Dudley Ryder (Lord Ryder).
1754 Hon. William Murray (Lord Mansfield).
1756 Sir Robert Henley (Lord Northington).
1757 Sir Charles Pratt (Earl Camden).
1762 Hon. Charles Yorke.

Speakers of the House of Commons

1713 Sir Thomas Hanmer.
1715 Hon. Spencer Compton.
1728 Arthur Onslow.
1761 Sir John Cust.

[1] It will be noted that the mastership of the rolls was then thought compatible with a seat in the house of commons.

SCOTLAND

Secretaries of State for Scotland

Sept. 1714 James, duke of Montrose, dismissed Aug. 1715.
Dec. 1716 John, duke of Roxburgh, dismissed Aug. 1725.
Feb. 1742 John, marquess of Tweeddale, resigned Jan. 1746.[1]

Lords President of Court of Session

1707	Sir Henry Dalrymple.	1754	Robert Craigie of Glendoich.
1737	Duncan Forbes of Culloden.	1760	Robert Dundas of Arniston
1748	Robert Dundas of Arniston		(the 2nd).
	(the 1st).		

Lords Advocate

1709	Sir David Dalrymple.	1746	William Grant of Preston-
1720	Robert Dundas of Arniston		grange.
	(the 1st).	1754	Robert Dundas of Arniston
1725	Duncan Forbes of Culloden.		(the 2nd).
1737	Charles Erskine of Tinwald.	1760	Thomas Miller of Glenlea.
1742	Robert Craigie of Glendoich.		

IRELAND

Lords Lieutenant of Ireland[2]

1713	Charles, duke of Shrews-bury.	Sept. 1737	William, 3rd duke of Devonshire.
Sept. 1714	Charles, earl of Sunder-land (never went to Ireland).	Jan. 1745	Philip, earl of Chester-field.
Dec. 1716	Charles, Viscount Townshend (never went to Ireland).	Sept. 1746	William, earl of Har-rington.
Mar. 1717	Charles, duke of Bolton.	Dec. 1750	Lionel, duke of Dorset.
Aug. 1720	Charles, duke of Graf-ton.	May 1755	William, marquis of Hartington (4th duke of Devonshire).
Oct. 1724	John, Lord Carteret.	Sept. 1756	John, duke of Bedford.
Sept. 1730	Lionel, duke of Dorset.	Mar. 1761	George, 2nd earl of Halifax.

[1] Tweeddale was the last secretary for Scotland till Gladstone's time. M. A. Thomson, *Secretaries of State*, 1932, pp. 35–36, shows that the attribution of this post to Lord Selkirk in 1731 is erroneous. See above, pp. 33, n., and 272.

[2] During the prolonged absences in England of these lords lieutenant they were represented by lords justices chosen from the chief officials in Ireland; see above, p. 293. In the exceptional case, however, of Sunderland and Townshend, who never landed in the country, two lords justices, the duke of Grafton and the earl of Galway, were sent from England in 1715.

Lord Chancellors

1710	Sir Constantine Phipps.	1726	Thomas Wyndham (Lord).
1714	Alan Brodrick (Viscount Midleton).	1739	Robert Jocelyn (Viscount).
1725	Richard West.	1757	John Bowes (Lord).

Archbishops of Armagh (Primates of All Ireland)[1]

1714	Thomas Lindsay.	1742	John Hoadly.
1724	Hugh Boulter.	1747	George Stone.

Speakers of the Irish House of Commons

1715	William Conolly.	1733	Henry Boyle (earl of Shannon).
1729	Sir Ralph Gore.	1756	John Ponsonby.

[1] Until Boulter came in 1724, William King, archbishop of Dublin, though only 'Primate of Ireland', was the most important prelate and generally a lord justice, after that Boulter and his successors always were.

INDEX

367 n. 4; as Prince of Wales, 38, 355 n. 5, 383.

George William, duke of Brunswick–Lüneburg (d. 1705), uncle of George I, 11.

Georgia, 95, 99, 136, 207, 209, 307, 309 and n. 1, 310, 318, 384.

Gerard, John (1545–1612), author of *Herbal*, 388.

Germain, Lord George, *see* Sackville.

Gibbon, Edward (1737–94), 52, 62 n. 5, 431; on Charles Emmanuel III of Savoy, 267 and n. 1; on William Law's *Serious Call*, 94; his aunt Hester, 93.

— — (1707–70), father of the historian, 93.

Gibbons, Grinling (1648–1720), sculptor and wood-carver, 402.

— Orlando (1583–1625), musician, 399.

Gibbs, James (1682–1754), architect, 401 f., 412 and n. 1.

— Joseph (1700–88), composer, 417.

Gibraltar, 173 f., 195, 198, 200, 207, 244, 307, 352.

Gibson, Edmund (1669–1748), bishop of Lincoln 1717–23, of London 1723–48, 72, 76 ff., 80, 82, 323, 394, 415.

Gideon, Sampson (1699–1762), 73 f.

Gilbert, John (1693–1761), archbishop of York, 81.

— William (1540–1603), and electricity, 382.

Gilboy, Mrs. Elizabeth, *Wages in Eighteenth Century England*, 127 and n. 2.

Gin-drinking, 44, 133–4, 384.

Girtin, Thomas (1775–1802), 401.

Gladstone, W. E. (1809–98), on Bishop Butler, 90; economic policy, 187 f.; revival of office of Secretary of State, Scotland, 273.

Glasgow, medical school, 385, 389; population, 274; rebellion of 1745, 255, 283, 414 n. 2; riots, 278; trade and shipping, 275–6, 285.

Glauber, Johann Rudolph (1604–68), chemist, 387.

Glover, Richard (1712–85), 22, 204, 421; with reference to Pitt, 128, 355 n. 1.

Godeheu, Director of French East India Company and successor of Dupleix, 328.

Godolphin, Sidney, earl of (1645–1712), 35, 420.

Goertz, Baron Friedrich W. von (d. 1728), 153.

Goldsmith, Oliver (1728–74), 62, 305, 407; *Deserted Village*, 109, 141; *Vicar of Wakefield*, 418.

Gonzales, Don Manuel, Portuguese visitor in 1730, comment on the poor, 130.

Gordon, Alexander (? 1692–? 1754), *Itinerarium Septentrionale* (1726), 395.

Gore, Sir Ralph, Speaker of Irish Commons (1729–33), 294 n. 2.

Goupy, Joseph (d. 1763), French painter, 406.

Grafton, Charles Fitzroy, 2nd duke of (1683–1757), 34; lord lieutenant of Ireland, 292, 301.

Graham, George (1673–1751), scientific instrument-maker, 382.

Granger, James (1723–76), 395.

Grant, Sir William, of Preston Grange (? 1701–64), 64, 273, 281, 283.

Granville, Earl, *see* Carteret.

— Grace, Countess (c. 1667–1744), 148, 204, 249 n. 2.

Gravelot, Hubert François (1699–1773), engraver, 406.

Graves, Richard (1715–1804), *Spiritual Quixote*, 97.

Gray, Stephen (1696–1736), electrician, 382–3.

— Thomas (1716–71), 129, 426, 429.

Green, Matthew (1696–1737), poet, 420 n. 2.

— Thomas, *see under* Ely.

— Valentine (1739–1813), mezzotint engraver, 414.

Greene, Maurice (c. 1695–1755), composer, 417.

Grenville, Hon. George (1712–70), 224 n. 3, 250, 353.

— Richard, Earl Temple (1711–79), 49, 147, 354, 370, 413.

Grenvilles, the, and Pitt, 346, 376 n. 1; opposed to Walpole, 204, 238.

Griffin, Thomas (d. 1771), admiral, 262.

Grimshaw, Rev. William (1708–63), of Haworth, 88.

Guadeloupe, 359, 364, 368 f., 372.

Guests, the, ironworks, Dowlais, Worcestershire, 117.

Gunning, Elizabeth (duchess of Hamilton and Argyll) (1734–90), 148.

— Maria (Lady Coventry) (1733–60), 148.

Gyllenborg, Count Karl (1679–1746), and Jacobites, 174.

Haddock, Nicholas (1686–1746), admiral, 210, 226, 229, 233 and nn. 2 and 3, 236, 240, 247.

Hadley, John (1682–1744), mathematician, 382.

Hailes, Sir David Dalrymple, Lord (1726–92), 287.

Hales, Stephen (1677–1761), scientist &c., author of *Vegetable Staticks*, 384–5, 388, 391.

MAPS

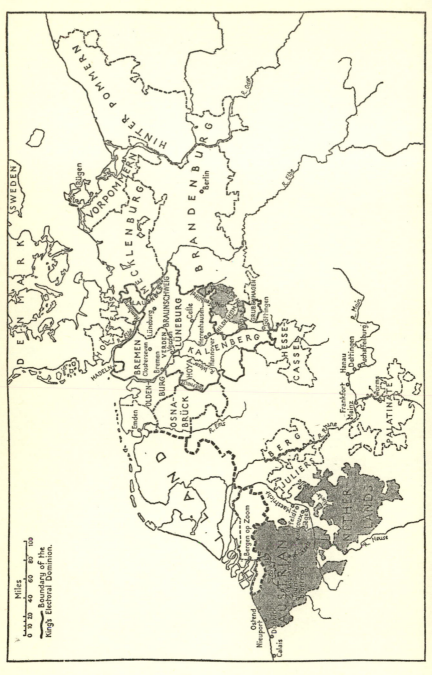

5. NORTHERN GERMANY, SHOWING KING'S ELECTORAL DOMINIONS AND OPERATIONS

Miles

0 50 100 200 300 400

✗ ✗ Barrier Fortresses
▨▨ Brunswick Wölfenbüttel

NORWAY
SWEDEN
FINLAND
St. Petersburg
Stockholm

IRELAND
ULSTER
Belfast
CONNAUGHT
Armagh
Tuam
Limerick
Dublin
MUNSTER
Cork
Waterford

GREAT
BRITAIN

Aberdeen
Glasgow
Edinburgh

Liverpool
Bristol
London
Calais

DENMARK
Copenhagen
HOLSTEIN
MECKLENBURG
POLAND
Thorn
Warsaw
LIVONIA
RUSSIA

DUTCH
Amsterdam
The Hague
HANOVER
Klosterseven
Berlin
Küstrin
Züllichau

Cologne
Frankfort
Mainz
THE
EMPIRE
Bergen
BOHEMIA
Prague
AUSTRIA
Vienna
HUNGARY

Cherbourg
Havre
Boulogne
Lille
Cambrai

Paris
Commercy
Luneville

BAVARIA
Munich
Füssen
SWITZERLAND
Geneva
SAVOY

Ushant
Brest
St. Malo
L'Orient
Quiberon
Belle Ile
Ile d'Aix
Basque Roads
Rochefort
Bordeaux

FRANCE
Lyons
Turin
PIEDMONT
Milan
VENICE
Verona
Trieste

TURKISH
Belgrade
Danube
EMPIRE

C. Finisterre
Ferrol
Santander

AVIGNON
Marseilles
Toulon
Hyères
Nice
CORSICA

Leghorn
TUSCANY
PAPAL
STATES
Florence
Rome
NAPLES
Naples

SPAIN
Madrid
Barcelona

Minorca (Eng)
Port Mahon
Majorca
Iviza
SARDINIA

KINGDOM
OF THE
TWO SICILIES

Lisbon
PORTUGAL
Seville
Cartagena
Cadiz
Gibraltar

SICILY
Palermo
Messina
C. Passaro

6. EUROPE, 1714-63

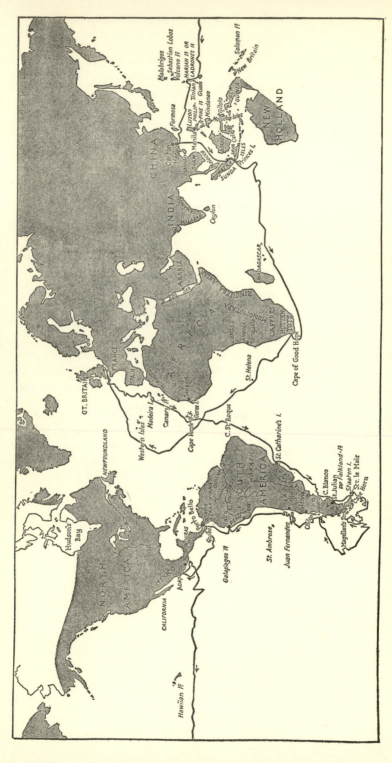

7. CHART SHOWING TRACK OF *CENTURION* IN ANSON'S VOYAGE

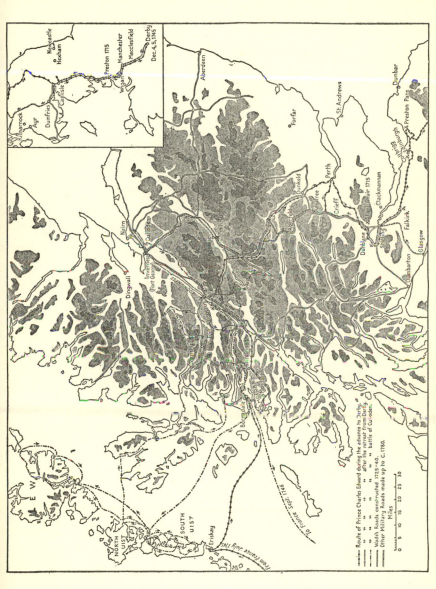

8. SCOTLAND, SHOWING WADE'S ROADS AND PRINCE CHARLIE'S WANDERINGS

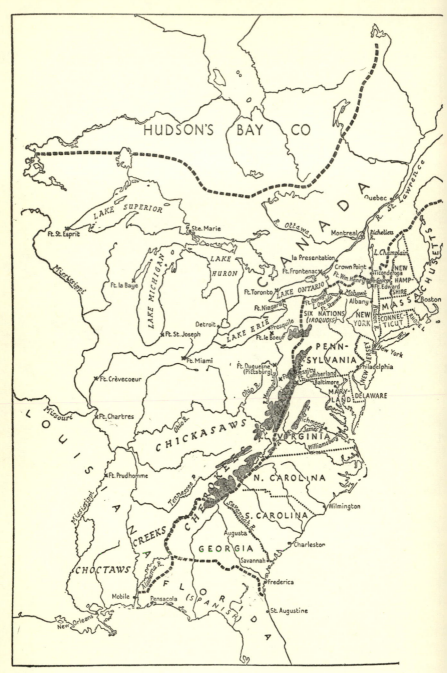

HUDSON'S BAY CO

CANADA

LAKE SUPERIOR

Ft. St. Esprit

Ste. Marie

R. Ottawa

Quebec

R. St. Lawrence

Montreal

Richelieu R.

L. Champlain

LAKE
HURON

LAKE
MICHIGAN

Ft. la Baye

la Presentation

Ft. Frontenac

Crown Point

Ticonderoga
L. George

NEW
HAMP-
SHIRE

MASSACHUSETTS

Ft. Wm. Henry

Ft. Edward

Ft. Toronto

LAKE ONTARIO

Ft. Oswego

L. Oneida

Mohawk

Albany

Boston

RHODE

Ft. Niagara

Ft. Stanwix

CONNEC-
TICUT

Mississippi

Detroit

Ft. St. Joseph

LAKE ERIE

Presquile

SIX NATIONS
(IROQUOIS)

NEW
YORK

Ft. le Boeuf

PENN-
SYLVANIA

New York

Ft. Miami

NEW JERSEY

Philadelphia

Ft. Crèvecoeur

Ft. Duquesne
(Pittsburg)

Ft. Necessity

Ft. Cumberland

DELAWARE

Baltimore

MARY-
LAND

LOUISIANA

Missouri

Ft. Chartres

CHICKASAWS

Ohio R.

Monongahela

Richmond
James R.

VIRGINIA

Williamsburg

Ft. Prudhomme

N. CAROLINA

Tennessee R.

CHEROKEES

Savannah R.

S. CAROLINA

Wilmington

CREEKS

Augusta

Charleston

Mississippi

GEORGIA

Savannah

CHOCTAWS

Alabama R.

FLORIDA
(SPANISH)

Frederica

Mobile

Pensacola

St. Augustine

New Orleans

9. NORTH AMERICA AND

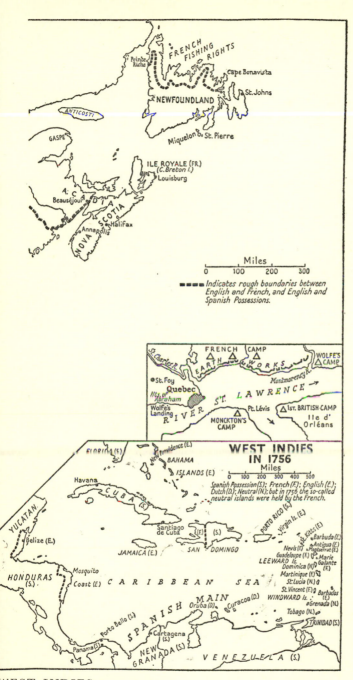

Miles
0   100   200   300

▬▬▬▬ Indicates rough boundaries between
English and French, and English and
Spanish Possessions.

**WEST INDIES
IN 1756**

Miles
0   100   200   300   400   500

Spanish Possession (S.); French (F.); English (E.);
Dutch (D.); Neutral (N.); but in 1756 the so-called
neutral islands were held by the French.

WEST INDIES

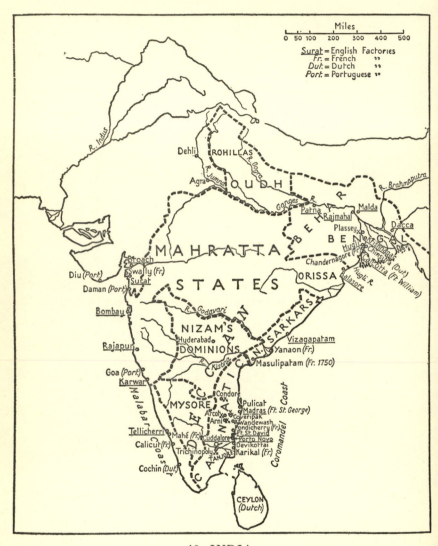

Miles

0 50 100 200 300 400 500

<u>Surat</u> = English Factories
Fr. = French "
Dut. = Dutch "
Port. = Portuguese "

R. Indus

Dehli   ROHILLAS
                        R. Gogra

Agra   R. Jumna   O U D H

                R. Brahmaputra

        Ganges R.   B E H A R
            Patna   Malda
                Rajmahal
                Plassey   B E N G A L
                        Hugli   Chinsura   Dacca
        Chandernagore (Fr.)   Chinsura (Dut.)
                            Calcutta (Ft. William)

M A H R A T T A

Broach
Diu (Port.)   Swally (Fr.)   S T A T E S   O R I S S A
        Surat   Hugli R.
Daman (Port.)   Balasore

Bombay   R. Godavari
                        D E C C A N
            NIZAM'S   N. SARKARS
        Hyderabad   Vizagapatam
Rajapur   DOMINIONS   Yanaon (Fr.)
                R. Kistna   Masulipatam (Fr. 1750)

Goa (Port.)
Karwar   Condore
                    Pulicat
        MYSORE   Madras (Ft. St. George)
            Arcot   Coveripak
            Arni   Wandewash
Tellicherri   Mahé (Fr.)   Pondicherry (Fr.)
Calicut (Fr.)   Cuddalore   Ft. St. David
        Trichinopoly   Porto Novo
                    Devikottai
                TANJORE   Karikal (Fr.)
Cochin (Dut.)   Coromandel Coast

Malabar Coast   C A R N A T I C

            CEYLON
            (Dutch)

10. INDIA